WHATEVER IT TAKES

By Jim O'Brien

The Continuing Saga of the Pittsburgh Steelers — II

In Memoriam *A share of the proceeds from the sale of our earlier book "Doing It Right," the story of the glory years of the Pittsburgh Steelers, was earmarked for the Art Rooney Scholarship Fund. On August 29, 1992, author Jim O'Brien presented Steelers' president Dan Rooney with a check for $20,000 — the largest check ever presented to this fund from an outside source. The fund provides financial aid to needy youngsters on Pittsburgh's North Side who want to go to college or continue their education.*

Published by James O'Brien-Publishing
P.O. Box 12580
Pittsburgh PA 15241
Phone (412) 221-3580

Portions of some of the chapters were originally published in The Pittsburgh Press, and are reprinted here with permission.

First printing

Photos by Bill Amatucci, Mike Fabus, George Gojkovich and others from the photo files of the Pittsburgh Steelers.

Manufactured in the United States of America.

Printed by Geyer Printing Company, Inc.
Pittsburgh PA 15213
Typography by Cold-Comp
Pittsburgh PA 15222

Photo reproductions by Modern Reproductions, Inc.

ISBN Number 0-916114-10-4

Dedication

For all my mentors and teachers, who showed the way.

To the memory of a Hall of Famer, Doc Carlson of the University of Pittsburgh, who wanted me to write in a positive manner, and taught me about "blessed boomerangs."

To the memory of another Hall of Famer, Steelers owner Art Rooney, who taught us all so much about life, and once said, "I never had a player I didn't like; I never had a player I didn't think was a star."

To my family and friends, especially those who have encouraged me and helped me turn my dreams into books about Pittsburgh and achievement.

And especially to my wife Kathleen and our daughters — Sarah and Rebecca — just for being there and sharing their love.

This book is for them. And for you.

—Jim O'Brien

Words of Praise

"Jim O'Brien has, by dint of a keen eye for detail and tenacious reporting, carved himself a nifty niche as Boswell to sporting Pittsburgh."

— Phil Musick, WTAE Radio

"Jim O'Brien is uniquely qualified to bring you these stories about the Steelers, whom he lived with and died with during the breath-taking '70s, the unforgettable decade that belonged to the Steelers, creating a heyday of excellence in Pittsburgh. And O'Brien, in his soft, inimitable style, puts flesh and bone onto his characters with a penetrating insight into his subjects. He brings these men alive as to what they were and what they are, which is a damn fine crew from Coach Chuck Noll on down."

—Pat Livingston
Former Sports Editor
The Pittsburgh Press

"If anyone qualifies to be described as Pittsburgh's sports historian, that person is Jim O'Brien. He knows his Pittsburgh teams. He writes with authority as well as with an affection for the teams and people he portrays."

— Myron Cope, WTAE Radio

"Doing It Right is not your typical football book that centers around games and statistics. It's a book about people — the people most responsible for the Steelers' four Super Bowl seasons in the '70s."

—Norm Vargo
Sports Editor
McKeesport Daily News

"To Jim O'Brien, whose writing I have read and admired over the years."

—Dan Rather
CBS-TV News

"Like David Halberstam's first-rate Summer of '49, Doing It Right *is less a recounting of thrice-told tales than a study of how men came together for a group purpose, driving them to the peak of their abilities. Over the years, no one's been a better, more committed sports chronicler than O'Brien. Some may have burned more incandescently, some have remained longer in the trenches, but no one's produced a higher volume of solid reporting.* Doing It Right *brought O'Brien back to the players, interviewing them in their homes and offices, bringing himself into the story as Roger Kahn did in the brilliant, elegiac* The Boys of Summer."*

—Abby Mendelson, SRO

"As the precocious editor and publisher of Pittsburgh Weekly Sports *in the early 1960s, Jim O'Brien was a trend setter. He provided a forum in Pittsburgh for a new breed of literate, humorous, hard-hitting sportswriters. Subsequently, during his years with* The Miami News *and* The New York Post, *O'Brien clung to his roots. Pittsburgh was always in his blood, and since returning here in 1979 he has been a knowledgeable observer of the scene. Like his previous books,* Hail to Pitt *and* City of Champions, Doing It Right *is a valuable addition to the archives. Part history and part memoir, it follows the Pittsburgh Steelers of the Super Bowl decade into the 1980s and their post-football lives, enriching the folklore."*

—Roy McHugh
Executive Report

*"*Doing It Right *can best be described as a unique behind-the-scenes story of what sets the Steelers apart from the pack, yesterday and today. Football fans and non-football fans alike are bound to benefit from the insight into how these men strived for excellence on and off the playing field. Jerry Kramer's* Instant Replay, *which chronicled Vince Lombardi's great Packer teams of the 1960s, has always been my favorite football book. Until now. This is the best football book on the market today."*

—Matt Marsom, Editor
The Football News

"*Jim O'Brien makes it easy to recall the glory days of the Pittsburgh Steelers.* Doing It Right *is loaded with colorful insight into the players, coaches, and management of that championship franchise. Painstakingly researched, O'Brien interviewed just about everybody associated with the team at that time.*"

—Nikolai Bonesso
The City Paper

"*What* Doing It Right *gives us is not so much the concrete and beams of the dynasty; rather, we get the flesh and blood. O'Brien has not put on paper X's and O's, much as a coach or quarterback chalk up winning plays. Instead, he chose to dip his pen into the heart of this team and its city. Couched within a 'sports book' is a 'feel' for Pittsburgh — its people, its tradition, its pride, its heart. It's a feel provided by one of its sons. You come away liking that feeling.*"

—Taylor Scott
Point Magazine

"*Jim O'Brien, the kind of sportswriter I admire, is really consistent. His book,* City of Champions, *was the best such book I had ever seen. Now he's written one about the Pittsburgh Steelers,* Doing It Right, *which is the best of its kind. Jim always does a terrific job of research, interviewing and writing and never resorts to mean-spirited innuendo. Great book about a great team by a great guy!*"

—Joe Browne
City Lights

"*I've been privileged to not only know Jim O'Brien, but also to have him as one of my teachers during my years at Point Park College. His motto always was. . . 'Make the reader think he was there.' It is a constant in all of his work. When you read a Jim O'Brien book, you swear you've been there with him.*"

—Bob Pompeani
KDKA-TV2

Contents

NOSTALGIA

STEELERS AT HEART

THE LONGEST SEASON

Steelers offensive unit poses before regular season finale in 1976.

"In order to win, and to be successful, we will do whatever it takes."

—Chuck Noll

"Whatever it takes, we'll get it all done."

—Bill Cowher

"When we didn't win, some people didn't think we were smart enough to come in out of the rain."

—Art Rooney

Libba Dudley

Author Jim O'Brien, left, visits with Steelers' legendary figure "Bullet Bill" Dudley at Farmington Country Club in Charlottesville, near the University of Virginia, in the summer of 1992.

"Many celebrated people are just folks when you get to know them."

—Charles Kuralt

Life on the Road

Preface
On the road with the Steelers

*"You went on the playground when the sun came up,
and you didn't leave till the sun went down."*
—Art Rooney

*"Success . . . seems to be connected with action. Successful
men keep moving, they make mistakes, but they don't
quit."*
—Conrad Hilton

I was telling a friend at breakfast one morning about an interview
I had just had a few days earlier when I visited the home of Chuck
Noll in our neighborhood. I spent several hours with Chuck and his
wife, Marianne, when both were in a relaxed and expansive mood.
Retirement suited them both just fine. It was the first time I had ever
been in their home, even though it is located only little more than a
mile from my own home. It gave me yet another insight into what was
so special about the Steelers' long-time coach and his family.

"I've been a Steelers fan for a long time," the friend said, "and
I take my son to every Steelers' opener. It's become a tradition in our
family. I would love to take my son to see Chuck Noll, and just sit down
for a few hours and talk with him. That would be a dream come true."

Several thoughts raced through my mind when I heard that. For
one thing, several Steelers who played for Chuck Noll expressed a similar desire. They had a deep need, it seemed, to spend some quality time
with their old coach, to get to know him better, to break through the
barriers they believed existed in a coach-player relationship that might
be removed now that they have all retired from the game.

Rocky Bleier, Andy Russell and Lynn Swann all sought such a get-
together with the man who coached them to Super Bowl championships,
yet always remained at a safe distance.

Noll had telephoned me in response to some notes I had left in his
mailbox. "When will you have some free time?" I asked. And he responded, "I have lots of free time now. When do you want to come?"

I set a time for that afternoon, lest he change his mind. I have always enjoyed talking with Noll.

My intent in writing my books about the Steelers, *Doing It Right*
and now *Whatever It Takes,* was because I wanted to talk to some of
my favorite Steelers through the years, to find out what they were up
to, how they were doing, and to share some stories with them. I thought
I could learn something, and I have not been disappointed. I could not
think of a better way to spend a day.

I have enjoyed my sojourns. It has always been my objective as
a sports writer to take others with me on my travels, to put them where

1

I have been fortunate enough to have been. To take them on buses and behind closed doors, for example, to Maui for mass on St. Patrick's Day with Art Rooney. And I got paid to do that.

I remember riding in the rear of a bus with the Steelers after a loss to the Colts in Baltimore, and sitting among Art Rooney, who was chomping on an unlit cigar, and talking to Terry Bradshaw, Mike Webster and Larry Brown about the ballgame. It was behind them now and though they expressed keen disappointment over the setback it wasn't long before they were smiling and laughing and enjoying each other's company. I thought it was my job to take my readers along for the ride. I grew up in Hazelwood, not far from Forbes Field and Pitt Stadium, where the Steelers played in my youth, and I have worked from the point of view that I was writing a letter back home to the kids I grew up with, and letting them know what it was like to travel and spend time with a big league ballteam.

In writing this book, I had an opportunity to spend time with John Brown and John Henry Johnson, Paul Martha and Ray Mansfield, Noll and the new coach on the block, Bill Cowher, and to talk with Frenchy Fuqua and Sal Sunseri, Terry Hanratty and Loren Toews, John Banaszak and Moon Mullins. It was always fun.

Martha is among those who credit his own experience as a professional athlete as a tremendous help in his career development, as an attorney and as an executive in sports, specifically the Pittsburgh Penguins, the two-time Stanley Cup champions.

"First, teamwork is a big part of the job and the competitive spirit transcends the rest of your life," he said. "Then there is a synergism with the business of sports and sports itself. Playing in the NFL gave me an enormous advantage; the business side is a lot different, so I'm able to see the total picture and relate well to the players. I've been there."

The most difficult interview was one with Sam Davis, one of Martha's former teammates and one of my favorites when I covered the Steelers for *The Pittsburgh Press*, who suffered neurological damage in a mysterious incident at his home to the north of Pittsburgh. Seeing Davis in a dulled state and in a psychiatric hospital setting was shocking to the senses.

The highlight, however, was traveling to Charlottesville, Virginia and interviewing "Bullet Bill" Dudley, one of the magic names from my boyhood days when football players and athletes were all larger than life. He is 70 and still sees himself as a Steeler.

"Let me ask you a question," said "Bullet Bill" at one point, turning the tables on me. "Is it true that today's ballplayers are only interested in themselves and in making money? Do they care about what people think of them, do they try to help out in the community, and do they see themselves as role models?"

I told "Bullet Bill" that I thought there were still many athletes, and the Steelers are still among the league leaders in that regard, who give of themselves unselfishly in the community, who make a difference with young and old people by their personal efforts, and who

2

genuinely care about their reputations. Some are still outstanding role models. Some still merit our admiration.

One of those, Gary Anderson, said he thinks Dudley is on to something, saying he has noticed a big change in the attitudes of the players when he first joined the Steelers 11 years ago, and the ones he works with today.

Those who misbehave, who do drugs or get into difficulty with the law or the league office, will get a lot more attention today than they did in Dudley's day. The media tracks their activities in a much more zealous manner, and scrutinizes their every move. The good doesn't rate as much attention, however, as the bad.

There are both elements in pro football. Many of the Steelers have been successful on and off the field. Many of them have followed the lead of their coach, and done whatever it takes to be winners.

Some good things are likely to happen with the Steelers in 1993. There is a good chance that both Noll and John Stallworth could be inducted into the Pro Football Hall of Fame in the same class. It promises to be another great pilgrimage for Pittsburghers and western Pennsylvanians to what has become a Steelers' shrine in Canton, Ohio.

It was Stallworth who said he wants his children to "excel at something." Stallworth was not only a great receiver, and a good human being, but he has been a huge success in the real world as well. He is the president of an aerospace engineering firm in his hometown of Huntsville, Alabama.

This book is about the successes as well as the failures of football players who have called Pittsburgh home. I want you to feel like you are sitting in on a conversation with all of them. I hope you will enjoy spending time with these Steelers and Steeler fans as much as I did.

Steelers owner Art Rooney schmoozes with Emil Boures, center, and Bryan Hinkle in clubhouse at Three Rivers Stadium.

3

Introduction
"Doing It Wrong"

My book *Doing It Right*, about the glory days of the Pittsburgh Steelers, was just off the presses at Geyer Printing in Oakland in the summer of 1991 when a series of negative developments left their biggest fans wondering what in the world had gone wrong with the Steelers.

It was enough to shake the faith of the Steelers' most fervent fans.

Some were suggesting to me that I better hurry up and write another book and call it *Doing It Wrong,* about the gloomy days of the Steelers. Then again, a Pirates' official had stood up at a sports luncheon, and jested that he heard I was writing a book about the Bucs to be called *Doing It Wrong.* So the Steelers weren't the only team in town to suffer setbacks.

Pitt's athletic department was giving the Pirates and the Steelers a run for their money. So were the mayor's office and city council in the play-for-pay department. It was a difficult year all the way around.

The first stunning story during the Steelers' summer stay at St. Vincent College was that offensive lineman Terry Long had tried to commit suicide at his home in the North Hills.

Tim Worley was once again unable to practice much because of one hurt or another, and then it was learned he had a drug and alcohol problem. The Steelers had a $3 million investment in Worley, a running back who was their No. 1 draft choice in 1989.

Worley was arrested on September 25 for driving under the influence of alcohol, and resisting arrest near Greater Pittsburgh International Airport. He entered Gateway Rehabilitation Center on October 21 for a month-long stay.

Both Long, who had tested positive for illegal anabolic steroids in July just before his suicide attempt, and Worley, who had a second positive test for cocaine, were suspended for four and six weeks, respectively, by the powers-that-be in the National Football League office. They were the only players in the NFL to be suspended for such reasons during the 1991 season, and the first Steelers to be set down for such infractions since the NFL instituted its current drug policy.

Worley told Ed Bouchette of the *Pittsburgh Post-Gazette* that he purposely used cocaine even though he knew he would get caught because of his concern over financial and football problems. "I was crying for help," said Worley. "I thought I was having a nervous breakdown."

He said his real problem was not cocaine, but the beer he drank to numb himself from the problems he was facing. "It's up to me now," said Worley, who would also be suspended for the 1992 season.

Commenting on the Worley situation, Steelers' president Dan Rooney remarked, "We're very disappointed. It was a blow to us. We're concerned for Tim because we know he has been having problems. He's on his way to get his life straightened out, and we hope he succeeds."

A former Steeler quarterback with a history of drug problems, Joe Gilliam, was arrested in Shreveport, Louisiana on July 19 for allegedly attempting a robbery at a mini-market while flashing a knife.

Hall of Fame cornerback Mel Blount came under fire by authorities for excessive disciplinary measures at the Mel Blount Youth Home in Washington County. Blount had been sincere in his efforts to make a difference in the lives of troubled youth, but he came off looking bad in this charge. He has more support now.

Blount believed it was a bad rap, but promised to improve the situation. The matter was cleared up.

Blount bounced back in a big way. On February 15, he received the 1991 Walter Camp Man of the Year Award at Yale University.

One of his most respected teammates, offensive guard Sam Davis, was hospitalized in September after a mysterious incident at his home on a farm in Zelienople. It was said that Davis had taken a terrible fall down a stairway in his home in which he suffered serious head injuries and neurological damage. His wife was away for the weekend and found him upon return. Police investigated the accident, but did not believe there was any foul play. Rumors persisted to the contrary. Some insiders believed that Davis had been beaten up by some overzealous debt collectors. Davis denied that when I visited him in the hospital. "I know what people are saying," he said. Davis has gone through a series of ill-fated business projects since his playing days. His most recent undertaking was an asphalt business. In any case, he has required extensive rehabilitation treatment, and does not seem like the same Sam Davis we all knew and loved during the glory days of the Steelers.

Former teammates and friends of Davis were distressed by his misfortune. "Sam's a great guy and was one of the true leaders of the Super Bowl teams of the '70s," said Joe Gordon, the Steelers' director of communications, in an article in the *Beaver County Times*. "He was respected by everyone and probably was one of the most popular players within the organization."

The 47-year-old Davis had visited the Steelers' training camp at St. Vincent several times just prior to his mishap. It was always a happy occasion because Davis has always been a guy who brought sunshine into the world.

Word came out of Cleveland that former Steelers offensive lineman, John Rienstra, had confirmed a report that he was an alcoholic. He quit the Browns during training camp, but returned a few days later. It sounded familiar to Steelers fans. "In the beginning, I was kind of paranoid about people finding out," Rienstra said, "but I've got some years behind me now. I don't think much about it any more."

Rienstra had been the Steelers' No. 1 draft choice out of Temple in 1986, but was a problem child during his roller-coaster ride with the

Steelers. He was often plagued by ulcers and stress-related unrest during his tenure in Pittsburgh. There was a period when he seemed to have his act together, and was a quality starter for the Steelers. Then he got into Chuck Noll's doghouse and, finally, the Steelers gave up on him. He became another No. 1 choice that went bad.

Huey Richardson, a linebacker/defensive end who was the Steelers' No. 1 draft choice in 1991, spoke to the media on draft day, but refused to speak to them again the entire season, for no apparent reason. This was strange behavior for a Steelers ballplayer. The team had always prided itself on being the most open organization in the league, and had been cited by national media for outstanding public relations.

The New York Times reported that Terry Hanratty had a book coming out in which he wrote of his comeback from alcoholic problems. He had gone through treatment at a rehabilitation center to set himself straight again.

After the Steelers got off to a 2-2 start, defensive line coach Joe Greene, one of the team's all-time greats, was quoted in newspapers across the country with this assessment of the Steelers:

"The record says we're mediocre. We were mediocre the year before, and the year before. We've only been able to be competitive with mediocre teams. I'm not saying that, the record is saying that."

Then Tunch Ilkin, the team's player representative, said, "I think everybody believes we're a pretty average, mediocre team. And we haven't proved differently."

If that wasn't bad enough, stories persisted about Terry Bradshaw's unhappiness with the Steelers, especially Noll, and Pittsburgh and its football fans. What, indeed, had gone wrong in Camelot?

The Steelers struggled to a 9-7 record and came up short of the playoffs and everybody's expectations for 1991. Bubby Brister spent the season bitching and bristling about Joe Walton's complicated and unproductive offensive system. It simply wasn't working out after a two-year experiment.

Noll, true to his character, remained steadfastly loyal to Walton to the bitter end.

The year ended with the media calling for Noll to give up the ghost. They enjoyed advising Noll that it was time for him to follow the advice he had always given his players and to get on with his "life's work." They succeeded in ruffling Noll's thinning blond hair several times during the stretch run. They were getting to him.

It appeared that team president Dan Rooney was ready to stick by Noll for another go-round, with certain changes being mandated, but Noll stunned the Steelers by announcing his retirement the day after Christmas. "He dropped a bomb on them," as one former Steeler put it.

I believe that Noll had simply had enough. Noll no longer needed the aggravation, from either the media or the members of his team who could not discipline themselves and dedicate themselves to giving their all on the football field. Too many things had gone wrong, and the cumulative garbage became a burden on Noll's back. Enough was enough.

Noll may have also known that he did not have a very good football team, and he lacked the patience to try and pull things together. Some insiders say Noll was no longer as strict and demanding with those who strayed, or were late for team meetings and the like.

In short, it wasn't much fun for him anymore. He was nearing his 60th birthday, was in good health, and decided it was time to take a break. It was time to go sailing, to improve his golf game, to sip some wine, dine on some gourmet food offerings, and to smell the roses.

This is not a book about *Doing It Wrong*. Such subjects don't hold much appeal to me. The Steelers have set higher standards than most for success in sports and in life, and there is still much to be learned from the examples set by people who have performed for or been associated with the Steelers.

I believe the Steelers' organization misses the presence of Art Rooney more than anyone realizes. His faith, compassion and good humor are sorely missed. He had a special charm, and so did the Steelers as a result of his influence. He counseled all the players. He lifted their spirits.

I was encouraged to write a sequel to the saga of the Steelers for several reasons. *Doing It Right* was the most successful regional book in western Pennsylvania during the pre-holiday season of 1991, right up there with some national best-sellers.

During a series of book-signings at book stores during the holiday season I received much positive feedback on *Doing It Right*. So many said they enjoyed it, or offered that it was the perfect gift for their grandfather, or father, brother or sister, uncle or cousin, or a friend who had moved away who remains a Steelers fan. I was particularly pleased when women said they enjoyed reading it.

"Anybody who wants to understand and appreciate the Steelers' organization, and its players, past and present, should read this book," wrote one reader.

Then, too, many wanted to know why I hadn't written more about this particular Steeler or that one whom they especially liked.

Bob Keaney, the president of Industrial Metals & Minerals Company in South Fayette Township, said, "I loved your book, but how come you didn't have more on Moon Mullins?"

"Thank you," I responded. "I will, I promise, in my next book. I'm working on it right now."

I later learned that Moon Mullins was Keaney's right-hand man and heir apparent at his company. Keaney had become a fan of Mullins during his playing days with the Steelers. No wonder Keaney wanted more on Moon Mullins.

I went out and interviewed a whole new cast of characters in the life of the Steelers, people like Paul Martha and John Brown, who preceded the Super Bowl days and have made their mark in the sports and business world of Pittsburgh. I interviewed John Henry Johnson, a legendary Hall of Famer, who now lives in Cleveland, and is fighting ill health.

I had several interviews with John "Frenchy" Fuqua, and could have written a book about him alone. What a character, what a storyteller. I found that former Steelers like Mullins, John Banaszak, Randy Grossman, Ted Petersen, Loren Toews and Ray Pinney could provide insights and a perspective different from the stars of those Super Bowl teams.

"Bradshaw is still a star, Swann is still a star, Joe Greene is still a star, Franco is still a star," said Grossman. "They really haven't had to do the things most of us have had to do to move on in our lives."

I asked more questions regarding their relationships with Noll because I wanted to focus on him more now that he had concluded his career with the Steelers. I am not convinced, however, for what it's worth, that Noll will not coach again somewhere in the NFL, or a college or prep school. His wife, Marianne, was not thrilled when I told her my theory about Chuck's comeback.

I went to North Carolina State University to learn more about Bill Cowher, the 34-year-old defensive coordinator of the Kansas City Chiefs and the kid out of Crafton, just outside the city limits, who had come back home to become the coach of the Steelers. He had left his mark and many friends on the Raleigh campus where he had been a gung-ho collegian. There was never any question that he was from Pittsburgh and that he rooted for the Steelers.

Cowher is careful to tell people he is not in Pittsburgh to replace Chuck Noll. He came back to coach the Steelers. It should be an interesting challenge. I signed a copy of *Doing It Right* and gave it to him as a welcoming gift. I thought it might help him understand the mystique of one of the greatest sports teams in history.

We can all learn something from the success stories and the not-so-successful stories of the Steelers.

When Worley got into trouble with drugs, Rooney scolded a generation in *Steelers Digest* when he said, "It begins with parents and how they raise their children. It begins in athletics in high school, where high schools have to realize those kids are not just athletes but also students.

"When you go to college, colleges have to realize athletes are students and they have to not only graduate them but also educate the whole person.

"Then in the pros, we pay them significant money. Maybe we should look at the situation to see how we can guide these young men so they realize they have a long life ahead, and they have a lot of people counting on them.

"All of us in society, including the media, have a responsibility to handle the situation properly.

"Everyone is responsible for his own actions. But this situation, as far as the impact on our society and our young people, causes us to reflect on what we can do."

With all that went wrong for the club in 1991, it is important to keep things in perspective. So many former Steelers are doing well in their "life's work" and have been good role models. The Rooneys and club officials don't want to see the team's image tarnished, or spoiled.

The Steelers weren't the only team in town that experienced problems in 1991 and 1992. The Pirates and Penguins both won championships, only to see financial difficulties and shakeups in the front-office and loss of star players, take the gloss off their great seasons. The Pitt athletic department, as well as the school at large, had a difficult period. Duquesne and Robert Morris were on the rebound from bad times. So the Steelers had lots of company in a distressed market.

Going back and interviewing some of the best of the best reaffirmed the positive feelings I have always had about the Steelers. Some of them have slipped for sure, some have just gotten old and gray, but they all had their day in the sun, and they still shine when they reflect on their seasons with the Steelers.

Even with all the problems, the Steelers are still special in many respects, and worthy of our study as well as our affection and admiration. Relive the glory days! Enjoy, enjoy those magic moments we all shared as Steeler fans.

Former light-heavyweight boxing champion Billy Conn, at left, entertains Art Rooney and Sam Davis during visit to Steelers' clubhouse. Conn, known as "The Pittsburgh Kid," was one of Rooney's all-time favorites.

Sam Davis
"I'm proud of being a Steeler."

"I'll be alright. I'm gonna make it. That's what being a Steeler is all about, right? That's what being a person is all about."

—Sam Davis, 1992

S am Davis was lying flat on his back on a bed, fully clothed but without any covers, in Room 503 of the Allegheny Neuropsychiatric Institute. A nurse announced that he had a visitor, and Sam smiled when he saw me coming through the door.

"Hey, howya doin'?" he asked. "Geez, it's good to see you, my friend. It's been too long. Howya been doin'?"

He smiled once more. It would be the last time he would smile during my hour-long visit.

He stood up and shook my hand, and held onto it for awhile. I was relieved that he recognized me right away. He looked much better than I had expected, even though he seemed smaller than when I had last seen him. He certainly looked smaller than when he played right guard for the Pittsburgh Steelers for 13 seasons, from 1967 through 1979.

He tried to play in 1980 and again in 1981, but had to give up the ghost. His knees gave out before his desire did. He was 37 when he retired. He was 46 when I called on him in mid-January of 1992 at ANI.

Seeing him sedated, so docile, it was hard to picture him pulling out of the line and leading the way for Franco Harris and Rocky Bleier on an end sweep.

He smiled less. The Sam Davis I knew always seemed to smile through an entire conversation. He had a glow about him. There was sunshine in his smile, a warmth to his voice, a compassion for his fellow man. To me, he had always been the wise old owl of the Steelers, someone who could explain the personalities and nuances of his teammates. He was kind of like a counselor, a father confessor, when I covered the club in his last two years with the team. He provided insights into the Steelers. He always had that reassuring smile.

But that was before his accident. Before his alleged bad fall. "Or whatever happened to him," as teammate Mel Blount put it. Or, as Sam's mother-in-law said, "It's still a mystery to me."

Sam supposedly took a bad fall in his home, and was KOd in the process. His wife, Tammy Davis, found him when she returned home after being away for a weekend. That was how it was reported in the Pittsburgh newspapers, but it never washed with me. I never thought the story rang true.

Rumors were making the rounds at Three Rivers Stadium that Davis had been beaten up for failing to pay off some business loans, but Sam insists that isn't so.

"There's no way he fell down the steps," said Blount. "Sam is too much of an athlete to get hurt like that in a fall down the stairs of his home. He knows how to roll, or how to break his fall.

"I saw him soon after he was taken to the hospital, and he had bruises and marks all over his body. His injuries were severe. He may never see right again. I've talked about it with some of the other guys, and we're certain Sam got beat up. I don't think you'd get any argument there. We think Sam must have borrowed some money for his business from some unworthy people, and they came to collect on the debt. Who did it? That's the big question. Someone who wanted to give him a message.

"The first time I went to see him, they had him on a dyalysis machine because his kidneys weren't functioning properly. I'll bet he got kicked pretty good."

Actually, I felt better when I saw Sam myself, and when he spoke to me. I had feared the worst based on conversations I had with his wife, Tammy, and with some of his former teammates who had been to visit him earlier in his convalescence. When his wounds were fresh, when his words were more difficult to come by. When he was hooked up to machines.

Then, too, in a lobby outside his room, I had come across about five or six other patients, and they appeared to be in a zombie-like state. Some just stared. One man was bent over badly and leaning against a wall. An old woman was distorted and slumped over in a wheel chair. Was Sam in this kind of shape? That's what I wondered as I walked past them and toward his room.

The treatment center, located in Oakdale, about 10 miles west of downtown Pittsburgh, just off the Parkway West which takes you to the Greater Pittsburgh International Airport, is an attractive place. It is a satellite facility of Allegheny General Hospital on Pittsburgh's North Side. Its appearance is clean and orderly. Its staff friendly, but firm. Its security is tight. I had been okayed for a visit by Sam's wife. I came during the regular visiting hours. While I was there, I appeared to be the only visitor on the floor.

Sam had been hospitalized for over four months, first at Allegheny General, then at Allegheny Neuropsychiatric Institute, or ANI as it's called, then The Rehabilitation Institute in Squirrel Hill, and back to ANI.

"They were having some behavior problems with him at The Rehabilitation Institute," Tammy had told me over the telephone. "He was getting agitated easily, and real confused. They were spending too much time trying to calm him down. So they sent him back to ANI. He's on medication and he seems to be coming along.

"The last couple of days he's been down and quiet, not as cheery as before. He needs to get back to rehab again."

Back on September 9, 1991, Sam said he had taken a terrible fall down a hillside at his 55-acre farm in Zelienople, and perhaps a subsequent one down the stairs of his nearby home when he returned there,

11

still groggy from the first mishap. It's difficult to determine exactly what happened. He told me he had struck his head against a tree stump, in any case, and doctors said he had suffered neurological, or brain damage. His memory was selective. He strained to see some things, and what he saw didn't always register right in his mind. His mind didn't always see the same thing his eyes saw, as Tammy explained it.

Frankly, I was surprised by how much he remembered. He apparently had been more battered and bruised a few months back, but had healed in the interim. He was so much better than I expected. But Tammy and John Banaszak, one of his teammates, had both told me Sam still thought he was playing football.

"He still thinks he's playing for the Steelers," said Tammy.

"Eventually, when I get well, I'll be able to do the things I did before," Sam told me at ANI, looking me straight in the eyes. "I want to play football again. The Steelers need me."

Many thoughts were going through my mind as I drove my car out to see Sam at ANI. I had mistakenly gone to Allegheny General Hospital, which is located midway between Three Rivers Stadium and the H.J. Heinz Company, where Davis — naturally No. 57 — had played ball and worked during most of his lengthy stint with the Steelers.

Before that, I had dropped off my daughter, Sarah, at the Music Department at Duquesne University, where she spent Saturday afternoons practicing with the Three Rivers Youth Symphony. She had been a cellist with the all-state orchestra the year before, and was back in similar competitive auditions again. This was her Super Bowl build-up.

I had told Sarah, then an 18-year-old high school senior, that I was going to visit Sam Davis, and talk to him for my next book about the Steelers, and I told her about his predicament. "Why do you want to interview him?" she asked. "Isn't that kind of cruel?"

Her comment caught me off guard. As an old friend, I felt sorry for Sam Davis. I wished he hadn't been hurt. I had prayed for his recovery. As a writer, I wanted to see him, and I wanted to talk to him, and I wanted to write about what had happened to a man, a special man at that, who had distinguished himself so valiantly for so many seasons with the Steelers when they were the best team in the National Football League, indeed, one of the greatest teams in sports history. How the mighty had fallen. It was a story, a sad story, but it could provide a lesson. And it is my hope that he will recover.

But Sarah's words stayed with me, and haunted me somewhat. As a journalist, my natural instinct was to observe and write about things that interested me. I remember that soon after I began an internship as a city-side reporter at *The Pittsburgh Press* in the summer of 1962, when I was 20, I watched an autopsy of a woman at the City morgue. I watched as a doctor from the coroner's office drew a scapel across the top of the woman's stomach, and lifted her chest back, like a large flap, toward her head. And I didn't flinch. I felt like a medical intern rather than a newspaper intern. But it was the beginning of a professional career of standing back and watching and writing about the human condition: the good, the bad, the ugly.

Seeing Sam in such sad shape was also a sobering experience. Sometimes we never realize how well off we are at times, how fortunate we are, and how so much can be taken away from us so fast. No matter how strong you are, no matter how much weight you can lift, no matter how many giants you can knock on their backsides, you can be struck down so fast you don't know what hit you.

I was listening to the radio as I drove the Parkway West toward Oakdale. In my youth, I knew Oakdale only as a Nike missile site. That was back in the days of bomb shelters and Civil Defense signs on street corners and inside buildings. Now I was going there to see how Sam Davis was doing at an extended care facility on Old Steubenville Pike. just down the road from Hankey Farms, across the road from the Fort Pitt Motel.

I was listening to stories about Muhammad Ali, who had turned 50 years old the day before. I had watched some TV features about Ali the night before, reflections and film highlights of his storied career, and it had brought back some special memories. I had never met or interviewed anybody quite like Muhammad Ali. He was larger than life.

During a nine-year stint as a sportswriter for *The New York Post* (1970-1979), I had covered many of Muhammad Ali's championship fights from ringside, especially the ones with Joe Frazier at Madison Square Garden. I had spent time at his training camps, slept in the same room as his trainer Angelo Dundee on the eve of one of his fights, and regarded it as a special time in my life.

I had been to Ali's 21st birthday party, back in 1963 when he was called Cassius Clay, which was held in the Sherwyn Hotel in downtown Pittsburgh a week before he was fighting Charlie Powell at the Civic Arena. He KOd Powell in the third round. I remembered how Clay kept calling Myron Cope "Mickey Rooney" at that press conference. The Sherwyn is now the main building of Point Park College on Wood Street at the Boulevard of the Allies.

Clay, or Ali, had first come to Pittsburgh during my junior year as a student at the University of Pittsburgh. It hardly seemed possible that 29 years had passed since then. Ali, at 50, had been suffering from Parkinson's Syndrome for several years, and spoke slowly, and not always lucidly, in recent interviews I had seen and heard. Time and too many blows to the head had not been kind to him, though he was still a handsome, nearly unmarked, fellow.

There was also much talk on TV and on the radio about the upcoming Super Bowl contest between the Buffalo Bills and the Washington Redskins, which was a week away.

That brought other Super Bowls to mind, ones I had covered when I was working for *The Miami News, The New York Post* and later with *The Pittsburgh Press.*

It had been 12 years since the Steelers had last played in a Super Bowl. They had beaten the Los Angeles Rams, 31-19, at the Rose Bowl

13

in Pasadena, California on January 20, 1980. It was their fourth Super Bowl triumph in a six-year span.

As I was driving to see Sam Davis, the sun was shining bright on a rare winter's day in Pittsburgh. The temperature was about ten degrees, but the wind chill factor made it feel like 17 below. The sun was shining every day, or so it seemed anyhow, 12 years earlier when the Steelers were staying in Newport Beach, California before Super Bowl XIV. The Steelers worked out at a nearby college football field.

I still have photographs from one of those workouts. I had taken most of them, and given my camera to a crony to snap one of me with one of my favorite Steelers — Sam Davis. I took pictures of the Steelers when they were between posing for an official NFL team photo. It's more casual than the official one. I caught a few of Chuck Noll smiling as he faded back to toss a football playfully. It was not your normal Noll photo, where he always seems so dour and serious. No, this was a fun time in his life and in the lives of the Steelers.

Could it have been 12 years earlier? Sarah was seven when she spent a night with me at the Steelers' training camp, the same season they won their fourth Super Bowl, the final pro season of Sam Davis.

Banaszak had been there, and he had prepared me for the worst. "It was awful difficult," he said of seeing Sam Davis after his accident. "He was just physically beat up. Emotionally, I was spent.

"When I walked in, he recognized me the first time. The second time he didn't recognize me. Another time he recognized me. He went to a therapy session and he came back and he didn't recognize me.

"I felt I was close to him; I thought he was close to everyone on the team. He was someone you could talk to if you had questions. He was someone you respected. He was one of the finest competitors around.

"I saw him last summer at a few golf tournaments, including my own. I thought he looked super. He looked ten years younger than his age. Now he looks 20 years older. It was just a terrible shock to see him."

Sam Davis sat on the edge of his bed in Room 503 of the Allegheny Neuropsychiatric Hospital. The room was sparsely furnished, spartan and Spic 'n Span clean. It reminded me of the room he had shared with teammate Jon Kolb at St. Vincent College in Latrobe when they were playing for the Pittsburgh Steelers.

Davis wore a gray sweater with wide horizontal red and yellow stripes across his still-broad chest. He wore stone-washed gray denim jeans, dark blue fuzzy wool socks, and blue-gray slippers. All very neat.

His hair was cut closer than I had ever remembered seeing it, and there were nicks and bruises about his forehead, skin discoloration spots. There was a lump and a bad bruise under his right eye. He looked like and spoke like a club boxer who had remained in the ring too long.

His hands were dry and chalky in appearance and he kept them clasped in his lap. He kept saying, "Yes, sir," when I would say something, or ask him questions. "Yes, sir." When he did this, he

Sam Davis and Ron Johnson ham it up at Newport Beach, California.

Line coach Rollie Dotsch and Sam Davis at Super Bowl XIV practice.

reminded me of the kids at the Mel Blount Youth Home who had been instructed to respond that way to their elders.

I mentioned to Sam that I had recently been with John Brown, who had been an offensive lineman with the Steelers when Davis first joined the team. Brown was now a PNB executive. He had retired in 1972. Brown told me he didn't go to see Davis because he didn't think he could bear it. Later, they would get together for lunch.

"If he can be quicker, he can make it," Davis told me, as if John Brown were still playing tackle for the Steelers. "Lookit what Rocky did. I'm going back after this year."

I brought along a copy of my book about the Steelers called *Doing It Right,* and showed Sam pictures from the book. When I heard about Sam getting hurt, I had wondered why I had not interviewed him at length for a chapter in my first book about the Steelers. He had, after all, always provided me with such insights into his fellow players. He had always been a pleasure to interview. He did a good job of identifying most of the players even though he seemed to be straining, and poking his head into the book to get as close as possible to the black and white images I put before him.

"He can see extra large print," said Tammy. "He complains about darkness. The eyes can see but the mind is not telling him what he sees. He might see a lamp and say it's a coat rack."

As I scanned the book for him, he mistook L.C. Greenwood for Joe Greene in one photo, and the statue of Art Rooney for Terry Bradshaw. But he correctly identified a shot of Bradshaw, as well as ones of Blount, Jack Lambert and Franco Harris.

He knew I was testing him and sometimes he grew impatient, and he questioned what I was doing with a raised voice. After he had told me he was eager to get well so he could get back to playing for the Steelers, I asked him, "Do you think you can win the Super Bowl again?"

He snapped back, "Why are you saying 'you' when you ask me that? I'm not the Steelers. Yes, sir, I think the Steelers can win it again."

I had been advised that it would be good to ask him questions, to help bring back the past.

"It's like trying to bring back thoughts and memories of someone cooking a pork roast for you," said Sam. "As soon as you smell it, even 20 years later, you'll remember what it tasted like."

I thought that was a pretty sound observation for someone who was having recall problems.

"Every so often there are glimpses of memories about his business involvements," Tammy told me, "but much of his memory centers around football. He'll say, 'I'm OK. I'll be ready to play Saturday.' His memory is mostly about football."

To help restore his memory, somebody had posted a four-inch wide white paper banner around the top of the ceiling of Room 503, like a paper molding at the top of two of the walls, with events and dates hand-printed with a Magic Marker pen.

It read like this:

1944 — Born July 4
1962 — Graduated Northwestern High
1963 — Married Thomasina Kelly
1965 — Tonya Born
1967 — March Divorced Thomasina
1967 — Graduated from Allen University
1967 — July Married Gladys
1967 — Vanessa Born
1969 — Tammy Born
1979 — Divorced Gladys
1981 — Began working at Heinz
1982 — Retired from Steelers
1983 — Opened "Only Happiness" Card-Gift Shops
1985 — Married Tammy Oct. 13
1986 — Began Sam Davis Construction
1986 — Began Sam Davis Group
1986 — Ruel Born August 4
1988 — Samantha Born May 7
1989 — Dorothy Born July 14
1990 — Sam Davis Construction Out of Business
1991 — Found Injured At Bottom of Stairs Sept. 9
1991 — In Allegheny General Hospital Sept. 9 - Oct. 15
1991 — Admitted to The Rehabilitation Institute Oct. 15

Some people, as I've said, have suspected foul play was involved in the injuries suffered by Sam Davis. They speculate that Sam may have borrowed money for some of his construction and corrugated box business, and was unable to meet his debts. They believe he was beaten up to teach him a lesson.

"I know people are saying things," said Sam during our stay, "but let me tell you what happened . . . Three men came to my house. They had been at my house before, with Jerry Parker, about buying boxes. It was during the evening, around six o'clock. There's a big park near my land that used to be used for hunting, but it's illegal now. You've been there."

I had never been there, but I just nodded.

"They said they wanted me to show them where the deer were on my farm. I told them I didn't want anybody taking any guns out, or shooting anything. I thought they had left their guns in the car.

"We started up a hill, and all of a sudden three deer appeared ahead of us. They started shooting. I was between them and the deer, and they weren't more than 10 feet behind me. I thought they were going to hit me. They did more than scare me. I was afraid I'd get hit. I thought I might get shot. So I jumped out of the way. I fell down a hill, and I hit my head on a tree stump.

"They helped me get back to the house. I didn't know what was going on around me. I couldn't figure out what happened. I thought I was OK. They didn't think I was hurt that bad, and they left. Later, I fell down the stairs into the basement of my home."

Who found you there?

"I found myself there. I thought I'd be OK. I was always able to work through pain. I learned that playing for the Steelers. My wife came home and we went to Allegheny General Hospital. That's what I remember."

John Banaszak had been to see Sam Davis several times. And I knew that Jon Kolb, his former roommate, had been to see Sam several times since he got banged up. I had heard that Mel Blount and J.T. Thomas had been to see him. Some other former teammates had told me they felt badly that they hadn't been out to see him, that they should, that they would. They winced when they said it. Some said that, after hearing what others had said about seeing him, they didn't want to go because they didn't think they could handle it.

Sam Davis didn't want to get into names. That wasn't important, he said. "I don't want to talk about who comes to see me. Players have donated finances to my wife to help pay the bills," he said.

"I had three different businesses of my own. People think there might have been a problem because I lived in the ghetto earlier on. I lived in the tough black district, out in East Liberty, for 12 years. People probably just think a lot of people are trying to hurt me."

Anybody who has ever met Sam Davis would have a difficult time believing that anybody would want to hurt him, unless they were lining up against him in an NFL battle. Certainly his former teammates would have a tough time thinking of anyone who would want to do harm to him.

"I've been fortunate to do more things for them than they might have ever expected," Sam said of his teammates. "I did it just because I love them. If a player called me now, I'd do anything to get out of here and go help them.

"I look at business as I look at people. I look at business as I look at one of my best friends. I'm trying to help people. I like to work with them. Business is about how you perform with each other."

I mentioned to Sam that Chuck Noll had recently announced his retirement.

"I think Chuck Noll will come back," he said. "He is a coach, and he ought to be coaching. I have all the respect in the world for him. I have all the respect in the world for the Steelers.

"He's never ever not going to be confident. He works hard at what he does, and he makes sure he does whatever he needs to do to survive. That's how all of us should work.

"I wanted to say everything I could say — from the bottom of my heart — about how great the team is. There's no team better than the

George Gojkovich

Sam Davis (57) looks to block for Rocky Bleier (20) between Terry Bradshaw (12) and Franco Harris (32).

Bill Amatucci

With line coach Dan Radakovich.

Davis leads the way on end sweep by Franco Harris.

Steelers. You take Art Rooney; he's like God to me. That's the way I feel. The fans are the best. I love them."

Davis saw a photo of Terry Bradshaw, and it sparked some thoughts. "He's a pro," said Sam. "He's stronger than most people give him credit for. Before a game, he always helped get us ready. Everybody was trying to do what they can to protect Bradshaw, to give him time to throw.

"Bradshaw was bright. He was born and raised in the country and he had an outlook that was different from most people. He was looking for certain things to happen, that even the coaches can't relate to. The coaches had other ideas. They did a good job with the way they trained him.

"He wanted to get the ball and drop back about ten yards, and the coaches said 'Two steps, that's it!' They got on the same page. Just look at the record.

"Terry's got a heart. If I wanted anything, he'd find a way to get it to me. If I wanted $5,000, he'd give me $10,000 to help me. All the players would.

"The whole team has shown me interest. The coaches, the whole staff, the owners. The organization has been good to me. They want me to get well. They're talking to me, hoping I'm doing well. They're doing what they can do to help me get well again. So I can get strong, so I can play ball."

I remembered that Sam was brought up in the Baptist religion, and I asked him if he prayed much for his recovery.

"I do that every day," he said. "As many minutes as there are in a day, I try and pray."

I asked him if he had learned anything through his association with sports and the Steelers that served him in good stead in his bout to get well again.

"I just feel like Sam Davis, the person, right now," he said. "Eventually, once I get well, and am able to do the things I can do, I want to play football again.

"I take pride in being a Steeler," he said. "Not because I was the captain, or a team leader. I was just proud that they took enough courage and enough interest in me to let me play for them."

I had heard that Bill Nunn Jr., who had gone from being a sports editor with *The Pittsburgh Courier* to becoming a full-time scout for the Steelers, was primarily responsible for bringing Sam to the Steelers.

"He came to sign me," said Davis. "He did a good job of convincing me I could play pro football."

Occasionally, one of the patients would holler out from the room on the other side of Sam's door. It didn't seem to bother Sam. "They're all my friends," he said. "They all know I play for the Steelers."

Sam Davis remembers one of the best moments of his youth. "It's when I got my first bicycle," he said during my hour-long visit at ANI. "I think I was about four years old. It had training wheels on the back of it. My parents got it for me for Christmas. I was so excited."

Davis was the only child of Ruel and Irene Davis. His father worked in the construction business. He was a tile mason. "My mother worked for the city and for the county," said Sam. "She was in maid service for awhile, and then she got involved in education programs.

"I started tagging along with my father when I was very young, maybe seven or eight years old, and stayed with him all the way through high school. My father found lots of things for me to do, whether it was picking up pieces of wood, or helping clean up, whatever. I liked working with my father, just like I like playing football."

Sam was born and raised in Ocilla, Georgia. His full name is Ruel Sam Davis. The family moved to Jacksonville, Florida, but Sam returned each year to work on an uncle's farm in Georgia. So, after his days with the Steelers, he went back to what he knew as a child — construction and farming.

"I first went out for football when I was in the tenth grade, but I quit the team," he told me in an interview back when I was covering the Steelers for *The Pittsburgh Press*. I still have the typewritten notes on two time-yellowed pages in my files.

"I thought the guys were too big, too tough. But I came back the next year."

He was small, at 5-11, and weighing 180 pounds as a senior in high school. A coach from Allen University in Columbia, South Carolina came through looking at another player. He was semi-interested in Sam before his senior season. "If he's that interested and motivated after the season," said the recruiter, "he could be useful."

So Sam ended up at Allen, where there were about 900 students at a small NAIA school. "I had a 50-50 scholarship," said Sam. "I worked for half of it, and played for half of it. I've stayed with that program the rest of my life, it seems. I've always been involved with some type of work outside of sports."

Davis, who was No. 57, was a natural to work for the H. J. Heinz Company and help peddle some of its 57 varieties. He worked with Heinz for eight years on a part-time basis before taking a full-time job upon retirement from the Steelers.

"At Allen, I did a lot of dirty work. I kept the halls clean, like a janitor, and took out garbage from the school cafeteria. I received no special privileges. About 300 people came to see most of our games. 1500 was a big crowd.

"So you can imagine how fortunate I felt when I was playing for the Pittsburgh Steelers. I was so damn happy to be with the Steelers. I was just glad to have made the big time. I had never been to a pro game in my life — only what I saw on TV — and all of a sudden I was there, in it. My concept was different from a guy who came from the Big 10, and was a top draft choice. I wanted them to know that I was just as good as they were.

"At first, I was just concerned about Sam Davis and Sam Davis being there. About my third year, I was more concerned about the team, and that's when Chuck Noll came along. It got different in a hurry."

When he was playing for the Steelers, he was still undersized as pro guards go, at 6-1, 255, but he was smart and agile, and perfect for Noll's trap-blocking schemes, for getting out ahead of Harris and Bleier and throwing blocks on end sweeps, and for standing tall and keeping bigger bodies away from Bradshaw on passing downs.

"Other people helped me," he said. "When I first arrived here, I didn't know much about technique. I had speed and guts and I didn't care what happened to me."

Late in his career with the Steelers, after he had cashed some Super Bowl checks, he bought a 55-acre farm in Zelienople. "I'm just a country boy at heart," he said then.

He was looking forward to a record-tying 14th season with the Steelers, but wrecked his knee in the pre-season finale at Dallas in 1980 and was finished as a player.

He was attempting a comeback the next year when we spoke. "I'm very positive about everything I do," he said. "A lot of things happen to you, I don't care how bad they are. But that's when it's time to work hard and go after it. I came to this team trying to make it, and if I leave trying to make it I'll be no worse off."

For most of his 13 seasons with the Steelers, Sam set a tone for the rest of the team to follow. He was known as "Tight Man" or simply "Tight." L.C. Greenwood, who was good at that sort of thing, pinned the nickname on him with a simple explanation. "Tight? . . . he keeps us together."

Once asked about his role with the team, Sam said, "An offensive lineman has to be strong inwardly as well as outwardly. There are things people don't see that enter into it. The frustration comes from many directions. You might be in pass protection, for instance, nullifying your man. The man might be slapping you upside your helmet, or grabbing your jersey and doing a lot of illegal things. But you can't lose your head. You have to keep your proper position and worry about technique, not the other man — even if he pulls your face mask.

"You can't let it get to you, and let it affect you. A defensive lineman loves to see an offensive lineman frustrated. To keep him off balance, you have to have control and confidence and be cool. You want to strike out, but you can't."

One of the highlights of Sam's career was the way he capped off a great 1978 season by nullifying Randy White of the Dallas Cowboys in the Super Bowl.

"To me, the Super Bowls were the worst of times. We had to be ready; that was pressure time. There was no tomorrow. We hadn't won that Super Bowl game yet; it still had to be done. The most competitive thing was playing in the Super Bowl."

Davis once discussed a problem many pro athletes have in adjusting to their post-playing days for a story in *The Pittsburgh Press*.

"College and professional athletes," he said, "are realy not aware of what people do for a living. They are put on a pedestal early in life, and looked after as long as they can play. It starts with the pampering, the special treatment, the recruiting, the scholarships, people doing favors for you, the things they do for athletes while they're in school. In some ways, athletes always have it easy.

"Most men have played some type of sports in their lifetime, and women are getting more involved these days. They can realize just how hard it is to be good in sports. There is respect for the athlete in that area, but from a business proposition there is not. Most people can't relate to the kind of money athletes are making these days.

"On the other hand, many athletes don't know what other people are making when they start out on jobs, and how long it takes to earn a significant salary. Athletes should prepare for their 'life's work,' as Chuck Noll puts it, while they are playing. You may have to put in a 16-to-20 hour work day to get anything done. Most athletes train hard, but they're not used to putting in that many hours a day. They should understand that when they go looking for jobs, people won't care what position they played. They'll want to know what they can do.

"Athletes can make the best businessmen available. In order to be successful at anything, you have to compete and be dedicated. If the athlete will just apply those things to other areas, he can succeed."

During the eight years that Davis worked part-time for Heinz, he had a hectic schedule in the off-season. "During the first four years, I lived out of a suitcase," he said. "I was all over the place every day for five months a year. It was crazy."

Maybe Sam should have stayed at H.J. Heinz, where his prospects looked good. But he wanted to go into business for himself, and he, unfortunately, had several business ventures go belly up on him.

It was time to say goodbye. Sam invited me to sit for awhile with his friends, and fellow patients, in the lobby area. I declined, as I was checking my watch, and had to get back to pick up my daughter Sarah after her rehearsal at Duquesne University.

"I'll be alright," Sam assured me. "I'm gonna make it. That's what being a Steeler is all about, right? That's what being a person is all about. You're not a Steeler and you have those qualities."

He gave me a great big bear hug in the hallway. "Thanks for your love," he said. "I love you."

John Banaszak
"I enjoyed every minute of it."

Cleveland Stadium is a special place, an aging sports shrine, a theatre for only the toughest breed of men, and it means even more to John Banaszak. For him, a native son, it is still a thing of beauty, an old-time ballpark that always brought out the best in him, and still brings back the best of memories. It's his Field of Dreams.

"Cleveland Stadium has character," observed Banaszak.

He first went there as a boy of seven or eight, clutching the firm hand of his father, Chester Banaszak, a Cleveland millworker who loved sports, and regularly took his son to see the Browns play football and the Indians play baseball. John cherishes the pictures that his mind draws for him even today.

Banaszak came back to Cleveland Stadium as a defensive lineman for the much-hated Pittsburgh Steelers, indeed, a member of the vaunted Steel Curtain Defense, from 1975 through 1981. And no one rooted for him more than his father and the Banaszak family, nearly heretical behavior because the Browns had always been their team.

"People are critical of Cleveland Stadium, and say it's ugly, a relic, and that it's outlived its usefulness," said Banaszak. "They knock the field, the facilities, the clubhouse, how cold it is when the wind and snow blow in off Lake Erie, those unruly fans in the endzone. It's always had a bad rap. But I always had a special feeling for the place.

"When I was a kid, I saw some great football teams there. I was at the National Football League championship game with my dad in 1964 and saw Frank Ryan throw four touchdown passes to Gary Collins as the Browns beat the Colts, 28-0. In 1968, I saw the Browns lose (34-0) to the Colts in the NFL title game when the winner would go to Super Bowl III. The Colts lost to the Jets in the Super Bowl that year. Jimmy Brown was the star in Cleveland back then. But the Browns, all of them, Vince Costello, Ross Fichtner, Bill Glass, John Wooten and Gene Hickerson, I loved them all."

Cleveland Stadium is where his love affair for football and for his father all began. "In my first game as a pro at Cleveland Stadium," said Banaszak, "I bought 49 tickets for family and friends. I was only making $17,000 as a rookie. You divide that by 16 games, and I don't think I made much money playing football that day. But it was worth it.

"It was quite an experience going into Cleveland Stadium and lining up against the Cleveland Browns before 80,000 fans. We had some tough games there. I enjoyed every minute of every game I ever attended or played in at Cleveland Stadium."

Of course, Banaszak could also say that about Three Rivers Stadium and just about every stadium in the National Football League. None of the Steelers played the game with any more zest or joy than John Banaszak.

24

Chester Banaszak with his son, John, in 1980.

The real Banaszak Bunch includes, left to right, Carrie, John, Mary, Jay and Amye at Christmas, 1991.

At 6-3, 244, not especially big for a lineman, he played behind Dwight White at the defensive right end position, for the most part, then shared the spot with White, and finally succeeded him there. Both played the game with great gusto.

Banaszak was popular in Pittsburgh. He's a big teddy bear of a fellow, full of fun, and he laughs easily. There was "The Banaszak Bunch" who brought banners to celebrate their favorite player. Pittsburghers liked his looks, the locks of dark brown hair he had to sweep off his brow, his style, his smile. He should have brought a lunchpail to the game. In every sense, he was a millworker. His dad worked for Lincoln Electric, and John worked for the Pittsburgh Steelers.

"Maybe they like me because I'm Polish," he said back them. "Being Polish is pretty important to me. I didn't have any choice in the matter, though. Both my parents are Polish. My grandparents immigrated to America from Poland, from a place near Warsaw."

Whenever he sacked a quarterback or hit a running back for a big loss, Banaszak really got excited and did what teammate Jon Kolb called "the Banaszak dance."

Banaszak never blushed about his reputation. "I play with a lot of emotion and enthusiasm," he told us midway through his seven seasons with the Steelers. He made the team the hard way, as a free agent from Eastern Michigan in 1975, and he was just happy to be a part of the program. "That's the way I've always played games," he explained.

"We're well-prepared and I'm going to have fun and enjoy it to the outmost. To me, it's still a kids' game. To me, Sunday is the fun day, when it's not so much a business as it is during practice. I want to be involved in it."

He played behind some much ballyhooed people for the better part of his career with the club, but seized every opportunity to shine. "Everyone on our defensive line can play football, and they can play it with the Steelers. So we must be pretty good," he said at training camp in the summer of 1979. "When your chance comes, you better prove you can do it. I got a chance in my second year when both Joe Greene and Dwight White got hurt."

He had some big moments in critical victories over Houston with an interception and several sacks during that 1979 season. He had a sack in Super Bowl XIV against the LA Rams to cap off that season. At the outset of that same year, at the climax of the previous campaign, he made a key fumble recovery on the first series of Super Bowl XIII against the Dallas Cowboys. So the rings remind him of some magic moments.

Though he was bypassed in the 1975 college draft, Banaszak was approached by five different NFL teams when he completed his career and graduated from Eastern Michigan.

"People told me I was crazy when I signed with the Steelers," said Banaszak. "They said, 'Hey, they just won the Super Bowl. They're loaded. Why don't you sign with the Lions? They need help. Or the Giants? They're awful. Or the Bills or the Patriots? Your chances are better.' But I thought I'd get an honest look in Pittsburgh.

"I can remember calling my father up to tell him I had signed with the Steelers. He knew I had talked to five teams altogether. I called him to let him know what my decision was.

"There was a silence on the phone for a minute or so. For the next ten minutes, I was shouted at and berated. You couldn't believe what I was hearing. How could I do this? How could I do this to him, and to all our relatives, our cousins, to everyone in Cleveland? How could he go to work on Monday? He would be ripped apart at work. It was like I was a traitor. On and on he went.

"I don't know if I got to say anything else or not. Finally, he said, 'OK, you made the decision. I guess I'm going to have to become a Steeler fan.' And he did. He made the weekly trip to see me play whenever it was at all possible. He couldn't make it to Pittsburgh for Monday night games, because of his work schedule, but that was about it.

"My father and Jack Ham's father became good friends. They were both Polish, and they were both so proud of their sons. I used to help my dad deliver coal at night in our neighborhood, just like Jack did with his dad in Johnstown. So we had a lot in common. They really enjoyed the Steelers' scene. They were big shots. That made me feel good. I provided my dad, my parents, with some enjoyment."

Banaszak spoke of his father on several occasions during my visit to his home in early January of 1992. Every time he did, I heard a hint of a break in his voice, like he was going to get choked up if he continued.

When he showed me all the framed photos he had on the walls on his basement office, Banaszak gave me some background. "Is that your dad?" I asked when I saw one photo, showing a proud man with his arm draped over John's shoulder. It was, indeed. John pointed out the Super Bowl ring on his father's hand.

"He had my first ring. Now my son Jay has it; he and my dad were very close."

Again, there was a break in Banaszak's voice. "He died a short while back," he began. "Geez, it was five years ago this month. We all miss him a lot."

Next to that photo was one of Bum Phillips, who coached the Houston Oilers during a stretch when they may have been the second best team behind the Steelers in the NFL. Bum was admiring one of John's Super Bowl rings in the photo.

There were photos of Banaszak with Mike Douglas, the TV star, after Banaszak and teammates Roy Gerela and Ray Oldham had won an NFL players' golf event during one of their Super Bowl seasons. "Golf, that's my passion now," bubbled Banaszak. There were photos of special friends on the Steelers, like Steve Furness and Gary Dunn.

"Boy, we had some good times together!" interjected Banaszak. "Moon Mullins and Dunn and I all had the same birthday — August 24. We had some great parties together. It was always a tough practice for us on the 25th."

27

There were photos showing Banaszak sacking or tackling the likes of Rams' quarterback Vince Ferragamo, the Oilers' Earl Campbell, the Browns' Brian Sipe. There were game balls, plaques, more photos, a scrap of one of the banners once brandished by "The Banaszak Bunch," and other memorabilia.

"I'm proud of all my accomplishments with the Steelers," said Banaszak. "All this brings back special memories. It makes this a nice place to go to work every day."

Banaszak is a partner and vice-president of Aeriss, Inc., responsible for marketing ceramic fiber insulation, refractory materials and related commodities to the steel and foundry industries. He operates out of his home office, but he is on the road a lot, out hustling, trying to sell his products.

He says his status as a former Super Bowl Steeler is still a door-opener. "My customers like to talk football with me," he said. "They talk to everyone about the steel business, and they want a break from that. That gives me a distinct advantage over my competition. But today's Steelers' team makes it difficult sometimes to talk about football. So I'm more comfortable answering the usual questions I get: What were Bradshaw or Greene or Lambert and those guys really like?"

Before that, Banaszak had his own business, three quick change motor oil units bearing his name, located in Bethel Park, Robinson Township and the North Hills, but he sold out to Valvoline when he got an offer he couldn't refuse.

Banaszak lives in a handsome home in McMurray, Pa., a suburb in Washington County about 20 miles south of Pittsburgh. On game days, it takes him about an hour to drive to Three Rivers Stadium.

His 18-year-old son Jay, who was attending a prep school, Western Reserve Academy, in Cleveland, was lounging in the family room watching a football game on TV. John's daughters, Carrie, 15, a freshman at nearby Peters Township High School, and Amye, 13, a seventh grader at the local elementary school, were visiting friends.

John's wife, Mary, was at work this day, providing drug counseling for federal inmates in the city in a project she initiated. I remarked to John how neat everything was in his home, after we passed a stairway where sneakers were all lined up in a row. "I cleaned the house today," said Banaszak, positively beaming. "That's my job here every Saturday morning."

At the time of my visit, John and Mary had been married for 20 years. "She was my high school sweetheart," he said. "We were married when I was still in college. Jay was born during my junior year. Mary worked and supported me through those years. After what she'd done for us, it was a great incentive for me to make it as a pro football player after I graduated.

"I'm very proud of my accomplishments. The Steelers gave me an opportunity to play pro football. I was a free agent from a small school, but they gave me a chance. I have to be thankful for that.

"Mary and I come from the same background. We never lived high off the hog even when I was making decent money with the Steelers.

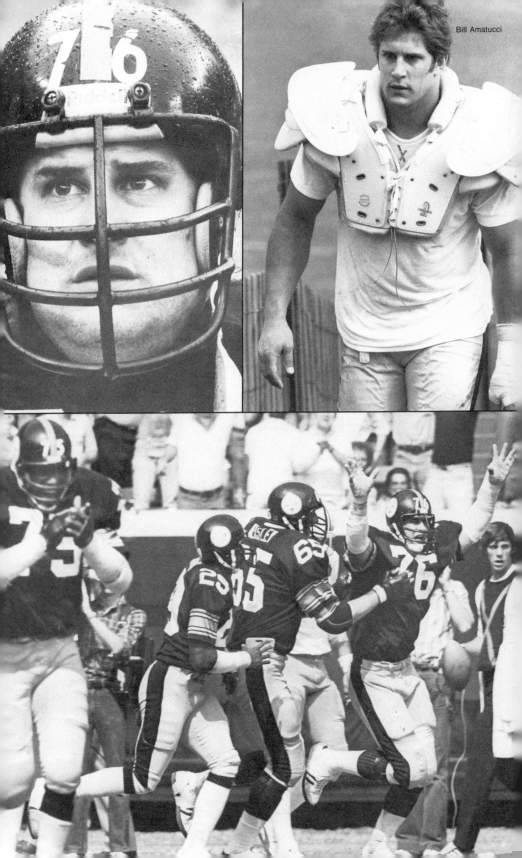

Bill Amatucci

We've never been flashy people. We're happy in our environment.

"We weren't frugal, but we tried to spend our money wisely. I didn't get involved in some of the stuff the other guys got into investment-wise. Some of them got stung pretty good. I lost money on some limited partnerships, just like everyone else. We were more conservative. It's paid off."

I was a little nervous when I first arrived at the Banaszaks' home. There was a big black dog chained in the front yard, and I couldn't pass him on the sidewalk without petting him. He was excited and darting around. He started out licking my hand, then biting at my hand lightly and playfully. He was frisky and friendly, at first, but I feared he might get a little more enthusiastic if I tried to pass him and go to the front door. I could feel his teeth pressing into my hand.

Banaszak came out, much to my gratitude, and talked to the dog. "Don't worry about Max," he assured me. "He's a friendly dog." Yeah, just like John Banaszak, I thought, but look what he did to opposing backs.

So Banaszak has a beautiful family in a beautiful home in the suburbs. Photos of his family members were all over the place.

"I've been very lucky. I remember how awful I felt when I drove home from St. Vincent College when I was cut from the team," he reflected, going back to a dark day in the summer of 1982. "I was so upset. But I was listening to the radio in my car, and that's when I heard the news about Doug Kotar of the Giants having an inoperable brain tumor."

Kotar had grown up in a community near McMurray called Muse, just outside of Canonsburg, and was a fine running back for the New York Giants. Kotar would soon die after a difficult hospital stay. "I had played in football and in softball games with Doug," said Banaszak. "That helped me realize that getting cut from the Steelers wasn't the worst thing in the world. It helped put things in perspective for me."

Cleveland was something John Banaszak had in common with Chuck Noll, his coach with the Pittsburgh Steelers. "We went to rival high schools," said Banaszak. "Chuck went to Benedictine and I went to Holy Name. We'd talk about it during Cleveland week. He'd come in the locker room before we'd play in Cleveland and say to me, 'We're going home this week.' He'd go and see his sister, who lived near the hotel where we stayed on the west side of Cleveland. I'd go home and have some good Polish cooking.

"I always thought I had a good relationship with Chuck. Chuck was always interested in my career outside the locker room. Chuck made it very clear that football was only a passing thing. 'This is not your future,' he'd say. 'This is only a stepping stone.' He talked a lot about it. We all benefitted from his constant reminders.

"My first off-season employment came in 1977 when I was working for the Dart Trucking Company out of Canfield, Ohio, as a sales rep. I wore a business suit to the Stadium one day, and was going to work out after I'd been working at my job all day. He came up to me and said, 'What are you doing?' When I told him I was in the trucking business, he beamed.

"He said, 'Trucking? Hey, when I was with the Browns, I had a job as a sales rep for the entire Cleveland area for a trucking company.' He started telling me about federal trucking regulations and other stuff. I was shocked he knew so much. He was genuinely interested.

"Probably the least known asset that Chuck brought to the Steelers was an interest in our lives beyond the football field. The public has no idea that discussions like that ever occurred. It was encouraging that he had an interest in us like that. If I go to see him today, he still inquires about my activity. When I had a string of quick-change motor oil places, he discussed that with me, too. He was fascinated by the operation. And he was one of my customers.

"When I think about Chuck, I always go back to my rookie year. We were playing the Colts in the first round of the playoffs at Three Rivers. I really thought that was going to be the last game I ever played with the Steelers because of something I did in that game.

"The Colts had a good team. They had Bert Jones and Lydell Mitchell and 'The Sack Pack' and a great defense. We kicked off to them and they drove down to our 35. It was fourth down and three and they're going to punt. Chuck gets everyone on our punt return team together on the sideline and says, 'Let's get after this one and block it.' J.T. Thomas and I had worked on a crossing rush to get their blockers mixed up. We crossed just like it was drawn up, and I got in free. I'm in midair in textbook fashion to block the kick, and I get knocked into the kicker.

"I'm on the 50-yard line and 50,000 fans are hollering. I look next to me and I see a yellow flag by my face. And I could hear Chuck hollering at me, over the voices of 50,000 fans. I wanted to hide under the carpet.

"He's trying to get at me when I come to the sideline and I ran the other way to get away from him. He runs down the sideline at me. He's hollering, 'What are you doing? How'd you do that?' I told him, 'Chuck, I got knocked into the kicker!' He screams back, 'You can't get friggin bumped into the kicker!' I heard him say that. I feel lower than a curb at this time. I'm saying to myself, 'If we lose, it's my fault. I'll be gone by Tuesday, I'm outta here.'

"But we won. That's the game where Andy Russell picked up a fumble and ran 94 yards for a touchdown. Yeah, that's the one where they took a commercial break during Andy's run. Russell and Mansfield have made a living off that story on the banquet circuit.

"I figured I'd get vindicated by watching the game film. I'm thinking he'll apologize to me for the way he hollered at me in the Stadium. Chuck was the special teams coach then, and it was the second play we had to watch on the special teams group. They broke down the film for each group to see what they needed to see and work on.

"Well, we see the play and J.T. Thomas was the guy who knocked me into the kicker. He'd come free, too. I'm waiting for an apology, and

31

Noll hollers out in the dark room, 'You can't get friggin blocked into the kicker.' He said it again. 'Next time, you'll be outta here!' It was like somebody shot ice water up your veins. You just wanted to die.

"Sometimes his expressions spoke louder than words. He could just look at you and melt you. Or he could look at you and instill confidence. I'll always remember that when we were coming off the field at halftime in Super Bowl XIV and we were losing to the LA Rams, 13-10, Chuck was smiling. Like we had them just where we wanted them. That made such an impression on me. He could just look at you and instill confidence stronger than any motivational speech that Lombardi ever gave.

"Chuck never really gave a motivational speech. I'm still waiting for his first motivational speech."

I brought up his personal disappointment over the way he was cut loose by the Steelers at their 1982 summer training camp. He and L.C. Greenwood, who had both started the previous season, were both cut at that camp.

Banaszak had started all 19 games in 1979 and had a streak of starting 42 straight games before he had a hamstring injury. He started 53 of 55 games in his last four seasons with the Steelers. That's why he was startled when he was released.

"L.C. was 34 and I was 32," said Banaszak. "If I go into camp and don't throw a hamstring, maybe I don't get cut. I didn't see any reason I couldn't have made that team. I started the year before. L.C. had a bad knee at that camp. We both worked hard during the off-season to get ready. I thought we were ready."

But if his days as a Steeler came to a crushing close, his start with the Steelers was something special as far as NFL training camps were concerned.

"One of the reasons I signed as a free agent with the Steelers was because I had a college relationship with Woody Widenhofer, one of the Steelers' assistant coaches. He told me, 'I'll see to it that you are in camp at least until the College All-Star Game.' That gave me two weeks to make an impression.

"I knew some guys in college who signed as free agents and they were home in two days.

"I think I had the team made after the 'Oklahoma Drill' the first day, though I didn't know it then. I was ready from Day One."

The 'Oklahoma Drill' used to be one of the highlights of the Steelers' training camp. A defensive lineman would go nose-to-nose with an offensive lineman. A running back followed his blocker through a narrow pit — blocking dummies were laid on their sides to provide a channel to contain the activity — and it was always a real collision course.

"I had to beat out two veteran defensive linemen — Jim Wolf and Charlie Davis — and I didn't know how I'd be accepted if that happened. Both of them were black, and the starting defensive linemen were all black. This was 1975, and there were still rumors about racial problems in pro football. But there was never a problem. I was accepted from the start.

"They kept putting me in the 'Oklahoma Drill' over and over again. They couldn't believe what I was doing. They had me do it eight times, which I was told never happened before.

"That was against other rookies and free agents. The talk was about how I'd fare against the veterans. I went up against Jon Kolb and Gordon Gravelle and Jim Clack and held my ground. Then it was just a matter of if I could play for the special teams. That's what you had to do in those days to stick with the Steelers.

"Chuck gave me a real opportunity. He told us free agents would be taken care of and looked at just like everyone else, and he was good for his word.

"Chuck and his staff treated free agents like equals on the playing field. Their decisions were not made on how much they had invested in a player. Look how many guys were second or third round draft choices who didn't make the team, and ended up playing for other teams. But Noll knew who he wanted on his team."

Banaszak remembered good times spent at Ron Demsher's Wagon Wheel on Washington Pike in South Fayette. "There were just regular fans there, the kind of fans that made the Steelers special," said Banaszak. "We'd go in there Friday afternoons following practice. There'd be five to eight, or ten to twelve of us, who'd meet there. This was at the height of our popularity in these parts — during our Super Bowl reign — and, at any other place, we'd have been mobbed. We just wanted to be treated like everyone else, and that's the way it was at the Wagon Wheel. Ron's a super guy and his customers respected us, and gave us our space.

"They had a guy in there called 'Spin-Out.' He had a saying that he was crazy and had the papers to prove it. At Christmas time, he'd go out and buy us all a bottle of whiskey. Just for the hell of it.

"The question I hear now the most is: 'Do you miss it?' I really don't miss it anymore. I played organized football for 25 years. There was no football left in my body when I was done. The competition has been replaced by the competition in the business world. I think I have successfully substituted the business world for the football world.

"Every day I go out there to make a sales call there are two or three other vendors right behind me. The competition is keen.

"I miss the locker room more than I miss playing football. I miss the camaraderie. That's irreplaceable. When I had the three motor oil quick-change units, I had 25 kids working for me. I'd visit the outlets and talk to them on a regular basis, and try to pep them up to always do their best. I was Chuck Noll to those 25 individuals.

"I'm feeling pretty good. My grandparents were immigrants. They came to this country for one reason: to give their children a better chance. That was instilled in me by my parents and my grandparents. So that's what I want to do now.

"My grandfather worked in the mills in Cleveland. It was J&L then, now it's LTV. My father struggled to put himself through college at night. He wanted me to have a better shot at life.

"I spent two years in the Marine Corps after high school so I could go to school on the G.I. Bill. It was just something I knew I had to do.

"Rarely will I get through the fourth period of a Steelers' game at the Stadium anymore. I'm outta there so I can get home at a decent hour for dinner. But I still tailgate before the games with friends who were part of the Banaszak Bunch. There's probably six to ten of them, sometimes as many as 12 of them whom I see regularly. We still have a good time together.

"Hey, I'm one of the few guys from our team who still goes to the games. I'm still a fan. I was a fan when I was eight years old, and my dad was taking me to the ballgames. I'll always be a fan.

"When fans think of me I hope they'll feel the same way I felt about my career. I enjoyed every minute of it. There's nothing I could look back upon and say I had a bad time or that was a disappointment, or that was work. I enjoyed every single practice, every single meeting, every single camp, every single game. I enjoyed the entire seven years in Pittsburgh as a Steeler."

George Gojkovich

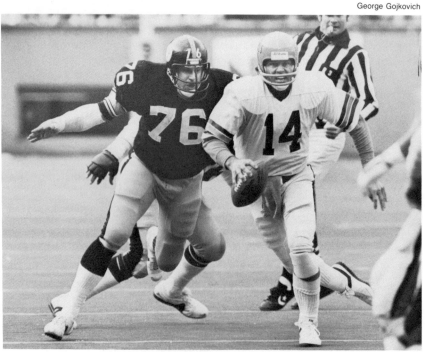

John Banaszak sacks Cincinnati Bengals quarterback Kenny Anderson.

Randy Grossman
"Football is a fairy tale."

"What's a nice Jewish boy like you doing playing football?"
—David Susskind

It was the summer of 1981 at St. Vincent College, and the Steelers were running around the outline of the football field in the notorious "350s" or "gassers."

Randy Grossman, as was often the case, was leading the pack. As he passed us on the sideline, Grossman couldn't resist shouting, "I'm still here . . . just for the record."

Grossman was always reminding reporters that they were wrong about him when they expressed doubts that he would make the team. In a pre-season preview, we had mentioned that there were rumors making the rounds that Grossman might retire, and he resented that.

But this was nothing new for Grossman. All his life people were saying Grossman wasn't going to be on the team. They were always telling Grossman he didn't measure up — to their standards, anyhow.

Who could blame Grossman for getting back at them?

David Susskind once asked Grossman on a fund-raising show that was staged in the Pittsburgh studios of WQED-TV, "What's a nice Jewish boy like you doing playing football?"

Grossman once remarked, "I could have been born rich and blond-haired, blue-eyed and Anglo-Saxon. I have a pretty good time as it is, and I'm curly-haired, brown-eyed and Jewish."

Well, sort of, just to throw everyone another curve Grossman had been telling people he was a Quaker, or, at least, that he had been married in a Quaker ceremony.

Another time, he said, "They say I'm too small, too slow, and too weak. But I'm like the guy in the decathlon who doesn't win any of the individual events, but who ends up winning the whole thing."

As Steelers' coach Chuck Noll once put it, "If you handicapped football players the way you do yachts in races, you'd have to put Randy in the Class C category. His size and speed wouldn't impress those computers the Dallas Cowboys use to grade those guys they have. All big, fast guys who'd be Class A.

"All Randy does is go out and win. His boat comes in first in the overall race. Those are the kind of guys we like to have on our team."

Grossman was good enough to stay eight seasons with the Steelers, contribute to four Super Bowl championships, and come away with four rings to add to his jewelry collection. He and Bennie Cunningham were a consistent tandem, often splitting time at the tight end position. It was a Steelers' strong point.

Noll never threw the ball that much to the tight end in the Steelers' offensive scheme, but both made their share of clutch catches when the

Steelers needed them the most. And both made big blocks when called upon. They were consistent and reliable.

At 29, Grossman, the most popular Jewish athlete in Pittsburgh since Sid Gordon of the Pirates and Marshall Goldberg of Pitt, retired from the Steelers to go into the restaurant business.

He was going to be the co-owner and co-manager of Bobby Rubino's Ribs at Station Square. Told he would be better off opening a deli downtown, Grossman grinned and said, "I really should; we could use a good deli here. But that's the story of my life. I've been making my living carrying a pigskin, and now I'm going into the ribs business. That's not really kosher."

From start to finish, Grossman was always his own man with the Steelers. He was a determined and dedicated clutch performer who made fools out of everyone who said he wasn't big enough — at 6-1, 225 — or speedy enough to play tight end in the National Football League.

His wit was All-Pro, for sure, but when he stopped smiling as much as he did early on he decided to call it a day. "I wasn't getting the same measure of satisfaction or enjoyment," he said.

He caught on with the club as a free agent in 1974, impressing the coaches during a stretch when the veterans were out on strike and he called it quits, ironically enough, in mid-July of 1982, when another player strike was on the horizon.

He joined Jon Kolb, Joe Greene, Sam Davis and Dwight White as long-time veterans of the Steelers' glory days who had retired after the 1991 season was completed. Rocky Bleier, Mike Wagner, Gerry Mullins and Steve Furness all were missing from that campaign, so the old gang had already begun to break up.

Grossman once listed his greatest thrill as making the NFL in the first place, realizing the life-long dream of a boy who loved the Eagles when he was growing up in Philadelphia, and later starred as a receiver at Temple University.

He started in 44 of the 118 games he played for the Steelers and caught 118 passes for 1,514 yards and five touchdowns during the regular season, and in playoff competition he caught 15 more passes for 186 yards and a touchdown.

"I'd like the fans to remember me for what I did," he said, "and for doing what I was asked to do when I was called upon."

Grossman had gone to his dressing stall following a press conference to clear out his stuff, and Dan Rooney was walking with his head down in a different direction, through the lobby of the club's offices at Three Rivers Stadium.

"You're losing another good one," I remarked to Rooney.

"We sure are," he said with a smile. "He was always making the team, and ending up a regular. I always had confidence when the ball was thrown his way. And I think everybody else did, too."

Lynn Swann spoke to Grossman in the clubhouse, warming up, it seemed, for his post-career work as a network sports announcer. "Every year, for eight years, they said you weren't going to make the team," said Swann. "And you did! And now you're leaving on your own.

I think it's great!"

Grossman admitted he was relieved. "I really didn't want to go to camp this time," he admitted. "I've been around long enough to know how tough it is. You have to have the primary goal of wanting to start for the Steelers. That's the only objective that ever appealed to me once I made the team. But I didn't feel that way anymore."

Funny thing, Grossman looked the same when he announced his retirement as he did at his peak as a player. He looked solid, firm, ready to run a short route and grab a bullet from Terry Bradshaw like it was a ball of pink cotton candy.

He appeared ready to go in motion behind the line, tap the center on his behind so he knew where he was, and then bury his head into the bodies before him to clear a hole for the backs in short yardage situations.

"I'm in good shape, I know," he said. "I'm probably in better shape than 95 percent of the guys on the team. I always was. But everybody gets just as sore because you push yourself to the limit. I know what I have to do and I just don't feel like doing it again."

The way Grossman expressed himself reminded me so much of another outstanding athlete, Dave DeBusschere, when he explained why he was retiring after playing for championship teams with the New York Knicks when I was working in New York.

In short, Grossman no longer felt like pushing himself to the limit, so he decided to step down on his own, and go from broken ribs to spare ribs. Such an injury caused him to lose his starting job in the first exhibition game in 1981.

Randy reached for a box above his dressing stall, and lifted it down. "After eight years," he said, pointing to the contents of the box, topped by a gray sweat suit, "this is all I have to show for it."

He was kidding, of course. He had four Super Bowl rings, and the satisfaction of fooling everyone, from high school and college coaches who shied away from him because of his size and speed — or lack of both — to the doubting sportswriters, the so-called experts.

It was the winter of 1991, the last day of 1991, in fact, and things were rather slow, as expected, at the offices of Kidder Peabody, the brokerage firm on the 37th floor of the USX Tower in downtown Pittsburgh.

The sky was clear, for a change, and you could see forever from a conference room. You could see Three Rivers Stadium if you walked to the other side of the building. Randy Grossman grinned as he sat at a long table in the front of the room.

He had a full, but neatly-trimmed beard, and there was more salt in it than you remembered from your last meeting, nearly a decade earlier. Grossman's grin was the same. It always gave the impression he knew something you didn't know. His eyes were as dark and bright as ever, and inviting a conversation.

Grossman was a great interview this sunny afternoon. He had been to hell and back business-wise since he left the Steelers, with some serious setbacks. "It's been tough," he conceded. "It's been real tough." Among other things, his marriage came apart after 12 years. "Football is a fairy tale," he said. "Real life sucks!"

This was a rather surprising summary, coming from Grossman. He certainly looked prosperous enough, as he always did. He cast a handsome figure. He still had that great grin. He is heard on local radio stations giving stock market reports from his Kidder, Peabody office. He still enjoys a high profile in the community.

But he had been sobered by some of his experiences since he had left the Steelers, perhaps a year or two prematurely after the 1981 season, and provided striking insights into the Steelers and the world of professional football and that of the professional athlete.

He was especially interesting when he spoke about the team's quarterbacks at the start of his career with the Steelers, namely Terry Bradshaw, Joe Gilliam and Terry Hanratty. Grossman knows that despite the problems he has experienced in his post-Steelers days, he has been luckier than most. Gilliam got into drug and alcohol abuse and, more recently, crime — armed robbery down in Louisiana during the 1991 football season. Hanratty had written a book about his bout with alcohol. All three quarterbacks had marriages come apart at the seams since their Steelers' heyday.

I asked Grossman if he had a clue as to why Bradshaw continued to badmouth Chuck Noll, as well as the Steelers organization and Pittsburgh sports fans.

"It's not a problem between two people, just one," said Grossman. "I don't think Chuck has a problem with Terry. But I don't have a clue as to the source of Terry's disenchantment. I don't know what the problem is. I can't talk from the team's perspective. From my perspective, Terry was given every opportunity.

"In 1974, our first championship season," Grossman continued, "there was a strike, and the veteran players stayed out. I was a free agent rookie that year. That helped me make the team. Gilliam came in. We were undefeated (6-0) in the pre-season, for whatever that was worth, because they were really exhibitions. Most teams didn't have their best players.

"Our veteran players came in late. We beat Baltimore easily (30-0) in the opener with Gilliam at quarterback. We go out to Denver and we score 35 points, which is pretty good, but Denver also scores 35 points, and we have a tie game. Bradshaw started the next game. Just like that. We lost that game (17-0 at Oakland), and then we continued on and won our first Super Bowl championship, and we're happy. Everyone but Joe Gilliam, that is. That season alone should have endeared somebody to a guy, talking about Bradshaw and Noll.

"Maybe Terry Bradshaw would still have what he has today. But his success with the Steelers made Terry Bradshaw what he is today. And it ruined Joe Gilliam. I'm not saying that Terry Bradshaw might not have been super anyhow, or that Joe Gilliam wouldn't have had his problems with drugs. But, anyhow, it was a big event in both of their lives."

38

Randy Grossman holds for placement kick by son Oliver with Rocky Bleier observing.

Randy and his father hold football in similar scene back in 1954.

Randy and his late father Joe in Steelers' clubhouse.

I told Grossman that Dwight White is still enraged by that decision of switching from Gilliam to Bradshaw. "The black players were all in shock," said White, a defensive lineman who is also in the investment counseling business in downtown Pittsburgh. "We couldn't believe it when Noll said Bradshaw was starting. As blacks, we felt betrayed. Gilliam had gotten national attention as a black making a breakthrough at the quarterback position. Noll is responsible for the ruination of Joe Gilliam."

I also mentioned to Grossman that Andy Russell and Mel Blount saw it differently, Russell saying that Gilliam wasn't doing what Noll wanted him to do — hand off the ball more frequently to Franco Harris rather than throwing the ball so much, and Blount saying that Gilliam brought a lot of bad baggage with him to Pittsburgh, that Gilliam had been fooling around with drugs while at Tennessee State, and having pro money only worsened his problem.

"I don't know about any baggage he brought with him, or that he had drug problems before," said Grossman. "I was shocked, that's all I know. I was a rookie . . . what did I know? I didn't see it as a black-white issue. I just didn't see how Joe was removed. All I know is that everything was going great with Gilliam at quarterback.

"I feel real indebted to Joe Gilliam. I don't think I'd have made the team without Joe. I'm very fond of Joe Gilliam. Joe was a throwing quarterback. He loved to throw the ball. I was a receiver and I could catch the ball. He gave me a lot of opportunities to catch the ball. As a rookie, especially as a free agent rookie, I needed all the opportunities I could get to demonstrate that I could, indeed, catch a football. He threw the ball to me a lot."

I asked Grossman, "How good a throwing quarterback was Joe Gilliam?"

"I think he was as good as Bradshaw," said Grossman, without hesitation.

"How good was Hanratty?" I asked.

"I didn't get to see him very much," said Grossman. "He stayed out during the strike. I only got to see Hanratty in practice.

"Hanratty was the smartest of the three. Now somebody doesn't have to be dumb for somebody else to be smart. Hanratty seemed to have the greatest grasp of the game. He seemed to be the most strategic. But, from appearances, he didn't have the physical capabilities of Joe Gilliam or Bradshaw.

"Joe and I just hit it off. Joe was a great guy. He got along with everyone. He was very considerate. He really seemed to be able to feel how others were feeling."

With that in mind, I asked Grossman how he reacted to the news a few months earlier that Gilliam had been caught and jailed after a robbery attempt in Louisiana.

"It hurts a bunch," said Grossman. "I don't know if Joe had continued to play whether he would have the same problems, or whether he'd had them before.

"The football world is a very small part of the real world. The real world can be very difficult on you."

I mentioned to Grossman that many people point to sportswriters accusingly and want to know why they don't expose drug use or alcohol abuse by athletes. I contended that you could be in the clubhouse every day, as a sportswriter or as a member of the team, and you might not know what another ballplayer was doing in that regard.

"You could be completely oblivious to it," Grossman agreed. "If that's not your thing, you might not be aware of what someone else is doing on their own time.

"But I look at that another way as well. If you want to write about sports, then write about sports. If you want to write about drug abuse, then write about drug abuse. If you want to write about sexual abuse, then write about that.

"If somebody writes about theatre, they write about the performance. They don't get into the personal lives of the actors and actresses, and write about AIDs or homosexuality. The sports page isn't what it used to be.

"All I know about Joe Gilliam is that he was one of the best at his craft when I knew him. It just happens to be a craft that doesn't last a lifetime. It's regretful.

"I don't know what more Joe could have done to retain his starting job with the Steelers, or to succeed with the Steelers. Most athletes who are successful in such an individual task don't know where to go when that task ends. You go, as the saying goes, from the penthouse to the shithouse."

Grossman grinned once again at his own sauciness.

Then he got serious again.

"Even after his demotion, Joe Gilliam remained a strong team player. And he was really very supportive of Bradshaw and the team. It was the same way at the start of the next season. He thought he would be competing with Bradshaw and Hanratty for the starting job. But it was Bradshaw's, right from the start. That was pretty evident to everyone.

"So Joe became unhappy. But they weren't going to trade him because he was unhappy. As an aside, that's why I was amused to read so many stories this season, or hear the sportscasters on the radio and TV saying the Steelers would have to trade Bubby Brister if Neil O'Donnell was going to be the No. 1 quarterback. Why? You want two good quarterbacks. You don't want one good quarterback and one bad one.

"So, if you're unhappy how do you get out? In any other job, you can quit and take another job somewhere else. But not in pro sports. The only way out is to be the bad boy, and become so bothersome that they don't want you around anymore.

"Joe wanted to be let out. I never asked Joe, but I think he would have gone elsewhere for less money just to play. There was a high frustration level. You just want to bag it. What can you do? He started misbehaving. The problem is he got caught up in the role. It just stuck with him.

"That's why there are alcoholics, drug addicts and thieves. That's not judgmental. In one sentence, the real world sucks."

"They say sports is a microcosm of life," Grossman said, getting into a more philosophic discussion. "For an athlete, his life is compressed into a 25-year period. He or she finds himself or herself climbing to the highest height. Then, their legs are cut out from under them.

"An athlete is like a 60-year-old person when they leave their sport. You have to be willing to start over as a grunt, to get new skills, in order to cope in the real world. Some go into coaching because it's something they know, something close to what they've been doing all these years. But in most cases that means coaching in high school, and for how much money? You have to build yourself back up.

"I don't watch football much anymore. I loved playing football. This organization was great, the players on our team were the greatest. I don't enjoy watching the game. I'm a terrible fan. I wanted to play; I didn't want to watch.

"You never have to completely grow up when you're playing sports. In the beginning, everybody plays games, whether it's kick-the-can, hop-scotch or pitching and catching a ball. You play games. Then you start picking teams. Certain guys get picked early, and certain guys get picked last. Then it's not fun for some of them and they drop off. Some guys fall away. They get into something else. Little by little more guys drop off. And you get down to a smaller number of people who are playing. There are usually more Little League teams in any town you can think of than there are Pony League teams. Less and less people participate as you get older. Professional athletes are the guys who are still playing games.

"Professional athletes don't have to deal with rejection until the end of their careers, or until they get cut, or until they retire and go looking to get into something else. All of a sudden they might come up short in what's necessary to get or to hold a job.

"Until I left professional football, I was getting paid to play. Then you have to adjust to the real world. Before, even though they say the competition is so keen in professional sports, in truth, you are competing with a very select group of people. In the real world, you have to compete with everybody.

"When you're out selling insurance, or selling cars, or selling manuscripts, or selling stocks and bonds, you're competing with a lot more people. The competition is much greater. There are fewer referees. There's no clock. The clock is supposedly 24 hours, but at the end of the 24 hours it doesn't end. It restarts. I find it much more competitive out here; I find it much more stressful."

Grossman has given this topic a great deal of thought, it is obvious. And this is coming from a guy who found training camp both a source of joy and stress. He loved playing football, but he always felt that he had to catch every ball thrown his way, and make every block, if he wanted to hold onto his job. He made the team as a free agent, somebody who was not selected by any team in pro football in the college draft, but was invited by the Steelers to try out for the team. There were no guarantees, not from the beginning. And every year he felt like a free agent. Most players who came to the Steelers as free agents in the first place — whether you are talking to Sam Davis, or Grossman, or John Banaszak or Donnie Shell or Keith Willis — will tell you they never shed the tag, in their minds anyhow, of being a free agent.

They always felt the pressure of sticking with the Steelers.

I mentioned to Grossman that I thought I was getting better insights into the Steelers and the world of the professional athlete from players like him, sometime starters, non-stars, than I had gotten in earlier interviews with the team's stars.

"The non-stars are the ones who are falling away now," he explained. "We are the ones who have fallen off to the side. Bradshaw and Swann and Franco and Greene are still stars. They're still in the same environment, they're still in the limelight. L.C. Greenwood is in TV commercials. They're still playing games, so to speak. They are playing it out until the end.

"John Banaszak and I had similar backgrounds. We were free agents from small colleges. Everyone comes to camp thinking or feeling they can play. The real difference is that someone like Swann, who came in the same year, was on the team from the first day. He had no second thoughts about making the team. When Banaszak and I came to camp, we thought we could play, but we weren't on the team.

"We were always wondering: what happens if we don't make the team? Every week people were cut from the squad. Hey, that could be me. It forces you to be more introspective. You are more opened up to what the real world is really like.

"Every year I had to make the team. That was my m.o. It was one of the most stressful things I had to deal with. They were always drafting new tight end prospects, looking for somebody as big as Bennie Cunningham who could catch the ball and block. For eight years, I couldn't make plans. I didn't know if I'd make the team."

Overall, though, Grossman doesn't want to paint too glum a picture. On the walls of the offices at Kidder Peabody, in addition to portraits of the firm's founders, there are beautiful paintings and prints of Pittsburgh from all points of view, some of them similar to what can be seen from the windows high atop the USX Tower.

Grossman can't forget the best of times. "I have real good memories of my days with the Steelers," he said. "That's one of the reasons I decided to stay in Pittsburgh. My whole adult life has been spent in Pittsburgh. My fondest memories are of me with the Steelers.

"But I don't look at the Stadium so much when I think about that. I have a much stronger pull toward Latrobe."

Funny, I thought, but I feel the same way. I find I like photographs for my books on the Steelers that were taken at training camp rather than during the game. I prefer to see the players up close, as fans did during the glory years, and you see them closer at camp. I like to see them without their helmets, in sweat-stained T-shirts, or after they'd shed their shoulder pads, trudging up the hill toward the locker room after a hard day's work. I liked to see them making the time, tired as they often were, to speak to some fans, to sign their names to whatever was shoved in front of them, offering a smile, a handshake, posing one more time for a photo.

For me, the days and nights at St. Vincent were the best, a trip back in time, a relaxing period where you could get away from the real world, and have more time to talk to football players and the coaches and the fans and the sports media, to get to know them better.

"Practice at the Stadium was like a 9 to 5 job, a more normal work-day," said Grossman. "At St. Vincent, we were completely removed from the real world. You were with a bunch of guys and you were sweating it out from morning till night. You didn't have to make your bed; some-body else did that for you. You didn't have to cook or make any sched-ule. You didn't have to worry about anything but football.

"It was much more intense there. You had two practices a day. I had to make the team. Once we got to Pittsburgh, I didn't have to worry about making the team. Every play at St. Vincent had great significance. At Three Rivers, it was just games.

"If Swann or Stallworth couldn't grab their head at St. Vincent they knew they'd be on the team. Everyone knew what they could do."

I asked Grossman what sort of relationship he had with Bennie Cunningham, who had been the Steelers' No. 1 draft choice out of Clem-son in 1976, and was usually the starting tight end when they were both on the squad. "We were friendly," said Grossman. " I had no problems with Bennie. I was supportive of him, and he was supportive of me. As competitors for the same position, we weren't close friends."

Grossman and Chuck Noll were never that close, either, but there was a mutual respect. "I wish he hadn't retired at this time," said Gross-man. "I think he's still the coach that he always was. Maybe he was just feeling frustrated.

"As complex as people say he is, I think he's pretty basic. You really find out what somebody's made of in times of stress. We had great years, but we weren't going undefeated. We had some problems to overcome along the way.

"One year (1976) Bradshaw was hurt and we had to go with Mike Kruczek, a rookie, at quarterback and we kept on winning, even though we didn't get to the Super Bowl that year. We had two starting run-ning backs knocked out, so we didn't make it all the way. But we were a great team that year.

"It wasn't always a cakewalk. We went through some tough times. Chuck's overriding philosophy was not to get fancier or trickier, but to get more basic. That was his catchphrase, as far as I was concerned. He's more famous for his 'Franco Who?' and 'Terry Who?' comments, and for always saying 'Whatever it takes.' But when we were in difficult circumstances, I can't remember him telling us 'we've got to do whatever it takes.' I remember him saying, 'We've got to get back to basics.' He said we had lost our focus, and we had to go back to the beginning and concentrate on technique, and the little things that got us where we were. He chopped away at what we were doing. We got more elementary."

I interrupted Grossman. What he was telling me only added to my personal confusion over why Noll turned to Joe Walton two years earlier to establish a too-complicated offensive system that was the source of controversy from start to finish.

Grossman agreed. "It seemed very out of character for Chuck," he said. "If you look back at nearly all the championship teams, the Packers and the Giants, you're looking at guys who were all basic guys who just beat you up.

"The flashiest team that ever won may have been the New York Jets in 1969, but that's because they had Joe Namath and all that hype. But if you get past Joe Namath the Jets had tough, basic guys.

"That's why I'm real curious to see how all this run-and-shoot stuff works out in the long run in football today. What Chuck instilled in us was that you didn't get it done by fooling people."

I asked Grossman if that didn't appeal to him in particular because he was a very fundamental football player himself, not especially big, not especially fast. "It fit very much into my mold," he said. "It fit our other players, too. Who were the flashy guys on our team? Franco wasn't that flashy. Maybe Lynn was a little, but he was mostly catching short passes across the middle, and that took a good work ethic and courage to consistently come up with the ball while taking a beating. He chipped away at you. Same with Stallworth.

"Our defense just beat you up. Our offensive line . . . I can't think of a more workmanlike group of guys. They were downright dull.

"Noll and I never really talked to each other much. But I never thought he was impersonal. I never once thought his door wasn't open. He wasn't obtuse. He was so blunt in what he wanted.

"If you did what he asked you to do then everything was great. One of his biggest attributes was his assistants. He used them as an extension of his personality. He had people who he could communicate through to his players. Maybe in a way he was not able to do.

"He had people like Lionel Taylor, who was responsible for the receivers. Lionel was a flashy guy. I always seemed to get my messages from Chuck through Taylor.

"We were getting down to the last cuts one year, and I didn't know if I had made the team. I went to Lionel and said, 'I'm really concerned. Am I going to make the team? Can I look for an apartment?' And he said, 'Don't worry. You're OK. You can look for an apartment. You're going to be here.' Now Lionel couldn't say that on his own. He had to be talking for Chuck.

"He had George Perles, who was a wild man, and a great coach, and he had Rollie Dotsch, who was different personality-wise, more reserved, but also a great coach. He was more conservative, as far as coaching was concerned than George, but just as enthused. No head coach is going to get it done unless he has the assistants.

45

"That may be one of the reasons they haven't been as successful in recent seasons. I don't know the guys now. When was the last time somebody from Pittsburgh went on to something bigger? Maybe Tom Moore did when he went to Minnesota two years ago, but it seemed like a parallel move to me. I don't know if it really was a move up. You can't coach all 40 guys yourself.

"I hope Chuck Noll comes back and coaches somewhere else. I would be a real loss for the world for him not to be coaching young men somewhere. The world needs good men."

Grossman was asked to give an account of his present situation and activity. "I still like to keep in shape, and to get exercise," he said. "I play racquetball. I've been in the brokerage business since '89. I live in Indiana Township, just outside of Fox Chapel. I've been there since '85.

"I have a 16-year-old son, Oliver, and a 10-year-old daughter, Lucy, and I have an ex-wife and a significant other."

When I asked him if he still professed to be a Quaker, he shook his head. "My ex-wife was Protestant," he said. "As a compromise, we were married in a Quaker ceremony. I was born a Jew and I'll die a Jew."

Three Rivers Stadium didn't seem so far off, not from our vantage point from the window on the 37th floor of the USX Tower. Did Grossman have any ghosts still running after passes at the Stadium? "No, not anymore," he said. "I feel light years from there now.

"I always look at that time period as laying the foundation block for my life. The time spent in the Rooney organization and all my experiences there were more than what I expected of life. I still strive to make my life that. But life isn't like that. It was an exceptional family, an exceptional organization. Life in the real world, outside the Rooney organization, is much more of a mediocre standard.

"You can never get back to that. A player is a kid. Even when he's done playing, he's a kid.

"No, I don't go to the games anymore. I'm not interested in watching. I hear few of the other guys go, either. They weren't watchers; they were players."

Grossman was starting to look at his watch, and he looked like a man who wanted to get back to work. We had talked long enough, I thought, and I didn't want to hold him up any longer.

But he paused after he stood, and held onto his chair, and said there was something else he wanted to tell me. "I have a picture that has a special significance I'd like to get to you," he said. "Do you remember how we used to bring our kids with us to practice on Saturday mornings at the Stadium? Well, someone took a picture one Saturday of me holding the ball for Oliver to kick. When my mother saw it she said she couldn't believe it. She said, 'I have the same picture of you and your dad.' She went and found a photo showing my father holding a ball for me to kick in our living room.

"That reminds me of something else I wanted to tell you. You know, Art Rooney was an old man when I first came to the team. I had been retired about two or three years, and I walked into the Steelers' office lobby one day, and I saw Mr. Rooney. I said hello to him, and he said hello, and he asked me, 'How's Oliver?' It blew my mind. Now how many kids ran through that place through the years? It left an amazing impression on me.

"Many people might say, 'How's your kid?' Or some might say, 'How's your son?' But for him to remember his name . . . it was unreal. I think Oliver's special. But for him to remember his name like that really knocked me out. That's why, I'm sure, everyone thought Mr. Rooney was so special. He remembered your name."

Randy Grossman with Lynn Swann and John Stallworth.

Grossman grabs one against Denver's Bill Thompson in 1978 AFC playoff.

Chuck Noll
Soon after fourth Super Bowl title

"Mamas, don't let your sons grow up to be cowboys."
—Waylon Jennings or Willie Nelson

"Mamas, don't let your sons grow up to be Cowboys
. . . or Oilers."
—Chuck Noll

Chuck Noll was in relatively good spirits, considering that he had an upset stomach, was on the Scarsdale Diet, had a fever blister on the right corner of his lower lip, a sports writer at his left side and was surrounded by hundreds of cheerful people wearing cowboy hats and red bandanas and feasting on fried chicken, barbequed ribs, wine and beer.

He smiled, was warm, and made pleasant conversation at a table for eight at a party tossed by ABC Sports at Marriott's Rancho Las Palmas Resort in Rancho Mirage, California, just outside Palm Springs where the National Football League owners' meeting was held in March of 1980.

Winning a fourth Super Bowl championship just a few months earlier can fortify a fellow for such assaults on his constitution, soul and pride, as I wrote in a special feature for *The Washington Post.*

The week before, Noll and his wife, Marianne, had led a Steeler contingent of coaches and wives to a post-Super Bowl vacation in Acapulco — a reward for a job well done — and Montezuma had exacted some more revenge at Noll's expense. It helped Noll's dieting, anyhow, although the problem persisted in Palm Springs.

Noll was not wearing any of the western paraphernalia that was passed out at the door. "That's not him," said Joe Gordon.

Gordon, the Steelers' publicist and his wife, Babe, and club president Dan Rooney's wife, Pat, all wore their cowboy hats and bandanas. They looked like the genuine article. But Dan and Chuck would have none of it.

When the scene was recreated to Noll several months later, he smiled and told us, "They got caught up in the spirit of things and I was still suffering from Mexico. I didn't wear a cowboy hat because I didn't want any extra wind resistance on the way to the bathroom."

Only a man who pilots his own airplane might put it that way.

That night was not a complete bummer for Noll, however. After all, he did hum a few bars from his favorite song, "Mamas, Don't Let Your Sons Grow Up To Be Cowboys," popularized by country/western giants Waylon Jennings and Willie Nelson. Only Noll has his own version. When he sings it, it goes like this: "Mamas, don't let your sons grow up to be Cowboys . . . or Oilers."

When these stories are related to some people who have dealt with Noll, they say, "That sounds out of character for Noll." Maybe they don't know Noll too well.

He has always been a private man, to begin with, but he does have a droll sense of humor. If you can catch him at the right time, he will even tell you a joke, and some of his stories are even better than Noll realizes.

At one point during that March affair at the NFL owners' meeting, Noll leaned across the table and asked Dan Rooney, "How come they never have parties with a hard-hat theme?"

Rooney smiled and shrugged his shoulders.

"I guess they do," said Noll, not missing a beat. "Only they call them Super Bowls."

That's vintage Noll. As fine as any of the wines and gourmet foods in which he indulges.

Now this was the summer of 1980, mid-August to be exact, and the Steelers were at their training camp at St. Vincent College in Latrobe, Pa., about 40 miles east of Pittsburgh. Super Bowls seemed like a long way off.

The Steelers had opened their training camp the month before, and Noll was never happier. More than anyplace else, he always enjoyed working with his team at training camp in Latrobe.

It is where he liked to be, at a retreat, so to speak, where he and his assistants had the full attention of the troops, time for two-a-day drills and teaching them how to play football the right way. Noll's way.

Noll always prided himself on being a teacher. He did not need a stadium, an opponent, frenzied fans, TV cameras and certainly not pre-game and post-game interviews by the media to make his job more enjoyable. At St. Vincent, he was a football coach, pure and simple.

Noll, at age 48 in the summer of 1980, was in the prime of life, as far as a football coach was concerned. His record was the envy of everyone in the NFL. He lost some weight during the summer, got his golf game in order, had a flattering tan and looked like a coach who had it made. He has always been smaller than most of his players, but there was no doubt about who was the Big Man on Campus.

He smiled a lot at St. Vincent.

He smiled a lot out in California that March at the owners' meetings, too, where he had to be an ambassador, a good winner and whatever else was expected of him. Sometimes he came up short of some people's expectations, but that was nothing new.

At that point in his career, even after winning four Super Bowls in six years, he had never been named NFL coach of the year by the Professional Football Writers Association, it was pointed out at Palm Springs by Joe Browne, the public relations director of the NFL.

"What do they want from him?" inquired Don Shula, one of Noll's former bosses at Baltimore and one of his biggest boosters as well, as Shula sat at poolside one day. "All the guy does is win Super Bowls."

It was a relaxing time for Noll and the Rooneys, a time to enjoy the fruits of their victories. The Steelers' staff commanded a lot of

49

attention and respect in those days at league get-togethers. Board chairman Art Rooney was already a revered figured in pro football.

And Noll always enjoyed working for the Rooneys. He confided that it meant a great deal to him that the Rooneys regard football as a full-time business — and that they were not relying on other businesses to bankroll the club.

"Very much so," said Noll. "We have common purposes, and that's most important."

Concentration is a key to success, Noll noted. He never liked distractions, which is one of the reasons he never cared for Raiders' president Al Davis, who was always embroiled in one controversy or another with the NFL and civic leaders in Los Angeles and Oakland. Noll always thought Al Davis' biggest problem was Al Davis.

Noll was never enamored with Davis. In fact, they were archrivals, stemming from the feuds both on the football field and in the league courts, between the Raiders and Noll. Davis was never one of Noll's favorites, far from it, even though Davis and the Rooneys remained on good terms, despite some philosophic differences. Noll could never stomach somebody on what he perceived to be an obvious ego trip.

One of Noll's former players, however, contends that the Steelers' coach is an egomaniac himself, only an "introverted egomaniac." Noll flinched at the charge. "I don't have an ego problem," he said. "Ego is something that never is satisfied. There's a big difference between ego and pride in what you do."

There was never any doubt that Noll took great pride in what he accomplished in Pittsburgh, and that was understandable. Yet he shunned the spotlight.

When asked to pose for a photograph with some players, he would often suggest that one of his assistants be in the picture instead. He had been approached to do commercials and he always rejected them — and hundreds of thousands of dollars — opening up opportunities for the players. "Their time is shorter," he'd say. "Let them have the ads." He did an ad once for a local bank, but regretted it later. He would make a public appearance every now and then, if prodded enough, but could easily get lost in the crowd. It was never his style to attract people around him. There are times he likes to lecture — he's an expert on many subjects — but will do so only with the right people. As a result, he has often been depicted — wrongly — as a dull man.

He is anything but. He doesn't mind, though. He is at peace with the world when tending the roses in the front of his home in Upper St. Clair, or when steering his boat out of its slip in Hilton Head, where he has a getaway place.

One of the varieties of roses he has is called "Charisma." So when you ask him if he thinks he has charisma, Noll will smile and say, "Yes, in my yard . . . where it belongs!"

Noll's celebrity status at league meetings was pointed out to him, but he quickly dismissed its importance.

"You're better off winning the games, not the league meetings," he said. "A lot of people are very competitive in this league. Everybody's trying to outdo one another out here. But there are no trophies for this."

It made me think of how many wives who attend these affairs try to outdress one another, on the tennis court, on the dance floor, in the hotel lobby. Some of the men are guilty of the same one-ups-man-ship.

There was no use, Noll insisted, in asking him to dwell on past accomplishments, either. Noll liked to refer to the four Super Bowls the Steelers had won in the previous six years as "antiques." To him, they had no relationship to what he was trying to accomplish at St. Vincent.

"One of the things you learn in football," he said, "is that you're only as good as your last outing. I don't like to reflect on what we've done in the past. I'm not a very good storyteller, for one thing. I'd disappoint you. When it's time, I'll talk about the good old days. But it's a sign of old age, reveling in the past."

Even then, he was antsy to get back to his office at Three Rivers Stadium, cut up game film from the previous season, rewrite the playbooks, prepare for the draft and training camp. He'd had his vacation and been away from it long enough to suit him. He wanted to resume his quest for excellence.

To an extent, he and the Rooneys — rich as they are — were out of place in Palm Springs. Noll looked all right — he once thought he would want to retire in California, when he was coaching there, but has since changed his mind — but he is from Cleveland and he has lived and worked in Pittsburgh, and he had been away from home too long.

In short, Noll was never your average football coach. He could be perplexing, he could be overbearing, he could be completely off base on some subject, depending upon one's own point of view, but he was never dull. And, as Shula said, all he did was win Super Bowls.

Shula is more at ease with people than Noll and not lost for words when writers approach him for interviews. He smiles a lot more. When we spoke in Palm Springs, Shula was amused by the fuss over Noll and how his former assistant puzzled people. Shula was one of the men, along with Upton Bell, who recommended Noll to the Rooneys when they were looking for a new head football coach before the 1969 season.

"He had a good grasp of the total picture," said Shula, in explaining his recommendation. "He was not just a position coach. And I thought he'd make somebody a good head coach. I thought he'd fit in well in Pittsburgh. And he has. There's so much more he could do, if he were a selfish sort of person. But he doesn't toot his own horn. He doesn't steal the show. And he's good to his assistants.

"We got him in the first place because Mike Sandusky recommended him to me when we were looking for someone to replace Charlie Winner, who went to St. Louis as the head coach. We liked him from the start. And I like the fact that when people asked him if he learned anything from me during his stay with the Colts, he always added that he learned a lot from Sandusky and Bill Arnsparger and the other assistants, too.

"Chuck prides himself on being a walking dictionary, and we'd try to stump him. If you correct him, he gets disturbed. Two nights before the Super Bowl (the Colts-Jets contest after the 1969 season) he got pretty loose with us when we were out one night, but basically he didn't run around with the assistants. He got along with everybody, but he had his own lifestyle.

"He was always under control. He had a good marriage, and family life was very important to him. He was very interested in Chris and Marianne. What amazed me in Baltimore was how he helped take care of his sister's kids. There was a death in the family, and Chuck really came through for them."

Shula didn't recall the details and Noll would never discuss such a personal matter. A decade later, Noll and his wife would show the same personal interest and concern when Shula's wife was terminally ill.

A friend of Noll was prevailed upon to provide some details on Shula's story about Noll's sister, Rita.

"His sister's husband died," the man disclosed, "and Chuck took over support of her children; I think there were four of them. He sent his one nephew, the oldest boy — his name was Kenny — to St. Vincent College — and Kenny ended up as the film coordinator for the New England Patriots. He had the oldest girl staying with him and Marianne while she attended school here in Pittsburgh."

Such a story wouldn't surprise George Pernicano, a colorful restaurateur in San Diego who first met Noll when Noll was an assistant coach on the staff of the Chargers and sees him from time to time when Noll visits his waterfront restaurant. Pernicano was a visitor in the Three Rivers Stadium press box during the 1991 season.

"He's such a great person," said Pernicano. "He's a hell of a family man; he doesn't go this way and that way. When he was with us, and even now when he stops by, it's always a happy time. He's always talking about food and wine, and he wants to go into the kitchen and discuss recipes with my cook.

"He's always sort of an inside man. I told Dan Rooney when he hired him, 'If you get this guy, you'll be happy with him. He's the same sort of guy as you and your dad.' He's a family man, a church-going man, and he fits the Rooney's mold. He's a different cut, not a flamboyant man. He and Marianne are just beautiful people. I've been on his side all the time. I have always loved the Rooneys and I love him."

Bum Phillips, the former coach of the Houston Oilers who always blamed the Steelers for setting up a roadblock for his team on the way to the Super Bowl, was also a visitor to the Three Rivers Stadium press box during the 1991 season.

"He's a guy who believes in what he's doing," offered Phillips. "He's himself, the same way every time. He's not counterfeit. He's a gentleman when he wins or loses. He doesn't like to sit around like I do, and shoot the breeze with sportswriters, but he's the genuine article just the same."

Jim Katcavage, a scout for the Philadelphia Eagles for many years, was a classmate and teammate of Noll's during his University of Dayton days. "He was always a more serious sort than the rest of the guys," recalled Katcavage. "He hasn't changed. He was never one to fool around much, even in our student days."

53

Walt Michaels, the former head coach of the New York Jets and the New York Generals, was a teammate of Noll for eight of Michael's ten seasons with the Browns. "He lived in Cleveland, his hometown, so it wasn't the same with him as the rest of us on the team," said Michaels. "Half the team would get together for a few beers after practice all the time, but he didn't come much. He lived at home, I think, until he got married.

"He was conservative. We called him 'The Pope,' because he was such a scholarly and sober type. It was just his nature. He studied hard. He didn't have the size — same as me — and he had to do it the way he did. He couldn't have been any different. He was more of a scientific player. He did a hell of a job with the body he had."

Mike Fabus

Miami's Don Shula shakes hands with former assistant Chuck Noll.

Chuck Noll
As a teacher in the early '80s

"It still takes good people."

Chuck Noll was known to greet a group of assembled reporters after a Steelers football game by saying, "My, isn't this a well-behaved class? Quiet, attentive, all set to take notes. That's nice."

Then Noll allowed a smile to slip out, maybe even a wink and, suddenly, he seemed more human. Like a favorite professor from college days. And Noll liked that image.

When he was coaching the Steelers, he could be stern, stone-faced, frustratingly private, bulldog stubborn, not given to free-wheeling conversation. He was most at ease when he was lecturing.

And Noll can lecture on just about any subject you can name.

Some time back, in the early '80s, when I was writing for *The Pittsburgh Press* and teaching a writing class one night a week at nearby Point Park College, I asked Noll to address my students and he agreed to do so.

My students were driven in an old-fashioned bus by Steve "Froggy" Morris of "Froggy's" — just around the corner from Point Park on Market Street — to Three Rivers Stadium for their evening with Chuck Noll.

Noll stood in a large meeting room in front of a green chalkboard covered with x's and o's and the mumbo jumbo of pro football, and spoke at length to these journalism students.

They sat in their school-like chairs, hanging on his every word — he loved that — as he spoke about the Steelers, synergism — that is, the whole is greater than the sum of its parts — loyalty, dedication, determination, success, sacrifice and, most of all, for those who were really listening, and reading between the lines, about life.

In the papers they were assigned to write after their interview with Noll, every student referred to him as a teacher. Noll would smile at the comparison. One of those students was Bob Pompeani, who now reports on Steelers' doings and other sports around Pittsburgh for KDKA-TV.

Noll was planning a teaching career when Sid Gillman offered him the last spot on the coaching staff of the Los Angeles Chargers of the American Football League. Al Davis of Raiders' fame was on that same staff.

After six seasons there, Noll joined the staff of Don Shula with the Baltimore Colts. He was there three years when the Steelers signed him as their head coach.

In 23 seasons, he compiled a record that put him on the all-time list of successful coaches, and it is expected he will be inducted into the Pro Football Hall of Fame in 1993.

His Steelers won four Super Bowls in six years, and were voted the Team of the Decade in the '70s.

Former New York Giants coach Allie Sherman saw Noll at work one day during a Steelers' practice session.

"He's teaching," Sherman said to us on the sideline. "These guys do it right. They go over all the points, from step one to step ten. Some coaches like to think they're teachers, but they're not. Noll is a teacher."

Here's a lengthy interview we had with Noll:

Why do you fancy yourself more of a teacher than a football coach?

"I was exposed to those kind of people. It's the only thing I know. Paul Brown was a teacher. I had high school and college coaches who were teachers. On the staffs I was on — with Gillman and Shula — teaching was very important. We're all trying to be the best we can be. I don't know any other way to do it."

How were you so successful in such a competitive business?

"The people we have here. Any success we've had is a team thing. Nobody does it alone. A lot of people say, 'Let's compare teams.' They want to know which team has the better tackle or who has the better guard. Some teams may have the better people, but they don't have the better team. A lot of people can't function well as part of a team. Some people function better as individuals."

As usual, you have side-stepped the real question. Why have you succeeded?

"It's not something you can talk about. It's tough to put into words. You have to live it. If it were easy to define, or easy to do, as my wife always says, everybody would do it. Why don't we just keep it a secret, how's that?"

You prefer to talk about the team, about other people. Why's that?

"It's a team thing. I haven't thrown a ball; I haven't caught a ball. We just tried to create the atmosphere; we tried to get people to grow. It still takes good people. It still takes people who are going to execute. It's not x's and o's."

You seem uncomfortable when the talk turns to your football feats, when anybody suggests you've been one of the best in the business, that your bust could be in the Pro Football Hall of Fame someday. How do you manage to take it all in stride?

"Before we won those championships, no one thought we were so great. Now everyone's a genius when they win. We had the kind of people, the talent, who could win."

You had to do something special with that talent. You talk about creating the proper atmosphere, yet you don't believe in motivating players. How does that fit?

"People tell me, 'My son has a lot of talent. If only he were motivated.' But motivation is a part of talent. If you don't want to use it, and work at it, you don't have any talent."

The game has changed in recent seasons, as it did in your playing days, and before that. How do you think your champion-

George Gojkovich

Chuck Noll in winter.

Hall of Fame

His mentor Paul Brown

George Gojkovich

Lighter moment for Terry Bradshaw and his quarterback coach.

ship teams would fare in today's football game?

"That's something you can't do. You can't take the present day and put it back. You'd make adjustments, that's what you'd do. There are always different problems to be dealt with. Who knows? Maybe we'd be better."

You always have said that football is a growing thing. What do you mean by that?

"Yes, the game develops. It's a growing thing, a vital thing. It doesn't stay the same. It changes and it has nuances. It's one of the things that makes it exciting. It's a dramatic evolutionary thing. You have to change to meet the challenge."

Have you grown, too?

"Just older. Football, basically, is still pretty much the same as when I got started. The things that aren't important have changed the most. The fundamentals haven't changed. It's still a game of blocking and tackling, knowing how to hit, being willing to. You try to create an atmosphere for these people to function best. You try to help them be the best they can be. You're talking about conditioning and techniques. About what to do and how to do it, creating good work habits."

How did you manage to keep on top of this for so many years?

"You're trying to improve every day. You're trying to get everyone on the same page. The team is the sum of what you have, but it can be greater than the sum of its parts."

That's synergism, right?

"When a football team or a group can work together and, in effect, rub off on one another, it's a real human experience than can only be understood if you've been through it. When the players have trust, faith and belief as a whole they are better able to inspire one another. If I spot a player who can't work with the group, he's got to go."

So how do you size up a prospect?

"You have prejudices about size and speed and other measuring sticks, but you have to be careful. Everybody's different. No two guys are alike. That's why I hate to compare people. We try to look for the guy who's the exception. They're all different. It's exciting, in a sense. And it's amazing. As many human beings as I've come in contact with, I have yet to find two exactly alike. What you want is good people."

Who were the good people who helped get you going so you could be successful with the Steelers?

"Joe Greene. Terry Bradshaw. Franco Harris. Mel Blount. L.C. Greenwood. Sam Davis. Andy Russell. Ray Mansfield. It's a long list. Just look at our rosters through the years."

What was it like that first year, when you won the first game, and lost the next 13 as a rookie head coach with the Steelers?

"It wasn't a hell of a lot of fun. But there have been difficult times every year. Somebody said he had an awful offense back then, that it was unimaginative and dull, and all those things. Then we won and some of those things worked out pretty well. When other people start

58

Chuck Noll is carried off field following 1972 game at San Diego which clinched first division crown. Steelers, left to right, include Gerry Mullins (72), Jon Kolb (55), Jim Clack (50), Ray Mansfield (56), Terry Bradshaw (12) and Frenchy Fuqua (33).

Quarterback klatch conducted by Chuck Noll in 1972 for fearless foursome: Terry Hanratty, Bob Leahy, Terry Bradshaw and Joe Gilliam.

copying what you're doing, it's something. You figure you might be doing something right."

You've changed things around in recent seasons, as the game changed. Is it that much more different these days?

"I don't think so. You have to have faith in what you're doing. What we've been doing is choosing people, and they have to be good people. You hope they'll end up maturing. You hope you don't have to watch them all the time. There's no way you can police them."

There are problems in pro sports today that didn't exist to the same degree during your most successful seasons. There's more money, more drugs, more agents and a more critical media. How did you adjust to those things?

"These are just other problems that have to be solved. We've had a staff that could solve those problems. It's not easy. One thing that's certain is change. As far as drugs go, there's probably a lower percentage of drug usage in the NFL than in society as a whole. A player really can't perform if he's on drugs. It'll show up."

Coaches like you and Don Shula, Tom Landry and Bud Grant stayed in the game a long time. But others dropped out, blaming their lack of enthusiasm for continuing on burnout. How do you figure that?

"Burnout is bullshit. We tried to be as efficient as possible in preparing our team. There's a point in practicing where you have diminishing returns. People can only concentrate so long. That goes for coaches as well as players. I never believed in sleeping at the stadium. I had a home for that. I tried to spend the month of June with my family, and nothing else, and that was very important time to me."

Bum Phillips once told me that you're not a 'sit-around, bullshit type of guy,' and he said the same of Landry. At league meetings I attended, you didn't seem to mix a lot. I didn't see you talking football with other coaches. How come?

"They're your competitors. So you don't want to give away anything, right?"

The Steelers had a losers' image before you came to the club. They were a tough, hard-hitting team, but they didn't win consistently. It's been said that you and the Rooney family were the perfect marriage, that you didn't try to hog the spotlight or steal the team away from them.

"When I first came here, I had to evaluate the situation. There were a lot of problems, but it wasn't ownership. It had to do with what you have to do to win. To win, you have to have the people. I wasn't competing with Art or Dan or any of the Rooneys, or them with me. We were working together. It's a team game."

Coaches like Landry and Dick Vermeil and Bum Phillips showed up in advertising and in TV commercials, yet you shunned that sort of thing, too. Surely, you could have cashed in on your fame during the four Super Bowl years?

"I didn't want to compete with my players, either. The players are in here for a short time and I thought I was in here for the long haul.

I thought those ads were theirs and rightfully theirs."

What did you learn from Art Rooney?

"I learned a lot from him. He was so great with people. I'd liked to have learned more."

What do you think the future holds for you and for the Steelers?

"I have no idea. If I could see into the future, I'd be at the race track today."

What do you think you'd like to be when you retire as a football coach?

"Be a teacher."

George Gojkovich

Training camp manager Bill Nunn Jr. lights up Chuck Noll.

Upbeat moment at retirement press conference for Chuck Noll.

Dan Rooney and Noll grow glum toward end of same announcement.

Mike Fabus

Chuck Noll says goodbye
"There has to be an end sometime."

It was the day after Christmas, 1991, and greeting cards were hanging from the black walls in the lobby of the Steelers' offices at Three Rivers Stadium. Chins were hanging everywhere in a funereal-like setting as staffers were saddened by the day's surprising news development in Steelerland.

Chuck Noll had come to the office that morning and told his boss, Steelers' president Dan Rooney, that he had decided to resign as coach of the team. That was it. No more. They talked for 20 minutes.

I spotted Noll's secretary, Pam Morocco, sobbing unashamedly in someone else's office. It hurt.

I felt strange as I sat with other members of the media waiting for Noll to come and announce his resignation as coach of the Pittsburgh Steelers after 23 years on the job.

The TV cameras had all been set up, and the cameramen were doing sound checks on the microphones, newspaper photographers were jostling for prime positions, and focusing their cameras, some of the reporters were testing their tape recorders, and others were talking to their offices on mobile phones. There was much clicking. There was much commotion in the room.

The crowd and equipment had increased considerably, and changed considerably, since Noll was announced as the new coach of the Steelers back in 1969 at the club's claustrophic-inducing offices at the old Roosevelt Hotel. There were no lap-top computers back then.

The room at Three Rivers Stadium for his goodbye press conference was certainly more spacious. It looked just like a college classroom, which suited Noll just fine as he has always seen himself as a teacher, something of a professor. The week's work schedule prior to the final game with the Cleveland Browns was still on the black chalkboard, as was a simple offensive play — a run off left tackle — that could have been drawn by Dr. Jock Sutherland back in the late '40s. That chalkboard, along with a large painting of a Steelers' helmet, would serve as the backdrop for Noll and Rooney to offer parting remarks.

A table, a battery of microphones and two chairs were all there waiting for their arrival.

I had been summoned to the Steelers' offices by a telephone call from Dan Edwards, the team's publicist, who called at 12:10 and told me there would be a press conference at 1 o'clock. I'd have time to shave, and make the half hour drive to Three Rivers Stadium. I didn't ask Edwards what the press conference was about. I knew better from experience. I knew in my bones that it was bad news. That Noll would no longer be coaching the Steelers.

I didn't want Noll to retire. I wanted him to stay and, hopefully, turn things around, and have a few good seasons before he called it quits. I knew Noll and I didn't know who the new coach would be — no one did — and, like a lot of people, I resist change. With Noll, you knew who you had to deal with, and what that was all about.

But it dawned on me just a few days earlier, a few days after that final game with the Browns, that Noll would not continue as the coach. I was driving home on Banksville Road, on a stretch on the other side of the medial strip from where Dan Rooney had been badly injured in an auto accident about a decade earlier, when it hit me that Noll would not come back.

I was listening to a sportscast on the radio and the announcer said something like "Noll is not sure what he's going to do. . ." He's gone, I thought. He had always told his players that if they were even thinking about retiring then that's what they ought to do. "If the thought enters your mind. . .," he had said on so many occasions. Noll would hear his own voice, I thought. He had no other choice.

He was 59, and he would turn 60 on January 5, 1992. He had been in pro football as a player and coach for 39 years. He had simply had enough of it. The season had been a frustrating one for him, on and off the field. He walked away from a $700,000 salary.

But I hated the idea of the Steelers without Noll as the head coach.

Noll's door was always open. I think he trusted me, and it took a long time to build up that trust. He was as accessible as anybody I had ever dealt with in the sports world. He wasn't the easiest or most entertaining interview, but he tried in earnest, and he was genuine and usually affable and accommodating. There was a calmness about him, a reassuring smile, and he had a better sense of humor than people gave him credit for. In short, there was a decency about him.

Best of all, he was a good man.

"Change is inevitable, Chuck always said that change was the one thing you could count on," Joe Gordon reminded me as we later spoke in the Steelers' office complex.

Gordon had joined the Steelers a few months after Noll was hired in 1969, coming over from the NHL Penguins to serve as the publicity director of the team, and had been an integral part of the team's dynasty. In more recent years, Gordon had been promoted to a more prominent executive position, with a new title each year, it seemed. He was, in short, one of Dan Rooney's top sidekicks and advisors.

This was a difficult day for everybody in the Steelers' organization. Dan Rooney looked grayer than usual, with his hair and suit of the same color. He looked like a priest. Noll wore a charcoal gray slipover sweater and matching slacks, an open white shirt, and shiny black shoes — nothing special — to the press conference.

Some of the sportswriters who had known Noll the longest were not even present for his final day on the job. Neither Norm Vargo of *The Daily News* in McKeesport nor Dave Ailes of the *Tribune-Review* in Greensburg, who had been on the beat the longest, were present. No one could contact them.

After all, it was the day after Christmas, and most were elsewhere enjoying the holidays. They didn't expect the news to come so soon. Tab Douglas of 3WS Radio brought his two children, ages 6 and 4, with him, and left them in the lobby for the receptionist to look after. "My wife's out shopping for leftover Christmas cards," he explained, "and I was home baby-sitting."

Rooney walked ahead of Noll through some reporters and sat down at the table. Dan Edwards asked the cameramen if they were ready.

Rooney started reading from a yellow legal pad on which he had hand-written his remarks.

"Chuck Noll is retiring as coach of the Steelers," related Rooney. "He is, and will be, a part of he team in the future. It has been a wonderful 23 years. Chuck is a great man, and he hasn't changed from day one. He brought dignity and integrity to the coaching profession, and that, even more than four Super Bowls, is what it means to be a Steeler.

"He and my father made the Steelers special, and they will always be special because of them. We in Pittsburgh are really fortunate. What a great time and experience. Pittsburgh has a great football tradition, and Chuck Noll has furthered that tradition.

"He ranks with the great coaches of the game. I always liked to compare him with Amos Alonzo Stagg. He ranks right up there with George Halas, Vince Lombardi and Curly Lambeau. I want to thank Chuck and Marianne for everything, especially being friends. The greatest compliment that I know is my wife said a long time ago, 'If anything happens to us, I would like Chuck Noll to raise my kids.' Thank you, and God bless."

Noll forced a smile, and looked up and checked out his audience, and measured them with his eyes. He paused before he spoke, strictly off the cuff.

"You know, it's much easier coming in than going out. The emotions that build up and the attachments that build up over 23 years are tough to, I guess, sever. That's probably the best way to say it. They're not going to be completely severed, but it's tough. It's been great for me. It's been great for my family, and it's been a good experience.

"The pluses and minuses have all been great experiences. Football, to me, is something special. The game of football is something special. And probably the thing that I appreciate the most about football is that it teaches you humility, because as soon as you start thinking you're pretty good . . . things can get tough.

"It makes you dig down deep and find out what things are all about. When you start thinking back, and this process has kind of forced me to think back, the only thing that I can say is, 'Thank you.' I mean this to everybody, to the city of Pittsburgh, to the coaches that I've been associated with through the years, to the players. Especially to the players, because those are the guys that make it happen on the field, those are the guys that made our success, and it's been great memories and it's been a real upbeat experience for me and my family. I'd like to again say thank you."

Then reporters began to ask questions:

Reporter: "When did you come to your decision?"

Noll: "Not easily. Time frame? I can't really say because it's been like this (up and down) and there's no one point where it came. This morning, if you want an actual time frame."

Reporter: "You must have talked about it with your family over Christmas."

Noll: "We talked about it for a long time . . . I couldn't avoid it because every time I'd come in I'd get a question. I think it was after the first Super Bowl (IX) victory. 'When are you going to retire?' So I've been thinking about it since then."

Reporter: "Why now, Chuck?"

Noll: "Well, 39 years in professional football is a goodly time. If you write for 39 years maybe you ought to think about it, too."

Reporter: "Chuck, you were quoted a couple of weeks ago saying that this was probably your most frustrating season, more so than any other. What compounded the frustration?"

Noll: "We had great expectations for this football team, and still at this point we're talking (that) we could have easily had 10 victories with this football team, but we didn't. That's the reality of it. And it would have been great to have had 10 victories and be in the playoffs and go all the way, and then say 'goodby,' but it didn't work out that way."

Reporter: "What do you do now, Chuck? What are your plans?"

Noll: "I put in for a government program so I could re-educate myself so I could do something, but I don't think it's going to come through. I think after 39 years in it I have to step back and see what the flowers smell like for a little bit."

Reporter: "If this season had no bearing on your decision, could you look back over maybe the past six or seven years?"

Noll: "There has to be an end sometime, and this is it. This is when it happened."

Reporter: "Would you label this burnout?"

Noll: "Natural death."

Reporter: "You had, until the last half of this season, never given any indication that you wanted to do this."

Noll: "Well, we wanted the concentration on the football. We want to win football games. That's what you're in there for. There's only one thing to do. I know there are a lot of people that think there are other things. Winning football games is what's important, and you work to do that. And you try to keep the concentration on that, not on some fat old man that is going to get into his life's work."

Reporter: "Chuck, since you've been doing your life's work, what comes after that?"

Noll: "That's the major question. The $64,000 question."

Reporter: "Do you still have a desire to coach, to teach football, or are you just at the point where you have no desire to do any of that?"

Noll: "Desire peaks and valleys as you go along. It's been that way throughout my life. I can remember running laps when I was in college, saying, 'What am I doing out here? This is terrible.' And then the next minute this is the greatest thing that ever happened. That's life. Right now I'm not planning on coaching any more, although I've been accused of coaching all my life, when I was playing or doing other things

. . . (On the) golf course. Nobody wants to play with me because of it."

Reporter: "Are you ruling out ever trying to coach again?"

Noll: "Probably . . . One day at a time."

Reporter: "Chuck, is this a sad day for you?"

Noll: "It is. I told you, it was easier coming in than going out. It's tough. It's been tough on my family, the decision, and I went back and talked to some of the people in the organization and we cried a little bit together. It's that time. It's tough."

Reporter: "So this is no spur-of-the-moment thing. It's thought-out, right?"

Noll: "It's thought-out. No anger, nothing involved, right. For you investigative reporters, there's no challenge."

Reporter: "When you took that seat 23 years ago, does that seem like yesterday to you in some ways?"

Noll: "There's no question about it. It seems like yesterday. Time, I guess, keeps going faster and faster. . ."

Reporter: "Chuck, in thinking back over the last couple of years with you and Terry and the comment about Franco — the Franco Who?' — do you have any regrets about how things ended with you and some of your star players?"

Noll: "Obviously, you'd like everything to be smooth, but termination is not easy, it's not usually smooth. I heard somebody tell me (philosopher Ralph Waldo) Emerson probably put it best when he said, 'Your actions speak so loudly I can't hear what you're saying,' and I'd like to keep it that way . . . You don't know what that means, I guess."

Reporter: "Are you planning to meet with any of the players that are on the team now and sitting down with them?"

Noll: "And reminisce? When we get in rocking chairs we'll probably do that. There are things to be done and I'm sure I'll be busy from that standpoint. And I'll miss all the guys. I'll miss the training camps, I'll miss the season, those types of things. That's going to be tough, but I'm sure you'll help me."

Reporter: "Chuck, did you have a sense after the game Sunday — you said there was some emotion — that it was your last game?"

Noll: "Well, the thought was there, but you keep vascillating back and forth. Sunday's game, afer the game, was a traumatic time, I guess. An emotional time. For our players, it was a good victory and for some of the comments back and forth it was tough. (Pause) And you've got enough now, before it gets tougher."

Noll gripped the arms of his chair as if to depart, and Myron Cope couldn't resist. "One more question," cried Cope. "Is it fair to say that over the 23 years you've changed, in other words, mellowed?"

Noll: "You'd have to ask somebody else that question . . . I think I've stayed the same. But who knows?"

67

I spotted Joe Gordon sitting in the back of the room. His face was flushed and buried in his folded hands, like a man saying prayers. This was a press conference he could have done without. "It hurts; he's a friend," said Gordon later.

I listened to Cope chatting with Doug Hoerth during Hoerth's afternoon talk show on WTAE Radio an hour after the press conference. WTAE is the flagship station for Steelers' game broadcasts, so Hoerth — who boasts of not caring one whit about football — was told to concentrate on the Noll story the rest of the afternoon.

Cope called in from the Steelers' offices, and they lined up some former Steelers to chat about Noll.

Cope recalled how Noll has a habit of gripping the arms on his chair late in a press conference, a signal that he's ready to vacate the premises. "He wanted out of there at a certain point, and I asked him another question — it wasn't such a great question, either," said Cope. "And I coulda kicked myself for asking one more question. Because he was going to cry."

Cope commented on a show later that evening on WTAE that Noll had left the building within minutes of the conclusion of the press conference. "He threw on his coat and he was outta there," said Cope. "That's when I got a gulp in my throat."

Former Steelers receiver Lynn Swann was contacted by WTAE and he offered a few thoughts an hour or so after the announcment. "I am surprised," said Swann, "that he decided to do it after what he termed his most frustrating season. Chuck is a very competitive fellow, and I thought he would want to come back and produce a winner before he called it quits."

In explaining Noll's manner, Swann later said something about how Noll built "certain walls between him and the players." Swann also said, "Something is going to be lost."

Cope coaxed Swann to retell a story about how he and some of his teammates once went, unannounced and uninvited, to Noll's home in Upper St. Clair on Christmas Eve in 1979.

"I went with Gerry Mullins, Jack Ham, Mike Wagner and Franco Harris," said Swann, "and we were standing outside singing Christmas carols. Chuck came out and invited us all into the house.

"Chuck got out a ukelele and started playing it and singing carols right along with us. Seeing him like that, and seeing some of the stuff that was on the walls of his home, pictures and stuff . . . it gave me a totally different view of the guy."

Cope told a story about how easy it was to work with Noll on all the pre-game shows they taped together through the years, and how understanding and cooperative Noll would be if any problems developed.

"We were in Cleveland once and we used to stay at this out-of-the-way hotel clear on the other side of Cleveland from the Stadium," said Cope. "They had just changed all the phones in the hotel, and we couldn't use the new kind to hook up our radio transmission lines back to Pittsburgh. Noll didn't get ruffled. He said, 'I have a sister who lives ten minutes from here, and we can go to her house and do it from there.'

68

Dan Rooney welcomes new coach Chuck Noll in January, 1969.

Let's Have a BIG HAND For CHAZ

Scoreboard message salutes Noll on 100th victory in December, 1979.

And that's just what we did. That's when I realized why we were staying in that faraway hotel, too. Because Chuck picked the hotels himself. He wanted to be near his sister's house."

Hoerth told Cope and Swann they were running out of time, and would have to cut the conversation, but Swann persisted. "I think there's a guy right here who could take Chuck's place, right here in this city."

Cope came back, "Are you talking about Joe Greene?"

"No," said Swann, "I'm talking about Paul Hackett at Pitt. He runs a pro offense, and he did just that for the Cowboys and the 49ers. Think about that."

It was starting to sink in. Bob Smizik, the sports columnist for *The Pittsburgh Press*, offered aloud that things might change for the worse when a new coach took over.

"Coaches make demands nowadays when they take jobs," he reminded the reporters around him. "A new coach might come in and see this room, and say, 'What's this?' When they tell him it's the media room, he might say, 'Not anymore it isn't.'

"We have one of the best situations here as far as accessibility, and that could change with a new coach."

Younger writers from *The Press* like Steve Hubbard and Gerry Dulac demurred, saying that would never happen with Rooney and Gordon around. But Smizik still wasn't so sure about that. "We'll see."

Others said Noll was not the easiest coach to interview, or to get information from, that he didn't, for instance, stand around on the field after practice, as some NFL coaches do, and talk to the reporters routinely after a workout.

"But you could see him when you wanted to," said Smizik. "You could have lunch with Dan Rooney if you wanted to. I hope that won't change."

It was the day after the day that Noll announced his resignation. The doors to the Steelers' offices were locked, and only a few staff members were at work. It was unusually quiet. Only three sports writers were in the media room. They were the two main beat writers, Ed Bouchette of the *Post-Gazette* and Steve Hubbard of *The Pittsburgh Press*, and Ron Cook, a columnist for the *Post-Gazette*. They were there hoping to sniff out some news regarding Noll's successor. They were debating about who was the best hockey writer in town. Noll was already old news.

Out of curiosity as much as anything else, I attended all of Noll's last press conferences with the Steelers. If he was going to retire, I wanted to be present at his last meetings with the media, to see how he would handle his critics.

At his final weekly press conference prior to the season finale with the Cleveland Browns, somebody started drilling him about the Bubby Brister vs. Neil O'Donnell competiton for the starting position at quarterback.

70

As the questioneer persisted, Noll became rankled.

Reporter: "You can't guarantee Bubby that he won't be a back-up then?"

Noll: "You're trying to make a story. There are no guarantees in this world. There are no guarantees in football. There are no guarantees."

That was vintage Noll. He not only responded smartly to what he considered an inappropriate question, but he made a teaching point — not about football, but about life.

To the end, Noll was Noll. He kept coming back with Nollisms.

Reporter: "I don't think he was looking for a guarantee. He just wants to know that the job is going to be open for competition at least going into next season."

Noll: "Next season will take care of itself. Right now we've got one game that we're concerned about and that's Cleveland."

Reporter: "You said you don't want to switch back and forth. Why, if you have two guys who are capable. . .?"

Noll: "It sounds like one of those questions. 'I don't know anything about football, but. . .' "

Reporter: "If you have two guys who are capable, what's wrong with going week-to-week? Does it create dissent on the team?"

Noll: "It has a tendency to divide, and you have people choosing. That happens even when you are not doing that. And that's something you'd like to avoid because you want one team, one goal, one purpose and that's not necessarily a story."

Reporter: "Are you talking about players or the stinking media?"

Noll: "I'm talking about everybody: coaches, fans, media, players."

Then the topic turned to another controversial subject: Tim Worley, who had been suspended during the season by the NFL office for drug abuse.

Reporter: "Are his problems over?"

Noll: That's a day-to-day thing. Anybody who has any understanding of that knows that — that's what it is."

Reporter: "Does he have a support group for this? Is there some way the team is involved in helping him?"

Noll: "The team has become very much involved in helping him. His support group, it's the whole ball of wax that you have to go through."

Reporter: "You don't want to say how involved?"

Noll: "Involved."

Reporter: "The team has become more involved in those kind of situations, helping players, than maybe they were 15, 20 years ago."

Noll: "Are they? Yes. We didn't have the problem 15 or 20 years ago that you have right now. Society didn't have the problem that it has right now. Society has gifted us with this problem and we have to face up to it. Our primary source of business is not rehabilitation, however, our primary source is to win football games and you have to make judgments based on that. That's an offshoot."

Reporter: "You were kind of outspoken when this first surfaced about Tim (Worley). You made some comments about his future on the team. You came across to some people as being perhaps cold and distant. Have you changed? Were you misinterpreted at that time? Have you been supportive?"

Noll: "In order to get somebody to get into rehabilitation, you sometimes have to be a little bit tough."

Reporter: "Did you see this coming at the time?"

Noll: "Yes."

Reporter: "And you were purposely that way?"

Noll: "It has to get done."

Reporter: "You have a chance of being 7-9. In light of everything that has happened with (Barry) Foster, injuries, left guard . . . is that a decent record with everything that's happened this season?"

Noll: "We'd like to have nine wins right now. We have the capability of having that and it's disappointing that we don't. Again, we hurt ourselves along that line, different areas at different times. That's disappointing."

Reporter: "Is there anything the young players, any players, can learn from what Worley has gone through?"

Noll: "I think that one of the things most people learn from is their own experience. You can tell stories. You can talk about other people, but until they experience it themselves sometimes it's tough."

Reporter: "You've said several times that the season has been a disappointment. Have you made up your mind what you want to do when the season is over?"

Noll: "No."

Reporter: "That's something that you don't give any thought to?"

Noll: "I don't think about it right now."

Reporter: "Is this year any different from past years when you make up your mind about what you want to do when the season is over?"

Noll: "Yes, it's different than any other year."

Reporter: "Why?"

Noll: "It's different."

Reporter: "Because you're a year older? Because of the losing record?"

Noll: "No. None of those things."

Reporter: "Desire still there?"

Noll: "Yes, pretty much. That has nothing . . . you got a deadline on this?"

Reporter: "Will you know Sunday when you run out on the field if it will be your last time?"

Noll: "No."

Noll's final post-game press conference, following the game with the Cleveland Browns, lasted about five minutes. I had been talking to Sam Nover, the WPXI-TV sportscaster, in the end zone near the end of the game, and I predicted that Noll would walk out in anger during the press conference. Nover said, "Oh, I don't think so. Chuck wouldn't do that."

"You watch," I said. "They're going to get under his skin, and he'll leave."

Noll opened up with some positive comments about how the Steelers played in their season finale, how well the defense had played, how the offense made too many mistakes, and that there were too many penalties.

No one was interested in the usual post-game fodder. Sportswriters were cracking one-liners before Noll showed up for the press conference. They sensed that this was the last time they would meet Noll under these circumstances.

Ed Bouchette of the *Post-Gazette* began to drill Noll.

Bouchette: "What are your future plans?"

Noll: "I don't know right now what's going to happen. It'll be later on."

Bouchette: "Do you know when you'll make your decision?"

Noll: "No, not really."

Bouchette: "Before Christmas?"

Noll: "I don't know."

Bouchette: "Why do you have to wait?"

Noll: "Well, there are some . . . We have to talk a little bit. There has to be some discussion."

Bouchette: "With whom?"

Noll: "Everybody. I'll probably talk to you. We'll take a vote and see how it goes."

Bouchette: "Do you have to talk to Dan Rooney?"

Noll: "That's one of the things that has to be done."

Bouchette: "Friday you said you made up your mind. . ."

Noll: "No, I didn't say that. I said 'this game wouldn't make a difference' and it doesn't — the win or the loss."

Then other reporters got into the fun.

Reporter: "Did you have any particular emotion today?"

Noll: "Yeah, there was a lot of emotion. It doesn't always show. You don't have to wear your emotions on your sleeve to have emotions. There was emotion."

Reporter: "Was it frustrating to finish one game out of a playoff berth?"

Noll: "We would have liked to have been about 10 wins and then we'd have no problem at all. We could have easily done that."

With that, Noll exited the room, and didn't look back.

Bill Cowher
"Whatever it takes, we'll get it all done."

B ill Cowher was 12 years old and playing peewee football for the
Crafton Little Cougars when Chuck Noll signed on to coach the
Pittsburgh Steelers on January 27, 1969. When Cowher was playing catch in front of his home on Hawthorne Avenue in those days he
didn't dare dream that someday he would be the head coach of those
same Steelers. Crafton is less than five miles from Three Rivers Stadium — which opened a year after Noll came to Pittsburgh — but it seemed
a lot farther for a young boy back then. Cowher had to travel a zig-zag
road to get there. It didn't take him very long, however, to reach his
destination.

He got there quicker than Noll, who grew up in Cleveland. Noll
was 37 when he was named the head coach of the Steelers. Cowher was
34 and would be 35 by the time the team went to training camp at St.
Vincent College. He is the youngest head coach of the Steelers since
they hired John Michelosen, 33, to succeed Jock Sutherland in 1948.

Dan Rooney chose Cowher to become the 15th head coach in the
Steelers' 60-year history, succeeding Noll, who retired on December 26
after 23 seasons at the helm. Rooney did so at the endorsement of Tom
Donahoe, the director of football operations, who oversaw the search
for Noll's replacement. The announcement was made in front of family
and friends, and a room full of media at Three Rivers Stadium on January 21.

"I want to thank the Rooneys and Tom Donahoe," said Cowher
in his opening comments, "for giving me an opportunity to fulfill a life-
long dream."

Cowher, with close-cropped hair parted in the middle, looked like
he had just come from a military academy. Another Major Dad. He held
his head erect, had a firm chin, and spoke with strong conviction. He
was serious, for the most part, respectful and to the point, but he smiled
at some of the off-the-wall questions, and he has a smile that goes from
ear to ear, one naked ear to another naked ear.

When he played football at Carlynton High School — Carlynton
is a jointure of the school districts of Carnegie, Roslyn Farms and
Crafton-Ingram — and North Carolina State, Cowher's ears were covered
with hair, lots of hair. One such photo from the family album appeared
in the *Pittsburgh Post-Gazette* the morning of the press conference. It
wasn't a very flattering photo. His parents had given it to the *P-G* upon
request.

"I'll tell you the moral of that story," said Cowher. "It's always
keep your parents updated with recent pictures."

Young as he is, Cowher knew the Steelers before they got to Three
Rivers Stadium. He had seen them play at Pitt Stadium, and his father,
Laird, told him stories about when they used to play at Forbes Field.

Mike Fabus

Kaye and Bill Cowher with new boss at hiring announcement.

Bill Cowher's family, from left to right, are brothers Dale and Doug, sister-in-law Janet, parents Laird and Dorothy, and wife Kaye.

Asked about his earliest memories of the Steelers when he was a kid, Cowher had to smile before responding. "I guess going up Heart Attack Hill, John Henry Johnson returning the kickoff, probably more than that, the hot dogs and popcorn at the stadium," he said.

He was referring, of course, to the steep incline alongside Pitt Stadium that is more commonly referred to as Cardiac Hill. Pro Football Hall of Fame running back John Henry Johnson did, indeed, run back kickoffs on occasion. Going to a stadium or ballfield with one's father and friends always seems to be a cherished memory for most men, and Cowher is no exception. Cowher has a heckuva memory, though, if he can remember John Henry Johnson returning kickoffs because Johnson's last season with the Steelers was 1965 when Cowher was eight years old.

Many of Cowher's comments that first day were a little fuzzy, and often in unfinished sentences, and he forgot to introduce his wife, Kaye, after he introduced everyone else present from the Cowher clan. Most of them were clad in black and gold ensembles for the occasion. Just like die-hard Steeler fans. But it was understandable if he was a little nervous in taking over such a monstrous assignment in his hometown.

When he was a teenager, the Steelers were the toast of the town, the Pirates were winning the World Series, Pitt had a national championship team, and Pittsburgh was hailed everywhere as "The City of Champions." So he has a healthy respect for the torch that has been handed to him, and he doesn't intend to drop it, or burn himself carrying it.

"The Steelers, I think for anyone who's grown up here," Cowher continued, "have been involved in the Renaissance of this city and I don't think there's any question that the '70s took this downtown area and it flourished and it grew from it. You take a little bit of that with you. I think you go back to some of the great coaches that have come out of this area. There's a work ethic. You know that nothing will be handed to you, that you have to work for it. I think it's what the City of Pittsburgh stands for: pride and tradition, nothing that comes easy."

Cowher was awarded a four-year contract to get started in earnest on his project. He had been the defensive coordinator and linebackers coach for the Kansas City Chiefs. His boss there was Marty Schottenheimer, a former Pitt center from Fort Cherry High School in McDonald, Pennsylvania, who had once been cut from the Steelers squad by Noll after a tryout late in his pro playing career.

"Bill was probably as well-respected by his peers as any player I've been around," said Schottenheimer in a telephone press conference conducted at the Steelers' offices soon after Cowher's signing.

"Bill is a very bright, hard-working individual. He has two qualities that we think are most important: He's a very fine teacher and very demanding. There will be no free lunches.

"There will be a purpose to everything that they do. It will be extremely well-organized. He's abundantly qualified to do the job. He's always been very detail-conscious, very thorough in everything that he does. Bill Cowher has but one negative in that he's never been a head coach before. Other than that, I don't know of anything."

Lou Holtz, the head coach at Notre Dame, recruited Cowher to come to North Carolina State when he was coaching there. "Bill is an outstanding coach and person," said Holtz. "I am really happy for his success. One does not accomplish at an early age all that he has without having a lot of things going for him. I feel sure that he will do very well."

Under Cowher, the Kansas City defense led the American Football Conference and was ranked second in the National Football League in 1989, his first as coordinator. In 1990, K.C.'s defense led the league in three categories with 60 sacks, 25 fumbles recovered, and 45 takeaways. The year before, it finished third in the AFC and fifth in the NFL as the Chiefs went 10-6 and claimed an AFC wild-card playoff berth.

Cowher began his coaching career in 1985 as special teams coach for the Cleveland Browns under Schottenheimer. He was one of Schottenheimer's first hirings. Cowher coached the Browns' special team units for two seasons before taking over the defensive secondary for the 1987 and 1988 campaigns.

Some thought Schottenheimer would have been an ideal coach for the Steelers, while others suggested Mike Ditka, another former Pitt star from Aliquippa. Neither was available as both were under contract. Cowher was asked if Schottenheimer had much of an influence on him as a coach.

"He's a fine football coach," came back Cowher. "He had a great deal of influence on me. I have a great deal of respect for the man. The one thing that I feel very fortunate about is that through my last 12 years in the National Football League, five years as a player, seven years as a coach, I've had an opportunity to be associated with some fine football coaches — Sam Rutigliano, Dick Vermeil, Marty Schottenheimer. And I feel that the qualities of those individuals, the good, the bad that we all have, have helped me grow as a coach, and I think they've all played a major part in me being given this opportunity today."

Cowher was asked what part growing up in western Pennsylvania played in the development of so many football coaches who came from this region.

"I think it's the realism that you're not handed anything," he answered, "that you have to work for things you believe in, things that you want."

Less than a week after Cowher was hired there was a full page profile of him in the Sunday edition of *The Pittsburgh Press* by feature writer Bill Utterback who checked out some of the people who knew Cowher as a kid, as a collegian, and as a young pro.

Lou James, a boyhood buddie and a high school teammate, said, "I remember the first day I met Bill. We were 8 or 9 years old and we got into a fight in the alley behind his house. I whipped him that day,

77

and then I hid from him. I can still see the look in his eyes. It was scary. He hates to lose. He gets so intense, and you can see the intensity in his eyes. They say Mike Singletary (of the Chicago Bears) has the most imposing eyes in football, but they can't be any more imposing than Cowher's."

Another classmate from Carlynton, Bill Ellsworth, told Utterback, "You would look at him in the huddle and he'd be so intense, so emotional, that there would actually be tears in his eyes."

That could be quite a contrast to Chuck Noll's eyes. In his book, *Looking Deep,* Bradshaw said, "When you look into Chuck Noll's eyes, you see nothing. They appear mysterious — cold and emotionless."

Ray Ellis, a former Browns' safety, told Utterback about Cowher in his Cleveland days. "We had a nickname for him," said Ellis, who also played with Cowher in Philadelphia. "We called him 'The Face.' Frank Minnifield named him. It had to do with the intensity we saw in his face. During a game, you would look over at him and he looked like a big, old, mean grizzly stalking and prowling."

Jim Ritcher, an offensive lineman of the Buffalo Bills, was a teammate of Cowher at North Carolina State. "Cowher was a crazy guy," related Richter. "He was one of the fun guys to be with. The people he hung out with, they'd break down doors, stay up late. He was the typical college football player. It is hard to picture him as being the coach over the players and having to discipline them and that kind of stuff. It's hard to see it."

Hey, hopefully we all grow up. Cowher might encounter difficulty getting confirmed as a Supreme Court judge, but Dan Rooney, as much a straight arrow as there is, thinks he has the right stuff to instill some spirit in the Steelers and help turn the team around.

"I am very excited about the Steelers future," Rooney said in his opening remarks at the press conference to announce the hiring of Cowher. "I am confident we are headed in the right direction. Our players will have the opportunity to do their best, because they will be in capable hands under excellent leadership.

"Bill is a very capable young man, with the experience and intelligence to be a successful coach in the National Football League. I am impressed by his strength, character and enthusiasm — his appreciation for the game.

"We are pleased that he will be the Steelers coach. He will be a credit to Pittsburgh, the Steelers, the National Football League, the coaching profession, and to himself."

For a tow-headed kid from Crafton, it can't get any better than that.

Cowher came back home with a bright outlook. Some critics thought he came off as too optimistic, perhaps unrealistic in his assessment of the Steelers' situation. Even Myron Cope, who wants to see the Steelers succeed more than anybody, questioned Cowher's scouting report on the team in a TV commentary he did the night of the hiring announcement. Cope felt Cowher put himself out on a limb.

"I've had aspirations of becoming a head coach," Cowher had said at the press conference, "and what the Steelers organization has given me is an opportunity. And the one thing that has excited me more than just coming back to Pittsburgh, which to me has been a big plus, is that I think there's a big opportunity to win here.

"Again, I think the tradition, the stability, the credibility of the front office and the wealth of talent that is on this football team is exciting to any football coach who can come into this situation, and I feel very fortunate to be given the opportunity to do that."

Cowher couldn't count the number of hands that went up with that remark. His interrogators wanted to know whom he was talking about when he referred to the wealth of talent.

"On defense, there is a lot of team speed. Offensively, you have great depth at the running back position, talented wide receivers, and two young quarterbacks who give you a chance for the future. And given those positions, and that type of talent, I think there is a great opportunity to win."

Eyes rolled among the skeptical media.

Cowher was asked what it was like following in the footsteps of Chuck Noll, one of the all-time great coaches and the only one to win four Super Bowls.

"Chuck Noll is a legend," he said firmly. "I know the word has been used to describe him as that. What Chuck Noll has done for this city is something I stated in my opening statement. He's brought tradition, he's brought pride to this city. And that's the thing I want to do also, in my own way. I have no reservations about following Chuck Noll, because what Chuck Noll did, he did for him and he did it in his way. Bill Cowher will do it his way."

Cowher was told that he came off differently than Noll, that people were used to a soft-spoken coach in Noll. How would he compare?

"Well, I can't answer that," said Cowher. "I'm going to be Bill Cowher. There are probably going to be some situations that come up that, as they do in a football game, you prepare yourself, you do your homework and you react. That's what I'm going to do. I'm going to be me. I think I prepared myself to handle adversity. I've prepared myself to handle success, and I think there's an unknown. There's an unknown that the Rooneys and Tom Donahoe have taken when they picked Bill Cowher as their head coach. My challenges, as have been put forward to me, as they have with every position I've accepted, are to prove that I can be the best at what I do."

Cowher was asked about his work habits.

"We will do what it takes," he said, sounding like you know who. "I don't want to scare any coaches away. We will do what it takes to get the job done, and again, my belief is that things have to be thoroughly done. I believe the best chance you have for success is that everyone has a true understanding of what's expected of them. If that means spending time until 2 in the morning, we will do it. If we can get that job done and be home by 8, we'll do that. If it means spending 2 1/2 hours on the practice field, we'll do it. If it means going out there and doing it in 1 hour and 45 minutes, we'll do it. So we will do what it takes to get it done."

Would working in his hometown, in front of family and friends, pose any sort of problem, or would it be a distraction?

"I'm able to deal with it. My parents may be in another situation. I think it's great. It's all in how you want to perceive something. If you want to let it be a hindrance to you, then it will be."

That also sounded a lot like you know who. It's scary.

"To me, it's a great opportunity for my family to be able to see their grandchildren, and us not having to fly in; so we can save some money. So I look at it in no other way than that. Because my job will be consuming enough. I think it's a great opportunity to come back to your hometown."

Cowher had said he would like to talk to Chuck Noll about the job. He sounded like some of the former Steelers when he spoke about his desire for such a meeting.

"I've had a chance to meet Chuck before on a very formal basis, down at the Senior Bowl," he said. "I have a great deal of respect for the man. Anyone who's been able to accomplish the things that Chuck Noll has accomplished in our profession has to be put in a class of his own. As for my conversation with him, I haven't sat down and document-ed exactly what I wanted to ask him. I have a great deal of respect for him. To be quite honest, I think it would be very enjoyable for me to sit down and talk with Chuck Noll."

Cowher confessed that he hardly got choked up when he learned that Noll had retired. It might have been an emotional moment for Noll, but not for Cowher. To Cowher, it was just another job opening, another opportunity. The year before he came up second in the interviews for the head coaching job in Cleveland, and he was hoping his time had come.

"To be honest, I think it was about the seventh job opening that took place at the time," said Cowher. "You know, we all can't stay in this business forever. Chuck's tenure in this league is well document-ed. Again, he goes down as one of the all-time great NFL head coaches. We are all going to retire at some point. I looked at it as nothing more than that. I think what he's been able to do for the game of football and, more importantly, what he's been able to do for the City of Pittsburgh, is something that is remarkable."

Cowher was asked to describe himself as a football player, and how his status might have affected his outlook as a coach.

"I would say I was not gifted athletically. I got by because I knew what I was doing, desire, good special teams player, always your 46th or 47th guy on the roster. Every year at training camp I had a fork road philosophy, because I knew at any time I could be heading down the other road. How has that helped me? It's helped me to understand that hard work and belief in yourself can allow you to obtain any goal that you set forth. It's not just talent that can get you someplace. If you make a commitment, and you believe in it, that you can obtain anything."

Asked if he had a soft spot in his heart for guys like that, Cowher was quick to correct any such miscalculation.

"Only if it doesn't compromise your chance to win," he said. "There are a lot of great guys out there, but if they can't help you win, you've got to be careful in how many great guys you have on your football team."

Everybody in the Steelers' offices was complimenting Chuck Noll on how good he looked, what a great tan he had, and they wanted to know how he felt and how he was doing. Noll did look good, and he did have a great tan, and I thought to myself that he had to feel strange and awkward — you just do when you return to an office setting where you once worked.

Noll was all smiles and short sentences and nods and more smiles. He was all browns and beiges, with an open-collared shirt, and a sportscoat and slacks. He was standing by the receptionist's desk in the lobby of the Steelers' office complex at Three Rivers Stadium, speaking to his long-time secretary, Pam Morocco. I had seen her crying unabashedly on the day her boss retired, nearly two months earlier. "I felt so bad that day," admitted Morocco. Now she was able to smile in response to his remarks. Noll was holding his mail in his hands, and he handed her some of it. Maybe he asked her to take care of it. He was, after all, still employed by the Steelers. In what capacity, nobody seemed to know.

Bill Cowher came by and spotted Noll and approached him, said something in the way of a greeting, and shook Noll's hand. Was I witnessing a historic moment — the first meeting of Noll and Cowher — since the grail had passed hands?

"No, that wasn't it," said Cowher when I visited with him in his office later. "Dan flew us both down to Hilton Head a week or so ago, with our wives, and we had a chance to talk. Nothing major. It was just a casual conversation. We talked about instant replay, and Plan B free agents, stuff like that. I wanted to have his input. We talked about some of the players."

You can bet that one of the players they discussed was the troubled Tim Worley, a $3 million investment by the Steelers that seemed to be going down the drain. In fact, Worley had also stopped in the Steelers' offices that same day. He was told Coach Cowher wanted to see him, but managed to duck out without saying anything to his new boss. Within a few weeks, Worley's name would be in the news again, this time for failing to take some drug tests, and he faced the possibility of being suspended for the entire 1992 season. That's exactly what happened.

Worley would be Cowher's first major challenge, no doubt. One thing was clear: Noll did not have to concern himself with such matters anymore. That's one of the reasons Cowher could say of Noll, "He looks relaxed. He seems at peace with himself. I have a lot of respect for him, and I value any knowledge he might pass along."

A few nights earlier, the Steelers hosted a reunion of former players in the same conference room where Noll's resignation and Cowher's hiring had been announced. There were no media present for this event, just plenty of beer and soda pop and hoagies. There was a great turnout of Steelers alumni.

"I sat down and had an opportunity to shake hands with everybody I'd rooted for all my life as a Steelers' fan," he said. "It was a fun time, and the best time I've had since I've been in Pittsburgh. I've been so involved with all my duties, I haven't had much time to enjoy myself.

"Seeing all those great players from the past had a major impact on me. For the first time, it really hit me that I was back in a town where I grew up, and that I was coaching the team of my youth, 16 years after I left high school.

"Seeing the players from so many different eras," continued Cowher, "it was a great night for me, almost from a selfish standpoint. It was an opportunity to see guys like Ray Mansfield and John Brown, the guys who laid the foundation for the Super Bowl teams, who went through some tough times. It was special. There is such great tradition here.

"When I was at Kansas City, they had a really good alumni organization called the Ambassadors Club. But there are so many more individuals who have stayed in Pittsburgh and made this their home, so the potential here is even greater."

Cowher had received congratulatory letters from many of those alumni who attended the evening get-together, and now he was signing letters of response that had been prepared for him by his new secretary. He dropped a note to all the alumni who attended the affair.

After Noll left, management moved Morocco to a different office and hired a new secretary for the new head coach. They hired Cyd Roman, whom I had worked with during my days in the athletic department at the University of Pittsburgh. Roman had served as personal secretary for Johnny Majors, Jackie Sherrill and Foge Fazio, but was replaced soon after Mike Gottfried got the job. She had since been working in the ticket office at Pitt. Friends from her days at Pitt, Les Banos, the Pitt sports photographer, and Kenny Bashioum, a sports-minded retiree who runs errands for the Pitt football office, were taking her out to lunch. She was in good company.

Some of the new assistant coaches Cowher had hired were walking back and forth past Roman's desk. It was a different scene, except for the familiar face of Dick Hoak, with its five o'clock shadow.

The office was the same where Cowher held forth, with framed posters of the Washington Redskins and Atlanta Falcons, for whatever reason, some x's and o's on the chalkboard, and NFL paraphernalia spread around the shelves. The only difference I noted was the family photos Cowher had put up on some shelves.

I asked Cowher to reflect once more on his earliest memories of going to Steelers' games at Pitt Stadium. "I was probably about eight years old," he said. "We didn't go to many games. But I remember walking up that steep hill. It seemed like it took forever to get there. I probably remember John Henry Johnson the most because I always thought that was such a good football name.

"In 1975, when I was in college, I followed them closely on TV. I was a proud Pittsburgh boy when I was down in North Carolina."

He was a linebacker at North Carolina State in Raleigh. "It was always hard to get tickets when I was in high school, so I saw more of them on TV," he said. "I remember we'd watch Notre Dame highlights on Sunday morning, and then the Steelers' games. Yes, I had some posters in my bedroom, of guys like Dick Butkus and Ray Nitschke, because I was a linebacker. As I got older, though, I took down my posters. Jack Lambert was my favorite Steeler; I just liked the way he played the game.

"I came here maybe two Sundays when I was in high school. It wasn't that easy to get tickets. I just enjoyed staying at home, and watching the football games on TV. I never really enjoyed going and watching a football game. I'd rather watch something like that on TV. If I go to a football game, I want to be playing in it.

"Those days came back to me, though, when we had all the players in the other evening. It was an opportunity to let down my guard. It was gratifying to see so many guys turn out for the affair. There was a very nice sense of nostalgia, people talking about old times. It was something very positive. You go through life and you go through something like this — and it goes so quickly — and all of a sudden it's over and you don't have a chance to reflect on what you experienced together. I would like to see us strengthen our alumni association. It would be great for our younger guys to meet these people, and to pick up some of their knowledge, and to learn about the business world. It could help our guys get jobs.

"They appear very supportive. They'd be supportive of anybody who accepted this position. Every player who played for this team wants to see the team be successful again. They're proud of what they've done, and they'd like very much for the team to be successful. Even the players who were here before the Super Bowl seasons shared in that accomplishment. I'm trying to broaden their involvement with our team."

I asked, "Was there any particular player you got a kick out of seeing?"

"Jack Lambert. Again, he was a linebacker, a great linebacker, and I was a great admirer of Jack Lambert. I liked the desire with which he played the game. I talked to him a little bit. I thought the guys they had here — Russell, Ham and Lambert — were the best linebacking trio maybe ever in the history of the league. They weren't that naturally talented, and they were undersized for their position, but they played it hard, smart and they were so opportunistic.

"Lambert was one of the last to leave the other night. I'm told he was the same way when he played. That he liked to hang back, have a beer or two, and just soak in the whole scene before he'd head home. Lambert still has that look; he can freeze people. I get a kick out of him. I wish we had a few Lamberts on this ballclub."

Cowher likes the Steelers scene, complete with all the team photos from the four Super Bowl winners, the Lombardi trophies, the large portraits of the past members of the team who have been honored in the Pro Football Hall of Fame, and all the other reminders of the team's tradition that are displayed on the walls of the office complex.

"To me, that is a motivating force," said Cowher. "To look up on the wall, and to know that they all played here, and that so much was accomplished here, right in Pittsburgh, right in Three Rivers Stadium. That should pump you up. You're so close to it.

"If you're able to accomplish something as great as the Super Bowl, it should be something for you to show off the rest of your life.

"You talk to any player, and the people stay in this game to win the Super Bowl. It's the only thing that measures success. You don't think about individual awards, and you don't think about statistical leaders — who remembers them, anyhow? — you think about who won the Super Bowl. That represents the best in the NFL.

"They can take your playing records away from you, but they can't take away your ring. That's what you want.

"You have to prove yourself every year," continued Cowher. "My motto is that you build for success. You can't live off the past. What happened here in the past was the result of a lot of hard work. But there was failure, too. As long as you stay focused on your goals, you can accomplish what you set out to do.

"Professional football isn't just getting the best players. It's getting the right mix of people. You have to overcome adversity and sometimes you have to deal with success — both have their own set of challenges — and move on. You do it with the demeanor that you expect to be good."

I asked him, "When you see some of those pictures, do you have to pinch yourself to see if you're really the head coach of the Pittsburgh Steelers?"

"I haven't seen the sun much since I've been here. We've been living out of a hotel, and I have been here most of the time," came back Cowher. "I don't even know if it's raining. I haven't thought much about what I have here. Maybe when we actually take this team out on the field for the first time...then it will hit me. When this job came open, I looked upon it as another possible opportunity for me to become a head coach in the NFL."

He eventually moved out of the hotel and into a $650,000 house in Fox Chapel. It's an easy commute to work. Whereas Noll's assistants tended to live in the South Hills during the Super Bowl days, the assistants in more recent years have bought homes in the North Hills. New roads have brought about a quicker commute out that way.

Since he spent so much time in the Steelers' shelter since coming on board, somebody should have cued Cowher when he was seated at a dais for a local program within two months after becoming the coach of the Steelers. He asked the woman next to him who she was, and what she did. It turned out to be Sophie Masloff, and she's the mayor of his old hometown. And a big Steelers fan.

Bill Cowher
Recalled by friends at N. C. State
"You just knew he was going to be a coach."

Bill Cowher concluded his playing career at North Carolina State University in a post-season game, appropriately enough, against the University of Pittsburgh, his hometown team. It was in the Tangerine Bowl, now called the Citrus Bowl, in Orlando, Florida following the 1978 campaign.

One of his former teammates and fellow linebackers, Dave Horning, recalls it was a personal showcase for Cowher, both in the clubhouse and on the playing field.

Horning, now the assistant athletic director responsible for academic support services at N. C. State, said, "Bill was always a team leader, and he gave one of the best pre-game speeches I ever heard before that Pitt game. It was right up there with Knute Rockne of Notre Dame.

"He was one of our captains, and this was his last team function, and he made the most of it. He was from Pittsburgh, and he was a real Steelers' fan, but when he went home he didn't want to hear any 'Pitt this and Pitt that' talk. His personal pride was on the line, and he let us all know that."

Just for the record, N. C. State knocked off Pitt, 30-17. That was in Jackie Sherrill's second season as head coach of the Panthers. He had a pretty good future pro linebacker himself in a sophomore named Hugh Green, and Sherrill would go on to post three successive 11-1 seasons at Pitt.

He also had a pretty fair coaching staff, which included Jimmy Johnson, now the head coach of the Dallas Cowboys; Pat Jones, the head coach at Oklahoma State; Foge Fazio, an assistant with the New York Jets; Joe Pendry, an assistant with the Kansas City Chiefs; Joe Moore, an assistant at Notre Dame; and Dave Wannstedt, an assistant with the Cowboys who came up second to Cowher in the Steelers' search for a head coach after Chuck Noll retired at the end of the 1991 season.

It does not surprise Horning that Cowher is again keeping company with those kinds of guys.

"He was a year ahead of me in school, and I can remember when I came out for team practices in my first year, he was the kind of guy who always took charge," recalled Horning. "He was a sophomore, and he wasn't a full-time starter yet, but he acted more like a senior.

"He had played a lot as a freshman, and lettered. He came right in and contributed. He was a starter his last two seasons. He was always up for games against Penn State, or Pitt, and North Carolina, our biggest local rival. He loved those games the best. When he didn't make the Philadelphia Eagles in his first pro tryout, he came right back to school and completed his studies. He got his degree in four-and-a-half years.

"When he came back, he served as a graduate assistant coach in our football program. It was my junior season, as I had been red-shirted. Bo Rein was our coach, and Bill worked real hard with him, studying film and reviewing the playbook. He was real serious, and when he talked to us and told us what to do, he knew what he was talking about. He was real earnest. I knew then that he wanted to be a coach.

"I think one of the reasons that he became a head coach in the NFL at age 34 was because he planned well. Bill took care of his school work. He was a fun guy, but he was all business on the field and in the classroom."

Horning said N. C. State spent $600,000 to establish a strong academic support program for all its athletes. "That was non-existent when I went to school," he said. "We went to school just like the other students, and we had to have a certain amount of street savvy. You had to know what was going on. You were thrown in with the rest of the students, and had to sink or swim pretty much on your own."

That particular evening, Horning was late for our date for an interview because a study hall session ran longer than he had anticipated. "We just came back from spring break," he explained, "and some of the guys weren't quite ready to get back into studying yet. You have to keep after them sometimes."

As he spoke, I couldn't help but wondering whether the athletes were better off, in the long run, when they had to fend for themselves academically in college.

Horning has offices in both the Everett Case Athletic Center and the Wiesiger-Brown Athletic Facility on the Raleigh campus. The last time I was there it was to interview Jim Valvano, the head basketball coach, just before his final season when controversial charges of NCAA violations were swirling above his handsome head. There was a void without Valvano because he was always a great host, and fun to be around. I missed seeing his red sportscar in the first parking space. I missed his smile, his stories, his jokes, his Jimmy Durante impressions.

Valvano would have enjoyed Cowher's company, no doubt. "Bill always knew how to have a good time," said Horning, coming quickly to Cowher's defense when I told him that some of Cowher's other former teammates made him out to have been a wild guy in his college days. "Bill Cowher knows how to separate business from pleasure.

"He knew when to play around and when not to play around. He had his schoolwork in line, he knew his plays, and he was never in trouble with the athletics department or with the law. He was not that type of person, or he wouldn't have been here.

"Jim Ritcher, who was on our team, and is now a Pro Bowl player with the Buffalo Bills, told me that he told some stories to the media about Cowher when he was in Minneapolis at the Super Bowl, but thought the stories made Cowher out to be some kind of crazy, misbehaving college jock. Jim said Bill was a little wild until he met his girl friend, Kaye, who became his wife. But we were all a little like that, right?

"Bill was probably the most serious football player on our team.

Bill Cowher, in center, during his linebacker days at N.C. State.

Linebackers Kyle Wescoe (57) and Cowher (54) were Wolfpack Pa. imports.

87

He did not like to get beat one-on-one, or to get beat as a team. He hated to lose. He didn't like to make mental errors. He was always prepared. He knew what Penn State was going to run on second and seven, or third and eight. He studied film and he enjoyed going over tendencies and stuff like that with the coaches."

I asked Horning if Cowher was a cheerleader for Pittsburgh and its teams when he was a student at N. C. State.

"I was from Kent, Ohio, where Jack Lambert played his college ball, and Bill and I were both big fans of Jack Lambert. Bill was an inside linebacker, and I was an outside linebacker. Bill also liked Franco Harris and all those guys. We had a lot of guys from Pennsylvania and Ohio, and he'd get after us pretty good, especially when Pittsburgh played Cleveland. We'd tell him the Browns were going to beat the Steelers, and he'd say there was no way that could happen.

"We had 19 kids from Ohio and Pennsylvania, and most of them dominated the starting lineup. We felt pretty good about that. Bill never really bought into southern living. Some kids go away and change their attitudes. Bill let you know he was from Pittsburgh and that he was proud of it. He was a big Pittsburgh Steelers fan.

"Bill was at N.C. State from 1975 to 1978, so he got there when the Steelers were winning their first Super Bowls. There wasn't a better time to be a Steelers fan."

It was early March and it was 80 degrees the day I visited the N. C. State campus to talk to old friends of Bill Cowher about his days with the Wolfpack.

It was easy to appreciate why this area of the country has such a strong appeal for young people from Pennsylvania and Ohio and other northern areas. Students were wearing shorts, and some were kicking their shoes off as they read books at benches. There were pickup basketball games and students playing tennis outdoors.

I had just come from Wake Forest, and would be visiting the University of North Carolina at Chapel Hill and Virginia Tech the next day. My daughter, Sarah, an 18-year-old high school senior, was being interviewed and doing auditions with her cello at these schools that had already accepted her for admission. She, too, wanted to go south and be warm in the winter. "You can't go wrong at any of those schools in that area," Cowher had told me before I left Pittsburgh. "It's a great place to go to school, and there's real sports enthusiasm down there."

It's also why Raleigh and the surrounding area are among the fastest growing areas in the nation. The beautiful, peaceful Blue Ridge mountains rise to the west of Raleigh, and to the east are wonderful beaches at Emerald Isle, and further south, Myrtle Beach, or the seclusion of the Nags Head, Cape Hatteras region.

Raleigh is a city of approximately 400,000, about the same as Pittsburgh, and both rank in recent studies by Rand McNally as among the top places to live in America. Raleigh is located next to the Research Triangle Park, the world's largest research center.

With a student population of 25,000 students, N. C. State is the largest school in North Carolina.

N. C. State has a wonderful sports tradition and history, and no one knows it better than an old friend named Frank Weedon. Weedon, the senior associate athletics director at N. C. State, was sitting behind a cluttered desk, looking very much like he was still the sports information director.

Weedon was about to start his 33rd year in the Wolfpack's department of athletics. Only his office is now in the Wolfpack Stroud Center, just across the way from the Wolfpack Club offices in what used to be a hotel complex, and his main concern these days is in the athletic alumni and fund-raising area. An alumnus, in fact, donated the hotel to the school. Student athletes reside there. Weedon is still the school's unofficial sports historian, however, and he was showing me some printed materials he had put together the year before in promoting the school's 100th year of football competition.

"He is so loyal to N.C. State," said Dean Smith, the basketball coach at the University of North Carolina, when I mentioned Weedon's name to Smith during a visit to the nearby rival school the following day.

When Weedon talks about some of N. C. State's former stars, like Roman Gabriel, Ted Brown, Mike Quick, Dick Christy and Jim Ritcher and coaches like Earle Edwards, Lou Holtz and Dick Sheridan in football, or basketball stars like David Thompson, Tom Burleson, Monty Towe or Rodney Monroe, or coaches like Norm Sloan and Jim Valvano his eyes positively glow.

They do the same when he chats about Bill Cowher. Weedon showed me a copy of a letter he had sent to Cowher congratulating Cowher on being named head coach of the Steelers, and the letter he received in response to it.

In his letter, Cowher wrote:

"I'm just so grateful for the opportunity to be the head coach for an organization with such a rich tradition, and I couldn't be happier to be in my own hometown. It's not going to be easy, but I'm really looking forward to the challenges that lie ahead."

In Weedon's letter to Cowher, he mentioned two bits of trivia, typical of the sports information director in his blood. He mentioned that Art Rooney Jr., the nephew of the late Steelers' owner, still holds three interception records at N. C. State: one game (three), a season (eight), and career (16).

Weedon also mentioned that Cowher had become only the second former N. C. State football player to become a head coach in the National Football League. The only other one was Alex Webster, with the New York Giants.

That brought back a personal memory. I remember small things that people in sports have done in my presence that provide some insight into the kind of human beings they are when they away from the spotlight. Little kindnesses.

When I was working at the *New York Post*, I went out to cover a Giants' practice one afternoon in 1972 at Yankee Stadium. I was accompanied by my father-in-law, Harvey Churchman, who was visiting our home on Long Island.

He is from McKeesport, Pennsylvania, and the Giants had an assistant coach, Jim Trimble, who was from the same community in western Pennsylvania. So I made a point to introduce my father-in-law to Trimble who, in turn, introduced him to Webster. Webster was like a big teddy bear, standing there on the sidelines.

After practice, I went into the Giants' clubhouse to interview Webster. I told my father-in-law to wait outside until I was finished. Webster started the interview by asking, "Where's your father-in-law?" I told him he was waiting for me in the hallway. "Hey, let's get him in here," Webster said. He called on one of his assistant coaches, Emlen Tunnel, a Hall of Fame defensive back in the glory days of the Giants, to go out and invite my father-in-law to join us. Just a small thing, perhaps, but a class gesture, I thought.

Judging by some of Cowher's early activity, he appears to be of the same old-fashioned solid stock as Webster. And he must have a little bit of Jack Lambert in him, too. Lambert always took pride in being old-fashioned.

"Bill doesn't mind getting bloody," said Weedon when I asked him what he remembered best about Bill Cowher. "He had a tough attitude. He was a real hard-nosed football player. He didn't mind getting into the middle of things.

"He married a very pretty girl, Kaye, one of the Young twins who played for Kay Yow on our women's basketball team. One of his buddies (Matt Miller) on the Browns married the other sister, Faye. Bill introduced them.

"Right after he got with the Browns, we heard they were surprised with his knowledge of football. Here, he had a knack for doing the extra. I'm not saying he was a student of the game, but you could tell he wanted to know what was going on at all times. He was never all-conference, but he played with good players like Ted Brown, and he managed to make his own mark. He was the captain of our 1978 team.

"He hung around with Ted Wescoe, another fine linebacker, and they became good buddies. He played with Jim Ritcher, who won the Outland Trophy as the nation's outstanding lineman when he was here.

"Bill was personable, a smiling-type kid. He never seemed to have a bad word for anybody. He could talk to the sportscasters and handle himself pretty well. He had that little extra."

David Vaughan, the equipment manager for the football program at N. C. State, was a student manager and hung around with Cowher during their student days in Raleigh.

Vaughan has only the best memories of Cowher. "He was a hard-nosed player," said Vaughan during our visit. "I've been working in this locker room a long time, and I've seen a lot of linebackers come through here. He was a competitor; he wasn't going to leave it in the locker room.

"We had a lot of players from Pennsylvania, and Bill was one of the ones I liked. I got along great with him. Bill loved to play the game.

"When he was the special teams coach in Cleveland, he used to insert *Playboy* photos, or shots from a Bugs Bunny cartoon, into the films he showed his players, something to lighten up the atmosphere. He wanted to be serious, but not too serious. He liked to break them up a little bit, too.

"He was a little wild when he was a student here. He liked to go out drinking — didn't we all? — but he was never in any major trouble. He'd just be out having a good time. He was a good man. I'll be rooting hard for him.

"I definitely knew he was from Pittsburgh. So when I heard he was hired as the head coach of the Steelers, I said, 'Hey, wait a minute. He's from Pittsburgh. He has to be happy about this.' You can't be happier than being back with a pro team you grew up with. He's a young up-and-coming coach. (Marty) Schottenheimer sure liked him.

"The Steelers have always had the tradition of being a tough, blue collar team. He'll continue that tradition. I hope Bill does well for you.

"He was a rah, rah guy. They'd start working themselves into a frenzy before the game, and by the time they got to the field he was dangerous at times. They didn't go out to play two-hand touch. He was one of the guys who liked to hit. We'd hit you when he was here. As a linebacker, he was calling our defenses, and you could tell he took pride in that.

"He was really up for our games with Penn State. He started a slogan that he and some of the other guys from Pennsylvania were 'Penn State rejects.' About half our players were from North Carolina in those days, and about a third from Pennsylvania. I ran into some from up there I'd like to send back to you, but Bill was a beauty.

"So is his wife, Kaye, in a different sense. I know her, too, because she played basketball here. Our coach Kay Yow, was the Olympic coach when we won the gold medal in Seoul, Korea. Bill and she started dating back here. They are good people. You pull for good people. You want to see them succeed."

Bill Cowher
N.C. State

His idol Ray Nitschke
Green Bay Packers

91

George Perles
The man who drew The Steel Curtain
"We were lucky to learn from the master."

George Perles looked comfortable, as he always does, lounging in a big, soft chair in the lobby of the Holiday Inn in Greentree, a suburb just south of Pittsburgh. Perles was patting the knee of his daughter, Kathy, who sat to his right, as he spoke about his days as an assistant coach with the Steelers. It was like he wanted to remind her that he knew she was there, waiting to talk to him. His other hand was dangling off the left side of his chair. It caught the eye.

Perles was wearing the ring from Super Bowl XIV, the one with a four diamond setting to signify the four NFL championships won by the Steelers in the '70s. Perles was a part of all four, as a much-valued aide to Chuck Noll and one of the leading architects of the famed Steel Curtain Defense.

"I only wear it during recruiting season," said Perles, almost apologetically. "It's so bulky, so heavy. But I wear it when I'm calling on high school prospects. The teachers, coaches, players and their parents all want to check it out. It gives you something to talk about."

Perles was beginning his ninth year as the head football coach at Michigan State University. His Spartans won the Big Ten title in 1987 and 1990, and the 1988 Rose Bowl, and went to post-season bowl games in six of seven years. Perles was named the 1987 Coach of the Year by *The Football News*. But 1991 was a down season, with a 3-8 record, and Perles was pushed to give up his duties as athletic director if he wanted to continue as coach. He was on a whirlwind tour that had brought him from East Lansing, Michigan to Florida, North Carolina and Pennsylvania in the final days of the recruiting campaign. He had just come from Erie, where he signed his final recruit.

"It could be our best class in ten years," said Perles, sounding like most coaches at the completion of a recruiting period.

The next day Perles would be speaking at the Coach of the Year Clinic at the Green Tree Marriott just down the road. Perles is a partner in the group that promotes the clinic, which was established 30 years earlier by Duffy Daugherty, who coached Perles at Michigan State, as well as Bud Wilkinson of Oklahoma, and Pete Dimperio, a legendary high school football coach at Westinghouse High School in Pittsburgh.

Interestingly enough, Perles preferred to stay at the Holiday Inn so he would have some privacy rather than checking out his investment. He wanted to have time alone with Kathy, 33, who still lives in Pittsburgh and is the manager for a Blockbuster Video outlet in Crafton. She has a bachelor's degree in English from West Virginia University.

Terry, 32, who holds degrees in chemical engineering from the University of Virginia and an MBA from the University of Pittsburgh, is a product manager for Strategic Minerals Corporation in Pittsburgh, which manufactures metals. Terry's wife, Tracey, is the community relations director for the Chambers Development Corporation in Pittsburgh. John, 29, who has an engineering degree from Michigan State, is a packaging engineer in Grand Rapids, Michigan, and is a partner in some real estate and restaurant enterprises. Patrick, 28, who also graduated from Michigan State, was seeking a college coaching position when I spoke with his dad. Pat had been a graduate assistant at Michigan State for two years, and was on the staff at the University of Toledo for three years. I remembered all three boys working as ballboys at the Steelers training camp at St. Vincent College. That's when Perles was called "Georgie Porgie" by Myron Cope.

"This is still my second home," said Perles. "I couldn't get my kids away from here. They liked it too much."

When we talked about his former boss, Chuck Noll, Perles said he and wife Sally had special feelings for him. "He was awful good to my family," said Perles. "Just the way he treated my wife and my kids. It's hard to put in words."

This would be important to Perles, considering one of his favorite comments: "If you have your good health, a good wife, a good family, then everything else is pure gravy."

An old friend, Dino Folino, accompanied Perles to Pittsburgh. Folino was an assistant coach at Pitt when I worked there as the assistant athletic director and sports information director in the mid-80s. He was an assistant on Foge Fazio's staff, and a likable fellow.

Folino is originally from Greenfield, where I spent a great deal of time as a teenager. It was the neighboring community to my hometown of Hazelwood. There was a dance there every weekend at one of its churches. So we knew a lot of the same people. Folino is good people. He and his wife, Anita, have nine children. She is a practicing attorney, and when she was working in Pittsburgh, she and Dino had to take turns driving the kids to and from his family's home in Greenfield where his parents looked after them.

Dino called me to confirm my meeting with Perles, changing the hour we were to get together, and he was making sure that all was in order before Perles got to town. Folino confirms what Perles says about learning how to treat assistant coaches and keeping things in perspective, especially when it comes to the families of staff members.

"I work for the best guy in football," Folino told me. "He's been so great to me and my family. When my mom was sick, he let me go home a lot. When she died, he gave me time to go home. I really miss her. I'm the original mama's boy. That's where I'm going tonight . . . to see my dad. He's doing OK. It was hard on all of us. But George understands that's more important than football."

Perles remains a cheerleader for Chuck Noll, who had announced his retirement six weeks earlier, closing out a 23-year stay with the Steelers.

93

Perles made a somewhat surprising prediction regarding Noll, one which I think has merit.

"I think Chuck Noll will enjoy a year of boating, golfing, swimming, sunning, tennis and a good time, and he and Marianne will travel, and spend some quality time with their son, Chris, and his wife in New Hampshire.

"Then he'll be ready to return to coaching. It's in his blood. He'll come back."

I told Perles that I had bumped into Marianne Noll only the day before, when she was having lunch with a friend at the St. Clair Country Club. I was at a nearby table with Art Rooney Jr. When I suggested to Marianne that Chuck would be back coaching in a year, she sighed. "Tell me why," she said with a smile. "I hope you're wrong. We're enjoying this already."

She told me they were leaving the next morning for their vacation home in Hilton Head, and that they would be away for a good while.

"I called over there today," said Perles, "because I had hoped to see them while I was in town. But I missed them."

Why did he think Noll, who had just turned 60, would come back to the rigors of coaching in the NFL?

"He'll be the hottest coach on the market a year from now in the NFL," said Perles. "People will create openings. He's still the classiest coach around, and he'll be the biggest guy coming back into the league. The only thing that ties it was Vince Lombardi coming back to coach.

"Chuck will be the hottest thing next year. He'll make the Bill Parcells thing look small. He's still in good shape, he's a young 60. He'll get all his boating and golfing and, when he comes back, hold onto your hat. He'll get his battery recharged. I'm saying that not just because it's my feeling — that's selfish — but because I believe it will be great for the game. He'll be away just enough to make him want to get full stride."

When asked to point out the highlights of his stay with the Steelers, Perles is predictable: "Mine's Mr. Rooney, Dan Rooney and Chuck Noll," he said.

"I always knew the presence of Mr. Rooney was special. I think his walking around and having coffee with everyone was good for the franchise. He was always so good with everybody, especially my wife and kids. He was equally good to me. With my three sons, I think I reminded him of his own situation with all his sons. I've always been quite an eater, and he liked that. He told me I might be the best knife and fork guy on the team.

"He liked Rollie Dotsch because Rollie smoked cigars. He told Rollie to come into his office anytime and help himself to a cigar. He had a humidor on his desk where he stored his cigars.

"He was a big booster of Chuck Noll, too. He liked to say to us, 'You know when I knew I had a good coach? In his first year we won one game and lost 13. He lost a lot of games but he never lost the team.

George Gojkovich

Defensive coach George Perles stirs up troops in "Oklahoma Drill."

Bill Amatucci

Perles fires up defensive linemen at Three Rivers Stadium.

That's when I knew I had a good coach.'

"Dan and Chuck had a super relationship. They were similar in age, and they had a lot in common. They were both good family people, and their Catholic religion meant a lot to them. They were both class acts. They were conoisseurs of wine. They loved to fly planes. So they had quite a relationship.

"Chuck was special. I was lucky to learn the profession from a guy like him.

"Chuck never told a coach how to run his life. He didn't give you any advice or noise about where you hung around. Most of the assistants enjoyed going out and having a good time together, while Chuck preferred to go his own way. I don't get into my coaches' private lives, either, because of the way Chuck dealt with us.

"With Chuck, you always had time for yourself and for your family. He didn't bother your private life.

"When we were discussing football, you better know what you're talking about. He was involved in all aspects of coaching."

I mentioned that I had been told by many former players that they thought the assistant coaches on Noll's staff back in the '70s were more apt to speak their piece, or to challenge Noll on strategy and personnel.

"He liked that," replied Perles. "He liked a good discussion, a good argument. Hell, he loved it. He loved a good discussion. When you're discussing something with him, though, your chances of winning were not that great. If you tried something new, it better work. Chuck taught me all kinds of techniques for linemen: the club, the slip, the uppercut, all the leverage moves, moves for pass rushes."

When I was covering the club when it won its fourth Super Bowl, the coaching staff consisted of Rollie Dotsch, offensive line; Dick Hoak, offensive backfield; Tom Moore, receivers; Paul Uram, conditioning; Dick Walker, defensive backfield; Woody Widenhofer, defensive coordinator; plus Perles, assistant head coach/defensive line.

"That staff may have been as good as it gets," pointed out Perles. "Rollie Dotsch was as good an offensive line coach as there was. Dick Hoak knew the system well and he could get along with the biggest celebrities like Franco and Rocky. They had great respect for him because he had done it himself. Tom Moore was special. Woody came to us at 27, with all kinds of ability to learn, and he had the right guy to teach him.

"There were good coaches on the staff before that, in Bud Carson, Dan Radakovich, and Lionel Taylor. But none of us brought a system with us. We all did it Chuck's way. He was one of the first guys who went for college coaches. He wanted teachers. He didn't want guys standing around with their arms folded watching practice. He always preached basics and fundamentals."

Perles joined the Steelers staff in 1972 and the team made the playoffs for the next eight years. At the time, the defensive line was the key to the Steelers' success. In 1978, Perles was promoted to defensive coordinator. A year later he became the Steelers' first-ever assistant head coach.

Before going to school at Michigan State, Perles spent two years in the Army. In college he was a starting two-way tackle. He earned a master's degree in physical education. His coaching career began in the high school ranks with a pair of two-year stints in Chicago and his hometown of Detroit. His late father was a long-time Ford Motor Company employee. George's first college job was as a defensive coordinator at Dayton in 1965. In 1967, he returned to Michigan State as an assistant and remained there until joining the Steelers.

"We were lucky. I got hired because I was recommended by John Sandusky, who had been a coach with Chuck on the Colts' staff and had been a teammate of his in Cleveland, and by Hank Bullough. Woody was an assistant with us at Michigan State. Chuck was excellent about asking his staff for recommendations. I had a chance my second year to speak up for Woody. I was with John McVay at Dayton. Wayne Fontes was on that same staff, as was Tom Moore. In 1976, we had an opening when Lionel Taylor left, and Woody and I spoke up for Moore. In 1977, when Rad left, Tom, Woody and I all spoke up for Rollie Dotsch. He was my classmate at Michigan State, and Tom and Woody knew him from their days in the Big Ten. In 1978, when Bud Carson left, Woody, Tom, Rollie and I spoke up for Dick Walker. He was at Ohio State and we had all worked together at camps, and had been buddies. We won two Super Bowls with that staff. Tony Dungy played for Woody and Tom when they were assistants at Minnesota. We all liked him. That's the thing: the whole staff were buddies. A lot of people didn't know that. That's the way Chuck operated.

"Then 1982 and all of a sudden the World Football League came along. I went to Philadelphia, Rollie went to Birmingham, and Woody went to Oklahoma within a year. We all went there along with another great friend, Hank Bullough (who coached the Pittsburgh Maulers).

"The guy who got me into the WFL was Chuck Fairbanks. I pushed for Rollie, and then Rollie and I pushed for Woody. We did the same thing in the NFL that we had done with the Steelers. When I went to the (Philadelphia) Stars, I hired Joe Pendry, and he's on the Chiefs' staff now."

I mentioned to Perles that I first met Moore in 1974 when he was an assistant with the World Football League's New York Stars, and I was covering the club for *The New York Post*. We had a good mutual friend in Dick Bestwick. Moore and Bestwick had coached together at Georgia Tech.

"So it went round and round," said Perles. "No one knew the wraparound effect. No one knew the chemistry. We went back years and years. It wasn't like we just all happened to hit Pittsburgh during the same period, and pulled it all together somehow. And we inherited Hoak. We were roommates for eight years. We got along great. We were like rats together. We went on vacations together. At camp, we went out together. We were close. We were at each other's homes, and went on vacations together. We worked together and played together. Hell, we used to go out at night together during training camp — that's no secret — and we enjoyed ourselves."

It wasn't difficult to get Perles talking about his former players. He likes to talk about how smart they all were. "Andy Russell invented the hug-up technique when he was an outside linebacker late in his career with us," said Perles. "He had slowed down somewhat, and he was scared he was going to get beat by some of the fast backs. Andy would fake a blitz to freeze the back momentarily. He didn't want to have to cover him one-on-one downfield. Andy was brilliant. He made up for his lack of speed with his recognition ability and his knowledge of the game.

"Jack Ham was the most demanding player on the field. He wanted to know everything. He wanted to know why we were doing what we were doing. What was behind the thinking. He wanted a dissertation on what he did. The Hammer, God he was something. He wanted criticism, but he hated to hear he had done something wrong. He was so proud. He wanted to do things right. He was one of everybody's favorites. A lot of people thought he was a real gentleman. They didn't know he was so mean on the field.

"If Ham screwed up, Lambert would be screaming at Ham. Ham would be laughing. Lambert would jump on everybody, even Joe Greene. One day in practice, it got pretty scary between Lambert and Joe. Another time in practice, some of the guys on the defense wanted to start holding hands in the huddle. Jack said there would be no hand-holding in his huddle. He hated quarterbacks. He suggested they put skirts on quarterbacks. That got a lot of play in the papers around the country. Lambert would put his head in his dressing stall before a game, and just sit there. He was in deep concentration.

"Those guys were brilliant. There wasn't anything they couldn't do or understand. Dwight White and Joe were something on that line. White was 'Mad Dog' and he was always on the officials. He gave them a fit. And we had Ernie Holmes. Guys like Gene Upshaw with the Raiders, good as he was, always were a little nervous around Ernie. They didn't know how to take Ernie. He had Upshaw worried.

"And Joe. I give Joe credit — besides Chuck and the Rooneys — for being the guy who put us in a position to win. He was an unbelievable defensive lineman. He was as valuable in the locker room as he was on the field. He set the tone for behavior on our team. He'd tell a rookie 'We don't play loud music in here.' Or, 'We don't say that to the trainer,' or 'We don't talk that way to the equipment man.' It was tough to win all those Super Bowls without a lot of envy and jealousy. He kept everyone under control in the clubhouse. He will go down as the finest captain in the history of the game.

"And we had L.C. He ran like a deer. He came up with a suggestion for what we should do on defense in that first Super Bowl with Minnesota. We were worried about Fran Tarkenton scrambling all over the place to pass. L.C. said, 'I'll stand in front of him in the throwing lane. He can't throw over me.' And he batted down about four passes. And we had guys like John Banaszak and Steve Furness to fill in on that line. Mel Blount was so great on pass protection. People couldn't get free from him. And Mike Wagner . . . what a great guy. He was tough just like Russell and Ham. Ron Johnson was something, too. He was a nose guard in high school and a walk-on at Eastern Michigan. When we played against Dallas in Super Bowl XIII, he was the first rookie to start at cornerback for a winning team in the Super Bowl."

Some say the Steelers stayed with those guys too long, that they didn't make the tough decisions to drop their superstars when they were no longer up to snuff. One personnel decision that came to mind was when the Steelers put Dwaine Board on waivers at the outset of the 1979 season. Board was a big defensive end from North Carolina A&T whom the Steelers selected on the fifth round of the college draft.

From the day he was drafted, Board became one of Perles's pet projects. He singled Board out as "the sleeper" in the draft. But the Steelers kept Dwight White rather than Board. Board went on to become a great pass rusher for the San Francisco 49ers and played on Super Bowl teams there. The Steelers spent the next few years trying to draft a pass rusher, but they never came up with anybody even close in ability to Board.

"We won the Super Bowl with White on that team," Perles points out. "He deserved our loyalty for one last shot at the ring. But it's a shame we couldn't have hid Board for a year. We knew he'd be a good one."

George Perles has been successful as Michigan State coach.

99

Sam Rutigliano
A rival coach who respected Steelers
"The only thing that's tough is death."

S am Rutigliano was a rival coach with the Cleveland Browns when I was covering the Steelers for *The Pittsburgh Press.* He was one of my favorites in the National Football League because he was such a regular guy, a good guy, a warm-hearted individual who never forgot his humble beginnings in Brooklyn. Rutigliano never regarded himself as a genius, or some god on high. He was for real, sentimental, compassionate and had a positive spirit. He had a good rapport with his players and the press. He had a good sense of humor, and was engaging and quotable. It has always been easy to spend time with Sam Rutigliano.

He reminded me of Foge Fazio, who was the head football coach at Pitt during most of my stay as assistant athletic director and sports information director from 1983 through 1987 at my alma mater. Maybe Italian football coaches are all like that: warm and friendly, sometimes to a fault. He might have been all the things Terry Bradshaw wanted in a head football coach.

Terry Bradshaw could have hugged Rutigliano, that's for sure. Rutigliano embraces everybody he comes in contact with; he just can't help himself. It's his heritage. He reads every book by Red Auerbach, another Brooklyn-born coach. Rutigliano has the Celtics' spirit. "Auerbach, to me, is the greatest coach-manager," related Rutigliano. "He's an amazing guy. If you've got quality players and Celtics pride you can win championships in any sport."

Rutigliano was the boss of the Browns from 1978 to 1984 and saw the Steelers up close when they were the best ballclub in the NFL, and saw them go into decline. Rutigliano still remembers why they were the best and has some ideas about why they went bust. He knows how those things go.

Art Modell, another go-go guy from Brooklyn, was his boss with the Browns. "One night at a banquet, Art got up and put his arm around me and told the audience, 'This is my guy. He's a winner!' He gave me a five-year contract. That was eight weeks before he fired me. I had a nice scholarship for a few years as a result of that. He had to pay me for the rest of the contract because I wasn't coaching anywhere else. Ralph Wilson offered me the job in Buffalo, but it wasn't the right offer. I had some other offers, too. I had to ventilate. That was the best thing I did was to take some time off from coaching. Coaches are always saying 'I gotta' and everyone thinks their desk is the most important place in the organization."

He said the nicest letter he got after he was fired came from — who else? — Art Rooney, the owner of the Steelers. Rutigliano remembered that Rooney wrote "a wonderful letter" in which he said

Sam Rutigliano

he had "never been around a coach who had as much dignity under pressure."

Seven years had passed since Rutigliano's stay in Cleveland. Rutigliano was beginning his fourth year as the head coach at Liberty University in Lynchburg, Virginia when he paid a visit to Pittsburgh in early February, 1992, as a featured speaker at the 30th annual Coach of the Year Clinic at the Green Tree Marriott near downtown Pittsburgh. Don Andrezjwski of the Marriott administrative staff makes sure everything is first class.

It is a nationally-renowned clinic attended by about a thousand coaches, mostly high school coaches, from the tri-state area that was originally organized by Duffy Daugherty, the late coach of Michigan State University, Bud Wilkinson of Oklahoma, and Pete Dimperio, the late coach of the perennial Pittsburgh city champion Westinghouse High School football team.

Dimperio was from my hometown of Hazelwood and was one of the most successful prep coaches ever. He was an Italian who was a great after-dinner speaker and would have gotten along famously with Rutligiano. His son, Pete Jr., is now in partnership with George Perles, the head coach at Michigan State who once served as an assistant coach with the Pittsburgh Steelers when they were winning Super Bowls.

Rutigliano invited me to join him for a leisurely Sunday afternoon brunch at the Green Tree Marriott, right after he had wound up the clinic with a "you can make the difference" motivational speech. He also invited two of his former football players at Liberty, namely Eric Green, the Steelers' No. 1 draft choice in 1990, and Green's former roommate Frank Fuller. Also at our table was Chuck Klausing, one of the most successful high school and college coaches in Western Pennsylvania history, who has been coaching at Kiski Prep and is on the advisory board for the Coach of the Year Clinic.

Klausing coached successful high school teams at Pitcairn and Braddock, near his hometown of Wilmerding, and was a big success as the head coach at Indiana University of Pennsylvania and Carnegie-Mellon, with stints as an assistant at Rutgers, Army, West Virginia and Pitt along the way. Klausing was going to drive Rutigliano to the airport after our interview meeting.

Sam showed up wearing a light blue warm-up outfit, with white and black piping, and a Liberty U. logo. His sunglasses were as dark as his curly hair and his humor.

"Hey, Eric, what do you weigh now — about 255?," said Rutigliano as we were strolling though a hallway at the hotel.

"Yeah, Coach, about 255," said Green, almost inaudibly.

"Sure, Eric. You weighed 255 when you were baptized," came back Rutigliano, chuckling over his own joke.

Rutigliano regaled us all with his stories and observations over lunch. When Green and Fuller pushed away from the table to go to the all-you-can-eat buffet line, Rutigliano warned the waitress, "You're going to lose money on this duo."

I asked him about going from the NFL to a little known school that was a Division I-AA program.

"Everybody asks me what I'm doing coaching at Liberty. 'Why aren't you in the NFL?' I'm coaching at Liberty because that's where I want to be. I heard Howard Cosell talking about his plans for the future on the radio the other day. He said, 'I'm going to be what I want to be be, not what they want me to be.' The same goes for me.

"Everyone at this clinic would like to be walking around with a tag on their breast that says 'Mike White — Los Angeles Raiders' or 'Bill McCartney — Colorado' but they can't. There's a niche for everyone, and you have to make the best of it."

Rutigliano always respected the Steelers and had a high regard for Chuck Noll. I knew he could provide some insights into the Steelers' success from a different perspective. It was a bonus to also enjoy the company of Green, who had gotten off to a great start as a tight end with the Steelers in his first two seasons, and Fuller and Klausing.

Then, too, Rutigliano was coaching the Browns when Bill Cowher, the newly-named head coach of the Steelers, succeeded in making the team and, in the course of our conversation, Rutigliano revealed that he was an assistant coach when Paul Martha played his final NFL season with the Denver Broncos. So Rutigliano was even more familiar with the Steelers scene than I realized.

"It would be interesting to find out what happened in their drafting process so that they went from doing the best job in the league to doing one of the worst," said Rutigliano.

When I said that basically the same people were involved in the scouting and decision-making during the ups and downs, he said, "Something had to be different. Who was making the choices?"

Rutigliano reeled off the names of all the great draft choices by the Steelers in the '70s — "You can't get two better No. 1 draft choices than Greene and Bradshaw," he said —and was either on the mark or pretty close when it came to naming the round on which they were drafted, and he can do the same for the Steelers' selections in the '80s.

"Then they took those two backs from Baylor (Greg Hawthorne and Walter Abercrombie) with their No. 1 choices, and Mark Malone, Keith Gary, Gabe Rivera — Rivera, that was a real tragedy — Darryl Sims, John Rienstra and Aaron Jones. Is Aaron going to make it? The only quality No. 1s they got during that span were Robin Cole, Louie Lipps and Rod Woodson. They laid about six or seven dinosaur eggs in a row."

Green asked his old coach a question: "What was wrong with Keith Gary?"

"Gary? With him you needed giant cans of Alpo at your training table," replied Rutigliano. "He was such a big dog. Eric, do you think Aaron Jones is going to be good? I'm sorry, I shouldn't ask you a question like that."

103

Rutigliano remarked that the Steelers seemed to do better when the draft was held a few months earlier than it was during the '80s and '90s. "It was the same way with the Dallas Cowboys," he said. "They had more information than the other teams when there was less time to prepare for the draft. They were ahead of everyone else. Now guys sell those draft lists to the other teams as soon as they're printed. Al Davis has everyone's list by the time the draft is conducted."

Rutigliano gave the Steelers high marks, however, for their scouting efforts, grading and selection of Green after his senior season at Liberty.

"They really did their homework. Dick Haley and Tom Donahoe made several visits to our campus to check Eric out. I remember we had this one terrible day weather-wise and we had to switch our practice to the University of Virginia and bus over to Charlottesville. Donahoe drove over about 60 miles and saw Eric in a seven-on-seven scrimmage session. I think he liked what he saw that day. I think that sold Donahoe on him.

"When the Steelers maneuvered to change their draft position, I knew they were going to pick him. Cleveland, Dallas, Kansas City and Washington all thought he'd be there in the second round. It's a good thing for Eric he didn't get drafted by the Redskins. He'd have been a blocking tight end, just like an offensive tackle."

Then again, if Green had gone to the Redskins, he'd be wearing a Super Bowl ring.

He missed the last five games of his second season with the Steelers after suffering a broken right ankle in practice. There's no doubt that he's one of the NFL's finest young players.

"When we went to spring practice in 1989," recalled Rutigliano, "I knew right away he was something special. I just hope he's competitive enough. He was always crying about something when he was here, and would allow himself to be sidelined by small stuff.

"The scouts needed to know what a big guy like him could do against big-time competition. It would have been easier for them to judge him if he was going up against Notre Dame and Miami. They weren't convinced that Central Florida and Youngstown State were really testing him.

"He showed in a 25-24 victory over Eastern Michigan that he had the right stuff. I knew then there was something inside of him. Still, there were quetions. He got kicked out of Liberty twice. But I told those scouts that if everyone in the NFL were students at Liberty they would all get kicked out sometime along the way. Liberty is tougher discipline-wise than West Point. They mentioned drugs, and there was nothing there. Everyone was looking for something to be wrong. But they were there. One day I had 12 scouts in my office. I told them, 'Hey, I can't talk to you all at once. You'll have to take a ticket.'"

While I was with them for brunch, Rutigliano told Green he would like to set up a city-wide clinic featuring them both in Savannah as part of a Christian Outreach program he is involved with. "It would be a nice way to give something back to the community and the kids there," said Rutigliano. "Eric's coach at Beach High, Ken Cannon, really believed in him and helped him when he needed it."

Rutigliano had just finished his recruiting efforts for 1992, and had wrapped up his travels by visiting Beach High School in Savannah, Georgia, the high school that sent Eric Green to Liberty University. "By the time I got there, I didn't have any scholarships to give," Rutigliano told Green. "I'd made an offer to a good kid there sometime earlier, but he was waiting to hear from Georgia Southern. That was his first choice. If Georgia Southern didn't come through, he might end up out in the cold. He waited too long."

Green and Rutigliano hooked up in Green's senior season at Liberty. Rutigliano had been working in TV as an analyst for the previous four seasons and collecting his full salary from the Browns during the same span. Green had gone largely ignored in his three years at Liberty. He had caught 34 passes in three years. With Rutigliano running the show in Lynchburg, Green grabbed 62 passes his senior season. "He should've caught 162 passes if I were smarter," said Rutigliano. "I should've thrown him the ball on every down."

Having a tight end who weighs 255 pounds plus is a good example, according to Rutigliano, of the evolution of players in pro football during the past two decades. "In 1969, the largest player on the Bears weighed 255 pounds," he said. "This year their lightest lineman on either side weighed 260."

Green said he felt underused at Liberty until Rutigliano came along. "I had a sense that I could do more," he said at our meeting.

Rutigliano also credits Green's development to having a fine receivers coach on his staff like Bob Leahy. "He used to play for the Steelers, and he wanted to join me at Liberty," recalled Rutigliano.

When the Steeler scouts came calling they knew that Leahy and Rutigliano had the background to make a sound judgement on a prospect. Leahy had been a backup quarterback for the Steelers in 1971. Rutigliano had a pretty terrific tight end in Cleveland with Ozzie Newsome. "I think I know a tight end when I see one," said Rutigliano. "And Ozzie could never block like this guy.

"As soon as we finished our first spring practice, I called Eric to my office. I told him, 'You don't realize what's ahead of you.'"

Despite the big numbers Green put together as far as receptions in his senior season pro scouts insisted on projecting him as an offensive tackle. "They were looking for another Larry Brown, a guy who played tight end at Kansas but ended up as a tackle with the Steelers," said Rutigliano.

"I think Dick Haley and Tom Donahoe had that in mind, at first. Then Dwain Painter, the Steelers' receivers coach, came down and spent some time throwing the ball to Eric. I told you the Steelers really did their homework on this guy. Even after the Steelers drafted him, Dan Rooney asked me, 'Sam, do you think he's a great player?'

105

"I told him he could do all the things you need in a tight end in the NFL. At Liberty, we just scratched the surface with Eric. If he had been a sophomore when I got there he'd have been illegal as a senior.

"I don't want to be critical of coaching, but I still don't think they realize what a blocker he is. I wouldn't move him around so much in motion. I'd move him around, but I'd walk him around. That is, I want him in a set position before the ball is snapped."

Rutigliano does not regard himself as a friend of Chuck Noll. They never had that kind of relationship. "Hey, the Steelers-Browns series was like the Army-Navy game, but I thought we got along fine," said Rutigliano. "We lost our first meeting with them in overtime. We met at midfield and shook hands after the game. Somehow we found each other. It never happened again after that. We just never sought each other out. It wasn't like the Sam Wyche-Chuck Noll feud. It was never a big deal; it just didn't happen, that's all.

"Chuck was unique. He was never involved or caught up with titles. Ego is the greatest defector in this business; one of the biggest problems. If people wanted titles they should have been dukes or doctors and lawyers.

"You could see how involved he was in every aspect of his team. Offensively, you could see what he learned from Paul Brown, Sid Gillman and Don Shula. You could see the imputing from those guys. Chuck even coached special teams for awhile, and he was the quarterback coach for some time. He had his hand on everything involving the Steelers.

"He reminded me of why delicatessens make so much money in New York. I never saw anyone at the cash register who wasn't 70 and wasn't a part of the family.

"That is why it was so out of character for Chuck to turn over his offense to Joe Walton. I remember when I was coaching in Cleveland, I had Paul Hackett working with our quarterbacks. He asked me if he could talk to Bill Walsh about an opening on the 49ers staff. I told him he could. Hackett came back to me and said Walsh offered him the job. He said, 'But I'll stay if you name me the offensive coordinator.' I said, 'I think you better go.' Then it would be his offense. And I didn't want that.

"I think if Chuck had a chance to re-do that again he wouldn't have brought in Walton and turned the offense over to him. When I saw Chuck standing on the sideline with a headset, letting other people make the decisions I knew something was out of whack. Who's smarter than Noll?

"He had to know the thing with Walton wasn't working out. But he has too much personal integrity to have fired Walton during the season. But he should've done just that. It ended up costing him his own job. I don't think he wanted to start all over again with another system. He probably figured it wasn't worth it.

"Chuck was just different from most of the coaches. At league meetings, he always had a sense of dignity about him. He never, never used his success and marketed himself. Ed Kiely, their old public relations guy, told me Chuck could have had everything from peanut butter to Hagar Slacks. But he felt that was for the players. I felt the same way, but I didn't win four Super Bowls. There are a lot of guys — Mike Ditka is a good example in Chicago — who market themselves in every way. They milk it for all it's worth.

"He was just as friendly toward me after I was fired as he was before that happened. That told me something about him, too. I think he's a tremendously misunderstood guy. He likes his privacy, that's all. At the league meetings or all-star games, you'd never find Noll in the lounge or restaurant. It's not his style.

"He's also good to work for as an assistant. He's like Al McGuire who says you don't need red eyes or sore eyes to win. He wasn't like Joe Gibbs or Dick Vermeil and into sleeping at the stadium overnight. He went home and his assistants did the same. They had a sane schedule.

"It was also interesting how he depended upon people like Perles and Woody Widenhofer with other staff hirings. Chuck didn't know a lot of coaches. If you were at the Senior Bowl or East-West Classic you wouldn't see Noll at any of the social events. So he didn't know who was out there. His assistants recommended other guys."

Rutigliano believed that the Steelers' scene would change in that respect, what with the hiring of Bill Cowher to succeed Noll as head coach. "Bill's into red eyes and sore eyes. Those young guys are like that; they only know one way. Bill will be a type A head coach. He was the first guy Marty Schottenheimer hired — as special teams coach — when Marty took over for me in Cleveland. Later, he became the secondary coach.

"Bill was one of those special team guys. He never played regular except maybe one or two games. But he was always ready to play. He always knew what he was doing. He wasn't fast, but he could cover those guys who could run 4.4s and 4.5s on the kickoffs, and they couldn't get by him. He covered well. He was originally drafted by the Philadelphia Eagles, but they waived him during the pre-season. He came to us the next year. He made the team not on talent but on dependability. It's hard to believe that, at age 34, he's already a head coach in the NFL. He's had a meteoric rise.

"If you have a 45-man roster it's important who you have as the 42nd through 45th guy. Bill wasn't going to be a frontline linebacker, but he was smart and tough. He was a coach's player. He was always ready."

Rutigliano is also a big fan of Schottenheimer, a former All-East linebacker at Pitt who was cut near the end of his pro football playing career by Noll. "I had Marty on my staff for five years in Cleveland," said Rutigliano. "He was a linebacker coach in Detroit when I got him."

I remembered that Rutigliano would always call for Schottenheimer whenever I entered the Cleveland clubhouse because he knew we had been students for a similar spell at Pitt. Rutigliano would do things like that. He was personable. "I turned out a few guys there who became head coaches," said Rutigliano at the urging of Klausing. "We had Marty and Dick Kotite and Dick MacPherson and now Cowher."

When I told him how Paul Martha was faring as a vice-president of the Penguins, Rutigliano said, "I had him in Denver. He was a tough cookie. He could've played a few more years, I'm sure, but he wanted to get back to Pittsburgh to be a lawyer. When he was with us, we played the Steelers in Denver and we beat them."

Assessing the strength of the Steelers, Rutigliano remarked, "For seven years, we'd line up against the Steelers and we knew if we didn't block Joe Greene then we could forget it. He was such a dominating force.

"I'm a big fan of Joe Greene. I really think he'll be the best coach in the league when the time comes. He has a sense of judgment like E.F. Hutton. When he spoke, people listened. He was the balance in the Joe Gilliam thing. Joe had taken Terry Bradshaw's place, and Joe helped make it possible for Bradshaw to get back his job without the black players going on mutiny.

"They always had so many class guys on the Steelers, with the exception maybe of Ernie Holmes. Ernie was a little off center. At the Pro Bowl, I was the coach one year and had Mike Webster, Jack Ham, Mel Blount, Franco Harris and Jack Lambert. They were all class guys, and they knew what they were doing.

"Someone told me in the Pro Bowl that I should use Earl Campbell and Franco Harris in short yardage situations. I said, 'Hey, I will if I can find them. They're hiding.' None of the guys want to get hurt in Hawaii. They just want to be in Hawaii.

"Lambert, to me, was the biggest nemesis. He knew everything. Greene tied up everybody in the middle, and it left Lambert free to make the tackles. And he made them. Russell, Lambert, Ham, Toews and Cole could all make the tackle. That's why it was tough to make a breakaway run on them.

"Lambert was always hollering and screaming at everyone, telling them what to do, and where they were supposed to be. And he'd cover backs coming out of the backfield for passes, and not too many linebackers did that then. Now they take out a linebacker and put an extra defensive back in there. Another guy who really hurt us was Mike Wagner. He didn't get proper credit. He was a great free safety. The same was true of Randy Grossman at tight end. He was tough."

I asked Rutigliano to compare the Steelers of the '70s with the 49ers of the '80s. "We played the 49ers in '81 and we beat them," he said. "I think the Steelers were more dominant defensively. I think they were better than the Redskins are now, too. I think they were the best. When you played the Steelers, you hated to give your team a scouting report. You knew you couldn't win. I told our assistants to be careful about how much of the truth to tell them. I didn't want them going into the game thinking we couldn't win.

"Swann and Stallworth could make the big play. They were so great because in the fourth quarter they could put you away. They had a great running attack, and they could control the ball. With Bradshaw, they had the ability to go up top for the big play.

"In that league, you had to have two things. I think in every playoff game Franco went over 100 yards. So they could control the game. And they had the big play quarterback with Bradshaw. Bradshaw looked more like a linebacker or a tight end. He could stand in there against the rush and not worry about taking a hit. He could handle it. And they had that dominant defense. Greene was never single blocked on a run or a pass. And L.C. was a great up-field pass rusher."

Hey, Sam, say that again. That adds up to three things, unless you use the same math as Yogi Berra.

I reminded Rutigliano of a difficult day in his life. It was on Sunday, January 4, 1981. It was a day Rutigliano left the most positive impression on me, but something less with fans of the Browns, and his boss, Art Modell.

The Browns lost to the Raiders in the AFC playoffs that day by 14-12 and they blew a last-minute opportunity to beat the Raiders. I didn't have to remind Rutigliano of any of the details of the final drive.

"We were down to their 13 yard line and it was second down. Brian Sipe threw the ball into the endzone to Ozzie Newsome. He should've thrown it to Dave Logan, who was wide open, or into Lake Erie, which was also wide open.

"We thought we'd try a pass for a touchdown and if we didn't make it we go for the field goal. A field goal was anything but automatic that day because Don Cockroft had missed three field goal attempts and one extra point. Cockroft told people we never gave him a chance to kick the game-winning field goal, but he doesn't talk about the ones he missed earlier. Sipe told the media it was my call.

"Mike Davis intercepted the pass to Newsome and that was the end of the game for us. That play follows me around like Ralph Branca's homerun pitch to Bobby Thomson. I was in Auckland, New Zealand once and a guy asked me, 'Why did you throw that pass?' I got hot and I said, 'Hey, I didn't throw that pass.'

"I'm at Liberty and we play a game before maybe 16,000 to 18,000 at Eastern Michigan, and there's a big sign in the stands that says 'RED RIGHT 88.' That was the play. I said, 'Those creeps from Cleveland have followed me here.' The same thing happened at Youngstown. It wasn't the same sign, but it said 'RED RIGHT 88.' That was it.

"Everything changed for me after that. It was like having a great marriage and you're caught cheating by your wife. It was never the same; they never forgave me for that. Art Modell made me vice president of the team soon after and I should have realized that was the kiss of death, not a vote of confidence. When the Raiders went on to beat San Diego and then Philadelphia it only made it worse for me. Art Modell would have given his liver to go to the Super Bowl that year.

He sees guys like Ralph Wilson going to the Super Bowl, and some of the newer owners and it rips his insides."

I have different memories of that day in Cleveland. The temperature was one degree, and the wind chill factor made it feel like 37 degrees below zero. The wind was blowing off Lake Erie. It was bitter cold. The media mobbed Rutigliano after the game to explain the Browns' strategy at the end.

"Those were all my plays, not Brian Sipe's, at the end," he was quick to tell everyone. He didn't mention that he had instructed Sipe not to force anything, or risk an interception if a receiver wasn't wide open.

"One mistake," said Sipe, "and there goes a dream."

As Sipe came to the sideline after the interception, Rutigliano reached for him, and clasped his hands alongside Sipe's helmet and looked straight into his eyes. "I told him I loved him," said Rutigliano.

He let that sink in a while, and added, "I say that to other people besides women."

A reporter persisted, and asked Rutigliano if it were the toughest loss of his life.

Rutigliano sighed and shook his head in the negative. "There are moments that you savor, and this won't be one of them," he said. "The only thing that's tough is death. Today is Sunday and tomorrow is Monday and life goes on."

I wrote in a column I did for *The Pittsburgh Press* a few days later than few NFL coaches understand that better than Rutigliano. His life's experiences have taught him how to keep things such as sports, and football games, in their proper perspective.

The "toughest loss" in his football career came on a New Hampshire highway 18 years earlier when he was an assistant coach with the New England Patriots. Rutigliano and his wife, Barbara, and their 4 1/2 year old daughter, Nancy, were driving home from Montreal. Rutigliano, after a long stretch at the wheel, dozed for a second and he lost control of the car. It went off the road and the car flipped over. Their daughter went through the rear window of the car and died from head injuries. It's something Rutigliano, understandably, won't soon forget.

"There was a total new outlook in terms of being able to carry on," he said. "It helped keep the problems of my life in order. Over the years I've tried, regardless of my hopes and dreams, to never really get down. After an experience like that, nothing else can get you down."

Some of the reporters were relentless and wanted to re-examine Rutigliano's last-drive strategy. Rutigliano realized he was going over familiar and uncomfortable ground, again and again.

"I know I'm sounding redundant," he apologized, "but so are some of the questions."

He looked around and asked everyone if they'd had enough of his time. Sensing they were semi-satisfied, he said, "Look, I want to thank you. And, listen, I hope you all have a happy new year."

Rutigliano really was a class act in the NFL.

Dan Rooney
His top ten thrills of the '70s

Super Bowl XIII in Miami ranks high on Dan Rooney's list of the Steelers' 10 greatest games of the '70s when the team was heralded as the pro football team of the decade.

The Steelers defeated the Dallas Cowboys, 35-31, to become the first NFL team to win three Super Bowls.

Even so, in the ratings offered by the Steelers' president, Super Bowl XIII ranks only second or third — he's not sure which — among the Steelers' greatest games of that decade.

He rates the Steelers' first Super Bowl success, a 16-6 victory over the Minnesota Vikings in New Orleans in Super Bowl IX, as No. 1.

"You never replace the feeling of that first Super Bowl victory," he said. "The first Super Bowl is a tremendous thing. It's just a great feeling — to be there and to win it."

Rooney's runner-up choice for his "greatest game" either is winning that third Super Bowl title in Miami, which brought immortality to the team by ranking it with the Green Bay Packers of the late 1960s, or the "Immaculate Reception" playoff game on Dec. 23, 1972, in Three Rivers Stadium. The controversial scoring reception by Franco Harris with 22 seconds left beat the Oakland Raiders, 13-7.

Rooney says he saw the play, something few others can actually claim, not counting the TV replay. "I knew right away that it was a good play, but I didn't know how it would be ruled."

Rooney would not list his team's greatest games of the '70s in any particular order. It was difficult enough, he insisted, to limit it to 10.

"The game we played after the 'Immaculate Reception' sticks out in my mind, for instance," Rooney related. "Even though we lost it. Miami defeated us, 21-17, for the AFC title. But it was a great game in that the people of Pittsburgh gave us a standing ovation when we came off the field."

Still, that game isn't on Rooney's ratings.

The Steelers qualified for the playoffs for the first time in 1972. A game in the drive to win the division championship remains vivid in Rooney's mind.

That was the Steelers' 23-10 victory over Minnesota in Pittsburgh. "We felt like we had knocked off a pretty good football team," related Rooney.

The Steelers went on to win their next three games — over Cleveland, Houston and San Diego — and finished with an 11-3 record.

Rooney regards that last game as an important one, too. "We were playing late that day, and we knew we had to win in order to win our first division championship," he said. The Steelers steamrollered the Chargers, 24-2. On Dec. 29, 1974, the Steelers defeated the Raiders, 24-13, in Oakland to win their first AFC championship and gain their first Super Bowl.

"What was so unique about that game was that it showed the character of Chuck Noll and the team," Rooney said. "Right before the end of the first half, Bradshaw threw a touchdown pass to John Stallworth, who was a rookie. The officials ruled that Stallworth was out of bounds when he made the catch. The instant replay proved otherwise.

"But we didn't cry or go into hysteria. Not the way (Oakland's managing partner) Al Davis did after 'The Immaculate Reception' two years before." The Steelers went on to defeat the Vikings for their first Super Bowl title.

One of the games Rooney had to scratch to get down to 10 games was a 42-6 victory over the Browns in Cleveland in October 1975. "There were fights in that game, but it showed how the Browns, who had dominated us for so many years, were frustrated by the turnaround in our fortunes.

"We had won the Super Bowl the year before, and we were really showing Cleveland that we were the team. We finished that season by defeating Dallas (21-17) for our second straight Super Bowl (X) championship."

The Steelers didn't win the Super Bowl the following year, yet Dan shares his father's expressed sentiments that the 1976 Steelers may have been the best football team in history.

The Steelers lost four of their first five games. Terry Bradshaw was hurt in the fifth game at Cleveland. Mike Kruczek, a rookie, replaced him at quarterback.

The Steelers won 10 consecutive games as the defense yielded just 42 points, ran up an incredible string of 22 scoreless quarters, didn't allow a touchdown in eight of its last nine regular season games, and shut out five of its last eight opponents.

Rooney chose a 7-3 victory over the Bengals on a snowy day in Cincinnati. "That may have been the best defense ever played in the National Football League," he said.

With some relish, Rooney recalls a 34-5 victory over the Houston Oilers in the AFC championship game at Three Rivers Stadium on January 7, 1979.

"It came up cold and rainy," Rooney said. "There were two inches of water on the field the whole game. And we just completely dominated Houston." From there, the Steelers went on to win Super Bowl XIII.

"This made us the first team to win three Super Bowls, which made it a big, big thing," Dan declared. "Others had won two. This put us at the top."

The next game Rooney mentioned was in the Super Bowl the following year, a 31-19 win over the Los Angeles Rams at the Rose Bowl in Pasadena.

Rooney didn't want to stop with ten games. He said, "There were just too many . . ."

Photo Days at St. Vincent College

View from rear rooms at St. Vincent College's Bonaventure Hall where Steelers stay at summer training camp. Over 450 Benedictine monks are buried on hillside.

Bill Amatucci

Steelers were welcomed back in big way after winning fourth NFL title.

George Gojkovich

113

George Gojkovich

Huge crowds gathered below Bonaventure Hall on Photo Day in July, 1970.

George Gojkovich

Players posed systematically for news photographers and fans.

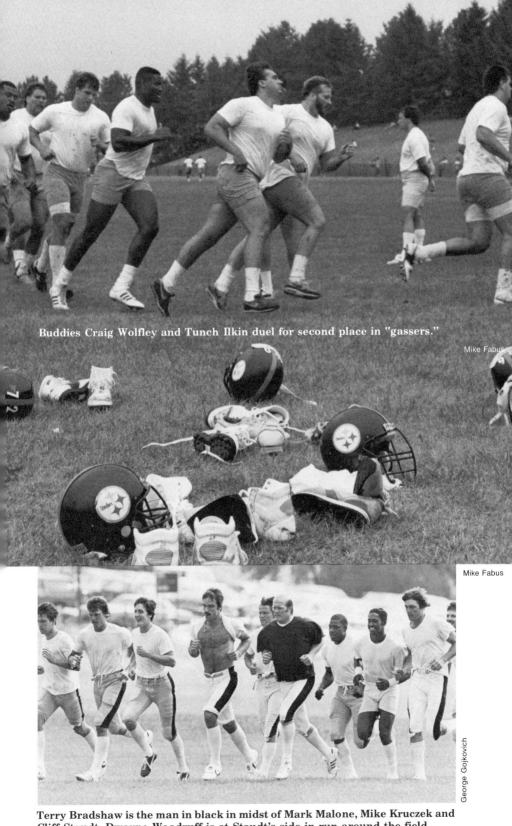

Buddies Craig Wolfley and Tunch Ilkin duel for second place in "gassers."

Mike Fabus

Mike Fabus

George Gojkovich

Terry Bradshaw is the man in black in midst of Mark Malone, Mike Kruczek and Cliff Stoudt. Dwayne Woodruff is at Stoudt's side in run around the field.

Crowds line path from clubhouse to field, swarm likes of Lynn Swann (88).

George Goji

George Gojkovich

George Perles, at left, and Ralph Berlin flank "Oklahoma Drill."

Bill Amatucci

See how many faces you can recognize in practice drill.

George Gojkovich

Terry Bradshaw signs autographs for fans following practice.

Bill Amatucci

Tom Donahoe clocks John Stallworth in 40-yard sprint.

Mike Webster, Gary Dunn wait for signal to start "gassers".

Bryan Hinkle and Gary Anderson are among pack leaders in "350s."

Bill Amatucci

George Gojkovich

Lynn Swann

George Gojkovich

John Banaszak

Players arrive for start of another summer at St. Vincent.

Mike Fabus

Dwight White lifts weights under watchful glare of Chuck Noll.

Bill Amatucci

Dark-shirted Jim Clack contests Joe Greene in blocking drill.

Bill Amatucci

Mel Blount breathes deeply while John Stallworth, Larry Brown wait turn at weight-lifting apparatus.

Dick Hoak has running backs go through their paces.

Franco Harris signs autographs.

Joe Greene as assistant.

Punter Bobby Walden holds for place-kicker Roy Gerela.

Terry Bradshaw, at left, looks on as Joe Gilliam gets off pass.

Ray Mansfield
Still at home on the range

"Mansfield had the perfectly shaped posterior for a center. He would stand up tall and his wide fanny made it easy to take the snap."
—Terry Bradshaw

R ay Mansfield is great company. I can't think of a better way to spend a wintry Saturday morning than drinking hot coffee and swapping stories with Mansfield. He is an exceptional storyteller. He lives about a mile from me in Upper St. Clair, a suburb 12 miles south of Three Rivers Stadium, the same community that Chuck Noll and Myron Cope call home.

Mansfield can tell stories about all his former teammates on the Steelers, and about Chuck Noll — he unabashedly tells you he loves Chuck Noll — and, before long, Mansfield is mixing John Wayne and Gene Autry into tales about Bruce Van Dyke and Joe Greene. He's good at it.

Mansfield is still in demand as a motivational speaker around the country. His popularity helps him sell insurance and group health plans for Diversified Group Brokerage of Pittsburgh. He and his partner Chuck Puskar have offices in Canonsburg, a community a little farther south best known as the hometown of singers Perry Como, Bobby Vinton and the Four Coins. I bump into Mansfield from time to time at ballgames at our local high school, and at sports luncheons and banquets — we have shared many a dais in our day — and I worked with him ten or twelve years ago on the board of the Pittsburgh chapter of the National Football Foundation and Hall of Fame.

He has been responsible since I can remember for managing the affairs of the Steelers chapter of the National Football League Alumni Association, and he takes his role seriously. As former teammate Rocky Bleier puts it, "He is the historian and storyteller about our teams. He is the keeper of the memories."

Mansfield played organized football for 25 years, 14 in the NFL, a rookie season (1963) with the Philadelphia Eagles and 13 seasons with the Steelers (1964-1976), and never missed a game. He took pride in being called an ironman. "There were times," he has said, "when you thought you would play forever."

Mansfield misses football more than most. "I had a lot of withdrawal problems," admitted Mansfield. He doesn't miss the blocking sleds, and the two-a-days at St. Vincent College, or studying film, or the aches and the pains. No, he misses the camaraderie, being out with the boys, being one of the boys.

"I can't believe I'm 51 years old," he said, shaking his head, during my visit to his home on the first day of February, 1992. "I still think

I'm 30. This will be the year when I'm out of pro football more years than I played.

"I can accept being 51 and looking 51," he continued. "It's how fast those last 15 years went that shakes me. Another 15 years and I'm going to be at retirement age. I hope they don't go as fast.

"I can't imagine slowing down. I never want to be on Social Security. I want to be out hiking in the Grand Canyon when I'm 70. I don't want to be out in the park feeding pigeons. I want to be on the other side of the mountain."

Mansfield and his good friend and former teammate Andy Russell have an annual ritual since they retired from football — their wives call it a "rite of passage" — in which they take on a physical challenge, like climbing a mountain, white water rafting, or going on a long hike. Sometimes they have taken another teammate, like Mel Blount or Mike Wagner, with them. They do it at a time just before they normally would have been going off to football training camp.

Mansfield loves to organize alumni functions, get-togethers, golf outings, fund-raisers, anything to assemble the Steelers for a good time, a good weekend.

Now that Chuck Noll is retired, Mansfield has a magnificent dream for a team reunion.

"I want to get Chuck to lead us on a hike," he said. "I want him to take us out in the wilderness. We can sleep out. Maybe carry a little whiskey and have a few sips at night. That sort of thing would be so wonderful."

Mansfield and his three mutts met me at the door of their home when I came calling. The biggest of his three dogs, Cleo, a red coon hound, jumped up on me as soon as I crossed the doorway. I am always a little nervous around big dogs, and I believe they sense that, and get even more aggressive.

Mansfield smiled at my discomfort. "Kill, Cleo! Kill!" Mansfield shouted, just for the hell of it. Mansfield's command startled me for a moment. Thank goodness Cleo wasn't a trained attack dog.

"I never said that before," said Mansfield, always the practical joker and kidder, somewhat apologetically. "I guess I shouldn't have done that. I didn't know what he might do."

That was reassuring. After the initial shock, I came to feel comfortable in a hurry in Mansfield's home. It was snowing outside, and I dropped my snow boots by the door. I was chilled when I came in, but I got warm in a hurry. First, we sat down in the living room, then Mansfield suggested it might work out better if I had a table on which to write my notes during our interview, so we moved into the dining room.

Mansfield wore a green ski sweater and eyeglasses, and got us some coffee, rich and black, before we began talking.

Three dogs — they looked like junkyard dogs to me — quickly settled in around my chair. Mansfield referred to them as "All-American mutts." Jasper, the youngest one, was lying alongside my shoes, and his mother, Lady, was to our right. Cleo was at my left and occasionally got up off the rug to sniff me out and, at one point, started licking my left cheek. "He must like you," said Mansfield.

The dogs were just loafing, as Art Rooney might have expressed it, and soon it looked like a slumber party. Mansfield has been surrounded by dogs since he was a little kid. I haven't had a dog in my house since I was about 20 or so. Mansfield and the dogs all looked contented. It was a familiar scene for Mansfield.

"Life's been good to me," Mansfield said at one juncture. "To me, life was good from the day I was born."

Mansfield was born in Bakersfield, California. He was quick to tell me that Frank Gifford and Clint Eastwood as well as Theo Bell, a former Steelers' receiver, were all from Bakersfield. I told him that one of my boyhood heroes, Ralph Kiner, also came out of Bakersfield to play for the Pirates. "A lot of good guys came from Bakersfield," said Mansfield.

"We lived in a labor camp there, the ones with the common bath house," said Mansfield. "My oldest sister, Merelene, got pneumonia there and died when she was seven. It wasn't easy. We lived in a Department of Agriculture camp. If you have seen the movie *The Grapes of Wrath* then you know what kind of camp I'm talking about. I watch that movie every time it's on TV, and I just re-read the book. That's the story of my family. We were hillbillies and fruit-pickers and we were proud of it."

Mansfield mentioned that he provided the eulogy a few years earlier at the funeral service for his brother, Gene, and that he read a speech from *The Grapes of Wrath*. It wasn't easy to do. "I don't know how I got through that," said Mansfield.

I had just watched parts of *The Grapes of Wrath* on TV myself during the previous two weeks when it was aired late at night. It's always been one of my favorite movies, too. I loved John Steinbeck's book even more. When I mentioned that to Mansfield it was his opening or cue. "C'mon, let's go into the family room," he said. "I want to show you something."

He showed me a remarkable family history on a video cassette that his sister, Shirley, put together, using a script that Ray's daughter Kathleen wrote with his help. It's one of the best home movies I ever saw, and I thought that Mansfield might get teary-eyed at any moment. I had him go back over a few sequences.

"I'm just such a sentimental bastard," he said.

The movie was mostly of photographs from family albums, tracing the history of the Mansfield clan back to its Arkansas origins and its movement from there to Missouri, and on to California, to Washington, to Arizona, back to Missouri, back to Washington. "My dad liked to move on," said Ray. The Mansfields went where they could find work, helping to harvest fruit and vegetables, and construction work of any kind. Toward the end of the movie there are some motion picture segments of the Mansfield family outings. It ends with a clip from the movie *The Grapes of Wrath* that captures the spirit of the Mansfield

Ray Mansfield's hair and clothes, plus the fired-up fans outside Three Rivers Stadium, signal successful '70s campaign.

Ray Mansfield's family during the Steelers' glory days included (left to right) Jennifer (7), Caroline (3), Jimmy (2), Kathleen (9) and wife Janet.

128

clan. Pa Joad says: "We've sure taken a beaten." And Ma Joad replies: "I know. But we'll go on forever, Pa, because we're the people."

There are titles and credits, and appropriate background music. It reminded me of the western serials I used to see on Saturday mornings at our local theatre.

The family history is entitled "The Long-Legged Guitar Picker From Arkansas." It's about Owen Ray Mansfield and his wife, Carmel, and their family. Ray's dad had four brothers and they had their own performing band that played at church dances and community events. His dad is usually seen wearing a cowboy hat, sometimes playing a guitar.

"My dad loved the west, he loved the cowboys," recalled Ray. "I'm thankful to my dad. He always wanted to see the other side of the mountain. That's why I'm the way I am. Gene Autry was his favorite. My brother Gene was named after Gene Autry."

And Gene Autry can be heard singing ("I'm Back In The Saddle Again") in several sequences of the Mansfield movie, and there are songs like "Red River Valley," which is the theme song in *The Grapes of Wrath*. "My dad was authentic," said Mansfield. "My dad was bitten by a rattlesnake and lived to tell about it. My dad's mother was one-fourth Indian.

"My dad learned to build roads working for the WPA during The Great Depression."

He learned carpentry and cement work. Ray came from sturdy stock. Some of the Mansfield ancestors appeared in Civil War uniforms. There were lots of pictures — still and in motion — of family reunions. You could see dogs and kids everywhere.

"In the pictures," mentioned Mansfield, "you can see the closeness, how the parents are always hugging the kids."

Ray Mansfield drove from Pittsburgh to Long Beach to visit his daughter, Jennifer, only a month before my visit, at the outset of 1992. En route, he drove through Gallup, New Mexico, where he knew his father had spent some time as a freight-hopping teenager.

"I pulled off in that town because I wanted to see it," said Ray. "It's an Indian town. A story came back to me about my dad nearly starving to death in that town.

"He hopped the freight cars when he was 18, back in 1928. He jumped on a car in Cabool, Missouri to start. There was a famous railroad detective in those days known as 'Texas Slim.' He was a notorious character. He was known to have shot a kid off the top of a box car. He had a real mean streak in him. He took milk away from a starving man and just poured it over the guy's head to humiliate him.

"My dad always told stories about 'Texas Slim.' My dad got caught with some other guys trying to hop a freight in Gallup. 'Texas Slim' caught them and told them to get out of town or he would put them in jail. Later on that night, my dad was hungry and went looking for work that he might do in exchange for a meal. He knocked on the door of one house and who should answer but 'Texas Slim.'

"At first, he was outraged. 'What are you still doing here?' asked the railroad detective. 'I thought I chased you out of town this morning.'

"My dad said, 'I was just looking for some chores to do so I could get my supper.' The man had a pile of wood in the backyard. He told my dad that if he split up all the wood he would give him his supper. My dad went to work and was out there quite awhile when 'Texas Slim' called him in. He said, 'Come on in here and get your supper, Slim. I didn't want that firewood cut; I just wanted to see if you would really work or if you were just a no-good bum.' He called my dad 'Slim' because he was 6-3 1/2 and weighed about 185 pounds.

"My dad got to California, and worked out there a few months, and then came back home. He was visiting some relatives and that's when he met my mother. She was teaching school in a one-room school house called Pine Hill. She was sitting on the edge of a well having lunch when my dad passed by. A relative of my mother had told her when she was a little girl that one day she would look in a well and see the man she would marry. While my mother was looking in the well, she saw my father passing by. She knew in an instant that was the man she would marry. Then, on August 18, 1932, they were married in West Plains, Missouri."

The thing I appreciate and admire about Ray Mansfield is the rich details and dates and names he provides when he tells stories. His recall is exceptional, and he inherits story-telling skills from his father.

"That was our entertainment when I was a kid," said Ray. "My dad would sit with his guitar, and sing us songs, and we'd have to identify the tunes, and then he'd tell us stories. My dad was so good at storytelling. Once in a while we'd have a radio going, but it would get busted, and we'd go a year without one. I was in eighth grade when we got our first TV set and, boy, that was a big deal."

His stories, even the simplest, are gems. For instance, I mentioned the name of Ray Mathews, who came from my wife's hometown of McKeesport, and was a star receiver with the Steelers in the mid-50s when I first became a fan. Mansfield came back with this anecdote:

"I told him one day that when I first came to the Steelers everyone kept calling me Ray Mathews. And he told me, 'Yeah, but after you were here awhile, everyone started calling me Ray Mansfield.'"

"I come from people who taught me how to work and work hard. That's what I'm proud of," said Mansfield. "I worked my ass off in training camp every summer. We had fun, but we didn't drink till we dropped, or cause any problems. We looked at a few girls — that's no secret — but when I was at practice there was no monkey business. I was always there.

"I remember getting up before school and working when I was a kid. My dad worked on a WPA project during the Depression. He could do anything. He was a mason; he could do plumbing, carpentry. If it was hard work, he could do it. In 1940, my dad worked in a farm labor

Ray Mansfield presents $5,000 check to Steelers president Dan Rooney for Art Rooney Scholarship Fund on behalf of Pittsburgh Chapter of the NFL Alumni Association.

camp in California building fruit boxes. He earned six cents an hour, 60 cents a day, and about $4 a week.

"Whatever jobs he had couldn't support a family. So we always did extra work, all of us. In Arizona, we picked cotton. When we got to Washington in '49, we settled in Kennewick. My dad hauled coal to people's homes. It was one of the worst winters in the history of the United States. The following spring, he still had little work, so he contracted our family to cut 10 acres of asparagus every morning before school. When I was in second grade, I was out there helping the family to make money. I did that through my junior year in high school. I'd cut asparagus, stooping over the whole time to do it, for about three hours each morning before school. It was strictly stoop-work."

I suggested that may have helped him later as a center. "You might be right about that. I think my muscles were well stretched out by that time from all that work in the fields. I was naturally flexible. It may have helped me."

One of the film segments showed a man named Willie Vaughn. He was a black man. He was the partner of Ray's dad in a cement work business. "My dad was way ahead of his time in that respect," said Ray. "In those days, back in the early '50s, not many white people associated very much with black people, and nobody went into business with them. My dad said Willie was a good worker, a good man and a good friend.

"The only thing that mattered to my dad was that they worked well together, and liked and respected each other. The partnership worked out well for them. He and Willie both had nine children, so they didn't have to hire anyone else to help them do the work.

"It all worked out of the best. All but one of my dad's children graduated from college."

Mansfield was a maverick, a throwback to a more free-wheeling era, when Chuck Noll came to the Steelers in 1969 and wanted to instill more discipline into the team — on and off the field.

Mansfield had a roommate named Bruce Van Dyke who had come to the Steelers in 1967 and stayed till 1973. He played in the Pro Bowl in his final season with the Steelers, and was traded away by Noll in the off-season.

"I think it bothered Chuck that Bruce was nursing a calf muscle strain for a long time, and missed games. Bruce was a teaser, and I think he got to Noll one too many times. I think Noll thought Bruce usurped his authority too often.

"Bruce and I were so bad we went out at night and after curfew during two-a-day drills. No one else went out during two-a-days. Everybody was dead tired. We always wanted to break the mold. Our room was at the end of the hall, close to the exit, so it was easy for us to get out after the coaches checked to see if we were in bed.

"We were out this one night, and I don't think we got back till 5 o'clock in the morning. They're having a drill where someone's holding the dummy bag, and we're working on blocking techniques. Chuck is working with the tight ends and the backs.

"I jumped up and grabbed the bag. Chuck was showing Larry Brown, who was playing tight end then, how to block a certain way. "When Chuck did it, I sort of drove the bag into him. I thumped it into Noll, just for the helluva it. I think he smelled my breath. Chuck eventually talked to Chuck Fry, who was our offensive line coach. Fry came over to me when we were doing stretching. Bob says, 'Chuck told me to start double-checking your room. He smelled booze on your breath.'

"The next day, Bruce and I were lying on our beds after the first workout, and we were talking about going out again that night. The next thing we know, Chuck's standing in the door. He says, 'I hear you guys like to go out after curfew. We're going to start double-checking this room.' And Bruce comes back with, 'Geez, we were just planning tonight's escape.' See, that's where I drew the line. I wouldn't go that far with the head man.

"It's a shame, though, because Bruce was the best pulling guard in the game. He was great at trap-blocking. He had worked with Vince Lombardi on the great teams at Green Bay, and he knew how to block at the head of the sweep. He blocked for Frenchy and Franco, and he was the best we had. Van Dyke was something. I sure missed him after he left.

"We were all hellions. But there were certain things we put ahead of everything else. The family was always No. 1. I was raised that way. You have to hand it to a wife. It's not easy having a husband in pro sports. If you want to sniff around long enough you're going to find problems. I've been fortunate. I have a good wife and I have a good family."

Mansfield also told a story about an incident involving Joe Greene that gives a glimpse of why Greene was the most feared defensive lineman in the National Football League.

"We were playing the Cleveland Browns, and their center, Bob DeMarco, kept chop-blocking Joe. It's an illegal block and it can be a career-ending block. Joe was furious with DeMarco, and kept warning him not to do it again.

"The Browns ran a screen pass to the left, and Bob had pulled out of the line and was out there on the screen leading the blocking. Joe ran about 20 yards and clothes-lined him, and knocked out some of his teeth. It's a wonder he didn't knock off Bob's head. Whenever I see Bob, he still bitches about that day."

George Perles told me about that same incident a few nights before, and added to it.

"After Joe knocked out DeMarco, he went over and stood in front of the Browns' bench, and got the attention of Nick Skorich, their coach. He told Nick, 'I'm the one that did it! I want you to know that!' Then Joe came over to me and told me what he had said to Nick. Joe said, 'I thought you'd get a kick out of that, Coach.' I said, 'You're right, Joe. That's just great,' " recalled Perles.

133

Mansfield admired Greene's passion for playing. "There were a few games Joe Greene played where nobody could block him. At Houston in 1972, he was a one-man demolition crew. If you looked at films, you couldn't believe how many guys were trying to block Joe Greene. They were so concerned with Joe Greene that it left everyone else in a one-on-one situation, and it left the other team vulnerable to blitzes. Joe Greene was the greatest."

One day I was driving by the tennis courts in Upper St. Clair and I spotted Ray's wife, Janet, playing doubles tennis, and her partner was Ginny Giusti, the wife of former Pirates' relief ace Dave Giusti. It struck me that Janet and Ginny had a lot in common. They were both married to highly-competitive fellows who had long and distinguished careers in major league sports. And the relationships have endured.

Ray and Janet started dating shortly after he had graduated from high school out in Kennewick, Washington. She is a nurse at Eye & Ear Hospital, right across the street from Pitt Stadium where Ray first began playing for the Steelers back in 1964. The Mansfields had been married for 29 years when I visited them early in 1992.

They have four children. There's Kathy, 27, who works for USAir in Orlando; Jennifer, 26, out on the West Coast who was trying to finish up her work for a degree in speech therapy; Caroline 22, who's still at home and was helping her dad at his office while attending a travel agency school, and Jim, a junior on the football team at the University of Hawaii.

Mansfield told me he had gotten angry with Tom Donahoe during the 1991 campaign because Donahoe had been critical of Chuck Noll for not giving the rookies more of an opportunity to play so they could be properly evaluated.

"I thought that was, in a sense, a betrayal, for him to say that to a media guy," said Mansfield. "Chuck never betrayed anybody. It really pissed me off.

"Two weeks later, I was on Bruce Keidan's radio show, and I said I was still angry about it — because I love Chuck Noll — and I don't know anything about Donahoe. I said the last time I saw him he was a ballboy for the Steelers. That's all I said.

"I got a letter from Donahoe, and he resented how I expressed myself. He said he had always admired me. He said he was also proud of his own career. He said no one admired Chuck Noll more than he did, and that no one's worked harder with Chuck Noll. He wished me a Merry Christmas.

"I wrote him back and I was still scolding him, I suppose. Chuck taught us one thing. You never air your dirty laundry outside the team. It can only hurt the team. I told him if he was going to be in the position he's in that he had to learn the same lesson."

134

Frenchy Fuqua
The Count is in the attic.

"Frenchy is either going to take his secret to the grave or write a book about it himself someday."
—Terry Bradshaw

John "Frenchy" Fuqua was reflecting on his starry nights at the Aurora Club in Pittsburgh's Hill District. Only the day before, in late December of 1991, somebody was shot and killed at the club's doorstep, and I mentioned this to Fuqua.

He didn't sound surprised by the shootout. He didn't sound surprised when I told him 40 shots were fired in all, according to the police report. "I know the Aurora Club well," he said. "Every Friday night there was always a fifth of Canadian Club, with ice, cherries and orange slices, waiting for me at the Aurora. Even when I didn't make it, they were ready for my arrival.

"Friday was a football player's Saturday night. We didn't have a curfew and we had an easy workout on Saturday so you could stay out late and relax and have some fun. That's before Doris (his wife) found out where I was.

"Yes, I knew the Aurora Club well. It was patronized by pimps and any other degenerates you can name. But it was the only place where you could catch a band playing after one o'clock. A lot of the guys on the team went there regularly. One should be street-wise going in there."

The Hill District is the black section of the city, an area between the Civic Arena and Pitt Stadium. Considering where it sits in relation to Downtown and Oakland and The Strip and Shadyside, it should be one of the city's most fashionable neighborhoods — like San Francisco's Nob Hill — but it is something less. It has its share of mean streets.

Fuqua frequently went there in the company of John Rowser, a defensive back for the Steelers ("Yowzer, yowzer, here comes Rowser") and a fellow Detroit traveler. They had grown up on the same street and both starred on the football team at Eastern High School. "We had the most dominant team in the city," interjected Fuqua.

"They never trusted Rowser and I, being from Detroit," recalled Fuqua of his Aurora Club days. "Detroit was leading the country in homicides and crime at the time, so they never trusted us. That was good."

Fuqua, always the fun guy, cackled over his own comment during our telephone conversation from his bedroom in Detroit.

"If you wanted night life in Pittsburgh," offered Fuqua, "you had to go to the Aurora Club. I usually traveled alone, but I'd bump into the other guys on the team there. Like L.C. Greenwood, Glen Edwards and Ernie Holmes. We even took Moon Mullins and Ray Mansfield there a few times. Believe me, I've been there."

135

So had I, as a college student, in the company of John Henry Johnson, another legendary figure in Steelers' history who was inducted into the Pro Football Hall of Fame in 1987.

John Henry caused a commotion that night at the Aurora by refusing to pay for our drinks. No one trusted John Henry, either. Thank God, nobody messed with John Henry, either. We escaped unharmed, backing out the door as I can best recall.

Frenchy would have loved John Henry. They were kindred spirits.

The news about the Aurora Club wasn't the only conversational cue that had come my way that day before I telephoned Fuqua. My youngest daughter, Rebecca, then 14, had cleaned the bowl for her goldfish that day, and I carried it to her bedroom for her. In his playing days, Frenchy Fuqua was famous for wearing shoes with large glass heels that had goldfish in them. Plus, his former coach, Chuck Noll, had announced his resignation that same week. They were all fodder for Fuqua's consideration.

I found Fuqua, at 47, still full of himself and something else. "I've always loved to bullshit," he said. "I can tell some stories."

And he did, disclosing a long-held "secret" about what really happened on "The Immaculate Reception" that brought fame to Franco Harris in the 1972 AFC playoff game against the Oakland Raiders, and wonderful tales about his teammates, especially his pal Ernie "Fats" Holmes.

Frenchy Fuqua is more famous for his flamboyant attire than for being a fine running back for the Steelers over a seven-year stretch, from 1970 to 1976. He was a member of two Super Bowl championship teams, and created a stir wherever he strode and spoke. He was often outrageous in costume and comment, and claimed to be the NFL's best dressed performer.

Fuqua flitted like a firefly across the Pittsburgh skyline in the early '70s when he was the best running back the Steelers had to offer before Harris hit the scene. Whatever uniform he was flashing, the black and gold or some got-to-be-seen-to-be-believed combination, Fuqua was both reliable and iridescent.

He once wrote a critical letter to the editors of *Esquire* magazine for excluding him from a list of the "Ten Best-Dressed Jocks," and it was later reprinted in the magazine.

"You express yourself with your clothes," said Fuqua during his flashiest period in Pittsburgh. "When you feel like a king, you dress like one. Clothes reflect the emotions. I always loved clothes."

Pat Livingston, then sports editor of *The Pittsburgh Press,* dubbed him as "a happy-go-lucky soul brother to all mankind."

Fuqua inspired other Steelers to follow his lead, and they were a bunch of dandies who drew stares at airports across the country. This prompted Tex Maule, the pro football writer for *Sports Illustrated*, to observe, "The Steelers are all by themselves in the threads league. No other team touches them."

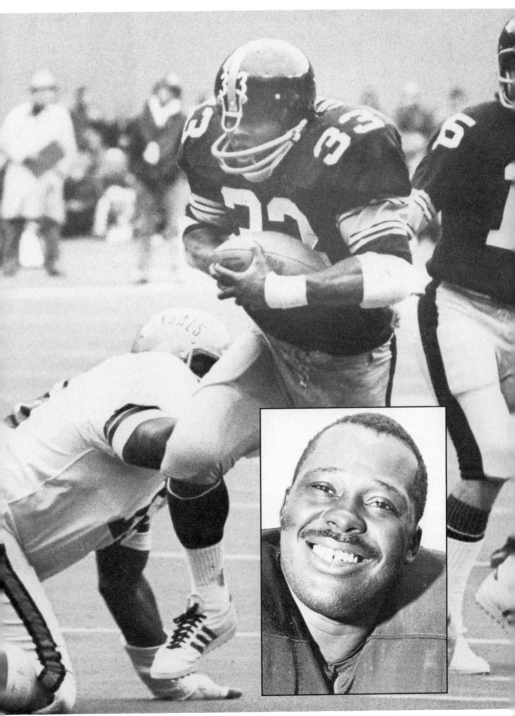

John "Frenchy" Fuqua flashes running form against Bengals.

George Gojkovich

137

Livingston asked Noll, then a 39-year-old coach, how he felt about his ballplayers dressing so outlandishly for road trips. "I don't care what people wear or how they cut their hair," Noll responded, giving an early clue to his concentration. "I'm concerned with how they play football."

Fuqua is a legendary figure for more than his daring dress. He was also the middle man in "The Immaculate Reception" sequence. Terry Bradshaw was throwing a pass down the middle of the field to Fuqua, one of the team's most sure-handed receivers, when Jack Tatum of the Oakland Raiders collided with Fuqua, knocking the ball back upfield where Franco found it and grasped it at his shoe tops and raced for a touchdown in the AFC playoffs on December 23, 1972.

It was a fourth and ten call at the Steelers' 40 yard line with 22 seconds left to play, and the Steelers trailing, 7-6. Bradshaw ducked a strong rush, but was flattened as he let the ball go and had no idea what happened afterward. A lot of people still don't.

"Frenchy likes to be coy about it," said Terry Bradshaw in his book, *Looking Deep,* in writing about what he termed the pivotal play in the team's history. "The glory days for the Steelers were still two years ahead, but we buried our past that day.

"If Frenchy did touch the ball first, then the play was voided. In those days, it was illegal for a ball to be touched first by another offensive player. John Madden and the Raiders felt they got shafted.

"Frenchy doesn't want to say and is either going to take his secret to the grave or write a book about it himself someday."

It's one of the most famous and frequently aired sequences in sports history, yet Fuqua is often a forgotten figure in it. He teases people about whether or not he or Tatum touched the ball because, if he alone had touched it, the catch and run by Harris would have been nullified by NFL rules in use at the time. Back then, the ball could not be touched simultaneously by two teammates on the receiving end. Today it can be.

Fred Swearingen didn't signal a touchdown right away. He checked a sideline camera to help him make the call. There wasn't any official review of plays at that time. Thus instant replay was born.

"I always have to tell that story," said Fuqua. "I tell them everything that happened, except who touched the ball and how. Jack Tatum had to hit it for it to have been a legitimate reception by Franco. But let's not beat around the bush. Jack didn't touch it. It's the only secret I have left in my life.

"That pass was coming to me from the get-go. Ron Shanklin and I had led the team in receiving (with 49 catches apiece) the previous season, and I was considered one of our most sure-handed receivers."

According to game reports, post-game commentary, and Bradshaw's book, however, rookie Barry Pearson was the primary receiver on that final play. But that was other people's version of the story, not Fuqua's.

"When Bradshaw went to the sideline to confer with the coaches before that play, I watched those blue eyes from the sideline to the huddle, and I knew he was going to throw the ball to me. Bradshaw eyed me all the way back to the huddle," said Fuqua.

"If the timing had worked out, and the pass protection hadn't broken down — Otis Sistrunk nearly got Terry — I was wide open. I'd have either gotten to the end zone or to the sideline, and Roy Gerela would have had an easy kick for a field goal to win it. I could have been the hero.

"But Bradshaw had to duck under and away from the rush — he ran to the right — and in the meantime Tatum left one of our wide receivers, Barry Pearson, and came up to cover me. The ball came my way. The ball was tipped and Franco caught it and ran away with hundreds of thousands of dollars I'd have made on that play. It took 1.8 seconds for the ball to go from my hands to Franco's hands.

"I've watched that play a hundred times. I have it on tape at home. Tatum wasn't near me, at first, when I went into my hook. I was around their 30 yard line and I'd have taken an angle, and we'd have been, at the least, in a position where Roy couldn't miss it.

"Franco should have been nowhere around that ball. But some players just have a nose for it. A guy like him is always at the right place at the right time. I'm glad he was."

Noll had said, "Franco made that play because he never quit on the play. He kept running; he kept hustling. Good things happen to those who hustle."

John Madden, the Raiders' coach, was protesting on the other sideline. Madden claimed that Fuqua, not Tatum, had touched the ball and the pass should have been ruled incomplete, having bounced from one offensive player to another.

"It's so disappointing," Madden said, "to come down to a whole season and have it end like this."

Fuqua begs to differ. "That play is shown on TV at least three times a year," said Fuqua, "and my boss always gives me a nod at the office the next day to acknowledge it. But what would have happened if Frenchy Fuqua caught the ball? But I was always a team player, and always thought in the team concept. If I had scored, though, I'd have given the reporters a better story than Franco. The controversy is what made that play."

Fuqua was the Steelers' leading rusher for two seasons, 1970 and 1971, succeeding Dick Hoak for those honors. Following Fuqua's reign, Franco Harris would hold that distinction for the next dozen years.

Fuqua's finest season was 1970, his first after being traded to the Steelers following his rookie season with the New York Giants. He gained 691 yards on 138 carries, a 5-yard-a-clip average, and scored seven touchdowns.

On December 20 of that 1970 season, at Philadelphia, Fuqua rushed for 218 yards, still a Steelers' one game record. He went 85 yards for a touchdown in that game, the third longest run in team history.

"It was a great day," gushed Fuqua over the telephone from Detroit, just about 21 years later. It was still fresh in Fuqua's mind. "When anyone questions my speed, I refer to the film of that game. The

Eagles had a defensive back named John Outlaw, a bona fide track star, and he couldn't catch me. Nobody was going to catch me that day. Not even Bob Hayes. Nobody.

"And I had just gotten out of the hospital; I'd had back spasms, and I was playing a different position, halfback instead of fullback. That's when I fell in love with the counter 15 trap play. Either Terry Cole or Preston Pearson were in motion, and Bruce Van Dyke, our guard, was pulling out and leading the way for me. Terry Hanratty was our quarterback and he kept calling audibles at the line of scrimmage. It all worked. We were unstoppable that day."

He was 5-11, 205, and loved to block, just like John Henry Johnson. He took his share of shots, and was often injured, but played with hurts that might have sidelined bigger backs.

"I believe in the old saying," he once said, "that it's not the size of the dog in the fight, it's the size of the fight in the dog."

Fuqua began working for *The Detroit News* when he was still with the Steelers, and continues today in the same role with what is now known as the Detroit News Agency. It's a combine involving the *Detroit News* and the *Detroit Free-Press*. He is responsible for recruiting newscarriers.

He started working part-time in 1975 and full-time in 1978. His family, including his 72-year-old mother, was living in North Rosedale Park — a "professional neighborhood," according to Fuqua, when we had a series of interviews.

He travels to schools throughout the city in an effort to interest young people in delivering the newspaper in their neighborhoods. Fuqua has always been good on his feet, and he gets the kids' attention in a hurry, no easy task in Detroit's inner-city schools.

"Good morning, students," he says. "I'm John 'Frenchy' Fuqua, and I was a running back for the Pittsburgh Steelers when they won their first two Super Bowls.

"I've been a member of the No. 1 team in the National Football League, and I want you to join the No. 1 team in Detroit."

Then Fuqua holds up his two Super Bowl rings for all to see. "That gets their attention every time," said Fuqua during our conversation. "They've never won a Super Bowl in Detroit, so it's still something special. That will quiet them down.

"Sometimes I pass the rings around. We had to lock the door one time. One of the students was hiding one of the rings. Can you imagine the scare that went through me before that ring turned up?"

Nowadays, Fuqua is turning his efforts to recruiting adult newscarriers, something that is being done in Pittsburgh as well. His talk plays even better with adults. "They can remember our team," he said. "I played for a team that they're still talking about twenty years later."

People close to the Steelers are still talking about Ernie Holmes, a defensive tackle for the team from 1972 to 1977, and one of its fiercest and most formidable members, on and off the field.

"Ernie wasn't crazy," said Fuqua, laughing before he got to his own punchline, "he was just damn out of his mind."

And Fuqua was Ernie's best friend on the team, indeed, the best man at his wedding at a church on Pittsburgh's North Side.

"I adopted Ernie," said Fuqua. "For awhile, we both lived in the same apartment, at the Washington Plaza Apartments across from the Civic Arena. I was always begging Ernie not to break the fingers of the women who weren't interested in his attentions. He had a bad habit of throwing them out of the door if they didn't go along with what he wanted to do, and he'd slam the door on their hands. He was always breaking their fingers in the door. I scolded him: 'If they say no, don't break their fingers!'

"Ernie and I had a rapport. He called me in Detroit before he had that incident on the Ohio Turnpike where he was shooting at passing trucks, and later at the police in a helicopter.

"He called me and he said, 'Frenchy, I'm having problems. I'm leaving my wife, and I'm broke. I don't have a penny.' I told him, 'I can lend you a thousand, but you've got to sign some papers so the club will pay me if you don't.' And he said, 'Frenchy, if you can just give me $300 to just get to Pittsburgh I'll be all right.'

"I told him he ought to get back to Pittsburgh where he could play for the Steelers basketball team in the off-season. At that time we were getting about $125 per game for basketball. I told him he could make some pocket money until he got straightened out.

"I was to meet Ernie when the incident occurred. No one knew he was hurting that bad to do something like that.

"I helped Ernie later on. He was working as a security guard and rasslin' out in LA when he called me after he retired. He said, 'It's tight out here. It's rough. I need a solid job.' I put him in touch with a guy we originally met in Pittsburgh who had some connections in Hollywood. He put Ernie into some Mr. T shows, and some commercials for awhile.

"I hear from Ernie every now and then. He calls me from his boat. I was one of the few guys on the team who wasn't afraid of Ernie. I respected his size — he was the largest guy on the team — but it wasn't his size that scared guys. It was the quickness of his feet. He was known as 'Dancing Bear.' People would size him up, for football or for a fight, and ask themselves, 'What would I do if I had to take on this guy?'

"One time he got mad at my wife Doris for driving our car on the edge of his grass, and messing up his lawn a little bit. He came over to our house and I knew he was coming, and I knew he was hot.

"I had a .32, a little pistol. I'm telling myself, 'If he hits my wife, I will destroy him. I will have to shoot him.' I figured I'd have to shoot him six times with that little pistol, then hit him with it on his head in order to stop him. And that might not do it. He was scary.

"You know the only thing that could stop Ernie? A trap block. That's how the other teams eventually stopped Ernie. They just let him shoot across the line like he liked to do, and they'd give him an opening, and then they'd have a 265-pound guard crack back on the side of his legs. They'd cut him down to size in a hurry that way.

"But I loved Ernie. I'd take him with me when I was out at places like Aliquippa, having fun with the ladies. I could handle myself all right, but if someone was bigger than me and giving me a bad time, I'd say to them, 'Why don't you discuss this with my brother? Ernie!' That would end that.

"I enjoyed Ernie. He was a lovable guy. He had to stay at Western Psychiatric Institute for awhile after his shooting incident on the turnpike. I may be talking out of school here, but I was paid by the team to visit Ernie at Western Psych on a regular basis. I stayed in town an extra three weeks to look after him. I would sneak him a pint of Courvoisier, a cognac he loved to drink. That would make him happy."

The news about Noll's retirement gave Fuqua pause for thought. "I felt sorry, in a way, and maybe that's not the right word, because I know how hard it is for someone to leave the game. Chuck Noll had become synonymous with the Steelers. At the same time, I feel good for him. There's not much more he could accomplish. I hope he'll enjoy the time that he'll have to do other things. I remember how his son Chris used to come to training camp. But he had to share his father with so many others. Noll had to be a father to, at first, over a hundred young men, then 40 or so when the season started. They all had different needs, and different personalities, all pulling for his time and attention.

"Can you imagine what kind of father-son relationship you have when a father has one son and then so many players to look after. When does he really get a chance to be with his son?

"Chris was Chuck's only child, but I wondered how much time he had for him and his family. When we came to the Stadium in the morning, Chuck was always there waiting for us, and when we went home at night he was still there.

"I remember him telling us at one of our meetings how his father-in-law was always talking about what he was going to do after he retired. He had all these things he wanted to do with his time after he retired. How one of these days he was just going to relax and go fishing. But he kept on working and working, and putting off his plans. Soon after his father-in-law retired, Chuck told us, his wife died. He never really got to do what he wanted to do. Why didn't he stop and take the time?

"Chuck's point was that we couldn't put off our dreams. We had to do it that day. We had to do it now. But maybe Chuck kept that same story in his mind regarding himself and his own plans. Maybe Chuck took that philosophy and used it himself."

I mentioned to Fuqua that I had heard Noll had bought an expensive boat and had it in a slip at Hilton Head. That he was really into boating. "See," said Fuqua. "I told you so."

"Frenchy" Fuqua

Fuqua gave that some more thought. "But I think it will be difficult for Chuck to give up football altogether. It's hard to get that out of your blood, out of your veins. We're in the same business, so to speak, the newspaper and writing business, and they say you have ink in your blood.

"Yeah, I missed it when I left the Steelers. But my personality changed the moment I hit the Ohio Turnpike on the way back here. I changed to the other side. My business card says 'Frenchy Fuqua' but I always introduce myself as John Fuqua. If you didn't know I played football, you wouldn't know it by the way I talk or behave these days. Just when I'm talking to you.

"When I retired, I was content, and glad to be away from it before I got a bad injury. I didn't watch a game for the first six weeks during the first season after I quit. Then one day I caught the Browns against the Steelers on TV, and I haven't missed a game since."

When I called, he was watching an AFC playoff game between the Kansas City Chiefs and Los Angeles Raiders on TV, along with his youngest son, Derrion, who was eight years old. "I just made him a super hamburger, one with two patties of beef," boasted Fuqua. "He's happy."

Fuqua has a daughter, Keylea, 18, who was in her freshman year at Morgan State University, his alma mater. He also has another son, John Jr., then 16 and a junior at Henry Ford High School in Detroit. Fuqua had gone to Detroit Eastern High, later renamed Martin Luther King High.

"My son's team made it to the playoffs," said Fuqua. "He's a defensive back, if you can believe that. All the knowledge I had to pass on to the chump, but they eat at McDonald's and do what they want.

"John Jr. is an excellent athlete. He's captain of the team and he's been starting since he was a freshman. I've talked to him, and next year I'll make sure he plays offensive back. He's a natural, just the way he runs.

"My legs kinda kicked out to the side when I ran. When you watch him running from the rear, you can't tell him apart from me. He had shied away from the comparisons, but he is a natural runner. I always thought defensive backs needed to be more smooth in their stride. I want him to be in the best possible position to help him get to college and get a scholarship."

Summing up his Steelers' career, Fuqua feels positive about it. "I think I had a fulfilling career," he said. "I'm one of the very, very few to experience world championships. I worked for a winner, I worked for a helluva family, especially The Chief. I benefitted from having student-of-the-game coaching, which comes from Chuck Noll. I learned football there. I met a parade of personalities from all over the United States that I will always be able to tell stories about.

144

"I was a fun-loving guy who took my football seriously. And I liked to bullshit a lot. Like my mom always tells me, 'If you died tomorrow, you'll have led a full life.' I feel that way, though I'm in no hurry to meet my Maker.

"I played for a team that's being talked about twenty years later."

Fuqua offered remarks about several of the Steelers who stick out in his mind, namely Ray Mansfield, Rocky Bleier, Franco Harris and Ron Johnson.

"Ray Mansfield could be a dirty sonuvagun. When he was going to get you, he got organized to get you. He used to say, 'I'm not going to get mad, I'm going to get even.' And he would. I see him every year at our alumni golf outing, and he's still the same. He's still running, still hitting and still getting even. I saw him sneak into games to keep his consecutive game playing streak alive when he should've been in a hospital bed. I call him 'Ironman' and he earned it.

"I saw Franco the first time on TV in the College All-Star Game. I was watching it with Rocky Bleier and Preston Pearson and some other running backs at St. Vincent College, and we were watching him closely. He didn't have that great a game. But he caught a pass and he kinda double-dribbled his feet. You could see the quickness in his feet. I told Preston, 'Hey, did you see that stutter-step?' He could come to a stop and then beat people. He could tip toe and then break outside. He picked well, and he had that great stutter-step.

"He wasn't impressive at practice. He was a different man in the game. Every day at practice when he took a handoff he would run the ball about 40 yards up the field. After practice, every day, you'd see him jumping rope. His legs were always in good shape. He took great care of his legs.

"Rocky and I go all the way back to 1970. I hung out with Rocky after practice when his foot was bleeding, the one that had been damaged by a hand grenade in Vietnam. I'd say, 'Rocky, you can't do this to yourself,' and he'd say, 'Please don't tell anybody. I'll be all right.' You could see the pain he was in. You could feel the work and the sweat and the pain. If there was ever a guy who was dedicated to coming back, to proving himself, it was Rocky. The way he came back is an inspiration for everyone, and it's a story he shares with so many in his motivational talks. He comes to Detroit from time to time and we get together. We stay in touch."

Fuqua says he often gets together with John Rowser and Ron Johnson in Detroit. They were at the Pontiac Silverdome when the Steelers played the Lions there during the 1991 campaign. He said Rowser owns a club called "The Sting." Offers Fuqua: "It's one of the top black night clubs in town."

He says he has known Johnson, who joined the Steelers the year after he retired, since he was a baby. "His family lived across the street from mine; I was a friend of his older brother, Wayne, who has since died. Ron always wanted to tag along with us, and we'd shoo him away. I can remember tossing little rocks at him to get rid of him. I see him about twice a month."

145

They called him "The Frenchman" and "The Count" when he was playing for the Steelers, and showing up for social occasions in capes, plumed hats, canes and color combinations you couldn't believe.

I asked Fuqua if he was still a fashion plate. "I'm quite conservative now," he said. "I wear business suits, white shirts and ties, sweaters. I may get a little jazzy every once in a while. The wife and I will get dolled up and go out for the evening.

"When I was in the limelight, it was all a part of showbiz. I told the IRS that, but they disagreed. I lost the case when they challenged my taking a business deduction for the clothes I wore. They wouldn't let me deduct it. When I went to banquets back in those days, people would have been disappointed if I didn't dress the part.

"The Count is alive and well, only he's up in the attic. The girls at the office get after me every now and then to get out some of my old threads. Here in my hometown, more people remember me now than when I was playing.

"They did a feature on me in one of those 'Inside the NFL' shows on HBO a few years back. They won an award for my 'Where Are They Now?' segment. Every now and then down at the office we'll have a Halloween party or a western party and the girls get after me to dress up.

"I wore my 'Superstar' outfit down there and took my cape and all for them. Most of that stuff is still up in the attic. I tried them on this year, and I was still able to get into most of them."

I told him that L.C. Greenwood was still stewing over the fact that Fuqua became celebrated for his clothes when L.C. insists it was he who introduced Fuqua to the world of fashion.

"Hollywood Bags . . ." began Fuqua, letting the name flow for awhile. "The audacity. I get a chance to see him every now and then when he's out here for a promotion. I'm the cause of Hollywood going to Hollywood. He and Mike Wagner and Chuck Beatty and Jim Clack tried to compete with me as far as clothes were concerned.

"I brought class to that organization. It was a trip for the guys to come to my room on the road and see what I had just bought. I give L.C. credit for getting some gold shoes, but that's the only thing he ever did that deserved some credit. The other stuff he purchased was stuff I turned down. But all that stuff is out of my budget now."

When Fuqua was with the Steelers, he used to lead the way in what was called a "dress-off" competition.

In 1973, he had a pair of clogs with six-inch heels and a goldfish in each heel. They didn't last long because of the mortality rate of the fish.

"After practice one day, I was going from Pittsburgh to Allentown," said Fuqua back then. "The fish never made it. All I know is they died somewhere on the way. They couldn't get oxygen.

"L.C. was known to wear blue hot pants and panty hose. Can you imagine a guy 6-6 with nerve enough to wear panty hose? Even so, I was the permanent king of the dress-off."

Franco often served as his valet for the competition in the clubhouse. "It was a lot of fun," Fuqua said. "It brought the team together."

There was the time Fuqua showed up in a skin-tight lavender jump suit, a pink cowbelt, white shoes, white gloves, a top hat and a glass cane. He usually wore oversized sunglasses and big hats.

On another occasion, he wore blood red knickers, black boots that came up over the calf. He had a coat of black velvet decorated with red stars. That was his so-called "Superstar" outfit. "I am the best-dressed player in the league," said Fuqua. "I feel flashy, and if you feel flashy off the field you're gonna feel flashy on the field.

"I think it was a privilege for the people to see the outfits I wear," he said. "Usually, there's a pretty big crowd outside the gate after the game. I try to shock them every weekend."

Fuqua explained the annual dress-off competition in detail to New York sports columnist Ira Berkow in December of 1972:

"It's an annual thing," said Fuqua, "and it's held about a month before the end of the season in the locker room after a practice.

"Everybody is fat-mouthin' about their rags until the moment of truth, when they meet The Count. Then they fall by the wayside. This year, Jim Clack was the white hope.

"You have all your clothes in your locker, hid. You put 'em on one at a time. We have an announcer who handles it like a prize fight. You start with the briefs. Clack broke out with powder-blue silk ones. I countered with my red bikinis.

"He pulled on some weird zebra stockings. Then I blew his mind; I laid my red panty hose on him.

"He broke back with some blue velour pants. I broke out in my pants with the new look of plaids. He tried to come on strong with some shirt that wasn't fantastic. He was fading, and I hadn't even got to the bulk of my dry goods. He knew it because already I was getting the oohs and aahs from the players. He broke out in a plaid bow tie. Nothing. A sweater vest. Zero. Blue clogs. Embarrassing.

"I hit him with the rest of my three-piece red suit with a blood-red turtle-neck. Then I had a sensational gimmick. From my vest pocket, I pulled out a watch. I looked at it, looked at him and replied, 'Your time is runnin' out, Clack.'

"Believe it or not, he began to sweat. He wiped his head with a towel. He said it was the lights."

Then Frenchy came on with his "knockout stuff": three-inch high heel white boots, a monogrammed coat and "broke down my white gangster-style hat on one side like only I can and that was it."

French was telling Berkow about his contest with Clack while his fiance Doris Moore was looking on. Fuqua kept referring to her as The Countess. As in "Right, Countess?"

He went on about his sartorial splendor. "It's very exciting after games," continued Fuqua. "I just feel good — when we win — from the top of my gorgeous head to the bottom of my curly toes. I hear the fans chanting when I come out of the locker room. 'Frenchy's comin',

Frenchy's comin', what's he got on?' I sign autographs from different poses, so everyone can get a good look at me.

"Then I jump into my Mark IV. The Countess is waiting for me. I blast on a tape, usually a jumpin' tune, and we speed off. And, you know, this may sound silly, but like 50 yards away I can still hear the fans. 'Ooh, did you see that — was he bad?' "

Somebody asked Doris Moore, who later married Frenchy, how she liked being "The Countess."

"It gives me a headache," she said.

John "Frenchy" Fuqua

The linebackers

"Today's game is like touch football."
—Jack Ham

"I was lucky to step into a job where I coached what had to be the best linebacking trio of all time."
—Woody Widenhofer
Former Steelers' coach

Jack Ham, Jack Lambert and Andy Russell played together for three seasons and were considered by many to have formed the best linebacking unit of their time (1974-76).

It was an era when the 4-3 defense — four down linemen and three linebackers — was fashionable in the National Football League. And the Pittsburgh Steelers were flexing their muscles.

They won their first two Super Bowls, IX and X, following the 1974 and 1975 seasons, but came up short in 1976. Steelers founder Art Rooney always regarded the 1976 team as the best in the history of the franchise. But, with running backs Franco Harris and Rocky Bleier sidelined by injuries, Pittsburgh lost to the Oakland Raiders in the AFC championship game that year by 24-7.

That year the Steelers shut out five opponents in an eight-week span. They had a dominant defense even though Ham (6 feet, 2 inches, 218 pounds), Lambert (6-4, 220) and Russell (6-2, 225) were not overpowering physically.

The Steelers had the wild, head-knocking rush up front and the versatile, highly-organized linebackers and secondary to back it up.

Ham, Lambert and Russell were formidable against the run and so quick and smart against the pass that the Steelers could leave them in man-to-man coverage against the backs and tight end and drop an extra safety deep as a second "center fielder." The famous Cover Two — two defenders deep playing zone and five defenders short playing tight man-to-man — was a critical factor in the Steelers' success.

All three linebackers were outstanding athletes with strong desire, dedication, and intelligence.

Russell and Ham both played 12 seasons with the Steelers. Russell retired after the 1976 season, and Ham quit after the 1982 season. Lambert lasted 11 years before a toe injury forced him to retire ahead of schedule following the 1984 season.

While together, they complemented each other extremely well.

Bob "Woody" Widenhofer, who had been Russell's backup at Missouri, became the Steelers' linebacker coach in 1973. Ham and Russell were the outside linebackers, and Henry Davis, who made the AFC-NFC Pro Bowl that season, was in the middle.

Davis suffered a concussion during the preseason in 1974. Lambert, a second-round draft choice out of Kent State, took over as a starter in the season opener and was named the NFL defensive rookie of the year.

"He was never really a rookie," recalled Joe Greene. "He just seemed to belong right from the start. He knew what he was doing, and he knew his place."

Widenhofer, who has been an assistant coach in recent seasons with the Detroit Lions after a disappointing stint as a head coach at his alma mater in Missouri and two seasons in the USFL, knew he had some studs at his service with the Steelers.

"I was lucky to step into a job where I coached what had to be the best linebacking trio of all-time," said Widenhofer.

Several NFL coaches during the '70s, such as Don Shula of the Miami Dolphins, Sam Rutigliano of the Cleveland Browns and Bart Starr of the Green Bay Packers, and some who became head coaches in the '80s, like Bill Parcells of the New York Giants and Joe Walton of the New York Jets, all felt Pittsburgh had the best linebacking in the 1970s.

When Russell retired, he was replaced by Loren Toews, then Robin Cole. The Steelers won two more Super Bowls, XIII and XIV, and continued to set the standard for linebacking in the league. In more recent times, they have boasted about several other fine linebackers, like Mike Merriweather, David Little and Bryan Hinkle.

"I'm not a believer in comparing teams or players," allowed Lambert. "It's like comparing Muhammad Ali and Joe Louis. Who can do it? Just to be mentioned as one of the greatest as a team or player should be enough."

Rutigliano, now the head coach at Liberty University where he helped develop Eric Green, often refers to the Steelers as the model when he is discussing football. Asked if he thought the Steelers had the best linebackers during the '70s, Rutigliano remarked, "Without question. Particularly with Russell.

"They had three great tacklers, three mobile people. I can go back and look at film of our games against them, and we had so many chances for big plays killed by those guys making open-field tackles when I thought we could break away for big gainers.

"I don't think you ever saw, collectively, three smarter guys at that position. They were rubber-stamp guys: all great people on and off the field.

"I had two of them — Ham and Lambert — when I coached the Pro Bowl (1981). I couldn't have been more impressed — with their talent and the way they accepted what we wanted to do, and then did it.

"Donnie Shell, Mike Webster and Franco Harris were the same way. It was easy to see why the Steelers had been perennial winners. Not everybody goes to the Pro Bowl and approaches it the same way. With some guys, we should've brought a carousel and some swing sets."

The Super Bowl and AFC-NFC Pro Bowl were showcases for the Steelers during the club's glory days.

At the end of the 1975 season, Ham, Lambert and Russell all represented the Steelers in the AFC-NFC Pro Bowl. Russell was selected six consecutive times in his career. Ham was chosen eight straight

150

Jack Ham, Andy Russell and Jack Lambert take a breather.

am snares Roger Staubach.

Russell with PNB's John Brown.

seasons, more than any other linebacker, until Lambert broke his mark after the 1984 season by making his ninth straight appearance.

Ham had 32 career interceptions, tying him at the time for second place on the all-time list for linebackers (The leader, Don Shinnick of the Baltimore Colts, had 37). Ham was the only unanimous choice on the defensive unit for the team of the decade for the 1970s.

Twice Lambert was named NFL defensive player of the year, and twice the Steelers' most valuable player. He led the team in tackling for ten seasons until he was injured in his final campaign.

"They all had strong points that were different," said Widenhofer. "What they had in common was they were great athletes and they were intelligent and they understood the game.

"Russell really studied. He wanted every edge. He could tell by the tilt of the backs, the formation, what was coming. Andy was on top of all that. Ham picked up that stuff later on. He was just learning at that point, but he was such a natural athlete.

"Lambert brought the intensity part. He was best known for his toughness. But he was also very smart."

Russell made the Steelers as a sixteenth round draft choice out of Missouri in 1963. He started as a rookie, spent the next two seasons as an officer in the military service, then returned to play 11 more seasons with the Steelers.

He played for coaches Buddy Parker and Bill Austin before Chuck Noll arrived in 1969. Parker's 1963 team nearly won the division title. Austin's teams were all losers — going 2-11-1 in his last year — and Noll's first squad was even worse at 1-13.

"I always enjoyed playing football and I had fun even on those losing teams," Russell said. "It's probably a greater challenge to be a linebacker on a losing team than a linebacker on a winning team because you get more support on a winning club."

It was nicer to be on a championship team, but he missed some aspects of what he was able to do in the bad old days.

"I used to blitz all the time," he recalled during our interview. "I'd just go on my own. Our linebackers would blitz one out of every three plays. A linebacker loves to blitz because it's the only time he knows where he's going. With the team Chuck (Noll) put together we had much more support up front and we blitzed once a game."

Russell never liked the idea of sitting back and reacting.

"I liked to think that I had talent for smelling out the play," Russell said. "I tried to guess what they were doing. A lot of of it was predicated on what you saw in the film all week. A lot depended on the down yardage. If I got burned on a play, I'd watch for the quarterback to call it again. The quarterback always comes back to what's worked for him."

How soon did Russell recognize that Ham and Lambert were special?

"I've been around around this game a long time, and always watched and studied linebackers, especially on film," Russell said.

"I don't have any reservations saying Lambert was the best middle linebacker I've ever seen and that Ham was the best outside

George Gojkovich

Johnson (29), Jack Lambert (58), Loren Toews (51) and
Beasley (65) hold Falcons' Bubba Bean for no gain during
h quarter goal line stand in 1978.

Rill Amatucci

Jack Ham with Penn State's Joe
Paterno at Hall of Fame induction in
1988 in Canton, Ohio.

Andy Russell

Pittsburgh Steelers

Pittsburgh Steelers

Steelers linebackers coach
Woody Widenhofer holds Jack
Ham's jersey up at retirement
ceremony.

linebacker I've ever seen." Ham was inducted into the Pro Football Hall of Fame in 1988 and Lambert followed in 1990. Some say Russell should have been similarly enshrined as well, but he is still waiting.

Ham became a copy of Russell. Ham read the other team's offense as if he had been in their huddle. He also took a cue from Russell and got involved in business during his playing days. He got involved in the coal business, something he had done in his youth, helping his dad deliver it in their Johnstown neighborhood to make some extra money, and he has continued in that field.

"I couldn't have fallen into a better situation," said Ham, who came to the Steelers as a second round pick out of Penn State in 1971.

"Andy, whom I consider the best linebacker I ever saw play, had been with the Steelers for eight seasons, and he played the way I eventually did. His specialty was diagnosing plays and reading tendencies. I think I may have been quicker and stronger than Andy, but I adopted the other things he did, and pretty soon I was able to diagnose plays almost as well as he could."

Ham felt his greatest asset was his ability to "ball-react," which means following a quarterback's eyes and trying to guess where he's going to throw the ball.

"Until 1982, it was no secret we played a stunt 4-3 defense," Ham said. "But in the secondary we disguised defenses in order to give a quarterback a bad pre-read.

"When a quarterback comes to the line of scrimmage, we'd try to get him thinking we're set up for zone coverage. By the time the ball was snapped we'd have shifted back into man-to-man or vice versa.

"The idea, of course, is not to give the quarterback an accurate look at the defense until he's dropping back. It really is like a chess game out there, especially when we faced guys like Roger Staubach and Bob Griese."

Rules changes opened up the game and put more emphasis on passing, and took away some of the Steelers' strong points, like the bump-and-run maneuver mastered by Mel Blount and the other defensive backs.

"Today's game," Ham said with a sneer, "is like touch football on grass. Toward the end, we were playing with our hands tied behind our back."

When the rules were invoked to protect quarterbacks from harm, Lambert protested. "They ought to put the quarterbacks in dresses," he declared on a Monday Night Football Game interview.

Dick Butkus of the Chicago Bears, Sam Huff of the New York Giants, and Ray Nitschke of the Green Bay Packers were Lambert's boyhood heroes.

"There are few guys who care as much anymore," said Lambert. "I played the same way I played in high school and in college. I always hated to lose.

"Middle linebackers aren't like they used to be. They are so much more involved with pass coverage. I don't think the defenses were as complicated as they are now. They didn't have to chase tight ends, or go one-on-one with wide receivers deep. You have to play a more controlled game now. You can't afford to be out there flying around. It's more of a thinking man's game."

Russell was asked for his thoughts about Chuck Noll. "Noll is a great head coach," he said before Noll announced his retirement. "He has the players' respect entirely. He doesn't make mistakes in the way he deals with players. He very seldom gets up in front of the team and says something meaningless. You always have the feeling he has put a great deal of thought into what he says. It's never just some inane comment you haven't heard since you were in high school. That was impressive to me. He doesn't make petty rules just for the sake of discipline. Chuck is a disciplinarian, but when he sets down a rule, there is some sense to it. It's not just some silly little rule a guy will lay down to say, 'Look, I'm boss and you're subordinate, so I'm going to tell you what to do.' Chuck doesn't operate that way, and the players respect him. Too many people in Pittsburgh have an erroneous opinion of Chuck. They think he's low key and not a disciplinarian. He keeps himself aloof from the players. He doesn't allow himself to become buddies with the players as I've seen some coaches do. Consequently, it's clear with Chuck that if you don't perform, well, you aren't going to stay around. It's not a matter of what you did in the past. You could have played great for ten years, but that doesn't matter. It's not even a question of how you played last week. It's how you will play this Sunday and the Sunday after that that matters with Chuck. That's the way it should be. That's how you build a winning football team. Chuck doesn't allow you to become complacent."

Former USX president and CEO David Roderick is flanked by (from left) Woody Widenhofer, Jack Lambert, Andy Russell and Jack Ham.

Jack Lambert
"I'm also a human being."

"Jack likes to hit hard. He likes to inflict pain.
And that's just when he's out on a date."
—Roommate Rocky Bleier, 1980

It was late February, 1992 and Jack Lambert had left his hideaway in Worthington, Pennsylvania, a 125-acre wooded tract where he and his family live, to spend a nostalgic evening with his former teammates on the Steelers and to meet the new coach, Bill Cowher.

Over 40 former Steelers showed up at Three Rivers Stadium for an informal get-together, some in sleek business suits, most of them in casual sweaters and slacks, including the new coach. Cowher was happy to see Lambert because Jack had been his favorite football player on the Steelers during the glory days of the '70s. Lambert was in a light gray business suit. Cowher wore a sweater that must have been sent to him by Looie Carnesecca, the Hall of Fame basketball coach at St. John's University.

Cowher played linebacker at Carlynton High School near his hometown of Crafton, and then at North Carolina State, and he did his best to play with the fire and fury of Lambert. He had only been on the job for a month as Chuck Noll's successor when he met these distinguished Steelers from the past.

When Cowher addressed the alumni, Lambert was at the head of the class, sitting in the front row of a conference room where the Steelers hold regular chalk talks and review films. Another Hall of Famer, Mel Blount, was in the back of the room. Jack Ham had stopped by earlier to give his regards to the new coach, but had to skip out because of another commitment.

Blount had been in the news in a negative manner during the 1991 season, drawing criticism for "excessive disciplinary measures" at his Mel Blount Youth Home in Washington County. But that was behind him, or so he thought anyhow, and he appeared prosperous and positively glowing in a dark business suit and a light cowboy hat.

After Cowher finished his comments, he asked if everyone would stand up and introduce themselves, say when they played for the Steelers, and tell what they are doing these days.

Lambert was the first to stand up. He did so in a studied and so-so serious manner. There has always been a lot of Ham in Lambert; he's a method actor. "My name is Jack Lambert and I played linebacker for the Steelers for eleven years, from 1974 through 1984," Lambert began, looking down at his shoetops. "And I'm the supervisor for discipline at the Mel Blount Youth Home."

A cowboy hat came sailing from the back of the room in Lambert's direction. Everyone in the room broke up laughing. It was vintage Lambert. He has always been able to get a rise out of his teammates.

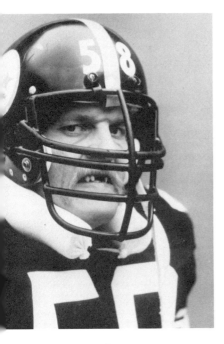

Jack Lambert

Jack Lambert lectures press prior to Hall of Fame induction in 1990.

"It was good to see him," said Ray Mansfield a month later. "We don't see much of Jack these days. Jack's a hermit now. They sent us a picture from that night. It's like a team photo with Cowher in the middle. Lambert's in the back. He's the one with the scowl on his face. He's always playing the hard-ass role."

Not always. Lambert is a kinder, gentler sort with his family: his wife, Lisa, and his two daughters, Lauren, 7, and Elizabeth, 5. When Lambert was inducted into the Pro Football Hall of Fame in the summer of 1990, he pointed to them in the front row by the steps of the sports shrine in Canton, Ohio, and said, "There, ladies and gentlemen, is *my* Hall of Fame." There has been an addition to the Lambert clan since then. On July 8, 1991, John Jr. was born. Jack loved to tell everybody that his son was born on his birthday — his 39th birthday — which just happens to be the Steelers' birthday as well. Art Rooney founded the franchise on July 8, 1933.

Lambert was showing pictures of his kids to anybody who would look as he moved among the crowd at Cowher's coming-out party. "I can't believe it," said a former teammate. "Jack Lambert showing baby pictures! What's the world coming to?"

When Lambert was about to be inducted into the Hall of Fame, he was asked what in the world he was doing in Worthington, Pa., wherever that was. "I've been changing lots of diapers. Keeping busy and playing golf," he said. "It's really something, I'll tell you. It's great."

He was also planting crops, building swing sets and working on a part-time basis, patrolling the woods nearby as a deputy wildlife conservation officer for the Pennsylvania Game Commission. "I'm really dangerous now," he said. "They've given me a badge and a gun."

He kept bugging Jack Ham to come up to visit him, but without success, according to a mutual friend of ours. Finally, Lambert sent Ham a card with an invitation, only it was signed by his daughter, Lauren. "Won't you come up and see my daddy and us?" she wrote, perhaps with some prompting from you know who.

Lambert comes to the big city only on occasion, and only for something he really enjoys. A few weeks later, he was back making an appearance at the Sport, Travel & Outdoor Show at the Expo Mart in Monroeville. Lambert also appeared in TV commercials to promote the event. He was dressed for duck-hunting.

Every so often I hear of a Lambert sighting. Someone will see him signing autographs at a sporting goods store in a Pittsburgh area shopping mall, or something like that. His movements are traced with the same zeal as those of his former coach, Chuck Noll, the California condor and the northern spotted owl of the Pacific Northwest.

Otherwise it's Worthington, 40 miles northeast of Pittsburgh, a sportsmen's paradise Lambert began developing during his latter days with the Steelers. There's a lot of Garbo in Lambert, too, and, like the old-time Swedish cinema star, he wants to be left alone. Or so he insists anyhow.

"I don't enjoy crowds or being the center of attention," Lambert told me in an interview back in 1981. "I'm simply not as outgoing as Lynn Swann and some other people on the team."

On another occasion, Lambert allowed, "My idea of a good time is to have some friends over, put on a fire, cook some food and suck some beers."

Or, some more lines from Lambert: "Life's too short to be taken too seriously. Sure, I jag guys and kid around, but the people who know me know where I'm coming from, and those who take me seriously are crazy."

There are photos from the past all over the place in the Steelers' office complex at Three Rivers Stadium. During a mid-March visit in 1992, I was asked by Bob McCartney, who has been with the Steelers for nearly 20 years and is the club's video and film director, to identify some of the older photographs where the jersey numbers were not visible. I recognized the likes of Lynn Chandnois, Pat Brady and "Bullet" Bill Dudley, alongside Jock Sutherland, Jack Butler and Dick Hoak.

There is a larger photo of Dudley on another wall in the complex, just to the left as you enter the front doors. It's the Steelers' Wall of Fame. Large portraits of all their Hall of Famers are displayed there. Across the way, are team photos of the four Super Bowl winners, along with game action photos by Mike Fabus from the previous season.

The Steelers' Wall of Fame includes the team's founder, Art Rooney, a former co-owner, Bert Bell, and Johnny "Blood" McNally, Dudley, Walt Kiesling, Bobby Layne, Ernie Stautner, Joe Greene, John Henry Johnson, Jack Ham, Mel Blount, Terry Bradshaw, Franco Harris and, at the end of the line, Lambert.

Just a few feet from the color photo of Lambert, looking for someone to tackle in his No. 58 jersey, were some of his old friends, some of the people who know him best, laughing and having a good time in the middle of a snowy afternoon. Connie Rose, the receptionist for 14 years, was behind her desk. Ralph Berlin, a team trainer going on 25 years, was sitting on the desk, and Tony Parisi, the team's equipment manager for 28 years, was standing by Berlin's side.

These are some of the people Lambert liked best in the Steelers' organization. "He liked the backend guys," Parisi said. "That's because we looked after him pretty good."

Parisi was speaking about the Steelers' support team, people who looked after things in the clubhouse and on the field, like the late Jack Hart, the team's long-time field manager and one of Lambert's best friends; Berlin and his training staff, Rodgers Freyvogel, who succeeded Hart and helps Parisi in the clubhouse, and the team doctors who put Jack back together again after injuries. Lambert thanked them all publicly at his induction ceremonies at Canton. He was always more comfortable with the so-called little guys in the organization.

I took a walk with Parisi down the black-and-gold striped hallway leading to the Steelers' clubhouse, and asked him some more questions

159

about Lambert. He, too, had been happy to see Jack at the Steelers' smoker for the alumni to meet the new coach.

When Parisi speaks about players from the past, he nods instinctively toward the dressing stalls where they once put on the black and gold uniform. He can still envision them in their stalls, just like thoroughbred horses at one of Art Rooney's stables.

"Jack calls every few weeks to see how I'm doing," said Parisi. "He'll ask me 'How's the family?' just like Art Rooney always did. He'll call a few days in advance to tell me when he's going to stop in. Jack Ham's like that, too; so is Lynn Swann. They never come over here that they don't stop in the backroom to say hello.

"Jack was funny about some things; I don't know if he was superstitious or not. But he wouldn't go out on the field for a game if I didn't adjust his pads and his helmet. He'd have me strap up his shoulder pads, and adjust them. He'd have me tighten the screws on his helmet, and make sure it was just so.

"I'd put him on. I'd be turning the screwdriver, and I'd say, 'Let me make it for hitting today.' And he'd smile. He'd give me one of his three smiles a year."

Parisi smiled at his own little joke.

"Another time, we'd be scrimmaging, and I'd see him sitting on the sideline, and he'd have a silly smile on his face. He'd give me that smirk. And he'd say, 'Boy, I really got dinged in there. The birds are chirpin'. They're really chirpin'.'

"He never said much in the locker room. When he came in here, he was ready to go. He dressed up for practice the same way he'd dress up for a game. He'd tape himself up the same way. He loved the game.

"He was never into too much horseplay here. He was serious about his football. I'd get him going. I'd eat some raw garlic, and go over to Jack and say something to him, and purposely breathe hard in his face. He'd holler out, 'Gawd, you stink! What the hell did you flush down that face of yours? Did you eat kitty litter for breakfast?' He was funny, too."

Parisi had played professional hockey for 16 years, and I first met him back in the early 60s when he was working with the Pittsburgh Hornets of the American Hockey League. He was a spare goalie and equipment manager. I mentioned to Parisi that Lambert liked to play hockey when he was a kid back in Mantua, Ohio, and that he wished he could have been a professional hockey player, too.

"He would have been something," Parisi said. "He'd have been a competitor. He'd have been an intensive guy on that ice. He'd have been a sight, I'm sure."

Parisi also remembers the day Lambert suffered what turned out to be a career-ending injury. Lambert suffered a badly dislocated left big toe on the second play of the first game of the 1984 season against the Kansas City Chiefs at Three Rivers Stadium.

"He came to the sidelines in great pain," recalled Parisi. "He pulled off the shoe and the socks, and it was bad looking." Parisi pulled back the thumb on his left hand to show the absurd angle at which Lambert's

Bill Amatucci

Mike Fabus

Lambert chats with Coach Bill Cowher.

Pittsburgh Steelers

Young Pro Bowlers Lambert and Noll.

George Gojkovich

Bill Amatucci

toe was sticking. "He tried to shove it back in place on his own. He was never the same after that.

"He says his knee and his toe still hurt him from time to time. Otherwise, he looks good."

Lambert was limited to eight regular season games in 1984 after suffering the "turf toe" injury. It never got better during the off-season, so he retired in July of 1985 at the age of 33 after 11 seasons with the Steelers.

During his prime, Lambert was the premier middle linebacker in the National Football League, a dominant figure in the famed Steel Curtain defense. He was known for his fire-breathing, piston-pumping, hard-nosed playing style.

Bud Carson, the team's defensive coordinator in Lambert's early days with the team, once said, "There never was a player who played with as much intensity as Jack Lambert."

"For some guys, sometimes it's tough for them to get up to play," said Joe Greene. "But Jack Lambert loved to play."

Team president Dan Rooney said, "Jack Lambert demanded total effort from everybody in the organization. He would tell everyone from me on down to the ballboy when he thought something was wrong. He took us to greatness. He was the symbol of our success in the 1970's."

Lambert was an all-pro choice seven times in a nine-year span between 1975 and 1983. He played in nine straight Pro Bowls, more than any other player of his era. He was named the Defensive Player of the Year both in 1976 and 1979.

Jack Ham, who played left linebacker next to Lambert for almost a decade, said, "Of all the middle linebackers — Ray Nitschke, Willie Lanier, Dick Butkus — what set Jack apart was his ability to defend against the pass."

Andy Russell, another linebacking teammate early in Lambert's tour with the Steelers, said, "Lambert was equally good against the run as those other great linebackers, but he was dramatically better than any of them against the pass. He called the defensive signals. He set the tone. He was intelligent, all business, a terrific leader."

Many remember his toothless snarl, the way he barked defensive signals, urged his teammates to higher levels, pumped his arms and legs before each play until the moment he could unload on an opposing ballcarrier or quarterback. He came to represent the Steelers, particularly to their blue-collar, shot-and-a-beer fans because of his aggressiveness and work ethic. More than anything, they loved his intensity. He was a badass among badasses.

Super Bowl X and a match-up against the Dallas Cowboys comes to mind. The Cowboys were leading, 10-7, in the third quarter when Steelers' placekicker Roy Gerela missed a short field goal. Cliff Harris, the Cowboys' safety, ran up and — in a patronizing gesture — patted Gerela on the helmet. Instantly, Lambert seized Harris and flipped him to the ground.

"It wasn't something I thought about — jumping on him — it was a split-second thing," said Lambert, "but I couldn't permit anyone to intimidate our team."

Lambert didn't arrive with a brash attitude, however. He knew his place, and showed proper respect to the veterans in the clubhouse. "When I went into the locker room at Three Rivers Stadium for the first time," he recalled, "I didn't say anything to anyone. I was awed. I always wanted to play pro football and here I was with all these guys I'd always looked up to."

The Steelers won an unprecedented four Super Bowls in Lambert's first six seasons. He played a major role in every championship season. His fourth quarter interception thwarted any hopes the Los Angeles Rams had in Super Bowl XIV.

Lambert had admirers throughout the league.

"The guy I admire the most on the Steelers is Lambert," said Don Shula, the coach of the Miami Dolphins, and a favorite of Lambert, when I interviewed him at an NFL owners' meeting in 1981. "He enables them to do so many things defensively.

"In one game against the Steelers last season, our quarterback, Dave Woodley, was scrambling and he thought his man was open, and he threw it down the middle. But Lambert stopped and dove back and stretched out horizontally and snared the ball with both hands fully extended.

"Woodley came over to me on the sideline and said, 'Coach, I wish we had some receivers like that.' He's just so mobile, and lets them play a different style of defense."

Another opposing coach who was a big fan of Lambert was Sam Rutigliano of the Cleveland Browns, who coached him in the Pro Bowl. "To me," said Rutigliano, "Jack Lambert *is* the Pittsburgh Steelers."

Lambert was involved in a lot of "celebrity roasts" for various fundraising affairs during his tenure with the Steelers. He was fair game himself, and he was pretty good at sticking the needle in others.

At one such affair in 1980, for the benefit of Big Brothers and Sisters of Greater Pittsburgh, held at the Hilton, Ray Mansfield roasted Lambert in this manner:

"When you first meet Jack Lambert, you can't stand him. But he grows on you, and after you know him for awhile, you hate his guts.

"I taught Jack a lot . . . how to tie his shoes, how to brush his fangs."

Rocky Bleier offered, "Jack likes to hit hard. He likes to inflict a lot of pain. And that's just when he's out on a date."

Said Joe Greene: "He didn't have to psych himself up. He didn't like you if you had a different color jersey on. Heck, he didn't like half the guys with the same jersey on."

Lambert would blast them all in return, and then go home, wishing he had never gone to the banquet in the first place.

In July of 1989, Lambert was among the featured speakers at a so-called "Farewell to Arms" roast to raise money for the Western Pennsylvania Spina Bifida Society and the Steve Courson Medical Trust Fund at the Sheraton at Station Square. The dais lineup included former Steelers L.C. Greenwood, Lynn Swann, Ray Mansfield and Mike Webster, Bob Golic of the Los Angeles Raiders, comic Jim Meston and sportscaster Myron Cope. I served as master of ceremonies. It is one of my fond memories of the real Jack Lambert.

Despite his protests not to make public appearances, Lambert has long been one of the best Steelers standing before a mike. He always comes prepared, usually brings appropriate props or costumes, and tailor-makes his talks for the occasion. He can be very serious — like when he's talking to young people about drugs — or very funny. He is never dull.

He may have been the best speaker when he was inducted into the Pro Football Hall of Fame in Canton, Ohio, not far from his boyhood home of Mantua, in the summer of 1990. He could have run for President that day, and, at times, he sounded like he was doing just that.

One night at the Pittsburgh Athletic Association, at a roast of Rocky Bleier, he was sensational telling the "true story" of Rocky's wartime heroics.

At the "Farewell to Arms" event, which featured Courson and Webster, hence the reference to their arms or bared biceps, Lambert was a blast. I saved him for next to last among the speakers, to precede Cope. I figured they were my stars, and I thought they could play off one another, as they had appeared together in TV commercials for Budweiser and Kennywood Park, and had become sort of a Frick 'n Frack team.

Lambert slipped a red T-shirt on over his dress shirt and tie that night. They were selling such T-shirts to raise money for Courson, who needed a heart transplant. When he was at the mike, Lambert scolded Courson, "You know we didn't always agree on everything," he said to Courson and the audience. "But you were my teammate. And I care about you. I love you." Lambert wouldn't let Courson off the hook about what he had done, but his heart went out for Courson just the same. He strongly urged everybody that they better go out and buy the T-shirts. Or else.

Cope decided to do something different on this particular evening. It was a bad decision. The event had been loosely-organized and the evening had already run too long when Cope came to the mike.

He started reading an excerpt from Ernest Hemingway's celebrated novel, *Farewell to Arms,* and it was going nowhere. He called Webster to his side and instructed him to read part of the dialogue. Many in the audience were beginning to nod off.

I wasn't sure what to do. I had known Cope since I was 14, and had always had a great deal of respect for him. But he was dying. And he was taking the program down with him. I also knew not to upset him. I didn't want Cope chewing me out in public, but I had to give him the hook. I also didn't want to risk his wrath in the aftermath of the event.

While Cope was going on and on, I left my seat and went down to the end of the dais to seek Lambert's help. "What the hell's wrong with Cope?" asked Lambert. "Has he gone crazy?"

"Look, Jack, you have to do me a favor," I said. "I want you to go get Myron and just flip him over your back and take him out of the hall."

I returned to my seat. Soon after, Lambert left his seat. He caught Cope by surprise. "What's up, Jack?" asked Cope as Lambert approached him. Lambert grabbed Cope, heaved him over his shoulder, and walked across the raised platform, with Cope's head dangling by Lambert's backside. The audience was howling. Most people thought this was all in the act.

I closed the program, and joined my wife in front of the dais. I was still nervous, worrying about Cope's reaction. Just then, Cope came back from the next room where he had been deposited by Lambert. He was smiling and in great spirits. "That was great!" cried Cope. To my wife, Kathie, he said, "Your husband done good! I decided I was going to try something different tonight, and I figured if it bombed that someone would save me!"

Getting Lambert to do my dirty work showed how far we had come from our first meeting at St. Vincent College ten years earlier, in the summer of '79. Lambert snubbed me several times at my first Steelers' camp. He refused to stop and talk with me. He wanted nothing to do with me.

He had come to camp infuriated with me because of a story I had written about him a few months earlier. Jack and I did not get off with each other on the right foot.

I had returned to Pittsburgh in late April of 1979 after working nine years in New York, and one year before that in Miami. When I came home, returning to *The Pittsburgh Press* where I had worked on weekends while in high school, and in the summer of my sophomore year at the University of Pittsburgh, I was given the Steelers' beat.

I wanted to be positive and upbeat in my coverage, having just left *The New York Post* because new ownership wanted us to dig up dirt every day about the teams we were covering.

I was back in Pittsburgh about two weeks when I learned that Lambert had been attacked in a downtown disco called The Happy Landing, located about two blocks from *The Press* in the Gateway Center. A notorious bad actor had taken offense at Lambert's mere presence in the night spot, and had blindsided Lambert as he left the bathroom. The man slammed a beer mug into the side of Lambert's head, splitting his ear. Lambert required four stitches to close the gash at Divine Providence Hospital.

The guy who did it has been in prison most of the decade since that incident for other activities. He was a known "hit man" for mobsters in Pittsburgh. He had threatened Lambert that he would cut his hamstrings so he could never play football again.

Our police reporter learned of Lambert's altercation. He saw it on the nightly police report for May 8, 1979. Our editor knew about it. The beat writer for the *Pittsburgh Post-Gazette* knew about it. Everybody chose to ignore the story. They sat on it.

I wasn't sure what to do. I tried to contact Lambert by phone at least three times, but he would not return my calls. I wanted his side of the story. I talked to Chuck Noll about it. He was unhappy about my interest. I sought his assistance and advice on the matter. "It's your decision," he said. Dan Rooney didn't want to discuss it, either, though he was aware of the incident.

I wrote the story, and soon wished I hadn't. It wasn't worth it. It didn't earn me any points with my superiors at *The Press*. Or with the readers. Lambert was such a big favorite with the fans that they didn't want to see his name smeared, either. Lambert had been in more than his share of bar scuffles before this. It got me off to a bad start with the Steelers in general, and Noll and Lambert in particular.

Rooney thought Lambert was a victim of his own reputation. "It's like watching the cowboy movies on TV, where it was important to determine who was the fastest gun in the west," remarked Rooney.

"Jack's been told to be more discriminating," Noll said after my original story appeared.

Joe Gordon, then the team's publicist, came to Lambert's rescue. "He's a target for guys looking to make a name for themselves in a hurry. Guys challenge him even when they have no chance, just to say they had the courage to take him on."

Lambert said, "Trouble has a way of finding me. Call me Darth Vader. No one will believe anything else." He didn't say it to me, but to a rival reporter.

When the veterans reported to the Steelers' training camp, a week later than the rookies and free agents, I approached Lambert to talk to him one day. "Don't you get near me!" he scowled, putting me down in front of fellow reporters.

This went on for a few days. Lambert blew a dragon's breath at me every time I drew near him. Finally, I said, "I have to talk to you."

He replied smartly, "We have nothing to talk about."

"We have to talk," I said.

I suggested we talk somewhere that was more private than the sidewalk outside Bonaventure Hall, where the Steelers are housed during training camp. Lambert agreed to meet me in his room. He was miffed, and there was no doubt about that.

I followed Lambert into his room. He had a room to himself, at the end of the hallway, close to the door in case he wanted to sneak out after curfew. The room seemed very small as we sat in chairs opposite one another. Lambert was staring a hole in my forehead, or so it seemed, anyhow. I was nervous, to say the least, but did my best to look him right in the eye.

We had a heated exchange and we came to an agreement. Lambert set the terms. "The next time you write something that upsets me," he snapped, "I'm going to kick your ass."

"Fair enough," I said. "As long as you don't stop speaking to me."

Lambert and I got along fine after that. Oh, he'd bitch about this

George Gojkovich

line or that line, or this quote or that quote, along the way. He still does. He was an avid reader of the sports page, and a strong critic of his critics. Lambert should have been a sportswriter; he had a calling. But he'd sooner sell his soul to the devil. Lambert, at best, suffered sportswriters.

He did his best to scare all of us.

Our relationship improved considerably after that. I tried to get him to be a guest speaker at the Curbstone Coaches monthly meetings at the Allegheny Club. These were football forums for the fans in which local pro, college and high school coaches, players and administrators spoke about what was going on in their little worlds. Bob Prince and I were the original emcees.

The Pittsburgh Brewing Company paid the Steelers who spoke at this noontime luncheon the princely fee of $250 for five minutes of mostly inane remarks. Lambert would have none of it. "But," he told me, "I will come and speak to your class at Point Park."

At the time, I was teaching a course in sportswriting every Wednesday night at Point Park College in downtown Pittsburgh. And Lambert brought his fiance, Lisa, with him when he appeared before a dozen college students, and talked to them for over an hour. He did that for free. And with no fanfare.

So did Sam Davis, Mel Blount and Gordon. Noll hosted a class in his office one night at Three Rivers Stadium.

Lambert would call me each off-season, just before he would conduct his own summer sports camp for boys in Hiram, Ohio, to meet for an interview at Three Rivers Stadium. We met in a few bars for interviews. He had me out to his home in Fox Chapel. He greeted me at the garage door, holding a shot gun. He had been cleaning it. But he held it just to throw me off guard, or to make me nervous. Seeing Lambert waiting for you with a shotgun is unnerving even in the best of circumstances. He took me with him one night when he went to the Millvale Sportsmen's Club in Wexford to do some skeet-shooting. Teammates Mike Wagner and Moon Mullins were there that night. They were all pretty good at shooting clay pigeons out of the sky. I had the idea that they saw the clay pigeons as their favorite sportswriters to aid their marksmanship.

Lambert would let me get close, and then he'd put me in my place. He was close to both of his parents, I knew, even though they had divorced when he was two. I asked him once if their split-up had affected him. "I'm sure it has," he said, "but it's none of the business of the readers of the Sunday *Press*."

Jack Lambert has always been an interesting study on the Steelers. There is the man and there is the image. He wants people to look at Lambert the man — "I'm also a human being, but people don't want to believe that" — yet he has always played the role and enhanced his image. He still does.

Others contributed to his image as well. In the Steelers' highlight film for the 1978 season, for instance, he was shown up close, snarling and hissing, and hollering, and hitting with the impact of symphony cymbals crashing together, and he was referred to as "Count Dracula in cleats."

But he was once called to breakfast by his mom back in Mantua, Ohio, and I always thought there was a lot of little boy in him, struggling to get out of the hard shell in which he had encased himself. Lambert wants to be loved — we all do — but he makes it so difficult for some to do that, with the exception of his family and select friends.

There are at least two Jack Lamberts, but it takes time, and patience, to learn about the other Lambert, the one few are privileged to know.

Greg Hawthorne, the Steelers' No. 1 draft pick in 1979, remembered his first impressions of Lambert.

"He's loose; he likes to do the same things as a lot of people here," Hawthorne said at St. Vincent in August of 1979. "He's very quiet off the football field. When he gets in those pads, things change. It's his game and he plays it rough. Down there on the field, he might be a psycho or wild. He's like Clark Kent and Superman. He surprised me. I was watching him signing all those autographs for the kids every day after practice, and I couldn't picture him doing that. I thought he wouldn't say nothing to nobody.

"I thought he'd be mad all the time. But he's an all right guy. I thought he was a roughhouse dude when I first saw him. Then on the first workout with the veterans, in the 'Oklahoma Drill,' he got into a fistfight with Thom Dornbrook, and I thought he sure is a wild and crazy dude, just like I had imagined. After a week or so, I learned that he isn't like that.

"He has that bold walk, with his chest out and his stomach sucked in, like a king of the mountain. He's up on his toes all the time. But maybe that's just the way he walks."

To Lambert, his hard-earned image became something of an albatross around his thick neck, a scarlet letter on his puffed-out chest, a mark on his forehead. He became a target for every tough guy, and punk, who wanted to make a quick reputation for himself.

In that summer of '79, Lambert shuddered when I told him what had happened to a former teammate, Joe Gilliam, who got his head caved in by some hoods in Baltimore. Lambert was always critical of Gilliam for fooling around with drugs, but he felt for him when he heard he was hurt.

I often reminded Lambert of his Happy Landing incident, or his not-so-happy-landing incident. He hated for me to bring it up; he'll hate for me to bring it up here. Lambert insisted he wasn't looking for trouble.

"I'm an old-fashioned guy," he said. "I won't walk away when someone gives me or my girl friend a hard time. To me, that's part of being a man. Nobody is going to bad-mouth me.

"Those things happen from time to time. It creates problems, depending on what kind of mood I'm in. Yeah, I could probably be described as moody. A guy has his girlfriend there and wants to impress her. These things are going to happen when people have a few libations. Sometimes

I can walk away from this, sometimes I can't. The last time I didn't walk out, I got hit with a beer mug and ended up with four stitches."

He is, indeed, a law-and-order man — a throwback to another era. He'd have made a good sheriff in Dodge City. He always liked to wear a ballcap with the Pittsburgh Police Department insignia on the front of it.

Lambert liked living in Pittsburgh and playing for the Steelers.

"There are a lot of good people in this city," he told me once. "They're mostly good people, but there are always a few exceptions. There is always someone who wants to take a shot. It's difficult for me, at times, to walk down the streets of Pittsburgh. It's because of that image, not because I'm a famous linebacker.

"Jack Ham is a famous linebacker and he doesn't have to go through the things I do. Jack doesn't get in fights; he'd walk the other way. I'm not knocking him for that, but I can't. I told you, I'm an old-fashioned guy.

"You know, I have two choices. I can go out in public or I could stay home and live the life of a hermit. And I won't do that. Nobody can tell me how to live my life, or how to show discretion, or whatever."

When Lambert was about to be inducted into the Hall of Fame, he said, "I'm very proud of the fact that people did feel I gave a hundred percent. That had everything to do with my popularity here in the city. There are a lot of hard-working people in this town. They know who is out there working hard and I think they appreciated it."

There's a soft side to Lambert, one quickly learned at the Steelers summer training camps. He has always been great with kids and senior citizens. He prefers them to those in between. He appreciates the innocence of children and the wisdom of older people. With the kids, with whom he has always been most patient, he said, "I can look at them when they're asking for autographs and feel something special for them." He reprimands them sometimes, reminding them to say "please" and "thank you" and keeping their place in line.

During his stay with the Steelers, Lambert served as honorary chairman for the Children's Hospital Ronald McDonald House, and was active in other youth-related activities.

"After practice every day, or whenever I get a chance," he said, "I'll sign autographs. It's not the thing I look forward to after a hard practice when I'm hot and tired, but it's worth the extra half hour or whatever it takes.

"I remember when I was a kid, standing outside the stadium in Cleveland, waiting for the Browns. I remember when I was a kid and when I'd get shunned. I know how it feels."

But some of the Browns stopped and signed their name for young Jack Lambert, and he says he still has those autographs somewhere in his mom's home. He still treasures them. He'd like to think that the kids still feel the same way about having his name on a scrap of paper, or on the bill of a ballcap, or their T-shirt or game program.

But then there are times he prefers to get away from the crowd. That's when he likes to go hunting or fishing.

"He likes to get on those plaid shirts and jeans," said Steve Szemes, the president of the North Side Deposit Bank, whose headquarters are on Federal Street, just a few blocks from Three Rivers Stadium. "I have a friend who used to take Lambert trout fishing north of here every year. Jack eats that up, I'm told. He thinks he's a real mountain man."

Once at Latrobe, Lambert told a friend of mine, Norm Vargo, the sports editor of *The Daily News* in McKeesport, why he liked to slip away from St. Vincent and go fishing in a nearby lake.

Happiness for Lambert was sitting in the middle of a boat in the middle of a lake. "My Uncle Chuck always took me fishing when I was a young boy," allowed Lambert. "Nothing like it. Great way to relax . . . I never heard of anybody asking for an autograph in the middle of a lake.

"I like to wade those isolated streams. Nothing but you, the fish, and Mother Nature out there. I fished some streams where it seemed like I waded for miles, and didn't see a soul. Now, that's relaxing."

Author Jim O'Brien interviews Johnny Blood and Jack Lambert, both members of the Pro Football Hall of Fame at Steelers 50 Seasons Celebration.

L.C. Greenwood
A long way from Canton, Mississippi

*"My parents thought football was a game
and there were a lot more important things."*

I love to listen to L.C. Greenwood. He has the greatest voice of all the Steelers. It's a rich bass voice that warms the ear and the heart. He's so big and lean and has always looked more like a basketball player than a football player. He talks like and laughs at his own stories the way Wilt Chamberlain always did. And Wilt Chamberlain was my idol long before I ever heard of L.C. Greenwood. I always wish there were a hammock nearby, so I could lie in it and just listen to L.C. Greenwood go on about his stories, and just stare at the sky and the trees overhead.

Greenwood was working out of a different building than he was when I interviewed him for *Doing It Right*. He had shifted headquarters early in 1991 from Bridgeville to Carnegie, a community best known as the birthplace and hometown of Hall of Famer Honus Wagner of the Pittsburgh Pirates. It's an old railroad and mining town, similar to Bridgeville, located close to both I-79 and the Parkway West, and experiencing something of a business boom since plans were announced for the new airport just west of Carnegie.

"I've added some construction and electric work to my portfolio," said Greenwood, who still has partnerships in two companies, one called Greenwood Enterprises and the other Monaloh Basin Engineers. "We're into engineering, highway work, coal, natural gas, you name it. Whatever it takes, you know. That's why I'm into five or six businesses.

"The recession has been a difficult period for everybody in my businesses. I'm doing good because my doors are still open. We're not making a lot of profit right now — business is slow but steady — and I figure if we can keep the doors open we'll be fine when things turn around. I keep telling myself that things are going to turn around. Things should get better."

I told him that I saw him in a series of Miller Light commercials shortly after I had interviewed him in late 1990 at his Bridgeville offices. "We did about seven new commercials back then, but we haven't done anything lately," he said. "So it's been back to the old grind.

"The only time you see me on TV now is when I'm doing something for free, like at a fund-raiser for some charity, or something like that. But I'm glad I still get asked; I hope I can still do some good for those things."

He misses the fun and games, and being a professional football player. "Where you can still do the kid thing, and run and jump and play," he said, then laughed at his own lines. "When you get out in the real world, you face a whole different animal."

172

L.C. Greenwood

L.C. Greenwood chases after Roger Staubach of Dallas Cowboys.

173

He knows things are going relatively well for him. All he has to do to remind himself of how well he has it is to think about his friend and former teammate, Sam Davis. Davis was a patient at the time at The Rehabilitation Institute in Squirrel Hill, still recovering from serious head injuries.

"I went to see him a couple of times when he was out this way (in Oakdale), and it was tough going," allowed L.C. "Seeing him like that. Especially when I just saw him at a golf outing shortly before whatever happened to him. I was with him on a golf course just a few days before it all happened. When I saw him, it was pretty traumatic. The last time I had seen him we were just swapping b.s., and now I'm talking to him and he's hallucinating. That was tough for me.

"So, overall, I'm feeling pretty good. My health is good. I think I'm pretty blessed. I'm the same old person: pretty easy-going, and I feel pretty good. I can't complain."

I asked him if he had been back home in Canton, Mississippi lately. "I got together with my family at Thanksgiving down in Atlanta, at the home of one of my four sisters," he answered. "I enjoyed us congregating there. And I'm looking for some excuse to get down to Canton to see my folks pretty soon. I'd like that."

To Moses Greenwood, football was a bunch of foolish nonsense. He could not understand why his son, L. C., the oldest of his nine children, spent so much time playing games when he should have been working.

"I had to help out a bit," recalls L.C., "but my dad wasn't satisfied unless I was working all the time. That's what he did. You had to understand where my dad was coming from."

Moses Greenwood was in the construction business in Canton, about 25 miles northeast of Jackson. Canton is a town where the Rev. Martin Luther King marched during the civil rights protests of the '60s. L.C. was away at college when that was going on. So he missed it. But L.C. has clear-cut memories of Moses Greenwood.

"He left home at 6 in the morning and he didn't get back until 6 in the evening," said his son. "And then, after dinner, he'd leave the house and go work somewhere else from 8 to midnight. Plus, he kept a farm for us, and he was a lay preacher on weekends. He wanted me to work all the time, too.

"Football wasn't important. Keeping the family fed was."

Greenwood was greatly disappointed when he and John Banaszak were both put on waivers the same day at the Steelers' training camp on August 30, 1982. He was nearing his 36th birthday and was the oldest Steeler on the team, but he thought he had another good year in him.

He was in good shape business-wise because he had already started two of his own companies.

An easy-going, super-cool operator on a football field, and sometimes lethargic-looking at practice, Greenwood has always been a workaholic away from the stadium.

L. C. Greenwood

"I never had football in mind as a career," he said. "Playing football was always a way to get out of work."

In his final season, Greenwood was paid about $275,000 by the Steelers. A guy would have to feel some pain over losing a paycheck like that. "You always want to be able to put food on the table," said Greenwood philosophically.

He worked in the cotton fields on the outskirts of Canton at age 8 and opened a bank account when he was 12.

"By the time I got out of high school, I had enough money to pay for four years of college," he recalls.

He made $2.50 a day, $15 for a five-day week, chopping cotton in the summer. He said. "I could take a quarter and eat lunch and be satisfied."

L.C. built his first home at age 15.

"I had chores to do each morning before I went to school — before the sun came up — and chores to do when I came home," he recalled. "As far as my father was concerned, football practice interfered with work I could have been doing at home, or with him somewhere.

"Football always came up during the time when harvest was the priority. My parents thought football was a game and there were a lot more important things.

"I wasn't able to convince my parents of the benefits of football until I was in the 11th grade. I wanted to play basketball and football, but my dad said it had to be one or the other.

"He wanted me to work all the time. I never really had time to study; I had to get my studies done in school. He was very persistent.

"I ran to and from school. I was wet when I got to school, and wet when I got home, just from sweating. I didn't play football until my junior year in high school. Football was a way to get a break in the action, a way to get out from under my father."

Greenwood was good on the football field and in the classroom. He planned on attending Clark College in Atlanta. He thought he wanted to become a pharmacist and return to Canton and open a drug store. Then some college football coaches came calling on him at his home in Canton.

"I never knew anyone who went away to college; I was dumb to anything like that," said Greenwood. "The coach would say, 'L.C., let's go down and have a steak and a beer.' But I didn't drink and neither did I eat out. I never talked to any of the coaches who wanted to take me away."

He had academic scholarship offers, but he accepted an athletic scholarship to Arkansas AM&N because it was the most attractive offer.

He kept up his studies at school, but switched his interests. He became a vocational education major and figured he would get into the construction business when he graduated. He knew he could build houses.

As a senior at Arkansas AM&N, Greenwood gained some national attention. He was named to an All-American team selected by *Ebony* magazine. He was the Steelers' 10th round draft pick in 1969 —

Chuck Noll's first season — the year that Joe Greene of North Texas State was the Steelers' No. 1 selection.

He and Greene were the pillars upon which the Steel Curtain defense was built. Greene was both a friend and an admirer of Greenwood.

"One of the things I remember about L.C. on the field was when we were out in Oakland for the AFC championship, right before our first Super Bowl," recalled Greene. "L.C. was sitting in the hall watching TV and some of the guys we knew from the Raiders, like Gene Upshaw and Art Shell and others, walked by and said, 'Hey, what are you doing?'

"L.C. just smiled and said, 'Just watching who we're gonna play in the Super Bowl.' That typified our attitude that day for the game. It was kind of nice."

Greenwood and Greene were both named to the Steelers' All-Time team during the Steelers' 50 Seasons Celebration.

"I never thought about being remembered," said Greenwood. "After I'm done in the game, I've just got to do something else. I'm still playing football because it's part of me. I'm trying to find things to replace football.

"Maybe they don't want me to play, maybe they want to make room for some young guy. Who knows? L.C. might be here for five years."

Just before he was to report to camp in July of 1982, L.C. found it difficult to sleep. "I might not be included," he admitted he thought. He would wake up at 4 a.m. and go out and run, even in the rain.

Two days before his departure for camp, his last camp with the Steelers, he said, "I'm going up there to work.

"I just run, run, run and if you pass out, you pass out. That's what training camp is for. I've been around for quite awhile, but I don't look at myself as some sort of dinosaur."

Steel Curtain defense featured, from left, Dwight White (78), Joe Greene (75), Ernie Holmes (63), Jack Lambert (58) and L.C. Greenwood (68) against arch-rival Raiders. L.C., at 6-6, was the tallest of them all.

Rocky Bleier
"I did what I had to do."

*"He was the tough little guy
with the big heart."*
—Terry Bradshaw

Rocky Bleier has been to the Super Bowl several times since the Steelers last appeared in the National Football League's championship game.

He has been invited to the site to speak to corporate executives and administrators, sales personnel, any group that might benefit from Bleier's comeback story and motivational message.

People who love football love Rocky Bleier, and they still enjoy his company. He is especially in demand during the playoffs and Super Bowl. He adds to the Super Bowl scene. They know that Bleier has been there, in the battle, in the black and gold uniform of the Steelers, and that he and his team came out on top all four times.

Fran Tarkenton, John Elway and Jim Kelly can tell you that it's not easy to do that. "I don't know why Buffalo didn't give Washington a better game of it," Bleier said after Super Bowl XXVI. "They had two weeks to prepare. Is there that much difference between the two teams? Washington is a good team, but they're not that good. The Bills never adjusted, they never picked up the blitzes, they dropped balls. You don't get there that often."

Bleier has known the bottom and he worked hard to get to the top of his profession. He has known despair when doctors told him he would be lucky to walk again normally after he suffered shrapnel wounds in his legs and foot during the Vietnam War. But he wouldn't quit. Even before that, he was told he was too small and too slow. One of these days, he figures somebody will tell him he's too bald for something.

But he had something special, and teammate Terry Bradshaw puts it best when he refers to Bleier as "the tough little guy with the big heart."

Only in America could a guy grow up in rooms over his dad's saloon — just like Steelers founder Art Rooney — and become the captain of the football team at Notre Dame and one of the inspirational leaders of the Super Bowl champion Steelers. Bleier has come a long way from his humble origins in Appleton, Wisconsin.

It's no wonder he has the best of all smiles, a Cheshire cat smile, a toothy smile, and that his dark eyes shine through eyeglasses, or sometimes over them, when he considers his career and his friends and his good fortune.

To see Bleier and his wife, Aleta, and their teenage children, Samantha and Adri James, at their spacious French Tudor home in suburban Fox Chapel, just north of downtown Pittsburgh, you would have to say he has it made. But he made it himself, by refusing to quit

George Gojkovich

when others told him that be the wise thing to do. Bleier actually blushes when you remind him of his success.

While he was in Minneapolis on personal business, Bleier did not stick around for the Super Bowl. He watched the first part of the game at the airport in Minneapolis-St. Paul, part of the third quarter on the drive home from the airport in Pittsburgh, and the fourth quarter on television at his home. Talk about running to daylight.

Bleier had been to Minneapolis where he "did a luncheon" for Duracell. Two days earlier, he spoke at a dinner in Dallas. He spoke to Duracell's senior staff and some of its best retail customers at a luncheon at the Windows Over Minneapolis restaurant at the top of the IDS Building. He greeted their guests, mingled with everyone, and previewed the Super Bowl for them, mixing in some anecdotes from his storehouse of Steeler stories. The Duracell group had just returned from viewing the Ice Palace in St. Paul, which was shown on TV many times during the week that preceded the showdown between the Buffalo Bills and the Washington Redskins. It was bitter cold in the Twin Cities in late January, but Bleier warmed everybody up in a hurry with his beaming familiar face, his theatric presence and his so-smooth program. This was not his usual motivational talk. Duracell didn't need anybody to charge its batteries, that's for sure. "Everybody has an opinion about this game," Bleier told them, "so I'll give you mine."

He told some behind-the-scenes and strictly-in-the-huddle stories about his days with Terry Bradshaw and Franco Harris and Joe Greene, and other related tales "hopefully with some humor," as he put it. He said there are about 130 plays in the average NFL contest, and that the outcome is usually determined by what happens on four or five of them. "It's always the unexpected, the things you can't count on," observed Bleier, "like interceptions and fumbles and big mistakes that weren't drawn up on any chalkboard, or talked about in any strategy sessions or scouting reports, that affect the final score and determine who wins and who loses."

He told the Duracell folks how the Steelers put in a play especially for their first Super Bowl meeting with the Minnesota Vikings, back in Super Bowl IX in January of 1975. "It was called a 'dive 34 sucker' and it was a counter play with me carrying the ball," said Bleier. "It was designed to take advantage of Doug Sutherland's quickness in coming across the line. Our linemen were to let their guys get through with brush blocks, and we faked it to Franco going one way, and I was coming the other way. I was to run against the grain in the gaps they left. We had never run a counter all season, and we did it on the first play of the game. I ran for 18 yards. Later, we ran the same counter play — dive 34 sucker — and I went for nine yards. We ran it two more times for solid gains. Later on, it's third down and six to go and Bradshaw asked the offensive linemen what they wanted to run. All of them called out 'dive 34 sucker' — see, they don't have to block. I protested. I told Terry that we couldn't run the play five times and expect Doug Sutherland to fall for it five times. But he did."

Rocky Bleier scores TD against Chiefs in 1980 Three Rivers finale.

Bleier went back to the next year's Super Bowl game, Super Bowl X in Miami against the Dallas Cowboys, for his next story. "There was about two minutes to go in the game, and we're ahead 21-17. It's fourth and eight on our 40 yard line. Chuck calls time out. Bradshaw goes out — he was hurt — and Hanratty comes in. We can't figure out why he's sending Hanratty in; we figure we better punt it.

"But Chuck was fearful that they might block a punt. They'd been getting to our punter pretty good that day. Hanratty calls a four right split-84 trap. That's me carrying the ball off right tackle. The thought of me doing that and gaining eight yards was beyond my wildest comprehension. As we broke the huddle, Hanratty says, 'Eat up time.' If anybody knew my style, they wouldn't think of me eating up time. I took handoffs and went right into the hole; I knew the shortest distance, in my case anyhow, was a straight line. If he wanted somebody to dance and take up some time, he should've given the ball to Franco. With me, five seconds elapsed, I gained a few yards, and we turned over the ball to Dallas. If we had lost that day, Chuck Noll and the Steelers might have come in for some second-guessing on that decision. But our defense held and we won the game."

Terry Bradshaw hates stories in which he comes off as a dumb quarterback, but Bleier has one of those, too. You have to pay close attention to appreciate this one. "In Super Bowl XIV," began Bleier, "we put in a special complementary pair of plays to take advantage of something the Rams did.

"One of their defensive ends, Fred Dwyer, was a slasher. He rushed the quarterback by slanting inside. Jack Youngblood, on the other end, would hook out and hold his ground on the outside, waiting for someone to come his way.

"So we had some trap plays, with pulling guards. On the one play, the guard pulls and blocks Youngblood from the blind side. On the other, the guard pulls the same way, but the ball goes the other way, and it's the job of the blocking back — me — to catch Dwyer on the side.

"Bradshaw never got it right in the first half, and we ran those plays about four times. He ran the wrong play to the wrong side every time. So now you have a pulling guard who can't get at a slashing defensive end, and you have a back trying to block Youngblood head on. Chuck was burning, and he took Terry to the chalkboard at halftime and went over the sequence again. On the second play of the second half, Terry ran the play, and he ran it the wrong way again. On the second play! I thought we were in trouble from thereon in. But Terry threw two big touchdown passes in that game, to Swann and Stallworth, and he was at his best, as always, in the big game, and we won. Terry was named the most valuable player of the game."

Rocky and Aleta had just returned from a visit to St. Francis Hospital on the Lawrenceville-Bloomfield border before our interview took place. Aleta is on the board at St. Francis. Her father, Dr. James Giacobine, was a pioneer open heart surgeon at St. Francis. Rocky was serving as the honorary chairman for the hospital's "Courage To Come Back" fundraising campaign.

Rocky introduced me to Aleta and the children before we retreated to the game room for our interview. Rocky Bleier's game room attests to the recognition he received for a special kind of contribution to the Steelers and pro football at large. There are trophies and plaques and citations everywhere.

In 1974, Bleier won the George Halas Award as the NFL's Most Courageous Player. In 1975, he won the Whizzer White Humanitarian Award — named after the former Steelers running back (1938) who is a Supreme Court Justice — and the Vince Lombardi Award from the Wisconsin Pro Football Writers. In 1979, he was selected as one of the 10 Outstanding Young Men in America by the U.S. Jaycees.

But don't overlook Bleier's on-the-field achievements. In his 12 seasons with the Steelers, the 5-11, 210 pound running back gained 3,865 yards. When we talked, he ranked fifth in rushing on the Steelers' all-time list, behind Franco Harris, John Henry Johnson, Frank Pollard and Dick Hoak. Near the end, he passed the likes of Frenchy Fuqua, Tom Tracy and Fran Rogel to rate that high. That's not bad for someone who was best known for his blocking ability and courage under fire.

The highlight of his NFL years was in 1976 when Bleier rushed for 1,036 yards — he was only the third Steeler to eclipse a thousand yards in a season. That year, he teamed with Harris to become only the second backfield in NFL history to have two runners exceed the 1,000-yard mark.

Also, Bleier and Harris teamed in 1976 to tie another NFL mark when the two rushed to 100-yard outings together on back-to-back weeks — only the fourth time any NFL backfield accomplished that feat. Bleier's first 100-yard game was in 1975, a 163-yard effort against the Green Bay Packers, his boyhood heroes.

In 1978, Bleier enjoyed another solid season with the Steelers. He rushed for 683 yards and scored six touchdowns — five rushing and one on a pass reception.

People remember that Steelers team well, and they want Rocky Bleier to know they saw him in action. They say things to him like "What great teams they were!" Or, "You were always one of my favorites!" It makes him feel good; it makes them feel good. He gets paid well to tell his own story, and that is essentially what he has been doing for a living ever since he retired from the Steelers.

"I am a better ballplayer today than I ever was when I played for the Steelers," he says with a smile. "The tales and the legends continue to grow."

Bleier was Audie Murphy in a Steelers' uniform, a war hero in the eyes of many. Bleier is understandably a little uncomfortable in that role. Hey, he went to Vietnam and he's proud of that, but he didn't do anything heroic there. He got shot and wounded in a rice paddy. It was what he did when he came home — his personal rehabilitation — that is his story of courage. He plays that down as well. "I did what I had to do," he says. "To me, there weren't many alternatives. I wanted to play pro ball, and I didn't have much else to fall back on at the time."

While in Minnesota for the Super Bowl in January of 1992, Bleier stayed at the Sheraton Park Palace in St. Paul. He was driven around town in a limousine and received first-class treatment. It was snowing, and Bleier said when he looked out the window of his hotel room at the scene on the streets below he thought about his hometown of Appleton, Wisconsin.

"From my window, I could see a man shoveling snow on the sidewalk in front of a little grocery store," said Bleier. "When my dad had his saloon somebody had to shovel the snow in front of it. Usually, it was iced over, and we had to scrape the sidewalk, and break up the ice. That's one of the things my kids will never know. They've never had to shovel snow off sidewalks."

There's lot of grass, but no sidewalks near the homes in Fox Chapel. It's an affluent community, one of Pittsburgh's most posh addresses, and both of the Bleier children have gone to private schools.

That brought something else to Bleier's mind. About a year earlier, soon after I had completed writing *Doing It Right,* the first installment on the saga of the Steelers in their glory years, Bleier and I were both chatting with Chuck Noll at the Steelers' offices one day. Noll asked me how my book was coming along, and I told him it would be coming out soon. "Now you have to do a sequel," said Noll, "and see how the second generation makes out. Most of our guys came up the hard way. And people who come up the hard way and become successful have a habit of giving their kids everything they want. I'll be curious to see how their kids make out, and how successful they become."

Rocky remembered that. "Noll's statement still haunts me," he said. "Let's see how the kids turn out . . . That's what's scary about Noll. I never would have thought out that comment.

"That's like a story he once told us about ballplayers who just followed the leader during a players' strike. He talked about players going like lemmings to the sea and to their death. Ninety-five percent of the guys on the team had to look up 'lemmings' in the dictionary.

"The only time I got in trouble — me and my big mouth — was when Chuck had called us something in a meeting. I can't remember what he called us now. Vito Stellino of the *Post-Gazette* was waiting for us afterward. He had a story in mind, and he was trying to substantiate it. He was probing; he was going down the wrong way. He got me mad. And I called out to Webster, 'Hey, Mike, what did Chuck call us today?' It was one of those things that didn't need to get out. It was in the paper the next morning. The headline said 'Bleier Said. . .' You always hate those headlines anyhow. I can't remember what it was that I said. But it was controversial. I was taping my wrists in the locker room, and Chuck came by. He looked at me and said, 'What is said in the family stays in the family.' And he walked on by."

I asked Bleier about the time he knocked Noll at a luncheon and it got on the wire services. "Oh, yes," he said. "You mean 'the

George Gojkovich

thousand-yard runners together.

Bleier always at his best against Browns.

Bill Amatucci

George Gojkovich

Sam Davis, Jon Kolb and Randy Grossman give Rocky room to run.

Monongahela fiasco,' as I call it. It was at a Rotary Club luncheon for about 30 people that a friend of mine asked me to do in Monongahela. I thought it was just an intimate affair, and I posed this question: 'Did we win four Super Bowls because of Chuck Noll or in spite of Chuck Noll?'

"There was a reporter in the audience, unknown to me, and he wrote about what I said. Looking back, I shouldn't have said it. I don't think we could have won those Super Bowls without Chuck. We might have won Super Bowls without Chuck, but we wouldn't have gotten to the Super Bowls without Chuck. And in the Super Bowls we wouldn't have won all four of them without Chuck.

"He stressed fundamentals. He told us it was not a complicated game. He was able to pull the guys together. That was a combination of Chuck and the assistant coaches. There was a synergism between the assistant coaches and Chuck and the players. We had overachievers, guys who needed pats on the back, and the assistant coaches were providing that. In those days, our No. 1 and No. 2 draft choices were becoming All-Pros. You can call it good fortune, you can call it lucky. Any draft pick is an educated guess. You hope they have the drive to win. He had those people.

"He had the assistant coaches. Chuck could be aloof. But his assistants were just like the guys, and they got along great. There were a lot of guys who had antagonisms toward Chuck. I always thought he hated me. He probably didn't even think about me. We, as a team, were driven to the assistant coaches. We had great assistant coaches. Not only as teachers, but as personalities. They weren't assholes or shits; they weren't going to take roomcheck and then run and tell Chuck you weren't in your room. There was a great bond between the assistants and the players. You played for those guys. Guys like George Perles and Woody (Widenhofer) were cheering you on and you weren't even one of their players. They were responsible for the defensive unit, and they liked to see us do well. Rollie Dotsch and Dick Hoak were our biggest boosters. They fooled around together. As much as you'd like some acknowledgment from the head coach, the assistants filled that void. Then that made it special when you got it from Chuck, too. It was important.

"I really liked Hoak, and so did Franco. Dick was a teammate of mine when I was there the first time — before I went into the Army. Dick was always quiet. But Dick knew the game and he respects guys who know the game.

"It was easy to talk to Dick. It wasn't easy for me to talk to Chuck. He frustrated me. Thinking about my relationship and my experiences with Chuck, I'd have to say they were not any better than anybody else's. Some of the things he said were interesting. I find myself quoting Chuck and his philosophies. They come back to you, they help you in other tasks besides football. My dad had a couple that come back to mind every now and then."

186

"It's amazing the impact your coaches and your teachers have on you throughout your life," Bleier said. "I was fortunate. I had important people in my life who made a difference.

"There was a man named Dutch Schultz who was my band instructor in junior and senior high school. This was a Christian Brothers school and the teachers were strict and demanding. My high school coach was a guy named Gene 'Torchy' Clark. He was one of those high school coaches who touched a lot of people's lives. He coaches basketball and football. In fact, he started the football program at Florida Tech, which is now Florida Central. He was a teacher. I had made all-state my junior year and as I entered my senior year I was the only all-stater coming back. I was the leading rusher in the school history. We're scrimmaging one day before the season, and I missed the count. I was late on a lateral. I was going half-ass and I didn't grab it. I fumbled the ball. He grabbed me in front of everybody and did this parody on me, like 'I'm an all-stater, look at me.' He made me look like a fool. I took it to heart. I told myself, 'He'll never do that again. I won't give him an opening.'

"I played trumpet in high school band. I had band practice first, then basketball practice. I would make it to the last half of basketball practice as a freshman. Remember, 'Torchy' was also the basketball coach. He said, 'You're going to have to make a decision. You'll have to decide what you're going to do, and whether you want to be on this basketball team.' He had a big impact on me.

"Tom Pagna at Notre Dame had a big influence on me. He told me, 'Everyone can run with the ball, but to be a complete back, you have to know how to catch a ball and how to block.'

"I remember we were playing Purdue one day when Leroy Keyes was a sophomore star. I coughed up a ball at their two yard line and Keyes ran 98 yards for a touchdown. It was on national TV. On the ensuing kickoff, Nick Eddy ran the ball back for a touchdown. He got me off the hook. I was standing on the sideline and I was watching Tom Pagna. He had tears rolling down his cheeks by the time Eddy was in the endzone. It showed me his passion for the game, and how much he cared about our running backs.

"And, of course, Chuck Noll gave me an opportunity to prove I could play pro football. My biggest regret is never sitting down and talking to him. I have mixed feelings about that. I'm sure there are a lot of guys who would like to do that. I saw Lynn Swann at Noll's retirement announcement. He told me he would like to get a bottle of champagne and go ring Noll's doorbell some day and say, 'Let's open this up and chat.' I think a lot of guys would like to be there with Lynn to share that moment."

> *"I was fortunate, I had important people in my life who made a difference."*
> —Rocky Bleier

Businessman Dwight White

Joe Greene and John Banaszak

Darryl Sims, left, with J.T. Thomas and Sam Davis at social gathering.

Family Album of Steeler Snapshots

Mike Fabus

Chuck Noll presents John Stallworth his second team MVP award. Noll and Stallworth are both strong candidates to be inducted into 1993 class at Pro Football Hall of Fame in Canton, Ohio.

Mike Fabus

Steelers Reunion: Former teammates gather to salute Donnie Shell and John Stallworth when they retired after 1987 season. From left, Mike Wagner, Moon Mullins, J.T. Thomas, Randy Grossman, Sam Davis, Shell, Stallworth, Tony Dungy, Roy Gerela, Jon Kolb and Lynn Swann.

Franco Harris

Mel Blount

Steve Courson

Mike Wagner

George Gojkovich

Bill Cowher chats with Andy Russell, Mel Blount, Steve Furness.

Joe Greene poses with Art Rooney amid Steeler greats.

Joe Gilliam

George Gojkovich

Donnie Shell

Pittsburgh Steelers

George Gojkovich

Mike Webster

Lombardi Trophy

Tony Parisi has looked after
equipment since 1965.

Dr. Steele, Ralph Berlin
and Bob Milie assist injured
John Stallworth.

Tony Dungy at St. Vincent

Placekicker Roy Gerela

Steve Furness

"By the end of the season, you felt like you'd had a lobotomy."

Steve Furness felt at home as soon as he entered the inner sanctum of the Steelers at Three Rivers Stadium. The official address is 300 Stadium Circle and the doors were different, and so were the glass partitions, floor and ceiling than when Furness was last there, in 1980, during the Steelers' 50 Seasons Celebration, as he recalled. The area had been refurbished, opened up, brightened up. Even so, it seemed the same somehow for Furness.

Connie Rose remained as the receptionist and her smile and friendly manner were reassuring. On the black wall to his left, he saw huge framed color photographs of some of his former teammates who had since been named to the Pro Football Hall of Fame: Joe Greene, Jack Ham, Terry Bradshaw, Mel Blount, Jack Lambert and Franco Harris.

"It's kind of intimidating, knowing they were your friends," said Furness, "and knowing that they're now Hall of Famers. You did stuff with them you were supposed to do, and some things you weren't supposed to do."

To his immediate right, there were four framed color photographs — team photos from the four Super Bowl championship teams (1974, 1975, 1978, 1979) — and the face of Furness was in each of those four team photos.

It was not like looking into four mirrors, however. The face in the photographs was fuller than the one that studied the photographs, smiling when he saw other all-too-familiar faces that brought back memories of good times, crazy times and bad times.

Furness had been on a physical fitness kick in recent years, watching what he ate and jogging, and had shed 35 pounds from his playing weight of 255. He wasn't doing any power lifting anymore or stuffing himself at the dinner table, as he felt compelled to do as a player. His hair was cut closer than it had been when last seen as a Steeler. His mustache was much neater, and no longer drooped down the sides of his mouth. He was trimmer all the way around.

He had been a defensive tackle for the Steelers for nine seasons. He had been a fifth round draft choice out of the University of Rhode Island. He overcame great odds to become a solid and committed contributor to the Steel Curtain defensive unit.

He had been one of the Steelers most ardent weight lifters, following the lead of Jon Kolb and Mike Webster, and working out with Larry Brown, Jim Clack, Ted Petersen and Craig Wolfley as well not far from his home in McMurray, a suburb 15 miles south of Three Rivers Stadium.

I was struck by the difference in Furness' appearance from when I had covered the team in the late '70s. I had seen a Christmas card

Bill Amatucci

George Gojkovich

George Perles provides instruction.

Fearsome foursome, plus one: Dwight White (78), Ernie Holmes (63), Joe Greene (75), L.C. Greenwood (68) and Steve Furness (64).

with the Furness family a month earlier that was posted on the wall in the office of one of his old friends and former teammates, John Banaszak. "Look at Steve," said Banaszak. "Doesn't he look great?"

Banaszak had no idea back then that Furness would be one of the first assistants hired by the new Steelers' coach, Bill Cowher. Cowher kept Dick Hoak, who had been the team's offensive backfield coach for 20 seasons, and hired Ron Erhardt, who had coached the previous 10 seasons with the New York Giants, as the offensive coordinator, to start his staff.

Hoak was the only holdover from Noll's staff. Many were surprised when Joe Greene was not retained as the defensive line coach. Greene was very popular in Pittsburgh, and had been promoted in the local papers as a major candidate for the head coaching job when Chuck Noll announced his retirement. Greene was disappointed he didn't get the job.

Greene would get a job on Don Shula's staff in Miami. It was ironic that Furness was filling the slot previously manned by Greene. When Furness first started to see action on the defensive line for the Steelers it was as a fill-in for Greene.

"I'm not here to replace Joe Greene," said Furness. "Just like Bill Cowher is not here to replace Chuck Noll. No one can take the place of Joe Greene. I am going to be an assistant coach responsible for the defensive line. No one has been a bigger fan of Joe Greene than I have been. You never know if you'll have the opportunity to return, so I'm grateful. I didn't know Bill when I came here for the interview. We had a mutual friend who got us together. It was an intense interview. I felt awkward, at first, but now I feel real comfortable."

Given a forum, Furness volunteered information about the violence of pro football, as well as the use of steroids. He admitted he had experimented briefly with steroids, as a player, but quit because of negative side-effects. It just came out naturally in his reflections. It was not something I promoted, but I was fascinated by how often he mentioned the violent aspects of the game, and the gang-tackling tactics favored by the Steelers. There is a fury in Furness that football permitted to come out without him getting into any trouble. It was true of many of his teammates as well.

Furness, 41 when he rejoined the Steelers, had been the defensive line coach the previous season with the Indianapolis Colts. He was looking for a job after the Colts changed head coaches, dropping Ron Meyers and hiring a former Steelers' quarterback, Ted Marchibroda, who had been the offensive coordinator for the Buffalo Bills.

Before that, Furness had served as a line coach for eight seasons at Michigan State on the staff of George Perles, who had been his position coach during his entire stay with the Steelers.

I asked Furness why he decided to leave the college ranks to return to the NFL. "I was tired of recruiting, and the long hours year-round that you keep as a college coach," he said. "My wife (Deborah) was operated on for cancer, and I couldn't be with her, and I had a son

(Zachary) who had a concert, and I couldn't be there. I was in Shreveport, Louisiana, and I'm baby-sitting a kid who has his hand out and wants money to come to Michigan State. And my family needed me. That's when I knew I had to get out.

"There aren't many college places better than East Lansing, Michigan. Maybe places like Notre Dame and Michigan and Southern Cal are as good, but not many. You can get real spoiled with the facilities you have to work with at Michigan State. It's all first class, and I had a great relationship with George.

"I had a great situation at Michigan State, too. I had the defense. I had to learn how the secondary played, and we had to make some adjustments in what we were doing. George didn't enjoy making some of those adjustments. We had some disagreements about what we ought to do. But he let me coach and we had some good results.

"George had the same attitude at Michigan State that he had here. But he had played that way and coached that way at Michigan State before he came to the Steelers, you should know that. His attitude was we're going to beat you up. We're going to belt you every chance we get, we're going to wear you down. Our relationship got better. I got to know George on a man-to-man basis. That was a whole different thing from when I was playing for him with the Steelers.

"I called Dan Rooney for advice before I left Michigan State for a pro job. I think the NFL is a more quality life, even though the hours can be demanding here as well. I'd rather be home more often during the year. Last year, I saw my son play freshman football, and I saw every game, which I wouldn't have been able to do the year before. My wife is well again. It's great.

"And it's even greater to be back here. We still have lots of friends here. It felt very settling to be back here. After I got through checking out all the rooms here, I felt a peace, like I belonged here."

Steve Furness would be the first to tell you he was not a star performer for the Steelers. Just solid, intense and consistent, and always ready to play. He was a fine pass rusher and recorded sacks in some of the biggest games, including Super Bowl XIV, the Steelers' fourth such triumph. He broke his ankle late in Super Bowl XIII.

He became a full-time regular in 1977, starting every game, but playing three different positions on the front four for the defensive unit. He led the team in sacks that season with a career-high 8 1/2 and topped all defensive linemen in tackles.

Prior to that, he had been a spot performer, playing mostly for Joe Greene when Greene was hampered by back and shoulder problems. In that role, Furness started six games in 1975 and played the entire second half of Super Bowl X, leading both teams in tackles.

He was on the taxi squad most of his first two seasons, but was outstanding on special teams when he made his breakthrough early in his career. He eventually lost his starting job to one of his best friends,

Gary Dunn, and was sorely disappointed when the Steelers traded him to the Tampa Bay Buccaneers before the 1981 season.

"I'm unhappy about it," said Furness at the Steelers' training camp at St. Vincent College back in 1981, as he departed the place in a huff, "and I guess I'll be bitter about it for a long time."

Time passes.

Soon after he was hired to be an assistant coach with the Steelers, Furness walked into the locker room where he was greeted by an old friend, Tony Parisi, the team's equipment manager for nearly 30 years.

"Tony Parisi told me the first thing former players do is to look at the locker space they used to occupy to see who's there," said Furness, "and that's exactly what I did. Tunch Ilkin is in my locker. He was a rookie my last year, and he's made an impact here."

Furness was asked when it would sink in that he was with the Steelers once again. "The first time we go out on the field in uniform," he said. "That was always a great thrill for me. When you were getting ready to go out, and you could hear the crowd. It makes your hair stand up. It makes you tingle. It makes my hair stand up and it makes me tingle just to talk about it."

Furness reflected on his first days with the Steelers, at summer training camp in 1972, a year that would climax with the Steelers making the playoffs for the first time in their history, with "The Immaculate Reception" TD catch by Franco Harris in a 13-7 AFC playoff victory over the Oakland Raiders, and, finally, a tough battle before falling to the Miami Dolphins, 21-17, in the AFC championship.

"It was intimidating to see the Steelers then, too," offered Furness. "I saw Mel Blount from the back and I thought he was a defensive lineman, not a defensive back, and Terry Hanratty looked like a lineman. He was lifting weights.

"I think about Lynn Swann. We've continued to develop a relationship over the years. He and I shared something together on the punt return team. Swann returned punts and I blocked for him. We had developed ties. Lynn was my friend on the special team before he became a factor in the National Football League. It took me a long time to be a contributor, not a factor. I have remained friendly with him. I saw him a few times when I was at Michigan State, and he was doing some of our games for ABC-TV. We went out to dinner together.

"The guys on the team at Michigan State couldn't believe he was really Lynn Swann. Here was this slight, small, physically unassuming guy, and he wasn't what they expected. It was the same when Jack Ham came to our practice. He looked too small to have been a Hall of Fame linebacker.

"And I'd like to see Swann on the wall out there, too, because he belongs in the Hall of Fame. We're not done yet. I hope to be here when they put a few more photos up on that wall."

Furness takes great pride in having been a part of the Steelers' Super Bowl squads. Even when he was coaching in the NFL at Indianapolis last season, he said several coaches quizzed him about his teammates. They wanted to know what Jack Lambert was really like.

Furness referred to a reunion of former Steelers that was hosted by Cowher the week before in the team's offices. "I'm told some of these reunions haven't been well-received in the past, that it would be Ray Mansfield, Lloyd Voss and Andy Russell, and that was it. But this was a great turnout and, hopefully, it's a sign of what's to come."

Furness was the fifth or sixth man for several years, playing behind the best known and most feared front four of the '70s in the National Football League, indeed, a front four that was featured on the cover of *Time* magazine (Dec. 8, 1975).

I asked Furness to reflect on those legendary characters who surrounded him in those days.

On L.C. Greenwood: "I never could see L.C. as the football player everyone made him out to be. He was likable, had a great sense of humor, was charming. L.C. looks more like a basketball player than a football player. I can't picture him playing a violent brand of football, not from what I saw when I first met him. I was amazed; he had such a happy outlook. As we got older, he respected me for my style of play. I was a blue collar worker who didn't make many mistakes. I got into a reckless, violent style and our personalities blended real well. He was a big, fluid guy who could run, and he could put heat on a passer, and he did what he did very well."

On Joe Greene: "I didn't know what he would be like. I heard about Mean Joe Greene. When he first shakes your hand you're taken aback. His hand is so big. But he is soft-spoken and you don't expect that. I saw tapes of him at his wildest. I also saw him at times enter into that other personality of his. There was no doubt about his status. He helped me. He grabbed me by my face mask once after I'd messed up. He said, 'Don't worry. You're out here because you can play. Don't worry.' As he got older, he tamed down. Before that, he was real scary when he lost his temper. I remember him throwing his helmet, and I remember him slapping and elbowing people, his own teammates, in our huddle. I remember the time he went after Bob DeMarco of the Browns and clothes-lined him and broke his nose in front of the Browns bench. I remember him and Dwight White shared an apartment once, and they were arguing about whether the room temperature was too hot or too cold. Finally, Joe swatted the thermometer right off the wall. He said, 'Now, there's nothing to worry about!' I remember him cutting the wires on a stereo set in our locker room because somebody didn't turn it down when Joe told them to do just that. I remember him playing a game in Houston once, where a guy got him upset, and Joe had five sacks and blocked a field goal and played like a man possessed. Guys who played against him always said you didn't want to piss him off. If you did, he'd make plays all over the place. He'd be a terror. People ask me what Joe was really like. Was he really mean? I tell them his school at North Texas State was called Mean Green, and that's how he got his nickname."

On Dwight White: "My first impression of Dwight was that he was a real confident, outspoken guy. He relished the role of being who he was. He was always a talker. He was always making all those remarks; he was real mouthy. It just made him play harder, to back up what he said. He was real entertaining, and he lightened up the drills. He liked the physical part of playing football. He liked beating up on people. He liked throwing his body around. There was no question about his courage. He carried false bravado off the field, but the guys who knew him knew he was OK. He'd talk funny to the new guys and get under their skin. But he was also introspective, and we knew when to give him his space. We had some good experiences together. I played next to Dwight for four or five years, and we had to learn to play together. He was a better pass rusher; he was faster. We enjoyed pounding people; we butted each other after good hits. But you left the violent part of your personality out on the field. He could put on glasses, a business suit, and look good. He could also put on shorts, smoke a big cigar, and look like a bum."

On Ernie Holmes: "I never knew what to make of him. I never really understood him. He was physically imposing. He was so thick; he was built like a rhinoceros. His game was a physical, straight-ahead power game. You can be a finesse player like L.C., you can be a technique guy and be aggressive like Joe, or you can play a physical and mental game like Dwight and I, or you can play a pound game like Ernie did. He was a great pass rusher. His locker was next to mine. I had Dwight on one side and Ernie on the other. By the end of the season, you felt like you'd had a lobotomy. Dwight was a joker, hiding your pants or your underwear, cutting up your ties. With Ernie, I never knew what he wanted. He was constantly changing, searching for his identity. He was a real likable guy, very pleasant. He could talk on a variety of subjects. He was probably one of the biggest reasons I got an opportunity to play. He ate himself out of the league. He played at 285, but he drifted into 290 and 300 and 310. You can't play and be an effective player as a defensive lineman at that weight. There's no place for guys over 300 in this game, unless you're a freak like Tony Mandarich when he came out of Michigan State. Ernie used to wear rubber suits to lose weight. But before practice he'd eat a plate of deviled eggs and then he'd get sick. He'd sweat like crazy when he wore those rubber suits and he'd stink like crazy. He's the person I ended up replacing. Then John Banaszak came in and I ended up at right tackle. Ernie had one sensational season where he had 13 1/2 sacks, and was physically dominating. He beat guys to a pulp. He didn't change his game. Joe changed his game, so did L.C. It was hard for Dwight and I to change. Ernie had some psychological problems. Later on, I'd see him on TV. I saw him as a wrestler. I saw him as a prison guard. But I haven't personally seen him since I left the Steelers. When your career ends and you're not prepared for something else, you have no place to turn. It has a paralyzing effect on you. It's a vicious cycle."

I mentioned to Furness that he made several references to the violence of football. I asked him what he was referring to. "Clubbing people with your arms and your fists," he said. "Throwing your man down, pounding him, getting up under his body and turning him backwards."

I asked him if he felt he could be a tough guy, and get nasty, knowing he was flanked by some especially tough guys who could come to his aide. "I could have done that on my own," said Furness, "but I drew strength from the other guys. We did it in practice, running to the ball. Guys might run 20 yards and butt you in the back. Wagner and Ham did it to me a lot. They'd come into a pileup and hit me from behind. They weren't trying to hurt me. We just wanted to get into a hitting mode.

"Sure, it was violent. When a guy got into the other team's backfield, the first guy stood up the ballcarrier, and the second guy rammed him. We weren't trying to hurt him, but we were going to wear him down. Some people referred to it as 'the criminal element' and playing dirty. There are teams today who play it that way, like Philadelphia and New Orleans. They play an aggressive, intimidating style."

I told Furness that when I was working in New York, from 1970 to 1978, that football fans and observers there felt the Steelers' style was a gangland, dirty style. When I came home to Pittsburgh, however, I learned that the real bad guys in pro football were the arch-rival Oakland Raiders. "They were always the bad guys," said Furness with a smile.

"Maybe it was just the black uniforms that made people see the Steelers and the Raiders as dirty teams. George Perles had a lot to do with instilling that style in us. Michigan State was always an aggressive, pounding defense when he was there. They had people like George Webster, who played as rough as they came. Perles brought that with him from Michigan State, and then we picked up the pace on our own. We picked it up and added to it. That was just our style.

"Jack Lambert set the tone in the huddle. We were like that from the first play of the game. He was in a rage the whole time he was out there. He was crazed when he was on the field. It would be the third play of the game, and I'm trying to talk to Dwight White about something we need to do, and Lambert would shout, 'Hey, I'm running this huddle!' And I'd think, 'Hey, forgive me.' And one of the defensive backs would chime in and say, 'Ooh, Bad Jack! Give 'em hell!' And Jack would say something like, 'Screw you, Shell. I'll get your ass, too!' We had a lot of fun out there.

"There was an aura about the Steelers back then. Everyone has their own stories about each other. They all have their stories. Some are printable and some not so printable. Some are heart-warming.

"Jack was something unique. He was washing dishes one day and he sheared his hand open pretty good. He should have had about 20 stitches in it. He patched it up somehow on his own. This happened the day before one of our games. He played, and the gash came open again. Blood was pumping out, I mean squirting all over the place. He had blood on everyone. You don't have players like that today. His hand was ripped apart, and he should have been stitched and sent home with a lollipop.

"Jack would come in and have this scowl on his face. Like Clint Eastwood. That was his form of humor. He could scare guys. If you didn't know him. Once you got in with him, you were in good. Our other linebackers knew how to pull his string. I never wanted to find out whether I could tease him or not.

"When I saw him at Coach Cowher's get-together last week, it was strange seeing him taking his kids' pictures out of his wallet. I remember him telling me once on a bus, 'All I want to do is settle down and have a family.' I told him not to let the guys in the media hear him, or he'd ruin his reputation. He'd ask me what it was like to be married.

"The second year I was with the Steelers, I roomed with a guy named Ed Bradley. He was a linebacker and he was a Jack Lambert type. Jack was a technician and very smart, and enjoyed the physical part, beating up people. Bradley was like that. We got along fine. We were roommates for two years. I had some interesting roomates. Rocky Bleier was my roommate on the road, and then Mike Webster."

Soon after he made the Steelers' squad, Furness found himself involved in an ambitious weight-lifting routine. "I moved to Washington, Pa., and Jim Clack, who was living there, helped me get a place," said Furness. "Jon Kolb was the leader of the weight-lifting pack. They worked out at Washington & Jefferson College all the time. They showed me the ropes. They started it before Mike Webster got here, and he only made it more intense. Jon was the catalyst to start with. When Larry Brown turned into a hulk as a tight end, we helped him as he made the switch to playing tackle. Then we moved our activity to the Red Bull Inn on Rt. 19, between Canonsburg and Washington. It was owned by a fellow named Lou Caringa, who was an avid lifter, and had a weight room in the basement of his restaurant. We were later joined by Ted Petersen, Steve Courson and Craig Wolfley. We'd lift and then we'd eat at the Red Bull Inn. We got a good price, but Lou couldn't have afforded to feed us, too. The way we ate, he'd have gone out of business.

"If it weren't for Mike Webster and Jon Kolb and Larry Brown, I couldn't have lasted as long as I did in the National Football League. I wouldn't have been as committed or as consistent. I was never a star, but I was strong and played with great enthusiasm. But you had to be strong to survive in the line. We had a team of regular guys, as Noll put it, and a few stars. It turned out, however, that we had more stars than we realized then.

"You have to have the strength. Unless you can pump the iron, you're out of here. It was very competitive. Mike Webster really pushed me. He used to say, 'You have to be whipped into shape.' I couldn't do what they could do, but I hung in there pretty good. I was hampered by long arms. Those guys went to another level. The offensive linemen, in particular, were into the bench press. It got depressing for me. When it was my time to max out — lift as much weight as I could — they had to remove weights from the bar. They would blow me away on the bench. They were around 500 pounds and I was around 400 pounds. It was absurd what they could do. Mike and Jon and Larry had a tremendous work ethic. They were disciplined and they had a very good lifestyle. The way they lived, their moral fiber, I benefitted from the association. There was a big difference between the offensive linemen and the defensive linemen. The offensive guys were more disciplined and more controlled. Seeing the side they had was insightful for me. Things that irritated me, they'd just go along with the flow.

"I wasn't blessed with the gifts some of them have. To see some guys with great physical ability just trash their careers . . . it makes me crazy. It's tragic. Why would you stay out drinking all night? Or doing drugs? You have to pay for what you put into your body. I've seen guys experiment with drugs in college and it just doesn't go with football. Some guys are going to fool around a little with drugs at a party, you know that's going to happen, but it can't be a way of life. That bothered me in college. I almost got into a fight in college over that; it's the only time I went after somebody as a coach."

Yes, but how about when he was with the Steelers? Steve Courson has charged in his anti-drug talks and in his book, *False Glory,* that some of the Steelers were using steroids to enhance their body-building efforts.

"I experimented with steroids when I was playing here, I'll admit that," said Furness. "I experimented with them. I wanted to see what would happen. I was pleased with the temporary results. But I didn't continue. My weight increased, my strength increased, my anger increased, my moods increased. When I stopped, I changed back to the way I was. That causes a depression, because you suffer mentally when you're not as strong or able to lift as much weight. After a while, I was satisfied with the way I was lifting. I'm glad I didn't continue because of long-time side effects.

"I knew Steve Courson was doing steroids. No one could tell him anything. It was like talking to Lyle Alzado. When you tell them, and they continue to do what they want to do, it's hard to feel sorry for them. I feel sorry for what happened to them. You can't save someone who doesn't want to be saved.

"The Steelers warned us about steroids and drugs. The league had people come in here and talk to us about the dangers. The popular view of the use of steroids is very distorted. It wasn't unlawful back then to take steroids. The NCAA wasn't testing for steroids. Courson said 50 to 80 per cent of the guys were doing steroids. It might have been true at one time, but as more information became available about the long-range dangers the use of steroids dropped off considerably. Guys didn't want to take the risk. The trainers started passing out booklets about the dangers of drugs, all kinds of drugs. Players today are properly forewarned. It's made a big difference for the better."

While Furness found much that was familiar to him upon returning to the Steelers offices, he noticed one major difference. Art Rooney, the team's owner and spiritual leader, had died in 1988. "I miss him not being here," said Furness. "I miss his cigar, or seeing him walking down the hallway once in awhile in his socks, without his shoes on, if his feet were bothering him. The people who are still here have taken their cue from him. The people who have been here carry that common bond with them.

"But he'd come by you on the airplane on the way back from a game, and tap you on the leg, and say, 'You OK? You'll be all right.' He would ask about your family; he knew your wife and kids by name. You were sort of his family.

"You can block everything out and be back with him again. I enjoyed it. I never realized what a big effect he had on everybody. We were lucky to have known him."

Bill Amatu

Steve Furness enjoys campfire chat with Jack Lambert.

Ernie Holmes
"I was a very large baby."

"He was a day-to-day problem . . . We had a spare couch for Ernie with his name on it."
—Chuck Noll, 1982

When he smiled, which was often, he flashed a gold tooth. When he frowned, which was just as often, the ends of his Fu Manchu mustache curled a certain way and he was downright menacing.

Grown men shuddered. Even when he smiled at them. Ernie "Fats" Holmes has always been a formidable figure. Even Jack Lambert kept a respectful distance. He didn't know what Holmes might do next. No one did. Especially Ernie Holmes himself.

"They don't know what to make of me when I smile at them, just when they're ready to beat on my body," he once said of his opponents in a report I did for *The Pittsburgh Press.*

When he shaved his skull, leaving only an arrow on top to point him in the right direction, even his best friends snickered.

After he was arrested for firing a revolver at truck drivers as he weaved along interstate highways in northeastern Ohio, and for wounding a policeman in a helicopter that pursued him, he was considered crazy. Steelers' president Dan Rooney and Chuck Noll, with the help of attorneys, got Holmes out of that and several other jams. They stood up for him.

Holmes had been depressed because his first marriage had broken up when, at age 24, he went on his wild shooting spree in March of 1973. He was arrested near Youngstown, Ohio.

"There was a lot of pressure back home," he said. "A lot of things on my mind."

He wounded a police helicopter pilot in the ankle when the helicopter came after him.

His problems were diagnosed as "acute paranoid psychosis."

Dan Rooney went to bat for him, promised continued employment, even starting status, which helped Holmes get put on probation rather than doing time.

Holmes had been helping high school students "academically and athletically" only a week before that incident.

Art Rooney visited him often, and sent teammates to see him, during his stay at Western Psychiatric Institute, just below Pitt Stadium. "If it was possible to add another member to your family," said Holmes in the aftermath, "I'd like to add him to mine."

Ernie Holmes had his own way of doing things, destructive to himself and opposing players in the National Football League, when he was playing defensive tackle for the Steelers in the '70s.

205

He once appeared on the cover of *Time* magazine along with Dwight White, Joe Greene and L.C. Greenwood as a member of the front four of the "Steel Curtain" defense. But he was the least celebrated of the bunch. Yet, for a brief spell, he was as great as any of them. "He was devastating," recalled Joe Gordon, the team's publicist.

Holmes did not sustain his greatness nearly as long as the other defensive linemen. But it was never really the "Steel Curtain" defense without him, either.

My last personal interview with Holmes was in 1982, when the Steelers celebrated their 50th anniversary. He did not come to town for that event, but I talked to him over the telephone. He was in Tucson, Arizona at the time.

The last time Holmes came back to Pittsburgh was probably in June of 1985 when he played in the annual golf outing of the Steelers alumni at Oakmont Country Club. He was then living in Compton, California.

Nobody associated with the Steelers has Holmes' present phone number. None that are any good, anyhow. Rooney and Gordon both keep the names, addresses and phone numbers of former players on a Rolodex in their offices. Neither could get hold of Holmes if they wanted to these days. Ray Mansfield, who looks after the local chapter of the NFL Alumni Association, doesn't have a current number for Holmes. They all have numbers for Holmes in Texas as well as California and Arizona, but they're all disconnected. I made calls to all the cities Holmes has called home since he left the Steelers, but came up empty.

"That's Ernie's fault," said Mansfield. "It's not easy to keep up with him. He's not the most reliable person in the world. Everybody on our team liked Ernie, and we enjoy seeing him. It would be nice if he let us know where he was once in a while."

"The last time I heard anything about Ernie," said Dwight White, "he was weighing 350 pounds and wrestling on the west coast."

Holmes, who turned 44 in July of 1992, has surfaced in the past as one of the "Redskins" in an American Express commercial with former Dallas Cowboys coach Tom Landry, in pro wrestling, as a security guard, as an assistant high school football coach.

"I've had a lot of jobs since I quit playing," Holmes told Pittsburgh sportswriter Ron Cook on June 10, 1985 when he was at the golf outing at Oakmont. "People ask me, 'What are you doing those lowly things for? You were a superstar. What did you do with all your money? Snort it away?'

"I try to tell them I don't do that stuff. I try to explain to them what's happened to me. But how do you tell my story?"

He was at his best when he was working or playing with kids. He has a way with them. He thought he had some understanding of why inner-city kids had so many behavioral problems. "If there was a little less sidewalk and a little more dirt and trees, there'd be a lot less crime," he said.

But Holmes has his own problems and they are complex.

Still none for the thumb as Ernie Holmes flashes Super Bowl rings.

Holmes' head was shaven clean when he signed autographs at camp.

He has had bouts with alcoholism and with drugs. He drew a sentence of five years probation after pleading guilty to three charges of assault with a deadly weapon for that incident on the Ohio Turnpike. A drunk driving charge and an acquittal on a charge of cocaine possession are also on his police record. In 1980, in the Los Angeles area, he was arrested for assaulting a barmaid who resisted his advances.

He had a stay at Western Psychiatric Institute in Pittsburgh. That was after the Ohio Turnpike incident. "I must have gone haywire," he said.

His history is not a pretty one.

The last time we spoke, he spoke in a rush, and he spoke about himself in the third person, for starters.

"Ernie's been trying to make it," he said. "I always enjoyed working with kids. I've always left the problems behind me. It hasn't been me reviewing my past; it's been the media every time. I'm not actually happy. I'm kinda struggling. But I'm satisfied with some things.

"I've always liked myself. I'm responsible for myself. I'm optimistic about everything."

Chuck Noll's eyes closed — almost automatically — at the mere mention of Ernie Holmes. His eyes closed the way Holmes' eyes always seemed to close.

Noll has never been so frank in discussing any subject as he was in reflecting on Holmes, and his behavioral pattern, when I asked him about Holmes.

Holmes played for the Steelers from 1972 to 1977 and was traded to the Tampa Bay Buccaneers the next year. His stay with the Steelers was memorable, but brief. Many people, in acknowledging Noll's coaching ability, point to his being able to have a Holmes and an Andy Russell on the same team, and being able to handle and blend the best of both kinds of athletes and people.

"Ernie couldn't play anymore, that's why we traded him," said Noll. "They blew him right out. He was — for two years — one of the best defensive linemen in the game. He had two years that were really great. Then there was a big change. Why the big change? I don't know. It seems like he was more interested in things other than football.

"He has a history of what he's telling you now. Sin and saving. Sin and saving. Ernie was a day-to-day problem. Up and down. One day he was great and the next day he was down.

"Ernie was a guy of excesses. He couldn't ever get enough of things. More, more, more. He was that way with food, drink, that way with everything. That way with love. And with hate.

"You never knew which Ernie Holmes you were dealing with that day. He was a problem. Ernie needed attention, and he would do anything to get it, whether it was to balloon to 300 pounds, or to shave his head, or to get into the Guinness Book of Records. Attention was important.

ith Joe Greene

Ernie Holmes

"There's a lot of con in him. He was never in touch with reality. George Perles and Dan Rooney and I all spent a lot of time with him. We had a spare couch for Ernie with his name on it. As problem players go, he was one of the larger ones."

Trying to explain his weight problems and how he first got the nickname of "Fats," Holmes once said, "I was a very large baby."

Holmes held his own when I asked him about his career with the Steelers.

"I didn't get much recognition, but I added another dimension to the Steel Curtain," he said over the telephone from Tucson. "I played strictly at my highest emotional basis. It meant something to me to turn the ball over to the offense. I played for Art Rooney. The Chief was my man. I played all I had for him.

"Art Rooney is one guy I don't hold anything against. He's the greatest man I ever met in Pittsburgh. I played the way I did out of love for him.

"I would have played if my leg was broken. When I was beating 260-pounders with one arm, for instance. Or when I had pain in my knee and continued to play. When those 260-pounders began knocking me down and running over my chest, I couldn't understand it.

"I played for the love of Mr. Rooney. Any time we were down, or badly bruised, I sucked it up for The Chief. He came to my aid when I needed help."

I talked to several of Ernie's old friends on the team about him at the team's 50 Seasons Celebration in 1982.

Former teammate Sam Davis was hopeful Holmes could turn things around. "There's no doubt he can make a comeback," said Davis. "Maybe it's starting to hit him. Athletes are trained like that: 'If we don't stop this guy here, we're going to lose.' When your back is against the wall — the way it is for Ernie now — he might just do it. Ernie has always been that type of competitor.

"He has to make a change, else he's going to crumble. The thing that hurt Ernie so much is drinking all that cognac. If he knows that, he's headed in the right direction."

Mel Blount, another former teammate on the "Steel Curtain" defensive unit, came to Ernie's defense. In the early days, Blount and Holmes, and Joe Gilliam and White used to dance to the music in the Steelers' clubhouse, and have a great time.

Blount said, "I think Ernie can do it. First of all, he has to want to do it. It's hard to say if anyone really does or not. If he wants to get his act together, he can. Ernie, in my opinion, was a good person. I think the pressure of the game got to him.

"He was surrounded by great athletes, and he was great, too, but he probably felt he wasn't getting his due, publicity-wise or financially-wise. I think Ernie could have been a different man, if he had been well paid and publicized. He was a high-strung kid."

Holmes had his best and worst days against the Oakland Raiders, the Steelers' fiercest rival.

His performance against Gene Upshaw, the Raiders' All-Pro guard, is something his teammates still talk about. The Steelers beat the Raiders, 24-13, in the American Football Conference championship game in 1974, and Holmes simply dominated Upshaw.

"I was scared after Fats hugged me," said his coach, Woody Widenhofer, following that game. "I can imagine how Upshaw felt."

Upshaw got his revenge two years later when the Raiders defeated the Steelers, 24-7, in the AFC title game. A few days before that game, Holmes had predicted, "We're going to have the intensity of a charging rhino and a herd of tanks. We'll be more pumped up than the U.S. blimp."

L.C. Greenwood recalled what happened after that game: "They beat us and Upshaw was walking off the field laughing. Fats saw that, walked up to him and challenged him to go back out and play again — just the two of them. Fats hated it when his man didn't hurt after a game. If they didn't bleed, or he hadn't knocked them down, he wasn't happy.

"Upshaw was frightened by Ernie; he didn't know what to make of him," said Greenwood at his office in Carnegie. "He looked to the rest of us to help him out of a sticky situation. 'Tell him the game is over,' Upshaw said to us. But, with Ernie, it was never over."

With Cook, Holmes concluded his conversation by saying, "I don't know if I had a good time or just a good drunk during my days here. I don't have any arrows to shoot or axes to chop on anyone's head. I just wish things could have been different.

"My mama always told me, 'Don't look over your shoulder. Somewhere, sometime things will be better.' The way I look at it, mama knows. Yeah, mama knows."

With me, Holmes had this to say as a summary: "I developed a bad drinking habit. I was an alcoholic. I drank too much cognac, to maintain an image, so I'd be what people wanted me to be. My head wasn't squared away."

There is no such thing as a former alcoholic. Holmes had to face that fact, too, but he refused.

"I still drink my beer," he said. "It's an occasional thing. I don't drink liquor at all. I consider myself blessed.

"The only thing I miss is the substantial amount of income. And I miss my friends on the team. I miss being with them in the locker room. Tell everybody up there I love them. The bitterness is gone."

"I've always liked myself."
—Ernie Holmes

Moon Mullins
"You have to have a heart"

"To measure the man measure the heart."
—Malcolm S. Forbes

G erry "Moon" Mullins gets mad when he talks about Terry Bradshaw. That's too bad because Mullins and Bradshaw were the best of buddies when they were teammates on the Steelers Super Bowl teams of the '70s.

Something went wrong with the relationship, just as something went sour between Bradshaw and the ballclub and other teammates.

You can almost see heat waves rising above the handsome head of Mullins as he talks about Bradshaw. His blue eyes, just like Bradshaw's blue eyes, dance when he talks excitedly.

"I haven't talked to Terry in nearly ten years," said Mullins, an offensive lineman for nine seasons (1971-79) and a starting guard/tackle for all four Super Bowl teams during that decade.

"I get upset with the Bradshaw and the Courson books about their conflicts with the Steelers," said Mullins. "It wasn't my experience with the club, and I talk to many of my teammates, and they don't share their dissatisfaction, either. I was there at the same time. Am I just naive? I just don't see it in the same light.

"I was his road manager, so to speak, when Terry traveled around the country on a country and western singing tour after one of the Super Bowls," said Mullins, smiling at the memory. "I was at his wedding. He was in my wedding. I thought we were real close.

"But you never really knew how you stood with Terry. He's different. But I made some comments a few years back that I thought Terry was making a mistake by being so critical and turning his back on Chuck Noll and his teammates. I mean these guys were part of your family. I think he's missing something."

Tony Parisi, the long-time equipment manager of the Steelers, told Mullins soon after that Bradshaw was upset with him for making such remarks that were reprinted in newspapers. "Terry thought I was stabbing him in the back," said Mullins.

"I don't really know what the source of his discontent is, and I never realized it was so severe until recently."

Mullins mentioned that he, Mike Wagner and Bradshaw once shared an apartment at the Mt. Royal Towers on the Parkway East, across from the WTAE radio-TV complex. The apartment building had just been constructed and wasn't even officially open at the time, but Steelers' publicist Joe Gordon got them in somehow.

"It was a pretty sparse enclosure, but we didn't care back then," said Mullins. "We were too busy having fun. But I remember that even back then it really bothered Terry that he couldn't go anywhere in the city without causing a stir.

212

Embracing Rocky Bleier

Bill Amatucci

Blocking for Terry Bradshaw

Moon Mullins

Blocking with Sam Davis (57) for Franco Harris

213

"He was like the Pied Piper. People swarmed over him when we'd go somewhere. That gnawed on him. He couldn't do what the rest of us could do. The people just wouldn't let him alone. He had no privacy. It forced him to be a recluse, which was not his personality.

"He was forced to hide out, and it really worked on his overall view of the city.

"The Chuck Noll thing mystifies me. It never knew it was as bad as it turned out to be. Terry and Chuck were working together a lot because Chuck was also the quarterback coach back then. The whole thing makes no sense to me."

Mullins looked great as he sat behind his desk at Industrial Metals & Minerals Company in South Fayette, less than a mile from the Bridgeville exit off I-79. He said he weighed the same 230 pounds as he did when he was an undersized lineman for the Steelers, but he appeared trimmer. At 42, and retired from playing football for 12 years, he looked prosperous.

He stood up and sucked in his stomach and puffed out his chest a little in self mockery and said, "You probably remember me at the start of the season when I'd be built up to 260 or something like that. Not the way I looked at the end of the season."

He looked comfortable in a burgundy ski sweater over an open-collared white dress shirt, and dark slacks. He looked sleek because he was clean-shaven, whereas he wore a mustache and often a beard as a ballplayer. Early in his career, he wore his hair long, and looked like a mountain man. He is the vice-president of the company which sells ores and minerals and industrial-related materials around the country. There are about eight people in the firm, which represents companies like Kennecott Copper and Dresser Industries.

His boss, Bob Keaney, says he is grooming Gerry to take over the operation of the company someday. They had been working together for 11 years when I visited their offices in early January of 1992.

"This is my life's work, as Chuck would put it," Mullins said. "When I look back on my football career, I'll always have great memories, but this is where I'm expending all my energies these days."

He was single again, having been divorced a few years earlier. He has an 11-year-old son, Michael, who was living with his mother in Pittsburgh.

I mentioned to Mullins that I was surprised by how many of his teammates from the Steelers had gotten divorced since they quit playing ball. "I don't know if it's any higher than the national average," he said. "I think people put too much emphasis on pro football players, and pro athletes in general, and have too great of expectations for them. Off the field, we're the same as everyone else."

Besides the obligatory office watercolor of the skyline of downtown Pittsburgh as seen from the homes on the hills south on the Ohio River, the walls are decorated with four plaques with miniature reproductions of the front pages of the *Pittsburgh Post-Gazette* the day after the Steelers

214

won each of their Super Bowls, and then, too, there are plaques with embossed squad photos of the four championship teams.

"That's so I can look back and check to see who was on each of the teams so I can appear smart when people ask me about them," said Mullins, always willing to poke fun at himself. He was not wearing any of his Super Bowl rings.

"Back in 1976, after our second Super Bowl, when we'd beaten Dallas (21-17) in Super Bowl X, Terry and I traveled around the country together. I was supposed to be his road manager, but I was just along for the ride. He went to Nashville and cut some country western records."

Mullins was responsible for travel arrangements, time schedules and hustled Bradshaw's record albums in the audience when Bradshaw would take a break from his singing during their road tour.

"We really did it for fun," remembered Mullins, "and we've got some great stories from those days.

"About that same time, Burt Reynolds did a dialogue on TV in which he depicted Terry as sort of a Li'l Abner, and made fun of him, portraying him as a dumb quarterback. It got a lot of play. To this day, Terry still hates that image. Burt was seeing Dinah Shore at the time. Terry was in LA to do her TV show.

"Burt felt badly for what he did — he blamed it on the writers who provided his script — and he invited Terry to come to Dinah's place so he could apologize. So we went to Dinah Shore's.

"Burt and Terry really hit it off. Burt had been a football player in college in Florida. He and Terry both had ranches and both raised horses. So they had a lot in common. Soon after, Terry was in a lot of Burt's movies and got him a TV pilot with country western singer Mel Tillis.

"And I was right in the middle of all that. We were having a great time. Terry and I remained close through the rest of my career. After he left Pittsburgh (following the 1983 season), he pretty much slammed the door behind him.

"I don't know if I should talk about it or not — I'm not here to beat up on Terry Bradshaw — but it still burns me. We were playing a flag football game and we had all the great players from our team, and we were going to play all the great players from the Dallas Cowboys at Three Rivers Stadium in 1988.

"That's the game in which Andy Russell, Franco and Frenchy Fuqua all got hurt. Andy and Ray Mansfield were spearheading the project. Roger Staubach was going to play for Dallas, and we wanted Brad to be on our team.

"I mean Andy and Ray really live in the past, and they wanted it to be the real thing. To them, this was going to be a real grudge match. Andy said he called Terry ten times. Andy asked me to call him. Andy said, 'C'mon, you're good friends.' But I didn't want to get in the middle.

"Bradshaw really blasted Andy about it. He had his secretary call and say that he was upset about getting all the phone calls, and that if Russell didn't stop it he was going to send some guys up here to break his legs, stuff like that. How could he do that?

"Terry Hanratty ended up playing quarterback for us, and he looked great. Physically, he looked fantastic and I'm telling you he was throwing the ball as good as I'd ever seen him throw it when he was playing here.

"But Brad turned his back on the players. He did it again two years ago when we had a special reunion of our '78 team, thought to be maybe the finest in pro football history. He said he was coming, then he changed his mind and stayed away. We have annual alumni golf outings at Oakmont that Ray Mansfield puts together, and we have a great time together. But Terry stays away. I think he's missing something. We're missing something, too, and that's Terry.

"He must have made a decision to close this chapter in his life. The truth is, after all he's achieved, he should appreciate what other people did for him. He's not on television now because he's some great announcer; he's on because he was the quarterback for four Super Bowl championship teams.

"We accomplished that together. I was a minor character in all that; I was not an important player. But I think he's making a mistake by not savoring some of that."

Mullins doesn't see many Steelers' games these days. He attends a couple a year with customers at Three Rivers Stadium, and watches some on TV. "I got burned out, watching film every day for ten years," Mullins explained. "That gets a little old."

Mullins had his moments in the sun. He was a tight end at Anaheim High School and at the University of Southern Cal back in the '60s, and was always thought to be a southern California kind of guy — laid-back and looking for the next wave to ride to the beach — during his distinguished stint with the Steelers.

With his free-flowing dark hair and mustache and beard, he reminded me of a younger version of singer Kenny Rogers.

As a player he'd get noticed when he pulled out of his right guard position and led a sweep to the left, tossing a block that freed Franco Harris for a touchdown jaunt. Otherwise, Mullins got lost in the crowd. That was cool with him.

"I'm pretty much of a laidback guy," Mullins told us back when we were covering the club for *The Pittsburgh Press.* "So it works out well being an offensive lineman. You can't get angry or strike out when somebody is beating on your head, or you'll make mistakes. You must stay under control."

He knew his playbook and his role well.

"We have a great quarterback and great receivers," said Mullins in the summer of 1979, just before the Steelers would embark on their fourth Super Bowl triumphant season, "and our job is to provide protection and make our passing game better. There's not a lot of room for personal glory."

That great quarterback, Terry Bradshaw, cared about his teammates back then. He bought the Steelers offensive starters oil portraits
of themselves to say "Thank you," and Mullins was most appreciative.
"I thought it was the greatest," said Mullins at the time. "You
know you're appreciated. It makes you want to work that much harder
for the guy. It's something he didn't have to do."

He was called "Moon" Mullins after a comic strip character, and he enjoyed a laugh as much as the next guy. But he was strictly business
on the ballfield. He had to pay attention.

Mullins was the Steelers' fourth round draft choice in 1971, a draft
that produced seven starters for the team. It included Frank Lewis, Jack
Ham, Dwight White, Larry Brown, Ernie Holmes and Mike Wagner.
Mullins became a starter his second season at offensive tackle.

"The nucleus of the team was built with that draft," said Mullins.

He was one of the unsung heroes of the Steelers' reign. He was
smart and he could play every offensive line position, He played as the
second tight end in short yardage situations, and caught a few passes
from that position. He was the outstanding offensive lineman versus
the Minnesota Vikings in Super Bowl IX.

He scored four touchdowns in his pro career. Two of those TDs came
as tight end with pass receptions against Cleveland in 1972 and Cincinnati in 1974. The other two were on fumble recoveries against Miami in the AFC championship game in 1972 and against San Diego in
1975.

The idea of lifting weights never did much for Mullins. He resisted the entreaties of fellow linemen like Mike Webster, Jon Kolb, Larry
Brown and Steve Courson to join their merry fun in the weight room.

"I never really rejected it; I just never got devoted to it like other
offensive linemen," he said. "I just did enough to get by."

Mullins was smaller than most of the people he had to block, but
he had good technique, good feet, good hands, and was determined to
carry out his duties.

"To play the game and be good at it," he said, "you have to have
a heart. That's the basis of the whole game. You can have all the physical ability in the world. But if you don't have heart. . ." His voice trailed
off.

Chuck Noll paid him the ultimate compliment on one occasion.
"When his life is on the line," noted Noll, "Moon will find a way to win."

Or, as his line coach Rollie Dotsch once declared in unorthodox
logic, "His number one strength is savvy and intelligence and competitiveness." Or, was that three strengths?

He was one of the most handsome ballplayers on the team, moving Mike Webster to remark, "To say he was one of the most eligible
bachelors in Pittsburgh would be a gross understatement. He's a legend
to some of the younger players."

That reputation ended, however, when he was married in February of 1980 to Pittsburgher Cyndi Cronauer, who was described by Terry Bradshaw as "gorgeous."

That's when Bradshaw thought Mullins was a great sidekick. "He's a funny guy," Bradshaw said back then. "I love being around him because he is fun. He was a lot of things I couldn't be. He was loose, a free spirit. He's not a jock. He loves the game, but he's not consumed by it."

Mullins was asked once by Vic Ketchman, the sports columnist for the *Irwin Standard-Observer*, to explain himself. "Football isn't my whole life," he told Ketchman. "Football has always been the priority in my life, but I've just never dedicated my whole life to it."

Franco Harris always appreciated the line play of Mullins, and frequently participated in the same poker game as Mullins on airplane trips. "If you want to learn more about Moon Mullins," offered Franco, "get a deck of cards and bring your money."

Mullins has always spoken his mind. Once, he felt the Steelers' offensive linemen were vastly underpaid and he complained to management.

"I was one who always spoke my mind when I didn't think something was right," he said with more than a hint of pride during our interview.

After his third season, Mullins went to management to complain when the Steelers traded away Bruce Van Dyke, whom he was playing behind. It opened an opportunity for him, yet Mullins thought the Steelers made a mistake.

"With all the socio-economic diversity we had," said Mullins when we visited him in January of 1992, "we had a close-knit group of guys. A lot of credit for that has to go to Chuck.

"I was fairly early in the equation for building the team. A lot of changes were made in 1971 and 1972. The final pieces came together in 1974, with that draft."

That draft included the likes of Lynn Swann, Jack Lambert, John Stallworth, Jim Allen and Mike Webster.

"I could see how talent was a prerequisite," said Mullins, "but I saw personnel moves made that were not based solely on talent. The outcome, of course, is well known to everybody.

"I saw some fairly talented people that were traded away. In Chuck's master plan, he was going to try and form a team that he wanted to work with. Chuck looked beyond pure talent.

"Chuck got rid of players like Roy Jefferson and Dave Smith simply because their personal chemistry didn't fit in. They were not what he wanted, personality-wise.

"One person who comes to mind, who was close to me, was Bruce Van Dyke. Bruce was a little counterproductive to the kind of team they wanted. But the year before he was traded he was a Pro Bowl player. They were rare on our front line in those days, and just as rare, except for Webster, when we were winning Super Bowls.

"Bruce and Ray Mansfield took me under their wings when I got here. Bruce and Ray really helped me, and motivated me. They told me what I had to do, like excel on special teams, if I wanted to make the club.

"I played a lot at guard as a rookie because of injuries to other guys. They moved me out to tackle the next year. I was playing alongside Bruce. I'm told the decision was made by Dan Radakovich, our line coach. So I replaced Bruce at right guard in my third year. We had Jim Clack as a backup center and guard then.

"Bruce was from the old school, and he was a fun-loving guy. He and Mansfield were always taking me out after curfew at training camp. So there was a conflict. Bruce was openly rebellious, and Chuck wanted to stress discipline.

"We still talk about this. Andy Russell had his 50th birthday party this past year at Froggy's Restaurant downtown. Andy confronted Radakovich, who'd come in for the party, about Van Dyke's departure from the Steelers. Rad told Andy he felt I was a better player than Van Dyke at the time."

Mullins believes he was more of a kindred spirit to Van Dyke and Mansfield than some of the other newcomers to the club. "I was more in their mold," Mullins said. "I was sort of a free spirit from California. That was always my calling card.

"I was a tight end, but I was told when I was drafted that I'd be in the interior line. I had to learn a new position. It was easy to me, though. I knew the playbook and I could get by without sitting in my room all night reading the playbook. I'd go out with Van Dyke and Mansfield.

"They appreciated that I was trying to be one of the boys. They rooted when I'd make tackles on the special teams.

"Bruce and Ray always roomed together, and they had the last room in the hallway, right by the stairway. As soon as the bed check was made by the coaches, they'd be down the stairway and out the door. They were gone.

"When Bruce left, I became Ray's roommate. Rad told me I was the only one who came in and complained after Van Dyke was traded. Rad liked me. He pushed me. I gave him a lot of crap, but he has to be given a lot of credit for developing our Super Bowl offensive line. We had talent, but he utilized it well.

"Mike Webster was the only star on our offensive line, and he'll be in the Pro Football Hall of Fame as soon as he's eligible, I'm sure, but we always had a group of offensive linemen who could hold their own with anybody.

"Rad wanted the line to be interchangeable, that's why we had to learn each and every position. He wanted us to be as good no matter who was playing where.

"I went along with the flow. To me, it was business as usual. It was serious football when you were down there at the Stadium, but people weren't looking over your shoulder when you were off the field. I appreciated that.

"I was always thought of as kinda loose. I had that California image. The front office always felt I was a little crazy. I was fun-loving.

I always spoke my mind if I was wrongly persecuted. But I always did what I was supposed to do on the field."

This may have been what appealed to Bob Keaney when he was checking around, looking for someone on the Steelers who might be interested in working for him at Industrial Metals & Minerals Co.

"I've been a Steelers' fan since Day One," said Keaney, whom I originally met in his volunteer role as the clerk of session at Westminster Presbyterian Church in Upper St. Clair and knew to be a good man.

"I realized we needed somebody young in here, somebody I'd want to turn the business over to someday. I lived next door to Bob Prince at the time. And I asked him if he could introduce me to Moon Mullins.

"I liked two things about Moon Mullins when I followed the Steelers. He was versatile. That appealed to me. When he finished up with the Steelers, he turned down offers to continue in Cleveland and Houston. He wanted to work here.

"Plus, I used to play golf with Chuck Noll on occasion. I asked him, 'Who are the smartest guys on the team?' He said, Besides the quarterbacks, the offensive linemen.' So I talked to Mullins. He didn't want to go to work right away. He wanted to take some time off, do some hunting and fishing, and go to work for me when he got back. We've been together for 11 years and it's worked out great.

"He learned the business fast. He's a quick study. He asked me how to make a sales call. I told him to wear his first Super Bowl ring on his first call. I told him to wear his second Super Bowl ring on his second sales call. And so forth.

"He rarely wears his Super Bowl rings. He's like Chuck Noll in that respect. And my customers tell me Gerry doesn't bring up the subject of football. They do. But the Super Bowl ring still works; it still opens up some doors.

"After all, how many people in the world have ever seen a Super Bowl ring?

"I remember once hearing an announcer say of Gerry, 'He's played in four Super Bowls and he's never made a mistake.' He's the same way here."

Terry Bradshaw
"There is a bond among us that can never be broken"

"I'm back in the saddle again,
out where a friend is a friend."
—Song by Gene Autry

Terry Bradshaw has always been bigger than life. He comes across that way on TV when he's on "NFL Today" for CBS-TV, and he was that way in the locker room after a Steelers football game. He dominates the picture, and he always has, the way he once dominated playoff and Super Bowl games.

Bradshaw likes to talk, and he's good at it. He commands your attention, and if your eyes or mind should stray, he'll grab you by the shoulder or the kneecap and squeeze to get your attention. He can squeeze hard.

He was always there in the locker room, whether he played well or poorly, and he never made you feel like you were holding him up. Others would stay in the showers long, or retreat to the trainer's room, when they had a bad day, but not Bradshaw. He was always willing to talk.

Bradshaw was born to be a quarterback and to talk about his role. Bradshaw was born in Louisiana and he talked sorta funny, at least to the Pittsburgh ear, with all those country-fried and down-home expressions of his. He had that hee-haw manner, that big ol' cowboy hat and boots, with big buckles on his belt, and lots of anecdotes, and he was fun to be around.

He would play pitch and catch with you on the sideline during practice, and show you how he held the football to throw it better, with the fourth finger on the rear tip of the ball. I could always throw a football fairly well, about 40 to 45 yards on a spiral, but not under pressure, of course. But I couldn't throw the ball the way Bradshaw showed me because my hand wasn't big enough. My fingers don't stretch as far as his. But he'd let you show him how to hold a football, too, and smile and have some fun about it. He'd pretend like he was learning something, nodding his blond head a lot.

He was willing to throw the ball under fire, and frequently was flattened after he released it. And you never thought he'd ever get up again. "We hated that," said Jon Kolb, speaking for the offensive linemen. "We used to say under our breath, 'Get up, Terry, you're making us look bad.' Bradshaw would get up, and stagger off the field. But he'd come back in a play or two, and be his old self. Bradshaw was always scaring people with his dead-man act." There were times when you thought there was no way he could return to action, and he did. He had more lives than Lazarus and a cat combined. Bradshaw was beautiful.

Boyish-looking Terry Bradshaw shows up at Three Rivers Stadium for the first time in 1970, shortly after he was drafted out of Louisiana Tech

I remember Bradshaw created a stir when he married Melissa Babish, who was from Pittsburgh and had been "Miss Teenage America." I had known her dad, Joe, who was a football and basketball official. That didn't last.

Then he married JoJo Starbuck, the ice skating star. Two things stick out in my mind about her. I once had occasion to sit next to her on a Steelers' flight to Dallas, where the Steelers were playing the Cowboys. We had a nice conversation. I remember telling Myron Cope, after we landed in Dallas, that she was nice to talk to. Cope made a sour face when I made that observation. "I can't stand the sound of her voice," came back Cope. Imagine Myron Cope being critical of someone's voice. Another time, I was working at the office of *The Pittsburgh Press*, when I received a telephone call from a reader. "Is JoJo Starbuck any relation to Roger Starbuck?" a woman wanted to know. It's too bad Bradshaw wasn't there to answer that question. I never met his third wife, Charla. They have two daughters and live on a 20-acre spread in Roanoke, Texas, about 15 miles from Fort Worth. Bradshaw says it was worth the wait.

My first sports editor when I made my debut as a full-time beat writer on the pro football circuit was a southern maverick named John Crittenden, who headed the staff at *The Miami News*. He once told me, "You can't write about the quarterback too often, and no one really cares about the center and guards, though they might pretend to. So they can sound like they know something about football." So I wrote a lot of stories about Bob Griese of the Dolphins, and Griese was good enough to eventually lead the Dolphins to an undefeated season and two Super Bowl championships.

But I was gone by then, to New York, where I loved interviewing Joe Namath of the Jets and Fran Tarkenton of the Giants, two of the best at their business.

I had always been attracted to quarterbacks in the first place. My earliest sports hero was John Unitas, the quarterback of the Baltimore Colts, who came from Pittsburgh, and had been rejected by Pitt and the Steelers in his youth. I loved the names of Norman Van Brocklin and Bob Waterfield and Y. A. Tittle and Chuckin' Charlie Connerly and Slingin' Sammy Baugh. In my early 20s, I spent time in a bar frequented by Bobby Layne when he was with the Steelers. One of the nicest men I've ever met was Bart Starr.

So Bradshaw had a great deal of appeal to me. I had been around the biggest of athletes, both current and past, during my nine-year stay in New York, but none of them had any more magnetism and charisma and ability than Bradshaw. He was like Muhammad Ali in so many ways. He was big, he positively beamed when he spoke, he was so animated, he had a lot of showbiz in his blood, he was controversial, he said anything that came to his mind, and — this was the real enigma — you never knew whether he really meant what he said, or whether he was just playing out a role. Bradshaw said some outrageous things. He still does.

George Gojkovich

And he goes back and forth on what he says. He still does. He can't seem to make up his mind how he truly feels about Pittsburgh, the fans, the Steelers and, most of all, Chuck Noll. He has offended a lot of Pittsburghers and former teammates with some of the things he has said, and his reluctance to return to the city where he was the star of the show once upon a time.

"What's with Terry Bradshaw?"

That's a question that has been posed to me by so many people while working on my books about the Steelers in recent seasons.

Bradshaw wasn't thrilled when the Steelers selected him as the first player picked in the 1970 draft. He had to check a map to see where Pittsburgh was located, and he heard it was a smoky city, an ugly city. Bradshaw would have been happier if he had been picked to play in Atlanta or Miami or Dallas or Houston, some place where the sun shined once in a while, and the people didn't talk so funny.

Terry Paxton Bradshaw didn't know how he was going to fit in when he got to Pittsburgh. Of his first meeting with Noll, he remembers Noll's "tight lips" and "seething eyes." It didn't do much to make him feel at home.

In his latest book, *Looking Deep,* which was written by Buddy Martin of the *Denver Post,* Bradshaw has a lot to say about Chuck Noll.

"When you look into Chuck Noll's eyes, you see nothing," wrote Bradshaw. "They appear mysterious — cold and emotionless."

He wrote of Noll's indifference when he needed someone to care, about how Noll needed to be in control. "Chuck knew what he wanted, and didn't want any dissenting views. That's probably why he brought in young coaches all the time.

"Chuck is only comfortable when he's in total control. I suspect that's why he always thinks he has to be an expert on everything he does."

Bradshaw remains critical of Noll, and perhaps understandably so, because he feels his coach didn't show him any empathy when he was hurt, especially when he was hurt just before he was forced to retire.

He praises Noll for knowing everything that was going on with the Steelers. "Noll paid attention to all aspects of the game," Bradshaw said. "He wasn't a specialist."

Bradshaw goes back and forth about Noll, and you're never sure just how he feels about his former coach.

"Chuck Noll was right in the way he handled me, because it made me a better quarterback," Bradshaw says at another point. "He knew how to bring out the best in me as a football player, although I always felt he didn't understand me as a person.

"Chuck was not the kind of person who knew how to deal with my feelings."

Then, with a big assist from Martin, I'm sure, Bradshaw points out in his book that "no coach in the NFL lost more games during the '80s than Chuck Noll." It is, however, a sobering statistic.

Talking to Pitt's Jackie Sherrill

Flanked by "Bullet Bill" Dudley and Mayor Richard Caliguiri in 1979.

But Bradshaw acknowledges that the '70s were special for the Steelers.

"Looking back now at the Steelers' accomplishments, my wish is that someday we can all enjoy them together. What the Steelers did in the mid '70s will probably never be duplicated — at least not in our lifetime.

"The Steelers of the '70s are broken up now and we never get together anymore."

But the Steelers have had reunions, and they have even teamed up again to play touch-tag football games against old rivals like the Raiders and Cowboys, and most of them were there for the funeral of Art Rooney. But Bradshaw was always missing, much to the chagrin and puzzlement of everybody.

Yet Bradshaw says in his book:

"I want to go back to Pittsburgh and walk out on the field at Three Rivers Stadium, stand next to Chuck, and tell him I'm there to support him. That may never happen, because Chuck isn't easy to approach. But that's how I feel. We all grow up."

Bradshaw wrote that, of course, before Noll retired. So the only way he is going to stand next to Noll on the field at Three Rivers Stadium is during a pre-game or halftime ceremony to honor those Super Bowl teams. He wrote something else in his roller-coaster self-examination.

"Now I regret every negative story I've ever said about my ex-coach and wish him nothing but the best."

In his book, Bradshaw made observations about many of his teammates. He was never close to Jack Lambert, but he was in awe of him from a distance.

"Lambert would ride around at night with cops," recalled Bradshaw. "One night that nearly got him killed. Lambert got into a scrape in a bar with a guy who turned out to be a member of a 'death squad' that killed for money.

"The guy hit Jack on the head with a beer mug, and his policeman friend had to pull a gun to quell the disturbance. Today, the guy is serving a life sentence for first degree murder.

"Lambert was nicknamed 'Scarecrow' because his blond hair was always sticking out from under his cap or his helmet, and he was on the thin side as far as football players went. He was the one Steeler I never understood and he remains a mystery to this day.

"Lambert was the inspirational leader of the team. I remember him hollering at Mel Blount in the clubhouse, and I thought there was going to be a riot. But they got each other going.

"I remember when Lambert came to training camp, and we had a ritual where the rookies had to sing their college fight songs. Lambert refused. He hollered back at everybody, 'Kiss my ass, I'm not singing anything!' "

On Andy Russell: "Chuck didn't like Andy because he was smarter and knew the defense better."

On John Stallworth: "The only receiver who'd come over and ask why he wasn't getting more balls thrown his way was Stallworth. He'd say, 'Am I doing something wrong?' John was the Quiet Man who was every bit as good as Swann, and in some cases better."

On Moon Mullins: "He was a mover and shaker who knew all the bars, all the barkeeps, all the women. I always hung around with people who were different from me. Moon was with me in Albuquerque when some crazed Cowboys fan pulled a gun on me. We had gone out to dinner when the guy stuck the gun in my ribs. I screamed, and several guys jumped the guy and beat him up.

"Moon was my main man. We hunted and fished together, and we double-dated a lot when we were both single. He's the one guy whose relationship I miss the most."

In summary, Bradshaw wrote, "If I saw all those guys I'd want to hug every one of them. There is a bond among us that can never be broken, regardless of any differences."

Bradshaw has done his best, however, maybe his worst, to break that bond by bad-mouthing the Steelers' organization, specifically Chuck Noll, and staying away from events such as the funeral of Art Rooney, and the dedication of a statue outside Three Rivers Stadium to honor his beloved boss.

Sometimes it appears that somebody has urged Bradshaw to be controversial for the sake of being controversial, or for the sake of better ratings for CBS Sports. Bradshaw is a big success on TV, no question about that, but he has been chipping away at any statues, real or symbolic, that might have been built in his name in Pittsburgh.

One of Bradshaw's biggest fans is Bob Rubin of *The Miami Herald*, a sports media-watcher for his newspaper and for *Inside Sports*.

One Rubin report contained this comment: "You will see and hear a lot of Bradshaw, and Bradshaw will have a lot of strong, sometimes provocative opinions . . . Bradshaw has come to be known for speaking his mind — and what comes out in that good-ol'-boy Louisiana drawl sometimes ticks people off."

When you are billed that way, you have to live up to your reputation. Rubin made reference to Bradshaw's need to be the best at whatever he does, and how he had been frustrated, as have others, in being outdone by John Madden, a former adversary when he was coaching the rival Raiders.

"In several ways, though," related Rubin, "Bradshaw's a country-style Madden. He's animated, extroverted, funny, down-to-earth, charismatic, and extremely sharp; he's able to inform, educate, and entertain in 15-second bites."

You can't get a much better review than Rubin's anywhere.

Ted Shaker, the executive producer of CBS Sports, said of Bradshaw back in 1990: "We feel there are a bunch of things Terry can bring to the studio. He has a very commanding presence, almost bigger than life. People want to hear what he has to say, and in this role he'll get to talk about the whole NFL, not just a single game."

Bradshaw blossomed in his eight years on the job at CBS. As former teammate Randy Grossman put it, "Bradshaw is still a star." Bradshaw loves the bright lights, and playing to the crowd, without being in the crowd. With his new show, he's always in control. And he insists he doesn't want to be branded a bad-mouthing troublemaker. He's no monster, and he wants no part of that role.

"If an issue arises and I have a strong opinion," he told Rubin, "I'll state my mind, but I'm not going into the studio to hammer everyone. That would be counterproductive — and I'd be gone."

So is he getting a bum rap? How come he's suddenly so controversial, so critical?

"It's just that nobody else says anything," he says, and then cackles at his own comment. He knew that would also get him in trouble with somebody.

"I let my emotions carry me. When I've become controversial (it's been because) I've had thoughts and not been afraid to say them. The worst whipping I ever got was for lying," he told another writer, Jeff Hasen.

"I enjoy it. I enjoy looking at 174 monitors and finding the game I like. I'm like a kid loose in a candy store.

"It's challenging to do some things on the set that nobody has ever done — the demonstrations (of moves like), how to drop back, how to sit in the pocket. The worst thing I do is ask questions. Asking athletes tough questions is the hardest thing in the world."

Unless you're a good sportswriter, that is.

Asked by Rubin to explain his progress after a so-so start, Bradshaw blushed and came back strong.

"I didn't take it serious, at the start," he said. "I figured I'd be in there a couple of years, get fired and move on. I'd seen Sonny (Jurgensen) and Johnny (Unitas) and figured that's the way it is. I never paid attention to how the job was supposed to be done. I just hee-hawed my way around the NFL my first year, having a grand old time.

"Anyway, I started to take the job very seriously and got hungry to be good. Real hungry. I kept wanting more. I wanted to be the best, No. 1. It became an obsession.

"As an athlete, the bottom line is being No. 1. How many rings you got? That's all people care about. So why should I settle for second when I've been trained all my life that being No. 1 is all that matters? I looked in the mirror and said, 'Man, it's never going to happen.'"

He's learned to live with being one of the best, if not the best. It's not a bad way to make a living. "It was just like Mr. Rooney used to say to me with the Steelers: 'You'll be great.' It made it easier for me."

Bradshaw was talking about the decision to switch from doing game commentary with his buddy Verne Lundquist to working in the studio with Greg Gumbel.

It must have made him happy. Richard Sandomir of the *New York Times* caught Bradshaw in the best of spirits during a visit to the studio in September of 1991.

Dr. Steele attends to Terry.

Bradshaw's patented passing grip

"Bradshaw walks into a CBS office singing and twanging the cornpone 'I Never Met A Man I Didn't Like,' from 'The Will Rogers Follies,' an apt song for a guy who had a brief career as a country crooner."

Bradshaw told him, "I'm having a blast! I love my Bradshaw Ball! I love my blackboard! I'm just having fun. Sometimes I forget I'm on television."

This calls for a timeout to explain what Bradshaw Ball is all about. Bradshaw thought some changes are in order for the NFL, and on the Oct. 13th edition of "The NFL Today" he appointed himself NFL commissioner for a day, and unveiled his proposed rule changes. He wants to encourage scoring, big plays, fan enthusiasm and make the game more fun, or the way Bradshaw believes he played it best.

He didn't say it was also an answer to John Madden's "All-NFL Team," which merits a lot of attention annually.

A select list of some serious and not-so-serious of Bradshaw's suggestions follow:

— Eliminate zone defenses.

— Allow "one foot in bounds" to qualify for a legal reception.

— Institute the two-point conversion.

— Return to the bump-and-run defense favored by the Steelers when they won their first two Super Bowls.

— Stop the clock after every play in the last two minutes.

— Make field goals inside the 20-yard line worth just one point and those kicked between the 20- and 30-yard lines count for two points.

— Award the defense one point for blocking a field goal.

— If a team is trailing by 14 points or more in the fourth quarter, the team behind gets the ball back after it scores.

— The ground can cause a fumble that puts the ball up for grabs.

— Eliminate fair catches.

— Enforce the most severe penalty in the case of offsetting penalties. If the penalty is against the defense, restore time to the clock.

— Allow the players to celebrate in the end zone after a score.

— Every player on the field is eligible to catch passes.

— The official who blows an "inadvertent" whistle has it taken away from him.

— Only one player per team can earn more than $1 million; the rest are salary capped.

— Eliminate sending in plays or signalling them to the quarterback and make coaches sit in the press box.

— Limit substitutions: players must remain on the field for at least four downs or wait until the ball changes hands.

— Change "roughing the passer" penalty to equal "roughing the kicker" penalty.

— Kickoff returners cannot down the ball in the end zone.

— Kickers don't count against the 47-man roster.

— Kickers can't wear face masks.

— No Super Bowls played anywhere the temperature gets under 75 degrees.

— Bring in college bands and cheerleaders.

— And last but not least: NO TEAM MEETINGS.

George Gojkovich

When Bradshaw was inducted into the Pro Football Hall of Fame in August of 1989, he talked about his rise and fall and rise as a pro football quarterback in Pittsburgh.

"People didn't basically say I was stupid," Bradshaw said in Canton, Ohio. "They said I was stupid, period. Or dumb. That's an insulting and haunting experience, no matter what the circumstance.

"I guess maybe my career was a different kind of success story. I was a guy on top who went to the bottom and came back again. I'm in the Hall of Fame now for one reason; I'm there because I won."

Bradshaw was inducted into the Hall of Fame along with teammate Mel Blount, a defensive back; Raiders lineman Art Shell and Green Bay defensive back Willie Wood. Bradshaw gained the honor just before his 41st birthday.

At the best moment in his life, he still dwelled on disappointments, like the time 15 years earlier when he had been benched in favor of Joe Gilliam. That came in the 1974 campaign, which would culminate with Bradshaw leading the Steelers to the first of their four Super Bowl championships.

"I had disappointments I never thought I would have," Bradshaw said. "I was a star in college. I was used to people babying me, to getting a pat on the back. All of that can give you so much confidence.

"People would say, 'I've never seen you throw like that,' and they'd say I was great and they were always behind me. I never was put in the position of having to please somebody until I got to the Steelers.

"I'd never played on a team that had another quarterback besides me. We had another good quarterback in Terry Hanratty. He was an All-American at Notre Dame, and he was from western Pennsylvania. He related well with the other players. He had polish. He was one of the guys.

"I was an outsider who didn't mingle well. There were no cowboys on the team, no one who liked to fish or do the things I liked to do. The other players looked upon me as a Bible-toting Li'l Abner."

Bradshaw signed a rookie contract for $25,000, with a $125,000 bonus, and was asked to bail a franchise out of a nearly 40-year tail spin. He had early clashes with Chuck Noll.

"He wanted me to be like Johnny Unitas," Bradshaw said of his former coach. "He wanted me to study the books, burn the midnight oil.

"People said I was dumb, and that was an insult that wouldn't die. It even followed me off the field and affected my getting endorsements, because people said they didn't want an idiot representing them.

"But it wasn't that I wasn't smart. I just didn't understand. My personality compounded things. I was a country boy, but I wasn't a country boy.

"I was just from the South (Shreveport, La., was his birthplace), but when you're from the South, and you talk with a Southern drawl, they say you're a country boy.

"I said silly and funny things and I enjoyed reporters and I enjoyed talking. When I did interviews, I gave them a story, and I said some of the countriest things."

The bottom line was not what he said, however, but what he did on the field. "If I was a great quarterback, it was not in the sense that I had great statistics," said Bradshaw. "My numbers weren't awe-inspiring. I just fit perfectly with a team.

"For four Super Bowl teams, I was the trigger guy, and that was when I played my best. It was almost like some other guy took over my body and my level of play went up several notches.

"I remember having a feeling, a personal and team feeling, of total control. Other teams feared us. We did whatever we wanted. We completed passes; we ran the football. And we weren't throwing flares or screens to the backs. We were going deep to Lynn Swann and John Stallworth, and they (opponents) knew we were going deep, and they still couldn't stop us."

Bradshaw enjoyed sharing his Hall of Fame spotlight with his wife, Charla. His family made it all worthwhile. They put the grin back on his face.

"Pro football taught me that sometimes all that matters in life is being productive," Bradshaw said. "In football, being in the Hall of Fame is the ultimate. What makes me happy is that I'm there now for absolutely the right reason — because I won."

All-star lineup: Franco Harris, Lynn Swann, Terry Bradshaw

235

Terry Hanratty

"Each day is a wonderful occasion."

"He must also compliment himself on his fantastic comeback. He's just never satisfied with himself. He's very quick to criticize himself."

—Ara Parseghian (in 1968)
Notre Dame Football Coach

St. Patrick's Day was a week away, and Terry Hanratty thought aloud about what was coming. Hanratty looked out the window of his apartment in Manhattan, and focused his dark eyes below on the fabled Fifth Avenue, a street that's been heralded in song.

"The St. Patrick's Day Parade will go right past here," he said. "If there is a St. Patrick's Day Parade, that is. They're thinking about cancelling it. The gays want to march in the parade, and the Hibernians say, 'No way.' It's gone to court. If they rule to let the gays march, the Hibernians are going to cancel the parade."

"Maybe it would be OK if the gays were Irish," I suggested. "Are they?"

"Are they?" repeated Hanratty. "They are, indeed. Oh, they're Irish, all right, Irish brogues and all. You should see them on TV."

"What do you do these days on St. Patrick's Day?" I asked, knowing that Hanratty had been on the wagon for a half-dozen years after a stay at an upstate rehabilitation center.

"I'm going to hide," Hanratty said. "I did enough of that at Notre Dame."

As it turned out, the gays were not permitted to march in the parade, and Hanratty stayed out of sight, as well.

Hanratty was a hero at Notre Dame, back in the mid-'60s, an All-American quarterback who set school passing records. Notre Dame had its share of great quarterbacks in its history. The long list that preceded Hanratty included George Gipp, Angelo Bertelli, Johnny Lujack, Frank Tripucka, Ralph Guglielmi, Paul Hornung, George Izo, Daryle Lamonica and John Huarte. But none put up the numbers that could hold off Hanratty in his heyday at South Bend, Indiana.

Hanratty had a sense of humor. He was glib. He was a practical joker. He was the life of every party. He enjoyed a drink more than most of his teammates. He was Irish. And nobody had a better time on St. Patrick's Day. Nobody felt like he had to have a better time on St. Patrick's Day. It was a role Hanratty had down pat. Like most of the plays in Ara Parseghian's playbook.

None of his heroics at Notre Dame, or during his spotty pro career back home in western Pennsylvania with the Pittsburgh Steelers (1969-1975), and none of his comebacks on the playing field, can match what Hanratty has done in recent years. He has saved his life, and resurrected a proud spirit. He is a new man. He is a recovering alcoholic.

236

"I've been sober for six-and-a-half years," he said. "No alcohol. Nothing. Zero. I've never felt better in my life. Each day is wonderful, and I'm taking them one day at a time. Each day is a wonderful occasion. Life is good."

Hanratty's heart-rending stories of his anguish as an alcoholic prompted me to think back to the first time I ever talked to him. It was during the summer of 1978, before his senior season at Notre Dame. It took place, of all places, at the bar of an Italian restaurant named Natili's in his hometown of Butler.

Terry had just turned 21 and I was 26. I was interviewing him for a story in *Sport* magazine. We were both drinking a beer, and Terry was smoking a cigarette. While we were talking, Ed Vargo, a National League umpire who also lived in Butler, came through the front door.

As soon as Hanratty spotted Vargo, he pushed an ashtray containing his cigarette over in front of me. "I don't want him to see me smoking," said Hanratty. "It would be bad for my image."

"How about my image?" I protested in jest.

Hanratty's hometown of Butler spawned three other pro football players, the Saul Brothers. Older brother Ron played at Penn State, and twins Rich and Ron at Michigan State, and all went on to play in the NFL. Their dad was a coal miner.

The memory of that night suddenly took on new meaning when I heard about Hanratty's drinking problem.

We also played pool that night. Hanratty, the hustler, was having a good time. My story in *Sport* started off with a sequence from that scene in Butler:

On the break, the balls skittered about the pool table, none of them dropping into a pocket. Now it was Terry Hanratty's turn and he moved in quickly for the kill. The young man who quarterbacks the Notre Dame football team had spotted the No. 13 ball hovering on the rim of the corner pocket at the far end of the table, and he had eyes for no other ball. Without even bothering to chalk his cue, he bridged his big left hand on the table and ran his cue stick back and forth in his outstretched fingers.

"There you go, Hanratty!" I hollered, as Terry drew back his stick once more. "There you go — right for the primary receiver without even looking over the rest of the field."

We were playing "eight ball," and Hanratty had his choice of hitting any ball on the table, but instead of setting himself up for good position on the next shot, he was determined to take the easy one first.

"When your primary receiver is open," Hanratty said softly, in an undertone, "you hit him!"

With that, Hanratty stroked his shot. It glanced off to the right of the No. 13 ball and nicked the No. 7 ball. "And sometimes," said Hanratty, surveying his errant shot, "you have interceptions."

Hanratty had learned to be philosophical about interceptions. The year before, 1967, his junior season, he had 15 on the football field, all

237

in the first five games. Notre Dame lost two of them, to Purdue and Southern Cal, for the only two losses in Hanratty's career at Notre Dame. As a sophomore in 1966, Hanratty had led the Irish to an undefeated season, marred only by that famous 10-10 tie with Michigan State. He and his favorite receiver, Jim Seymour, had been pictured on the cover of *Time* magazine.

Heady stuff.

Even so, Hanratty wasn't satisfied. He wanted perfection. Parseghian thought Terry was too tough on himself. "He must also compliment himself on his fantastic comeback," said the Notre Dame coach. "But I guess he's just never satisfied with himself. Maybe that's good. He's very quick to criticize himself."

Following his senior season, Hanratty was the Steelers' No. 2 pick in the 1969 draft, right behind Joe Greene of North Texas State — the first pick in the overall draft, the first pick for Chuck Noll, the new head coach of the Steelers.

Hanratty was popular in Pittsburgh, a handsome local kid with Notre Dame after his name, and most fans rooted for him over Terry Bradshaw, the first pick the next season out of Louisiana Tech, and Joe Gilliam, a gifted thrower from Tennessee State who showed up in 1972.

This was when Noll was building the ballclub that would dominate the '70s in the National Football League, but it was a difficult time for the franchise — "We had a pretty bad team back then," said Hanratty in all honesty — and everybody associated with it, and it's left scars that are still sore.

Hanratty had hoped to make it big in the pros, especially in Pittsburgh, near his hometown. Hanratty was hungry. Back in Butler that night before his final season at Notre Dame, he had told me, "I'd like to get some money. I want to have the things I've never had. I'd like to see how the other half lives."

It never happened the way Hanratty had envisioned.

Hanratty had his heroes. When he was in high school in Butler, Hanratty worshipped Roger Staubach, Navy's All-American quarterback. He also looked up to Johnny Unitas of the Baltimore Colts.

He had good reasons for choosing Unitas as a model of perfection. "First off, he's from this area," said Hanratty, "and he had it rough as a youngster." Right there, Hanratty could empathize. Unitas' father died when he was five, and he was raised by his mother. Terry's parents separated when he was in high school.

Hanratty had a chance to meet Unitas during his junior season at Notre Dame. "He's a real down-to-earth guy," said Hanratty. "We really had a nice conversation. But you know, he's a lot smaller than I expected."

Unitas had been my boyhood hero as well — I wore No. 19 for a sandlot team called the Hazelwood Steelers — and mimicked his movements. As an adult sportswriter, however, I had found him a difficult, and not particularly enjoyable, interview. Sometimes our heroes come up short of our expectations.

"My father was an alcoholic," said Hanratty, sitting in his Manhattan apartment in March, 1992. "I have a brother and a sister, and they might have a drink once a year, for some special occasion. That's it." Affecting an Irish accent, he added, "I was the one blessed with the Irish curse, me boy."

After Hanratty hit rock bottom in 1985 — he dreaded going to work each day as a stock broker — he sought help at a rehabilitation center called Arms Acres in Carmel, New York, about an hour-and-a-half drive upstate from New York City.

I had worked in New York myself from 1970 to 1979, and it was a glorious time to be a sportswriter in New York. So many championship teams in so many sports. There was an electricity to the city. I loved the place, I loved the pace.

It was the only place where you could see, as I once did on a St. Patrick's Day, Presidential candidate Jimmy Carter campaigning on one side of town, and tennis star Billie Jean King campaigning for equal pay for women's tennis players on the other side of town. East Side, West Side, all around the town. Within the same hour. Or you could run into Joe Louis and Joe E. Lewis on the same street, as I once did, or Dustin Hoffman and Woody Allen.

I remember getting seats in the mayor's grandstand for an aunt and uncle of mine for a St. Patrick's Day parade, and being proud to show them the sights. "We really got I.V.P. treatment," my aunt told everyone upon returning to Pittsburgh. It was fun to be in New York back then. Especially if you were an I.V.P.

Nowadays, I find New York too demanding, too difficult, too dirty, always challenging, and I have no desire to return to live there. I have good friends there, I like to visit, but I believe it's changed and the quality of life has deteriorated somewhat since I lived there. Maybe it was the difference between going there at 29 and going there at 49.

Hanratty is still on a high, however, for the madness of Manhattan, only in a different sense than when he was often in a stupor at night, after too many drinks, or in the morning, after too few hours in bed.

I asked him if he finds it difficult to avoid drinking. I stopped drinking any alcoholic drinks for six-and-a-half years after I had done an extensive series of articles on Sudden Sam McDowell, the former American League all-star pitcher, and a recovering alcoholic. He openly revealed all the problems he had encountered as an athlete who was an alcoholic. I had been a classmate of McDowell for two years at Central Catholic High School in the late '50s, and his story threw a scare into me. I was covering the New York Yankees when he pitched for them late in his career, when Bill Virdon, his manager, had to send someone out to the outfield during the pre-game activity to get Sam before he got killed by a fly ball. He was in a fog from drinking. McDowell finished his career with the Pirates, and was dropped by GM Joe Brown after Sam broke a contract agreement regarding his drinking.

"I feel sorry for guys like Steve Howe in baseball, and now Pasquel Perez," said Hanratty. "Guys I work with wonder how Perez could blow a million dollars in salary by fooling around with drugs. They don't understand that the addiction becomes the most important thing in your life. When you've got an addictive personality, everything else is secondary."

When I stopped drinking any alcoholic beverages, I found friends would make remarks, or be uncomfortable in my company, if I ordered a Perrier with a slice of lime, or a Diet Coke. It still happens. Some will buy you a beer, even after you say you don't want one. "I don't trust anybody who doesn't drink?" so many of them will say. Or, "I'd hate to think when I get up in the morning that that's as good as I was going to feel the rest of the day."

Hanratty has heard all of those lines. "I've heard all of the great lines," he said.

"Most people respect what I did. People who object should take a hard look at their own life. Some of my old drinking buddies just don't call me anymore.

"Since I went into rehabilitation, I'll bump into friends I used to drink with. Everything is very cordial. 'We'll get together,' they'll say. But, boom, they're off and never the phone should ring. Some people are uneasy around people who don't drink.

"I had to stop. I think it definitely saved my life."

When Hanratty was playing for the Steelers, his nickname was "Rat." Just before he went to the rehabilitation facility in Carmel, he was weighing 163 pounds, down from his playing weight of 190. He had bad color in his complexion. He looked like "Ratso" Rizzo in the movie "Midnight Cowboy." A down-and-out bum. "I looked like hell," Hanratty conceded.

"You're in an environment where there's a lot of pressure on the job, and a lot of entertaining and parties and drinking is a big, major problem. I was sprung loose in that Wall Street atmosphere. Lots of parties, lots of drinking. Over the years, it caught up with me. I either went into rehabilitation, or lose everything."

I asked him if he had lost anything, as he saw it, because of his drinking habit. I knew he had been divorced about ten or eleven years earlier, after ten years of marriage. Had drinking been a contributing factor to the split-up? "No, I wouldn't say that," he responded. "But that's something we're instructed never to do. You can't look back. You can't change anything. You have to deal with today."

He has three daughters. Kelly, 21, was in her senior year at Notre Dame. Becky, 19, was in her junior year at Notre Dame, and her twin, J.J., 19, was a junior at Indiana. "It was natural for Kelly to go to Notre Dame; she always liked the school," he said. "Becky went to Georgetown originally, but wasn't happy there, and transferred to Notre Dame."

Hanratty had more to say about alcoholism. "I think for every alcoholic there's a bottom," he said. "For some, it's death. Everybody's bottom is different. Once you get to that point, you have to do something. A lot of people stop drinking for different reasons. I had to stop.

"Looking back, it was scary. My whole body was just tired. I was sick and tired of being sick and tired. Each day it was so difficult to

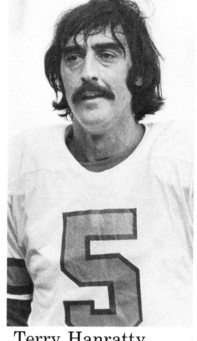

Terry Hanratty

With Terry Bradshaw and quarterback coach Vito "Babe" Parilli in 1971

get up. Each day you're eating lunch at your trading desk, and you never get away from your work. And you have no place to hide. You're going to be miserable all day.

"My body felt saturated. If someone put a band around me I thought pure scotch would pour out of me."

"Dewars was my drink when I was traveling with sports teams," I said. "Dewars and soda. Or just a beer."

"J&B was mine," Hanratty said. "J&B on the rocks."

To hear him talk, Terry Hanratty was on the rocks. "Terry Hanratty had to get help," he said. "I had a couple of friends who had gone to rehabilitation. People I talked to started to point me in the right direction. The people on Wall Street couldn't have been nicer. You hear about so much greed. But my associates, my customers, they were so helpful. The company I was working for at the time couldn't have been better. They just wanted me to get well.

"I go to some social activities now. There's so much entertaining going on. It just gets boring a lot quicker. I just don't stay as long. The same people are going to say the same thing after I'm gone, so I'm not going to miss anything."

"Did you need to be in a crowd? Did you need an audience, the attention? Was that intoxicating?" I asked.

"I never clamored for that," said Hanratty. "I never felt like I needed that."

The so-called luck of the Irish is a myth or blarney, most would insist, but you have to wonder when you consider what happened to Hanratty just over a year earlier. He shared his story of good fortune when he joined his former Notre Dame teammates for the 25th anniversary celebration of the 1966 team. I had read an article about it by Dave Anderson of *The New York Times*, and I asked Hanratty to recount it for me.

"I was leaving my apartment one evening," he recalled. "It was in January, a year ago (1990). I was returning a video to a store nearby. And I found this wallet on the ground in front of my apartment building. There were lots of credit cards in it, and a Massachusetts driver's license. It belonged to a Kelly Donohue. I called information, but there was nobody at the address that was on the license; she had moved. So I called American Express. The next day I got a call from Kelly in Boston, and she arranged for me to drop off the wallet to a girl friend of hers. I did that. She sent me a thank you note. She's a CPA in Boston. I got in touch and told her I went up to Boston on business a lot. She suggested we get together for dinner. She is Irish-Irish. Her mother and father are both Irish. Next Tuesday (St. Patrick's Day) should be a good one for their family. We hit it off, and we've both been on that shuttle from New York to Boston and Boston to New York a lot this past year. We're getting married on June 20. If I had still been drinking, I would have fallen over her wallet that night, and never seen it."

242

Hanratty, at 44, is an institutional broker at Sanford Bernstein in the General Motors Building at 59th and Fifth Avenue in midtown Manhattan. His clients include Mellon Bank, PNC and Federated Investors, to name a few, and this enables him to get back to Pittsburgh on business trips about every two months.

"We do block trading. Our average order is about 25,000 shares, where the average broker might be dealing with 500 shares," he said. "We're working with a lot of pension funds. We're the semi-sane people who tell the people on the floor what to do.

"We're on the 22nd floor, and there are about 15 of us. Most brokers are in midtown, hooked up to Wall Street, which is a relatively small area real estate-wise. We're very well known within the industry, if not on a national basis the way Merrill Lynch is. It's a beauty and the beast existence. No day is the same. It's a very competitive environment. There are a lot of guys on Wall Street who played football. You have to have high energy, and make quick decisions. I find it invigorating."

Chuck Noll is another subject near and dear to Hanratty's heart. "I disagree with those who think the game has passed him by," said Hanratty. "It's really a simple game. Some things change, and there's a herd mentality. You watch different games, and you see people all doing the same things.

"They make too much of the game these days. They spend too much time analyzing it, making it into *War and Peace*. Chuck coached nearly every aspect of our team. The Steelers won four Super Bowls, and none of his assistants were ever asked to be head coaches elsewhere in the NFL. That's unreal. Bud Carson became a head coach after being with some other teams. And the other guys who became head coaches in the USFL don't count because that was a minor league. But it points up how important Noll was in the Steelers' scheme of things."

I told Hanratty I heard he was the smartest quarterback of the bunch during his days with the Steelers, but that he just did not have the athletic ability of Bradshaw and Gilliam.

"To this day," Hanratty said, "I'll go to the chalkboard with anybody. Noll or Shula or anybody. I'm totally amazed by what some of these announcers tell people on the TV and radio games. I'm amazed at what Bradshaw tells people. I hear people talking about what he said on Monday, and I say, Hey, it's the exact opposite of what happened.

"A quarterback can take control of a game in a lot of ways. It doesn't always show up in the stats. One of the greatest games I played with the Steelers was against the Philadelphia Eagles (on Dec. 20, 1970) when Frenchy Fuqua rushed for 208 yards (still a club record). I called audibles at the line of scrimmage all day, and nothing showed up for me on the stat sheet. Yet it was one of my most satisfying games.

"Today, they're breeding quarterbacks who can't read defenses because they don't have to. An assistant coach does it for them upstairs in the press box. They're breeding quarterbacks who don't watch film.

You don't study films with the same intensity when you know on Sunday that somebody is going to send in the plays.

"Another thing I hate is special situation substitution. Why would a quarterback allow it to happen? We had such an intricate game system, but you didn't have to call plays in the huddle. Sometimes you didn't know what to do until you saw their set-up when you came up to the line. So you'd say, 'Check with me on two,' and line up. You still had 20 or more seconds to call a play. That's all you need.

"The offensive team should be offensive. You should set the tempo. So many offensive teams wait for the defense to put in six defensive backs and then they still throw a pass. I couldn't permit this mass substitution. Plus, I don't like it from a defensive standpoint, either. I want my best players in there, and I want them in the flow of the game."

I asked Hanratty if he could understand the ongoing criticism by Bradshaw of Noll, the Steelers' organization, and the fans of Pittsburgh.

"No," said Hanratty. "It's one of the most ridiculous things I ever heard in my life. Terry was Chuck's boy from the get-go. If anybody had a bitch, it was me. I figured if they wanted to go with Bradshaw or Gilliam, then fine, but why keep me around? Trade me.

"After my second or third year, I wish Chuck had come to me and said, 'Listen, Terry, we're going to give you a shot to play elsewhere.' My No. 1 dream was to stay and play in Pittsburgh, but if that wasn't going to happen I would have preferred going elsewhere. There were teams that were interested in me. I could have been a starter in the right situation.

"In your first four years, if you're not playing all the time your timing gets fouled up. You get stale. The game you've been excited about since you were a kid doesn't hold the same interest for you anymore.

"Chuck spent hours and hours with Bradshaw, some for football, and some for his personal life. He was in there with Chuck all the time in his first marriage, and in his second marriage. He was always talking with Chuck about his personal life, seeking advice and understanding. He was always in his office. I was there, and I know.

"I retired at 29. I had really lost my enthusiasm for the game. I had been playing since I was nine. I had been hurt so much. Back in those days, we weren't making the kind of money where it was tough to go out and get a job. You could step into another line of work and get back on the same financial level pretty soon. I figured I had to get on with my life.

"I have no bitterness toward Noll or the Pittsburgh Steelers. That's why I don't understand Terry badmouthing Noll or bad-mouthing Pittsburgh. Terry has dug a lot of holes for himself back there. He has in his contract that he won't ever have to go to Pittsburgh. That's so stupid.

"I side totally with Noll. I was in those meetings. I saw how he was treated."

"What's your personal appraisal of Noll?" I asked.

"He has a wonderful football mind," said Hanratty. "Chuck ran the whole show. He did it his way. He wasn't out there in front of the public, either, and I admired that. He stepped back and gave the players all the credit. He never went on a speaking tour, and he could have commanded so much money after winning four Super Bowls. He was never doing commercials. He would have been an ideal representative, someone with integrity and credibility, like Tom Landry, for a lot of major corporations. He was a strong, good-looking guy with a solid reputation. He saw no need for that. He turned down radio and TV shows in Pittsburgh as well.

"I was very fortunate in my football career. I had the best possible coach at every level, with Art Bernardi at Butler High, Ara Parseghian at Notre Dame, and Chuck Noll with the Pittsburgh Steelers.

"I am always in awe of the lack of coaching on some teams. There are not that many good coaches out there."

"If Noll was such an outstanding coach, how come the Steelers have been unable to win for such a long time?" I asked Hanratty.

"Talent, that's why. It's a basic ingredient for good teams. When you see the talent that was there in the '70s you can appreciate that there's no comparison with the Steelers of today. Chuck molded that talent. There were some strange personalities on that team, and he turned out winners. Your No. 1 and No. 2 choices have to be impact players every year, and you've got to get lucky on the late rounds once in a while."

Hanratty said he was looking forward to coming back to Pittsburgh on August 8 for a game between the alumni of the Cleveland Browns and the Steelers before a pre-season contest at Three Rivers Stadium. "I love those oldtimers' games," he said. "I shouldn't say oldtimers' games. That sounds so old. It's for players 30 and over."

Hanratty said not to tell anyone, but he had borrowed a football from Tony Parisi, the Steelers' equipment man, so he could practice throwing the ball with his buddies at Central Park. One of Hanratty's former teammates, Ray Mansfield, told me Hanratty was throwing the ball better in the last oldtimers' game than he did when he was playing for the Steelers.

"He looked great and he was really zinging the ball," said Mansfield, the player on the Steelers Hanratty admired the most ("I don't know of a player who had more heart than Mansfield. He could suck it up better than anybody.").

"This season is the 60th anniversary season for the Steelers, and I want to look good," said Hanratty. "Some of those guys will be telling me before the game that they haven't handled a football in years. And I'll piss them off when they see me throwing the ball. I'm working out every night. I've got to start zinging the ball. I'm getting a little bit of the ol' zip back." That game, by the way, never came off.

He walks 17 blocks on Fifth Avenue from his office to his apartment each day. He lives on the same street where he works. "How'd you feel on that walk tonight?" I asked.

"Wonderful," he said. "I feel 25. I have a quick step. I feel a little bounce in my feet. I have a clear mind. As good as I feel coming home, I feel even better when I'm walking to work in the morning.

"That's the big thing. I used to dread mornings. Now it's wonderful to be up and about. People in the office say, 'How come you're always so happy?' I say, 'Hey, a lot of people didn't get up this morning.' I should be happy about that."

George Gojkovich

Terry Hanratty — Butler's Pride and Joy

Loren Toews

A linebacker from Cal-Berkeley

"The rings mean more to me now."

L oren Toews was thought to be something of an intellectual when he played for the Pittsburgh Steelers. Toews (pronounced Taves) was just different, sort of a high brow who got lost on his way to the library and ended up in the locker room.

At least that's what I thought, but then again I never talked to Toews much when I was on the Steelers' beat. He suffered sportswriters begrudgingly when they happened to stray his way, and wanted insights into the Steelers' latest battle, and he seemed to have a superior attitude.

"That was the line on me," agreed Toews, "and I did little to alter it."

He roomed with Randy Grossman for nine years and often played chess with him on road trips, whereas most of the guys played poker.

He played, for the most part, in the shadows of stars like Jack Ham, Andy Russell, Jack Lambert and Robin Cole and had to wait until the latter part of his 11 seasons (1973-1983) with the Steelers to become a full-time starter, but he was also one of the reasons the team won four Super Bowls. Few NFL teams had players of the caliber of Toews waiting in the wings. He was 6-3, 222, and there was little or no dropoff when he came into a game. He was often sent in on passing downs.

Toews was a thinking man's ballplayer.

He graduated from Cal-Berkeley, the nation's preeminent public university, with a degree in biological sciences. This set him apart from the pack, for starters, because most of the Steelers were phys ed students in college, or majored in marketing, hotel management, business or communications.

He was a National Football Foundation Scholar-Athlete Award winner, and was feted along with the nation's other elite athletes with high q.p.a.'s at the sponsoring group's annual dinner at New York's Waldorf-Astoria, which is attended by all living Heisman Trophy winners and collegiate and corporate leaders.

Toews also lettered for three years at California in rugby, a head-knocking, free-spirited sport he enjoyed even more than football. Toews didn't bring the same passion to football as say Lambert, but he thought it was a great way to make a living, a means to an end career-wise, and was more like Ham and Russell in his cerebral approach to athletics.

This man had a soul, however. He was active in the Fellowship of Christian Athletes, and lent his efforts to many civic activities endorsed by the Steelers in their many outreach programs. He often joined Jon Kolb in advocating Christian values and an appropriate lifestyle to young people as well as teammates.

While playing for the Steelers, Toews attended the Graduate School of Business at the University of Pittsburgh, and picked up an MBA

Loren Toews

degree in 1981. In that respect, he followed the lead of Russell, who has an MBA from Missouri.

Asked who encouraged or motivated him to pursue an MBA, Toews told us over the telephone from his home in Los Altos, California, "No one in particular. Fear was the motivation there."

Toews worked at Equibank in the off-season in 1983.

Today he is a commercial real estate broker for Cornish & Carey Commercial Real Estate. He is involved with the leasing and sale of corporate real estate facilities.

"It's a tough market right now," he said in January of 1992. "You have to believe that things will get better."

When Toews was playing for the Steelers, he lived in McMurray, a suburb about 15 miles south of Three Rivers Stadium. He and his wife, Valerie, had been married 17 years when we talked. They have three children, Aaron Josef, 16; Jocelyn Marie, 13; Cassie, 9.

I mentioned to him that I was surprised by how many marriages among the Steelers had ended in divorce. "To me, marriage is a life-long commitment," said Toews. "It's one I intend to keep."

When Toews returned a questionnaire I had sent him, he offered some interesting insights into himself and his days with the Steelers.

His personal highlight was the first Super Bowl win. "I played half the game," wrote Toews, "which was, by far, more than I had played in any game in my previous two years with the team."

His most cherished memory: "Our field manager, Jack Hart, cold-cocking Art Rooney Jr. after a game. Art tried to get into the locker room, and Chuck Noll had told Jack not to let anyone in — and he didn't!"

The player he admired the most on the team was Jack Ham: "He combined flawless execution of his trade with humility and graciousness. He imparted inspiration by performance."

What he learned from his experience with the Steelers that serves him in good stead today: "The pressure to perform well on a consistent basis was so intense that everything I've had to do since then has seemed like a piece of cake."

That's Toews for you. Few Steelers would have expressed themselves quite like that.

Toews had turned 40 just a few months before we spoke at the outset of 1992. He was eager to talk about his experiences with the Steelers. It seemed to mean more to him now than it did when he was too busy doing what he did to reflect on it.

"It was more than a job," said Toews. "It was something I did well. I enjoyed playing football. Sports were never a passion with me. I had fun doing it. I never expected to play pro football. I didn't set my sights that high. When the opportunity presented itself to play for pay, and the kind of money we were making, it was a no-brainer to continue to play.

"I probably enjoyed playing rugby more. In football, you're pretty compartmentalized — even more so today than when we were playing — whereas in rugby you get to do a little of everything. You can run with the ball, score touchdowns and tackle people."

I mentioned that his alma mater, California, had a good football season in 1991. "I was tickled to see them do so well, and finish high in the rankings. Cal plays like a pro team. They had poor teams when I was there.

"It's a real good experience to go back to the campus now. You know so much more now. I see these kids who are on the team, and it struck me hard about how they are. They're no more adults than I was at the same time in my life. Playing at Cal was a great experience.

"That's something I've grown to appreciate with time. My Super Bowl rings mean so much more to me today than they did when I got them. I can probably count on my hand the number of times I wore any of my Super Bowl rings when I was playing. You know, they're really not great jewelry. The onyx is cracked on one of my rings. Others have come apart. Even so, they mean more to me now."

I asked Toews what else meant something to him from his days with the Steelers.

"Being associated with, and being a part of a great team," he replied. "Having that opportunity means more to me with each passing year. We had something special. I can remember when Gordon Gravelle got traded to the Giants. He came back later and told me there was a big difference between the two organizations, and how well he thought he was treated by the Steelers."

Toews, like many of the ballplayers from his era, suspected some things had changed in the Steelers' organization in recent years. "I have heard things," said Toews, "about certain guys on the staff having more control than when I was there.

"I can't believe some of the behavior I read about on the part of some of the players. The Chuck Noll I knew back then wouldn't have put up with that crap. Certain things wouldn't have been tolerated."

Toews thought the Steelers had so many talented players when he was on the team, and that people like himself —not quite so athletically gifted — benefitted from the company they were keeping.

"You can't help but learn," said Toews. "I appreciated the talent of the people around me. I had a lot of time to observe. I played more when guys got hurt. They were just starting to replace linebackers with defensive backs on passing downs when I got out. I wasn't one of the guys who made the team great, but I believe I made the best contribution I could."

He played mostly on special teams his first four seasons and excelled there in latter years when he was also spelling other linebackers, or starting when the Steelers went with a four linebacker scheme. He could play every linebacker position. He was awarded a game ball for his standout performance on special teams in the AFC Championship game with the Houston Oilers in 1979, which led to the Steelers' fourth Super Bowl triumph. He got heavier, stronger and more aggressive later in his career.

In 1977, he started all 14 games as a replacement for Andy Russell, who retired after the previous season. He started ten games in 1978, and in the strike-shortened season of 1982 he started in all nine games. He and J.T. Thomas were the only two of the 1973 draft class to earn roster spots. He has a brother, Jeff, who was a lineman for the Miami Dolphins.

"The difference between our team and the other teams was that we had great players at the skilled positions, like Terry Bradshaw, and Lynn Swann and John Stallworth," Toews told us. "Chuck Noll had great confidence in our receivers. I remember him telling Bradshaw 'if no one's open, throw the ball up there and Lynn and John will get it.' And they did. They were hardly ever intercepted when they went up for a ball. I don't know if they perceived the same kind of confidence, but it was there.

"Our team capitalized on opportunities, and that's a lesson for life. Looking back, now I know how fortunate we were. We went to the Super Bowl four times and we won four times. You look at a team like Denver that got there three times and came up empty, or the Minnesota Vikings who got there four times and came away with nothing.

"To me, Terry Bradshaw was the best example of a guy who seized the opportunity. He may not have been the best quarterback of his time, but I can't remember a playoff game where he wasn't great. He always came through. The one major difference in our team was Terry in the playoffs. I don't know if he necessarily was the most important player on our team in the regular season, but he certainly was in championship contests.

"That's why it really bugs me . . . some of the things that Terry and some of the others have said in their books, or in public, complaining about this or that in regard to their days with the Steelers.

"You never really knew where you stood with Terry. When he chose Verne Lunquist to present him at the Pro Football Hall of Fame I couldn't believe it. C'mon, give me a break. I don't see why he couldn't have picked someone from the Steelers, even if it wasn't Chuck. I hate to see that.

"Once when Chuck was getting knocked by some of the former players, and they were saying the Steelers won despite Chuck, I dropped Chuck a line. I wrote to him and let him know I disagreed with that opinion. He wrote to me and said thanks. He said he appreciated my letter.

"To me, he represented a standard, a degree of excellence. Chuck represented what the Steelers were all about. What mattered most to Chuck was what you did on the field. He didn't worry about things that didn't matter.

"When it came to picking his team, he didn't care what round you were drafted on. A good example was Dave Brown, a defensive back from Michigan they drafted on the first round in 1975. Chuck traded him, and he played a long time in Seattle, but he felt he had better defensive backs.

"He was a bottom line kind of coach. I still send him a Christmas card. I can't remember when I was playing anyone having a gripe with Chuck.

"To me, the memory of my days with the Steelers is really dear to me."

In sharing other impressions of the people he played with, Toews pointed to Jon Kolb as the one who had the greatest personal impact on him. To hear Toews talking, the difficult personal experiences Kolb has encountered over the past 20 years have left him even stronger than all the weights he was notorious for lifting.

"His house burnt down, the problems his sister had, taking care of her children as well as his own, and never complaining. He always seems to have time to help other people with problems. Just like he is now with Sam."

Toews was referring to Sam Davis, a former Steelers' teammate, who had been hospitalized for several months with severe injuries and impairments, including loss of memory, from an alleged fall he had taken in his home. Kolb had been visiting him regularly, and assisting him in his comeback.

"He's raised some money for Sam's benefit," continued Toews. "But he's helped even more so just by being a friend and being what a friend is all about.

"He was a real inspiration to me," said Toews. "Jon doesn't like to talk about himself; sometimes you have to drag it out of him. Jon has done some wonderful things in the time I have known him.

"He has a strong faith. It's a faith that shows in his daily behavior. He has a genuine concern and help for others. With Jon, he lives his faith."

Toews misses many of his teammates, but he likes being back in his home area, taking on new challenges in life.

"The toughest thing for players going from high school to college, and from college to the pros, is that you have to elevate your game. You have to be a fast learner. It's the same thing when you're out of football. You have to readjust. You have to reprogram yourself to do something else.

"In the four playoffs in which we won Super Bowls, we raised the level of our game each time. The business world is a difficult one, and you have to do the same thing.

"I'm in my life's work now. I have no complaints. Business is real tough. The lending institutions have made it tough to borrow money. Confidence is low. It's tough to move property. But it will get better. We'll be all right."

Jon Kolb
Cutting loose from football

"If the Super Bowls were the greatest thing in my life,
then that means I died when I was 34."
—Jon Kolb, at 44

"Hence I remind you to rekindle the gift of God that is
within you through the laying on of my hands;
for God did not give us a spirit of timidity
but a spirit of power and love
and self-control."
—Timothy, 2:6-7, New Testament

Jon Kolb kept tugging at his tie, and lowering the knot. He looked like a man with a noose around his size 17 1/2-inch neck who was afraid he would be strangled. Kolb wore a light blue button-down collar shirt, with a dark blue tie, and dark blue slacks. The top button on the shirt was open. "I'm just not comfortable with this yet," he said. "Some of my friends have been surprised to discover that I own a coat and tie. I don't know how to take that."

Kolb has never been sure how to take a lot of comments. He is a somewhat shy, sensitive, insecure type, too thoughtful for his own good sometimes, so he often reads too much into everything that goes on around him. But he has to break out of his old shell, and shed some of his working habits in his new challenge. At 44, he was out of the football world for the first time since he turned ten.

He was searching his Bible to find something to assuage his fears and sense of disenfranchisement.

After 23 years with the Pittsburgh Steelers, 13 as an offensive lineman, and 10 more as an assistant coach and strength and conditioning guru, Kolb was working in a different field.

He was completing his second month at his new desk, as a rehabilitation services manager for Nortim Corporation. Nortim (short for Northern Timberlands) is a contract management company providing risk management service for timber harvesting operations in Pennsylvania and other states.

Kolb was to analyze rehabilitation centers being used by Nortim throughout the state and coordinate and monitor treatment protocol. In short, he was to implement some of the conditioning and rehabilitation methods used by the Steelers through the years with loggers in a wellness program, and try to cut medical and time-loss costs for Nortim's customers.

It was the day after Easter, and Kolb looked like he had just come away from an Easter Parade. He looked, in the words of Art Rooney, like a real dude. His clothes emphasized his anvil-like build. He is broad-shouldered and trim-waisted. "My wife, Debbie, tells me she's pleased that I'm wearing white dress shirts to work now," he said with a smile.

As Kolb talked about his new task, I couldn't help but notice that he had a nice view from the window alongside his work station. It formed a beautiful backdrop. With the Steelers, not even the Rooneys or Chuck Noll had a nice view or a window where they worked. Kolb had the blinds rolled up, so he had the most open view possible.

"It's great; it's one of the real perks of this job," said Kolb. "When I'm talking to my wife, I can tell her, 'Hey, it's raining out.' All those years I was with the Steelers, I never knew what it was doing outside."

Kolb's comment reminded me of something Art Rooney Jr. had said about the welcomed change in his suburban offices at the eastern end of Upper St. Clair.

Kolb can see plenty of trees from his window in a relatively new and very attractive office complex called Summerfield Commons at the western end of Upper St. Clair. When Kolb is out of the office, which is often, he will be seeing plenty of trees, too, as he tours logging sites to see how the men are working, and where he might be able to help them in being physically more able to perform their tasks.

Kolb could hear a woodpecker outside his window, and he said he had spotted a bluejay a few days earlier. "I might have to call Chuck Noll and find out what the best birdfeed is and put out some feeding stations," said Kolb. For a fellow who grew up on a farm in Ponca City, Oklahoma, and had a farm of his own in Washington County when he was playing ball for the Steelers, this is important. It also points up his respect for the Renaissance man who was his boss.

A window, a view of the nearby woods, passing traffic, the sights and sounds of birds and squirrels, beautiful artwork and area rugs, a computer . . . Kolb was surrounded by all sorts of new things in what has to be a more pleasant working environment than he had been accustomed to for more than two decades. On the wall in front of his desk was a map of Pennsylvania with red and blue pins all over it, denoting the location of rehab centers and logging sites under the Nortim umbrella.

There were no plays diagrammed on any of the surrounding walls, and there was no playbook to work from. In fact, one of Kolb's assignments was to develop a playbook, so to speak, of how Nortim could best approach this new fitness program.

"Jon Kolb will be asked to apply the principles of sports medicine and strength-and-rehabilitation conditioning activities to the cutting edge of Pennsylvania's important forest products industry," said Patrick Fleming, president of Nortim. "Jon's role will be a pioneering one, like many of Nortim's education, safety, training, certification and follow-up activities."

Kolb, who has cut down some trees himself on weekends on his farm and in the National Football League, can put up a brave face with the best of them, thanks to his NFL training. But he concedes, "I'm scared, and that's on the record. I'm learning a lot every day about what

254

Kolb Clan includes (clockwise from Jon's left) Tanner, niece Cyndi, Eric and wife Debbie. There's also Caleb, 2½.

Trainer Ralph Berlin, left, and Dr. Paul Steele, right, accompany injured Kolb to sidelines.

I'm going to be doing, and, with this computer, for instance, I'm learning a whole new language. Sometimes it's scary.

"Pat is a bright man, and he's a lot like Chuck Noll. He knows so much, and I have to ask him to slow down when he starts showing me what to do on this computer. It's all new to me. See that telephone? I've been on it more in two months than I was ever on a telephone in my life. I have to call people, and make appointments to see them, at their convenience. I never had to do anything like that when I was with the Steelers. I will be making calls and writing letters, and it will be a new communications challenge for me."

The new Steelers' coach, Bill Cowher, chose not to retain Kolb's services as strength and conditioning coach. Some thought Cowher wanted a more vocal coach, more of a motivator in the muscle-building business. Cowher also has added Nautilus equipment to the Steelers' strength program, whereas it had been strictly free-standing weights in the past at Three Rivers Stadium. Kolb checked out a few other job possibilities around the NFL, but was not thrilled with the idea of moving if an opportunity had opened up elsewhere.

"I've basically lived in two places all my life, Oklahoma and here," he said. "After Chuck retired, I was talking to some of our other coaches, and I was shocked by some of the stuff they told me. Dwain Painter had been coaching for 27 years, and had never been in one place more than four years. Bob Valesente lived in 11 different places. John Fox had been at seven different colleges in ten years.

"That's not for me," he said. "There was a lot about football that I liked, and a lot I didn't like. I never liked training camp as a player or as a coach. I don't think football's that important — I'll get some people mad at me now — to take people away from their family all week, week after week.

"I didn't like watching film in dark rooms and dissecting them. During the off-season, it got to me being indoors so much of the time. When you didn't get to go out on the practice field, you never saw daylight unless it was a weekend."

But he knows he's going to miss it.

Kolb can clearly remember the phone call he received from Chuck Noll early in the morning the day after Christmas, the day Noll announced his retirement.

"He said, 'Jon, it's over,' and then there was a long silence. I wasn't sure what to say, so I said, 'I'm sorry.' And he said, 'Well, Jon, it was time.' I don't think he signed it in his own mind until that morning. I sorta sensed it was over for me, too.

"There's a sense of finality about something like that. You've done it for 23 years. It's something you have to put behind you. That is the final chapter of that portion of your life.

256

"There were certain things I could do at Three Rivers Stadium," conceded Kolb, "that I could do in my sleep. Here, every Monday morning like this, I am going to be stretched. But I am excited. I have a chance to develop something new. I'll be on the road a lot, but I'll be home most nights. Pat is good about that; he's concerned about the family, too.

"In my mind, when I was in college, I thought my life would be like setting a tread mill in motion, and that I would set it steep and fast for the first 25 years, and then level it out and maybe set it for downhill after that. But here I am, at 44, and I still have it set for steep and fast. I have to."

Kolb was also convinced that Noll was not having any difficulty accepting his new lifestyle. He disagreed with George Perles, the former Steeler assistant who is now the head coach at Michigan State University, who predicted Noll would make a comeback in a year or so as an NFL coach.

"Chuck has so many interests," said Kolb. "He is not bored, I can tell you that. And I believe he retired because he saw too many things happening — with the players and the front office — that were beyond his control."

Kolb talked about how he, at long last, finally got up the courage to go into Noll's office more frequently, and without being summoned, to ask him questions about football. "My last option before that was to go into his office, and I wasted a lot of time through the years trying to get the answers elsewhere," he said.

"But even during a break, I never found him idle in his office. He'd be reading a book about electronics or about boating, or stuff that I had no interest in whatsoever. If he saw these computers, he'd have the manual out and be testing their capacity, and their intricacies, and want to know what made them work. He's like that."

But what about Jon Kolb? Why is he like that? Why did he always seem nervous around Noll, as if he were going to be cut, when he was a player, or chewed out or second-guessed, when he was a player or as a coach?

"I guess it was my own insecurity," said Kolb. "I couldn't shake that. I was always afraid he was going to ask me a question and I wouldn't know the answer. I remember being in a car with him once at the Senior Bowl, and he started talking about Saddam Hussein and how the Arabs thought about certain things. I thought I held my own in that one. I was pleased. Then he asked me if I wanted to go out to dinner. He winced when I told him about a Kentucky Fried Chicken place that was near our hotel. We went to a restaurant of his choice instead, and it was really classy. And I got messed up with the menu, and didn't understand something where he took me. I felt out of my element. I have simple tastes. I'm still a farmboy from Oklahoma."

Though he feared him somewhat, Kolb was always a big Chuck Noll fan. "The thing that always impressed me was that he had the same standard for himself that he held up for everyone else on our team," said Kolb. "I don't think people have stopped to think about that.

"Sometimes he'd talk to me about his son, and I enjoyed that because I have three sons. He told me how his son bought an old house in New England and was restoring it. But I'd bring it up the next day, when we were on our way to football practice, and he'd act like we had never discussed it before. His mind was now on football. I learned that you didn't mix socializing and football with Chuck. He had tunnel vision when it came to football."

He did think Noll changed somewhat in recent seasons. He didn't think he hollered at players in recent years the way he had hollered at players in his day, or the way Noll had hollered at him in particular.

Kolb recalled a time when he fractured his ankle and missed the first game of the season. He was fearful that he would lose his position, so he came back to practice before the ankle had healed. He had it taped by Ralph Berlin into what amounted to a cast. Steve Furness, one of his friends on the team, ran over him in practice, and his ankle was killing him. "Noll ran over and started shouted, 'On the ball, do it again!' Noll spent what seemed like two hours chewing me out when it was only two minutes. I wanted to kill Furness and I wanted to kill Chuck at the same time.

"Another time, there was a story in the paper before the tenth game of the season that I had not allowed a sack to date. It wasn't the kind of thing you wanted to call attention to. I knew it was so, but it was like when a pitcher has a no-hitter going. You're not supposed to bring it up. Well, at our next practice Jack Lambert was giving it to me pretty good about my no-sack streak. He said I had it because I never had to block anybody like him. He got to me pretty good. Jack can get under your fingernails pretty good. So, during practice, at one point, I told Lambert to get down in Dwight White's place over me. White was happy to move out. Now Jack was skinny and fast, and I figured he would try to slip past me on the outside. So I sat back on my heels, so I could catch him on whatever side he attacked. But he lowered his helmet and came right over me. He ran right over me, and knocked me flat on my back. Well, Chuck came running over and started hollering at me before I could even get up. 'On the ball, do it again!' he hollered. You know how he used to holler that. I was mortified.

"In recent years, I saw guys missing their blocks and I'd look for Chuck to criticize them, and he didn't do it. When I looked, I usually looked into the eyes of Tunch Ilkin because he used to be subjected to that sort of ridicule, too. Only now, Chuck wasn't saying anything. I don't know if he decided it wouldn't do any good with some of the guys he was working with, or whether it wouldn't work with today's attitudes. Or maybe he thought they were doing their best. But it was a change, no doubt about it. He stewed, but he didn't say anything to guys who came late to meetings. I'd cover up my eyes waiting for him to drop the bomb on somebody, but he didn't."

Kolb recognizes that he is something of a bull in a china shop, but he welcomes the change. "What's in front that I can accomplish?" he said. "It sounds like I'm building monuments, but if the Super Bowls were the greatest thing in my life, then that means I died when I was 34."

This is not the first drastic change in Kolb's life. Shortly after the 1981 season was over, Noll called Kolb to his office one day and made him an offer he could not refuse: To retire as a player and become a coach.

Kolb had played 13 seasons, the second most by a Steeler to that point, and his 177 games played were the third highest in team history at that time behind Ray Mansfield (182) and Joe Greene (181), and the sudden role switch shocked Kolb.

"I went through two red lights on the way home that day," Kolb told me in an interview for *The Pittsburgh Press*. "For the first time in my life, I wasn't a football player anymore."

Kolb had become the strength and conditioning coach for the Steelers, replacing Paul Uram, who had been on Noll's staff for nine seasons and had left to resume teaching on a full-time basis in the Butler school system.

Since then, Kolb has coached the Steelers' offensive line, returned to his duties as the strength and conditioning coach, and stayed with Noll until his boss retired after the 1991 season.

After that day when Noll first called him to the office, Kolb was still a Steeler, but Kolb knew it would not be the same. "I would no longer be able to contribute directly to the outcome of a football game," he said. "I couldn't keep Harvey Martin of the Cowboys away from Terry Bradshaw, and give him time to throw the ball."

Jon's wife, Debbie, can recall that day even more vividly than her husband because she did not observe it through glazed eyes.

Debbie accompanied Jon when he appeared at a press conference at Steelers' headquarters to formally announce his new role. She sat quietly and did not say a word during the question-and-answer session. But she shed lots of light on the subject afterward.

"He was in a daze when he came through the door at home that day," Debbie recalled.

"I asked him, 'What's the matter?' because he looked like a zombie. And all he could say was, 'I'm not a player anymore.' We had talked about retirement so much, but he never knew it would hit him that way."

Kolb had been plagued during his last two playing seasons (1980 and 1981) with aches and pains in various parts of his seemingly indestructible body. He was often unable to participate in practice sessions during the week, and stood on the sideline on Sunday when the offensive unit was on the field for the first time in his career. It was difficult for Kolb to accept that.

In 1971, he became a starter and was one of the most durable players in the National Football League. He earned an "Iron Man" reputation by playing in 156 of 157 games in his first ten seasons. At one stretch, he started 112 consecutive games.

He started in all four Super Bowls. He was one of the strongest players in the league, and one of its first weightlifting fanatics. He could bench press 550 pounds and competed in several weightlifting contests, winning the NFL strongman competition in 1980.

But he had trouble, recalled Debbie, doing simple tasks when they were living at a farmhouse in Ninevah, Pa. . . . things like reaching a shelf over the kitchen sink.

"There were times he couldn't lift up his arm," she said. "Nobody knows how much pain he played with because he didn't talk about it, being quiet and humble the way he is. He wouldn't let anybody know about it."

Kolb did admit at his retirement press conference that he remembered wincing at a pre-game meeting during the 1981 season when a certain play was advanced in the game plan. It called for Kolb to use a blocking technique he knew would cause him pain.

"I had four hours to think about how much it would hurt," he said. "I don't know if you've ever had a pinched nerve in your neck. But it feels like someone is sticking a hot poker in there."

Debbie said she and Jon discussed the possibility of retiring before the 1981 season because he was having so many problems with an ailing ankle. "But he didn't want to give it up," she said.

Then Debbie Kolb made the most honest assessment of her husband's situation, one that even Steeler coaches couldn't offer in the case of Kolb, or Joe Greene, or Sam Davis, or any of their aging warriors back then. "The plain truth," declared Debbie, "is that, physically, he didn't have the abilities anymore."

She sat nervously, as her husband explained how he had reached his decision to quit playing and start coaching. She thought he handled it well. "I'm so happy for him," she said. "As the strength coach, he will still be involved in the game, and he can pave the way for the younger players to reach their potential.

"I have an antique desk in our game room, and I used to have my bills and coupons and papers spread out on top of it. But Jon's sort of taken over it lately. He'll come home from the office at six, eat his dinner, and then go to that desk right after dinner. He's charting out his graphs on all the guys, going over what they're doing in their workouts, and sometimes he stays at it till midnight.

"He's just so excited. I hope that enthusiasm doesn't wear off."

She said she and Jon talked to other Steelers they had been friendly with, such as Mike Wagner and his wife, Cathy, and Gerry Mullins and his wife, Cindy, and asked them what life was like after their Steeler days.

"They said it was a real adjustment," said Debbie, "but they cherish it as a good memory."

For whatever it's worth, the Wagners and Mullins would split up a few years later, and join the list of former Steelers whose marriages had come apart at the seams.

Debbie, Jon's second wife, was looking forward to a changed environment. "It'll be a lot nicer at home," she explained, "because he won't have his game face on. By Wednesday every week, he would change into a different person. He would just get so serious."

I once asked Sam Davis how Kolb could be so friendly and chat one day, and walk by you the next day without a word. Davis said, "I've roomed with Jon for a long time, and there are days he doesn't talk to me, either. Before a game, he gets 'tunnel vision,' that's all."

Debbie knew better than Davis about that. "I'd be talking to him, and he was looking at me, but he wasn't listening," she said. "So I just stopped talking to him."

She looked across the room where her husband was being interviewed by a TV sportscaster. Kolb's face was brightened by powerful lightbeams. Debbie said, "He looks happy, doesn't he?"

Soon after Jon Kolb learned that Chuck Noll had new plans for him, as an assistant on his staff and not as a player, Kolb's mind went into a whirl.

"You would need a whole newspaper to put down my feelings about retiring as a player," said Kolb.

"When I saw Joe Greene walk out of here after he announced his retirement, I saw the Steelers walking out of here. I felt the same way with Sam Davis. To me, Joe Greene and Sam Davis are the Steelers."

Kolb said that Franco Harris held a party for players only at Christopher's Restaurant atop Mt. Washington to mark the retirement of Greene, Davis and Kolb, and showed a highlights film called "Team of the Decade."

"A fan watching that might have seen the Steelers in action," recalled Kolb. "But I saw Rocky Bleier and Dwight White and Sam Davis and Joe Greene and Steve Furness and Mike Wagner and Franco Harris and Terry Bradshaw. To me, they are the Steelers. When they're all gone, there will be another Steeler team. The new Steelers."

L.C. Greenwood was going to go to training camp, a mistake on his part, as he had to be told to give up the ghost, and it was embarrassing for him, as it was for John Banaszak the same summer. "Now that Sam Davis is gone, we gave L.C. the nickname of 'Riggy,' which is short for rigor mortis," said Kolb. "Now he's the old man of the team. We kidded him about that."

Mel Blount came up to Kolb at Chris Passodelis' showcase restaurant and asked, "How come you're not gonna play?" Kolb said he really couldn't answer that. The thought of not playing still hadn't sunk in yet.

Kolb said he saw a movie called "Chariots of Fire" in which a former athlete stands at the top of a stadium, looking down at track and field action, and observes, "I know I made the right decision, but I'd like to be down there." Kolb said he could relate to that remark.

"I thought I could play till I was 60," claimed Kolb.

Kolb and his colleagues on the offensive line always worked out during the winter, usually in the basement of the Red Bull Inn on Rt. 19 near Washington, Pa., near where many of them lived.

"The Steelers were among the pioneers in pro football to use weights to make guys bigger and stronger," said Kolb, "but other teams have passed us, as far as their year-round programs are concerned. Our

261

offensive linemen have been second to none as strength goes, but some of the guys at the so-called 'skill' positions — oh, how I love that term — could use more work. It will help them."

Kolb was looking forward to his new challenge. "I get up every day at six o'clock and come in here," he said, as he sat in the Steelers' weight room at Three Rivers Stadium. "I can't wait to get to work."

If Kolb had to quit football cold and retire to his farm in Ninevah, Pa., he might not have been so thrilled. "It would be tough to make a living as a farmer," he said "I know that."

When Kolb came off the playing field at the final home game, he was crying. "I was upset about us losing, but we've lost before and I didn't cry," he said. "So, yes, I guess I was thinking that it might be my last game here.

"Way back at high school graduation in Ponca City, Oklahoma, I remember how sad some of the guys felt because it was over for us. But I had signed a letter of intent to attend Oklahoma State, so I was looking forward to that. Then when we played our last game of the year in my senior season against Oklahoma, some of the guys felt real bad, but I was looking forward to playing pro ball. Toward the end of last season, I started to think that maybe my time to cry was coming soon."

Jon Kolb

Ray Pinney
He went home to Seattle

"Pro football is a game of extremes. There's a lot of work and a lot of glory. In the working world, you don't get that. You're just working."

R ay Pinney played wherever Chuck Noll needed him. He had a strong sense of duty and professionalism about him that appealed to Noll, and he contributed in a quiet and distinguished manner to much of the success of the Steelers in the '70s.

Pinney was seldom praised, by his coaches, to hear him reflecting now on those days or to review his printed comments in the thin file of newspaper clippings about him to be found in the Steelers' publicity offices, or by the media. He did not enjoy a high profile in Pittsburgh.

His real name was Raymon Earl Pinney, Jr., and somehow that fit him even better than his snug football jersey.

Understand, however, that Pinney's plaintive comments and bleatings are not unique among his fraternity of offensive linemen. I never met an offensive lineman who didn't feel overlooked and unappreciated. It goes with the job.

Pinney was never a particularly good interview. He was not one to seek the attention of sportswriters, nor was he a particularly enthusiastic analyst in post-game give-and-take. He held his head high, too high for some, appeared aloof, and was satisfied to just do his job. I can't recall ever having a casual conversation or flip exchange with him during the nearly five years I covered the club. It simply wasn't his style. He had what TV's Archie Bunker would call "a constipated look" on his face.

Al King, a sportswriter for the *Indiana (Pa.) Gazette*, wrote of Pinney: "Sometimes, he's about as exciting as mold but, like that substance, he kind of grows on you."

King conceded in the same column, however, that "because he can play all five positions along the offensive line, Pinney is like a Navy blue sweater. He goes with everything and looks good doing it."

Pinney was only a stickout when he did not play well at whatever offensive position he was assigned that particular day, and he commanded attention, it seems, only when the likes of Bruce Smith of the Buffalo Bills or Leonard Marshall of the New York Giants were getting by him and sacking the Steelers' quarterback late in his career. Otherwise, he was often ignored.

Pinney was never a star, except when he left the Steelers to play three seasons in the United States Football League, where he was twice first team all-USFL, but he performed with solid skills and equanimity at every position on the offensive line when he was with the Steelers.

He did not always have a position to call his own, but offensive linemen are injured a lot and there was always an opening somewhere to be filled.

"The guys ahead of me were always a little better than I was, so I was moved around and learned all the positions," he once said.

He was 6-4, 265. He was agile and knew the playbook well. He was a center at the University of Washington in his hometown of Seattle when the Steelers made him the first of their three second round draft selections in 1976.

But the Steelers had Mike Webster entrenched at center, so they tried Pinney at other positions up front.

With the Steelers, Pinney started out at tackle, then played guard, and moved back and forth between the two positions, and played center as a long snapper for placement kicks and punts. When the Steelers were in short yardage situations, Pinney was the second tight end, and caught four touchdown passes over a ten-year span in that scheme.

"Starting in Super Bowl XIII and playing well, and catching four TD passes were the highlights of my career," said Pinney when we spoke during the holiday season in 1991.

"Pro football is a game of extremes. There's a lot of work and a lot of glory. In the working world, you don't get that. You're just working.

"I miss sitting around in the locker room, the camaraderie with my teammates. Randy Grossman was a good friend, and all the guys on the offensive line. I don't stay in touch; I'm too far away out here, and I don't hear from them. Hey, if you talk to Tom Beasley or any of those guys, please tell them I send my best."

He mentioned how much he had enjoyed a recent reunion with Dan Radakovich, his line coach his first two seasons with the Steelers. "He came out here with the Cleveland Browns, and we got together," said Pinney. "It was nice to see him."

He was also fond of Rollie Dotsch, who succeeded Radakovich as the Steelers' offensive line coach, before Dotsch became the head coach of the Birmingham Stallions in the USFL following the 1981 season. Dotsch died of cancer a few years back, so there will be no reunions with him, much to Pinney's disappointment.

Pinney was speaking on the telephone from his home in suburban Seattle. He grew up in Seattle and stayed there. He starred at Shorecrest High School and at the University of Washington. He always went back home during the off-season and often expressed a desire to play for the Seattle Seahawks. Pittsburgh was a place where he worked, that's all.

Unlike the majority of the Steelers, he never really became a Pittsburgher. That probably hurt his popularity as well. He wasn't that visible in the Pittsburgh community.

He just didn't excite anybody. He was a quiet, soft-spoken sort who got lost in a crowd. He was a studious guy; indeed, he had been the top scholar on his college football team. He was a highbrow in the truest sense, as no one on the team had a higher brow than Pinney. "I'm always concentrating," he once said to defend himself. "Maybe one of the reasons people think I'm lackadaisical is because I'm always concentrating."

Ralph Berlin, the team trainer back then, remembers Pinney as "appearing to be scatter-brained."

He was valuable in the Steelers' scheme of things. He was smart — he had been an honor student while majoring in finance and business in college — and he was resourceful and versatile, qualities Noll embraced and endorsed. He played chess with Grossman and Beasley during airplane trips. That, too, would be something Noll would note with approval.

"In 1978, I played guard in the playoffs, and the next week I was playing tackle in the Super Bowl," recalled Pinney of the peak of his playing days with the Steelers. "I didn't have enough experience to come in and dominate at any one position. There was always somebody there who was better than me. I had to learn as much as I could so I'd be ready wherever they needed me.

"Noll doesn't like people to make mistakes. I made them, but I kept them to a minimum."

Pinney was one of the unsung heroes of the Steelers' third Super Bowl victory. The only way you would have seen him on your TV screen in January of 1979 would have been if his man — Ed "Too Tall" Jones of the Dallas Cowboys — had blown by him and nailed Terry Bradshaw for a big loss.

That surely would have been good for a series of instant replays.

"Too Tall had been so dominant in all the films we saw before the Super Bowl," declared Dotsch after that game. "So we were concerned, and we considered Pinney and Jones a critical matchup. But Jones wasn't even a factor in the game."

Which means that Pinney's pass blocking, once considered a shortcoming as far as his skills were concerned, was a factor in the Steelers' success.

"I watched him on the first four plays of the game," recalled Dick Haley of the Steelers' scouting department, "and I knew we were in good shape after that."

Pinney became a starter during the 1978 season when Larry Brown suffered a severely sprained ankle in the fifth game. Pinney moved to guard for Gerry Mullins in the first playoff game, then back to tackle for the final two.

"I'm not in the limelight and I don't expect to be," Pinney said the following summer. "I got great satisfaction from the Super Bowl because we won and I blocked my man.

"There are only so many accolades that can go around after a game, and people look for sensational things. I had just as important a job as the people who did the sensational things. As long as I get the job done, I'm satisfied. This is my fourth year and I hope to be around here to contribute to a few more Super Bowl championships."

That wasn't to be, however. He missed the entire 1979 season because of a stomach ailment, and the Steelers never got back to the big game again after they won that fourth title.

"I had an operation to remove my appendix about three weeks before training camp opened in 1979," said Pinney during our long-distance interview. "I lost about 35 pounds. I was never really right at training camp."

Pinney was kept out of the early workouts at St. Vincent College, and then restricted to non-contact drills. Even so, he was in agony. He had constant stomach cramps. "I wasn't worried about football; I was worried about my health," he recalled.

Pinney was originally dispatched to the nearby Latrobe General Hospital, and then was transferred to West Penn Hospital where he underwent further intestinal surgery. He was unable to play during the 1979 schedule. "It was a long year," said Pinney. "I can remember coming out of the hospital after the surgery. A few guys had died in the same wing while I was there, so it put things in perspective. Seeing the sunshine was my highlight of the year. I logged 38 days in the hospital. I didn't have a lot of fun in '79. I had played well in the Super Bowl, and thought I had a chance to start. So it was a real bummer."

When Pinney returned to action for the 1980 season, he replaced Sam Davis at left guard in the starting lineup. Davis went down with a career-ending knee injury in the final pre-season tuneup at Dallas. Pinney started all 16 games that season, and 36 of 41 games over the next three seasons before he jumped to the USFL.

When he returned from the USFL, he bumped Monongahela native Pete Rostosky from the starting lineup, and played all year. So he was not one to settle for being a reserve, no matter what he was getting paid.

During one off-season early in his pro career, Pinney worked as a collector for long overdue debts for a bank back home in Seattle. His background, plus his degree in finance, may have led to his being selected by the other offensive linemen to be the treasurer for the so-called "Spike Fund" that helped lighten up their otherwise so-serious work duties.

In Steelers' jargon, a "spike" was a mistake. Make one and you contributed to a kitty set up for the offensive line. A penalty cost a lineman $1 for every yard lost. If someone sacked the quarterback, that was a $5 fine, plus $1 for every yard lost. Even if someone annoyed the quarterback it would cost an offensive lineman $2. Any mental error that could be detected on the game film was a $5 spike. When the Steelers rushed for 175 yards in a game, Dotsch, the offensive line coach, had to kick in $10. The idea was to make the coach contribute the most. Dotsch didn't seem to mind one bit.

Pinney could add and subtract, which was one of the reasons he got the job as treasurer of the fund. "But I really believe they picked me," he was fond of saying, "because I have an honest face."

Each position on the offensive line demands a different technique and assignments. Some players can't master one position in the offensive line, so Pinney's ability to play wherever there was a need was appreciated by Dotsch.

"Having him around gives you a good feeling of security," said Dotsch.

Noll appreciated Pinney, too, and the likes of Emil Boures and Craig Wolfley, who also were versatile, and willing to move around as the need demanded.

"The toughest thing in the world is to teach an offensive lineman all the things he needs to do," said Noll, who had played offensive guard and linebacker for the Cleveland Browns. "In college, all they do is straight block. We'd like them to do more.

"Pass protection, the way it's done in the pros, is entirely new to them. Passing in college calls for aggressive blocking, mostly on options. It's damn near impossible to draft an offensive lineman. The greatest college tackles bomb out a lot in the pros. Give me the guy with the right size and the right speed and agility, and we'll teach him."

Pinney was proof of that. He was a center in college, and the same could be said of Jon Kolb and Jim Clack and Tunch Ilkin and Mike Webster. Larry Brown and Gerry Mullins were tight ends in college. "Centers are usually the most intelligent offensive linemen, as a rule," noted Noll. "And you have to know what you're doing to play up front for us. We ask you to do a lot."

There is respect, but little warmth, in Pinney's voice when he talks about Noll. "He was fair," said Pinney. "Chuck rated your performance on the field. I thought I was consistent in my job. Nothing glamorous. I just did what they asked me to do. I never gave him or the Rooneys any trouble off the field."

Pinney did disappoint the Steelers, however, when he left the team after the 1982 season to sign with the Michigan Panthers of the USFL. "It was a no-brain decision," said Pinney. "When you can double your salary, and you have it guaranteed, it's an easy decision."

Pinney was paid about $110,000 by the Steelers during the 1982 campaign, and reportedly made about $250,000 each year in the USFL.

Another offensive lineman, Tyrone McGriff, and a wide receiver, Jim Smith, and backup quarterback Cliff Stoudt all skipped out on the Steelers in favor of greater compensation and opportunity in the USFL. George Perles, the Steelers' defensive coordinator, joined Dotsch in departing the club in favor of a head coaching position in the USFL. Before Perles reported to Philadelphia, he changed his mind and took a job as head football coach at his alma mater, Michigan State University.

The Steelers have never really recovered from the departure of Dotsch and Perles, as well as Woody Widenhofer two years later. They brought a knowledge and spirit to practices, especially scrimmages, that has been absent ever since.

Pinney came back to the Steelers after the USFL folded. The USFL played a summer schedule, so Pinney played the equivalent of five seasons in little more than three years. He came back to the Steelers at a salary of $250,000 per season.

"I fit well into the offensive line," said Pinney. "They had made some changes, and there were some new faces, but I picked up on it pretty fast, I felt anyhow. When I first came back I visited Chuck in his office. I asked him what he wanted me to do. He said he wanted me to play guard behind Terry Long. He said I might play some center. He knew I wasn't a center. I just said, 'Oh, yeah.' It typified our relationship. I did whatever Chuck asked me to do.

"But I remember when I was hurting at camp in '79, and how he was just such a know-it-all about the whole thing. He diagnosed my stomach problem in the hallway of the dorm one night. He didn't sound too sympathetic.

"He could be strange. I think he was in heaven when we were on strike. He could coach all those guys who didn't know the techniques, and the more he could teach you the happier he was to be coaching.

"He was not sociable with his ballplayers. He was not the kind of guy, like some other coaches I've known, who would put his arm around your shoulder, or pat you on the back."

While I never considered Pinney a good interview, I found that he was telling me interesting information, and providing some real insights into the Steelers' scheme of things. Like many, I may have misjudged Pinney.

Pinney's opinion about why Noll and Terry Bradshaw have bad blood between them was different from most I've heard.

"Terry is a hang-loose kind of guy and didn't want to get too serious about anything," said Pinney. "His style was not Chuck's. Chuck was a real teacher and Terry wasn't a good student. It's hard being a head coach. You have so many personalities to deal with, over 40 guys who want your personal attention and approval. But you have to be yourself, and Noll was that.

"We also had Mike Kruczek and Cliff Stoudt and Mark Malone behind Bradshaw, and they were the students. Mike would holler out the defense from the back of the room when we were studying films of our opponent. Bradshaw wasn't into that business. Chuck wanted them to be more like students.

"I got along fine. I wasn't looking for a father figure. I thought Rollie Dotsch was a great coach, and he was also a nice guy. We got along great. Same with Dan Radakovich. He drafted me, and he worked hard with us.

"I think part of the reason the Steelers haven't done as well in recent years is that they haven't had as good of coaches as they used to. You look at the assistants of the '70s. They had their own strong opinions, and they'd confront Noll if they didn't agree with him. Few of the assistants in recent years would stand up to him."

Pinney points to Mike Webster as the Steeler he admired the most. "He set the tone for the rest of us," said Pinney. "He was an outstanding player, and so consistent. He worked so hard, and he was real respected. He trained hard and got the most out of the talent he had. He was a real rock in the clubhouse. I had to try to keep up with some of the guys, and I just wasn't as crazy about lifting weights as they were. I didn't have the numbers they had, as far as how much weight we could lift. I couldn't relate to those guys in that respect. I was just a different kind of player.

"Overall, I have pleasant memories of the Steelers. I liked being a Steeler. I always did."

Pinney prefers Seattle to Pittsburgh, however. It's where he is from and, to him, where he belongs. He is a commercial insurance broker with Pettit-Morry Co.. He has two boys, Raemon, 10, and Darren, 6, when we spoke, and he keeps busy coaching them in the sports and being involved in their Indian Guides activity.

"The lessons learned in football, like dedication, consistency and hard work, apply in all walks of life," said Pinney.

Pinney said he was not surprised that Noll retired after the 1991 season. "It seemed like it was time for a change," he said. "He needed a new challenge. I can't see him hanging around the Steelers' offices. I can't see him living off his 23 years. He should go out and do something else, like he always told us. Maybe he has to get into his life's work."

While Pinney is proud of his professional football career, especially his stays with the Steelers, he sounds like a man who is moving on with his life. "We recently moved into a new home," he said. "So most of my football stuff is packed away. I pulled out a few of the photos of our Super Bowl teams, and put them up in the game room.

"But that's about it. You won't find any football shrine in our house. I have a bunch of game balls I was awarded, and I had them displayed for awhile. But I left them in the box after we moved. It's in the past; I have other things to do.

"I'd rather have the kids trophies on display, and their pictures on the refrigerator door of what they're doing in school. They belong in the spotlight now."

Larry Brown

Recognition was a long time coming

*"I don't know that Chuck Noll
ever had to yell at Larry Brown."*
—Jon Kolb

L arry Brown looks as uncomfortable in a business suit as does his friend and former teammate, Jon Kolb. But he's getting used to it, and chuckles at the thought of Kolb's discomfort. "I'm sure he'd like to be into something more casual," said Brown, "but I've talked to him, and he's taking on his new task with the same kind of zeal as everything else he takes on. That's just the way he is." The same applies to Brown. Like Kolb, he labored in anonymity for most of his career as an offensive lineman for the Steelers.

It took the 12th of his 14 seasons with the Steelers for Brown to be named to the Pro Bowl. Brown, a lovable brute from Starke, Florida, and the University of Kansas, came to the Steelers as a tight end, and bulked up into one of the biggest and most able tackles in the National Football League.

He has lost most of that weight, but not his constant smile or easygoing manner. It suits him well as a partner with former teammate J.T. Thomas in three Applebee's Neighborhood Bar & Grill outlets in North Hills Village, Edgewood Town Center in Swissvale and in the Bourse Shops in Scott Township. The latter is near the corporate headquarters office where Brown and Thomas are most often found.

"It was gratifying," Brown recalls of being chosen to the Pro Bowl late in his career. "Better late than never, I suppose. Everyone gets into something, whether it's as a sportswriter or whatever, and wants to do the best they can do. They do it for some sort of validation, some kind of feedback, as some measure of how well you are doing. You hope you will be as good as you can possibly be.

"With the Steelers, and on other teams in the league, there were a number of poeple who never got that kind of validation. Some never got it who deserved it more than some who did, or more than I did perhaps. But any time in your profession certain things occur that are nice, and that was one of them." It brought back memories.

It was the kind of cold that ripped through your ribs, no matter what you were wearing. It was 32 degrees. Freezing. The wind that swirled around Three Rivers Stadium made it seem even colder.

Coffee or hot chocolate could not warm you up. Nor could the Steelers clubhouse, not right away anyhow, warm as it was when the players filed in after practice.

Larry Brown slumped onto a stool in front of his dressing cubicle. Brown stared briefly at his outstretched fingers, battered and chalky black. They were trembling. An ankle also bothered him, but somebody else provided that information.

He was listed as doubtful for the upcoming game, and could be giving way to Tunch Ilkin as a starter, but Brown didn't bring up the subject as I approached him as the beat reporter for *The Pittsburgh Press.*

Brown was the sort of guy who no matter how painful the injury might be that he was nursing — offensive linemen are susceptible to nagging injuries — he would always put up a brave mask. "Don't worry about me; I'll be OK," he would say.

He apologized for extending a cold hand — which was so much like him, always so courteous and kind — when he was congratulated on the news that he had been voted to the Pro Bowl by the players in the National Football League.

For the first time in 12 seasons with the Steelers, Brown had been acknowledged by his peers as one of the best.

"It's about time," said Lynn Swann, who occupied the next stall in the Steelers clubhouse.

Brown seemed embarrased by the attention. He seemed to take it in stride, like he does most things. It wouldn't affect him for the final regular season test of the 1982 campaign against the Cleveland Browns at Three Rivers Stadium.

"It's a nice honor," he said. "I didn't make a big deal about not getting it, but when you get it you don't apologize for it."

During his 14 seasons (1971-84) with the Steelers, Brown never made a big deal about anything, which was a large part of his charm. It's also one of the reasons, no doubt, why he was overlooked so long.

There were many times when he prized his anonymity. To be singled out wasn't always a positive experience. "A lineman only gets his name mentioned on the p.a. system when he does something negative," Brown told me on more than one occasion. "The referee yells your number over the p.a. system when he's calling a penalty against you. No one says your name when you block your man."

As we spoke to each other, Brown tried to remove his black practice jersey and his shoulder pads in one motion, but they got stuck over his shoulders. He was struggling and needed help. For a brief time, he was a headless lineman. It was an appropriate image.

Here's a guy who was one of the Steelers' strongest people — he could bench press 500 pounds — but he couldn't get his shoulder pads over his head without the help of a sportswriter. "Those muscles make it even harder," said Brown.

During the team's glory years, the Steelers had so many stars — Swann, Terry Bradshaw, Franco Harris, Joe Greene, L.C. Greenwood, Mel Blount, Jack Ham, Jack Lambert, Donnie Shell, Mike Webster and John Stallworth — who were voted to the Pro Bowl, but offensive linemen like Brown, Sam Davis, Moon Mullins and Kolb got lost in the shuffle. Their teammates talked about their contributions to four Super Bowls, but they were largely unknown by the general public.

272

Larry Brown

1983 Pro Bowl class poses with local lovely in Honolulu: from left, Jack Lambert, Donnie Shell, John Stallworth, Mike Webster and Larry Brown.

273

"That's another reason why I never felt slighted," said Brown. "There were so many other offensive linemen on our team who were playing as well or better. My attitude has a lot to do with it. I'm not trying to minimize it. I could very well have not made it. To think as an individual, though, is contrary to what we're trying to accomplish here."

Brown was listed during the same period in a national publication, *Football Digest*, as one of the NFL's 11 most under-rated players.

At 33, and after a dozen years in the NFL wars, he was finally getting recognition. "I always felt I was appreciated in this room," said Brown, "and that I was recognized. Gary Dunn didn't make it to the Pro Bowl, but everybody here knows the kind of job he's done this year. The same is true for Steve Courson and Bennie Cunningham on my side of the line."

Brown's main concern was to be healthy enough to do proper battle with the Browns. Two weeks earlier, Brown came away from a 10-9 setback to the Browns in Cleveland with a swollen left eye. Marshall Harris had gotten a fist through Brown's face mask.

He didn't complain. "We might have lost the battle, but we didn't lose the war," said Brown. "I felt beaten up, but I didn't feel defeated. I didn't feel all was lost.

"I never look at this as a grudge game, or getting back at anybody. I just want to compete and win, and keep us going in the right direction. I don't look at this game as a redemption."

After the game in Cleveland, Brown was more concerned about the condition of Webster, who has having difficulty breathing and felt sick.

That's typical Brown, to hear Ted Petersen talk about him. "He's had a lot of physical problems in the last few years," Petersen said, "but I never hear him complain about it. It's only human to say I hurt here or there. He's always looking out for your well-being. He's always asking how you feel."

Other Steelers routinely offered similar sentiments about Brown, a gentle giant at 6-4, 270, and one of the most respected people in the clubhouse. They call him "Bubba" and it seems to fit.

"Everyone who has seen him make the transition from tight end to tackle here appreciates what he's accomplished," said Swann. He could have added that Brown only played one year of high school football.

"I'm happy for him," continued Swann. "Here's a guy who has gone through a lot, ups and downs, but has never complained. You never hear him say, 'I,I,I.' He never looks at anything like that."

Blount, like Swann, was disappointed he wasn't going to the Pro Bowl with Brown. But he was happy for a friend.

"He's been a great, great superstar for a long time," said Blount. "I wish I were like him. I can't be as humble and nice as he is. I guess I've got too much arrogance and egotism. Everybody admires him."

Ted Petersen
"There's a fire burning inside."

"Odessa is the setting for this book, but it could be anyplace in this vast land where, on a Friday night, a set of spindly stadium lights rises to the heavens to so powerfully, and so briefly, ignite the darkness."
—From *Friday Night Lights*
by H.G. Bissinger

Trinity High School sits on the crest of a hill high above College Field, where the Washington & Jefferson College football team plays its home games in Washington, Pennsylvania. I have been there in the fall, to watch W&J play, and it is an idyllic setting at that time of the year. It is an Ivy League backdrop. But this was early March, the trees were gray and bare, and so was the sky.

Trinity pays $25,000 a year to play its home schedule on the same field. A stranger might confuse Trinity with Washington & Jefferson because it has the look, a mix of old and new architecture, of a college building, and stretches long and low across the landscape. The Old Main building to the far right was originally an Episcopal school for boys. Thus the Trinity origin. It is a great campus setting.

It is raining lightly on this Friday morning as I pay a visit to talk to Ted Petersen, who played offensive line for the Pittsburgh Steelers during the glory years of the '70s and the not-so-glorious years of the '80s. Petersen's smile, as I approached him, had a warming effect. "It's like a little college," Petersen said as we surveyed the scene.

Petersen was approaching the completion of his second year as a teacher at Trinity, where he is the head coach of the football team. He is a formidable figure in the school hallways. He is 6-5, and about 235 pounds, about 10 to 15 pounds under his playing weight. He looked even taller, and athletic, because he was wearing a sleek warmup suit, white with light blue and red trim, and white sneakers. He is a handsome fellow, with an inviting smile, so the school kids are comfortable with him. But they know not to get too frisky, either, because he knows where to draw the line even if they are not always sure. He commands attention and respect, but in a nice, unintimidating way.

His full name is Ted Hans Petersen, III. He is a blond, blue-eyed Dane, and those glacier blue eyes reveal a seriousness, a sincerity, that one can recognize right away as the genuine article. "The one thing I demand when I'm talking to the players on my team, or to the students in my classes, is that they look me in the eyes when we're talking." Petersen said in a soft voice. "I demand that. If I find someone talking out of turn at one of my meetings, they're going to know I'm unhappy about that. They have to take it seriously. I teach them respect."

Petersen always struck me as a strong, silent type, a pleasant fellow who didn't seem to have a mean streak in him. Most of the Steelers' offensive linemen were soft-spoken, easy-does-it individuals. He is friendly, and quick to smile.

"I'm very much like my father," Petersen said, shrugging off my personal appraisal. It apparently had a familiar ring to it. "People who knew my dad think he's a real angel. But my dad — he's Danish, and he can fly off the handle — had a temper when I was growing up.

"I'm patient, but I lose it once in a while. When I get ticked off, they know there's a reason. It has more effect that way. I don't abuse it, or use it to get my way. I don't flip out before every game. It's real, not phony."

Petersen and I had spoken for nearly an hour during a free period in an office normally occupied by Frank Vulcaro, a school administrator who also serves as defensive coordinator for the football team. Vulcaro had been a small college All-American at nearby California (Pa.) University. There was a sign on the wall that read: "WE ALWAYS HAVE TIME TO DO THINGS RIGHT."

Now it was the next period, and Petersen was standing in the front of a classroom in Room No. 18, with about 20 students present, spread across five rows. He was passing out a test for them to take that morning. He teaches health education. One of the young women had been absent the previous three days, and Petersen told her she could take the test on Monday. Others, seeing an opening, asked if they could do the same. Petersen smiled and squelched those suggestions. He gave instructions for the taking of the test, telling them they could use their own notes, but not a set of keys he had given them. He wanted those keys turned in before they started their test. "Why can't we use our keys?" one young woman inquired. "Because it would be too simple," Petersen said. A young man asked, "What if we have the keys written in our notes?" I thought to myself that this was not a smart question to ask, even if it was an honest one. "I'll trust you not to use them," Petersen said. "You know what's right, right?" Some of the students snickered, as if to say, "Sure, man, sure."

He retreated to the rear of the class where he could monitor the test activity and continue our conversation at the same time. If there was too much talking among the students, he'd silence them. When most of them had completed the tests, and were talking too loudly, he hollered out, firmly, "Let's quiet down, please. We have a guest with us today!"

In short, let's all be on our best behavior.

Petersen played for the Steelers for eight seasons altogether, from 1977 through 1983, and then briefly in 1987. In 1984, he played ten games with the Cleveland Browns, and five more with the Indianapolis Colts. He sat out the 1985 and 1986 seasons, and came back to play three games with the Steelers when the veterans were out on strike at the outset of the 1987 season. And three games counts as a full season on the NFL players retirement plan. It gave him nine NFL seasons to his credit. It was a real bonus for Petersen. In several ways.

Ted Petersen

Petersen poises to block for Franco Harris.

"I was doing construction work, and thinking all the while that I should still be playing pro football. I thought I was in good condition," Petersen said. "When the players were out on strike in '87, and the team was looking for players to fill the roster, I asked my friends on the team how they'd feel if I came back. I wouldn't have jeopardized my friendship for that. But they urged me to do it; frankly I could use the money as I was just scraping by at that time.

"I had more fun for those three weeks playing football than at any other time because there wasn't a lot of pressure. Other teams were putting makeshift teams on the field, too. But I was so banged up physically, and it was a real education. It underlined how important it is to be in proper condition to compete in pro sports. I thought I was in fairly good shape, but I wasn't. I never could have lasted 16 games. So it was nice to put those thoughts of continuing to play pro ball to rest for good."

During his original stay with the Steelers, Petersen was a versatile performer. His prime position was left tackle, but he also saw service at right tackle and guard and center on the offensive line, and he could have filled in if needed at tight end, his original position at Eastern Illinois University.

"I was never a big offensive lineman," Petersen said. "I was a suped-up tight end without the talent to play that position in the pros."

He worked through two seasons of physical problems to earn the starting job at left tackle for the 1983 season. He started the first 13 games in place of Ray Pinney before a foot sprain in a game at Detroit shelved him for the season.

He had started in that same slot in Super Bowl XIV against the Los Angeles Rams when the Steelers won their unprecedented fourth NFL title in January of 1980. Two weeks earlier, in the AFC title contest with the Houston Oilers at Three Rivers Stadium, Petersen started at right tackle. I can still picture Petersen throwing a fine block to help open a hole for Rocky Bleier to score the final touchdown in that contest. I was among the media standing behind the end zone, getting into position for the post-game interviews in the nearby clubhouse.

In 1981 and 1982, Petersen played only nine games while rehabilitating from surgery to remove a benign tumor from his right hip. He saw action mostly on special teams his first two seasons, then had six starts in 1979 and nine starts in 1980.

He was drafted on the fourth round in 1977 after being the first player in the history of Eastern Illinois to be named Division II All-America. He was co-captain as a senior and earned a bachelor's degree in health and physical education, as well as a teaching certificate.

Petersen and his wife, Linda, have two sons, Teddy, 11, and Garrett, eight. The Petersens continue to live in South Fayette Township, where they resided during his playing days with the Steelers. It's 17 1/2 miles, or about a 25 minute drive, from there to Trinity High School.

Petersen was born in Kankakee, Illinois, and played high school football in his hometown of Momence. His mother has a clerical job there at the Baker & Taylor Company book distribution headquarters. His father is a trucker, having leased the family farm on which Petersen grew up.

Washington, Pennsylvania is about 35 miles south of Pittsburgh. You can get there by traveling on Route 19 or Interstate 79. As a child, I remember going through what was then usually referred to as Little Washington on our way to Wheeling and Bridgeport to visit relatives.

On my way to see Petersen, I went on Route 19, passing several large farms and landmarks enroute: the Meadowlands harness racing track that was developed by Del Miller and friends such as Ed Ryan of Ryan Homes and Joe Hardy of 84 Lumber; the Cameron Coca-Cola Bottling Plant owned by their friend Pete Cameron; Millcraft Industries owned by another of their friends, Jack Piatt; Jessop Steel, where a friend and neighbor of mine, Carl Moulton, serves as president, and the *Washington-Observer Reporter* owned by brothers Bill Sr. and John Northrup. A long truck was delivering a half-dozen rolls of newsprint when I crossed Main Street, just below the building that houses the area daily newspaper. Washington is a world unto itself, quite apart from Pittsburgh, with its own set of movers and shakers and noble establishment. Like a lot of Western Pennsylvania towns, it has known better times and is showing its age. Then I saw the outskirts of the campus of Washington & Jefferson College, a fine liberal arts school where several of the grandchildren of Steelers owner Art Rooney have been educated and have played football. Petersen, and several of his Steeler teammates, used to lift weights and work out in the gym there.

I spotted a railroad trestle and crossed railroad tracks, and drove around a lot of curves before I hit Park Avenue and another familiar landmark, College Field, a 4,500-seat stadium where John Luckhardt's fine W&J football team plays NCAA Division III football on a nationally-ranked basis. On the hill behind the grass field, of course, you can see Trinity High School. The school teams are known as The Hillers.

Petersen had put together records of 3-7 and 6-4 in his first two seasons as the head football coach at Trinity. The school team had posted respective records of 2-8 and 1-9 prior to Petersen's arrival. He came from Canon-McMillan High School in neighboring Canonsburg, where he had taught and served as an assistant coach for two seasons after retiring from the National Football League.

"We missed the playoffs by one game last year, and we play in the strongest conference in Quad A, the biggest and best competition class in western Pennsylvania," Petersen said. "We lost to all playoff teams last year, and we were blown out by only one team, Mt. Lebanon. We're getting there.

"My first year here we had 42 kids come out for the team — that was disappointing — and we ended up with about 35. Last year, we started out with 52 and ended up with about 48. This year, if everybody comes back, we'll have 73 kids. You do need numbers to compete at this level. You need depth.

"We had an eighth grade team that was undefeated this past season, playing against the best schools in the area. We had so many kids out for the team, in fact, that we had to have two teams, a Blue and a White team. That's a good sign."

He said he had Tunch Ilkin come out to speak to the students at a rally to interest them in participating on the football team. Ilkin replaced Petersen as a tackle in the Steelers' offensive line. He said he was thinking of inviting another former teammate, Craig Wolfley, an offensive lineman who spent the previous two seasons with the Minnesota Vikings, but still lived in nearby Upper St. Clair, to come and talk to his team the next time around.

"We're trying to build up the program here," Petersen said. "We have several midget football teams that feed players into the Trinity program. There's real potential here."

Strangely enough, there is another high school that you can see from the hilltop at Trinity. That's Washington High School on nearby Jefferson Avenue. "It's about a half mile from here as the crow flies," Petersen said.

Washington draws most of its students from the inner-city, and Trinity draws from a wider region, the suburbs and surrounding countryside. Trinity gets some farm boys and coal miners' sons.

"Traditionally or reputation-wise," explained Petersen, "Trinity has the size, and Washington has the speed."

Then, too, football and basketball both take a backseat to wrestling in Washington County. "We have an outstanding baseball team, too," Petersen said. "What's important is what the people in the community place value in. If they placed value in a strong music program, then we'd have a strong music program. Individuals who really care deeply about something can make their interest a point of pride at a school, too. You see that at a lot of different places."

I asked Petersen how he came to be a coach. "I was a physical education major in college, and I minored in driver's education and health," he said. "But then I saw how much time was spent in coaching on a high school, college and pro level, and I was relatively certain I didn't want to coach. I'm a family man. I have two boys and I didn't want to be away from them more than I had to be.

"But Bill Vosel, who's from Bridgeville, had become a good friend. When he returned as the head coach at Canon-McMillan, he asked me if I would be interested in helping him out as an assistant. That was in 1988. We took a group of kids who weren't exceptionally talented, but were excited and aggressive and they were good friends. They had played together for years. They had won only two games the year before, but we went 6-3-1 and just missed the playoffs by one game.

"Coaching is like a disease. It gets in your blood. I might do this differently than Vosel, though I had no problem doing it his way when I was with him. I found my own personality coming out. From an offensive standpoint, I was always drawing up plays. In our second year at Canon-McMillan, we were 3-7. So I had a taste of winning and of losing. I didn't feel I was ready to be a head coach, but then this opening came about. Friends urged me to go after it; they said it would be good to apply, and to go through the interview process. It was something I could build on.

"I was a speaker at a banquet one night at Trinity, and some people there asked me to apply. Then I did a banquet at Canon-McMillan, and John Luckhardt from W&J was also speaking there that night. He encouraged me to apply at Trinity. He thought it was a good opportunity for me. And I got the job.

"I would not have taken the job unless I had a teaching position as well. I feel strongly about that. I need to be close to the kids. I need to watch their grades, and look after them. I was teaching at Canon-McMillan. I'm a loyal person. I hated to leave. You get attached to the kids and their families."

In addition to passing out his health education tests, Petersen presented me with a white paper as well. It contained his "game plan" for the Trinity High School football program. It is something he has given to his assistants and to all the players. It reads like this:

"OUR PURPOSE:

"To give our athletes every opportunity to be successful in life. To be the best we can be individually and collectively by stretching our abilities physically and mentally during practice and game situations. We believe that by playing the game of football we will be better prepared to successfully overcome adversity in life.

"OUR VISION:

"To develop an exemplary program characterized by great competitiveness, winning seasons, and playoff games.

"OUR PHILOSOPHY ON WINNING AND LOSING:

"We do not believe in the win-at-all-cost philosophy! This attitude is directly responsible for cheating, and unethical behavior. We do, however, believe wholeheartedly in preparing to win by hard work and discipline within the framework of the rules. We also believe the only 'losers' in life are those who never attempt anything challenging in life. Therefore, (they) never know victory or defeat!"

I had spotted Petersen several weeks before at the Green Tree Marriott where he was among district prep football coaches attending a Kodak Coach of the Year Clinic, put together by Pete Dimperio Jr.

He said he had spoken to Sam Rutigliano, the former coach of the Cleveland Browns who is now at Liberty University. Petersen played nine games for Rutigliano in 1984 before he was fired. Marty Schottenheimer replaced Rutigliano, and put Petersen on waivers after one more game.

"Sam invited me to come down to Liberty this spring," Petersen said, "and I'm going to do it. I want to learn more about his offense."

Petersen said Lavell Edwards, the head football coach at Brigham

Young University, told the coaches at the same clinic "you need to get everybody with the same frame of mind. You've got to get players thinking about making a contribution. You want to make them feel like they don't want to do anything to pull down the team. When I was with the Steelers, you never wanted to be a detriment to the team. I wanted to contribute. With the Steelers, there was a lot of talent, but none of us wanted to make a mistake."

Reflecting on what Edwards said prompted Petersen to think about Chuck Noll, his coach with the Steelers. "That was Chuck's philosophy, too," he said. "You've got to get it done. Whatever it takes. You have to be prepared mentally and physically to play."

"Didn't you profit from being around some super motivated individuals such as Mike Webster, Jon Kolb and Larry Brown?" I asked. "Didn't they push you beyond limits you might have thought were possible for you?"

"It's a fact," Petersen said. "I wasn't in the same league as those guys. I could do some things physically well, but I got better because of the company I was keeping. It's the same way for students in school, for people in the business world.

"I had to learn a new level of intensity. I thought I was intense in college, but there was a big difference. I got that intensity from Chuck Noll. Whatever he described to us, he was intense. It was the same way with (our offensive line coach) Rollie Dotsch."

During the 1991 football season, I sat in the stands with Petersen one evening when he was scouting a game at Upper St. Clair between the Panthers and neighboring Chartiers Valley. Steve Courson, another of Petersen's former teammates, was supposed to be there, too, but hadn't shown yet. Petersen sat with some older assistants, and he was asking them a lot of questions.

Courson served as an unpaid assistant to Petersen. He was supposed to be a paid assistant, but failed to get the necessary paperwork turned in on time to school officials. He might have been too busy writing his own book, *False Glory*. Courson had been in a lot of controversy since his days with the Steelers.

Courson had abused steroids and alcohol during his stay with the Steelers, and was suffering with a diseased heart. He needed to have a heart transplant, but it wasn't easy to find a heart for a man his size, 6-1, 285, and it hadn't yet become a desperate need, so he wasn't high on the hospital's priority list.

In his book, Courson charged that Steelers players were abusing steroids during the 1980s and that coach Chuck Noll knew about it and did nothing. Although his book doesn't give any details on his accusations against Noll, Courson said, "What disappoints me about Chuck Noll is that he absolved himself of any knowledge or approval, no matter how tacit."

Noll strongly denied the allegations. "It's not true," he said. "I gave lectures against using that stuff. There was no turning my head from it."

In any case, Petersen was not a party to that treatise. He thinks that Courson respects Noll as a coach more than he might lead on in his lectures, interviews and in his book.

"I'm told it scares you sometimes how much you sound like Noll, or do things like Noll, as a high school coach," I said to Petersen.

Petersen smiled. "Steve Courson and I laugh about it. Sometimes I'm on the practice field, and something comes out of my mouth, and I look over at Steve Courson and we smile. 'Did I really say that?' But Chuck Noll and I are on the same page about a lot of things regarding football and life. Chuck Noll is right-on about a lot of things. I'm different in my approach, and I'm my own person, I believe, but I say some things that Chuck or Rollie might say when I was with the Steelers. Steve would be the first one to tell you that he learned a lot from Chuck. Steve may be bitter about the way some of the things were handled, but after coaching for a year I think he'd concede that there were some positive aspects to his stay with the Steelers.

"Steve coaches the offensive line for us. It was something I used to coach. But he and I are so alike in our thinking with offensive line play — to the letter — that when he speaks he speaks for me. It comes from being drilled so well with the Steelers. We were so well taught. At the time, it made me sick. We had guys who were 26 and 30 years old, some older, and we'd go over and over the same plays. Every week, we would cover the game plan like we had just learned it, over and over. That's why we made fewer mistakes than most teams; we knew what we were doing.

"There's something I do differently. I try to explain why we're doing certain things, as much as I can. I wanted to know why we were doing something a certain way."

"I was told that Chuck Noll did not like players to challenge his thinking," I said to Petersen." People like Paul Martha and Andy Russell say Noll did not like to be questioned by anybody about what was going on."

"No. Chuck just wanted you to do what he told you to do, or what his assistants told you to do," Petersen said.

"And he and they told you over and over again. I mean it gets to you. How many times do you have to go over the fake-toss 32-trap? We ran it against every defense. It was always in the game plan. It was sort of a bread-and-butter play in our offensive scheme.

"It was a fake toss to Rocky running outside — not too many teams took that seriously after awhile — and it was a quick trap up the middle, giving it to Franco going underneath. We could have done it in our sleep.

"Even when it comes to conditioning, I let my players know why we're doing certain exercises, or training routines. There's no easy way. We do this because we don't want to be cowards on Friday night. I want them to be stars on Friday night. Vince Lombardi was right: fatigue makes cowards of us all. I can remember the burning sensation I felt late in some games. You're tired and you think you're going to bust a gut. And you've got someone like Lyle Alzado or Howie Long across from you, and it's the fourth quarter, and you've got to keep them off the quarterback. You have to suck it up. But it sure helps if you're in the best possible condition to go the distance.

"I was proud of the way our team played last year. We didn't blow many assignments. We kept our mistakes to a minimum. So the drilling pays off. The Steelers' system was extremely complex. We can use some of the basic plays, but we couldn't coach it to these kids; it's too much."

"What was the highpoint of your career with the Steelers and what was your lowpoint?" I asked Petersen, believing I knew what he would say in answer to the second part of the question.

"The highpoint was not any particular game," Petersen responded. "But I remember how I felt in my second season with the team, in 1978, when we were going to the Super Bowl. All of a sudden, I heard Joe Greene saying we were going to end up at the summit. 'The what?' I asked. The Super Bowl, I was told. Joe told us we'd be going there. I only contributed on special teams that season, but I felt a part of it all.

"The Dallas Cowboys had shown a great deal of interest in me before the draft, and they went to the Super Bowl my first year, and I thought, 'Ah, I missed out on a Super Bowl ring.' Then I ended up winning two Super Bowl rings over the next two years. What's amazing is that Pittsburgh did it twice — back-to-back.

"The lowpoint for me was in the offseason, between the '80 and '81 seasons. I was doing a heavy dead lift in the weight room and I felt a burning sensaton in my right buttock. I also realized I couldn't run very well at times. I had pain I couldn't overcome. I couldn't gut it out.

"I came to camp, and underwent a physical exam. And they found a benign tumor in my right hip. Dr. (Paul) Steele, one of our team physicians, checked it out. He took X-rays and, eventually, he drilled it out. But I wasn't able to resume playing right away.

"People don't talk about Chuck's compassion, but I want to tell you this, so people know that Chuck Noll did care about us. He called me into his office. He said, 'You just get this taken care of. There will be a spot for you here when you come back.' He didn't have to do that. It was reassuring, and I needed that. After the operation, nothing felt different. I still couldn't play without pain. I was on an emotional rollercoaster. I know how Mario Lemieux feels."

Lemieux, the superstar forward for the Pittsburgh Penguins, had been plagued by a bad back the past two seasons, and his career was thought to be in jeopardy.

"It's so frustrating," Petersen said. "Some days, I'd get into a three-point stance, and I couldn't come out of it. I couldn't fire out without pain. I went to five different doctors and came up with five different opinions. It was definitely the hardest thing I had to deal with during my days with the Steelers.

"I never feared that I had cancer. I think the media did, though. They were always asking me, 'How do you feel?' I came back for two games — it was during a strike year — and then they put me on injured reserve for good. I came back in '82 and '83, but I was never the same again. I had my days when I could play pretty well, but I had days when it was difficult to do things properly. There was still pain.

"Right now, I have crushed discs in my back. There are two discs that have become narrowed. They've lost some of their cushion. I feel that from time to time. Last year, two days after the football season was over, I had pressure from my vertebrae on a sciatic nerve. It was so bad I couldn't walk in the school hallways. My toes were numb for several days. I know I'm looking at surgery down the line."

In the meantime, he wants to become the best high school football coach he can be. He wants the kids at Trinity to have the same pride in their program as he had in the Pittsburgh Steelers. He doesn't want to bore them with war stories, either. It's a different time, a different day.

But he believes the basics don't change. "I was critical of Tim Worley last year," he said. "I was against all of the things he was saying. I didn't like his selfish attitude. Then it came out that he was messing around with cocaine and alcohol. Then he said he was sorry, and that he would work within the program. I was pleased to hear that. But one of the assistant coaches on the Steelers told me it didn't mean anything, that Worley was — like most people who are on drugs — a con man, and that he would say whatever anybody wanted to hear. Drugs do that to you. They turn you into a liar."

It was easy to see that Petersen was upset by what Worley, the Steelers' No. 1 draft choice in 1989, was doing to waste away what could have been a promising career as a running back with the Steelers. Worley was in the news again because he had failed to take two drug tests, and was eventually suspended for the 1992 season. He had been suspended by the NFL the previous season for failing repeated drug tests.

"Players' attitudes have changed with the big money," Petersen said. "If I had made what they're making today I could be coaching as a hobby. I've met players who signed for a bonus of $850,000 and they're talking about retiring at the end of a four-year contract.

"When I was playing, we were so afraid of losing our jobs. At St. Vincent, me and Tom Beasley and Steve Courson and Moon Mullins would sit around before a cutdown date, and try to figure out who we thought they might cut. We were nervous. Now the rookies come in and act like ten year vets.

"I hear stories about players showing up late for team meetings, and getting away with it. That's a real problem. I was never late. Jack Lambert was never late, ever. No one was ever late. It wasn't the $25 fine. You didn't want Chuck Noll looking at you with those eyes. I don't know if he lost that or what, but it's been different in recent years.

"I signed for a $13,000 bonus, and my first year's salary was $25,000. I made about $135,000 my last full season with the Steelers, and about $150,000 that year with the Browns and Colts. If I had stayed that last full season with the Steelers (in 1987), I would have earned $215,000.

"When I was with the Steelers, we always felt we didn't do as well financially as players on other teams. But the Steelers organization treated you extremely well, personally, so it was hard to play hard ball with them. They were very fair, and they were good people to work for.

"I'm a very emotional man," Petersen said. "There's a fire burning inside. My wife likes to laugh, and have a good time, and so do I. I have great aspirations. My emotions show more out on the field.

"Football is a very violent game and only the strongest survive. That's what motivated me to play hard. I wanted to keep my job. That's the way it's supposed to be done. I could feel good about myself.

"I hated to be blasted in front of the whole team. That may not be the best way, but it sure kept me honest. There was a fear of failure. Within the framework of the rules, I wanted to beat the guy across the turf from me.

"But I wasn't trying to end anybody's career. Some coaches might tell you when you're in a certain position that you could blow out a guy's knee, or render him a career-ending injury. I let that go in one ear and out the other. That wasn't me. I didn't approve of that. I don't coach that way.

"Football is a game for aggressive people, and you should be as aggressive as you can be within the framework of the rules. I have my own philosophy about doing it right, and I stick with it.

"We play good football on the high school level in western Pennsylvania. We're right up there, just behind Florida, Texas and California. But we're right in there with some of the best in the country. What proves that is the number that goes on to college and to the pros. People take their football seriously around here, and I think the Steelers had something to do with that. We set high standards."

Photos by Stan Diamond, Washington Observer-Reporter

Trinity coach Ted Petersen with
one of his players, and (right)
with assistant coach Steve Courson.

Rick Moser
California beach boy was special

"Those Super Bowl rings mean more
to me now than ever before."

Rick Moser is a real muscular, baby-faced brute with brown curly hair, bright eyes and a mischievous look that can melt women with a wink. When he was with the Steelers, he always struck me as more of a lifeguard or beach bum than a football player. That was my problem, not his. But Moser had some magic moments, usually going downfield under a kick-off, and he melted more than a few kick-returners in his time, too.

If he, indeed, looked like a surfer from California, an opposing kick-off return unit was just another wave to challenge him. He rode that wave for all it was worth and then some.

In fact, during his first two seasons with the Steelers, in 1978 and 1979, he graded the highest on the club for performance on special teams, especially on kick-off coverages. He saw action in 31 of 32 regular season games his first two seasons. And he claimed two Super Bowl rings during that same spectacular stretch.

Not bad for a No. 8 draft choice out of New England.

Moser and teammate Steve Furness, a defensive lineman, shared the distinction of being the only NFL players from Rhode Island University, and Moser admittedly says he was lucky to get drafted by the Steelers. They had a star-studded lineup that didn't require him to run the ball much, but appreciated his talents at tackling kick-returners or breaking down their blocking as a role player.

Moser managed to put in two stints with the Steelers, in fact, coming back after a spell in the USFL and several short stays with the likes of the Miami Dolphins, Kansas City Chiefs and Oakland Raiders, to play in Pittsburgh in 1981 and 1982. Altogether, Moser stuck around the league long enough to qualify for a pension, and to pick up some valuable insights about what life was like in pro ball.

He has parlayed that into two successful careers. He was the technical advisor, and often had a bit role as an actor for five of the six seasons that HBO's "First and Ten" sitcom about pro football was on the air. When we spoke, he had just turned 35 in December of 1991, and he was working as a salesman for records management and office products for TAB Products of Houston.

"I've been very fortunate," said Moser. "Those Super Bowl rings mean more to me now than ever before. I'm in sales and it's a great tool. People like to reminisce about those days. I don't scratch my face so they'll see my ring, but those were also the Houston Oilers' best days, so they get noticed.

"Bum Phillips, who coached the Oilers then, had a healthy respect for the Steelers, even though he always said they blocked the Oilers' road to the Super Bowl. We liked them. We respected him and Earl Campbell and that crowd. Those two are still the most respected guys in town. There was a mutual respect between the Steelers and the Oilers, and the fans from Pittsburgh and Houston. So it works well for me here.

"I go to the games only on business. I don't care to go to football games as a spectator. In fact, I hate it. I did it once when my shoulder was broken when I was with the Steelers. I got drunk with the fans and I hated it. I couldn't concentrate. You can see it better on TV, and I guess I just don't see myself as a fan."

Working with the cast of "First and Ten" had to be a blast. "It was canceled the year after I left," he said, with more than a hint of merriment in his voice. "It was just like what happened to the Steelers. I left and they stopped winning Super Bowls."

Asked to explain his behind-the-scenes responsibilities for producing "First and Ten," Moser said he spent a great deal of time with the writers, and often suggested changes in dialogue to make it ring more true.

"In one scene we did, the actual Steelers' game plan for one of the Super Bowls was posted on the bulletin board in the background. I'd kept a copy of it. It was the real thing. You couldn't read it if you were watching on TV, but it was there just the same.

"The Steelers were there a lot in spirit. Some of the guys I played with inspired some of the characters on the TV show, though the TV characters were usually overdrawn."

I told Moser I had been talking to Frenchy Fuqua on the telephone, and he had been telling me Ernie Holmes stories. "I could see where those two, and somebody like Lambert and L.C. Greenwood, could provide models for the TV show," I said. He agreed.

"It was a very real show, with the locker room type of pranks you'd have in the NFL. The football part was pretty realistic. A lot of times the writers didn't know the correct terminology, or what people said in huddles, and I'd make it more realistic.

"The head coach was a little hard to swallow. No NFL coach could act like that. At first, we did it for a public that didn't know any better. We did it the first two years without O.J. Simpson. When O.J. came in, we made it more realistic and serious."

I mentioned to Moser that I had read where New York police when polled to pick the TV show that most accurately depicted what they did named "Barney Miller." I thought "First and Ten" wasn't always that far-fetched, either, in its depiction of pro football.

"I played a gay tight end in several episodes," said Moser. "That in itself was an unrealistic look at that situation. My character was openly gay. Not a flamer, but pretty open about it. There were a lot of innuendos and jokes in the script about it. I'm sure there are some gay pro football players, but they're in the closet, believe me. Deep in the closet. If a pro football player admitted he was gay, they would beat

Rick Moser

the hell out of the guy. There probably were some when I was playing, but you're not going to know about it.

"They did some other unreal stuff that was funny, but far from the real thing. They had naked girls frolicing with the football players in the showers. They were from the cheerleading squad. It was fun filming those scenes, but it was so unrealistic."

He mentioned Bubba and Jethro, two of the biggest bad actors on "First and Ten" who were linemen who loved to party. "Those two were a little overweight for pro football players," said Moser. "I had to work with Bubba. He was a bus driver in LA, and he kept driving a bus when he didn't have shows to do. But he got a good contract and he was able to give up being a bus driver. I had to spend an hour with him, at first, just to get him down into a three-point stance.

"We had to find doubles for the entire cast for the football-playing part. Everything in the football games was choreographed. It was harder than a real football practice. Everybody knew what they were going to hit, and how. I'd draw up the other team's plays.

"I ended up doing what I did in Pittsburgh. As a reserve running back with the Steelers, I was always posing as one of our future opponents. We were trying to give our defense a look at the other team, and what they liked to do, and what their tendencies were.

"Every week with the Steelers, I was pretending to be somebody else, like an Earl Campbell. Dick Hoak, our backfield coach, would hold up the play on a large card, and then we'd run it. Well, that's what I did when we were filming the show. I'd hold up the card off-camera. It showed everybody what they were supposed to do. It was tedious. We'd run the plays over and over again, until we got it just right.

"With the Steelers, at least you're practicing with a purpose, for a reason, to get ready for the next game. With us, it was just work. There was no glory."

I asked Moser what it was like to work with Delta Burke, who later starred in another TV sitcom called "Designing Women."

"She was really a nice person," recalled Rick. "She had a good presence as the owner of the pro football team. When she gave us speeches, like to go get 'em and stuff, and to kick some ass, she sounded believable. She actually could give you a chill in your spine. The show had a few women after her, and it didn't work. Shawna Reed — she's on 'Major Dad' — didn't come across in that role as well."

I asked him about O. J. Simpson. When I first covered pro football for a daily newspaper, the Miami Dolphins for *The Miami News* in 1969, I had several opportunities to interview Simpson when he was starring for the Buffalo Bills. To me, he was just like Julius Erving, or Dr. J, a superstar who was so genuinely cooperative with the press. Simpson struck me as a good guy, right from the start.

"He's still that way," said Moser. "He's genuinely a good person. Off camera, no one had a better time."

I mentioned to Moser that I had heard that Simpson was quite the ladies' man when he was on a stage set. "I never saw anybody quite like him," admitted Moser, "but I'd rather not get into that. He disappointed some people in that respect. But that's for his book."

Rick Moser didn't regard himself as a super prospect, or even a realistic prospect, when he first came to the Steelers' training camp in Latrobe before the 1978 season. He came to the right team, he says, he was fortunate.

"Having so many great players around you has to help," recalled Moser. "They do elevate you to be a better player. I was in the right place at the right time. At Rhode Island, we were lucky to have 5,000 fans at our home games. At St. Vincent, in those days, we'd get that many or more at our practice sessions on weekends.

"My roommate at Rhode Island, believe it or not, predicted I would be the Steelers' eighth round draft choice. After the first pre-season game, I went up to Hoak, and told him, 'I guess that's it for me. I think I'm wasting my time here.' He told me a story. When he was a rookie, he left camp for two days and went home. He said he came back and stayed ten years as a player. That story stuck with me.

"You can get discouraged during camp when you're in a situation like mine, surrounded by so many great players, and wondering just where you're going to fit in. Pre-season is not the most fun time of year in a big-time football setting.

"You're there working on football 24 hours a day for six weeks. Once you make the season, it's all downhill from there. There's a lot of pressure on you at camp, but you have to keep trying to make a positive contribution. The pre-season was my time to shine. I'd get to carry the ball a lot in the pre-season games.

"I'd get more nervous going into the game as a running back than I did going in on special teams. On a kick-off, for instance, you could put everything into one play."

He was a reserve behind Rocky Bleier, whom he came to admire for many reasons. "When we made the movie about his life, that's how I first got into Hollywood," said Moser. "A lot of us Steelers were in the movie to make it realistic. I went up to the director and asked for more — I didn't just want to be a background prop — and I basically got a part playing myself. I was making $1500 bucks. The other guys were making $135 a day as extras, and they were doing all the hitting. The last two days of shooting they went on strike for more money. They got it; it was the funniest thing.

"That's also when I learned what Rocky's life was all about. I hadn't read his book (*Fighting Back*), and I came to realize that his comeback as a professional football player was quite a feat."

During his stay with the Steelers, Moser had off-season acting credits in TV shows such as "B.J. and the Bear," and "Different Strokes" and "Mr. Merlin," and for movies like "Fighting Back" and "Lovely But Deadly."

Moser maintains a great deal of respect for Chuck Noll as well as Bleier. "You'd go into a meeting with Coach Noll and you'd always come out with a new word to add to your vocabulary," said Moser. "He's a true Renaissance man. He knows something about everything."

The Steelers had something special for them, according to Moser. "They were very confident. We felt that we were supposed to win. I came

291

in and was playing with legends. All of them were trying to make you a better ballplayer. I never really followed football that much before I came to the Steelers. I didn't live and die football when I was in college. But I learned to appreciate the company I was keeping."

In Moser's third season with the Steelers, he was lost to the team through strange circumstances. The Steelers were preparing to play the Miami Dolphins at Three Rivers Stadium on November 30, 1980 and Moser and Thom Dornbrook, an offensive lineman who grew up in the North Hills, were both on injured reserve. The Steelers tried to sneak them both through waivers, believing they could recall them if any team claimed them. But Thanksgiving somehow got into the middle of the proceedings, changing the rules of the game somehow, and Moser and Dornbrook were both claimed by the Miami Dolphins. The Steelers had made a mistake.

"The funny thing about that was that it was Friday when I learned that Miami now owned our rights," recalled Moser, "and we were playing Miami in two days at home. Dornbrook and I had to move our equipment from the home club's locker room to the visitors' locker room that same Friday.

"I talked Don Shula into putting me into the game on the kickoff team. The guys on the Steelers were joking around with me. I made Greg Hawthorne fumble on the second or third kickoff of that game. But Pittsburgh won that game.

"I went to Miami, and I hated it there. I was spoiled by the Steelers, that's for sure. The position coach means a lot in football. Hoak was a great guy, but my coach in Miami was not. His nickname was Weasel. I didn't respect him. I finished out the season with Miami.

"The next year, in pre-season, my lower back was hurting me. I had Shula waive me on a failed physical. I was picked up by the Raiders. I went to the Raiders' training camp. I didn't play a down in pre-season, just on special teams. Tom Flores, the coach, told me to come in and bring my playbook. They waived me and I went home.

"It's seven weeks into the season, and I've got an acting part in a Tom Cruise movie called 'Losing It.' It was to be shot in Tijuana. It was a good part and the money was good. The day before I was to report to start production, I get invited by the Kansas City Chiefs to come there for a tryout.

"I was contracturally obligated to Hollywood, but they let me out. A fellow named Rick Rossovich got the part. He's the brother of Tim Rossovich, who played for the Philadelphia Eagles. Kansas City needed a guy because Art Still was on injured reserve. They needed a guy for two weeks, and then they let me go. Rick Rossovich got some real good parts after that movie. That might have been my big break. Who knows?

"In early November, I'm driving into Hollywood, and I hear on the radio that Cliff Stoudt had broken his hand on a punching bag in a bar after a game in Seattle. I had my agent call the Steelers right away. And I went back to them for the rest of the 1981 season.

"The next year I went to pre-season with the Steelers and made the team. But they waived me at the end of camp. Nobody picked me up and I stayed with the Steelers. Late in the season, we're playing Buffalo in Buffalo. I'm the blocking back on a punt, and I let my guy go too early, and he blocked a punt by John Goodson. I was in the doghouse over that.

"One of the quarterbacks got hurt, and they needed another quarterback. I was let go. As soon as they dropped me, I got picked up by Tampa Bay. I finished out the season there. That was the last stop.

"I got there on Friday and John McKay put me in the game on Sunday. I made three tackles on the special teams. He told the team that maybe he should bring more guys in from Pittsburgh and not practice them before a game. I came back to Tampa Bay the next year, and didn't make the team.

"So I gave the USFL a quick shot. I got a good contract to play for the New Orleans Breakers, but that didn't work out and they sent me to Woody Widenhofer — who knew me from being one of Noll's assistants in Pittsburgh — and now I was with the Oklahoma Outlaws. But they signed Sidney Thornton, who'd been a teammate of mine in Pittsburgh, and I was gone. But I got back to Pittsburgh for another shot with the Steelers. I was credited with five years in the NFL to gain a retirement pension. It was a good run. I was lucky."

Moon Mullins (72) pulls out of line to lead blocking for Rick Moser.

Jim Clack
Spreading the word down in Dallas

"I have my own goals for this year. I go over them every morning before I begin working. I've been as low to the bottom as you can be. And I've been at the top. The top is better."

Jim Clack was back on a familar road, on a route often referred to as Tobacco Road. He was back in Greensboro, not far from his roots in Rocky Mount, delivering an inspirational message to the Chamber of Commerce.

This was in early March of 1992. He told me he had been back the month before as well, to address the marketing directors for all the schools in the Atlantic Coast Conference. Clack is an ACC alumnus, having been graduated from Wake Forest, where he was honored the year before by being inducted into the school's Sports Hall of Fame.

So some of the faces and certainly the backdrops were familiar to Clack. He had been to Raleigh, as well, to talk to the folks at BTI, a small telephone company.

Jim Clack can talk. He has had to talk his way out of a few difficult times in his life, and a few scrapes along the way, but he has a good story to tell — about overcoming adversity at several points in his life — and about some good old-fashioned values he learned along the way while playing nine years (two on the taxi squad) with the Pittsburgh Steelers, and four more with the New York Giants. He made the Steelers on his third try.

He started for the Steelers in two Super Bowls (IX and X), and was nominated for NFL Man of the Year in 1976. He was named the team's most valuable offensive player in 1978-79. He was the offensive captain of the Giants. He became a successful businessman, and was on the board of directors of the American Heart Association and the Rocky Mount Boys Club.

He was as big a hometown hero as you can find.

Then he took a tumble. His personal life and his business world came apart at the seams, and he was in an auto accident in which he was nearly killed. So he had to mount another comeback.

His story has touched thousands of people and encouraged them to achieve and continue to strive in spite of obstacles. He has a reputation as an inspiring and heart-warming speaker. His topics sound like some of the stuff former teammate Rocky Bleier has been doing, about desire, goal-setting, achievement and winning through hard work. In fact, he told me he had bumped into Bleier back in December.

That was in the Bahamas, where other former NFLers like David Robinson, Ron Bergey, Isaac Curtis and Larry Little were also present for a special promotion.

Jim Clack

Clack has been working as a motivational speaker in recent years for The Brooks Group. Their offices had been in Greensboro, but in 1991 they shifted their base of operation to Dallas when Bill Brooks was offered a position as president of UGA, a company they had done consulting work for in the past. Brooks wanted to keep his own company going, so he asked Clack to come with him, and look after his company.

"It's been a great opportunity for me," said Clack, when we spoke in North Carolina. "I'm traveling around the country, speaking more, and keeping out of trouble. It's like being at training camp at St. Vincent all over again. I'm at work from 7:15 a.m. till 7:30 p.m. most days. Then I go and work out.

"I like working with Bill Brooks. He's a great motivational speaker himself, and you get obsessed with what he wants us to do. We're preaching a lot of what I learned in Pittsburgh, about doing it right. I have a great relationship with Bill Brooks, and we both do whatever has to be done, no matter what time of night it is.

"That's a lot like what Chuck Noll expected from us. It gets ingrained in your mind. To be successful, you have to work at it. Every team in the league is essentially equal in talent, I truly believe that. It's what you do with your work time, and how badly you want something, that make the difference.

"Playing pro football was not just a means of making money. Obviously, we didn't make big money in Pittsburgh. But we wanted to be the best at what we were doing.

"Our focus in our seminars is on teammwork and commitment. I wonder where that came from? Companies are laying off people, and people have slimmer staffs. They have to get more out of people. They have to get more dedicated performers. We help them do that.

"I have my own goals for this year. I go over them every morning before I begin working. I've been as low to the bottom as you can be. And I've been at the top. The top is better.

"I have been given an opportunity to run a company, and I feel very, very positive about it. But you just can't talk about it. I remember when I was with the Steelers that Noll was never a rah, rah kind of guy.

"I remember one time we were getting beat at the half, and Lee Calland, a defensive back, started yelling as we were coming out of the locker room for the second half. Chuck said, 'Hold it right now.' He called us back into the locker room. Then he read us the riot act. 'I don't believe in false chatter,' he cried out. 'Let's go out and do it!' Noll never believed in con jobs. He wasn't into a lot of talk.

"The great teams have been like that. Miami and the 49ers and the Giants were solid fundamentally, and they got the job done. You can look at films of the great teams. They were all together. They were all the same, not a lot of rah, rah or high-fiving.

"What happened to the Steelers toward the end of Chuck's coaching career was that they got into the false chatter, and the clowning in the end zone stuff. That's not the Steelers. But I saw this on TV.

"If a guy makes a good tackle, he shouldn't spend the next five minutes celebrating. You get paid a half million dollars to do that in some cases. If you knock someone's helmet off, maybe you have cause for celebration. But you have to know when to celebrate.

"Swann and Stallworth scored touchdowns and they handed the ball to the officials. What does Jerry Rice do? He puts the ball down. That's it. That's the key."

Clack said he continued to remain in contact with some of his former Steeler teammates. Some of them told him Noll had changed, that he had relaxed some of his laws a bit. "I'm told that guys come in late for meetings and it's no big deal," said Clack, shaking his head at the thought. "I never saw a lot of bullshit on the sideline before, but you see it now. I hear things and see things that Noll never would have tolerated when I was there.

"Maybe he lost some of his motivation. Maybe I will when I get to be 60. Who knows? How many games did he lose in the last ten years?

"He used to tell the players, 'Hey, guys, your career is through. It's time to get on with your life's work.' Well, maybe the time has come for coaches to practice what they preach. His time is due.

"It happened with Tom Landry. If they don't win, why should they be there? Did they keep Franco Harris after he had passed his prime?

"They didn't want to pay him for what he had done for them. They need some new spark there. They've got to lighten up the atmosphere. Dan Rooney is like a funeral director. He can't get excited about anything. They miss The Old Man. He'd come in the locker room, and he'd say, 'Hey, Jim, come here and talk to me a sec.' Everybody liked him. They felt he cared about him. That's why we played for the little bit of money we played for.

"We do a profile on companies, and we see how workers react to different things. It's not always money that turns people on. It doesn't have to be material possessions. We enjoyed doing what we did because the Steelers were special, and there was a special atmosphere. We were the lighthouse of the league.

"When Gordon Gravelle went to the LA Rams, he told us how different it was. Their owner said she treated the players just like she treated her thoroughbred horses. Now how'd you like to hear that?

"We used to be encouraged to bring our kids to practice on Saturdays at the Stadium. It's sad to hear how the team doesn't get together. Other championship teams get together. The teams bring them in. With the Steelers, Ray Mansfield has to do it himself. The events are not really team-sponsored.

"They've been living off the past. They haven't won anything lately."

"Noll never believed
in con jobs."
Jim Clack

Dale Dodril (1951-59)

Ernie Stautner (1950-63)

These were Steelers..

Joe Bach (1935-36, 1952-53)

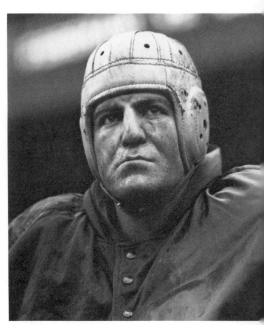

Leo Nobile (1948-49)

Chuck Cherundolo (1941-42, 1945-48)   **Fran Rogel (1950-57)**

John "Zero" Clement (1946-48)

These were Steelers . . .

Bobby Layne (1958-62)

Lynn Chandnois (1950-56)

Johnny "Blood" McNally
(1934, 1937-39)

Jock Sutherland (1946-47)

"Bullet Bill" Dudley
A true Renaissance man

"I believe Bill Dudley was as good as any football player who has ever played in the National League. He wasn't fast, but nobody caught him. He couldn't pass, but he completed passes. He was one of the top kickers in the game. The best all-around ballplayer I've ever seen."
—Art Rooney

"Games played with the ball, and others of that nature, are too violent for the body and stamp no character on the mind!"

"Error of opinion may be tolerated, where reason is left free to combat it."
—Thomas Jefferson

There is a beauty and strength and grace about Bill Dudley and his wife, Libba, and they are to be envied and admired. They are a throwback to another more chivalrous era, of Southern gentlemen and Southern belles, when it was important to be pleasant and polite, and to have honor and integrity. They represent the best of their generation. They are a class act.

"I've always been proud of Bill," allowed Libba, which is short for Elizabeth. "I've always been Bill Dudley's wife. People kid me about it. But he's still my favorite fellow. He is positive, and has many strengths, and I admire him for that."

To me, he will always be "Bullet Bill" Dudley, a legendary figure, a special name in football lore, a name that I remember from my earliest youth, when I first became fascinated with sports figures, and collected bubblegum cards, and read every sports magazine I could get my hands on.

I was born the same summer — August of 1942 — when Dudley reported as a rookie All-American from the University of Virginia to the Pittsburgh Steelers' training camp in Hershey, Pa. He was the team's No. 1 draft choice, the first player taken in the draft because the Steelers had finished last in the league the year before. So we both showed up in Pittsburgh the same year, and perhaps that adds to my fascination. He played only three seasons (1942, 1945-46) with the Steelers, interrupted by a 2 1/2 year stint as a pilot and instructor in the Army Air Corps during World War II, yet he remains one of the most famous and popular Steelers of all time. He later played with the Detroit Lions and Washington Redskins, and was elected to the Pro Football Hall of Fame in 1966.

As a rookie, playing both ways, he led the league in rushing and lifted the Steelers from last place to second. He was 5-10 1/2 and weighed 170 pounds. That's the same size as Gary Anderson, the Steelers' placekicker, which points up the difference in the times. His nickname — "Bullet Bill" — was a misnomer. It sounded good, but in the training camp of the College All-Stars in Chicago he consistently finished dead last among all backs in sprints. Yet he was special. He even kicked extra points and field goals, with an awkward style, like everything else he did. In 1946, he led the Steelers with 10 interceptions in 11 games, including one he returned 80 yards for a touchdown, and was named the NFL's MVP.

"He was the best all-around ballplayer I've ever seen," Steelers' owner Art Rooney told Myron Cope for a wonderful 1970 book called *The Game That Was.*

I was introduced to Bill Dudley by Mr. Rooney, whom he visited on occasion at the Steelers' offices through the years. They were the best of friends. I cherish the memory of a private dinner party the Dudleys attended, along with Jerry Nuzum, Joe Gasparella, Lynn Chandnois, and their wives, and Fran Rogel at the P.A.A. in Oakland back in 1982. They were all boyhood heroes of mine. My wife Kathie and I were both especially impressed with the Dudleys. They were different. They had a special Southern charm about them. It wasn't just their accent, but what they said and how they said it, that set them apart from most people. I remember that Libba wore an elegant black dress that night, and had her champagne blonde hair pulled back tight and tied with a black ribbon. "I wore it with a French twist then; that was some time ago," recalled Libba when I mentioned the memory to her during our most recent meeting.

I had just had a bountiful breakfast with the Dudleys in the dining room of the Farmington Country Club in Charlottesville, Virginia. The food and the conversation were special, and I felt privileged to be in the company of this couple that are still very much in love after 45 years of marriage. She fussed over Bill and I with equal relish.

The young waiter was unaware of who he was serving. He was too young. "How do you spell your name?" he asked. "Is that D-u-d? And l-e-y?" Just about every other person in the room stopped by the table to say hello to the Dudleys. They remain a celebrity couple in Charlottesville.

Both looked well. Bill wore a blue blazer with a University of Virginia lapel pin, and a yellow golf jersey and beige slacks. His face was bronzed and his hair parted with a precise cut as always. Libba wore a violet blouse and a floor-length blue and violet skirt. Her hair was cut shorter than when I last saw her.

Bill had left Libba and I behind to attend a meeting that was part of the weekend schedule for a reunion of an organization he belonged to at his alma mater at the nearby University of Virginia grounds. She and I sat on a veranda overlooking a beautiful golf course, and continued our conversation. It was the weekend for The Masters, and if you couldn't make it to the Augusta National this was not a bad runner-up. Libba said Bill was hoping to play golf later in the day.

The clubhouse was once a mansion on a rich man's estate. It has been beautifully restored. Buildings where slaves were once housed were pointed out to me, as were buildings where horses were once kept. This was the South, no doubt about it.

There was a rich aroma about the grounds from the flowers that had just bloomed. There were daffodils, paper whites, magnolias, and jonquils, as Libba identified the flowers for me. "There's a delicious fragrance to them," she said.

When I mentioned to Libba that Bill was so upbeat and positive, she said, "He's always been like that. When things go in the wrong direction for him, he still has the will to turn things around, that he'll do what's necessary to change the course of events. He knows the way out."

I inquired about his health. He had coughed, and cleared his throat harshly and continually during our conversation.

"He hawks all the time; I tell him about it, but he doesn't notice it any more," she said, smiling. "He had his nose flattened several times. There's no cartilage in his nose. It's just wishy washy if you touch it. He had a deviated septum. He's got a terrible sinus drip, and he has to clear his throat all the time."

Dudley, of course, played football before players wore face masks or nose guards. "I'd never know him if he had a pretty nose," said Libba, with one of those lines that distinguishes her conversation.

I also noticed that when we descended stairs to go into the dining room that Bill held on to a handrail and placed both feet on the same step before advancing, the same way my mother, who was 85 then, would do it.

"His knees are in terrible shape," said Libba. "He had arthroscopic surgery on them about eight to ten years ago, in the early days of such surgery, but now he's Mr. Hippety Hop. His one leg is shorter than the other, and it causes him to have back pain now and then. I wish he'd go and get new knees; they're having so much success with that now. I'm so afraid he won't be able to play golf; he enjoys it so much.

"I'd like him to do it soon so he's young enough to recover and get used to replacement knees. As it is, he can't stand for a long time without having pain. He's Mr. Parentheses, you know. He's always been bow-legged."

"How old is Bill?" I asked.

"Bill had his big one on December 24th," she said. "He turned 70."

"My mother's birthday is also on Christmas Eve," I came back.

"Bill's mother and his grandmother were also born on Christmas Eve," she said. "His mother, God willing, will be 99 this coming Christmas Eve."

I mentioned that Bill seemed to have great affection for the University of Virginia. That was an understatement.

"When he left the Steelers, he thought he was going to coach here," she said. "But then the Lions offered Bill a three-year contract, so he continued in pro ball.

"Charlottesville and the University have a real mystique for Virginians. I am from Lynchburg, where we still live, and Bill is from Bluefield. There's so much history here, and the atmosphere is magnificent. This is Thomas Jefferson's university. The University has grown up since Bill was a student here, but it's kept its charm. They've been able to keep that the same. It's like they have crystalized that in time. So it's something special. Virginia is a special place.

"Bill is a special man. He is a remarkable man in so many ways. He is a man of many hats. But he's always worn a small hat. His head has remained small. He has handled all his achievements and the attention it has brought him in the most humble way.

"I've never seen him think he's better than another person. He has a great deal of compassion and empathy. He's a very religious person. He has great spiritual depth. He has very firm religious convictions; he had a strong foundation from his family. They were Baptists. My family is Catholic, and Bill has become a Catholic.

"He has been a loving husband and father, but a father who disciplined his children. Whenever he said something, the kids knew he meant it. He doesn't mince words if he thinks anyone's wrong, maybe to a fault."

I received a letter at the outset of April from Bill Dudley, on his company stationery. He has been a sales representative for 31 years for The Equitable Life Assurance Society, working out of the Allied Arts Building on Church Street in Lynchburg. He does estate planning, for the most part. He has been in the insurance business, altogether, for 41 years.

He also served eight years in the state legislature (1966-73), and served a similar span (1974-81) as a member of the Board of Visitors at the University of Virginia. He is a statesman in the tradition of Thomas Jefferson, the school's founder.

"Appreciate your letter of March 16 and am sorry to be so late in answering," Bill began his letter, "but I had a brother-in-law, who was very sick and passed away and then my mother had a stroke. Anyway, will try to answer some of the questions you posed and will enclose a picture or two.

"Am still working, not pushing as hard as I used to but still in the office by 8:15 a.m. or 8:30 a.m., pushing paper, etc. Needless to say, during football season, I always think about my days with the Steelers as being possibly the happiest I spent in pro football, particularly the 1942 season, even though it was my first. I particularly enjoyed the train rides to and from games.

"You have heard me state before that the fans were fantastic and my opinion has not changed. One of the highlights of my career was my acceptance by the Pittsburgh community. I would have loved to have finished my career with Pittsburgh, but at the time it just wasn't in the cards and, thus, you make the best of the hand that is dealt you.

John Henry Johnson, Chuck Noll, Lynn Chandnois with Bill Dudley.

Dudley leads the pack at 50th reunion of 1941 Virginia grid squad.

Art Rooney and his family — the best. An employer-employee relationship began in 1942 and turned into a friendship that lasted a lifetime.

"The player I admired the most on our team was Chuck Cherundolo. He was a leader. He played all out. He was a real team man, one you could count on in every circumstance."

Coincidentally, Cherundolo, a center from Penn State, may have been the first Steeler I ever met in person. He was a salesman for a wine company when my mother worked in a state store that sold liquor and wine in our community. Cherundolo called on the store from time to time, and that's where I met him.

Dudley was coached by Walt Kiesling in his rookie season. When he returned to the Steelers following World War II, the Steelers were coached by Dr. Jock Sutherland, the tough disciplinarian who had previously directed the Brooklyn Dodgers and University of Pittsburgh football team. Sutherland and Dudley dueled from the start. They just didn't get along. So Sutherland traded Dudley during their second season together.

Back to Bill Dudley's letter of March 30, 1992:

"Since 1982 (the Steelers' 50 Seasons Celebration), I have become a grandfather two more times and have a granddaughter who will attend the University of Virginia this fall, and two grandsons, 12 and 10, who will be playing soccer. One regret: I was never married when I played football with the Steelers. As a result, my wife has only gotten to know a few of the people in Pittsburgh who were so good to me during my brief career in the City.

"I have had the privilege and pleasure of watching pro football grow up from the days of practicing when you couldn't see the sun until noon or later. Trips were taken by train in day coaches, Forbes Field with its wooden floors in the dressing rooms as well as holes in the boards. You brought your own pads to training camp, etc. Yet, when I played my last years with the Redskins, it was first class hotels, plane travel, whirlpools, concrete or marble floors, etc., in the stadiums. Could go on and on, but you have enough information, etc.; and, hopefully, will look forward to saying hello this fall."

While I was visiting with the Dudleys, my oldest daughter, Sarah, an 18-year-old high school senior, was participating in a special orientation event for prospective students for an honors program at the University of Virginia. We had attended a similar program the day before at the University of North Carolina at Chapel Hill, and I thought she now had her heart set on going to North Carolina. It was an idyllic day, with temperatures in the high '70s, and fresh flowers and shrubs signalling the start of spring. Teachers had taken their students out onto the lawns for classes. Everyone was wearing shorts or sundresses. It was more of the same in Virginia. "Chapel Hill just drips with Southern charm," allowed Libba, "but I think you'll find Virginia someplace special.

"Wait till she sees The University," warned Libba. "You must let us know what she decides."

Soon after he had sat down to breakfast, Bill began to discuss the merits of the University of Virginia. "I personally feel it's special," he said. "Very much so. I'm prejudiced, I know, but the University has a flair about it, just a little different feeling. Most of its graduates feel the same way."

Libba interjected, "We were just talking about it last night. Most who attended the school still talk about it with awe."

"There's so much tradition," said Bill. "Thomas Jefferson is still there, in a lot of ways, still establishing guidelines for proper behavior. It's not only physically attractive, but there's a philosophy that's appealing. They have an honor system. If you look over the grounds, you'll feel it."

At The University, they don't call it a campus. It's called "the grounds." There are no freshmen or sophomores. They are first-year and second-year students. There are no seniors, because Jefferson said you are never finished being educated. Professors are addressed as "Mr." or "Mrs." or "Ms." rather than as "Dr." because Jefferson did not have a doctorate, and no one could have a higher status than the school's founder and architect.

As I toured the grounds, and listened to professors and school administrators talk reverently about the school's spirit later that same day, I kept hearing references to honor and integrity, and these are things that Bill Dudley had discussed at our meeting. At 70, he is still adhering to the school's philosophy. He is a great walking advertisement for its virtues.

"When I went to Notre Dame for the first time last summer, for an NFL Alumni Association golf outing," declared Dudley, "I was given a tour by Johnny Lujack and Creighton Miller, two of their former stars. We were walking around, taking it all in, a real cook's tour, and Lujack was just beaming."

"Bill, have you ever seen a more beautiful place?" Lujack, at last, asked Dudley.

Miller, who knew Dudley longer, turned to him and said, "Bill, forgive him, he's never seen The University."

And no one was more of a Notre Dame man than Miller. His dad had been one of the original "Four Horsemen of Notre Dame." But he also knew how much Dudley loved Virginia.

I wanted Bill to talk about his days with the Steelers. Libba led him on. "You always said Pittsburgh fans were not only good fans, but they were knowledgeable fans," she said.

"They could pick out the loafers," said Bill.

I told him that Pete Rozelle, the former NFL Commissioner, had said he had never heard the word "loafing" until he met Mr. Rooney. "Oh, that's a word we used when I was working on the farm," said Dudley. "I knew it before I ever got to Pittsburgh."

I asked him if any of the veterans gave him a hard time about being called "Bullet Bill" when he showed up for his first camp. I remembered how "Mercury" Morris had taken so much heat about his nickname when he first came to the camp of the Miami Dolphins.

"Every ballplayer is skeptical about somebody who shows up with a reputation," Bill came back. "It doesn't mean they don't like you. They want to see what you've got. I'll never forget there was a fellow named Andy Tomasic. He was from Temple, and he was a good boy. He talked in his own inimitable way. He greeted me by saying, 'I saw some of your movies and I didn't think you were so hot.'

"I always felt . . . I never thought I could do anything special. I always felt I had to prove myself. A lot of the ballplayers today seem to think they're the greatest football player who ever lived. Is that true? Um, um. I always felt I had to work a little harder than the other fellow. I tried harder."

"Did you do the same thing in business?"

"Yes, sir. I still felt I had to prove myself. I still felt I had to work harder than the next guy to succeed."

"How do you account for all your success?"

"Luck . . . and effort," said Dudley. "I've always had a strong work ethic. Most people who were brought up when I was growing up had a strong work ethic. You were given something to do, and you did it, or you got your ass beat."

Libba blushed at Bill's bluntness. "You shouldn't. . .," she said.

"Well, it's the truth," Dudley continued. "I can't remember not working. I never heard of anybody dying from overwork. When you're overworked, you're tired and you go to sleep.

"My father, at first, was a meat salesman in Bluefield. That didn't last. Then he got into the life insurance business in 1932 or 1933. We had a couple of cows at our place. We all milked cows. We had a big garden, and we tended to that, too. Yes, I milked cows. I got up in the morning and delivered papers. I did that for about five years. It was the *Bluefield Daily Telegraph.* I'd leave home at a quarter to six to deliver the papers, and I'd get back at seven. Then I'd go out and milk the cows and I'd get back home at seven-thirty. I'd eat breakfast, and then I'd walk to school. I'd get there about eight forty-five. My older brother, Jim, did it before me. My younger brother, Tom, did it after me. There were four of us. I had an older sister, Margaret, but she died when she was 71."

I asked him how he had met Libba, and their faces both lit up. They needed little prodding. This was obviously one of their favorite stories. The Dudleys delight in retelling it.

"We had four sets of dances a year at Virginia," said Bill. "We had The Openings, the Midwinters, the Easters and the Finals. We always had big bands come in to perform at The University.

"I was standing on the side of the dance floor in 1942. I had been drafted by the Steelers, and I had also enlisted in the Navy Air Corps. I was talking to the captain of the football team. He was on his way to his senior season, and I was trying to get him to come back to school. He had already enlisted in the Marines. And Libba walked by with the fellow who brought her to the dance. I looked at her, and then I looked at her again when she walked by. Yes, I looked at her twice.

308

With Jock Sutherland.

"Bullet Bill" at Virginia

ırly Lambeau
dskins Coach

Sammy Baugh
Redskins QB

"The fellow I was talking to said to me, 'You like that.' I said, 'Yeah, you know her.' He said, 'I do. She's from my hometown in Lynchburg.' I asked, 'Can I meet her?'

"I danced with her, and when we were done, I said, 'Listen, sister, if you're here when I come back from the service, I'm going to look you up.' She said that was fine with her."

"I was 16, sweet 16, and just a senior in high school," recalled Libba. "I'd come up here with a Lynchburg boy. I didn't go to school here. I went to Randolph-Macon College, a women's school in our community. I had the best of both worlds. When I was behind that gate at school, I was as far from my family as I wanted to be. When I wanted to go home it didn't take me long to get there. And I took friends home with me. I was still in college when we had our first date."

"When we started dating," said Bill, "I knew what I wanted. I was lucky and persistent. I didn't have any communication with her for several years, but I called her soon as I got back from the service. She was very popular then, and dated about ten or twelve fellows. I couldn't get a date. It took me five or six weeks just to get a date. I prayed to the Lord to bring her to me.

"I started dating her in July of 1946, just before I reported to the Steelers' training camp. She told me soon after that she was becoming engaged to a fellow named Paul. I said 'I was sorry to hear that, and I hemmed and hawwed. I'll be around till the whistle blows,' I told her. I called her in the fall, and she said she wanted me to meet Paul. And I did. And I told him, 'I congratulate you, but if I can still beat your time, I will.' I used to go to bed and pray. I'm a believer. I said, 'Lord, I know you know how I feel. I want to make her my wife.'

"I hurt my leg in the last game of the season, at Philadelphia, and I stopped by to see a doctor in Charlottesville on my way back to my home in Bluefield. Then I stopped in Lynchburg to say hello. She called me and told me Paul couldn't take her to a Junior League dance, and asked if I would escort her. It was December, and I drove through a snowstorm to get to Lynchburg and take her. Later, I got a Valentine's Day card from her. She just said hello, nothing else. I called and told her I'd like to see her. She said that was OK, but that we couldn't go out or anything like that. So she and I sat and talked at her house, and we took a walk.

"I called her up and said, 'I'd like to see you again. You know the way I feel. I haven't changed.' After that, I went down to see her every other weekend.

"Next thing I know, she calls me and tells me she is breaking her engagement. It was in May. We got engaged on July 4th, and we were married on the 29th of July. I just knew what I wanted."

"And," interjected Libba, "we've been happy for 45 years. We got married when I was 21 and Bill was 25. Bill was very persistent. I was all set to get married to another young man. We had the invitations ordered, and we had linens monogrammed. I decided I was going the wrong way. I'm glad I changed my senses. I broke my engagement and became engaged to Bill. And three weeks after that, we got married. My mother got our wedding together in two weeks."

"When she broke her engagement, I was away that weekend with Mr. Rooney at the Kentucky Derby," said Bill. "He took me there a few times. We announced our engagement the first weekend in July, and we were married July 29th."

I asked Dudley what he thought of Chuck Noll. "He is a damn good football coach," declared Dudley. "He is one of the best. And he had a damn good team. He was a disciplinarian. That's needed to win championships. And that's what it's all about.

"I never really got to know Noll. I just followed his coaching. I think Paul Brown was probably the most outstanding coach in my time, frankly, and I think he had a great influence on Chuck Noll. I learned an awful lot of football from Paul Brown just from having him coach me on two All-Star squads.

"You must be respected in your job. Players don't have to like you, but you must have complete respect for the individuals you work for. If you like them and respect them, all the better. The same is true in business. For a boss to get the best out of you, and vice versa, you have to respect him.

"I go back to when I was a coach with the Redskins in 1953. We had Curly Lambeau as our head coach. He thought he knew a lot about football, and he did. But he didn't want to look at films. All the assistant coaches would look at the films, and tell him what they saw. He'd say 'I know that,' no matter what we told him about the other team. He was starting to take some things for granted, like a lot of us do when we've been in a job for a long time. And he did know 90 per cent of what was going on. But he could have known the other 10 per cent as well, if he would have only listened to what his assistants had to say. From what I can gather, Noll listened to what his assistants had to say. He was in charge, no doubt about that, but he listened. And I'm told his players had input, too.

"When I first joined the Steelers, our coach was Walt Kiesling. He was a very good assistant coach. But he was never meant to be a head coach. He didn't have the personality for it. There's a big difference between being an assistant coach and a successful head coach. There have been an awful lot of assistant coaches who turned out not to be good head coaches."

"With that in mind," I said, "do you think the Steelers took a big risk in hiring an assistant coach to be their new head coach?"

"You always take a chance," said Dudley. "People took a chance when they hired Noll. Someone took a chance on Don Shula and Dan Reeves, and I think they're good head coaches. The most successful coaches, as far as I'm concerned, were George Halas, Paul Brown, Vince Lombardi, Don Shula and Tom Landry, along with Noll. They were all disciplined individuals to begin with, and most of them didn't put up

311

with any horseshit. I've watched them all. You have to have the personnel. I never played on a championship team, and I'd have given my eyeballs to have done so. I played for nine years, and I played for nine different coaches. So people might ask, 'How the hell does Dudley know so much since he was never on a championship team?'

"I think Noll developed Bradshaw, and he had a great supporting cast. When you talk about any dynasty, there's going to be a lot of talent on the team, a lot of Hall of Famers. The Steelers had great talent, but they had to have someone pull it all together.

"The biggest thing about a football coach is he has to know what he needs. He has to take what he says he needs and win with it.

"Things are more sophisticated today, with the scouting and all, and the new technology, but I don't know that the athlete's approach is any better. A lot of us felt every time we went out on the field we had something to prove. Sammy Baugh was the best football player I've ever seen, yet he always wanted to prove himself. I don't mean to be derogatory about today's players, but I think society has made them different. When we were growing up, you felt like you were underprivileged. You wanted to make the most of your opportunities to play this game."

"A lot of things are different," I said. "For instance, you went into the military service. You signed up on your own."

"Well, I figured I was going to get drafted, so I wanted to beat them to it," he said. "I signed up for the Navy first, but I didn't hear from them, and so I signed up with the Army Air Corps. I wanted to fly. I wanted to shoot down Japs. That sounds awful today, forgive me, but that's what I wanted to do. I only got to fly two missions, and they were supply missions. I never saw a Jap plane. I was an instructor most of the time. I was sent to Saipan to play football. A big war was going on and we all wanted to be a part of it. All the bases had football teams, but everybody was itching for some real action."

I asked him about his friendship with Art Rooney.

"Why or how that developed one never knows," he responded. "I don't know if I was one of his favorites or not. I always looked at him as a friend. In the nine years I played in the National Football League, what I cherish most are the people I got to meet. I regret not having played all my years with Pittsburgh.

"But I got to meet Mr. Rooney, and Mr. Bell, and Mr. Marshall, and Mr. Mara, and Mr. Halas. They were great owners; they were great people. I got to know them all on a first-name basis." While he said that, it was interesting to note that he still, at 70, referred to them by their surnames.

"My relationship with Mr. Rooney helped me get to know all those people," he added. "We used to get postcards from him all the time, especially when he went to Canada. Art was a tremendous people person.

"I thought Art Rooney was a man of his word. Where I growed up, my word was always my bond. That's the way Mr. Rooney was. One time he was supposed to have sent a wire to bookies at race tracks around the country, and he could place a bet for several thousand dollars, and

312

it was honored. They knew he was good for the money. I don't know if that's true or not, but that's what I understood."

I asked Bill how he felt he fared in his 70 years. "The Good Lord blessed Bill Dudley," he said. "I've always worked. I've never seen anything wrong with it. I grew up with a different social attitude. Most ballplayers have to get a job, and they ought to prepare themselves for that while they are in school, and during the off-season. Only a few are fixed for life, and even they need to find a purpose in their post-playing days. Even some of the ones who make so much money are going to find a way to blow most of it. They're going to have to earn a living the next fifty years of their lives. They should be more concerned with life after football. No one loved the game more than I did, but you can't play forever.

"As for what's ahead . . . I'm taking it a bit easier. I don't make the calls I made ten years ago. I'm not a wealthy man, but we have a nice life, and I feel rich. Libba and I had four wonderful children. We lost a son, Little Bill, who died of leukemia when he was 5 1/2. You don't forget that. He took sick July 16th and died July 22nd. So we have three living."

When Libba looks at Bill, she reflects: "I often wish he'd slow down, and smell the roses. He's a demon for time. His days are filled every day, months ahead of time. I guess that's good in a way."

Bill looks back gratefully upon his years as a professional football player.

"It gave me everything," he said. "It gave me something to do when I came out of school, it gave me the start. Athletes at the University always knew they weren't here just to play ball. I think Virginia is the greatest place in the world. It gave me an opportunity to get me an education."

As I left Libba at the entrance to the clubhouse, she stood amid the flowers she had identified for me earlier. I went down the driveway and got into my automobile. As I was driving back toward the entrance, I saw Libba standing there, holding a paper white flower in her hand. I felt like I was in a movie. I stopped, and she came over and handed me the flower. "Something to remember us by," she said.

During my tour of the University of Virginia grounds later that day, I went off by myself to University Hall, where the University of Virginia basketball team plays its home games. I was told there was a hallway where plaques and photos and school sports memorabilia were on display. There was a wall in the hallway outside the main arena where plaques were posted of all the football players whose jerseys were retired. Dudley was the first to be so honored. His plaque, however, was hidden by T-shirts which had been hung out for display. There was a Christian concert for teens going on inside and they were selling appropriate paraphernalia at the entranceway.

The vendor removed the T-shirt so I could read Dudley's plaque:

35 Bill Dudley (1939-1941)
5-10   170 lbs.
Bluefield, Va.

313

Two-time All-American performer . . . Led nation in points scored (134 points) in 1941 . . . College Football Player of the Year in 1941 by Washington Touchdown Club and Maxwell Club of Philadelphia . . . Inducted into National Football Foundation's College Football Hall of Fame in 1956 . . . NFL MVP in 1946 . . . Named to Pro Football Hall of Fame in 1966 . . . B.S. in Education.

Down the hallway were other framed certificates from various All-America teams, and one for the Virginia Sports Hall of Fame, in which Dudley was inducted in May of 1972.

I took some pictures with my camera, and then raced to rejoin my daughter. As I drove across the grounds, I decided I wouldn't tell Sarah anything the Dudleys had said about the school because I didn't want to influence her decision in any way. If she wanted to go to the University of North Carolina at Chapel Hill that would be fine with me. And I was sure her mother would approve.

As we left Charlottesville and headed north to our home in Pittsburgh, Sarah turned to me and said, "Dad, I want to go to the University of Virginia."

I had a feeling that either Bill Dudley or Art Rooney were pulling some strings somewhere and smiling.

Jim O'Brien

Libba and Bill Dudley at ease in Charlottesville.

Ernie Stautner
The Steelers never had a tougher player
"I never was a good loser."

There was a special atmosphere with the Steelers in the '50s, even if it wasn't a winning atmosphere. Ernie Stautner hated the losing, but he loved the Steelers. They were a lot of fun and they played football hard, if seldom outscoring the opposition.

"I know I wasn't a loser," said Stautner, 67 and an assistant coach in his second season with the Denver Broncos, when we talked at an NFL Alumni Assn. golf outing at Oakmont Country Club June, 1992. "To me, a loser is a guy who is caught on a losing team but doesn't really care much. You know what I mean?

"The team will lose and lose and lose, and the guy will just drift along, putting in his time and never once showing any pride in himself and standing up to say, 'Something's wrong around here.' A loser is a guy who can laugh and tell jokes as he's leaving the field after dropping a game. I could never do that.

"I mean we lost a lot when I was playing for the Steelers, but I never got used to it.

"Every summer when I reported to training camp, I felt the Steelers were going all the way to the championship. I'd say to myself, 'I know we've had bad years, but that's in the past. This is a new year and a new start. This time we're gonna do it.'"

Stautner was an All-NFL defensive end and tackle with the Steelers, and played in the Pro Bowl nine times. Altogether, Stautner played 14 seasons with the Steelers, establishing a team record that was surpassed only by Mike Webster, who spent 15 seasons with the Steelers (1974-1988), and two more with the Kansas City Chiefs. Stautner was a player-coach that 14th season with the Steelers.

He stayed on as an assistant one more year, and then put in one year with the Washington Redskins before he joined Tom Landry's coaching staff with the Dallas Cowboys, where he coached the defensive line 23 years (1966-1988). He was the defensive coordinator for 21 of those years. He was one of the architects of the "Doomsday Defense."

He lost his job there when Tom Landry was fired. He was the head coach of the Dallas Texans in the Arena Football League, and was named coach of the year in 1990. Then he was offered the post of defensive line coach in Denver by Dan Reeves, a long-time Landry aide and former Cowboy in Dallas. "The lure of the NFL pulled me back," he said.

Stautner was one of four Steelers from the '50s named to their All-Time team, the only players voted to the lineup who did not play in a Super Bowl. The others were Jack Butler, Elbie Nickel and Pat Brady.

Stautner was a stalwart with the Steelers from 1950 through 1963 and has become a legendary figure in the team's history — he and his buddy Bobby Layne — for on-the-field and off-the-field shenanigans.

With Dan Rooney at Canton ceremonies.

At Oakmont C.C. in June, 1992.

Ernie Stautner

With "Big Daddy" Lipscomb

He was named to the Pro Football Hall of Fame in 1969, his first year of eligibility. Layne was elected in 1967.

Stautner says that Nickel and Butler both belong in the Hall of Fame as well, and that Brady was one of the best punters of his day. "His career was cut short by injury," he said.

"There's no way you can tell me that Nickel couldn't play tight end for us today," said Stautner over the telephone in an earlier interview. "Some of the catches he made were fantastic. They'd hit him in the back and it never fazed him.

"Butler was in the class of the top defensive backs, along with 'Night Train' Lane, Jack Christiansen, Emlen Tunnell and Yale Lary."

Stautner also said it was too bad there wasn't room on the All-Time team for John Henry Johnson. "He was a tough nutter," said Stautner. "He took nothing from nobody, and he'd be hell on wheels today, too."

Stautner said he wasn't faulting the voters for the oversight, and their choice of Franco Harris and Rocky Bleier as the all-time running backs on the club. Harris and Johnson have since both been named to the Pro Football Hall of Fame.

"The more-recent activities overshadow what happened once upon a time," said Stautner. "Everyone has a different view. It's hard to compare. It's very difficult to keep in mind what the old guys did. You can't expect everybody to know about the old days. I think it's great to have the fan participation in the voting. It's better for the game."

Stautner was the only so-called old-timer to crack the Steelers' famed "Steel Curtain," joining Joe Greene, L.C. Greenwood and Dwight White on the defensive line.

"The reason for that," said Stautner, "is that the older you get the more explosive you get. The game has changed considerably since then. It's gotten much more complicated, much more sophisticated, and much more demanding. The hitting hasn't changed, though, that's for sure.

"The defense is more limited today by the rules. Playing today would be extremely frustrating for a defensive lineman; I know because I coach them."

Stautner still has a smashed-in nose, square jaw and a look that would ward off would-be muggers. He looks like he could still handle himself in NFL wars. He appreciates the compliment, but he knows better.

"A guy my size (6-0, 218, when he came out of Boston College) wouldn't even get drafted today," said Stautner, "or they would want to switch me to linebacker. I was told I was too small by Frank Leahy when I tried out for Notre Dame, and they said the same thing when I went to the Steelers.

"The game has progressed. The scouting and coaching has improved. They use the computers now. You have to know more."

Something has been lost along the way, though. Stautner surely recognizes that as well as anyone, even more so than most because he has bridged the old days and current days in his pro football career.

"A lot of the camaraderie is lost today," said Stautner. "We used to go to the South Park Inn after practice and drink beer and eat those big fish sandwiches, and hamburgers, and we'd run together at night. We'd get together at Dante's in Whitehall."

As a 21-year-old sportswriter, I used to frequent Dante's because the Steelers and the sportswriters like Myron Cope, Pat Livingston and Bob Drum would be there. Stautner and Layne once gave my dad and brother a bad time, and I had to drive the getaway car to get my dad and brother back home in one piece. Stautner scared off a few people in that place. Stautner smiled when I reminded him of that.

"Now, everyone is involved in their own business deals, and they head to some office as soon as practice is over," he said ruefully. "You don't have that type of relationship anymore.

"I try to promulgate that. I invite my linemen to my house for fish fries, or take them out to dinner. I think you can have two different relationships with your players: All business on the field and yet have some fun off the field."

Dwelling on his days in Pittsburgh, Stautner said, "It was a great atmosphere, starting with the Rooney family right on down, but I'd trade it for the four Super Bowl rings, and the winning atmosphere.

"The worst thing in sports is to be a loser. The 15 years of losing with the Steelers started to make me doubt myself. I realize it was no fun being a loser. I knew it then, not just by comparison with what I experienced with the Cowboys.

"I didn't want anybody to beat me. The greatest motivation was not to be embarrassed. I loved to get ready to play against a real top player."

The closest Stautner and the Steelers came to being winners was in 1963. I was a senior at Pitt that year and started a tabloid newspaper called *Pittsburgh Weekly Sports*, along with Beano Cook, then the sports publicist at Pitt.

The timing was perfect. Pitt went 9-1 that year and the Steelers nearly won an NFL title.

"I never had as much fun as I did in 1963, which is the year we went right down to the final game in New York," Stautner told Ray Didinger when he was a sports columnist for the old *Philadelphia Evening Bulletin*.

"I had waited my whole career for that kind of opportunity, and when it came, it was one of the biggest thrills of my life. Oh, sure I felt the pressure the same as everybody else right before we played the Giants, but it was good pressure.

"I welcomed it. After all the years of finishing out of the running, it was a beautiful feeling to be down to the final game of the year and know all the chips were right there on the table, waiting to be taken.

"The pressure of a game like that didn't rattle my nerves or anything, if that's what you mean. It's like the old saying: If you can't take the heat, get out of the kitchen. Well, the same thing applies. I'd hate to think I was the kind of player who is fine for ten years while he's playing for a tailend ball club, but when he is asked to produce goes to pieces. I don't think I was.

"After that game, I felt dejection. Frustration. And anger.

"It's no secret, but I was terribly angry at our quarterback, Ed Brown. I never saw a quarterback have such a bad day. We had more scoring chances than I could count, and Ed fluffed just about every one. Oh brother, was I angry after that game.

"I was angry at Buddy Parker, too, because he was the man who made Bobby Layne retire at the end of the previous season. I have no doubt that if Bobby Layne was our quarterback in 1963, we would have beaten the Giants and probably won the world championship.

"That's what I had been working toward for all those bad years. It's not a very nice thing to admit, but I held a grudge about that for quite some time. That was the most crushing defeat of my entire life, and I didn't take it too gracefully. But as I said, I never was a good loser."

Did he ever wish the Steelers would have traded him so he could have played for a contender earlier in his career?

"To be honest, I would have loved it," Stautner told Didinger. "See, the one thing I wanted most in my entire career was to be a winner. I wanted to play on a championship team.

"If the Steelers had come to me and said I was traded to a contender, I would have been out of town so fast they would have never seen my tracks. I never went to a coach and asked to be traded, though. That's one thing I never would have done.

"I respected Art Rooney too much to do anything like that. Art was probably the finest, kindest man I'd ever met. I feel privileged I was able to play for him all those years. I would have felt I was slapping Art in the face to request a trade out of Pittsburgh, so I kept my mouth shut.

"But I thought about a trade, and as I said, many is the day I would have welcomed one."

Ernie Stautner on sideline with assistant coach Buster Ramsey.

Bill Jerome/Pittsburgh Weekly Sports

Pat Brady
The best punter the Steelers ever had

*"Anybody who's ever been a Steeler
has to be a Steeler fan."*

Pat Brady is bald now, but he has a handsome smile, and still enjoys a good time at his Bonanza Casino in Reno, Nevada. He's 64, and still behaves like a left-footed kicker.

This is a guy who signed contracts with three different pro football teams as a free agent when he came out of college. He stuck with the Steelers, but for only three seasons. He won the NFL's punting championship two straight seasons, in 1954 and 1955. His average kick was 44.5 yards.

He tore an Achilles tendon in the 1955 exhibition season and that ended his career. That was too bad. The Steelers never had a better punter. "Who could punt better?" asked Art Rooney Sr. during the Steelers 50 Seasons Celebration of 1982.

Pat Livingston, the former sports editor of *The Pittsburgh Press*, covered the Steelers for over 40 years, and he says Brady was the best punter he ever saw.

"They would bring other kickers in (to training camp) and let them kick alongside Pat," Livingston related. "When they saw how high he kicked they would leave on their own accord.

"He was quite a character, always the practical joker. He was probably the finest kicker the Steelers ever had. He was the only left-footed kicker and maybe the first. When he punted the ball, it was always coming to the returners on the opposite side. The Steelers got a lot of fumbles that way."

Brady's best punt is as clear in his mind as the numbers on the playing cards at the casino he operates in the town where he played ball at the local branch of the University of Nevada.

"We were playing the Packers at Lambeau Field in Green Bay, and we were leading by 21-20 in the season opener," said Brady.

"There were about four minutes to go in the game, and we were backed up at our own goal line. The Packers had a good field-goal kicker from Clemson — Fred Cone — and he could have won it for them if they had any kind of field position."

Brady kicked the ball 88 yards in the air on a spiral, according to a report the next day in *The Pittsburgh Press* by Livingston. It was caught on the fly. Brady was credited with a 72-yard punt, one of the longest in the club's history. The Steelers held on to win the game.

"I just had to get it out of there," said Brady. "I know they gave me the game ball. It was the personal highlight of my Steelers career."

Brady also remembers the worst punt of his career. That's the one where he tore the Achilles tendon.

Pat Brady

"I will never forget that Fred Broussard was the center and he snapped it high," recalled Brady.

"I went up to get it. I guess my leg was extended. I felt like somebody clubbed me in the leg. Or that somebody had kicked me. I looked to see what the ref behind me had done.

"I was told later that I shouldn't have been able to walk, but I got the kick off. Not a very good one, but I got it off."

Dr. Phil Faix was the team physician in those days for the Steelers as well as the Pittsburgh Hornets hockey team.

"He had done about 12 operations on the heels of hockey players — that was before they wore the steel plate in the heel of their skates — so I was lucky that he knew what he was doing," said Brady.

"But I never came back after that. He told me if I came back it could happen again, and it might leave me with a limp. I spent the entire season (1955) in Mercy Hospital."

Brady served as athletic commissioner in Nevada for about eight or nine years, and oversaw 18 title fights. "Billy Conn and I used to run around together when he was out there working," Brady said, referring to the former light-heavyweight boxing champion from Pittsburgh.

"I started out in Seattle," said Brady, explaining how he got to Nevada in the first place. "I went to the University of Oregon as a quarterback. But they had a guy named Norman Van Brocklin, who wasn't bad, and I didn't think I'd get to play much. So I went down the road to Reno. It seems like I've been here ever since.

"I still follow the Steelers. I was so happy for the Rooney family and for the Steelers when they won all those Super Bowls. People here in the casino can tell you I was rooting for them to win one for the thumb. I still am. Anybody who's ever been a Steeler has to be a Steeler fan," said Brady.

"My most cherished memory of my association with the Steelers was knowing Art Rooney and his family. He was quite the man. I used to call him Prez. He used to stay right at camp with us, kind of like a father. It wasn't the type of situation you have today where everyone is so impersonal. I felt like one of his own, and we developed a great Irish friendship. I'll never forget him."

Brady takes great pride in his Irish roots. He was once arrested in Reno for painting the white street lines green on St. Patrick's Day.

"I just thought people here weren't doing anything for St. Patrick's Day," he told Merlisa Lawrence of *The Pittsburgh Press* for an article during the 1987 season. "I guess I got their attention. They've had a big celebration ever since."

Among the players on the Steelers he admired the most, Brady picked Jim Finks, the current front office boss of the New Orleans Saints. "I admired his excellent leadership ability and his down-to-earth, easy-to-get-along-with manner. He was always interested in other players."

Brady also follows the careers of two other former teammates, Ted Marchibroda, the new head coach of the Indianapolis Colts who had great success as the offensive coordinator of the Buffalo Bills in recent seasons, and Ernie Stautner, a defensive coach with the Denver Broncos.

"From my experience with the Steelers, I learned the capability to work well with people," said Brady, "and the inspiration to help better the community."

Brady was a major force in the formation of the National Championship Air Races in Reno — the largest air race of its kind in the world — and has served as a trustee since the event was started in 1964.

He is a director of Fun Camp, Inc., enabling underprivileged area children to have the experience of summer camp. He is an integral part of the Reno chapter of the NFL Alumni Association, as well as Ducks Unlimited. He has been inducted into the Hall of Fame at both Bradley and the University of Nevada.

He was once Nevada's state printer, appointed by former Governor Dan O'Callaghan.

Aside from being the owner of a busy and demanding business, he serves as master of ceremonies at many functions in Reno. He is also an avid fisherman and bird hunter.

He and his wife, Odile, whom he met while attending Nevada-Reno, have five children, three daughters and two sons, whom he says have all been successful in their chosen fields.

"It would be impossible to describe his integrity or personality," said his secretary, Lyla Ferrel, "but I'm certain that few people would disagree that he leaves a lasting impact with his witty and happy nature."

Asked if he had any advice for today's players, Brady said, "Play not only for monetary gain, but for the pride and pleasure of your personal accomplishments as well. Be assertive and strive to uphold the reputation of all the fine things the Steelers represent."

Pat Brady

Elbie Nickel
"I always had a job."

"Life becomes sufficient unto life;
the rewards of living are found in living."
—Richard Wright
Author of "Native Son"

Elbie Nickel is not sorry he missed the big money in pro football. He had fun playing football from 1947 to 1957 for the Steelers and he worked in the off-season. The off-season job eventually made him financially well off.

In fact, his long-time involvement with the J.H. Butt Construction Co. turned out so well that he was able to enter semi-retirement before he was 60. At 69, he was retired and comfortable in his home in Chillicothe, Ohio, about 45 miles south of Columbus, when we last spoke in the spring of 1992.

He has his basement fixed up, and he has souvenirs from his playing days in high school, college (University of Cincinnati) and with the Steelers in the pros.

"I always had a job," said Nickel. "It makes you appreciate playing football more, and I had something to fall back on. I knew I couldn't play football the rest of my life. My first job was working for my father who had a business of his own. I worked with him during the off-season and enjoyed it.

"Being a football player wasn't too important. We didn't get much publicity. But it helped me get started in life."

He listed his greatest thrill as being selected to the Steelers' All-Time Team in public balloting by fans as part of the club's 50 Seasons Celebration back in 1982.

He was especially grateful because he was one of only four players from the '50s who made the team. It's something that should have impressed his son, Joe, and daughter, Susan, and more so his five grandchildren. Since then, he has picked up three more grandchildren and one great-grandchild.

Nickel has enough stories to tell them about his glory days with the Steelers.

"I can remember the time (in 1954) we beat the Cleveland Browns, 55-27, at Forbes Field in a Saturday night game," noted Nickel. "And another game (1952) in which we beat the New York Giants, 63-7, at Forbes Field.

"Lynn Chandnois returned the opening kickoff for a touchdown against the Giants. Their quarterback, Charlie Conerly, got hurt early in the game. Tom Landry finished the game at quarterback.

"Their coach, Steve Owen, had a book come out a few weeks before about this special 'umbrella' defense he had concocted. Our game was not good publicity for his book."

324

Elbie Nickel

The Steelers could roll up scores like that, yet they finished 5-7 in 1952 and 1954. They had only two winning seasons in Nickel's 11 years.

In his rookie season of 1947, the Steelers, under Jock Sutherland, went 8-4 but lost an Eastern Division playoff to the Philadelphia Eagles. That was as close as the Steelers ever came to winning a conference crown until 1972. Sutherland died after that 1947 season, and Nickel played the next four years under one of Sutherland's disciples, John Michelosen.

"We were the last team in the NFL to play the single-wing, and I was the blocking end," said Nickel. "So I was what was later called a tight end. I didn't have the speed these guys have today. The first three years I was there, I also had to play defense."

In the single-wing, the quarterback is a blocking back. He lines up directly behind a guard or tackle on one side or the other. The side on which he lines up is called the strong side, and is usually the side to which end sweeps — with lots of blockers out front — are run. The tailback takes a direct snap from center and stands back the way quarterbacks do now in the "shotgun" formation.

I told Nickel that Art Rooney used to tell me he thought Sutherland was a great coach, and that the Steelers would have been more successful earlier if he had lived.

"That single-wing was getting pretty old," said Nickel. "We couldn't draft anybody who played it because the colleges were all playing the T-formation. It was about over the hill. His defense was pretty standard stuff. He'd have been behind in that, too."

Nickel played for five different coaches in his stay with the Steelers. Michelosen succeeded Sutherland. Then came Joe Bach, Walt Kiesling and Buddy Parker. "We didn't get the coaching like you do today," noted Nickel. "Buddy Parker had some pretty good ideas. I was over the hill myself by the time Parker came. I was with him only one year. He was a good modern day coach. He was a little rowdy once in a while, but he was all business when it came to football.

"Sutherland was the most demanding. We had two workouts a day. One went three hours in the morning, and then we went four hours in the afternoon. The afternoon session was in pads. There was lots of contact. With Michelosen, it was more of the same.

"I was pretty lucky. I sprained my ankle once, and I was kicked in the back once, but that was about it. And I don't have any old football injuries plaguing me today. I'm grateful for that."

Those were difficult days in some respects, but Nickel has no negative thoughts in reflection.

"I enjoyed my stay there; it was a good town," he said. "We didn't win too much. One year (1952) we scored 300 points (to 273 for the opposition) and we won only five of 12 games.

"We were always a little short someplace. We had Jim Finks, Lynn Chandnois, Fran Rogel and Ray Mathews; we had as good a backfield as anybody. But we were thin on the line, and Jack Butler was our only good defensive back. My best friend, Bill McPeak, was a good defensive end. He was my roommate for eight years. He passed away about two years ago.

"Finks was a smart quarterback. He didn't have much to work with. We had a couple of 190 and 195 pound guards. He took a beating. Finks, McPeak and Butler were great players, but got very little credit for what they did for the Steelers."

Butler says Nickel was a great receiver. At 30, Nickel caught 62 passes to rank second to Pete Pihos of the Eagles who caught 63. Pihos is in the Pro Football Hall of Fame.

As far as the money went, Nickel said, "I made as much as $10,000 the last few years. Hey, you couldn't make that much working in a year. We were rich in other ways. Art Rooney was one of the finest men you'll ever meet, and there wasn't a better boss to be had.

"Art was like a father to me. He took me to the Kentucky Derby for thirty years. I think I started going with him in 1948 or 1949. They used to drive a lot and they'd come through Chillicothe and pick me up on their way down to Louisville. That's a couple hundred miles from here. Joe Tucker, Ed Kiely, Jack Sell and sometimes Bob Drum would be with Art. He loved the sports announcers and sports writers. And they loved him, too.

"You never knew when Art was winning or losing. He could win a bundle or lose a bundle and he'd be the same mild guy. You'd never hear him root for a horse when it's running, the way most people do.

"He seemed to like everybody. I didn't know of a player who disliked him."

That's why Nickel was pleased to see the Steelers win all those Super Bowls in the '70s. "I took a lot of pride in that, being an old Steeler," said Nickel. "I got a lot of publicity around here during that period because I had played for Art Rooney and the Steelers.

"I liked Bradshaw as a quarterback, and Swann as a receiver and, defensively, I liked Lambert and Blount.

"I live close to Cincinnati and I still go down there to see the Steelers whenever they come to town. I still root for them. I go there when the Browns play.

"I used to go to Wilmington and see the Bengals at their training camp. That was about 60 miles from here. I knew Paul Brown real well, and I'd talk to him when I was there. Now he's gone, too."

In 1988, in consecutive months, Nickel suffered two great losses. In August of that year, his dear friend and former boss, Art Rooney, passed away, and in September his wife of 43 years, Roberta, died as well. Nothing, no matter how good, lasts forever.

"My advice to the young players today is to enjoy their playing days because they don't last very long," said Nickel.

"I'll be 70 in December, and I'm in good health," he continued. "I feel good. I still bowl regularly, and I'm still competitive. I like to go to the race track. I go to Beulah Park in Columbus and River Downs in Cincinnati. I learned that from Art Rooney. He made a horse player out of me."

327

Jack Butler
A scout who stayed close to home

"You can lose with great talent,
but you can't win without it."

Jack Butler stops by the press box at every Steelers' home game. He says hello to all his old friends, shakes hands, smiles and engages in a few animated conversations. He is as friendly as they come, and has always felt fortunate that he has made a living — indeed, a life — in a game he loves.

Butler shares a box and observations at Three Rivers Stadium with long-time pals like Art Rooney Jr. and Rip Scherer, all pro football scouts in their day. Jack's wife, Bernie, sits in another box with Kay Rooney, the wife of Art Jr. There's a strong belief in the Rooney clan, almost a tenet in the Rooney religion, that "women corrupt serious football," according to Art Jr.

I talked to Butler about the Steelers' scouting and drafting fortune of the '70s during one of his visits to the press box midway through the 1991 campaign. Butler has been the head of the league's Blesto scouting combine since the mid-60s. He was 65 as we spoke, but said nothing about retiring.

"They drafted so darn well," Butler began. "They got Jack Ham and Franco Harris, and guys like that when everyone else wasn't as sold on them. Franco was kind of criticized by some scouts his senior year at Penn State. Then they drafted the big kid out of Kent State.

"L.C. was a late pick. They were lucky there. They had such great people and they had the coach to put it all together. What a great defensive line they put together. You can lose with great talent, but you can't win without it."

As you may have noticed, Butler speaks in a scout's shorthand. "The big kid out of Kent State," of course, is Jack Lambert.

"I went down and saw the middle linebacker at Kent State — what's his name? — and I liked him a lot," Butler continued.

Anyone who was put off by Chuck Noll's "Franco Who?" and "Terry Who?" remarks might get a similar mistaken impression of intent if they heard Butler going on about "the middle linebacker at Kent State" or "what's his name?"

"I liked him, but I never thought he'd turn out as great as he was with the Steelers," said Butler, still not mentioning Lambert by name.

"I watched him as a junior and as a senior, and I liked him every time I saw him. I thought he could play for somebody. But I felt he had to play on the outside. His body didn't look like it could hold up in heavy traffic. And look what happened to him. A lot of luck goes with it.

"It's the intangibles that set him apart from the pack. You could tell he liked to play. You get fooled, too. You think guys like it; they end up quitting."

328

Butler believes the pro teams have too much time these days to decide who they are going to draft. The draft used to be held earlier in the year.

"There are too many tryouts, too many tests, and you get carried away with numbers," said Butler. "That's the big thing today. Hey, you're looking for football players."

It's doubtful that Butler's numbers would impress any of the pro scouts today, yet he put in nine stellar seasons with the Steelers from 1951 through 1959, and remains one of the team's all-time interception leaders and a candidate for the Pro Football Hall of Fame.

"He belongs, but I don't know if he's ever going to make it," said Pat Livingston, the former sports editor of *The Pittsburgh Press*, who used to be on the nominating committee.

Chuck Noll figures to get into the Hall of Fame the first time he is eligible, which is the Class of 1993, and Butler knows Noll belongs.

"I think the guy really has something," said Butler, not knowing it was Noll's last season as the Steelers' skipper. "I can't put my finger on it. How many guys really have it? Landry had it. Shula has it. The guys on the team know if they do what he says they'll win.

"Chuck didn't make many mistakes when it came to keeping the right players. Not too many guys around who he let go who are still playing."

Butler bounced around in making observations about the Steelers during their glory years of the '70s.

"There was maybe one year when Fats Holmes was the best defensive lineman they had. Just for that one year. God, that was a great football team. See, I'm an old defensive back and I keep thinking defensively.

"You take a guy like Rocky Bleier, who was very limited. And look what he did. He rushed for 1000 yards one year. That team was as good as any team every was.

"Wagner was a good football player. He was smart, tough. He was always in the right place. Yes, he was a good football player. He was a part of that team. It's the team that matters. It still takes a whole team.

"You watch Ham play. You didn't know how he ever did it. He wasn't that physical. He wasn't smashing guys. He just made the play. He had great instincts. I don't know what the hell he had, but he had it.

"They were different. Some of them were so damn physical, like Holmes and Greene. And some of them just played smart, like Russell and Ham. They played a 3-4, and the middle linebacker made all the plays.

"The guards and tackles for the other team can't get to you; he was protected. He did the job."

Notice Butler still hadn't mentioned Lambert by name.

"Russell wasn't so physical, either, but so smart.

"Stallworth was something else, too. Play in and play out, I always thought he was better than Swann. But Swann made great plays. He won games. We had the best receivers."

With Pat Brady and Elbie Nickel.

Steeler coaches in 1961, left to right, are Butler, Mike Nixon, Chuck Cherundolo, Buddy Parker, Thurman McGraw and Dick Plasman.

Jack Butler

Pittsburgh area pro football players work out together (left to right) in 1956 at Brentwood High Stadium: Butler of Steelers, Lloyd Colteryahn and George Radosevich of Baltimore Colts, Ted Marchibroda of Steelers and Joe Schmidt of Detroit Lions.

Steelers set to depart Pittsburgh for training camp at Olean, N.Y. in 1953 included, left to right, Butler, Bill Walsh, Jim Finks and Dick Hensley.

Pittsburgh Steelers

1959 lineup includes (from left) Butler, Ray Mathews, Jimmy Orr, Bobby Layne and Jack McClairen. This team posted 6-5-1 record.

I asked Butler to pick the most important player on the Steelers in the '70s.

"You gotta go with Bradshaw," he answered, without hesitation. "Bradshaw was great. He was the kind of guy who won a lot of games for you. He might've thrown some stupid passes, and do some dumb things, but he won games for you.

"Marino has a better feel for the game. He's quicker to recognize things. I know he was schooled better, especially just coming out of college. He's been the whole team for five years. They don't have anything to go with him. Danny Marino has innate talent.

"I don't know what Bradshaw has that Marino doesn't have. Bradshaw might have had a stronger arm. He'd knock you over some times with his passes. Marino has more control. Marino played big-time college football and Bradshaw did not. He worked with a pro offense in college. Bradshaw was at little Louisiana Tech. A defensive back can get away with that kind of background, but a quarterback can't.

"Bradshaw didn't have as good a background as Marino and Montana and some of these other guys. But his arm was so great."

Asked about Bubby Brister, who bounced around in college and finished up at Northeast Louisiana, Butler said, "He holds the ball too long. He doesn't see enough."

Talking about coaching and solid backgrounds, Butler looked around the press box, as if he expected Joe Bach or Walt Kiesling to come back from the grave and haunt him, and said, "I hate to say this, but I can't ever remember being coached when I was with the Steelers.

"You just went out there and covered your man. Nobody ever told me anything about my footwork, or what to look for to determine what another team was doing. I was never coached. Kiesling didn't tell me anything."

How many times has Jack Butler been told by somebody that he belongs in the Pro Football Hall of Fame? It must ring hollow to him after all these years.

But Butler isn't the kind to either blow his own horn, or to issue any kind of plaintive call. The Hall of Fame call is out of his hands.

He was excited back in June of 1982, however, when he was selected to the Steelers' all-time team that was chosen to help mark the team's 50 Seasons Celebration.

"That's pretty nice in itself," said Butler, sitting behind his modest desk at Blesto, Inc., the NFL scouting combine he heads that is located in the Commonwealth Building.

Butler is a silent type who likes to mind his own business. So he's not about to complain about not being properly acknowledged.

"I enjoyed playing, and that's enough," he said. "Pro football has been good to me. It's kept me from having to go to work."

Butler, then 55, was a sometime receiver and fulltime cornerback for the Steelers during the decade of the '50s. He and Mel Blount, the other cornerback on the Steelers' All-Time team, shared the club career interception record back then with 52 apiece, but Blount went on to pick off five more opposing passes to grab the top rung for himself.

Blount also holds the team record for most interceptions in a season with 11, set in 1975, one more than Butler seized back in the 1957 campaign. Going into the 1992 season, Butler still held the Steelers' record for most interceptions in a game with four against the Washington Redskins on December 13, 1953.

The Steelers managed to find film from that game, and they screened it during the 50 Seasons Celebration dinner at the David L. Lawrence Convention Center. They also posted huge photos of Butler — No. 80 — in an exhibit there that honored great Steelers of the past.

Butler also recalled a big moment as a receiver. "We were playing the Giants in New York and I went in on offense late in the game and caught a touchdown pass from Jim Finks and we won it," he said.

Looking back, Butler said, "I don't think we were as smart as the kids are today. We just never looked at it as a job or anything. I enjoyed playing the game. We were paid, but that wasn't usually a good part of it. Kids are so much more knowledgeable today about everything, especially the football and business aspect of it.

"They are better coached, better conditioned and they know more about techniques, tendencies, and stategy and that stuff. We weren't as sophisticated.

"I think everybody looked at it as a fun thing. It was a great atmosphere, from the Rooneys on down, just from the people you met. There was great camaraderie.

"When we played, there weren't any outside activities. We never had anybody coming in with the *Wall Street Journal* under his arm, or, after practice, running to an office. Your attention was all on football.

"It wasn't more carefree, not when it came to football. It was the only thing you were concerned about. It was something you did, though, before you had to go to work. We looked at is as delaying the inevitable.

"When the season was over, you wondered what the heck you were going to do until the next season came around."

That sort of explains how Butler became a Steeler in the first place.

Butler was born in Oakland, grew up in a sports atmosphere near Forbes Field, and went to prep school with Frank Thomas, a neighbor who became a big home run hitter for the Pirates. One summer Butler was home from St. Bonaventure University, where he had played football and was then attending graduate school.

"I fully intended to go back to school," said Butler. "Fran Fogarty called from the Steelers and asked me if I wanted to try out for the team. I thought, 'Hey, this is a terrific way to spend my summer. I won't make the team, but it will be a great way to pass the time.' I never went back to school.

"Job-wise, I didn't know what I wanted to do, but I knew what I didn't want to do. I guess what I didn't want to do was to go to work."

Butler's ballplaying career was cut short by a disabling knee injury. That's one game he remembers all too well. It happened in a game against the Philadelphia Eagles at Forbes Field.

"It was a freaky thing," said Butler. "It happened on a play away from me. It was a little slot pass. Pete Retzlaff stumbled and fell and hit me on the knee on his way down. He hit me right below the knee. That was it. I'd been hit a lot harder many times."

Butler has had a gimpy knee ever since to remind him of Retzlaff. But he has more good memories than bad ones.

He has lived in large house in Munhall — one in which my sister-in-law Diane Churchman previously lived with her family, the Thomases — and he and his wife Bernie raised eight children there. "Four boys and four girls," boasts Butler. "Perfect planning."

His best salary with the Steelers was about $12,000. "I thought I made a helluva lot of money," he said.

During the off-season, he worked with electricians, started an exterminating business with his brothers, a restaurant and bar in West Mifflin ("It didn't really have a name," he said), and sold bar supplies.

"I bought a house, I built a building, I had no financial problems," said Butler. "Like I said, pro football's been great to me."

Pittsburgh Steelers

Jack Butler

Buddy Parker
"He took losses too hard."

Buddy Parker provoked some smiles, even hearty chuckles, at the annual National Football League owners meeting in late March of 1982, and that would have pleased the talkative Texan who coached the Steelers in some of their best times.

Parker had also coached the Cardinals in Chicago and the Lions in Detroit before Art Rooney dug deep into his pockets to come up with the money that lured Parker to Pittsburgh in 1957. Parker left all three places suddenly, surprising the people who knew him best, and they are still telling stories about him.

"He was different," said several of the NFL folks we spoke to that week at the Phoenix Biltmore after learning of Parker's death, at age 68, in a hospital in Kaufman, Texas. He had undergone surgery earlier in the month and died from kidney failure.

"He was a brilliant coach," remarked Rooney, when I called him on the hotel telephone to inform him of Parker's death. "Geez, he was such a young man, too."

Everything is relative, of course. When you are 81 someone who is 68 is young.

I had caught Rooney just before he was to go out for the evening to dinner with his family at the Arizona resort, one of the finest in the nation.

I apologized for interrupting him, but he said he enjoyed taking about Buddy Parker, one of his favorites. He also went on to tell me that he had a great day, and how many different people interviewed him, and how some young woman talked to him at length who said she was writing a book about the early days of pro football. He also told me how much he liked my wife, especially with a name like Kathleen, because his wife and daughter-in-law and granddaughter all had the same name. That was typical Art Rooney. But back to Buddy Parker.

Parker had always been a hard-working, hard-drinking individual. When he departed this time, he didn't surprise anyone. "I knew it was just a matter of time for him," said Rooney. "He'd been quite ill."

Others enjoyed the opportunity to take a break from the deadly serious discussions at the owners meeting to reflect on Parker, a one-of-a-kind character in NFL history.

"I really liked Buddy," began Art Modell, the owner of the Cleveland Browns, a team that was a fierce rival for Parker's teams at both Detroit and Pittsburgh. "We were at a league meeting in Palm Desert in 1964 and I was coming into the hotel one night with Vince Lombardi when we bumped into Buddy. He was at the bar and he was in pretty good 'spirits' — that's 'spirits' in quotes — and he and Vince got into a lively argument.

"Buddy said, 'Vince, let me tell you something about football. You give me a player loaded with fear and desire and I'll show you a winner.' And Vince replied, 'Buddy, my wife is loaded with fear and desire, and she can't even throw a pass.' That was one of the best exchanges I've ever heard in this business."

Parker's name was mentioned by Modell in the same breath as Lombardi and others compared him to Paul Brown as football brains go.

"I know Tom Landry always considered Parker to be one of the three best coaches in the business," related Wellington Mara, the owner of the New York Giants, who recalled sharing a motel room with Parker for four days at the first Senior Bowl in Jacksonville, Florida, back in 1950.

"He was a character. He hated to lose. I remember we beat the Steelers in New York in a big game at the end of the schedule, and their business manager, Fran Fogarty, God rest his soul, was up in our office settling up after the game. Fran told me, 'I hate to think of what it's going to be like on this trip back home.' Buddy could get rough."

They tell stories about Parker cutting off his tie on an airplane after a difficult defeat and how he was apt to come roaring down the aisle, shouting at players, picking them apart, and even challenging them to fights.

The one story that brought the most smiles to the coaches convening in Phoenix was the one about Parker and his sidekick, Buster Ramsey, getting the team trainer to tape their hands, the way pro fighters do, before they conducted bed check at the Steelers' training camp one summer. "They were ready to punch the players if they had to," recalled one man.

Parker was a throwback to another era, the old-time football coach who did whatever he wanted to, if he thought it might help win a few football games. He was a real taskmaster.

But it was a different ballgame then, more fun than big business, something college players looked forward to as a way to extend their light-hearted days before they had to get into the serious business of earning a living.

Parker was the head coach of the Cardinals in 1949. He quit that job and the next year joined the Detroit Lions. He led them from 1950 through 1956 and produced championship teams in 1952 and 1953. He quit that job, too, announcing he was leaving at a "Welcome Home" dinner for the Lions.

"I told you he was different," said Modell. "Most people say 'hello' at a function like that, and he said 'goodbye' instead. I like a guy who's different like that; he was his own man. He's the last of an era. I had tremendous respect for his football knowledge. He was a master tactician. But there was something different about the man."

Paul Martha can vouch for that. Martha was in Phoenix as legal advisor to the San Francisco 49ers. He broke in as a rookie under Parker in 1964 and played two seasons for him.

"I remember coming back to camp one night at St. Bonaventure after we'd been beaten pretty good by the Giants in an exhibition game

Ed Brown with Buddy Parker on sideline.

Walt Kiesling, Lenny Dawson, Buddy Parker and Ted Marchibroda at 1957 training camp.

at the Yale Bowl," recalled Martha. "I was rooming with 'Rooster' Fleming and we were right across the hall from a room shared by John Henry Johnson and Clarence Peaks. Parker was upset with both of them and he wanted to tear into them.

"You could hear him and Buster Ramsey coming down the hall together. They had been drinking and they were shouting obscenities. They stopped right outside our door. I hadn't played well and I was scared to death.

"They started hollering for John Henry and Peaks to open the door, but both of them had gone into Manhattan for the night. Eventually, Parker and Ramsey kicked down their door and they went into their room and waited for them to come back. They gave up at about 3 a.m. and went to their own rooms. John Henry and Peaks didn't come in until about 6 a.m. It's a good thing those four didn't meet up.

"Gary Ballman told me stories about Parker and Ramsey taping their hands before bed check as if they were going to come in and start punching the guys. He said 'Big Daddy' Lipscomb grabbed Parker by the front of his shirt one night during such a mission and advised him to return to his room before he got hurt."

Rooney related such stories, too, and laughed heartily as he told each one of them.

"The only bad thing about Buddy was that he took losses so hard," recalled Rooney. "He'd start drinking, and he didn't know how to drink. He always quit after a loss. We just didn't pay any attention to him."

During his stay with the Steelers, Parker produced the best seasons until Chuck Noll came along. He brought Bobby Layne in from Detroit to quarterback his ballclub, and they came up with a 9-5 season in 1962, good enough for second place in the Eastern Division, and a 7-4-3 record in 1963. He resigned as the Steelers' coach after losing three exhibition games before the 1965 season.

"He was different, much different," observed Jack Butler, the former Steeler who heads up the Blesto scouting combine. "I had a lot of respect for the guy. He could do things, make adjustments, or devise strategy to meet situations. He'd do different things. He was just a different individual."

Landy, who was coaching the Dallas Cowboys, said, "Buddy was one of the real fine coaches in the game. He had a great rapport with his players, which is to be admired. Ernie Stautner is on my staff, and he respected Parker a great deal. Buddy was one of the boys, but he was a disciplinarian. Ernie loves to tell Buddy Parker stories, but he also tells Ernie Stautner and Bobby Layne stories. They must've had some fun together."

Stautner remembers how things changed when Parker reported to the Steelers. "Right away you could tell he meant business," said Stautner. "There was this aura about Buddy. I guess you could call it a winner's aura. You could tell this guy knew his stuff.

"Nobody was what you'd call secure with Buddy around. he had us all worrying."

Andy Russell recalls Parker: "Parker was a very dynamic guy. He was quick to get angry, a bit unpredictable. The players didn't quite know what to expect of Buddy. Under Parker, we nearly won it all."

Buddy Parker represented Bobby Layne at his 1967 induction into the Pro Football Hall of Fame in Canton, Ohio.

John Henry Johnson
"My job was to block and run the ball."

"John Henry told the Captain
A man ain't nothin' but a man,
And if I don't beat your steam drill down
I'll die with a hammer in my hand
Lawd, Lawd
I'll die with a hammer in my hand."

He once dealt destructive blows to anybody foolish enough to get in his way on a football field, as well as a few other places. He struck them with fists, fierce forearm shots, elbows, you name it. He was known to break jaws. With his pile-driving knees, he did worse. This John Henry had hands that were hammers and he, too, was a hard-working black man and a legendary figure.

With John Henry Johnson, from the first whistle blown by the referee, he was at work. He was at war. He was among the last of the two-way performers in the National Football League, and he liked to knock people down. It didn't matter whether he was carrying the ball or they were carrying the ball. Either way, it could make John Henry's day.

He was accused of slowing down sometimes and letting a tackler get near him so he could whack the guy. He liked to rough up tacklers. He was an old-fashioned football player.

One of his teammates with the Detroit Lions, Carl Brettschneider, once said, "John Henry will rip you apart if you're not looking."

He was a multi-threat, as he could throw the ball, return punts and kickoffs. He would do anything he was asked to do, and then some. He played safety, cornerback, linebacker and even on the front fours in goal-line situations. He was a streetfighter who wore a helmet and pulled his chinstrap tight.

Sportswriter Jim Scott once wrote of Johnson: "He was 215 pounds of malice strung out on a 6-2 frame, a man who intimidated tacklers and runners alike as Sonny Liston once evil-eyed his ring rivals."

John Henry once told his teammates, "You've got to scare your opponents. It sorta upsets their concentration. I find I can run away from a lot of guys after I get them afraid of a collision with me."

He took some shots, too. Once, while playing for the Steelers in a game against one of his former teams, the Detroit Lions, Johnson was left with an eight-inch gash over his eye and a mild concussion while fighting with Wayne Walker in a Playoff Bowl in Miami at the end of the 1962 season. There were many casualties that day. The game was called "The Sixty Minute War."

One of the first memories the Steelers' new coach Bill Cowher has of seeing the Steelers in action as a youth was of John Henry Johnson returning a kickoff at Pitt Stadium. "I just always thought John Henry Johnson was such a great name for a football player," said Cowher. And it still is.

When I mentioned this to John Henry, he positively cackled and came back with, "I went down under some kickoffs, too. I wasn't opposed to playing on the kickoff teams."

John Henry was a handful. He scowled a lot, he smiled a lot. He had an easy laugh, and it was infectious. Nobody had a better time, on and off the field. There was a joy about John Henry. He played when there were few blacks on any of the ballteams — you could count them on one hand — and he paved the way for others to follow. There were few like him.

One of his former teammates on the Steelers, defensive back Brady Keys, who became a very successful businessman, was critical of Johnson back then. He thought Johnson should have behaved himself better — he was notorious for staying out late, drinking, playing cards, flirting with women, and partying — to help blacks like Keys gain more respect in professional sports.

"I could see that he was an angry black man," Keys said. "He was very, very angry. I can totally understand that anger now. John was angry that there were so few blacks in the league. He was angry that blacks were paid peanuts. He was one of the best players in the league and he was paid peanuts."

Johnson's top salary with the Steelers was $38,000, and he worked hard for his money. He, indeed, played with a passion. He fought off would-be tacklers with a fury, he met all challengers head on. And, boy, could he block. It was a role he relished as much as running off tackle.

"John Henry is my bodyguard," said Steelers quarterback Bobby Layne, who was a lot like Johnson on and off the field. "Half the good runners will get a quarterback killed if you keep them around long enough. But a quarterback hits the jackpot when he gets a combination runner-blocker like Johnson."

On another occasion, Layne allowed, "He went three ways — offense, defense and to the death."

When I was 19 or 20, and a student sportswriter at the University of Pittsburgh, John Henry allowed me to tag along one evening when he went to the Aurora Club, a late-night jazz joint for blacks in the city's Hill District. He caused a furor that night and we were lucky to get out alive.

In my early '40s, I used to bump into John Henry once in a while in a downtown watering hole like Froggy's, or at some golf outing or reunion sponsored by the Steelers' chapter of the NFL Alumni Association. At the time, John Henry was doing community relations work for the Columbia Gas Co. It didn't take long for John Henry to start singing a sad song about how he should have been in the Pro Football Hall of Fame. And he was right.

After a 13-year NFL career with four teams, including a six-year stay with the Steelers from 1960 to 1965, Johnson ranked as the No. 4 ranked ground-gainer in NFL history when he retired. One of the better fullbacks of his time, he was tops at his position for protecting the quarterback, and leading the blocking on end sweeps.

"Jim Brown was the only fullback better than John Henry at that time," said Dick Hoak, a former teammate who is the Steelers' backfield coach. "Jim got more recognition because he played for a better team."

Pittsburgh Press sports editor Pat Livingston pushed for John Henry a long time among the Hall of Fame voting panel, and sportscaster Myron Cope, who succeeded Livingston as the local representative on the board, picked up the baton.

Cope can tell some great stories about Johnson. "I remember the time the Steelers were playing the Rams, and they weren't too happy about a block that John Henry had thrown at one of their guys, or something like that; I'm not certain of the details," recalled Cope. "They were coming after him like an army. He picked up a yardmarker on the sideline and started swinging it at them like a madman."

A lot of his former teammates zero in on that incident, only with about a half dozen different versions of the story.

Here's the same story as told by Hoak to Ron Musselman of the *Valley News Dispatch:*

"We were playing Los Angeles in my rookie year, and a big fight broke out near the end of the game. Somebody hit John Henry from behind, and he turned around and nailed the guy, broke his jaw. The guy (Bill Jobko) attacked him and John picked up a yardstick and swung it at him. I got the heck out of there. I didn't want to get hurt, too."

Well, Cope said he wasn't certain of the details.

"Another time (in 1955)," continued Cope, "John Henry busted up the great Charley Trippi's face something awful. Trippi was a great back for the Chicago Cardinals, and John Henry made him a real candidate for plastic surgery." For the record, Trippi suffered a fractured jaw and a broken nose, and the injuries hastened his retirement.

"The mob in Chicago was ready to come after John Henry. Trippi had to call them off," cried Cope. "It's a true story. The mob was ready to put a cement bathing suit on John Henry.

"He was a great runner, but he was an even greater blocker for a back. He would get so low to the ground, and then come up like a cat. He would just spring at people and he would just crunch people. He was the greatest blocking back I ever saw.

"He had a picturesque running style. He had a long, galloping motion. He would leap over people, and across fallen bodies. He was a real colorful performer."

If John Henry was so tough, how come he had to grab a yardstick to fend off Jobko? "Because I didn't have my pistol with me," Johnson said with a laugh.

Finally, after too long of a wait, John Henry was voted in by the oldtimers' committee, and inducted into the Hall of Fame in 1987, joining Joe Greene at ceremonies in Canton, Ohio. John Henry was introduced by Art Rooney, whom he greatly admired, and Greene by Chuck Noll. The Steelers have never been better represented at the Hall of Fame ceremonies.

etting handoff from Ed Brown.

John Henry Johnson

h Paul Martha in bus promotion.

John Henry, left, with Bobby Layne, Dick Hoak and Buddy Dial.

John Henry Johnson was a second round draft choice of the Steelers in 1953, right behind Ted Marchibroda, a quarterback who had played at the University of Detroit and St. Bonaventure and is now the head coach of the Indianapolis Colts. Johnson also played at two schools, St. Mary's of California and Arizona State.

Johnson didn't sign with the Steelers, opting instead to sign with the Calgary Stampeders — that sounds like a team John Henry should play with — in the Canadian Football League. Though the Stampeders finished in last place, Johnson was named the league's most valuable player.

He joined the NFL after the San Francisco 49ers acquired his rights in a trade. The 49ers sent the Steelers their fourth round draft choice, a defensive back named Ed Fullerton of Maryland. The Steelers put Fullerton on waivers after a three week trial.

After Johnson signed a contract to play for the 49ers, team president Tony Morabito asked him where he preferred to play.

"Don't make any difference," answered John Henry.

"Well, do you like to play offense?"

"Yes, sir."

"How about defense?"

"Like that, too."

"But John Henry, you must like to play one place better than another?" insisted Morabito.

"Look, Mr. Morabito, I just like to play football!"

Johnson finished second in rushing in the league with 681 yards, a 5.1 yard average, in his NFL rookie year (1954). He was a member of the 49ers' "Fabulous Foursome," which included Y.A. Tittle, Joe Perry and Hugh McElhenny. Johnson was the last member of that backfield to enter the Hall of Fame. It may have been the best backfield in the history of the game.

There was a sequence that stuck out in his tour with the 49ers. His savagery was best epitomized in a nationally-televised game at Chicago. The Bears were leading, 17-14, in the third period when Perry broke loose for a 54-yard scoring run. After Perry had rushed five yards on that scamper, he was about to be dropped by the Bears' McNeil Moore when suddenly John Henry shot out of nowhere to level Moore with a thundering jolt. Moore was knocked back about five yards by the collision.

Phil Bengston, later the head coach of the Green Bay Packers, was an assistant with the 49ers back then. He called it the greatest individual block he had ever seen. "I played against Bronko Nagurski," said Bengston, "and the Bronk never threw one that hard."

Johnson was traded in 1957 to the Detroit Lions, whom he helped win the NFL championship. Two years later, he was dispatched to Pittsburgh, where he enjoyed his finest seasons, rushing for over 1,000 yards twice. He was 30 by the time he got to the Steelers, and they were the first team to feature him in their running game. With the Steelers, he had season rushing totals of 621, 787, 1,141, 773 and 1,048 yards, and was a three-time Pro Bowl performer.

"I was the first player over 35 to rush for 1,000 yards in a season," he said with more than a hint of pride.

He was the first Steeler ever to rush for 1,000 yards. He succeeded Tom "The Bomb" Tracy as the team's top runner, and led the Steelers in rushing four straight seasons. He is second to Franco Harris on the Steelers' all-time career rushing list.

His 87-yard touchdown run against the Philadelphia Eagles in 1960 is second only to Bobby Gage's 97-yard TD run against the Chicago Bears in 1949.

His 200-yard outburst against the Cleveland Browns was topped only by a 218-yard effort by Frenchy Fuqua against the Eagles in 1970.

Johnson closed out his 14-year professional career in 1966 with the Houston Oilers. At the age of 37, unreal for a running back, he ran for 226 yards in 70 carries in 14 games. When he left, he was the fourth-best rusher at the time. He had racked up 6,803 yards and 48 touchdowns.

"I was a John Henry Johnson rooter," said Steelers' owner Art Rooney. "He was a free spirit. He fit right in with me."

John Henry, at 62, and his wife, Leona Marie, were living in her hometown of Cleveland when I interviewed them in February and again in March of 1992. They have a condominium apartment there. Cleveland has never had a better running back in residence since Jimmy Brown retired, and Johnson was a better blocker than Brown.

John Henry looked much better than I had expected, sitting in the living room of his apartment on East Boulevard in the University Circle section of the city, not far from Cleveland Stadium, the scene of some of John Henry's finest hours.

I had spoken to one of his long-time pals in Pittsburgh, a street sportsman named Ducky Lewis, who had said, "John Henry is in bad shape. He's restless and he just don't walk right. He's stooped over, moves slowly, and doesn't remember things too well anymore. We were real tight, and we hung together a lot, and I hope he bounces back. He ain't been calling me."

Maybe John Henry just got up for this interview, like it was a big game. But he seemed to be doing all right. He speaks hoarsely, but he always did, like the words were coming through cobwebs. Maybe it was more muted than I had remembered. The burning dark eyes were dimmer, faded in the manner of Muhammad Ali. It's a shame, but some of our heroes just get old. Johnson seemed like more of an old fighter, a former boxer, than a football player.

John Henry has been married to Leona Marie, his second wife, for 27 years. They have one child, John Jr., 26 at the time. His first marriage ended in divorce in 1958, the year after he was traded from San Francisco to Detroit. He had five children by his first wife, and one of them died of a drug overdose, which was a tragic setback for John Henry. It came at a time when John Henry was unhappy with his job — he long pined for a job as a coach, or in some capacity with a pro club — and struggling with personal problems.

Leona Marie is a magnificent hostess and a big booster of John Henry. She fills in any blank spaces in his reflections. "He did real well, answering all your questions," she said after I had spoken at length with John Henry. "I'll have to tell his doctors. He does better with stuff from the past. His memory of recent events isn't so good.

"The doctors think his problem comes from too many blows to the head. He's doing much better these days. He nearly died in November of 1990. He was hospitalized quite a while. He had blood clots on his lungs, and he had a pulmonary embolism. He's a very lucky man. For awhile, he was going back and forth to doctors in Pittsburgh and Cleveland before they found out what was wrong with him. For awhile, they thought he had a heart problem, or a pancreas problem, or even cancer. He's doing much better now."

In his book, *The Glory of Their Times,* about baseball stars, Lawrence S. Ritter, a professor at New York University, marveled at the detail that his baseball players were able to bring to recollection of events long gone, but he was reassured by psychologists "that it is not at all unusual as one gets older for the more distant past to be remembered more clearly than what happened three weeks ago, especially if the distant past was particularly memorable."

Leona Johnson said her husband had been experiencing a shortness of breath a few years back, and had lost 43 pounds during his prolonged illness. She said he was back up to 216 pounds, about four pounds under his playing weight, and was in much better spirits.

There are many photos, trophies and mementos on display in one room of their apartment in tribute to John Henry's history in football. "I call it my trophy room," allowed Leona. It was shown in a "Where Are They Now?" special flash-back feature on former pro football stars on HBO's *Inside The NFL* during the 1991 season.

She said that some friends and former teammates of John Henry — "they all love him" — were planning to have a dinner in his honor in Cleveland in August. She had just been talking to Joe Perry, one of John Henry's backfield mates with the 49ers, and planned to talk to Y.A. Tittle. "I'm getting calls from all over the country," she said. Among them was Peter Castanza, from John Henry's hometown of Pittsburg, California, who negotiated his first contract with the 49ers. She and John Henry were also making plans to attend the NFL Players' Association convention in Las Vegas the following month, in April of 1992.

"They are trying to improve the pension for players who played when John Henry did," she explained. "He was lucky to have played past 1959 — the cut-off year for former players under the present pension formula. They call them the pre-'59ers, and they're trying to get more money for those guys. He gets a pension, and it helps, but it's nothing like guys get in some government jobs."

John Henry's hair had more gray than the last time I saw him.

346

"What was your fondest memory of your days with the Steelers?" I asked, for openers.

"They were special," he said. "The special bunch of guys I played with . . . And you had The Old Man. Mr. Rooney. He was a good owner. You could go in and talk to him. You could talk to him about salary. He had an open-door policy with his players. Bill Ford was a good owner in Detroit and Tony Morabito in San Francisco. But Mr. Rooney was extra special. I could always get something extra from him. He figured I deserved it."

"What was your best salary with the Steelers?"

"It was too long ago to remember."

"How would you describe your relationship with Mr. Rooney?"

"I believe I was one of his favorites. I thought I was one of his boys. But he made everybody feel that way. He'd always talk to you. You could talk to him about any problems you had."

John Henry was a hell-raiser, and was known to blow money in a hurry. So I asked him what kinds of problems he discussed with Mr. Rooney.

"I don't remember the problems I had," he said. Sometimes it's convenient to get old. You can blow off questions you don't want to deal with.

"What about Bobby Layne?" I said. "How come you guys hit it off so well? He was such a big booster of yours."

"Bobby Layne liked guys who hustled and could protect him," Johnson said. "That made me special to him. He gave me an opportunity to carry the ball. He would call the game. He was in charge. He called my number a lot. He just wanted you to do your job. If you didn't get it done, he'd tell you.

"My job was to block and run the ball. I enjoyed blocking. I enjoyed seeing a guy go down. It made you feel good. It made you feel important."

Johnson also liked his coach with the Steelers, the storied Buddy Parker. "When Johnson feels like running, there isn't a better fullback in the game. He's like Jim Thorpe," Parker once proclaimed.

"Buddy Parker was one of the best coaches I ever had," Johnson said. "He was an honest man. He liked guys who hustled and worked hard. If you did that, he was happy. He was a no-jive coach."

And exactly what was a no-jive coach?

"I liked to have a good time, and I stayed out late," Johnson said. "As long as you showed up every day at practice, and played the game hard, you had no problem with Parker.

"I liked the way he used me. I liked to run the ball, but blocking was my forte. My greatest feeling came from knocking the guy down, so Bobby could throw the pass."

Parker gave Johnson the ball more than any coach since Johnson had played in Canada at the outset of his pro career. He gained 1,048 yards in his fifth season with the Steelers and 1,141 yards in his third season. He played in the NFL All-Pro Bowl in 1962-63-64, when his career should have been over.

I asked John Henry about his reputation for running over people rather than around them.

"I enjoyed it; that's the idea," he said with a smile. "That's the way the game was meant to be played. The shortest distance between the backfield and the endzone was a straight line."

That was his style. But it certainly wasn't the way Franco Harris did it when he starred for the Steelers in the '70s. "Our styles were different," Johnson said. "He was effective the way he did it. Jimmy Brown was the best I ever saw at running the ball. Some others came up and looked good, but they disappeared."

When I asked him about the 49ers' "Fearsome Foursome," and wanted to know why the team was not more successful, he said, "We didn't have the defense or the depth to win a championship."

Getting into the Hall of Fame gave him great satisfaction. "That was a good feeling," he said. "It was something I thought I deserved for a long time."

He asked Art Rooney to introduce him, and he was further honored to have Joe Greene go in with him. "Mr. Rooney was an easy choice; he was an easy one to pick," he said. "Being there with Greene meant that I was one of the best among my peers."

His wife, Leona, had a story to tell about Canton, Ohio. "Soon after they built the Hall of Fame, the Steelers played the Cleveland Browns there (in 1962)," she said. "All the players had their wives and girlfriends come to the game. We won and everything was fine. The next year we played the Baltimore Colts there, and again all the wives and girlfriends showed up. Only this time the Steelers lost (48-17), and Buddy Parker was so angry. We had a party scheduled there after the game, and all the players were coming.

"Parker had a right-hand man named Boots' Lewis and he came and chased me and the rest of the wives and girlfriends away. We didn't know what was going on. Buddy Parker chewed out all the players. He hollered, 'You guys looked like Hannibal's Army, bringing all those women with you. Hannibal had all those women traveling with him, and that was his ruination!'"

Speaking of wives, Johnson was originally married when he was in college to Barbara Flood of Oakland, a sister of Curt Flood, who was a fine baseball player, best known for suing organized baseball over player control. They were married in 1950. After five children, they were divorced in 1958.

Even though he played with five pro teams, one in Canada, and four in the United States, Johnson considers himself a Steeler. "That's the way I think of myself," he said. "They come to mind first."

He grew up in Louisiana, in a place called Waterproof, near Natchez, Mississippi. He got into football when his family moved to Pittsburg, California. "I got into football when I was in junior high school," said Johnson. "I started out playing linebacker. Then I became a back. I could play both." He wishes Parker would have played him both ways. "I would have enjoyed it," he said.

John Henry Johnson

With Joe Greene at Three Rivers before 1987 induction into Hall of Fame.

John Henry usually shows up each year for the golf outing held by the Pittsburgh chapter of the NFL Alumni Association. Ray Mansfield, who organizes these get-togethers, enjoys John Henry and tells great stories about him. He told Bill Utterback of *The Pittsburgh Press* this one:

"John Henry was one of the best blockers that ever played the game," said Mansfield. "John could hurt you. He could break your jaw."

In Mansfield's first year in the NFL, he was a defensive lineman with the Philadelphia Eagles. He remembers encounters with John Henry, the blocker.

"He would get way down low in his stance and when you rushed at him, he wouldn't look at you," offered Mansfield. "His eyes would be off in the distance somewhere. You thought he didn't see you.

"As soon as you turned your eyes away from him, he would pop straight up and put his helmet under your jaw. You would eat soup for a week after one of his blocks."

When John Henry was about to be inducted into the Pro Football Hall of Fame in 1987, Chuck Noll spoke to a group of reporters at an informal press conference at St. Vincent's College. Joe Greene was being inducted in the same class, along with another former Steeler, quarterback Lenny Dawson.

"You only remember the guys who hit you hard; the guys who beat the hell out of you," said Noll, recalling his playing days with the Cleveland Browns. "John Henry did that to me and I'll never forget it. My head was spinning and I was dizzy for a couple of minutes.

"I remember him hitting me upside the head with a forearm. I was rushing the punter, and he was the guy protecting the punter. I came in and he unloaded on me more than most guys you had back then."

John Henry had a method to his madness. "It was my revenge," he said. "Every time I carried the ball, people beat up on me. They stepped on my hands. They hit me and knocked me down every chance they got. Blocking was my chance to get back at them. I liked to see their head snap back and their eyes roll a little. I'd flip guys in the air, knock them off their feet, boom!"

Maybe John Henry Johnson enjoys living in Cleveland because that is where he had his best days as a Steeler.

Clendon Thomas, a former Steelers' defensive back, told Bill Utterback of *The Pittsburgh Press* that Johnson seemed to play his best against the Browns.

"He used to love playing against Cleveland," said Thomas. "It was like he saved his best games for the Browns. Every game it seemed like he would outrun, outcatch and outblock Jim Brown. I think John Henry wanted everyone to know that he was a pretty good fullback, too."

The Browns were 3-0-1 and the Steelers were 2-2 when they played in Cleveland before more than 80,000 fans on October 10, 1964. John Henry was as old as his number, 35, that year, but he carried the ball 30 times for a club-record 200 yards as the Steelers won, 23-7.

Johnson scored three touchdowns in that game, powering his way up the middle 35 yards for one touchdown, taking a pitchout and sprinting past everybody for 45 yards for another, and he also scored on a five-yard bolt.

"John Henry just ran the ball down their throats," team president Dan Rooney recalled for Utterback. "It was an important game for us and he completely dominated it. He got almost all the yardage by himself.

"John was a tremendous runner . . . one you really loved to see play."

Johnson remembered his 200-yard effort well. "I might say that was the highlight of my career in Pittsburgh," he told Utterback. "I didn't care about the yards, but I enjoyed beating the Browns. I enjoyed playing against the best teams and players.

"I remember how loud the crowd was. I remember how hot it was that night. I remember we were big underdogs. I remember Coach Parker saying, 'Keep running it, we found their weakness.' We just kept moving up and down the field."

Johnson's memory played tricks on him when he calls the Browns' series. "They were perennial championship contenders," he said, "and we never won anything, and we used to beat them all the time." Not quite. During Johnson's six-year stint with the Steelers, his team's record against the Browns was 4-8.

Former teammate Lou Michaels said, "Nobody worked harder under adverse conditions. If we were down by two touchdowns or if we were playing one of the better teams in the league, John Henry was at his best.

"I've been around a lot of great athletes and most of them will quit when the odds are against them. Not John Henry. He was at his best when his back was to the wall."

Here's another tall tale they tell about John Henry Johnson: Following a football game between San Francisco and Green Bay in 1956, Johnson's last season with the 49ers, he was sitting on the bench, wiping blood and sweat off his body with a towel. There were cuts on his legs and arms. His cheek was bruised and swollen. His backside muscles were in spasm.

Johnson extended his arm toward teammate Leo Nomellini. "Pull it, Leo," Johnson said. "I want to pop my shoulder."

Nomellini, a Hall of Fame lineman who also wrestled professionally, did as asked. "John Henry," said Nomellini, "you'd better ease up. No sense in killing yourself. The way you're going, you won't last five years in this league."

Johnson just laughed. "I can't play any other way, Leo," he said. "Out there, it's either me or him. And I always dish out more than I take."

Nomellini had the highest regard for Johnson. "Let me put it this way," he said. "If I was going down a dark alley where hoodlums hang out late at night, I would rather have John Henry with me than any-one else on earth. He was just a helluva nice guy. But he hit like a tor-nado — all over you at once. And he was absolutely fearless.

"We had just the right nickname for John Henry. We called him 'Sweetpea!' John didn't mind. Hell, he was a rather sweet guy off the field."

When he got into the Hall of Fame, 17 years after he had become eligi-ble, Johnson was relieved. "I felt cheated," he said. "Every year, I'd see guys make it ahead of me who had worse statistics. I couldn't be-lieve it.

"I figured eventually when the Hall of Fame ran out of other peo-ple, they'd vote me in posthumously."

Art Rooney shared his dismay. "He belonged from the first day he became eligible," said the Steelers owner.

When he spoke to the media before enshrinement ceremonies in Canton, Ohio, Johnson said, "I ran over guys if they got in my way. But I had a few moves. I was confident, and I thought I was kind of elu-sive, but they taught me to run north and south, and I didn't fool around too much.

"Respect is all I wanted, and today I feel I have that respect.

"I want to be remembered as a man who loved the game."

John Henry and presenter Art Rooney at Hall of Fame in 1987.

352

J. R. Wilburn
Still in the record books
"I'd like to cling to a little something."

J. R. Wilburn has a single line that remains in the Steelers' record book, and it's his legacy. Going into the 1992 season, he still held the record for most receptions in a game with 12, which he established on October 22, 1967 in a 24-21 defeat by the Dallas Cowboys at Pitt Stadium.

"I'm always waiting for someone at a cocktail party to ask who holds that record, because I know the answer," said Wilburn over the telephone from his home in Midlothian, Virginia, where he is an account executive for Reynolds Metals Company, a job he has held since his playing days with the Steelers.

J. R. Wilburn, a wide receiver from the University of South Carolina, played five seasons for the Steelers from 1966 to 1970. He played three seasons with Bill Austin as the coach, and two for Chuck Noll, thus he can make comparisons.

I always liked his name. It had a certain ring about it, like one of those characters in a Dan Jenkins novel (*Semi-Tough*) about pro football. The Steelers have had more than their share of players with special names, starting with William Shakespeare, their first-ever No. 1 draft choice, out of Notre Dame in 1936.

The lineup would have to include Byron White, Byron Beams, Johnny Blood, Gary Glick, Chuck Cherundolo, Buddy Dial, Johnny Lattner, Lynn Chandnois, Buzz Nutter, Dean Derby, Paul Cameron, Val Jansante, Bobby Gage, Dale Dodril, Jim "Popcorn" Brandt, Johnny "Zero" Clement and Art DeCarlo. You probably have your own favorites.

But J.R. Wilburn was right up there with the best. His full name is Johnny Richard Wilburn, from Portsmouth, Va. That, too, has a nice ring to it, but it would take up too much space in the Steelers' record book.

"Yes, I still take pride in catching the most passes of any Steeler in one game in the team's history," he said. "They've had some great receivers there. It's the only thing I have left in the world of football. I'd like to cling to a little something."

Only a few days earlier, Chuck Noll had announced his retirement after 23 years as the head coach of the Steelers. It had been 21 years since Wilburn had played for him. Noll traded him after two seasons to the San Diego Chargers, but Wilburn holds no grudge about that.

"It shocked me that Noll was leaving," said Wilburn. "I saw it on ESPN. It seemed like he had weathered every storm. He was unwavering.

"I remember when he came in. He changed all the coaches and he had a definite plan in mind. It seemed to me he had a method to his madness. Whether it included you or not, it looked like he stuck with it.

"His whole attitude was always so positive. He'd take things step by step, and he would go over things so many times. His practices were so precisely planned out. He would have to get so much out of every practice. He truly believed that you did in practice what you did in a game. He was very methodical.

"You either fit into his scheme of things or you didn't. He never socialized with the players. He'd make one or two wisecracks a week, and that was the highlight. It was the best you could hope for.

"He had assistant coaches, but he seemed to handle everything himself. He liked to keep his hands on everything. He put his nose into everything at practice. He does it his way."

Wilburn can remember the day he learned he no longer fit into the Steelers' scheme of things. "I was at work at Reynolds Metals when I got the call. 'This is Chuck,' the voice at the other end of the phone said. 'How many Chucks do I know?' I thought. He got right to the point, and it was still the longest conversation we ever had. He told me he wanted more speed in the receiver ranks, and that I would fit in well with San Diego's emphasis on passing. I appreciated the fact that he called me himself. He didn't leave it to anyone else. I knew he was not a real sociable person, but he was a stand-up guy."

In that respect, Noll provided quite a contrast to Bill Austin, who had come to the Steelers for the 1966 season after serving as an assistant to Vince Lombardi on the great Green Bay Packers championship teams. He lasted three seasons, and Wilburn says they were all long seasons.

"He was a very good offensive line coach," recalled Wilburn, "but he was a facade as far as being a head coach. He tried to emulate Lombardi, and he wasn't Lombardi. If he had said, 'Hey, I'm Bill Austin' and just taken some ideas from Lombardi he'd have been better off.

"He tried to impersonate him — all the mannerisms and the same lines — and he didn't pull it off. There was an inconsistency to him. He looked like he was playing Lombardi one day, with a hard line on everything. The next day he'd be Bill Austin, and he'd mix with the players. You never knew whether Austin or Lombardi would be around any particular day.

"Noll brought the same person out every day. He had the same face every day. Bill Austin did not. One day Austin would be partying with the players at a local bar. The next day he had his Lombardi stuff on. He just wasn't cut out to be a head coach.

"Everything was a quote from Vince. 'We did this and we did that in Green Bay.' All his quotes came from Lombardi. We recognized the quotes. Lloyd Voss had come over from Green Bay, along with Tony Jeter and Ron Smith and Bruce Van Dyke. They'd make comments and comparisons. After awhile, Austin had some real problems racially. Roy Jefferson didn't care for Austin and he had a following. Before long, there were some real racial issues, and Austin had lost the team completely.

"Noll did not see black and white. Absolutely. Noll judged people strictly on ability. He never had any problem with dissension. Noll showed a sign of strength right away. Roy Jefferson pushed him real soon, showing up late for practice and team meetings, stuff like breaking curfews. Noll told everyone he would not tolerate anyone being late for anything, and that meant everyone.

"He gave away Roy Jefferson, who was a helluva ballplayer and easily one of the Steelers' best players. At that point, you could see he was not going to let things get away from him.

"You knew who was running the show. That was the turning point; he harnessed everybody. They found out right then that that kind of stuff was not going to go down with him. That trade was good for Jefferson and for Pittsburgh. To me, Jefferson thought he was getting a raw deal, but he was splitting the team down the middle and Noll simply would not have any of that. I thought Noll handled it very well.

"Bill Austin and Roy Jefferson had some shouting matches and shoving skirmishes. Chuck never had a confrontation with Jefferson, not in front of anybody, that I know of. He'd call roll, and just pass Jefferson's name up if he wasn't there. Austin would say something about what he was going to do with Jefferson as a punishment, and then not do it. He'd be somewhere having a drink, and he'd make a critical statement about Jefferson or someone else, and it would get back to Roy or the other party. They were both very emotional.

"I've seen it work both ways. Noll did not have two standards. There were several standards in San Diego, where Sid Gillman was the coach. He was a lot like Austin was in Pittsburgh. He had three standards. John Hadl could do anything. You could be drinking with him, and Gillman might fine you and the next guy, and ignore Hadl. That caused problems. I thought I was back in Pittsburgh with Bill Austin."

When Noll retired, Wilburn hoped it would work out best for his former boss. Noll had gotten rid of him, but Wilburn still respected Noll. "I think he's a good coach," said Wilburn. "If I said he wasn't, I'd be a damn fool. I thought he was very fair. That's the biggest thing I could say about him. He didn't see black and white. He just saw talent and how you fit into his scheme of things.

"He was looking for speed on the outside. I didn't have that. He explained it to me. He explains to you why you're gone. When he first addressed our team, he told us most of us would not be good enough to stay with his team. He told us that most of us would be gone in a few years. I just didn't think he was talking to me at the time."

Among the memories Wilburn cherishes the most are scoring his first NFL touchdown against the Philadelphia Eagles in 1967. Unfortunately, he couldn't recall the touchdown until he saw the game films. He had been knocked out earlier in the game by teammate Ray Mansfield, and had memory lapses about what happened thereafter.

"Ray put the hardest hit on me I've ever had in my life," recalled Wilburn. "Most of my passes were short passes. I caught one and one of the Eagles hit me, and then the lights went out altogether.

"Ray was trying to help me, I later learned. I was giving up ground, trying to cut up the field, and Ray was trying to throw a block for me. I didn't know what hit me. His helmet hit mine, and I was no match for his noggin. I got a new helmet after that, one with more protective padding in it.

"I lost a half day there. It was like the Nixon tapes. I had a few erasures, including that TD catch. Mansfield messed up my whole day. He's a piece of work.

"He was an incredible competitor. He still is. I know when you line up to play golf with him these days it's still there. He has an enthusiasm, a will to win, more so than any person I've ever known. He'd try anything once, just to see if he could do it."

Wilburn also remembers Rocky Bleier. "I never got to see Rocky when he was in the Super Bowls, but I saw him when he first came in. He was the last draft choice, out of Notre Dame, and he was nothing much to look at, at first. We ran down on kickoffs together a few times. That's when I could tell he was a tough piece of leather.

"I was staying with Terry Hanratty. It was during a strike-delayed season. Rocky had gotten shot up in Vietnam and he was really looking bad. He was trying to get in shape. He was also staying at Hanratty's place. If you could just see him; I was just hoping he'd be able to walk normally. Everyone was turning their head and wincing when he first tried to play.

"Hanratty would rub his injured foot. He had a special massage treatment. Rocky wore the same pair of jeans and a light shirt every day. That's about all he had with him in the way of clothes. Everything else in his bag was protein pills and vitamin pills. If it didn't have anything to do with working out, it wasn't in his suitcase.

"We'd run at a nearby school field and he'd be dragging his leg along. It's damn near a miracle that he could ever play again. But he was phenomenal. When I saw the Steelers on TV when they and Bleier were at their best, I wasn't sure it was the same Rocky Bleier. He wasn't just playing, he was starting.

"That was a far cry from when he'd first come back from Vietnam and appeared along with other alumni of the team at a halftime ceremony in 1969. He had a handlebar mustache and he walked with a cane, and he didn't weigh 175 pounds, but he got a standing ovation when he walked across the field.

"When he came back to practice with us, he was in agony every day. Terry told him, 'Hey, you don't have to do this; you don't have anything to prove. You're out there just killing yourself. Just cool it. Nobody is expecting you to do this.'

"But Rocky refused to quit. It's amazing to me. That's the biggest lesson I learned with the Steelers: You can never give up. I tell my son that every day.

"My son had to have open heart surgery this past year. He's had a heart problem, and it got worse. Rocky sent him a copy of his book (*Fighting Back*), and he wrote out a list of seven or eight principles that he lives by. One of them was to never give up."

Brandon Wilburn, 16, had a heart that beat too fast. "It would just take off whenever he exercised in any way," his dad recalled. "He doesn't have the problem now. He's going out for the football team next fall. It will be his senior year at Midlothian High School. I just want him to be healthy. Whatever he picks out, I just want him to do it well."

The Wilburns have a daughter, Mason, 19, a sophomore on the diving team at James Madison College in Harrisonburg, Va. The Wilburns have been married for 24 years. They were high school sweethearts.

"Leslie lived down the street from me," said J. R. "We dated for nine years. We've been good for each other."

He believes he learned a lot from his years of athletic competition that have served him and his family in good stead ever since.

"You need some type of inspiration," he said.

"You have to have something inside of you to make you tick. It can be brought on by adversity. Sometimes negative stuff drives me on; that's been my story, anyhow.

"I was always very small and very slow when I was in school. I grew four to five inches between my sophomore and junior year. I was a blocking dummy until that point. A coach really singled me out one day. He was an assistant coach — this was at Cradock High School — and he told me I'd never make a pimple on an athlete's ass. It was a stupid thing. He embarrassed me in front of everybody.

"I went back to that high school this past year because they were closing it. I saw a lot of my buddies. But I could still remember the sting I felt that day when that coach got on me in front of everybody.

"It happened out on the field. I wasn't paying attention; I wasn't playing at the time. I was probably goofing off. He stopped everything. And the whole world, everybody, saw it. At that point, I told myself, 'You either have to fish or cut bait.' I got a little help from somewhere, and I got bigger. And I found my place on that team.

"It's been mostly negatives that I've responded to. I was always too small, or too something. I was always trying to prove somebody wrong. That's why I liked Rocky Bleier. I have no idea of what he went through, but I always admired him, and I still do.

"I came back and played for our team after that coach had put me down so badly. It wasn't easy. We had two ends who both made all-state in my junior year, and I backed them up. Then I started as a senior.

"It would have been so easy to quit, and say he's right. 'Golly, he's right. And I'm folding my tent.' But things seemed to happen for the best after that.

"When I got to college, I was weighing about 172 pounds, and I was supposed to play major college football. I knew that wouldn't work. So I started lifting weights and I ate a lot, and I waited till everyone got hurt and I had my chance. I outlasted them, that's what I did.

"I've coached football a little bit. To me, football is just an extension of life. The one thing I got from Bill Austin is that if you're going to do it then do it a hundred percent. I don't know if that came from Lombardi or not, but it's a good rule to live by."

J.R. Wilburn and Dick Hoak get together to reminisce about their playing days with Steelers at NFL Alumni Association golf outing at Oakmont Country Club in June of 1992.

Bill Austin

"J.R."

Paul Martha
Always the All-American Boy

"It would be a shame if the sports tradition of this city were allowed to die. Things can be done to prevent Pittsburgh from becoming a ghost town as far as sports are concerned."
—Paul Martha, 1992

Paul Martha's ominous warning about Pittsburgh's bleak sports future was fresh in my mind as I motored through the once-bustling milltowns of Rankin, Braddock, Duquesne, Munhall, Homestead, Hays and my hometown of Hazelwood.

It was an overcast gray day in January of 1992 and the landscape did nothing to brighten my spirits. I had been spending time the previous few days near my old neighborhood attending a funeral in our family, and I was in a funk.

Passing through ghost towns will only darken your mood.

So many empty buildings, so many rust-coated roofs and equipment, rusty skeletons, an eerie stillness in the railroad yards below, whole units of once-familiar and foreboding mills missing on the horizon. Where were the proud buildings and busy, soot-stained, lunch bucket-toting, hard-hatted workers of my youth?

There was some white smoke in the sky over the USX Edgar Thomson Works in Braddock, but that was about it. No one in decades had referred to Pittsburgh as "the steel capital of the world," "Steel City" or "the smoky city," unless they were ill-informed travel writers or politicians just passing through and failing to check out the skyline.

Mesta Machine Company in West Homestead, where my father and two of my uncles and my brother Dan all worked, was gone, having given ground to Sand Castle, a water-ride amusement park along the Monongahela River. Some of Mesta remains with a new name.

In my youth, I used to pass through all these milltowns traveling on a streetcar from Hazelwood to Kennywood for summer picnics, and it was always an impressive view. The mills loomed so large on the western Pennsylvania horizon back in those days.

I recalled how a few years earlier, I had taken John Underwood, one of the nation's top sports authors and a former featured writer at *Sports Illustrated,* on a similar tour.

Underwood had telephoned me from Florida to ask if I would be so kind as to take him around the mill areas to do interviews and research for a book he was doing about religion and the dying milltowns. He said he remembered that I had been "a good guide" in driving him around Pittsburgh back in 1963 when he came to town to write about Pitt's highly-successful 9-1 football team, led by Paul Martha, an All-American running back, and the school's chancellor and most renowned cheerleader, Dr. Edward Litchfield.

I first met Martha in 1960 when he was the star of an undefeated (6-0) freshman football team at Pitt. That was the same fall when Billy Mazeroski hit a ninth inning homerun to beat the New York Yankees in the seventh game of the World Series right across the street from the Pitt Student Union at Forbes Field. Martha and I were in the same freshman class, and occasionally were in the same classrooms in the Cathedral of Learning over the next four years. We sweated through several Spanish classes, I recall. For me, Spanish class was equivalent to working in the mines or Mesta Machine Company.

Martha was always one of my favorites. He was a fine infielder on the school's baseball team, started for a freshman basketball team where the other four starters went on to start in the NCAA and NIT tournaments as upperclassmen, while he concentrated on football and baseball. He came through in the clutch with touchdown runs to win games for the Panthers. He was successfully boosted by Beano Cook, Pitt's sports publicist, for national honors. He was a writer's dream.

He was easy to promote. He was always smart, handsome, well-connected, fun to be around, and a tremendous competitor. He could mix with the poorest and richest people in Pittsburgh and never miss a beat.

He had been wearing a white warm-up outfit when I visited him earlier that day in his well-appointed formally-furnished office at the Civic Arena, and he was scheduled to play tennis afterward at the Racquet Club in Monroeville.

He looked good, as always, even if he, too, was in a bit of a funk, still distressed by all that had gone down in his life during the just-ended 1991. He looked in great shape, though he said one of his knees was aching from an old football injury. His heart was aching a little, too. His role at the Civic Arena had recently been diminished, and he wasn't sure where he stood in a lot of respects.

"1991 was the worst year of my life," said Martha. "My mother died in August. We won the Stanley Cup, but the real joy of such an achievement was stolen away because I knew beforehand that the team and the Arena operation were going to change hands. I knew in December of 1990 that, because of negative economic developments affecting the real estate business, the DeBartolos wanted to sell the team. I had a falling-out with the DeBartolo family, and they blocked my bid to be one of the owners of the Penguins. I lost my position as head of the Arena, and I'm no longer associated with the 49ers. And our coach, Bob Johnson — one of the greatest guys I've ever known — died in October as we were starting a new season. 1991 was just awful, as far as I was concerned. After all that we had gone through to build what we built here, and then to have to give it all up. Spectacor, a Philadelphia group, took over control of the Civic Arena in Pittsburgh. That just shouldn't happen. Some people got fired. It was very disruptive. People I was close to got fired."

He was retained by the new owners as executive vice-president of the Penguins. For one season, as it turned out.

"Paul has been an integral part of the Penguins leadership team for many years," new owner Howard Baldwin told Tom McMillan, the

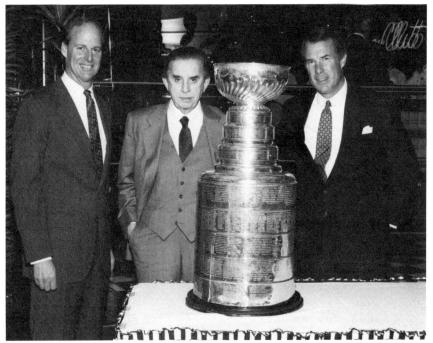

GM Craig Patrick, owner Edward J. DeBartolo and Martha proudly pose with Pittsburgh Penguins' 1991 Stanley Cup.

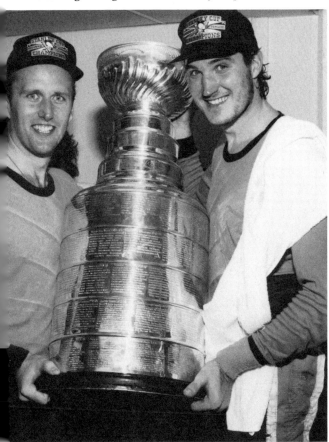

Bob Johnson
Head Coach

Tom Barrasso, left, and Mario Lemieux show off Stanley Cup.

hockey writer for the *Pittsburgh Post-Gazette*, "and I felt his experience, his management skills and his knowledge of the Pittsburgh area would be invaluable to us as we begin operation of the club."

Martha believed a letter of agreement with Baldwin, dated August 23, 1991, gave him and his group of Pittsburgh-based investors a legal right to buy 50 per cent of the hockey team.

A group led by Baldwin and Morris Belzberg had negotiated a deal to buy the Penguins from Edward J. DeBartolo Sr. for $31 million. Baldwin backed off his original agreement with Martha.

Then Martha detailed the financial problems of Pittsburgh's pro sports franchises — the Pirates, Penguins and the Steelers — and predicted that teams here would have a difficult time competing with teams from bigger markets like New York, Chicago, Los Angeles, Boston, Philadelphia and Atlanta.

Then, too, Martha thinks that Pittsburgh lacks the kind of inspired political leadership to lift the city and its sports franchises out of their doldrums. "David Lawrence and Richard Caliguiri could get things done in this city," said Martha. "They knew how to get big business behind their projects.

"The Pirates couldn't sign Bobby Bonilla and it's unlikely they can sign Barry Bonds. They're losing their best players." He said it was hard for the Penguins and Steelers to generate the kind of revenues needed to keep up with the ever-escalating salary structure in pro sports.

"We don't have a collective bargaining agreement now in hockey," he continued. "Some hard decisions have to be made, if we're going to maintain some sort of economic sanity. Right now, we don't have a collective bargaining agreement in hockey or football. That means there can be no free agency compensation and there can't be a draft. The salary escalation in baseball could kill all of us. It has a trickling-down effect in every professional sport.

"I'd like to see the business of professional sports put in a structure so a city like Pittsburgh can maintain its sports tradition. It would be a shame if the sports tradition of this city could be allowed to die."

There could come a day, he emphasized, when the stadiums and arenas are abandoned by some of our pro teams. They would be unused and empty. "You're really close to that with Three Rivers Stadium," said Martha. "Can you imagine Three Rivers without the Pirates' 81 home games? That could really happen in the '90s. I know the business."

If that doomsday prediction sounds outrageous, just think about all the abandoned mills along the three rivers. Looking back twenty years ago, did that ever seem possible?

I remember a conversation I once had with Art Rooney Sr. He said the Pirates were more important to Pittsburgh than the Steelers. "They have so many more dates at the Stadium than we do," said Rooney, whose first sports love was baseball. He loved to walk to the Stadium from his home on the North Side to see the Pirates play. He liked the fact that they played so often because he enjoyed getting out and being around people as frequently as possible.

"Without the Pirates, there wouldn't be big league baseball in Pittsburgh," said Mr. Rooney. "But even if the Steelers weren't here you'd still have big-time football out at Pitt."

Martha said there was a time in 1983 when DeBartolo wanted out of hockey. "I went to the mayor and other civic and county leaders and we got things done that enabled Mr. DeBartolo to remain here," said Martha. "So I know how to do what needs to be done.

"You need people who realize what sports means to a city's major league image and its quality of life. Once upon a time here, you had Davey Lawrence and Richard K. Mellon, and they got great things accomplished. You had the Renaissance, and Dick Caliguiri got the corporate support to pull off Renaissance II. Things can be done to prevent Pittsburgh from becoming a ghost town as far as sports are concerned.

"People have to recognize it is a serious problem. Pittsburgh has huge potential. With the new airport and the opening of the European common market, I think Pittsburgh will become an international hub. It's already an international city. You see more and more foreign-owned companies setting up shop here. The Germans love Pittsburgh; they're bringing companies here, like Miles. We need to put some shine back on the skyline."

Dan Rooney and Paul Martha were the most important people in the settlement of the NFL's 57-day player strike back in mid-November of 1982.

"I'm very proud of Danny and Paul," the Steelers' owner Art Rooney told us at the time. "They're both Pittsburghers. This is a laboring town, and they know what labor negotiating is all about."

Then the horsebreeder in Rooney came out, as well as a few bits of his cigar, which he rubbed away from his lips. "Danny has good sires in that respect," he said. "His grandfather on my side was a coal miner, and his grandfather on his mother's side was a steelworker.

"Martha's from management's side. Isn't he one of those rich kids? From what I've heard, anyhow. Martha came into the negotiating just at the right time. Danny told me Paul did a fantastic job.

"I remember the first day I met Paul," Art Rooney said of Martha, who was the Steelers' first draft choice in 1964 after an All-American career at Pitt.

"He was that type of person. He was easy to know and easy to associate with, both physically and mentally. I used to call him 'Star' and till this day I still call him 'Star' when I see him.

"Paul comes over here a lot. He's with Danny an awful lot. When we go to the league meetings, it seems that every time you sit down you sit with him. He's easy to be with. Like he's yours. Pittsburghers are like that. They have a special feeling for each other."

Then again, Mr. Rooney always said you could recognize a Pittsburgher's handshake. "There's a special warmth to it," he insisted. "You can feel it."

363

"I think the economic mechanisms have to change for a city the size of Pittsburgh to compete," said Martha. "The Pirates have become a minor league team for no other reason than they can't compete with bigger economic markets."

After Carl Barger resigned as president of the Pirates in 1991 to lead an expansion franchise in Miami, the Pirates interviewed Martha to fill the void. "It was a no-win situation," said Martha. "They interviewed me and Mark Sauer, and that was it. I hope he realizes what he's gotten into."

Martha had similar foreboding feelings when media speculation mentioned him as a candidate for the vacant athletic director's position at Pitt during the same period. Martha loves his alma mater, but has been distressed at the decline in standards for the sort of student now representing Pitt in athletics, and the lack of leadership and commitment to return the school's programs to what he regards as achievable lofty levels.

"Plus, I'd have had to take a major slash in salary," said Martha. "Pitt doesn't have the financial resources right now to do what's necessary to become competitive again. But the school has such a strong medical program — more organ transplants are done there than anywhere else in the world — and other fine professional schools, and they should be using them as bait to attract the finest student athletes in the world. There's a great opportunity there to do something special. You can't guarantee grad school acceptance to athletes when you recruit them — it's against the NCAA rules — but there should be slots open that are earmarked for athletes if they are qualified.

"I was on the search committee when they hired Paul Hackett, and I strongly endorsed him. He had been an assistant to Bill Walsh early on with the 49ers. I think he wants to do things right.

"I think football players should go to school and do well. When I was on that selection committee, I was disappointed when they laid down the guidelines for the kind of players they wanted on the football team. I felt Pitt was being compromised. Maybe I was naive."

Paul Martha has long epitomized the best in Pittsburgh sports. He first made his mark at Shady Side Academy, where he starred in several sports. He was a true student athlete at Pitt, and was good enough to be the Steelers' No. 1 draft choice in 1964. He played defensive back for the Steelers in the NFL from 1964 to 1969 while attending law school. He obtained his Doctor of Law degree at Duquesne University in 1969 and played one more year of pro ball, with the Denver Broncos in 1970, before retiring to practice law on a full-time basis back home in Pittsburgh.

Martha, 49 as we spoke in January of 1992, joined the Penguins' organization during the summer of 1978 after the DeBartolo Corporation assumed control of the franchise. He was named vice-president prior to the 1978-79 season and has handled the club's legal matters as general

Butler's Bill Saul, Martha's roommate.

Paul Martha

Dave Fleming
Martha's Pal

Martha (20) in action against Green Bay in 1969.

counsel since that time, and also served on the NHL's Board of Governors.

Martha wore many hats in his service to the DeBartolo family. With his background in law and professional football, he was selected to serve as neutral arbitrator for the NFL in 1982. He and Steelers' president Dan Rooney were credited with having a big influence in resolving player-owner differences that year and settling a 57-day strike that had halted play.

He also served as president of the defunct Pittsburgh Maulers in the USFL during their one season of operation — the Rooneys were really upset about their existence — and he has handled legal work for the San Francisco 49ers of the NFL. He became involved with the Major Indoor Soccer League as well, serving as vice president for the Pittsburgh Spirit. Spirit owner Frank Fuhrer is his cousin ("He's certainly made his contribution to the Pittsburgh sports scene," said Martha).

Before the DeBartolos sold their rights to the operation of the Civic Arena in 1991, Martha served as vice president of the Civic Arena Corporation and headed day-to-day operations of the entertainment facility. "I ran the whole thing," he said.

He and his wife Bobbi reside in Fox Chapel and are the parents of three sons, J.P., Christopher and Richie.

I recall a Saturday afternoon in September of 1991 when I took my wife Kathie and our daughters, Sarah and Rebecca, on a lunch/shopping trip to Shadyside. While walking on Walnut Street, we bumped into Bobbi Martha.

It was only a few days after the news first broke that Bob Johnson had brain cancer. He had undergone emergency surgery to remove part of a brain tumor on August 29 at Mercy Hospital. Within a few days, it was disclosed that there was a second tumor. "It doesn't look good for him," she told us. "Paul talked to the doctors and they are not very optimistic."

In Pittsburgh, a prayer vigil was begun by fans for "Badger Bob," a lovable figure.

No coach was ever more closely tied to a team's success than Bob Johnson, who lifted the Penguins to a Stanley Cup championship in his first and only season in Pittsburgh. The Penguins grabbed hockey's Holy Grail with an 8-0 victory over the Minnesota North Stars in Johnson's hometown of Minneapolis on May 25.

"Bob's the reason we were able to win the Cup, but he meant more to us as a person," said defenseman Paul Coffey. "I've never met a better man."

Johnson, indeed, was a bubbly sort who pumped up everyone's spirits. He made former Pirates manager Chuck Tanner come off as a gloom and doom guy by comparison, and you recall that Tanner was knocked for being such a positive person.

"It's a great day for hockey," Johnson liked to say, with the same spirit and smile of Ernie Banks, the one-time great of the Chicago Cubs

who always said, "It's a great day for a doubleheader."
Both put sunshine in other people's lives.

Johnson was 60 when he died at his home in Colorado Springs, Colorado. "He'll always be the Penguins' coach," said Scotty Bowman. "What he's done for this city and this hockey club in one year is pretty incredible," team leader Mario Lemieux said. "Nobody would have thought we'd win the cup last year, but with Bob Johnson everything was possible."

Edward J. DeBartolo Sr., of Youngstown, Ohio, is one of the nation's richest men. His DeBartolo Corporation is the nation's largest developer and manager of shopping malls, and he owns and operates many sports enterprises, especially thoroughbred racing tracks.

The San Francisco 49ers, led by his son, Edward Jr., won four Super Bowls in the '80s, succeeding the Steelers as the sport's most successful dynasty.

Martha worked with the father and son for 14 years. "I now have a strained relationship with the family, it's unfortunate," said Martha. "I had a signed deal with Howard Baldwin to be a partner in the new ownership picture, but Mr. DeBartolo Sr. blocked that. He didn't want an employee being part of management."

Asked how Mr. DeBartolo Sr. had been so successful in his business endeavors, Martha said, "He's a hard-working tenacious businessman. He's inexhaustible.

"I'm thankful to him for giving me the opportunity to develop a career as a sports and entertainment executive, which is very enjoyable. I have been exposed to so many different situations. I know this business. There have been a lot of good times, and there have been some bad times."

How about his relationship with Eddie Jr.? "He and I were good friends," said Martha. "We, in some way, will always be good friends. We went through a lot together. We went through some things we won't soon forget."

Martha will miss being associated with the 49ers and the NFL. "I felt I was a part of it, particularly in the beginning," said Martha. "I remember the hard times that Eddie Jr. and I went through.

"I was involved with selecting Bill Walsh as the coach. He was the perfect coach for the 49ers, a local guy who had coached at Stanford and been in the pros. He fit in perfectly in the community. He enabled Eddie to win the Super Bowl four times."

One of the most upsetting aspects of the 1991 campaign was the illness and death of Penguins' coach Bob Johnson. In his only year as coach of the team, Johnson directed the Penguins to a Stanley Cup triumph, the first in the history of the franchise.

"There are certain people you meet in life," said Martha, "and after a period of time you know they're very special. I didn't know him that well, at first, but I got to know him. He and Craig Patrick and I played golf together a few times, and we spent some time together.

"He was a special human being. He always found good in every-thing. He totally astounded people, particularly the players, because somehow he could find something good in a 9-to-nothing blowout. It made him a special person.

"My father-in-law was a special person."

Martha's deceased father-in-law was Edwin H. Gott, who had served as president, chief executive officer and then chairman of U.S. Steel, now called USX after a merger with Marathon Oil.

"He was a very honest, forthright person at a very difficult time in U.S. Steel's history," noted Martha. "He went to Peabody High School, and worked his way up through the ranks at U.S. Steel to become its top executive. I learned a lot from him. He had integrity; I remember him being very critical of some of the perks that went to top executives. He didn't think it was right.

"Art Rooney Sr. was a special person. All of his faults aside, you realize that he was special. Bob Johnson was that way, too."

Then Martha paused a moment, and said, "I would be remiss if I didn't mention my parents. My dad, Al, and my mother, Dorothy, had a lot to do with my success, as well as the success of my sister and our brothers."

His sister, Lynda, was a national baton-twirling champion during her high school years. His brother Richie was a running back at West Virginia University. He has two other brothers, Albert and David.

"Our parents came to all our games and activities, and carted us all around in their cars so we could do all those things," said Martha.

Switching subjects, I asked Martha what it was like to win the Stanley Cup after so many frustrating seasons.

"It was an interesting experience," said Martha. "It's something I'd like to do experience under different circumstances. The ownership problems and sale of the franchise and the management position at the Arena took the glow off what could have been an exhilarating ex-perience."

In short, with everything that was going on, he couldn't enjoy it. "No, I couldn't," said Martha.

What was he thinking as he saw the Penguins skating around the ice in Minnesota on May 25, 1991 after winning the clinching game?

"I was thinking it's really too bad because next year somebody else will own this team."

There was a book about the topsy-turvy financial world on a table near his desk called *Going For Broke.* It could have been the title for the Penguins' Stanley Cup campaign.

"This is all a little unbelievable," said Paul Coffey in the midst of the ownership squabble in November of 1991. "I've never seen a cham-pionship team be involved in the turmoil that's faced our team."

It wasn't too long before Coffey and Mark Recchi, two of the team's top stars and popular players who had big roles in the Penguins' Stan-ley Cup championship, were traded away. The Penguins struggled all season long just to qualify for the playoffs. Just when the playoffs were to begin, the NHL players went on strike.

Sometimes Pittsburghers take their own for granted. Paul Martha is one of those. He is a Pittsburgh treasure, yet he is often more valued and commands greater respect on a national basis than he does in his hometown.

Martha is often mentioned when top jobs come open in the sports world, and it doesn't matter whether you are talking about football or hockey or even baseball. He is regarded as somebody who can run a sports ship in a storm. He was regarded as a possible NHL commissioner.

Martha has lunch just about every day of the week with his long-time friend and fellow attorney, Steve Stepanian II, who has a law degree from Harvard. They once worked together at Reed Shaw Smith & McClay, Pittsburgh's top law firm.

On this particular day, Martha drove me in a blue Cadillac to the Gateway Towers where Stepanian lives in one condominium apartment and has an office in another apartment on another level. For lunch, Martha picked the Grand Concourse Restaurant.

This is a unique restaurant, another Pittsburgh treasure. It is set in the Edwardian splendor of the Pittsburgh & Lake Erie Rail Road terminal built in 1901. It's part of the Pittsburgh History and Landmarks' Station Square restoration. It's on the Monongahela River just across the Smithfield Street Bridge, with a grand view of the Golden Triangle.

Japanese businessmen took up three nearby tables. It pleased us to see that they all ordered Iron City Lite draft beer, and toasted with it. "This is becoming an international city," said Martha, repeating a favorite theme of his. "The sooner we realize that the better off we'll be.

"If Japanese interests wanted to buy the Pirates and keep it here, we should never turn our backs on such an offer."

At the time, Japanese interests were running into a snag in their bid to buy the Seattle Mariners of the American Baseball League because baseball commissioner Fay Vincent felt that it was not in the best interest of America's so-called favorite pastime to have foreign ownership. He later changed his mind.

"We can't be isolationists," said Martha.

"The Pirates just signed two ballplayers for a total of $9 million, and for one year in both cases," he said, alluding to new contracts for Barry Bonds and Doug Drabek. "That's bad business. Next year they'll be back for more, and the Pirates can't afford to pay more. We might need somebody to come in and buy the Pirates because the local corporations who own it now will not want to stay involved."

The Edwardian splendor of the Grand Concourse must have reminded Martha of what he had been reading lately. He talked about a book he was reading by Winston Churchill, and was in awe of Churchill's precise use of words, and the extent of his vocabulary.

Martha pulled out a slip of paper of words he had written down just that morning from Churchill's book. He tested us on a few of the words to see if we knew the meanings. Martha likes to read in the morning before starting his workday.

Stepanian is also a voracious reader, and said he had just re-read a book by Jimmy Breslin, one of my favorite writers, on Damon Runyon, a legendary Broadway columnist whose characters inspired shows like *Guys and Dolls.*

It was easy to see from the conversation why Martha and Stepanian get along so well. "Our wives accuse us of spending more time with each other than we do with them," said Stepanian, who serves as an advisor to Martha and helped him put together the group that wanted to buy the Penguins.

"We had a signed agreement to purchase the Penguins," said Stepanian, "but DeBartolo couldn't stand the idea of an employee buying the team from him. So he blocked the deal. It's too bad, because the team would be better off with local investors."

Then they started talking about baseball. Martha is a man for all seasons.

Back in 1982, Martha and Dan Rooney received a great deal of attention and respect for resolving differences between the owners and the players in the NFL and settling a league-wide strike.

I asked Martha what made Rooney so special. "He's probably as powerful right now as any owner in the league," said Martha. "He's so well respected because he's been consistent, honest, forthright, and he's been objective. He's been that way for a long time now.

"He's not the personality that Art was, but in a very quiet way he's been a steady force in the NFL. He has such a different style of ownership. You have people who have spent $140 million for a franchise, and here in Pittsburgh you have people who spent $2,500.

"So obviously they're going to have varying perspectives on the business of pro football. With Dan Rooney, there has been a growth. He's gained tremendously among his peers in respect and in power."

Martha spent his sixth and final season with the Steelers with Chuck Noll as the coach. Previously, Martha had played for Buddy Parker, Mike Nixon and Bill Austin. Martha never played for a winner with the Steelers. The best mark was 5-8-1 under Austin in 1966; the worst was 1-13 under Noll in 1969. The overall record during those six years was 19-62-3. He would have liked being a part of the turnaround.

"Noll traded me to Denver, rightly or wrongly, so that kinda colors my opinion of him," said Martha. "In Denver, I had the best year I ever had in pro football. I enjoyed Denver; I was happy there. I should have stayed another year or two, but I had already been an attorney for three years and I was thinking it was time I better begin my legal career in earnest, or get on with my life's work.

"Besides, my wife Bobbi had a collapsed lung, and she felt it was caused by the high altitude in Denver. If I had stayed with the Steelers, though, I'm sure I would have stayed in pro football longer because I could have remained involved with a local law firm while playing ball for the Steelers.

"I was at Reed Smith working as an attorney when Chuck Noll called me and told me I'd been traded to Denver. It was a real shock. I wasn't really prepared for it. I had no inkling he was thinking of getting rid of me. I don't think Noll was that crazy about me or Andy Russell. We'd ask questions just so we knew what was going on. Noll did not like being asked questions. He didn't want to be challenged.

"He was a good coach, I can't take that away from him. I don't know how he'll be ranked when they establish the final list, but he'll be up there."

While Martha respects Noll, he gets that steely look in his narrowed eyes when he talks about him. He has probably never forgiven Noll for not thinking he was good enough to stay with the Steelers, and be a part of the team's resurgence.

"You can't just be a good football coach," added Martha. "You have to have talented ballplayers, and you have to have enough of them to win consistently. The Steelers had a lot of talent when they won those four Super Bowls. There's also always a certain amount of luck involved — in any sport.

"When I reflect back, we weren't that bad a ballclub when I was playing here. We finished up the 1967 season with a win (24-17) at Green Bay when they were really good.

"When we came back to camp the next year, we were scrimmaging one day, and Austin got mad. So he put us in a 10-yard line drill, the first team offense against the first team defense. It was a real bloodbath. Four guys got hurt. Bill Saul was never right after that. I got hurt, Cannonball Butler got hurt, and Ken Kortas got hurt. It was a silly thing. We never came back from that."

Martha mentioned that he had been talking the day before to Dave "Rooster" Fleming, a boyhood friend of mine, and a local legend for his streetfighting and football heroics. Fleming always refers to Martha as "Rat" when he talks about him.

"We still talk to each other about every two weeks," said Martha with more than a hint of pride. "He's got two great kids, and one of them is a star running back at Central Catholic."

His friendship with Fleming tells you a lot about Martha, too. Fleming can often be seen in courtside seats at basketball games at the Civic Arena, courtesy of his buddy.

Back in 1964, Martha's rookie season with the Steelers, he shared a room at training camp with Fleming. Talk about an odd couple. Martha was the Steelers' No. 1 draft choice. Fleming was a free agent. Martha went to Shady Side Academy. Fleming was in the first graduating class of Gladstone High School. Martha was an All-American at Pitt. Fleming didn't go to college. They were from different sides of the tracks.

Martha was fascinated with Fleming, and his non-stop unorthodox workout habits, as well as his incorrigible alley cat behavior. Fleming was getting a tryout based on his ability and reputation as a running back for the Pittsburgh Valley Ironmen of the Atlantic Coast Football League, a minor league circuit. I served as the team's publicity director and arranged with the Steelers to have Fleming, and three other

371

members of their taxi squad, play for the Ironmen.

Fleming was a tough nut, though, a fearless performer. Fleming feels to this day that he was shafted by the Steelers, that he should have made the team. He also failed in a tryout with the New York Jets. He had to be satisfied with a ten year career as a defensive back for the Hamilton Tiger-Cats of the Canadian Football League. Fleming does some football scouting when he's not conducting clinics for younger guys on how to loaf on his favorite street corner in Hazelwood.

I remember Martha coming to a party in Fleming's honor at the Hibernian Club in Hazelwood back in the mid-'60s. One of Fleming's friends stood in front of Martha and deliberately and slowly poured whiskey on Martha's shoes just to see how he would react to the challenge. Martha smiled, shook his head and walked away.

I also remember when Martha got married. I was at his bachelor's party and at his wedding reception. Both were memorable events. His bachelor's party started out at his home in Wilkins Township and shifted to the Democratic Club on the North Side. Baldy Regan was known as the "Mayor of the North Side" in those days, way before he became a city councilman, and he was the unofficial host at the Democratic Club. Regan and a fellow named Jim Scanlon bought chocolate cream pies for the occasion, and were the first ones to start flinging them at the guests. "We bought 197 cream pies," Regan recalled this past year. "We kept going to this bakery on Brighton Road and buying every pie they had. That room got pretty slippery. People were falling down." Martha was grateful that his father-in-law, Mr. Gott, wasn't there, and hoped his future brother-in-law wouldn't go home and report the activity. "They had to bring in the fire department the next day to wash the joint out," said Martha.

"It was difficult for my father-in-law in the first place to accept me," Martha remembers. "I was a Catholic, and he was a real WASP. He wanted to make sure his daughter married the right guy."

Bobbi Gott was a beautiful bride, too. She had been a cheerleader at Penn State.

I was invited to the wedding reception at the Fox Chapel Country Club. Like a dolt, I brought along a buddy of mine, Bob Wishnev, who had not been invited. "You know Paul; it'll be OK," I said. Of course, I had never attended a formal sit-down wedding dinner before and, obviously, I had never been to the Fox Chapel Country Club.

Wishnev had the good sense to disappear soon after we arrived. I should have done the same. I remember there was an eight-piece orchestra in black and gray tails — all very formal.

I also remember being seated at a table with several beautiful young women, some of whom I knew from a distance at Pitt. I was enchanting them with my stories, waving my arms about to accent my tales, when I smacked a tray that a waitress was holding overhead. A parfait dumped unceremoniously into my lap. Thank god, it missed my Madras jacket. After all, it was the only Madras jacket in the joint. Every other gentleman wore a suit.

None of the women at the table ever asked me out on a date, and

I haven't had dinner with the Marthas since that spectacle. What the hell. What did I know?

In my hometown, you believed you were invited to a wedding reception if you recognized the name of the bride or the groom when their wedding announcement appeared in the local church bulletin or local newspaper.

"Hey, I know her, let's go to that wedding reception," one of us would say. And we'd stand at the bar in the reception hall, places like the Hungarian Club or the American Legion or Moose Club, and drink Iron City out of the bottle, and badmouth the bridesmaids and their attendants.

I remember Fleming's wedding reception was held at the Hungarian Hall. There was a shuttle service — I am deadly serious — between the hall and the No. 4 police station in Oakland. The police hauled out one drunk after another, if they became unruly at the party, and took them for a ride for a night in the cell of a castle-like jail just a block away from Pitt's Cathedral of Learning.

I remember sitting on the front steps of the hall, lecturing a boyhood pal named Patty Murtha that he was going to break his mother's heart if he didn't start behaving better. A few years later, when I was away in the U.S. Army in Alaska, Patty was walking home from a nightclub, staggering along on the Glenwood Bridge when he was struck by a bus and killed.

Paul Martha would have liked Patty Murtha.

There was a glass-encased model of planned buildings that would surround the Civic Arena in Martha's office. It's an ambitious project, one launched by the DeBartolos. Does Martha feel any sense of civic pride or civic duty to see it realized? "I feel I have an obligation," he said. "I have a power to do it. If I didn't, I'm letting a lot of people down."

What drives Martha to keep climbing new mountains?

"I don't know if there's one thing that drives people," he responded. "Other people telling them they can't accomplish things, I suppose. I was told I couldn't play major college football, then I was told I couldn't play pro football. I was told I was too small."

When Noll dispatched him to Denver, I asked, did he regard it as a rejection? "I wasn't able to completely celebrate the championships the Steelers won because I was disappointed I still wasn't a part of it," he said. He would feel the same way when the Penguins repeated as Stanley Cup champions in 1992.

"I had been there with Joe Greene and L.C. Greenwood, Andy Russell, Rocky Bleier and Ray Mansfield. They were still there when the great things started to happen, and I wasn't.

"Andy had trouble with Chuck. I had trouble with Chuck. Mansfield had trouble with Chuck. He was intellectually combative. He didn't like it when we challenged him about anything. Maybe he was correct in that; he was the coach."

Martha said he thought Noll's wife, Marianne, was a super lady. "I really like her," he said. He told a story of how he and Bill Walsh wanted to play tennis with Noll at the NFL owners' meeting one year. They knew Noll played the game. But Noll would have none of it.

"I asked Marianne why Chuck wouldn't play," said Martha, "and she said, 'He might lose.' I really liked her after that."

Martha and I had played tennis together, against each other and as partners, several times at the owners meetings. I told him I had asked Noll on several occasions if he and I could play some tennis together. "I'll hit with you," he'd say, "but I don't want to play."

Then Martha offered a few personal thoughts regarding the retirement of Noll, which had been announced only a few weeks earlier.

"The media here accelerated the retirement of Chuck Noll," he said. "The most surprised person was Dan Rooney. They really didn't plan on this. He didn't expect that. Rooney wasn't ready for it.

"Noll knows the team wasn't that good. He knows the team will be mediocre for another two or three years. He was not going to get bashed by the media any more; he'd had enough of it. It wasn't worth it to him or his family.

"He dropped a bomb on the Steelers. Now they need somebody to come in and create a new image. They had a Chuck Noll Era. It's over. They need to find that again. You can't find another Noll any more than you can find another Bob Johnson. But there are good men out there, and you've got to get the right one. It won't be easy."

Martha is flanked by Dick Hoak and Bill Cowher at 1992 social.

John Brown
Banking on another comeback

"He was one of the best, in so many ways.
There's a guy who always knew how to handle money."
—Ed Kiely
Retired Steelers' publicist

John Brown just beamed as our eyes met when the elevator doors opened. Brown was bent over, supporting his large body on aluminum crutches, trying to make his way out of the elevator and into the fourth floor lobby of the Allegheny Club at Three Rivers Stadium.

He hardly looked as tall and robust a figure as he had when we last had lunch there several years earlier. Back then, he appeared in a business suit and looked like the banker he is, indeed, a district manager for Pittsburgh National Bank.

Now he looked like an old football player, wearing a warm-up suit from Syracuse University, his alma mater, and he was obviously paying the price for all the battles he fought on behalf of the Orangemen, the Cleveland Browns and the Pittsburgh Steelers.

"When you're 20, you say 'What the hell.'" he had told me over the telephone a few days earlier. "When you're 52, you say, 'What did I do to myself?'"

His knees had been shot for some time; he had hobbled in pain since his last days with the Steelers. Players who played with John Brown remember that he had bad knees. It could be worse, some say. Look at Jim Otto, the old Oakland Raiders center. He can hardly walk. Brown didn't look much better off on this particular day, but he was hopeful he would be walking on his own in short time.

I had been waiting for Brown's arrival, passing the time by talking to Nellie Briles, the former Pirates pitcher who now works in the team's sales and marketing department. "I don't play in old timers' games," said Briles just before Brown arrived. "Right now, everything feels good on me, including my arm. I don't want to lob in one of those here's-one-you-can-hit pitches and get knocked down with a line drive. It's not worth the risk. I feel too good."

I had told Briles about Brown, and how he had just undergone surgery the week before to get two artificial knee replacements. "Our baseball alumni association has been after Mickey Mantle to do that," said Briles, "but he's deathly afraid of having surgery."

Old jocks don't just fade away; sometimes they come apart at the hinges. Joe Namath would soon get new knees, too.

It took an eternity, or so it seemed anyhow, for Brown to reach us. He was accompanied by his son, Ernie, a junior football player at Syracuse University, and Ernie's girl friend, Lori, a 20-year-old pre-med senior at the University of Akron who planned to attend Ohio Medical

College. They had come along, Ernie driving the family car from their home in the Swan Acres development of Ross Township, to help John get around town.

After Brown introduced them to us, I introduced Briles and Brown to each other. They talked about bad knees and new knees. Nearly 200,000 people a year in this country had total knee replacements last year. The most common cause of damaged joints is arthritis, but injuries and bone disorders also can cause damage. "The arthritic pain is gone," said Brown with an obvious sigh of relief. "Not having that anymore is a blessing in itself. It'll take me awhile to rehabilitate myself, but I'm thinking positive. I'll be back playing racquetball by June."

John Brown is big on comebacks. He has been making them all his life. He says the single most important thing he learned from playing football was the ability to overcome obstacles. For that same reason, Rocky Bleier is the former Steelers' player he admires the most.

Brown performed with honor at offensive tackle for 11 seasons in the National Football League, the first five (1962-66) with the Cleveland Browns, and then six seasons (1967-72) with the Steelers. He was the offensive captain of the Steelers.

Brown has been in there with the best of them. He played in two NFL championship games with the Browns, in 1964 and 1965, and he was there to help Chuck Noll establish the foundation for what became the best team in the NFL for the '70s.

He came out of a broken home in Camden, N.J., where he had knee surgery for the first time at age 14 as the result of a football injury, and starred at Syracuse under Ben Schwartzwalder in the early '60s, where he underwent several more surgeries on both knees. He hurt his knees as a freshman and sophomore flying down the field on kickoffs in scrimmages, and getting cut down by blocks.

I had seen him play against Pitt at the old Archbold Stadium when Ernie Davis was an All-American running back for the Orangemen, and I was the sports editor of the campus newspaper at Pitt. "I still have a photo at home I took of Davis in the dressing room after that game," I told Brown. "I got good pictures that day because it was cloudy overhead, it rained, and it was damp. The colors came out richer."

Brown smiled at my observation. "It was always cold and damp at Archbold Stadium," said Brown. Or so it seemed, anyhow, to a young man with bad knees.

But he persevered. He missed only four games in his first ten seasons in pro ball.

"I had two or three operations at Syracuse," he said. "The pros probably wouldn't have drafted me today. There's too much money involved and they wouldn't want to take the risk. They don't know what you have in your innards."

People who have been around Brown know, however, and they know he has always been something special, both on and off the field, as the father of a fine family, as an executive with PNB — he is responsible for eight banks plus a drive-in facility — as a ballplayer and team leader.

There was a search on for leaders at Three Rivers Stadium this Monday afternoon in early January as we talked over lunch. We had an overhead view from the top of the terrace at the Allegheny Club of the green playing field and the red seats of Three Rivers Stadium. There were patches missing in the artificial turf, where areas around the pitcher's mound and the bases had been removed. It looked like a puzzle with some pieces missing. "There are pieces missing out there," observed Brown, philosophically, "and, yes, there are pieces missing in the clubhouse."

Brown was talking about the Steelers, but he could have been referring to the Pirates as well.

The Steelers were searching for a new coach to replace Chuck Noll who had announced his retirement 12 days earlier. Unknown to both of us at the time, the Pirates had just dismissed Larry Doughty as general manager that morning. The Pirates had won the National League East title the previous two seasons with Doughty at the helm, but he was fired by new team president Mark Sauer who was not satisfied with his efforts.

The Pirates had called a press conference to announce Doughty's dismissal. "The Pirates' assessment was my errors far outweigh my successes here," Doughty said.

Two tables away from where Brown and I sat were Dan Rooney, the Steelers' president, and Dan Edwards, the team's publicity director. They were discussing a briefing Rooney would offer the press in a half hour about how the search for Noll's successor was coming along. They would also announce that Tom Donahoe, who was coordinating the search for a new coach, had been promoted to director of football operations. Only a few years earlier, Donahoe was disappointed when he failed in his bid to become the head football coach at suburban Mt. Lebanon High School. Now he was calling the shots for the Steelers. He had advanced himself in a hurry.

Rooney came over and said hello, and asked Brown about his knees before parting. "Are you ready to start running?" Rooney asked Brown.

"If you sign me," said Brown.

"I remember when they were looking for a coach to replace Bill Austin back in 1969," said Brown when Rooney retreated. "It won't be easy. There's a lot of pressure on Dan to come up with the right guy. Noll has spoiled us; he had so much success."

But, like Doughty perhaps, not lately.

Before I met with Brown, I had visited the Steelers' offices to do some research. Ed Bouchette, the beat writer for the *Pittsburgh Post-Gazette,* was in the media room and was talking over the telephone with one of the candidates for the head coach's job, Dallas Cowboys' defensive coordinator Dave Wannstedt, who grew up in the Pittsburgh suburb of Baldwin and had played and coached at Pitt.

Wannstedt was a favorite with most of the Steelers' officials — everyone but Dan Rooney, that is — but would later lose out in the job selection to another local candidate, Bill Cowher of Crafton, the defensive coordinator of the Kansas City Chiefs. Rooney favored Cowher.

377

"Lump" Jones, whose face still bears the flush of fighting fires for 20 years before he retired, stopped in the Steelers' office complex that morning to put in a pitch for his pal, Woody Widenhofer, an assistant with the resurgent Detroit Lions and one of Noll's former aides when Widenhofer and Jones first became buddies. "It'll be a crime if my man Woody doesn't get interviewed for this job," said Jones. "They gotta be kidding about some of the guys they're bringing in here."

Ed Kiely came by, and offered us two items of interest. Kiely was the Steelers' publicist when Brown first joined the Steelers and prior to the hiring of Joe Gordon. Kiely remained on as a p.r. executive and constant companion of owner Art Rooney. He became an ambassador for the Steelers.

I told Kiely I had been talking to "Frenchy" Fuqua, one of his favorites. "I got a call from Sears once about Frenchy owing them some money," recalled Kiely. "I didn't want to get in the middle of it. 'Hey, I'm not interested in being a collector for Sears,' I said to the guy who called, 'but I'll speak to Frenchy about it.' And I did. Frenchy told me, 'As far as bills are concerned, after two weeks I've reached my statute of limitations.'" Kiely chortled at his own story.

Then I mentioned I was having lunch at noon with John Brown. "He was one of the best, in so many ways," said Kiely. "He was always a class act. There's a guy who always knew how to handle money. I asked him a couple of times to come in and talk to the players about their finances, and to make a pitch to them about preparing for their careers after football. He'd do it, and he had so much to offer, but it was so disappointing because maybe one or two guys pursued it beyond that day, and got back to him."

Brown is a booster of Kiely as well, so it is a mutual admiration duo. "Ed Kiely was responsible for me getting to PNB," said Brown. "He wouldn't tell you about that, but he made the necessary calls. PNB had someone from the Steelers before me who didn't take it too seriously, but Ed went to bat for me.

"They help you; that's one thing you could always say about this organization. You have to lend something positive to the equation. You can't be out beating up on people, or getting arrested. But it's a good organization; that's why people don't want to leave it.

"In time, the guys who were disenchanted, or have expressed dissatisfaction, and you know who I mean, will come to realize what it meant to them to play for the Steelers.

"Take Bradshaw. He was raw when he came here. He needed a father figure, a coach, and a warden all at once. When he sits down someday and counts up the pros and cons, the prodigal son will return.

"Franco will, too. L.C., too. They have some bitterness — maybe that's not the right word — or resentment about what happened to them toward the end of their days with the Steelers. We're talking about three guys who were so super. Then the plug was pulled on them before they were ready to pull it. They resented it.

Ernie Brown and his proud papa.

ie Davis

John Brown

Jim Brown

"Coming from Cleveland, I saw it the other way. I remember how Jim Brown got mad at management and he quit after nine years, at the peak of his career, because they gave him some heat about going to England to make a movie. He left and it created an opportunity for Leroy Kelly. And the Browns went on. But Jim Brown had pulled the plug on them before they thought they were ready.

"I started working part-time at PNB in 1970. I worked during the off-season and was paid. But I continued to work for them during the season on Mondays and Tuesdays. I didn't get paid during the season but I didn't want to forget what I learned. And it was a wise investment on my part. They knew I was serious about working at the bank.

"The players aren't too smart when it comes to money. The sad part about it is that all the players have agents. Unless you're one of the No. 1 draft picks, you don't need an agent. They know what they're going to pay you across the board. All a ballplayer needs is a good attorney and an accountant. He can go to a bank trust company, and they can manage his money for him. I might be prejudiced, but I truly believe that.

"The top guys need agents because they have other things going for them. But the rest should be paying a fee for proper counsel, but not ten or fifteen percent of their salaries. It's like having another income tax.

"I can't imagine what it must be like for a guy like Bobby Bonilla to get paid over $29 million over five years, but I know his lifestyle won't be any better than it could have been if he remained here in Pittsburgh for what the Pirates were willing to pay him.

"Money doesn't go as far in New York, or Chicago, or LA, or a lot of other cities as it does in Pittsburgh. Plus, he was with a winning team and playing for a manager he liked. He'll miss that.

"Football players don't make what baseball players do, but they make a lot more today than we did. Today, some of these guys get a million dollar bonus and then $600,000 a year. If they took that million, and paid their taxes and put the rest into a sound conservative and solid investment they wouldn't need to touch that first million. You don't need to invest in get-rich quick schemes. You take a guy like Rod Woodson, who's making more than a million a year. He should never have to work the rest of his life if he looks after his money carefully.

"But I remember guys getting into cattle and grain, risky stuff they knew nothing about, and oil and gas exploration, and six-to-one return stuff, or so they were promised, and it blew up in their faces. They were left holding the bag.

"Some guys don't make as much as others, but their egos get in the way, and they have to have a Mercedes if the guy next to them has one. Their egos won't allow them to have less. When I left the Steelers, people asked me if I still hung around with the guys. I couldn't because I couldn't afford to hang around with them. You have to completely divorce yourself from that lifestyle. Besides, you're living in a 9 to 5 world, and they're not. You're on a different agenda."

John Brown wanted to talk about his impressions of some people who were special to him when he was with the Steelers.

"Joe Greene and I were roommates," he said with pride. He said that Bill Nunn, one of the team's scouts and the director of its summer training camp operation, suggested they room together.

"Before that, every roommate I had was released," recalled Brown. "But when I saw Joe, I knew he'd be here after I was gone.

"You know, I saw some of the real greats, and went up against some of the best in the business, guys like 'Big Daddy' Lipscomb, Alex Karras, Rosey Grier, Doug Atkins, Merlin Olsen, Big Buck Buchanan, Jim Katcavage, Willie Davis, Deacon Jones and Carl Eller. I had never seen anyone with the natural ability Joe had.

"A lot of guys you have to teach them and train them, but you saw him and wow. You'd ask yourself, 'Where'd he get all the ability?' I just never saw anyone like Joe Greene."

Then Brown pulled a name out of his cap of an oft-overlooked hero of the '70s.

"Of all the offensive linemen we ever had," he said, "one guy I really had a lot of respect for was Moon Mullins. He had great feet. If he had been bigger he'd have been All-Pro. He was just a little guy who was so tenacious."

He lists his two greatest thrills during his stay with the Steelers as Franco's "Immaculate Reception" and "meeting Mr. Rooney."

Brown is a booster of the Steelers' organization. "They taught me how to play the game," he said, "and I mean the game of life.

"I came here from Cleveland. I left Cleveland under questionable circumstances. I had arguments there about salary. When I got here, Dan (Rooney) came to my room, and said, 'Here's what we'll pay you. Here's what we expect of you. You're starting clean with us.' I'm sort of a second-hand Steeler because I didn't start out here. But his dad, Mr. Rooney, developed a relationship with me. It was always, 'How's your family?' We went to church at St. Peter's Catholic Church on the North Side, so that made it easy to see him. He'd say, 'John, I saw your son at mass. Have him come over to see me when he's there.' I'd say, 'He doesn't want to do that.' Things like that. When they had the 50 Seasons Celebration, Art and Dan Rooney asked me to participate. Heck, I had never been a big star. When they had the statue fund to build the memorial to Mr. Rooney, they again asked me to participate. That means a great deal to me. I'm on the board here at the Allegheny Club, and I know Ed Kiely had something to do with arranging that.

"They respected me; I respected them. I tell guys if you're going to play for a team then you should live in that city. You should get involved and keep yourself clean. You can't cause them any embarrassment."

Brown nodded in the direction of the stadium field, and said, "People think the only thing you learn out there is football. But you learn how to live."

One of Brown's all-time favorites was Ernie Davis. They had been teammates on a national championship team as sophomores at Syracuse in 1959. They came from Syracuse to Cleveland for the 1962 campaign.

Davis had won the Heisman Trophy his senior season and was thrilled when he was drafted by the Browns. Now he would have an opportunity to join his idol, Jim Brown, in the Cleveland backfield.

"Ernie and I were roommates in Cleveland and we became great friends," said Brown. "If Ernie Davis had lived he would have been greater than Jim Brown because he was a greater person than Jim Brown. Jim Brown was a great player, don't get me wrong, but Jim was always such a hardass.

"Athletes have super egos, but Ernie was just like another person. Even with his superstar status, he was easy to be with, and to talk to. He cared about you. When I was at Syracuse, he made me become a better student. I followed his lead. I had a brother, but I had a fragmented family because of certain circumstances, and he was truly like a brother to me.

"It was about the time of the All-Star Game in Chicago that we learned that Ernie had leukemia. When he was ill during my first year in Cleveland, Art Modell wanted him to play, but Paul Brown did not want him to play. I was having difficulty adjusting to playing offensive line in the pros. It was so different from what I'd done in college. It was a big adjustment. I was feeling sorry for myself. But I took heart from Ernie. His exact words were, 'I may not make it, but I don't have to give up trying.'

"He'd shave and he'd end up bleeding profusely. He had to have transfusions all the time. He had sores around his mouth. He'd sneak away for treatments. He didn't want anyone feeling sorry for him.

"I was with him once when a guy came up to him and said, 'Hey, aren't you Ernie Davis?' And Ernie just shrugged his shoulders and wagged his head to suggest he wasn't. 'You're lucky,' the guy said, 'because Ernie Davis is dying of cancer.' Ernie just looked at him. He'd stutter when he'd get excited and he said, haltingly, 'I am Ernie Davis . . . and I'm not . . . going to die.' "

After a 16-month battle, Davis died on May 18, 1963.

I remember being told about Davis' life-threatening illness by an NFL publicist in the presence of Chester L. Smith, then the sports editor of *The Pittsburgh Press*. We were asked not to write anything about it. In those days, that was good enough. It was in respect to Ernie's personal wishes.

"My son is named after Ernie," said Brown. "Ernie Davis's mother is my son's godmother. I told my son, 'You brought joy to her life and her husband's life, and you might have extended someone's life.' Her name is Mrs. Marie Fleming — she's in her '70s — and she and her husband still live in Elmira, N.Y. They go to most of the Syracuse football games. They bring Ernie boxes of food, real Care packages for him, when they come to the games.

"Ernie is a junior defensive tackle, and he gets to play a lot. We go to all the games. I have four weeks vacation coming to me now at

PNB. I take one week for a vacation and I take the rest one day at a time. I'm gone on Fridays. I tell them at the office, 'Don't look for me on Fridays in the fall.'

"My wife, Gloria, and I really enjoy seeing Ernie playing. My older son, John, who's 24, never played football. He's at the Monterey (Calif.) School of International Studies. He didn't want to play. He didn't want the burden of being my son as a football player, the comparisons and stuff. He went to Central Catholic and was a drum major. He didn't want football. He said, 'Dad, I don't want to do that.'

"Even Ernie didn't play football until his senior year at North Catholic. His peers got after him to play football. Ernie had been playing basketball up until then. Originally, he was going to either Arizona State or West Virginia. I told him, 'We can't afford to follow you to see you play at Arizona State. I can't pay $800 to fly there. But we can get down to West Virginia to see you play.' I told him, 'I'm not going to try and tell you where to go to school. But you'd make me proud if you would attend Syracuse.'

"I think his godfather talked him into going to Syracuse. Do you know Gus Kalaris, the guy who sells ice balls at the stand in West Park?"

I did not. But I later spoke with Gus. His stand, often frequented by the Steelers and their families as well as workers at the nearby Allegheny General Hospital, is called Gus and Yiayia's. The "Yiayia's" part of the name is Greek for Grandma. That was Gus's mother. His parents first opened the stand back in 1934.

"When I first came here," Brown continued, "we lived at Allegheny Center, and my oldest son worked for him. He liked my kids, they were always around his stand. He's the godfather for John."

I asked him how that came about.

"My son John went to St. Peter's on his own. I'm a Baptist and my wife's a Methodist. Then our youngest son went to St. Peter's, too. And they got baptized there."

Gus Kalaris calls John "Jay." And adds, "I was close with Ernie, too. John called me up at 1 a.m. one time to tell me he needed my help to get Ernie to go to Syracuse. I thought he would be a natural there, with his name, like he had to go there, rather than Arizona State. I thought he'd be an instant success. Both boys helped us out when they were teenagers. We liked them from the start.

"We like our stand, and the people we meet there. Franco stops by once in a while. Frenchy Fuqua used to stop. Dwight White was a regular, with his little girl Stacey, for our snowcones. Vic Damone came here. Art Rooney and his grandchildren. All his kids bought off us."

Brown is eager to stand on his own, and then to run and jump on his own. "I want to play racquetball again," he said with a smile. "I was good. I won't be able to play at that level again, but I want to play for fun.

"My knees were like those of a 75-year-old man. They looked like cauliflower on the x-rays. I had my first knee operation at 14. I forged my mom's signature on the permission form. (Hall of Famer Ernie Stautner did the same). My mom didn't want me to play.

"At Syracuse, in my first game as a freshman, we were playing Cornell, and I got hurt. I was flying down on the opening kickoff when I was cut down. They just put it in a cast, and immobilized it.

"I was out for spring ball that same school year. Then we were playing Army in an exhibition at the beginning of my sophomore season and the same thing happened. That was the end of my defensive career. I was red-shirted that year. I was never really sound after that."

I asked Brown about the strain being a pro athlete puts on marriages, especially during the post-playing period. So many of the Steelers are divorced. "I think it's tougher on the wives," said Brown. "Their whole identity is tied to their husband being a pro ballplayer, unless she has a career of her own.

"All the perks and recognition she has received are gone now. That can be pretty traumatic, unless she has her own career.

"My wife, Gloria, is a school teacher. She has been teaching for 17 years, first as a substitute, in the first grade at Northview Heights Elementary School on the North Side. It's a tough area; the kids mostly come from projects. We have been married for 27 years. Her maiden name is Gloria Brown. I think we got married a month after we met. She went to Central State in Wilberforce, Ohio and we were introduced by friends. Her father is a minister and he married us. I don't know how he got through it."

Brown likes the banking business. He went back to school after he began his career at PNB, and has a degree from the Stonier Graduate School of Banking at Rutgers. He had to work hard at it. "Writing papers was hard to do, until I found a good editor out at Pitt, near my office. We all miss being ballplayers," he said, staring out at the ballfield one final time. "I don't care who you are. It's tough out there in the real world. We were playing pro football; we were their dream. You start out playing football when you're a kid and you make it all the way to the granddaddy of them all. You don't want to give it up — nobody does — but you have to be pragmatic about it. When I quit playing pro football, you know how I felt? I was scared."

John Brown is an indefatigable booster of Chuck Noll. I asked Brown to compare Noll with Paul Brown, since both had played for Paul Brown in Cleveland. "I played for Paul Brown and for Blanton Collier in Cleveland, and then Chuck Noll here in Pittsburgh," said Brown. "The one in between was not in the same class as the other two.

"Paul Brown expected his players to take football seriously. On the first day at camp, you took an eight-hour test, just like a college board exam. If you couldn't pass it, Brown felt you couldn't understand his offense and defense. That seemed to be what Chuck Noll was all about. You had to know the game to be effective for him.

"Brown thought that even if you weren't the most physically gifted or athletically talented individual that you had a certain edge if you understood and knew what you were doing. He also gave tests on individual plays and you had to know what the people beside you were supposed to do. If you understood the concept of the play — I'm speaking strictly from an offensive standpoint — then you had a chance to execute it properly.

"Chuck Noll did not remind me of Paul Brown in his mannerisms or what he said as much as in his overall approach to the game. Chuck was truly a dedicated coach, in the same sense that Paul Brown was. Paul was a teacher and so was Chuck a teacher, and despite what some people say who played for them, I liked them both. They both made you better.

"Chuck and Paul demanded respect. If you played for them, you had to give them respect. That was their way of controlling the team. They felt if they couldn't control the team they couldn't win consistently.

"I remember once that Jim Brown had gained 1800 yards the year before (1,863 in 1963) and we were watching film of a pre-season game and Jim Brown missed a block in a sequence we were watching. And Paul said, 'If you can't block, you can't play for me.' That struck me. No one was getting off the hook with him. Now if Blanton Collier tried to reprimand Jim, well, Jim would just turn his back on him. Nobody turned their backs on Brown or Noll.

"Paul didn't yell at people. Chuck didn't yell at people. I don't recall them ever yelling at their players.

"This last group of Steelers . . . I don't think they really understood what they had. It's a different mentality. They didn't understand what type of man they had. The guys are different today, the agents are different.

"Somebody was in my office the other day, and they saw me having difficulty getting around with my new knees. And they said, 'John, hey, would you do this again?' And I have to say, 'Yes, I would.' It was a way of life. It was a sense of achievement. There were only 36 guys or 42, I'm not sure which, on a team when I came into the league. I was doing something no one else could do.

"Today, it's getting the most money I can. Today, it's not doing the best job I can. Maybe I'm speaking from an oldtimer's point of view, but I don't think this team will appreciate what they had until they're my age, and sitting back and reflecting on their experience with the Steelers.

"Hey, we had a helluva guy there. I'm not taking anything away from the new coach — I never played for him, so I have no way to judge him — but Chuck Noll is not going to be replaced easily in Pittsburgh. He did so much for this city."

Quarterbacks
The Steelers had them all

"We're the experts on quarterbacks."
—Art Rooney

"They make the biggest salaries in their business, and deserve them. Every play starts with them. Nothing happens till they take the ball from center."
—Jimmy Cannon

'The test of a quarterback is where his team finishes."
—Paul Brown

Terry Bradshaw was the best quarterback in the National Football League when he was leading the Steelers to those four Super Bowl triumphs.

He was the team's No. 1 draft choice in 1970, the first player taken in the college draft, and his success didn't surprise Steelers owner Art Rooney.

I treasure a post card that Mr. Rooney sent to me when I was working in Miami early in 1970. He wrote: "We're not sure what we're going to do with our No. 1 choice. I hope we do the right thing."

That's when they turned down some trades and took Bradshaw. The Bears then took Bobby Douglass, another quarterback.

"If anybody knows anything about quarterbacks," said Rooney, poking fun at his own franchise, in a story I wrote for *Pro Football Digest.* "it should be us. We're the experts on quarterbacks. We've had the best come through here."

Trouble is, few of them stayed long. That helps explain why the Steelers went 42 years before they won their first playoff game and 44 years before they won their first championship.

The Steelers once possessed Johnny Unitas, Jim Finks, Bobby Layne, Lenny Dawson, Jack Kemp, Earl Morrall, Bill Nelsen, and the rights to Sid Luckman, before Bradshaw showed up. And when they had Bradshaw, they had two pretty good quarterbacks beside him in Terry Hanratty and Joe Gilliam.

Only Layne and Finks played for the Steelers for any significant stretch before Bradshaw, and the Steelers gave up on both too soon.

Buddy Parker pushed Layne into retirement and the next year they needed him to put them in the playoffs. They had a good enough team to get there in 1963, but quarterback Ed Brown blew it in the big game against the Giants in New York in the season finale.

Finks left after seven seasons to become an assistant coach at Notre Dame. The booing fans at Forbes Field got under his skin.

Ted Marchibroda   Earl Morrall

obby Layne with Tom Tracy   Jim Finks

Layne, Luckman, Unitas and Dawson are all in the Pro Football Hall of Fame.

Kemp became a U.S. Congressman and later a member of the President's Cabinet, and has a bright future in politics.

The AFL quarterback stars were all NFL castoffs back in the '60s, namely George Blanda — who is from Youngwood, Pennsylvania and is also in the Hall of Fame — Dawson, Tobin Rote and Babe Parilli before Joe Namath made a name for himself and the league.

The Steelers were all set to draft Luckman in 1939, but Chicago Bears owner George Halas talked Rooney out of it, swapping him several players for the Steelers' No. 1 draft choice. Luckman became a Bear and quarterbacked the team until 1950. He tied Sammy Baugh for NFL passing honors in 1945 and was voted into the Hall of Fame in 1965.

Everybody is familiar with the fairy tale story of Unitas, a scrawny Lithuanian kid who came out of St. Justin's High in Pittsburgh, and was rejected by Pitt and Notre Dame — he led Louisville to its share of victories — and then was turned away by the Steelers.

The Steelers made Unitas their No. 9 draft pick in 1955. On the 11th round, they drafted another quarterback, Vic Eaton of Missouri. They already had Finks and Ted Marchibroda.

Unitas used to play catch on the sidelines at training camp with Art Rooney's sons, including the current president, Dan. The kids told their dad he was a terrific thrower, but Walt Kiesling cut him just the same. The Steelers kept Eaton as their No. 3 quarterback because he could do other things.

Unitas turned to playing quarterback, second-string quarterback at times, for the Bloomfield Rams on the Pittsburgh sandlot circuit for $7 a game.

Then Weeb Ewbank telephoned him when the Baltimore Colts came up short on quarterbacks, and Unitas led the Colts to NFL championships in 1958 and 1959. He was enshrined in the Hall of Fame in 1979.

"All I was trying to do was score touchdowns and win football games," Unitas said during a TV interview before the Super Bowl in 1992.

"When I was in eighth grade, I knew I wanted to play professional football. But I don't know why."

Bill McPeak, a former Steeler, once said when he was the head coach of the Washington Redskins: "John Unitas is more willing to sacrifice himself for the sake of the contest than any quarterback I know. None combine his savvy, his reflexes and his great spirit as a competitor."

Asked if he missed the cheering, Unitas said, "I don't miss the cheers. I miss the camaraderie of the players. I played with some greats."

Asked if he had his pick of quarterbacks for a starter in the Super Bowl today, Unitas said, "I'd like to have a Dan Marino or a Joe Montana."

The Steelers made Dawson their No. 1 draft choice in 1957. He had played at Purdue and before that at Alliance, Ohio.

Bill Nelsen

John Unitas

Ed Brown and George Blanda

Dan Marino

"That was in the years when all the teams were in the same room during the draft," recalled Ed Kiely, the public relations man of the Steelers back then. "When we took Dawson, Paul Brown of Cleveland stood up and slammed his fist on the table. He wanted Dawson in the worst way. Then he took Jim Brown. That's the way the draft works."

That same season the Steelers picked up on waivers a 20-year-old quarterback named Jack Kemp, who came out of Occidental College in California. He stayed one season with the Steelers.

Three years later, he was signed by the first-year AFL's Los Angeles Chargers. Kemp was the all-AFL quarterback that season and led the Chargers to the championship contest where they came up against Blanda and the Houston Oilers.

Kemp later quarterbacked the Buffalo Bills to the AFL title, defeating his old team, the Chargers, who had relocated in San Diego, in the championship game.

In addition to Dawson and Kemp, the Steelers also had Morrall in 1957, trading a fine linebacker, Marv Matuszak, to the San Francisco 49ers to get him.

One-time Steelers end Elbie Nickel recalled that period in Pittsburgh pro football history.

"We had lots of good, young quarterbacks back then," noted Nickel. "But they didn't have all those summer mini-camps like they have now, and they didn't scout them that well. You only had a week to make the team, really.

"They kept Eaton over Unitas because the third quarterback had to be able to play defense. We could keep only 33 men then. Unitas didn't get picked up right away. He got a break with Baltimore. He just didn't get a chance to prove himself in Pittsburgh. They were trying to win exhibition games then, to stir up some interest, to sell some tickets.

"Kemp was just a kid at the time. Dawson was another one who never got a chance to play. He could throw the ball well, but he had no experience. Dawson would make a mistake and he'd be back on the bench. He didn't prove himself until later on.

"Hey, they almost ran Bradshaw out of town before he could prove himself. He wasn't too popular when he was competing with Terry Hanratty, a hometown boy."

The Steelers kept Dawson for three seasons, then sent him to the Cleveland Browns. But Dawson didn't shine there, either.

Hank Stram related a story about how he obtained Dawson when he was coaching the Dallas Texans.

"I was in Pittsburgh at a clinic," recalled Stram, now an NFL analyst for the CBS Radio Network, "and I met with Lenny and 'Pittsburgh' Joe Litman, a good friend of mine. I told Lenny I'd love to have him on my team, but he said he was still under contract to Cleveland, and he couldn't get out of it.

"Then one day Paul Brown called me and tipped me off that he was going to put Lenny on waivers. He thought Lenny might clear them, too.

"He did, and he came to Texas. Everybody thought he was through because he had a sore arm," Stram said. "And if I hadn't known him from when I was an assistant to Jack Mollenkopf at Purdue, I probably would have cut him. Lenny was a quiet leader, but you had to recognize that. You had to be patient with him. We kept him, of course, and the rest is history."

Dawson became the all-AFL quarterback in 1962 and 1966. He directed Dallas to the AFL championship in 1962, when the Texans defeated the Houston Oilers, 20-17, in the league's first overtime title game.

In 1966, after they had moved to Kansas City and became the Chiefs, Dawson led them to another AFL title and then to the first Super Bowl — it wasn't known as such then — where they lost to the Green Bay Packers. Dawson led the Chiefs to a victory over the Minnesota Vikings in the Super Bowl at the end of the 1969 campaign.

The Steelers landed Southern California's Bill Nelsen on the 10th round in the 1963 draft. He had bad knees and the Steelers had bad teams, for the most part, during his stay. They sent him to Cleveland in 1968, where he enjoyed great success.

The Browns got into the NFL championship game that season, losing to a Colts team that was quarterbacked by — get this — Earl Morrall. It was the final happy hour for Morrall who had done such a great job backing up the injured Unitas. The Colts lost in the Super Bowl to the Jets, who were led by another fair quarterback, Joe Namath of Beaver Falls. Namath was named to the Pro Football Hall of Fame in 1985.

Nelsen quarterbacked the Browns to the NFL title game again the next season, where they lost to the Minnesota Vikings, 27-7.

"Nelsen was as good a quarterback as we ever had," Art Rooney said. "We should've kept him."

Terry Bradshaw and Terry Hanratty in early '70s.

Joe Namath
The pride of Beaver Falls

"Joe Namath realizes he is a football player, and that's why he is in the wheelchair. He will try to play football again when he gets out of it. There isn't any other way for him. It all comes down to a man being great at something."
—Jimmy Cannon
New York sports columnist

"Joe Namath's not only the best athlete I've ever coached, but the best athlete I've ever seen."
—Bear Bryant
head football coach
University of Alabama

What do Joe Namath and Paul Martha have in common? The obvious answer would be that they both played high school football and basketball and baseball in western Pennsylvania, Namath at Beaver Falls and Martha at Shady Side Academy.

Another would be that they were both No. 1 draft choices when they came out of college.

The more obscure answer, however, is that both roomed as rookies with Dave "Rooster" Fleming, a boyhood friend of mine and teammate on our hometown Hazelwood Steelers sandlot team.

Martha shared a dorm room at camp in 1964 with Fleming with the Pittsburgh Steelers of the National Football League, and Namath the next season with the New York Jets of the American Football League.

Fleming failed both tryouts, but became fast friends with the more famous All-Americans, Martha and Namath. Fleming had not gone to college, but could play football and was as tough as dirt. He ended up playing ten years as a defensive back with the Hamilton Tiger-Cats of the Canadian Football League, and later coached sandlot football teams in Pittsburgh, and did some scouting for the CFL.

Namath was a soul brother of Fleming. They had common roots and instincts for misbehavior. While Namath was the best paid pro rookie in history when he came out of the University of Alabama where he played for Bear Bryant to join the Jets where he played for Weeb Ewbank, Fleming was a free agent. Everyone in this paragraph is in a college or pro football Hall of Fame except for Fleming.

As rookies, Namath and Fleming both went to the World's Fair at Flushing Meadows, just outside Shea Stadium, and rather than pay for tickets they simply took a running start and hurdled the turnstiles together. It was more fun. They were no angels.

George Gojkovich

I didn't get to New York to work until 1970, but being a boyhood friend of Fleming served me in good stead with Namath. He trusted me, and thought I had to be OK if I was a friend of Fleming. Back home, a lot of people thought the exact opposite.

But I used this edge to my advantage. Paul Zimmerman, the highly-respected Dr. Z who has been the pro football guru for *Sports Illustrated* the past decade, was on the Jets' beat for *The New York Post* back then. But Namath did not like him. He was upset with something he had written about him, and he would not talk to him.

So Joe Namath became my beat one day a week. On Zimmerman's day off, I would go out to Shea Stadium to interview Namath. We had to have a story on Namath at least once a week; he was that big in the Big Apple. Otherwise, I covered Monday Night Football.

Because I was from western Pennsylvania, and knew who Larry Bruno was — he was Joe's high school football coach — and could tell "Rooster" Fleming stories from a first-hand basis, I couldn't be all bad in Namath's green eyes. Being a sportswriter for *The New York Post* was the only knock against me.

Namath was the most colorful quarterback I had ever covered. Then again, the only other quarterbacks I had covered with any consistency until then were Ed Brown and Bill Nelsen of the Steelers and Bob Griese of the Miami Dolphins. Griese had always been a begrudging interview. He felt about me back then about the way Namath felt about Zimmerman. Namath prepared me for Terry Bradshaw with the Steelers. Neither was ever dull.

I rooted for Namath, and no one was happier than when he was selected to the Pro Football Hall of Fame in 1985. He had starred for the Jets from 1965 through 1976, and finished up — some people forget this; Joe would like to — in 1976 with the Los Angeles Rams.

The Pro Football Hall of Fame could have a separate wing for quarterbacks out of western Pennsylvania. Namath was a controversial selection with some conservative types among the sports media because of his much-publicized free-swinging life style, too free-swinging for some tastes, and a run-in he once had with NFL Commissioner Pete Rozelle when he was forced to sell a bar called Bachelors III in Manhattan because of the type of customers it attracted.

But Namath was most deserving.

It was the winter of 1969 that the citizens of Beaver Falls showed Namath their true colors. He had managed to put the sooty mill town on the national map, so they put up green and white banners on every block of the main street, and had a parade in Joe's honor on Seventh Avenue.

They put up a sign at the corner of Seventh and Eighth Street near the Club Naturale. The sign proclaimed:

Beaver Falls, Pa., The Home Of
Joe Willie Namath
Super Quarterback

394

Namath went to New York and signed for $427,000, and learned all about satin sheets and llama rugs, Johnny Walker Scotch, and how to get a date with Racquel Welch for the Oscar cememonies. But he never got Beaver Falls out of his blood. He came back home often to see his mother and his father, who were separated, and he never forgot where he came from.

It is an endearing quality in every man.

People in Beaver Falls wouldn't let him forget when he was the strongest and most accurate rock thrower in gang fights in his youth, but he loved them and suffered their stories of his wiseacre days as much as possible.

He was proud of coming from Pennsylvania and it showed.

He picked up some strange accent while at Alabama, but, at heart, he remained true to his high school.

Joe Namath single-handedly saved the American Football League when it was floundering, and he made the merger imminent with the National Football League.

He brought the upstart league publicity and credibility from the moment he came out of Alabama to sign as the Jets' No. 1 draft choice in 1965.

The merger of the warring pro leagues came about the next season. At the end of the 1968 season Namath — after publicly guaranteeing a victory ("The Jets will win Sunday. I guarantee it!" he said) — led the Jets to a 16-7 victory over the Baltimore Colts in Super Bowl III in January of 1969 at the Orange Bowl. He was named the game's MVP.

Weeb Ewbank became the first coach to win the title in both leagues, having accomplished an earlier championship as coach of the Colts.

"I was privileged to coach Johnny Unitas in Baltimore and Joe Namath in New York," said Ewbank, a Hall of Famer himself. "Now they're in the Hall of Fame, and they're equally deserving."

Unitas, the pride of Pittsburgh, grew up on Mt. Washington. He was enshrined in 1980. George Blanda of Youngwood and a star quarterback and kicker in the AFL and NFL, was honored in 1981.

Namath ranked right up there with the best of pro passers. He completed 1,886 of 3,762 passes for 27,663 yards and 173 touchdowns. He did that in 13 seasons.

The real mark of a quarterback is how he performs when it comes down to the last few minutes, with his team behind and the fans booing and the wind blowing, etc. Namath was known as a "crises quarterback." He could get the job done under the toughest of circumstances.

So could Y.A. Tittle, Bobby Layne, Unitas, Otto Graham, Sammy Baugh, Terry Bradshaw and Norm Van Brocklin, just to name a few. In the Jets' Super Bowl year, Namath brought them from behind in the dying minutes of four games, including the AFL championship with the Oakland Raiders. He loved it.

It's been said that Namath did not see opposing players on the field. He saw x's and o's playing a rotating strong side zone defense that day in Miami.

He was a student, of football that is. He knew the plays and he could read defenses better than anybody. Ewbank gave him a complicated system and left him in charge. It was his show, almost all the way. Ewbank had Unitas 11 years before, and he knew a good quarterback when he saw one.

Paul Zimmerman, writing in *The New York Post*, observed: "People who knew him through the quotes about his hair and his mink coat, his great passing arm and quick release, saw a scientist at work that day. It was a textbook job, a clinical study on how to beat the strong-side rotating zone defense."

Buffalo sportswriter Bob Curran authored a book about the founding of the AFL and its early days, and the title tells you all you need to know about Namath's impact on pro football. It was called *The $400,000 Quarterback* with the subtitle of "The League That Came In From The Cold."

Namath reportedly signed a three-year contract worth $427,000. The Jets also signed another quarterback, John Huarte, a Heisman Trophy winner at Notre Dame, to a three-year contract for $200,000 that same year. That was big money.

Namath was an immediate national hit. The AFL was big league overnight. "With that kind of salary," said Bob Hope in a TV monologue, "Joe Namath will be playing quarterback in a business suit."

Jets' attendance averaged 54,877 in Namath's first season, up from 42,710 the year before, the first year that Sonny Werblin owned the club, and up from 14,792 the year before that, and 5,165 the year before that. Werblin also made a big difference.

Here's how Curran captured Namath's magnetism or charisma, whatever you want to call it.

"The press was impressed with Joe's smoothness and his looks. Standing 6-2 and weighing close to 200 pounds, Namath could be a great hit as a crooner, if healthy-looking crooners ever got back into style. To women, he looks like a Frank Sinatra with muscles, and for New York there could be no better way to look."

Namath was named the AFL's Rookie of the Year after the 1965 season. He completed 164 of 340 passes for 2,220 yards with 18 touchdowns and only 15 interceptions.

Years later, in one of his biggest days in pro football, Namath passed for 496 yards and six touchdowns as the Jets defeated Baltimore, 44-34. Namath and Unitas set an NFL combined record for passing yardage (872) that day.

Namath made his mark and so did the AFL. His place is solidified in pro football history. And in the heart of everybody back home in Beaver Falls.

"He could go down as the best passer who ever played," said Sammy Baugh. "He's the fastest on his feet I have ever seen."

Paul Brown, the former Cleveland Browns coaching great, said, "He can really wing that ball in there. He has strength and accuracy and you'd better get to him or he will run you out of the park. He already is in a class by himself."

Joe Namath

George Gojkovich

Joe Montana
"Maybe it's the Iron City beer."

"I suppose that to appreciate the quarterback in football you should have at some time knelt in the middle of a bunch of sweaty faces and drawn out a play in the dirt, then turned that design into a real thing — like a virtuoso takes notes and turns them into pure melody."
—Murray Olderman
Author of
The Pro Quarterback

This was in Pontiac, Michigan and it was before the San Francisco 49ers were to win the first of their four Super Bowls to rate comparisons with the Steelers of the '70s as one of the greatest football teams of all time.

This was in January of 1981 before Super Bowl XVI at the Silverdome, and someone reminded Joe Montana of another quarterback named Joe who once guaranteed the outcome of a Super Bowl. This was the week before the 49ers were to clash with the Cincinnati Bengals in the biggest football game of the year.

"I'm not going to do that," remarked Montana, shaking his light-haired head and rolling his blue eyes.

That other quarterback, of course, was Joe Namath of the New York Jets. Back in January of 1969, before Super Bowl III, Namath boldly predicted that the Jets would beat the Baltimore Colts, a 17-point favorite, and he made good on his word.

I moved to Miami that same year to cover the Miami Dolphins, and covered my first Super Bowl at the end of the 1969 season, a victory by Lenny Dawson and the Kansas City Chiefs over the Minnesota Vikings. The last Super Bowl I covered in person was the Bengals-49ers match at the Silverdome when I was writing for *The Pittsburgh Press.*

I was particularly interested in Montana because he came from Monongahela, Pennsylvania and was a hometown boy as far as readers of *The Press* were concerned.

When Namath made his famous pre-game boast, Montana was a running back for a midget football team called the Monongahela Little Wildcats.

"Joe Namath was my favorite football player at the time," recalled Montana, "because he was such a big success and he was from the area."

Namath, of course, grew up in Beaver Falls, and was an all-sports star there, as Montana was in Monongahela, 30 miles upriver from Pittsburgh, and at Ringgold High School. Montana turned down a basketball scholarship at North Carolina State, when Edgewood's Eddie

Biedenbach was recruiting for them, to accept Ara Parseghian's offer to play football at Notre Dame.

As a youngster, Montana used to pretend he was Terry Hanratty throwing the ball to Jim Seymour. When he was in high school, Montana adopted Hanratty as his idol. Montana would throw a football through a swinging tire in his backyard, just like Hanratty had done back home in Butler.

While his parents took him to Penn State to see that campus, and he had been to Pitt on many occasions to see the Panthers play, Montana wanted to go to Notre Dame, just like Hanratty.

Montana turned a program around at Ringgold High School. In 1974, he led a team of Pennsylvania high school all-stars on a 70-yard drive in the final minutes to beat Ohio, 14-7, in the annual Big 33 All-Star Classic.

At Notre Dame, he was known as "The Comeback Kid" for all the rallies he ignited, and he led a Dan Devine-coached club to a national championship.

He never forgets where he came from, or his early fantasies and influences in football.

Namath remains No. 1 in Montana's mind. Montana even had a dachshund named "Broadway," as a tribute to Namath.

Going into his first Super Bowl battle, the 25-year-old Montana was the most talked-about and talked-to young man on the Pontiac scene.

He was the cover boy on that week's issue of *Time* and *Sports Illustrated*.

He seemed to be handling the media crush as cooly as he does a pass rush. Montana tries and is most cooperative, but he is not very colorful. He doesn't have much to say. He's light-hearted and has been accused of being light-headed — does that sound familiar? — but he's for real. He reminded me of Namath in many ways, though he wasn't nearly as glib, and he didn't have Bradshaw's showbiz instincts.

This was only his third year in the NFL, but already his coach Bill Walsh was saying he would soon be the best quarterback in pro football. "By the middle of next year," Walsh said then, "he will be running the show."

Walsh knew what he was talking about, that's for sure.

Coming from Western Pennsylvania, Montana was well aware of the magnitude of the Super Bowl. But, for him, it had always been something that Terry Bradshaw and the Steelers were in, not Joe Montana and the San Francisco 49ers. This was the first time for both. Montana said he aimed to make the most of it.

After Montana led the 49ers on an 89-yard touchdown drive in the final five minutes of the NFC title contest with the Dallas Cowboys, and connected with Dwight Clark for a spectacular scoring pass in the final minute, and a 28-27 49ers' victory, Tom Landry, the coach of the Cowboys, said, "Montana has to be the key. There really is nothing else but him."

Montana took exception to Landry's remark. "I don't know how he could say that. It takes more than one man to defeat the Dallas

Cowboys twice in one season," said Montana.

Another highlight of Montana's season was when the 49ers defeated the Steelers, 17-14, before his family and friends at Three Rivers Stadium. It was the first time in his life that Montana had ever been at Three Rivers and he made the most of his visit.

"They have a lot of young people," Bradshaw observed of the 49ers that afternoon, "and they probably wanted to beat us because they'd seen us win all those Super Bowls. I know I would've felt that way."

So did Montana. This was exciting stuff for Montana, a blond, blue-eyed Italian. "My mother is a full-blooded Sicilian," he said, "and my dad's family is from northern Italy."

Joe's name sounds like something dreamed up by a Hollywood script writer, but it's for real and comes from northern Italy where it was Montani. He is also one-sixty-fourth Sioux.

"This is the ultimate," said Montana, as he surveyed the scene at the Silverdome. "I like being in this situation."

After that game, won by the 49ers, 26-21, Walsh, the 49ers coach, was talking again about Montana.

"Montana was the last pick in the third round. He's an excellent athlete, very quick on his feet. He can avoid the rush. He has a strong arm and good movement. And he's a great competitor.

"I'm not sure he'll ever be a great touch passer," Walsh went on, "but his passing percentage was the highest in the league and he had the best rating among the rookie quarterbacks. I regard him as a rookie because he hardly played his first season."

Walsh had worked out Montana two days before the draft and liked what he saw. But other scouts weren't so high on him. And Walsh would have drafted him earlier if he knew what he would be like as a pro.

"People felt he was too inconsistent," said Walsh. "He was a scatter-type thrower, not extremely accurate. But they were too close in their pre-draft line. They didn't allow for improvement.

"I thought he was in same mold as Brian Sipe and Joe Ferguson and that in two or three years he would be one of the top two or three quarterbacks in the NFL."

Then Walsh talked about a game the previous season in which he became firmly convinced that Montana was the young man to lead the 49ers out of the wilderness to the NFL's promised land.

"It was one of the greatest performances of the season," said Walsh. "We came out in the second half and we were behind, 35-7, and we beat New Orleans in the second half. We're still looking for an NFL game that was a greater comeback than that. We won, 38-35. Joe just played error-free football in the second half. We gained 450 yards in the second half. He's just one of those incredible quarterbacks. But even at Notre Dame he had a history of being a come-from-behind ballplayer.

"He has a special enthusiam for what he does. He doesn't study films enough, but put him on the field and he's at his finest. He just has a special resourcefulness."

Joe Montana

George Gojkovich

Montana was merely the latest in a long line of great quarterbacks to come out of Western Pennsylvania, along with Namath and Hanratty and the likes of Johnny Unitas and Danny Marino from Pittsburgh, George Blanda from Youngwood, Babe Parilli from Rochester, Johnny Lujack from Connellsville, Arnold Galiffa of Donora, Tommy Clements and Chuck Fusina from McKees Rocks, Richie and Kenny Lucas of Glassport, Joe Zuger of Homestead and Jim Kelly of East Brady.

Paul Zimmerman of *Sports Illustrated*, who saw most of them play, asked Unitas why western Pennsylvania produced so many fine quarterbacks. Zimmermann rates Unitas the best quarteback of the bump-and-run era and Montana tops of the modern breed, with Marino close behind.

"Toughness, dedication, hard work and competitiveness; a no-nonsense, blue-collar background," said Unitas.

"It was never easy. There were coal mines and steel mills, and boys would grow up and take jobs there. It was expected. You never thought about a different kind of lifestyle. We didn't have drugs or fancy cars. We had sports. That's all. And if you were good enough at playing football, maybe you could get away to see different things."

"Maybe it's the Iron City beer," explained Montana, trying his hand at coming up with a theory.

Zimmerman provided his own answer: "The most logical answer is tradition — and focus. If you're a kid with athletic ability in western Pennsylvania, you've probably got a picture of Montana or Marino on your bedroom wall."

Their fathers might have had something to do with it, too. Montana, Kelly and Marino all have fathers who helped fashion them as football players, and single-mindedly as quarterbacks.

They were zealous in their attention to their gifted sons. I can remember how Dan Marino Sr. used to be the lone figure sitting in the stands at 56,000 seat Pitt Stadium during the Panthers' practice sessions, watching his son go through his paces.

Montana's father, Joe Sr., put a ball in his son's hands when the kid was just starting to walk well and said, "Throw it."

Montana's father told Zimmerman, a former co-worker of mine at *The New York Post*, about those early days, and it sounds an awful lot like the stories of Marino and Kelly.

"I played all sports in the service," said Joe Sr., "but when I was a kid I never had anyone to take me in the backyard and throw a ball to me. Maybe that's why I got Joe started in sports. Once he got started, he was always waiting at the door with a ball when I came home from work.

"What I really wanted to do was make it fun for him. And I wanted to make sure he got the right fundamentals. I read books. You watch some quarterbacks, sometimes they need two steps to get away from the line of scrimmage. I felt the first step should be straight back, not to the side. We worked on techniques, sprint out, run right, run left, pivot and throw the ball.

"You know, I've been accused of pushing him. I don't think that's right. It's just that I loved it so much, and I loved watching him. And I wanted to make sure he learned the right way."

Joe was an only child. His parents left their modest middle-class neighborhood on Park Avenue in Monongahela and moved to California in 1986.

"Joe had problems with his dad," recalls a former 49ers official. "His dad was around all the time. He didn't have a job. His job seemed to be being Joe Montana's dad."

The Montanas turned off a lot of people, for one reason or another, back home in Monongahela. Joe just wasn't the kind of hometown hero they could embrace. When his parents were living there, Joe often paid visits without any local fanfare, ducking in and out and not wanting any fuss.

Like Terry Bradshaw, he had difficulty dealing with the crowds that mobbed him during his team's Super Bowl success string. He had problems going out in public.

Then, too, Monongahela's economic fortunes took a nose dive like many other Mon Valley communities when the steel mills and other allied industries started closing down. When people get squeezed for a buck they often have difficulty warming up to someone like Montana who makes millions to play football and endorse products in commercials.

Many people in Monongahela remain fierce fans of the Pittsburgh Steelers. They didn't want the 49ers to win a fifth Super Bowl.

"Hey, you're in Steeler country," Elinor Johnson told *Sports Illustrated*. "They don't want Joe to beat Terry Bradshaw's record. You can get your man in the street, your man in the bar, he'll tell you that."

Unitas believes rules changes in the NFL have helped Montana and Marino put up some astonishing statistics.

"Montana and Marino are head and shoulders over anyone else in the league," Unitas said a few years back when Montana was healthy and on top of his game. "If I had his personnel, I'd go with Montana. But if I didn't have that overall personnel, in a key game, I'd probably go with Marino."

Bradshaw is a big Montana fan. "It took me awhile to realize it takes a special person to run any successful system," said Bradshaw, alluding to the system employed by Bill Walsh when he was coaching the 49ers to NFL championships. "I don't think I could have mastered the 49ers system, because I don't think I would have had the patience. They attack linebackers. We attacked safeties. But we won, and they won. And it's Joe, more than anything. He makes the big throw. He leads the great drive. He never loses his cool.

"When you retire, no one cares how many yards you threw for, how many touchdown passes you had, or any of that. They just want to know where the damn rings are. That's the bottom line. They want to know if you won.

"They can talk about all the other guys out there. When they're done, all Joe's gotta do is say, 'Here are the rings, boys.'

403

"When I'm grading quarterbacks, the first thing I always check is their poise under pressure. Joe Montana has tremendous courage. No matter what situation he is in, his talent will shine through because of his courage."

Coming from Bradshaw, that meant a great deal to Montana. Growing up in Monongahela, Montana was a big Bradshaw fan. Back in 1988, Bradshaw visited with Montana in his role as a CBS broadcaster.

"He kind of kept me happy when I was down," recalled Montana. "He told me to stay with it. He said, 'Don't let them mess with your head.' He told me I was a very good quarterback. It helped keep me going."

Jim Finks, another former Steelers quarterback, and now the president-general manager of the New Orleans Saints, says, "Joe Montana has all the skills and poise and physical ability. And he has won how many Super Bowls?

"So I don't know what else you would rank a guy on. He's always high in passing. He always quarterbacks the team to a winning season. I've seen Joe now for too long. Every time we get a 17-point lead on that guy, I say he's got us where he wants us.

"They have a fine football team, but he's the triggerman. Just look at the championships, the skins on the wall. He's got 'em. That separates the men from the boys."

Hall of Famer Otto Graham, the great quarterback of the Cleveland Browns, told Ira Miller of the *San Francisco Chronicle*, "I'm a strong believer that the athlete of today is better than the athlete of my day. There's no question that if you look at Joe Montana's record over the years, he should be rated No. 1, as far as I'm concerned. You have to rate him the best of all time."

Bill Walsh, who was called a "genius" during the San Francisco reign of terror, claimed that he and Montana were "the best quarterback-coach tandem of the '80s, perhaps ever."

Walsh explains it this way:

"As soon as I saw Joe's beautiful footwork, quick natural steps I knew we could develop the disciplines in him that would have been difficult with someone slower or less athletic.

"Joe is the best in football at reading defenses. He has the basic insticts for sports. Probably by the age of 10, he was better than other people. He has that one great asset so many athletes lack — instinct."

Randy Cross, who played guard and center for the 49ers in Montana's first ten years with the team, and provided analysis for the 1992 Super Bowl as part of the CBS-TV team, said this of Montana in an interview with Dave Goldberg of the Associated Press:

"Joe marches to a different drummer as far as motivation goes. If you knew what motivated him, you'd have 11 guys like that on the field.

"People want to make something special out of him. They figure just because Joe is such a great player he's a special person. Joe is just like anybody else. He's not like a Joe Namath. He's not out running the streets, associating with a different group of people and doing different things. He's just a guy with a wife and kids and the same problems as anyone else."

Jeff Petrucci, the head football coach at California (Pa.) State University, was the quarterback coach at Ringgold High School when Montana was the team's All-American star. A few years ago, Petrucci was sitting in an endzone seat at San Francisco's Candlestick Park, watching Montana throwing passes.

When Petrucci returned home, he told his wife: "The kid has not changed. It's still just a game to him. Even though he's paid a lot of money, it's just a game, as if he's still playing back in the streets of Monongahela."

George Gojkovich

Joe Montana

405

Jim Kelly
Taking the right road
from East Brady to Buffalo

*"We're the leaders out there, and we have to go out
and win the football game."*
—Jim Kelly, 1991

*"I don't care if we're just playing showdown for a nickel
a hand. I want to beat your brains in."*
—Bobby Layne, quarterback,
1948-62

I remember the first time I laid eyes on Jim Kelly. He was home
on a break from college. He had more hair then and it was not as
slicked back as he combs it now, ala Jack Nicholson or Michael Douglas or Richard Gere.

Kelly came into the media room at the Steelers' office complex at
Three Rivers Stadium that day just to say hello to the local sportswriters
and to see what was going on. He was a tall kid who was curious about
the Steelers' scene. We were waiting for Chuck Noll to appear for his
weekly press conference. Joe Gordon, then the Steelers' publicist, introduced him to everyone assembled: "Fellas, this is Jim Kelly from the
University of Miami."

Kelly nodded and grinned, looking a little awkward. Some of the
sportswriters were courteous enough to return the smile. A few saluted
him. Nobody really spoke to him. Nobody knew how big this kid Kelly
was going to become in the world of football. Kelly quickly blended into
the background that afternoon at Three Rivers.

He was a good story even then, however, but nobody bothered to
interview him. After all, college football wasn't their beat, and he hadn't
become a star yet.

If Kelly had come into that same room during the 1991 season he
would have been stormed by the same sportswriters for interviews. Kelly
had become one of the premier passers in pro football, and his Buffalo
Bills one of the best teams.

Kelly came from East Brady, about 50 miles northeast of Pittsburgh along the Allegheny River, and he had been a Steelers fan all
his young life. He was a quarterback at Miami, just a junior, and he
was a big fan of Joe Namath and Terry Bradshaw.

He had been in the Steelers' clubhouse that day talking to Bradshaw. Years before, when he was a Pop Warner football player, Kelly
had his picture taken with Bradshaw. It was a picture he cherished.
He loved being around Bradshaw. And Bradshaw loved having a big,
talented kid like Kelly seeking his counsel, and hanging on his every

word. Bradshaw felt the same way when Pitt's quarterback Danny Marino, or his coach, Jackie Sherrill, came to the Stadium to see him. He loved to talk about football with them.

Bradshaw was also a big fan of young quarterbacks like Kelly and Marino, and boosted them often in the local papers. It was a mutual admiration society.

Kelly had quarterbacked Miami to a victory over Penn State as a freshman. After his visit to the Steelers' office that day, Kelly would return to Miami to lead the Hurricanes to an upset victory over the No. 1 ranked Penn State team, and to their first post-season bowl appearance in 14 years. Nowadays it's hard to imagine Miami not being in a major bowl.

Kelly saved a sinking Miami football program, and the Hurricanes have had a string of great quarterbacks and top rankings ever since. He started the streak that gained the school the name of "Quarterback U." He wore No. 12 — the same number worn by Bradshaw.

The Steelers were still one of the NFL's most admired teams when Kelly came to the Stadium. They still had the aura of a four-time Super Bowl winner, and they still had Bradshaw.

In mid-September of 1991, Kelly was on stage at Red Jacket Academy in South Buffalo for a press conference conducted by about 200 students. He was there in conjunction with *Kidsports* magazine, a *Sports Illustrated* spinoff for youth, for which he was the coverboy for its September-October issue.

"My favorite team growing up was the Pittsburgh Steelers," Kelly told the students who ranged in age from eight to 15. "But one of the reasons I went to college in Miami was to get away from the cold weather. So I'm not going to stand up here and lie to you. My initial feeling was 'Oh, no, not Buffalo.'"

Kelly wanted to impress the kids with the importance of family, and how everyone back home shares in his success as a millionaire football player.

"I owe everything to my mother and father," he said. "And if it wasn't for my parents and my five brothers being there to share with, none of this would be any fun.

"I'm doing it for myself and to make my family proud. Think about it. Wouldn't it be neat if someday you threw a touchdown pass and you could go to your dad or your brother and talk about it?"

Kelly may not have realized it, but he sounded just like Terry Bradshaw talking to similar student assemblies when Bradshaw was the star of the Steelers' Super Bowl teams.

In a 20-minute talk preceding his question-and-answer session, Kelly hit home with the students, stressing the importance of getting good grades, staying away from drugs, valuing family and working hard. The 31-year-old Kelly spoke from the heart.

"I come from a family," said Kelly, "that didn't have anything growing up. We scratched for everything. Believe me, for me to be up

407

here today and talking to you, never in my wildest dreams did I think I could do this, to make the money I make ($3 million per year), to be sharing it with my family.

"When I look back on it, I just say, 'I'm glad I listened to what my mother and father had to say.' I'm lucky I took the right road instead of the wrong road.

"Believe me, there are many people out there who have the ability to do what I do, to do what other successful people are doing, but there's so many people who decide to take the wrong road. So think about what you want to do with your life and start thinking about it when you're young."

He told the students that when he was in fifth grade he would practice signing his autograph.

"I used to say, 'Boy, someday this autograph's going to be worth something.' I set my dreams high."

He came from a small town where there were only 23 players on the high school football varsity roster so it wasn't always easy to think big.

"Everybody told me, 'Jim, you're not going to make it. Nobody's going to know who you are.' But they did because No. 1, I had people who cared about me, helping me along. And No. 2, I put in my mind the thinking that said, 'Hey, if you want it bad enough, work hard, study, do the things it takes, you'll get there.' "

Kelly confessed that his brothers do their best to keep his head size from swelling by reminding him of his interceptions rather than his touchdown passes.

"Everyone else says, 'Jim, you make $3 million a year, you're single and you have all these girlfriends,' " Kelly said. "Well, if it wasn't for my mother and father and my brothers . . . to share my success with, it's not worth it. That's what family's for. To support you, straighten you out, keep you down to earth."

Kelly concluded his speech by saying, "If one or two of you listen to me, that's great, but I hope a lot more of you listen and you take the right road."

Deborah Smith, the school principal, was impressed. "I was eager to see if he was a real honest, down-to-earth person and after meeting him and hearing him I'm convinced he's just a normal guy who made it big. He's got time to give to kids, kids in real need. There was a special feeling in the air. The kids were so excited."

Leo Roth, who reported on the school visit for the *Rochester Times-Union*, wrote, "He didn't preach or condescend."

Roth's review concluded: "The entire scene vividly demonstrated just how far Kelly, who suffered from a negative image early in his Buffalo career, has come as an athlete and person."

Kelly told Roth, "If what I said today sinks into one or two kids, it was worth it."

There is a big billboard that welcomes visitors to East Brady, Pennsylvania, known for "Brady's Bend," a big curve on the railroad track that used to be a busy stretch for trains, and as the home of Jim Kelly. East Brady has known better times. There are just over 1,500 residents and the unemployment figure is about 20 percent. It's always been a good sports town, and it's always been a big Steelers' town. Today, however, there are divided loyalties.

Everyone still roots for the Steelers, mind you, but not everyone does if the Steelers are playing the Buffalo Bills. Some of the citizens can't root against Jim Kelly. Then again, some of his biggest fans can't find it in their heart to root against the Steelers, either.

Art Vasbinder, co-owner of the Bachelors II tavern, a big sports hangout in East Brady, is a good example. He is a good friend of Jim Kelly and was his basketball coach in sixth grade. He travels to Buffalo for about four or five games a season.

But when the Bills were playing the Steelers, he begged off predicting a winner. "I'm rooting for Jimmy to do well and the Steelers to win," he finally said.

East Brady brings back a lot of boyhood memories for me. My favorite uncle, Rich O'Brien, married a nurse named Mary Sutton who came from East Brady. My Uncle Rich drove a blue Plymouth, but the only place he ever seemed to drive it was to East Brady to visit his in-laws. It was like it was the only road he knew.

I went to East Brady for a few funerals in my youth. St. Mary's Cemetery sits atop a hill there, high above the Allegheny River. It was a pretty town, I recall, with lots of churches and white frame homes, and lots of hills and steep, narrow roads climbing from the river. I remember my Uncle Phil Blotzer blew out a tire en route there once in a funeral procession. The tire just burned up on him and smelled terrible. I remember that us kids laughed about that, and drew baleful looks from the more somber adults. After all, it was a funeral. Another time, I was a passenger in the back of a car driven by my brother-in-law's father, and he kept going off the road and scaring the daylights out of us.

My Aunt Mary had a sister named Moonie and a brother named Sonny, as I recall, and they were friendly, country kind of people. Moonie had lots of grandkids. My Uncle Rich was always telling me about this local guy named Frank Fuhrer. "He's quite the golfer, and he's smart, too, with a real head for business," my Uncle Rich often related.

As an adult, I got to know Frank Fuhrer well, as the owner of the Pittsburgh Triangles of World Team Tennis, the Pittsburgh Spirit of the Major Indoor Soccer League, and other sports and business promotions. Fuhrer made a fortune in the insurance business, and then branched out into other entrepreneurial activities. More recently, he has promoted the Family House Golf Invitational, one of the country's leading fund-raising professional golf events.

So Fuhrer and Jim Kelly are the best known sports celebrities to ever come out of East Brady.

Football on every level has always been serious business in East Brady. The East Brady High Bulldogs have always been a tremendous

410

source of community pride. "Nothing brings back brighter days than those days as a Bulldog at East Brady," says Kelly. It's a blue collar town and Kelly's accomplishments have given it the same kind of boost that the Steelers provided Pittsburgh back in the '70s when the steel mills were closing down. Most of the mills and industry around East Brady have been shut down for some time.

"I'll tell you what Jim Kelly done for East Brady; he put it on the map," said a local businessman named George J. Pawkovich in an interview with Gene Warner of *The Buffalo News*.

"If you went out of town, even to Pittsburgh, people'd ask where East Brady's at. Now you mention East Brady and people say, 'Oh yeah, Jim Kelly's town.'"

Gerald Hunter, a retired Pittsburgh factory worker, said of East Brady: "It has no future. There's no place for people to work. Young people have to leave here and go where the work is. It's a shame because it's one of the most scenic towns I've ever seen."

None of the local kids have fared as well working elsewhere as Jim Kelly. But the local citizens love to tell stories about how he's still the same kid they knew when he was playing peewee football. How he still addresses his elders as "Mr." and "Mrs." and how he's still polite, respectful and deferential in their company.

"He hasn't changed at all except he has more money," said Marcy Hiles, whose husband Jim went to school with Kelly. "He comes to the house like he always did. He makes himself at home. He goes to the refrigerator and gets an Iron City. And he plays with my little boy. He's a little bit bigger and a lot richer, but he's the same Jimmy Kelly."

Notice how everybody in East Brady calls him "Jimmy" rather than Jim — just like in those "Nupe It" ads he does with tennis star Jimmy Connors. It's an ad for a pain-reliever that another Western Pennsylvania quarterback product, Joe Montana, did earlier with Connors.

Jim's father, Joe, a retired machinist, believes Buffalo is just a bigger version of East Brady, so it suits his son fine. "Buffalo's a working town like we are," says Joe. "Buffalo people are just regular working people. They're close-knit, like we are."

"Everybody's family," chimes in Joe's wife, Alice Kelly.

Jim Kelly can remember wearing jackets handed down through three older brothers. Then he would pass his on to two younger brothers. Ahead of him were Ray, Ed and Pat, and behind him came the twins, Danny and Kevin. Jim remembers cutting grass and shoveling snow to supplement the family income, and he remembers, all too well, dinners of peanut butter and jelly sandwiches.

"I still think Jimmy likes it best," says his father Joe. "The first thing he has is peanut butter and jelly. I went to the store for him, and he made me get it. He sure eats enough of it, two to three sandwiches a day. His favorite jelly is grape."

411

Jim's father worked for 32 years as a machinist at Damon Industries, repairing parts for steel mills — when there was work. We had something in common. My father worked the same period of time as a machinist — a drill-press operator — for Mesta Machine Company in Homestead.

"A lot of times I'd be out of work, and have to get two or three odd jobs, mostly carpentry or plumbing, to put food on the table," said Joe Kelly. "The boys helped out selling newspapers and things.

"We didn't have like some people — what do you call it? — a big entree for dinner all the time. It was usually mashed potatoes, beans and some kind of ground meat. At Christmas, we might have a turkey or a ham. If we had steak, well, it must've been a big celebration."

Jim Kelly can remember the competition at the dinner table for an extra helping. "Me and my brothers would be fighting over food at the dinner table. Many times we went to bed without too much to eat. The things that my mother and father went through . . . I never want to go through again. I'm just happy now to be able to give them what they need."

Most of the Kelly kids were big and were good at playing sports. Their father had been a Navy boxing champion. Jim was just a little special, and he showed great promise early. By the time he was ten, Jim could throw a football 40 yards and he was competing against boys a few years older and holding his own. He was a semifinalist in the national Punt, Pass and Kick competition.

Joe strung a clothesline in the backyard and had Jim throw the ball at it, over and over again. "He'd stand 20 or 30 yards away," remembered Joe Kelly. "I'd have him roll right and throw, roll left, drop straight back. He hit that clothesline pretty good.

"He said he had this dream about one day becoming a pro quarterback. I said, 'If you are really serious about that, you are going to have to work awfully hard.'

"Every day during lunch hour, he would come home from grade school and I would have him practice his dropbacks and his spinouts," Joe recalled. "I had him throw to different spots. I was interested in accuracy. I wanted him to be able to make all kinds of different throws without even thinking about them."

Sometimes they would get so caught up in the practice routine that Jim would go back to school with an empty stomach. "I regretted it at times," said Jim, "but now I'm glad my dad pushed me. He told me I'd thank him for it someday, and he was right."

Whenever his sons got out of hand or too spirited for the confines of the house, Joe Kelly would take them out to the garage and have them put on boxing gloves and football helmets and let them wale away at each other.

"We'd beat the dogspit out of each other," recalled Jim Kelly.

That story brought back some personal memories, too. There was a guy in our neighborhood named Pat Baine, a milkman with two sons and two daughters, and all the kids in the neighborhood had to box in his garage. It wasn't something he promoted. He just provided the

12 Jim Kelly

gloves. We would box on top of old bed mattresses, which did not provide the best footing, but were welcome when you got jolted by a punch, and knocked down. We also wrestled on those well-stained mattresses. Somebody was always challenging somebody else to a bout — either a boxing or wrestling skirmish. It established a pecking order, for whatever purpose, of who was tougher than who in the neighborhood.

Nobody was better at football than Jim Kelly in his neighborhood. By the time he was a senior, college coaches came calling at his door.

Lou Saban sold him on trading snow for sun and going to Miami. Joe Paterno wanted him to come to Penn State and be a linebacker. Paterno, by the way, is sick of hearing about that. Kelly never showed any interest in nearby Pitt.

"It wasn't a tough sell," said Saban. "When I told him we were interested in him as a quarterback and not a linebacker, his eyes lit up. I think the fact that it doesn't snow in Miami didn't hurt our cause, either."

Saban stayed around for two more years at Miami, and then Howard Schnellenberger took over as head coach. Schnellenberger succeeded in turning the program around.

"There was a lot of talk about dropping the program, the way they did with basketball," said Ron Steiner, who was the sports information director at Miami at the time time. "When Schnellenberger took over as coach, the talk was if he didn't do it, that was it for Miami football."

Schnellenberger gives Kelly proper credit for saving the day. "He is the single-most important person in the revival of Miami football," said Schnellenberger, now the head coach at the University of Louisville, where Steiner serves as his administrative assistant. "If he hadn't come along, there might not be any Miami football today."

Schnellenberger and one of his assistants, Earl Morrall, who had played quarterback briefly for the Steelers among other NFL teams over a long pro career, worked closely with Kelly.

Schnellenberger had coached Joe Namath at Alabama, and Schnellenberger said Kelly "reminds me of Joe to some degree. They're of different ethnic backgrounds, but both have that terrific confidence and approach football like a Mississippi riverboat gambler. They know how to win and they have the understanding that all this isn't as important as everybody else thinks."

When pro football people talk about different draft classes, they always point to the 1983 class as the one that produced so many terrific quarterbacks.

Kelly and Marino were the two most successful members of that vaunted class. Both have become two of the best paid football players in pro football history. Marino signed a contract in 1991 worth $25 million over five years. Kelly has a seven-year deal worth $20 million, ranking them one-two on the list of the NFL's highest salaries.

Both trace their roots to Western Pennsylvania, and both grew up wanting to play for the Pittsburgh Steelers someday. "I feel very

414

fortunate," said Marino. "Growing up, you never think you can make that kind of money."

There were six quarterbacks selected in the first round of 27 picks in 1973. The first pick was John Elway, and the class included Todd Blackledge, Tony Eason and Ken O'Brien.

"It's probably the best group of quarterbacks that ever came into pro football," said Gil Brandt, the former scouting guru of the Dallas Cowboys. "It was just a fantastic group of players and when you consider that Marino was the lowest pick of the group it's even more fantastic."

The Steelers, much to their chagrin now, passed on Marino and instead drafted defensive lineman Gabe Rivera of Texas Tech. Rivera, of course, was severely injured in an auto accident during his rookie season. At age 30, he remains confined to a wheelchair and, as reported in August of 1991, he has been attending the University of Texas at San Antonio, hoping to get a degree and become a high school football coach.

The only recent class that can rival the 1983 group was the 1971 group that included Jim Plunkett, Dan Pastorini, Archie Manning and Lynn Dickey. "That was a pretty good group," said Dick Steinberg, the director of player personnel for the New England Patriots, "but it was nothing like the 1983 group. There's never been a draft like that one."

Kelly is a close friend of Marino and he can appreciate what Marino must endure in regard to the demands on him to justify making the kind of money he is paid.

"As quarterbacks," said Kelly, "we have to take the field no matter if we're making a million dollars per year, or three million or four million. We take the field with the same things on our mind — we're the leaders out there and we have to go out and win the football game.

"I don't worry about stats, I worry about wins and losses. When you have big stats, your team is usually winning. That's all I worry about. I'm into team goals. It's nice to have the individual stats and everybody praising you, but you want to win.

"The money never put any more pressure on me. The only pressure you have is the pressure you put on yourself. I get paid to have fun, and that's what football is all about."

Believe Kelly when he makes a comment like that. He is not only having fun, but he remains a football fan, a sports fan. He collects sports memorabilia, and has impressive displays in his home.

The walls of his gameroom are covered with shirts straight off the backs of some current greats — like Marino, Montana, Elway and even Chicago Bulls star Michael Jordan. Each jersey bears its wearer's autograph and a special personalized message.

"I only collect people I really admire and those who are good friends of mine," he said.

Among the retired players whose shirts have joined Kelly's collection are Pro Football Hall of Fame quarterbacks like Namath, Bradshaw and Roger Staubach, and Hall of Fame linebacker Jack Ham. He also values the Seattle Seahawks jersey of the NFL's all-time leading receiver, Steve Largent.

What Kelly enjoys doing the most with his money is improving the quality of life for his family, despite their frequent protestations.

"Dad always wanted a Lincoln, so that's what we got," said Kelly. "Dad and Mom always wanted a Hawaiian vacation, so that's what they got. Brother Dan always wanted college tuition, so that's what he got."

He fixed up the Kelly home on Purdum Street in East Brady, giving it a facelift with new windows and siding. He offered to move his family to a new home, but they wouldn't hear of it. They are comfortable right where they are in a house that is nearly one hundred years old. And you couldn't get the Marinos to move from their Parkview Avenue house in South Oakland. They are comfortable there.

Jim did give his father a credit card, saying, "Buy whatever you want, Dad, including the world if you want it."

Jim feels indebted to his dad because Joe was raised in an orphanage by nuns and used to swear nightly to his wife Alice that his family would stick together through thick and thin.

Jim purchased a specially-equipped van for his parents. His mother has emphysema and needs an oxygen tent nearby at all times. She was a heavy smoker for over 40 years and is now paying the price.

The Kellys use the van, which is equipped with enough oxygen to take care of the entire family, to travel from East Brady to Buffalo for the Bills' ballgames.

Lots of times, when Alice isn't doing well, she stays in the van with her husband, and they watch the game on TV in the parking lot outside Rich Stadium. Sometimes, she just stays home.

"I want to take care of my family," says Kelly with more than a hint of pride, "and I'm having a damn good time doing it. You take things for granted when you're growing up, but I don't these days.

"Every once in a while, it smacks me upside the head and says, 'Wow, look what happened.'"

In an interview for *Sport* magazine with Milt Northrup, whom I know from days we spent on the NBA beat together, Kelly said, "I never in my wildest dreams thought it would ever come to this. I mean, I dreamt about playing in the NFL, and you always wish you could win the Super Bowl, but I never thought about having all this.

"I'm happy I'm able to treat my family the way I have. I surprise them. I'm Santa Claus in June. I'm Santa Claus in March. I'm Santa Claus at Christmas."

Mercury Morris
Growing up the hard way

"Success is getting what you want,
but happiness is wanting what you get."
—From "Field of Dreams"

"Some men outshine the sun."
—From "Pippin"

Back in 1969, the Miami Dolphins trained at a private boys' academy in Boca Raton, Florida. It was only the Dolphins' third season in the American Football League and it showed. The camp was primitive, and it always seemed to be hot and sticky. The mosquitoes swarmed out of the nearby swamps every night.

Eugene "Mercury" Morris blew into camp like a fresh breeze, too fresh for some of the established players. He was so buoyant, a cocky kid, yet likable. He said outrageous things, and was every bit as quotable and refreshing as the league's top media stars.

Morris was a writer's dream. He had a smile and a laugh that could move palmetto trees.

Morris was a No. 3 draft choice out of West Texas State, where he had set national rushing records, eclipsing those of O.J. Simpson.

We collaborated on a column called "Diary of a Rookie" three times weekly in *The Miami News,* and that helped get him into more hot water. His outspoken manner and brashness were even bolder in print. I was a rookie on the NFL beat, and didn't use the best judgement, either.

I have many memories and images of Mercury Morris. I had moved to Miami from Pittsburgh to take my first full-time newspaper job, and my beat would be the Dolphins in their last season in the AFL.

Morris grew up in Pittsburgh, with his maternal grandparents in Ben Avon, and his parents lived in Manchester, not far from the site where Three Rivers Stadium would be built. He played high school sports at Avonworth High School. He had always been a big fan of the Pittsburgh Steelers. So we had some common roots, and we developed a fast friendship.

He had roomed in college for a while with Simmie Hill, a gifted basketball player from Hank Kuzma's Midland state championship basketball team, another of my favorites, and Morris delighted me with stories of their relationship, like the time Hill had turned a snake loose on him in their dorm room. Morris told me he was running scared, jumping on and off the bed to get away from Hill and his pet snake.

Morris was full of good stories about Hill and himself. He smiled a lot. He laughed a lot. And he made others do the same. He was flip, and infuriated his coaches and teammates at times. They thought he was too mouthy for his own good. He was a cocky kid, too cocky for some of the veterans on the Dolphins. But he would back up the bravado.

417

He had talent and he had huge statistics to confirm his running skills. Yet the first thing the Dolphin coaches did was to alter the way he lined up in the backfield and the way he took his first step. At West Texas State, he simply sat in a crouch. At Miami, they insisted he take a three-point stance. At West Texas State, he crossed one foot over the other when he made a move to the side, to take a pitchout or to sweep the end. At Miami, they demanded he take that first step with whatever foot was in the direction he was going. They wanted no cross-over step. He balked about this. Why were they messing around with Mercury Morris?

Gale Sayers, a great runner for the Chicago Bears, sided with Morris. "When you have a great running talent like him, you should leave him alone," said Sayers, when I asked him about it. "If he wants to do a flip-flop before he takes the handoff, you should let him."

There, thought Morris. Even Gale Sayers knows I'm right. Morris had strong opinions about everything, so he was a natural for a feature that was suggested by my sports editor, John Crittenden, a man who also had strong opinions about everything. It was Crittenden's idea for me to do the diary column with Morris.

Together, Morris and I threw off a lot of sparks during that 1969 summer training camp at steamy Boca Raton. We both thought we knew everything.

It took a few years for things to click, but Morris and Larry Csonka and Jim Kiick combined to give the Dolphins a devastating running attack, and he was a winner. Not that first season. The Dolphins finished 3-10-1 under George Wilson. Don Shula came in the next year and the Dolphins finished 10-4. It wasn't long after that the Dolphins were dominating the NFL and winning Super Bowls.

Talking about memories and images . . . I remember his speed and swiftness, his cutting ability. He was quick to cut up field. He was quick to cut up. He had an easy running style. He had an easy smile. He was a joy.

I have this other memory I wish I could shake, the way he did would-be tacklers, but somehow I can't.

I remember one night that he invited my wife, Kathleen, and I to join him and his wife for a night out on the town. His wife was cute. She had a much lighter complexion than his, and freckles around a button nose. She was an airline stewardess. We were sitting in a dimly-lit cocktail lounge and the conversation was easy. She was also about eight months pregnant with their first child.

At one point in the evening, she and Kathie accompanied each other to the ladies' room. While they were gone, I said, "She seems real nice, Merc. You're a lucky man."

He shrugged off the compliment like I was a cornerback coming up from behind him. "I'm not that thrilled with her," he said. "I'm not going to be staying with her. It won't work."

I remember feeling uncomfortable with that comment. How could he just abandon this young woman who was going to have his baby?

I asked him about that this year, and he said, "I hate to rehash that. I wasn't getting married until I was done with pro football. And the next thing you know, I haven't played a down yet, and I'm married and I've got a kid on the way. I wasn't ready for that yet."

I remember thinking about it one night when I was in Miami, on January 20, 1983. It was nearly 14 years after our first meeting. His pro football career was behind him. I was in Miami on assignment from *The Pittsburgh Press*, and I was covering the American Football Conference championship game between the New York Jets and the Miami Dolphins.

I turned on the television set in my hotel room and saw Mercury Morris, wiping tears from his eyes, when he learned he had been sentenced to 20 years in prison for cocaine trafficking. For the first 15 years of his sentence, the TV reporter said, there was no legal provision for parole or early release.

That hurt. I liked Mercury Morris better when he was smiling.

Mercury Morris, a valued member of the '72-'73 Dolphins teams that won back-to-back Super Bowls — beating his hometown Steelers to the one-two punch — was going to prison. Morris was arrested in mid-August of 1982 by Florida law enforcement officials at his home in South Miami and charged with nine counts of drug-related offenses.

Two pounds of cocaine were confiscated, and he was one of five men charged with trafficking in drugs. Firearms and a box of $50 and $100 bills were found. Morris faced a maximum sentence of 100 years if found guilty on all counts.

"I can't feel sorry for Morris," said the Steelers' Mel Blount back then. "Nobody has to go that route. You don't have to get that desperate. It was pure greed. Lambert and I were talking about it, and we both believe that if he did what they're saying, then he should be prosecuted to the fullest."

Ironically enough, I bumped into another Pittsburgh sports hero when I was in Miami that week. Dan Marino, a senior star at the University of Pittsburgh, was at the game with his agent, former Dolphins captain Nick Buoniconti, and he was talking about signing before the NFL draft with the Los Angeles Express of the United States Football League. Marino was tempted to follow the lead of another Western Pennsylvania product, Joe Namath, in signing with a new pro football league. Marino could do for the USFL what Namath had done for the AFL, and make more money at the same time.

There had been rumors that Marino had been fooling around with drugs during his Pitt playing days, but they were never validated. Foge Fazio, the Pitt coach, said that Dolphins' coach Don Shula was the only NFL coach to call him directly and ask him about those rumors. Fazio said there was no problem. Most of the NFL teams, including the Steelers, passed on Marino in the first round of the NFL draft, and the Dolphins got him and the rest is history.

The Steelers selected Gabe Rivera, a defensive lineman from Texas Tech, on the 21st round. Rivera turned out to have an unreal appetite for food and booze, and busted himself up in an auto accident which left

419

him paralyzed late in his first season with the Steelers. He was charged with drunken driving and reckless endangerment that rainy night.

Marino and I had sat next to each other on the airplane trip from Miami to Pittsburgh after the AFC title game in 1983 and talked about his future, and Mercury Morris' future. Marino just shook his handsome curly-haired head when I mentioned Morris and his crime and punishment to him that day.

I remember the next day after I had seen Morris sobbing on TV about his drug conviction. Morris was more composed, even smiling like his old self, when he and his attorney, Ron Strauss, met with a gathering of reporters at the Dade County Jail.

Morris held up two sheets of paper which showed children's sketches of an athlete — wearing a Miami Dolphins uniform No. 22 — in a moment of glory.

They were drawn by the children of Strauss, who insisted that Morris was entrapped and enticed by a state undercover agent to commit an act he otherwise would not have committed.

"Mercury has never denied using or abusing drugs," said Strauss, "but he never sold drugs until the agent sought him out and asked him to get the cocaine."

It was late January and it was supposed to be a good time for those who follow professional football. It was a time when talk turns to Joe Namath and Terry Bradshaw and Johnny Unitas and Lenny Dawson and Weeb Ewbank and Chuck Noll and Don Shula and Tom Landry and Al Davis, past playoff heroics — "The Immaculate Reception" by Franco Harris — and Super Bowls. No one enjoyed these times more than Mercury Morris when he was a Pro Bowl running back with the Dolphins and they went to three straight Super Bowls and won two of them in the early '70s.

Seeing Morris in his dilemma made that seem so long ago.

"I'm probably the best message in the world of what drugs can do to you," Morris said on this Friday in Miami. "What started out as a groove turned into a rut . . . I was about to get out of the whole mess when this whole mess started."

It was so much fun at the start, the start of Mercury's career. He had everything going for him.

There was an affinity from the start, a trust and understanding. You were both reckless, flippant. You were two little guys from Pittsburgh who wanted to take on the world. Was the world ready?

He was the Dolphins' third round draft choice. He talked a big game and offered lots of opinions in that column you collaborated on in *The Miami News.* "I feel like a new gunslinger in town," he said for openers.

He said a lot of other things that made the head coach, George Wilson, wince more than once and wonder what he had on his hands. Some of the observations Morris made left Larry Csonka sneering and Jim Kiick kicking.

Miami Dolphins

Mercury Morris

Miami Dolphins

Mercury Morris follows Paul Warfield on end sweep at Orange Bowl.

He had a few run-ins with the coaches at camp. From the start, Morris always thought rules were for someone else.

He was good. In the opening game of his rookie season, Morris returned a kickoff 105 yards for a touchdown. The Dolphins lost that game, however, and they went 3-10-1 for the season.

Wilson was fired and replaced by Shula. Shula had them in the playoffs the next year with a 10-4 record — talk about a turnaround — and in the Super Bowl two years later. Morris was among the many heroes when the Dolphins went undefeated (17-0) in 1972.

He held, when he left the league, the all-time second best yards-per-carry average (5.1 yards) in the NFL.

Going into the 1992 season, Morris still held several of the Dolphins' rushing records. He had the best single game rushing total with 197 yards on 15 carries, including a 70 yard touchdown, against the New England Patriots on September 30, 1973. Later that season, he also rushed for 144 yards against the Baltimore Colts.

He was second to Csonka on the team's all-time rushing list with 3,877 yards, compared to Csonka's 6,737. Morris rushed for 1,000 yards right on the nose in 1972, averaging 5.3 yards per carry. He was second to Csonka in touchdowns with 29 to Csonka's 53. Morris had the most touchdowns in a season with 12 in 1972, scoring three in each of two games against the Patriots.

Morris was high on himself and life back then. It had been all downhill since the Dolphins dealt him to the San Diego Chargers after the 1975 season. He hardly played during his one season with the Chargers and he came crashing to earth when the end came to his pro football career.

"The only thing I didn't have was a game plan," he said. "When you leave professional football nobody hands you a game plan for the next week, or the next year, certainly not for the rest of your life. At the time I retired, I had done three basic things in life: play football, have fun and make money."

Morris was 36 at the time he met reporters to discuss his drug-related arrest. He looked in excellent shape. He always looked like a weight lifter. He was a well-toned 195 pounds, nearly 20 pounds more than he was when he was first jailed in the summer of 1982 after selling 456 grams of cocaine to an undercover agent. Anyone convicted of trafficking more than 400 grams of cocaine in Florida receives at least a 15-year prison term without parole.

"I no way feel this thing is lost," said Morris. "No. 1 in my mind is to prepare my appeal. This is my problem and I'm going to work it out."

Talking about drugs in general, he said, "This era is a drug-oriented era. It is a satanical force."

Talking about jail, he said, "In jail, you are going to get prison officials and inmates alike who simply don't like Mercury Morris."

He was planning to come home to Pittsburgh that same month — in the company of two marshals — for an overnight visit to see his

422

mother, Jacquelyn Revis, who was dying from ovarian cancer at St. Francis General Hospital.

Some reporters, believe it or not, asked Morris for his prediction on the upcoming AFC title game beween the Dolphins and the Jets. "Two words: Don Shula," said Morris. "Our goals were both the same — winning — he being a Capricorn and born one day before me.

"This team doesn't have any superstars. I think this could be the end of the thought that Don Shula can only win with big people."

The Dolphins did defeat the Jets, 14-0, and went on to play the Washington Redskins in Super Bowl XVII, where they would come up short in their bid for a third NFL title.

Morris was once among the biggest of Shula's stars. There is a line from a song in the stage show "Pippin" that goes like this: "Some men outshine the sun. . ."

Mercury Morris was such a young man.

You could not condone what he did and you did not buy into the line that hard times are to blame or an excuse for kids stealing, or dealing in dope, or mugging old people. But you still felt bad for an old friend.

The 1992 conviction for possession of and trafficking in cocaine was deemed not constitutional by the Supreme Court of Florida in 1986. Rather than hold a new trial, it was easier for him and the state to call it a tie. He had given them 3 1/2 years on a 20-year sentence, and they sent him home.

Morris had said he was railroaded on that trafficking charge, though he has always readily admitted — "always has, always will," as he put it — that he was definitely in possession. He said he had been using cocaine on and off for three years. He said he had been "free-basing my brains out." He had spent untold amounts of money on what we now know as crack.

His name had been cleared, in some respects. It couldn't change some things. His mother died a week after he was sent to prison. His father died a week after he left prison. "I never had the chance to be the sort of son I wanted to be," said Morris

When people in Pittsburgh asked his mother why he didn't visit more often during the period prior to his conviction, she would excuse him by saying, "You wouldn't want to see him the way he is now. He's not the Gene you remember."

He is now living in South Miami. He goes to one Dolphins game a year. If he's bored, he leaves at halftime.

He never gets the urge to try drugs again, he says. "The urge for what? A 20-year sentence? My kids? My wife? No."

His wife is Bobbie Morris. She is his third wife. She married him in December, 1979. That was after his days with the Dolphins and before his mighty fall. She visited him once a week at Florida State Prison, and brought the kids. There are six of them. She was loyal. And she prayed a lot. She must be a saint.

She had stayed with him during his drug-dependent days when Morris became a monster, a revolting figure. When a newborn daughter needed formula, he spent the money on cocaine. While his 10-year-old sons were playing in the house, he was free-basing behind closed doors. "They knew what was going on," Morris wrote in his book. "Dad was wasting himself." When his wife asked him to do one thing at Christmas — that he get the tree — he kept himself in a stupor until the wee hours and then, when the lots had closed, he climbed a fence and stole a tree.

According to the book, however, he never touched drugs after his arrest.

Morris spent a lot of time in prison lifting weights and reading the Bible. He became more spiritual. He had to.

Amy Wilson, a staff writer for the *Orlando Sun-Sentinel*, asked him about his glory years with the Dolphins.

"Those weren't the glory years," he said. "These are."

After his pro football career was behind him, Morris tried various business ventures, but they all went sour on him. Then he became a heavy user of cocaine, eventually switching to free-basing.

"People get cocaine and they get real smart," recalled Morris. "I chose that lifestyle. I had a lifestyle that led to the pinnacle of success and then one that led to the pits. I can't give the pigskin credit for my success any more than I can give cocaine the blame for my demise," Morris told newspaper writer Bill Ward when he was promoting a book about his life called *Against the Grain*, published by McGraw-Hill.

"Cocaine cannot come down your chimney and say, 'I'm going to make you a complete fool.' There isn't a reality to why one gets involved. What was once a groove became a rut. You don't drown by jumping in the water; you drown by staying in it."

Morris described himself as "not just a person seeking sobriety, but a person seeking to be saved from himself."

Morris wrote in his book: "When you're sitting in a jail cell staring 15 years in the face, you learn about priorities real fast. All my energy was devoted to getting out, not getting high. I quit. It wasn't a difficult task. It was fourth-and-one again. But this wasn't a game. My family, my freedom and my life were on the line. My days with cocaine were over."

On the drug overdose deaths of Len Bias and Don Rogers, which occurred just after Morris was released from prison, he wrote in his book: "You can't blame cocaine for the deaths of Len Bias and Don Rogers. Perhaps some . . . think I'm being unkind to the memory of these two men. But fact is they chose to adopt a lifestyle. Rogers overdosed in late June. You're supposed to be ready for the upcoming training football season then. What was he thinking when he took that cocaine? We all have a choice. You learn from your mistakes and move forward but you have to acknowledge that they are your mistakes."

Morris went on to say some things he has said more than once when visiting schools and speaking at assemblies. "Drugs are not good or bad. Cocaine, Jack Daniels, a .357 magnum. They have no inherent value.

But the choice to use them creates consequences that can be terrible. You get a speeding ticket, you can't blame the gas pedal, just like I can't blame cocaine. The problem is not drugs; the problem is attitudes.

"Politicians use buzzwords. They say, 'We've got to save the children.' Shoot, our children know a lot more than we give them credit for. Tell kids the truth — not the popular truth, the real truth.

"If you were to send off to Washington for a list of the most dangerous drugs — and emphasize 'dangerous,' not 'illegal' — you know what is at the top of the list? Alcohol. But there are acceptability factors in our society. Alcohol is legal, so it's acceptable."

He's not a big football fan anymore, but he still speaks with football references. "I fumbled early," he said of his life, "and came back to score the winning touchdown late in the game."

He said he had suffered a broken neck while playing for the Dolphins, and that he started to use cocaine to offset the pain in his neck. But he realizes now that wasn't the answer.

In the book, Morris and co-author Steve Fiffer wrote, "Did I know what I did wrong? Yes. Why did I do it? Because I was operating in a surreal society where right and wrong weren't always the litmus test for behavior. Because I was in the midst of a free-basing haze . . . I was messed up and so were my values. And who knows? Maybe deep down inside, I realized that the only way I could stop the downward spiral was to get caught doing something wrong. In crossing the line between mere use of cocaine to play the new role of middleman, I was inviting disaster. Maybe I realized that Mercury Morris couldn't jitterbug his way out of the corner he had got himself into; that Gene Morris needed some disaster to start him on the road to ruin."

Although he said he respected Shula as a coach, Morris painted him as man "who was uncomfortable" dealing with the changing teams of the early '70s in the NFL.

He had legendary battles with Shula. He still believes he should have started in the backfield with Larry Csonka, now in the Pro Football Hall of Fame, instead of sharing the other slot with Jim Kiick.

In his book, Morris tells how inmates smuggled sides of beef and chicken into their cells at the Dade Correctional Institute in Florida City. He tells of prisoners making wine out of Lysol. "You got drunk and disinfected all at once," said Morris, showing he had not lost his sense of humor.

He also says he is a strict father. He says he is rarely fooled by his kids. "I let them try," Morris said. "But they know they can't get away with much."

Morris sounded so good when I spoke to him in early April, 1992. His voice was so strong and vibrant, he was never more articulate. Many of his lines, I am sure, were well rehearsed. But he sounded good, especially when he laughed. And he laughed often. He sounded like the old Mercury Morris, even better.

"I've been on the lecture circuit for six years, ever since I got out of prison," said Morris. "It's an enjoyable business. And I've got a little consulting firm here in Miami.

"I've been working for 11 months on a growth and development package that I have been trying to sell to the National Football League. The athlete of today and the owner of today need to be on the same level. There's a vast difference between who these people are. This is a generation where having is more important than winning.

"Society is different. They come out of a different society. Where are we going in society? Statistics now make role models. It's strange to see the amount of cash that makes people go.

"I look at two dates, in my mind, that show me what has happened in pro sports. I marvel at what's happened, and how much difference there is between 1974 and 1984. Dan Marino signed with the Miami Dolphins for $1.4 million a year in 1984. In 1974, coming off two back-to-back world championships, the Dolphins' entire payroll was $1.4 million. Look at the difference.

"Jim Brown . . . the most he ever made was $55,000 a year with the Cleveland Browns. I was the highest paid player on the San Diego Chargers in 1976, and I was making $125,000 a year. Marino makes more than that in one game now."

Morris grew up with the Steelers, and still pulls for Pittsburgh ballteams, but he also takes pride in the fact that the Dolphins were winning Super Bowls before the Steelers did. "Look at our 1972 team," said Morris. "The Dolphins might not have been the best team on paper, but they were the best team every Sunday. Nobody beat the Dolphins.

"Then they came up with a computer game where the Steelers beat our '72 team. How could they do that? How could they factor in the intangibles?

"I remember seeing a 15-1 sign when we came to Three Rivers Stadium to play the Steelers in the AFC championship game in 1972. They thought the Steelers were going to beat us. My mother and father were in the stands; my people were in the stands. It was one of the highlights of my life. The game meant so much. We beat them 21-17.

"We won the Super Bowl, and our rings had a cluster of 16 small diamonds around one big diamond. The Steelers ended up being a part of that cluster of 16. How's that sound? After I said that, I thought of that article we used to write together in Miami.

"They said we couldn't win 17 in a row, so they made us underdogs in the Super Bowl, but we won that, too."

Morris started laughing.

I told him he sounded good.

"It's very simple," he said. "Sometimes when you make an F, you have to make and A just to get a C. I've been to the Super Bowl and I've been to the can. I've had the best and the worst. Now I'm somewhere in the middle."

Morris had appeared on a cable network TV show the week before with Roy Firestone, talking about the Mike Tyson story, after the former world heavyweight boxing champion was sentenced to six years in prison for raping an 18-year-old beauty pageant contestant in a hotel in Indianapolis.

I mentioned to Morris that I had just read an item in the newspaper in which a prison official said that Tyson was "adjusting to incarceration very well."

Morris changed his tone. "Whoever said that, they made it up," he snapped. "They're not there. If Tyson has any salt whatsoever, he'll be living out of the possibility of winning an appeal. You'll be hearing a lot about him. You'll hear so many stories, the trouble he's in. Everybody there will try to make Mike Tyson like everybody else. They will try to bring him down to their level.

"When I was at Raiford, a guard used to ask me, 'Mercury, how does it feel? You've been to the top, and now you're here.' And I'd say to the guard, 'I'm here with you.' I was a first-time offender and they had me with the worst. There are gangs there. If he starts to assimilate himself, he's in a real trouble.

"Here's a guy who has an opportunity now to become a human being. He's now into a survivor of the fittest mold. There will be people there who don't like him being there. He could steal their thunder. There's always going to be some asshole there — it could be one of the guards or one of the inmates — who will cause him trouble. The guards are going to look for something to brag about when they go home. They might say, 'Inmate Tyson, you need a shave.' Or 'Inmate Tyson, your shoes are untied.' I went to jail when I was in prison, and that'll happen to him, too. Human beings have a tendency when they get a dog down to kick him.

"The guards are just like the guy who goes into the lion cage at the circus. He walks around in there like he's in control. He's got a chair and a whip and a bullshit gun. But any second . . . he's gone. The guards know that."

Morris is not critical of Tyson. "He's still a viable human being," he said. "If I could have six months with Mike Tyson, he'd be a polished speaker. He'd understand it's important to communicate with people and to be understood."

Morris has two sets of children. He refers to them as "Star Trek" and "Star Trek — The Next Generation." His oldest sons, Eugene and Marco, are both adults and trying to find their way as a singer and a musician. He has a stepson Duke living in Atlanta. He has been married to Bobbie, his third wife, for 14 years. They have a daughter, Tiffany, 10, and twin boys, Jarrett and Elliott, whom he said would be 5 in June. "They have given me an opportunity to grow up myself," he said. "Sports does not provide a way for you to grow up. It only provides a way for you to grow old. What you have out there, too often, is the same 11-year-old kid who first started playing football. What they lack in life is coaching."

Morris remembers his early days in football. "My parents lived and died on the North Side, but I was living with my grandparents in

Ben Avon, a nice suburb just north of Three Rivers Stadium.

"I was a Steelers' fan, and they stunk. They had uniforms I hated, with yellow shoulder strips. I knew John Reger. He caused me to miss two games in my senior year at Avonworth High School. He hurt me playing touch tackle football at Bellevue Memorial Park. I was playing in a game with him and George Tarasovic, who had played for the Steelers but was with the Philadelphia Eagles at the time. I juked them a few times and they didn't like it. You know a lineman's mentality. So they got me."

He laughed at his own story.

"I liked John Henry Johnson, naturally. I liked Big Daddy Lipscomb. I liked Brady Keys — he opened up a chicken place and did well for himself in business, I'm told. I remember Bobby Layne and Earl Morrall. I can remember trying to sneak into a game in 1957 or 1958, and Earl Morrall was the quarterback. Now that's when I was a kid kid. I went to games at Forbes Field and Pitt Stadium."

Morris still insists he was set up by the police when he was arrested for drug trafficking. "And I was a willing participant. They put money under my nose and they didn't have a right to do that. I want people to know the truth. I want a chance to set the record straight. I'm not interested in revenge.

"But if you learn from your mistakes, you're better off. You live out of who you are. I'm trying to raise my children to be responsible people. I was guilty of being an asshole ten years ago, but I was not guilty of being a drug dealer.

"As far as football is concerned, I want people to check out my record, too. There are three guys who carried the ball over 700 times who averaged five or more yards a carry.

"Jim Brown is first at 5.2 yards per carry. Mercury Morris is second at 5.14 yards per carry. Gale Sayers is third at 5.0. When you're sandwiched in between guys like that, you must have been pretty good.

"I did that because I had to in order to stay on the field. It had to be at least second and five for me to stay in the game. I'd come in at third and nine and run for 11 yards, and come out.

"I was talking to Jim Brown about this just this year. He said there are guys today who gain a thousand yards, but they also carry the ball a thousand times. But I guess when you talk like that it's just a sign that you're getting old. Now I'm in Star Trek — The Last Generation."

Two of Mercury's favorite Steelers.

Brady Keys   Daddy Lipscomb

John Bruno
He left his mark

"I was in awe. I just couldn't believe our son was wearing a Steelers' uniform."
—Alfrieda Bruno

"His Steelers' jersey is still upstairs. He managed to hold onto that jersey. It meant a great deal to him."
—John Bruno, Sr.

Being a Steeler, no matter how briefly, is something special. For some, it is a medal of honor. It was that way with John Bruno who died from cancer at age 27 in April, 1992.

He used to like to tell a short story about his short stay with the Steelers. Just so people would believe he had been there. That was during a players' strike early in the 1987 campaign, and Bruno was one of the ballplayers brought in to represent the Steelers on a replacement squad in three regular season games.

"Mr. Rooney was coming through the locker room one day just as I came out of the showers," said Bruno. "I was just putting my underwear on when I turned around and there was Mr. Rooney, right in front of me.

"I was taken aback a little, but I managed to say, 'Hi, Mr. Rooney.' And he said, 'Ah, Bruno . . . Penn State . . . punter.' I didn't have my uniform on, or my number. But Mr. Rooney knew who I was."

That, of course, was the charm of Mr. Rooney, Art Rooney, Sr., the owner of the Pittsburgh Steelers. He was 86 at the time, and it would be the last season he would be a magic presence in the Steelers' locker room. He didn't need a program, even during a strike situation with a replacement squad in the locker room, to know who was playing for the Steelers.

"John used to feel ten feet tall when he told that story," said his father, John Sr.

It was a confirmation from the Steelers' patriarch. It certified that Bruno had, indeed, played for the Steelers. You can look it up. In the Steelers' official team guide, there is a Steelers All-Time Roster — from 1933 to 1992 — and there is a listing that reads like this:

Bruno, John (P), Penn State . . . 1987

That's it, right between Fred Bruney, a back from Ohio State, who played two seasons with the Steelers (1956-57), and Hubie Bryant, a wide receiver from Minnesota and Penn Hills High School, who played one season (1970).

John Sr., 56, a manager for product and market development at J&L Specialty Products, was unable to attend any of the three games in which his son punted for the Steelers. The Steelers won at Atlanta, lost at Los Angeles, and won at home against the Indianapolis Colts in that stretch. John Sr. was out of town on a business trip that last weekend.

Young John's mother, Alfrieda, was able to attend that game at Three Rivers Stadium. She didn't remember who the Steelers were playing that day, when we spoke. It didn't matter. She remembers seeing John punting the ball.

"I was in awe," she recalled. "I just couldn't believe our son was wearing a Steelers' uniform."

When the strike was settled, Bruno was one of several players from the replacement unit who were kept on during the transition period, but he was waived one week later. He was invited to come to camp the following summer, but he was cut after two pre-season games and a poor punting performance against the Philadelphia Eagles. The Steelers stuck with Harry Newsome as their punter for the 1988 season, and Bruno was back in the stands.

Newsome had an NFL record six punts blocked that year. "Some of my friends said to me that year that I should feel lucky that it wasn't me getting those punts blocked. But I said, 'the heck with that.' I would have loved wearing a Steelers' uniform all season, even if I had all of my punts blocked," said Bruno.

Bruno's agent, Mt. Lebanon lawyer Ralph Cindrich, arranged for a tryout with the Buffalo Bills, but Bruno also failed to make the grade there. So he returned home.

"No one expected me to punt at Penn State in the first place. I'll keep doing this as long as the opportunities are there," said Bruno.

"His Steelers' jersey is still upstairs," said his father when we spoke the week after John's funeral. "He managed to hold onto that jersey. It meant a great deal to him."

When he was a teenager, John Bruno's bedroom had Steelers' posters all over the walls and that wasn't long ago.

The Steelers were searching for a punter in the winter of 1992. Dan Syrzysinki had reportedly reneged on a verbal agreement to remain with the Steelers after they had put him on the Plan B free agent list, and signed with the Tampa Bay Buccaneers. The Steelers, in turn, signed Mark Royals, who had punted for the Buccaneers the year before. Royals' record was suspect, so the Steelers might have been interested if John Bruno wanted to make a comeback. After all, he was only 27.

A couple of Bruno's friends told him he would have been a worthy candidate, small talk to cheer him up.

But Bruno was not well. He had learned in December that the skin cancer that had been originally detected when he was a student at Penn State University, and was thought to have been cleared up, had come back. And it had come back with a vengeance. "Melanoma can be insidious once it gets going," said his father. The cancer had spread, and doctors had detected three inoperable tumors.

John Bruno of Upper St. Clair and Penn State.

Bruno knew he was in big trouble.

I learned about Bruno's illness within two months after I had heard about a young woman in our neighborhood having cancer. She was a few years behind Bruno as a student at Upper St. Clair High School, but they had walked the same halls at the same time. It hurts everyone to hear about young people with such serious illnesses. Both families were among the best people I know in our community. Why? That's a word that was on a lot of people's lips when they learned about it. It made everyone feel vulnerable. It shakes your faith.

I spoke to young John one day on the telephone, but he was not in the mood to talk much. I could appreciate that.

John succumbed to cancer on Monday, April 13 at Montefiore University Hospital in Oakland, just below Pitt Stadium where he had once performed for the Penn State football team. "It was at 5:40 p.m.," said his father. They are dates and numbers he and his wife will never forget. And the father impressed me with his memory of dates and details in his family's history.

The father remembers the Saturday night that preceded it, and what went on in Room 287 at Montefiore University Hospital.

"I'll never be able to replace the last night with him. He had lost most of his bodily functions, but his brain was still sharp. He looked so weak as he was lying in his bed. But he said, 'Dad, I want to stand up.' I helped him to his feet. And he just fell against me and I was holding him up. He hugged me. He gave me a big bear hug, the best he could muster. He wanted to get up just so he could do that.

"We had hugged, as a father and son will do on occasion, but the only other time we had hugged like that was when we met after the Fiesta Bowl back in 1987. He had come out of the locker room, and he had hugged his mother, and then his sister, and then I heard him saying, 'Where's Dad?' And he spotted me and came running over, and gave me a great big bear hug."

When John's dad shared that story with me, tears came to my eyes. That was the first time that had happened to me during any of the interviews for my books on the Steelers. It happened again as I wrote this. Bruno's dad told me that story in a measured, soft-spoken way, and it pointed up the depth of his love and his loss. His eyes were wet as well.

Some thought Bruno should have been the MVP in that Fiesta Bowl triumph that clinched a national championship for Penn State. Bruno punted nine times for a 43.4 yard average in the Lions' 14-10 victory over Miami and angled several punts inside the 20 to pin Miami's potent offense deep in its own territory.

"When we won the national championship against Miami we wouldn't have won it without him," said Penn State coach Joe Paterno. "He was good in the clutch. He was as responsible as anyone for bringing Penn State its national championship."

Aside from his punting feats, Bruno may have been best known for his performance as the master of ceremonies at a steak fry dinner a few days before the game. He was reported to have done a "David

432

Letterman-like monologue." Fran Ganter, Penn State's offensive coordinator, remembers the scene well. Ganter's wife, Karen, was Bruno's second cousin.

"It was a team function," Ganter recalled. "And one of the Miami players said, 'When we play Penn State, it'll be like the Japanese bombing Pearl Harbor.' "

Bruno later replied when he had the mike, "I may not have been a great student, but I know a little history . . . Didn't the Japanese lose the war?"

The Miami team exited the steak fry in a huff, but they had planned on departing early, anyhow, as part of their psychological warfare game. They were all wearing camouflage fatigues to enhance their tough guy image. But Bruno had already gotten the best of them. "I thought we were supposed to have some fun here," he said.

Said Ganter: "He had a true sense of humor."

Bruno had spared no one with his wit, making fun of both Miami coach Jimmy Johnson and his stiff-sprayed hairdo ("Clairol would like to thank him for doubling the hair spray profits") as well as his own coach, Joe Paterno. "He was quick — a great mimic," Paterno said. "A lot of guys said he did a great (impression of) me."

Bruno was a popular player, a natural team leader. He had a good time, but he gained the respect of his fellow players, and everyone who associated with him. He was different, and marched to the beat of a different drummer, like most kickers.

There was something special about him.

It was Good Friday and it looked the part. It was overcast and gray, and it looked like it might rain at any minute. I was in Irwin to pay my respects to the Bruno family. Young John was on view at the Vincent Rodgers Funeral Home at 805 Pennsylvania Avenue in Irwin.

I had arranged to meet a good friend for lunch beforehand at Angelo's Italian Ristorante on Route 30. I knew Bill Priatko would want to go to the funeral. He, too, had played one season with the Steelers, as a linebacker back in 1957. He had put in parts of seasons with the Cleveland Browns and Green Bay Packers as well. He is a great admirer of Art Rooney and Chuck Noll, and feels a special kinship with anybody who has ever played football or sports in general.

He lives in North Huntingdon. His wife, Helen, has had a long battle with cancer. One of his four children, a son, Danny, was left partially paralyzed in an auto accident soon after being graduated from West Point, but has waged a tremendous comeback. The Priatkos are great people, with great faith, and they know many of the same people out in Westmoreland County who count themselves as friends of the Bruno family. I knew Bill knew his way around town, and he would be a good scout.

After lunch, Bill took me into business district of Irwin, and introduced me to his barber, Dave Anderson, who was giving a middle-aged man a buzz-cut, and local shopkeepers, like Mike Javor, who owns a men's clothing store, and some citizens I had met the summer before at a Norwin Rotary luncheon, like Bill Snyder, a funeral director, and Will Bailey, a retired businessman. All of them knew about the Brunos. They pointed out a place where John Jr.'s grandmother once owned the Western Avenue Restaurant. The Brunos had strong roots in the community.

I stopped in at the First Presbyterian Church. It's on the corner of Main Street, right across the way from the John Irwin House, built in 1914, once the residence of the man the town is named after. There was a warmth about the church, even when it was empty, that was inviting. The pews were padded in burgundy cloth. The pews rose on an incline toward the rear of the room. It was like a small off-Broadway theatre.

The service was held there the next day at 11 a.m. Dr. Laird Stuart, the pastor of Westminster Presbyterian Church in Upper St. Clair, where the Brunos have been members for years, conducted the service.

He read a poem called "To An Athlete Dying Young."
"The time you won your town the race
We cheered you through the market place
Man and boy stood cheering by
And home we brought you shoulder high
Smart lad, to slip sometimes away
From fields where glory does not stay
And early though the laurel grows
It withers quicker than the rose
Eyes the shady night has shut
Cannot see the record cut
And silence sounds no worse than cheers
Rich earth has stopped the ears

John Bruno Sr. said the first person to show up at the funeral home in Irwin for the initial viewing period on Thursday night was Dennis Fitzgerald, the former special teams coach of the Steelers when young Bruno was on the ballclub.

There was a basket of flowers from Dan Rooney and the Steelers, and the Brunos received a beautiful sympathy card from Art Rooney, Jr., with a personal note. Their father taught them well.

Once inside the Rodgers Funeral Home, I recognized several young athletes. There was Joey David and Alex Kartsonas, whom I knew from the days they were athletes at Pitt. They had played sports with Bruno at Upper St. Clair High School. The hallway was full of husky young men who had played football with Bruno at Penn State. Todd Moules, Don Ginnetti and Mike Russo were pointed out to me.

John's sister, Cheryl, 30, who is also a Penn State graduate, spoke to many of them. "I thought John was going to beat this," she said, "because he was such a fighter."

Tom Bradley, who handled the special teams when Bruno was at Penn State, was also there. "He was very well liked by a lot of people," said Bradley. "He was always good fun. He was a practical joker, but not at anyone else's expense. Just his whole attitude . . . he was a guy you liked being around.

"He and our place-kicker, Massimo Manca, were both terrific. We weren't just coach-player in our relationship; we went golfing together, we were really friends.

"When Bruno was playing for Jim Render at Upper St. Clair, Ganter told me to check him out. After all, his wife is a Bruno. John played wide receiver and was a punter. I told Fran, 'I don't think he can play wide receiver for us, but he could be an excellent punter.'

"The first year (at Penn State), he sat behind George Reynolds. He got the job as a sophomore when Reynolds graduated and George Montgomery transferred to Michigan State. Now Montgomery punts for the Houston Oilers. John got drafted by the St. Louis Cardinals in 1987. He was taken on the fifth round, and he was the first punter drafted.

"A lot of our instructional punting tapes that we show kids at our summer camps have John in them. John used to work at our summer camps, and he was great with the kids. I just wish we had recorded what he said for a voice-over. It will be tough to watch those films now.

"Our whole team knew John well. He never had a bad day. He had a certain grin, like an I'm-gonna-get-in-trouble grin. He was a good spirit. A lot of times it's hard for kickers to be a real part of the team. But he was our Good Humor Man. I was OK till yesterday, but I lost it when I saw him here last night."

Joe Paterno attended the funeral service, along with Bob Phillips, one of his top assistants and once the head coach at Montour High School. Paterno offered his condolences to the Bruno family.

"I've known Joe since 1953," said John Bruno Sr. "He was the quarterback coach, an assistant to Rip Engle, when I was on the team. I was no big deal; I was on the team, that's about it."

He lettered as a wingback in 1956. He wore No. 11, which his son would later wear for the Lions. "Our teams were better known" said John Sr., "for having Lenny Moore, Rosey Grier and Milt Plum."

It meant a lot to the Brunos that Paterno and some of his assistants, and about 25 Penn State players attended the funeral. "There is something about the sports community," said John Bruno Sr. "We've had unbelievable support these past few months. Joe Paterno is a very private, personal guy, but he comes through for his players. People don't appreciate that, but he's special that way. These last few months have been difficult, but it helped to have people caring. John's friends and former teammates came to see John at the hospital and at our home. And he had a good time when they came to visit."

Paterno was proud to have known John Bruno and his family. "Everyone in the Penn State football family is saddened today," said Paterno. "John was an outstanding person and an outstanding athlete. He was always positive and had the kind of engaging personality that made him a pleasure to be around.

"As long as they play football here, people will always remember John's brilliant punting performance in the Fiesta Bowl. He was a great kid and a delight to be around. He was loved by everyone and he was a fun guy. It's a terrible loss."

Those sentiments were echoed in a letter I received from L. Budd Thalman, the associate athletic director for communications at Penn State. As a student sportswriter at Pitt, I knew Thalman when he was the sports information director at Navy during Roger Staubach's days, and as a pro football writer I knew him when he was the publicity director of the New England Patriots. He has always been a class act.

"Since the 1986 team was my first at Penn State, it will always have a special place in my memory," wrote Thalman. "John Bruno was such a happy-go-lucky young man that it's hard to understand why he has been taken from us.

"In looking through John's file to come up with the photographs you requested, I found a lovely letter from his mother, written after we had sent a copy of a program article to the family. It's obvious from the note that John came from a very loving home, with parents who had a real interest in him and what he did."

Bruno still holds Penn State records for punts in a season (79 in 1984); punting yardage in a season (3,273 in 1984), and ranks behind only Ralph Giacomarro in season punting average with a mark of 42.9 yards in 1985. For a career, Bruno's 41.7 average is topped only by George Reynolds (43.0) and Giacomarro (41.8).

He left his mark in more ways than one at Happy Valley.

John and Alfrieda Bruno had buried their son the previous Saturday, the day before Easter. I knew them too well to write about their son without their blessing. They wanted to share his story, it was good to talk about him, and they wanted to celebrate his life. They wanted people to remember him. They said their son would be honored to have his story in the same book as some of the greatest of the Steelers.

There was a painting of a lion at rest in a jungle setting behind the couch where they sat. There was a gold lion figurine atop a nearby television set. This was a Penn State home, no doubt about it. There was more of the same in the gamerooms downstairs.

It was dank and drizzling outside, but the Brunos were both smiling, and they warmed the room in a hurry when I came to talk with them. Like them, I knew exactly where I was the previous Saturday at 11 a.m. I was standing on the frontsteps of the home of ex-Steeler Terry Long in Franklin Park. We had scheduled a meeting. Long was not there, however. There was a Howard Hanna Realtors "For Sale" sign on his lawn. A few days later, I called him to see what happened, and his telephone had been disconnected. When I had telephoned him several times the previous month, I always connected with an answering machine that ended with this message from Long:

"Always believe in your dream. And may God bless you."

The Long no-show disappointment contrasted greatly with what I was doing on the same day the week before, having breakfast with

Steelers legend "Bullet Bill" Dudley at a country club in Charlottesville, Virginia, which was a thrill. What a difference a week can make.

"Thank God we have our faith," said Alfrieda Bruno. "It helps us carry on after something like this."

She is from Herminie and her husband is from Rillton, little communities just outside Irwin. His father was also named John Bruno, John Currie Bruno for the record, and he was a legendary coach at Sewickley Township and Yough High School.

"My dad was a coach for 35 years," said John Bruno.

He explained how there was once a Norwin High, and then a split into North Huntingdon and Irwin, and then a merger back to Norwin High. In between, Irwin had a Class B state championship basketball team that put the community on the map. Sports were always important. I mentioned that I liked the look of Irwin, and that it seemed like a nice place to live.

"Our first house was in Irwin, and young John spent time there in his boyhood," said his father. "I moved around a lot in my job at J&L, to Atlanta and to Cincinnati — John followed the Falcons, but we never became Bengals fans — before we came back to Pittsburgh, and moved into Upper St. Clair. We came here at the height of the Steelers' success.

"In his last two years, John spent a lot of time back in the Irwin area. His girlfriend, Karen Kortas, told us he often took her there, to point out his grandmother's house, and to show her the football field that was named after my dad.

"It was the original Sewickley High School field, but now it is used by midget football teams."

I asked him if it was true that his dad died while he was coaching.

"It happened on October 16, 1970 at Brentwood Stadium," he said. "We were living in Atlanta at the time, and I got a phone call at nine o'clock in the evening. The assistant coach, Allan Smith, called. He called me 'Currie' because there were too many Johns in our family. He said, 'Currie, we're at the South Side Hospital, and you need to talk to your mother.' He put her on, and that's when I was told that my dad had died.

"My dad had his team say a prayer in a huddle on the field before every game. He was about 5-7 1/2 or 5-8 and a full-blooded Italian, and he wore a hat. He was known for always wearing that hat. He was coaching at Yough High at the time. He had his hat over his heart during the playing of the National Anthem, and someone took a picture of him like that. Five minutes later he was dead. He was 58 when he died of a heart attack."

Alfrieda added a footnote to that story: "He wore the same hat all the time. My mother-in-law had it bronzed."

"My mother was English," said John Sr. "Her maiden name was Cook."

The Brunos shared a letter they had received from Dr. James A. Whiteside, director, medical aspects of sports, at the Alabama Sports Medicine & Orthopaedic Center in Birmingham. Dr. Whiteside was at Penn State when a dark mole was first discovered on Bruno's back, just under his left shoulder blade.

He wrote of his reaction to reading in the newspaper about the death of their son.

"My office notes from July 19, 1985, reveal an entry on John's chart about a pigmented nevus (colored mole) on his back that concerned me. Then its removal and later the wide excision by Dr. Perri in Pittsburgh. My conversation with Mrs. Bruno and Coach Paterno are noted. The relief when John punted for the first time thereafter 8/28/85 is expressed.

"Since my return to Birmingham in 1987 to work with James R. Andrews, a noted sports orthopedist, many former players' names and persons have crossed my path. None caused a greater stir in my heart than the news about John. Why? I guess I had considered him well. John made me proud in ways not obvious to others."

In the stories about his passing, John Bruno Jr. was always referred to as a walk-on punter at Penn State. But he didn't just show up for practice one day to anyone's surprise. He had been invited to come to Penn State, even though he was not offered a scholarship initially. "Joe called him a run-on," said his father. John Jr. had also visited Louisville, Marshall and Lafayette, who had expressed an interest in him.

His parents shared a copy of an essay young John had written to officials at Lafayette:

"An achievement that stands out in my life are the honors I have received in football during my senior year. All my life, I have been brought up around football. My father played football at Penn State University and his father was a high school football coach.

"As long as I can remember, I have been taken to football games on the high school, college and pro levels. I always loved to play football in schoolyards and parking lots. My father encouraged me to practice football among other sports in the backyard.

"I always dreamed of playing football in high school. Since I started playing organized football in middle school and on through to high school, my games were always viewed by my parents and a few relatives.

"It was always encouraging to know my family was watching me play. I felt like I owed them something in return. I always tried to play as hard as I could for them. All the practice and encouragement paid off when I received various honors for football in my junior and senior years. As a junior, I was named to the Western All-Conference team as punter. As a senior, I was named to the All-Western Conference, the All-South and All-WPIAL all-star teams as a split end. Earning these awards was my way of showing my family how much their encouragement meant to me. Accomplishing these high school honors was once a dream. However, I now have a dream to play football in college and I hope my family will be behind me to help make this new dream come true."

His dad remembers when John made up his mind about his college choice.

"John made the decision to go to Penn State on the way back from a visit to Lafayette. We stopped at Penn State to see someone. John and I walked around the campus, and he said, 'Dad, I'm going to go here.' That was it. He was there for five years. In his last two seasons, we never missed a game, home or away. They won 23 of 24 games during those two years, losing only to Miami in the Orange Bowl."

Young John once explained his preference for Penn State. "I've always been a Penn State fan. My father played for Penn State and my sister went to school there, too. I grew up in Pittsburgh, but I was never a Pitt fan."

Thinking about her son's last few years, Alfrieda said, "We were wondering what direction he was going to take over the last two years. He never seemed interested in a nine to five job. He never found his calling. He was an analytical type, and we thought he might get into finance. I thought he was such a great speaker that I was hoping, as a mother might, that he would become a minister. I saw him in that light."

He was working in sales with golf equipment at Cool Springs golf complex in Bethel Park before he got sick.

"Then we learned about his cancer and we knew the odds were greatly against him," said his father. "We never saw him shed a tear, except for the first day that he was told about his condition. You called him early when he was still having difficulty accepting what had happened to him. But any time his friends came around, he was upbeat. It was only Alfrieda, and his girlfriend Karen, and I who saw him in bad moments. We were trying so hard to believe he would be all right.

"He had some operations, like on his colon, and he was not in great spirits after those. But he'd bounce back fast."

"He never complained," added Alfrieda.

"It was tough for us," said John Sr., "to realize how sick he was. I knew early on, from the doctors, that he was gravely ill. His effort to do whatever the doctors wanted him to do was admirable. He never complained, as Alfrieda said. He had an analytical mind. He knew what he should do, what to eat, and he made every effort to do what was asked of him.

"He taught me that nowhere in my life should I ever complain about what's ailing me. When I think of all the tests he went through: the CAT scans, the liquids he had to drink . . . he just accepted it, and did it. I don't know how he did it.

"We have a lot of paperwork to do to get his affairs in order. I wrote to Joe Paterno and thanked him. I just wanted to make sure we recognized all the efforts of the players on the Penn State team. The sincerity and deep faith expressed by all those guys was overwhelming. I think it's the same type of thing that carried those guys through those last two seasons at Penn State when they lost only one game. The leader of that team was John Shaffer. He was the quarterback. He never made it in the pros, but he is a fantastic guy. He was a good quarterback and he's an even better person."

439

The Brunos put on a brave face and comforted those who came to comfort them.

Said Alfrieda, "I kept thinking he was going to get well. On the Friday night before he died, John was asked how he felt by Dr. Stuart Silverman, a physician at Montefiore. He and John Kirkwood were his main doctors. And John said, 'It's not over till it's over.' He always gave us hope."

The Brunos called and invited me back to their home a few nights later. They wanted to show me something. When I got there, John Sr. and Alfrieda, led me downstairs to the gamerooms they had spoken about at our first meeting.

There was a pool table in the center of the first room. There were trophies John Jr. had been given that filled up one corner of the room. There were family photos and portraits of the Brunos from way back, but everywhere there were more photos and plaques of John Jr.

Then they took me into the next room. This room was loaded with Penn State paraphernalia. "You'll have to forgive me for bringing you into rooms with all this Penn State stuff," apologized John Sr. "I know it's got to be tough on a Pitt man." There were more plaques and pennants and photos of John Jr.

"Our daughter, Cheryl, always called this 'John's shrine' when she lived here," said Alfrieda.

Then I was taken upstairs to John's old room. His Steelers' jersey — with BRUNO and No. 10 on the back of it — draped his bedspread. Behind it were three different Penn State jerseys — with BRUNO and No. 11 on them — and they were folded neatly in a stack.

There were boxes all over the floor, filled with game programs, letters, scrapbooks. There were newspaper clippings of every Penn State game and preview stories from the years John Jr. was on the team. Wherever his name was mentioned, even in the boxscore, his mother had highlighted the name with a yellow marker. They were all pasted so neatly under cellophane. A mother's handiwork was evident.

There were yellowed newspaper clippings about his grandfather, too, the legendary coach at Sewickley Township and Yough High School. I read an article about how his grandfather had fashioned football teams with the sons of coalminers in central Westmoreland County. His record as a head coach was 150-70-15, a .633 winning percentage.

One story, written upon the coach's death, alluded to him as someone "who always seemed in such good spirits." Sound familiar?

"His mother kept everything for him," said John Sr. "John always thought it was too much. But I think it's something he might have enjoyed if he were able to sit down, say ten years from now, and look through all this. It's a little overwhelming."

Sal Sunseri
He came so close to being a Steeler

"When I came out of surgery, and first opened my eyes, I saw my family. And right behind them was Mr. Rooney."

It would have been quite a success story: Hometown Boy Suceeds With Steelers. But it didn't quite work out that way for Sal Sunseri. He came close, closer than most kids who came up at the same time as he did during the glory days of the Steelers, and wanted to be just like them.

He was a year ahead of Danny Marino at both Central Catholic and the University of Pittsburgh. He grew up in Greenfield, on a hilltop across a valley not far from Marino's home in South Oakland, and won All-WPIAL honors for the Vikings. He stayed home and went to Pitt, where he was a captain and an All-America linebacker in 1981, and one of the school's most popular performers in years.

Sal had been named the defensive MVP for the North squad in the Senior Bowl, and had captained the East defense in the East-West Classic.

At the urging of owner Art Rooney, the Steelers selected Sunseri as their tenth draft pick in 1982.

Sunseri had a sunshine personality, could talk a blue streak, his family had an Italian food store in The Strip, and he was perfect for Pittsburgh and the Steelers. He was undersized, for sure, at something less than six feet, but he had a big heart, and he was determined to make the Steelers.

He was feisty, and he got into a fight the first day of "Oklahoma" drills at St. Vincent College, and people were aware of his presence. He was a self-promoter in the best sense, and the sportswriters loved him and were rooting for him.

But he sprained his right knee at training camp, and spent two seasons on injured reserve. He never suited up for a game, pre-season or otherwise, for the Steelers. So close, yet so far.

He returned to Pitt and became an assistant coach for Foge Fazio, who had urged him to come to Pitt in the first place, and he was the only assistant to stay on when Mike Gottfried got the job. Now he is on Paul Hackett's staff and is regarded as one of the program's top recruiters. Before spring practice began in March of 1992, Sunseri was named assistant head coach by Hackett.

Somewhere in between, he married Roxann Evans. They have three children, Jaclyn, 5, Santino, 3, and Vinnie, five months at the time we interviewed their father in late March. "Roxann came to Pitt on a gymnastics scholarship, and I came as a walk-on for the football team," said Sunseri. "And I was really a walk-on; I didn't have to walk too far to get here."

Sunseri is especially good at selling local kids and their families at staying home, and having family and friends in the stands at Pitt Stadium when they are playing college football. That's always been important to him.

"I feel I'm lucky and fortunate to have been able to experience all that I've done here in my hometown and to have been able to stay in one place, and to have my family and friends watch me grow," said Sunseri when we spoke. "My goal is to become a head coach someday, and to go to a bowl game, and to have my parents there, and to have them tell everyone around them, 'Hey, that's my son out there!' "

On a clear night you can see forever, or at least you get an impressive view of Pittsburgh, standing outside Sal Sunseri's boyhood home in Greenfield.

His home is just above the Parkway East near the Murray Avenue Bridge. From high atop Welfer Street, the sort of steep incline that made San Francisco famous, you can see a side of the city that is not often caught on canvas, or with a camera. But it didn't escape the eye of Sal Sunseri's mother.

"That's why we bought the house here," she said. "On a clear day you can actually see the river rolling. It's so pretty."

At night, this particular night anyhow back on June 29, 1982, you could see the U.S. Steel Building, now known as the USX Tower, straight ahead. You could see the Cathedral of Learning to the right. If the lights were on, you would be able to see Three Rivers Stadium on the far horizon.

"You can't actually see the Stadium, but you can see the light in the sky over it," said Ann Sunseri. "It glows when a game is going on there."

On that starry night, Sal could see himself playing for the Steelers in that stadium some day. It would be a dream come true for a young man who always followed Foge Fazio's exhortation to dare to dream.

There was a party at the Sunseri home that June night to celebrate Sal's good fortune. That same day, the second of a two-day National Football League draft process, he had been selected by the Steelers on the tenth round.

Typical of Sal, he not only invited family and friends and school chums, but he personally invited just about every member of the sports media in Pittsburgh to his place. With Sal, it seemed natural enough. To him, they were all his friends. Any publicity it might stir up would simply be more icing on his homemade cake.

There was a glow about the faces of Ann Sunseri, her husband Anthony, a wholesale food broker, and, most of all, their youngest child, Sal.

"This is a dream come true," said Sal, a high-spirited soul whom one Pitt official labeled the best football team leader at the school in 15 years. "I want to make that team so bad. I've just got to do what I did at Pitt."

442

University of Pittsburgh

Sal Sunseri as All-American linebacker at Pitt

Art Rooney, who frequently attended games at Pitt Stadium, recommended Sunseri to Chuck Noll and his staff — "He'll just give you everything he's got," he told them — and Sunseri had a chance to play for a team, and along with a player, Jack Ham, he had idolized since his days at Central Catholic.

His mother said it was rough on the first day of the draft when her son was not selected. "You wish for your son," Ann Sunseri said. "Sal's a good boy. He handled it better than I did. I never in my wildest dreams could've expected Pittsburgh to pick him. I can't believe it happened."

Sal Sunseri's friends figured it had to happen. After all, Sal had been living under blue skies all his life. So Jimmy Morsillo of Ambridge, a former teammate of Sal at Pitt, carried a case of champagne into the Sunseri home, and there were plenty of hands to help lighten the load.

Family and friends filled the house. Pitt coach Foge Fazio came early, with several of his assistants, including Dino Folino, who grew up and was still spending a great deal of time in Greenfield.

Danny Marino, the All-America quarterback who was just a junior at Pitt, joined in the festivities. Steeler fans will cringe when reminded of what he said that night. "I envy Sal," said Marino. "I wish the Steelers would select me. I'd love to play for them."

Art Rooney would have seconded that motion. That same year, he had told us, "We've got to find a way to keep that kid in Pittsburgh. He could be Terry Bradshaw's successor."

Emil Boures, who was the Steelers' seventh round pick, was there, along with Tommy Flynn, J.C. Pelusi, Phil Puzzuoli, Rob Fada, Bill Maas and Ron Killen from the Pitt football team.

It's interesting to reflect back now on who was there that evening. It was thought that Pitt might have a national championship team the next season, but it turned out to be a relatively disappointing one, considering the talent that was on that team. Present day pros like Jimbo Covert, Bill Fralic, Jim Sweeney, Chris Doleman and Carlton Williamson were also on that 1982 team.

Marino's sister, Cindi, an 18-year-old freshman at Pitt the night of that party at the Sunseri home, would marry Maas, but it would be a short-lived marriage, ending in divorce. Marino would marry Clair Veazy, who was then dating Gusty Sunseri, Sal's older brother, an attorney and Marino's original agent.

That night in Greenfield, several of the Pitt guys were watching a video tape of Pitt's Sugar Bowl victory (24-20) over Georgia. "I want Georgia with five points," joked Marino during the first quarter.

Lloyd Weston, who had come out of Westinghouse High to play at Pitt, and had remained on as an academic advisor to athletes, was at the party.

When Jimmy Pol's "The Steeler Fight Song of 1980" was played on the record machine, and those familiar refrains about Franco and Rocky were sounded, Weston shouted, "Next year they've got to get Sal's name in there!"

Sportscaster Myron Cope was dancing with Danny Marino's mother, Veronica, and WTAE's Bill Hillgrove, "the voice of Pitt," was tapping his feet to the music.

"Only in Pittsburgh," exclaimed Alex Kramer, an administrative assistant to Fazio at Pitt. He could have said, "Only in Greenfield."

The Sunseris bring sunshine into everybody's life with whom they come in contact. So, after a two hour visit, you get a kiss goodbye because you've become a part of the family.

Art Rooney had told everybody that Sal Sunseri would be a star on the Steelers' special teams. "Some of those hotshots today don't want to play on special teams," Rooney remarked during the second day of the 1982 draft. "All Sunseri will give you is everything he's got."

Sunseri showed up at the Steelers' offices soon after he was selected. He had his sleeves rolled up and he was ready to go to work. He bumped into Steve Courson in the parking lot outside Three Rivers Stadium, and they had already set a date to get together to lift weights.

"Donnie Shell signed as a free agent and he was a demon on special teams," said Sunseri, showing his awareness of Steelers' history. "I'd like to be the leader on the special teams."

Inside the door of the Steelers' offices, the first person Sunseri saw was Rocky Bleier. That was appropriate. Bleier had been a 16th round draft pick in 1968 who made it big with the Steelers, despite seemingly overwhelming obstacles.

"I can't compare myself to him because he's already proven himself," said Sunseri. "But he's an inspiration because they said all the same things about him when he came out of Notre Dame — that he was too small, too slow, all that stuff."

That's the same thing they said about Dick Haley when he came out of Pitt back in the '50s, but he was a fine defensive back and kick returner for the Washington Redskins and Steelers. Haley headed the Steelers' scouting department in 1982. He's now with the Jets.

Talking about Sunseri and Boures, both considered on the small and slow side, Dick Haley said, "We've made a living here on guys who weren't tall enough. Mike Webster wasn't big enough or fast enough, either. They're football players and that's what we're after."

Sunseri was sporting a New York Yankees jacket and a San Francisco 49ers ballcap when he showed up at the Steelers' offices, but his heart had always been with the Steelers. To him it was the next natural step in his career.

"I played my high school ball at Central Catholic, and then I played my college ball at Pitt," he explained. "The Steelers are the next step in football in this town, right?

Sunseri was seated in his office at Pitt Stadium, in an office complex built during the Johnny Majors years under the seats in the endzone

445

closest to downtown Pittsburgh. Spring practice for the 1992 campaign was under way, and Sunseri had recently been promoted to assistant head football coach on Paul Hackett's staff.

Sunseri was a survivor. Assistant coaches had come and gone during the previous ten years, as had two head coaches — Fazio and Gottfried — yet Sal stayed on, and was moving up in the collegiate football world, well ahead of his personal timetable.

"I'm only 32, and this gives me a chance to become what I wanted to become from the first day I got into this," he said. "My goal is to become a head coach.

"I'm excited about my new position. If Paul Hackett isn't around, I'm running the ship. It gives me a chance to get more acquainted and involved with the administrative end of things, to learn about budgeting and academics and to broaden my horizons."

When I mentioned how he had survived the turmoil and the change of coaches, he said, "I look at it as a positive. I've done a good job, and people have recognized that. And Hackett has just put the icing on the cake."

Sunseri believes in what he is doing. "You have to sell something, and Pitt is something I can sell," he said. "I have the strongest local contacts on the staff, and for us to be successful we have to keep the best high school players in western Pennsylvania right here.

"I started out as a grad assistant for Foge. He gave me my first opportunity. Then he put me in charge of the defensive line. Mike Gottfried came in and kept me. He put me in charge of the linebackers. Alex Kramer, our administrative assistant, was the only other holdover on the staff."

I reminded Sunseri of the events of the draft of 1982 when he and teammate Emil Boures were both selected by the Steelers. Boures was a versatile performer who could play every offensive line position and won early favor with Chuck Noll, and stayed five seasons. Sal spent two seasons on injured reserve, and never suited up for the Steelers in any kind of a game. So Sunseri is not listed in the Steelers' all-time roster. He came so close, and somehow he feels like he was a Steeler. In some respects, he will always feel like a Steeler. Just as Pitt will always be a part of his heart.

"To me, it was fantastic getting an opportunity to be with the Steelers," said Sunseri. "A local guy growing up in the city, and being here when they won the Super Bowls, and going to Pitt and being drafted by the Steelers . . . what more could I ask for? When I went with the Steelers, I thought I had a chance to go to a Super Bowl with them.

"One of the most impressive things was the way Mr. Rooney treated me. He knew everything that was going on. He knew every single player; every single player was important. Everybody in the stadium was important, from the guys on the ground crew to the top brass. He took care of them. He said hello to everybody. He knew everybody's name.

"When I got hurt, he talked to me. I was operated on at Divine Providence Hospital, and he was there. I know why he was successful.

When I came out of surgery, and first opened my eyes, I saw my family was there. And right behind them was Mr. Rooney.

"I hurt my right knee at training camp. It was in the second or third week of practice. It was a rainy day. And we were scrimmaging. The offense ran a short trap, and Tyrone McGriff was pulling out to block. I tried to take him down. He was so big, I knew I had to go low. He fell on me, and someone slid in from behind. I heard my knee pop. When I heard the pop, I knew it wasn't very good. I can still hear that popping sound.

"After the surgery, they put me on an extensive rehabilitation program. I got back late in the season. The Steelers made the playoffs that year. They were getting ready for the final game of the season against the Cleveland Browns. I worked on the 'scout team' to show our offense what the Cleveland defense would look like. Cleveland had a small nose tackle in Bob Golic. So they put me in there to be Golic. I'm going up against Mike Webster and Steve Courson. That was some experience. I learned what it was like to play nose tackle against those monsters. On one play, they picked me up and the next thing I knew I was ten yards downfield.

"The Steelers were very classy. They gave me every single opportunity to show what I could do. The following year, I felt good. They had been patient, and I thought it was going to pay off. I was up at camp at St. Vincent, and I was coming off the field one day. Somebody called my name. I turned to see who it was and my knee just went out on me. That was it. I was finished. I was on I.R. for another year.

"In my eyes, the Steelers showed me so much class. They were going to give a local kid a chance to play in front of family and friends. They gave me a long time to get better. They tried to fulfill the dream of a local boy. Who knows? Why did the Lord say it's time to get on with your life's work?

"But it gave me a chance to get into football coaching early. Now I'm in a position I probably wouldn't be in at my age, had I put in five or six years in the pros. I would have loved to have played for the Pittsburgh Steelers. But it's worked out just fine. At the time, it was frustrating. Now I don't feel so bad about it.

"I had a chance to line up with Ham and Lambert and Loren Toews as a linebacker, and go against Mike Webster and Franco. For a guy who grew up here and idolized all those guys, it was a real fantasy trip.

"I can remember when the Steelers came back from their first Super Bowl victory. It was January of 1975, and I was 15 and a sophomore at Central Catholic, and I rode out to the airport with some other guys from Greenfield to welcome them back. I remember I couldn't believe how big Ernie Holmes was. I couldn't believe how big and lean L.C. Greenwood was.

"That went through my mind when I was at the Steelers' camp. Here I was with so many of those guys who got off the plane that day. Now I'm with them. Maybe some day I'll be getting off the plane with the Steelers. But it wasn't meant to be.

"Just watching Ham and Lambert. They taught me how to play the game, how to think the game. I learned so much from them, and so much from Chuck Noll. He was big on teaching, and he taught the fundamentals.

"I have to be thankful. How many young men went to Central Catholic and the University of Pittsburgh, and got to be with the Steelers the way I did? Not too many people have stayed in Pittsburgh the way I have and had all these thrills.

"I can remember when I was in grade school at St. Philomena's in Squirrel Hill, and we were at the Kentucky Fried Chicken outlet on the Boulevard of the Allies in Oakland, right by the Playhouse, and I saw Terry Bradshaw and some other Steeler sitting on the corner eating chicken. I went over and asked Terry for his autograph.

"Years later, when I wasn't able to practice with the Steelers, I'd be standing on the sideline, and Terry would throw passes to me. Now I used to catch passes from Danny Marino, so I thought I was up to the task. I dropped the first three balls Bradshaw threw to me. That spiral was so tight, and it came at you so hard . . . I felt a little foolish. But then I started holding on to them.

"Just catching passes from Bradshaw was a big thrill for me. The whole thing was an unbelievable experience. I was paid for two seasons and that helped me get started. It made it possible for me to afford some things, and get married when I did. I wouldn't change it for the world.

"Chuck Noll taught us not to get caught up in that game of what might have been, what could have been, what should have been. I mean, I kid my dad about it. I tell him, 'If you were only 5-6, I might have been drafted higher.' But he wasn't. So I was 5-11 1/2, 220 pounds when I was with the Steelers.

"After I was drafted, I felt so good walking around the city. 'That's Sal Sunseri,' someone would say, 'He's with the Steelers now.' There was so much pride. I felt so special.

"The Steelers have struggled since then. They haven't been the championship team that they were. But they're still special. And one of the happiest days of my life was when I became a Steeler."

Assistant Coach, 1991   Pitt Captain, 1981

Terry Long
"I'm always worried about keeping my job."

*"The bottom line is tragedy is going to strike you
in your life. It's going to strike everybody,
nobody is immune."*
—Chuck Noll

*"I am always with myself,
and it is I who am my tormentor."*
—Leo Tolstoy

Terry Long tried to commit suicide on July 24, 1991 when the Steelers were conducting their summer training camp session at St. Vincent College.

First, he left the engine running on his car inside the garage of his Franklin Park residence, with the garage door still down. His girl friend, Denise, discovered him in time and foiled that attempt to kill himself. Then Long went into the house and swallowed some sleeping pills and gulped down a handful of rat poison pellets, according to police reports. He was taken to Allegheny General Hospital, where he recovered, and he was kept in the psychiatric unit for several days.

Long was home rather than at camp because he didn't make the trip to a scrimmage with the Washington Redskins at Carlisle, Pennsylvania, because of a hamstring injury. Long was worried that third-year lineman Carlton Haselrig was going to take his job while he was out of action.

Everybody associated with the Steelers expressed surprise and shock when they learned what Long had done.

But they should not have been that surprised or shocked. The 32-year-old Long, one of the NFL's strongest players, had been sending them signals from the start of his career with the Steelers that indicated that he was a high-strung, troubled, insecure individual who was always worried about his job status. Like most people who attempt to commit suicide, or those who succeed at it, Terry had long been crying out for attention and help.

Long was worried because he had failed a drug test that showed he was taking illegal anabolic steroids — and this disclosure would soon be made public — and he was facing suspension from the powers-that-be at the National Football League front office in New York. Then, too, he feared he might not make the team, and that his pro football career would come to a crashing halt.

As a pro football lineman, he was making about $265,000 a year, and was set to make $277,500 for the 1991 campaign, according to the NFL Players Assn. salary report. Long is a guy known for pinching pennies. He had tried some business pursuits outside football, but found he couldn't make a go of it, and wondered what would become of him if he could not play pro football.

One year he drove a bus during the off-season for the North Allegheny School District for $7.90 an hour. "I'm doing it for fun," he said. "I like being around kids."

In December of 1988, he started TL Sports Nuts, and had different kinds of peanuts shipped from his hometown of Columbia, South Carolina to Grove City where they were packaged. Long drove around western Pennsylvania distributing the packaged peanuts himself. There were some early encouraging signs, but Long was unable to sustain it. He also tried to get a real estate license, but failed the test.

On November 5, 1990, he was driving a new Nissan Pathfinder on a rainy highway in the North Hills and failed to negotiate a turn. He flipped the van over on its wheels and suffered a mild concussion and cut lip.

Anybody who checked his file of press clippings in the Steelers' publicity office would have discovered that Long had left a trail about his problems. Long had never been big on interviews with newspaper reporters, and was thought to be a reticent, leave-me-alone performer, a strong, silent type. He was a man of few words, but when he had spoken he had opened up his heart and soul and told much about his personal concerns and fears, and about an early life which was difficult, and where it was up to him to shoulder the load for others.

Interestingly enough, more than two-thirds of the clippings in Long's file are from the summer of his suicide attempt. Most of the rest are from his earliest days with the team. There is little in between. He did not have much to show for his other seven seasons with the Steelers.

Long was a super weightlifter in the military service and later as a student at East Carolina University. He was so strong, in fact, that he was a top prospect to represent the U.S. in the 1984 Olympic Games. But he passed on that opportunity because he didn't want to take any chances when it came to making the Pittsburgh Steelers football team. There was no way he could perform in the Summer Olympics and attend the Steelers' summer training camp at the same time. If he missed the camp, it had been strongly hinted by Steelers' officials, Long's chances of making the team would be sorely diminished.

"I have no regrets," he said that summer about his decision. "If I make it in the National Football League that'll mean more to me than a gold medal in the Olympic Games.

"I have to support a family. And I can't do that sitting out a season, or at least part of it, just to compete in the Olympics. I'm the seventh child in my family, and the oldest male. My father died when I was 15 and I have a wife and mother to support. There was no other way I could go when the Steelers made it plain they'd draft me. I've always wanted to play in Pittsburgh. Now I have my chance."

At his first camp, he was struck in the chest by a teammate's helmet, and felt an immediate burning sensation. He later spit up blood. Two days later, he was admitted to Divine Providence Hospital.

Craig Wolfley, Mike Webster and Gary Dunn at ling camp.

*"Only men of iron
would remain."*
—Will McLean in Pat Conroy's
Lords of Discipline

ry Long

Long sets to block for Mark Malone.

It was discovered that a ligament had been knocked loose in his chest. "The doctor told me as loose as it was, it could have fallen through my heart valve," said Long at the time. "I probably would have choked on my own blood."

A few days later, however, he was back in the thick of things at training camp. "I know people might think that's crazy," he said upon returning to action, "but I want to make this football team. That's what is important to me right now.

"If I can't do what I want, then my health is not important to me. I mean it's important to be living. But I want to make this football team. That's very important to me."

You may wish to re-read the paragraphs above. I suggest it offers some insight into what makes Long tick. No one is tougher on Terry Long than Terry Long. "I'm really a very friendly guy, once you get to know me," he has told wary sportswriters.

As a high school senior in Eau Claire, South Carolina, Terry Long worked two part-time jobs to help support his mother and six brothers and sisters. He was 15 when his father died. At 18, he quit school and joined the U.S. Army to be all that he could be.

He enlisted in the 82nd Airborne Division of the Army's Special Forces at 5-11, weighing about 160. He could bench press only 135 pounds and he could run 40 yards in a poky 4.95 seconds.

With the help of a sergeant schooled in weight training, he built himself up to a muscular 245 pounds, and then 260 pounds. He was bench-pressing 405 pounds, and he was running 40 yards in 4.8 seconds, excellent for a man his size.

By his second year, he was averaging 20 tackles a game as a noseguard for the camp football team at Fort Bragg. He played two years of service football and was voted the best lineman at Fort Bragg.

He has horror stories to tell about his Army days. Like when officers made an example of him when things weren't going right. "They used to hold me down and beat me up because I was bigger," said Long. "And it took four or five men to do it. When I'd fight back, somebody would kick me in the face to quiet me down. It wasn't pretty, I'll say that."

He obtained a high school equivalency degree during his days in the service, and went to East Carolina University upon completing his military service obligation. At East Carolina, where he was a 5-11, 272-pound lineman, he was promoted during his senior season with full color posters billing him as "college football's strongest player," a title earned at the North Carolina Powerlifting Championship in 1983 in the super heavyweight division.

He has bench pressed 560 pounds and once deadlifted 865 pounds, only 39 pounds less than the world record.

The 24-year-old Long beat out Nebraska's Dean Steinkuhler for first-team Associated Press All-American honors at guard during the 1983 season.

Even so, Steinkuhler was the second player chosen in the 1984 NFL draft, while Long languished until the fourth round when the Steelers selected him. Steinkuhler was 6-3, 260, and was thought to have the "correct" size for the NFL, whereas Long was regarded as too short to be effective. Long felt he should have been a No. 1 draft choice, too. "My size hurt, I know that," he said, "but I can play this game."

Long had some impressive numbers and had some incredible feats to his credit at East Carolina, however, such as lifting a Cadillac, fully equipped, off the ground. His nickname on campus was "Mr. T." That's when someone wasn't calling him "Baby Huey" or "Black Hulk."

When he was a freshman at East Carolina, he asked coach Ed Emory if he could parachute into Ficklen Stadium before the start of a game.

Long had run the 40-yard sprint in 4.77 seconds, and had jumped vertically 36 inches — that's up. With the Special Forces at Fort Bragg, he had over 60 jumps from airplanes to his credit. With or without a parachute, this was a human refrigerator that could jump.

"I don't want to sound cocky or anything," he said, "but I don't think they make them any faster than me."

As a weight-lifter in college, Long could squat 837 pounds, bench press 501 pounds and deadlift 865 pounds. He came to camp with a 54-inch chest, a 40-inch waist, 30-inch thighs, 21-inch biceps and a 20-inch neck.

There was something intriguing about him. The Steelers had gone their own way throughout the Super Bowl salad days with undersized offensive linemen who were quick and could trap-block bigger people.

It figured that he would appeal to a veteran weight-lifter and workhorse zealot like Mike Webster, who became his roommate on the road. "I needed a roomie because Larry Brown retired," Webster said, "so I picked Terry. He is so strong, I think he surprises himself sometimes."

Terry Long dreaded the day the Steelers selected John Rienstra of Temple as their No. 1 draft choice for the 1986 season. "Anytime they draft a guy at your position," said Long, "you feel threatened.

"I had a lot of recognition for the bad stuff I've done in the past, like penalties or mistakes," allowed Long. "People have written that I'm too short or not fast enough. Some nights I can't sleep because I worry so much."

Rienstra became a quality starter in 1989 before falling into disfavor with Noll because of another round of injuries and illnesses. Rienstra had difficulties handling the stresses and pressure of pro football. He was often in mental distress. During the 1991 season, after he had gone to the Cleveland Browns, he admitted to being an alcoholic.

In his first two seasons with the Steelers, Long looked confused at times when called upon to perform on the offensive line. Then again, so did Mel Blount and Terry Bradshaw and many other Steelers stars at the same time in their careers.

In February of 1991, Long was placed on a Plan B free agent list by the Steelers, leaving him free to negotiate with other NFL teams for a future contract.

"It's a bad feeling," he said. "It leaves you a little hollow. I thought I had maybe a couple of years left in me.

"You have to face it. I'm getting old. I'm not doing some of the things they want me to do. Only the fortunate ones get to leave when they want to. I probably won't get to leave when I want."

"Always believe in your dream.
And may God bless you."
—Message on answering machine of Terry Long

One day after telling teammates the NFL caught him using steroids, Terry Long started a car in a closed garage at his Franklin Park home in an apparent suicide attempt.

He later denied he had tried to take his life, but police said they found a torn-open package of "Just One Bite" rat poison pellets in the kitchen. They said Long was groggy when they arrived.

Patrolman Jim Bennett told *The Pittsburgh Press*: "He finally admitted to this officer that this was a suicide attempt as he feels his career is over."

Chuck Noll was upset with this turn of events. He said he had warned his players against the use of steroids because they can lead to "early death," as he put it. "I do know that long-term massive doses of steroids will kill you," said Noll. "All the Russian weight-lifters who were big-time into steroids died in their 30s."

As to what drove Long to do what he did, Noll said, somewhat angrily, "Terry kept reading all over the place other people's opinions. What you have to do is have the resolve to go out and earn the spot. Competition shouldn't put you in the tank. Competition should be a spur. If it's not, you've got a problem."

When I heard about Noll's response to what happened, I kept thinking that Noll was not someone who could relate to Long's problems. And Long obviously had a problem. Noll is neither a psychologist nor a psychiatrist. He is a person who prides himself in always being in control, and may have difficulty understanding why someone else might come unravelled in such a situation.

"The whole thing is in Terry's hands," Noll would say later on. "Terry has to do something. It's up to Terry."

In a question and answer report in *Steelers Digest*, Noll was asked how it affected him when one of his players, like Long, encountered personal tragedy.

"The bottom line is tragedy is going to strike you in your life. It's going to strike everybody; nobody is immune.

454

"It's also going to strike you on the football field, and if you learn anything from football, it's that there are going to be screw-ups, there are going to be mistakes, tragedies, a loss, but you can't let it get to you. You have to focus on what's important, and you make those decisions early on, and you have to stay with it.

"The old saying is, 'Suck it up and let's go.' You try not to let it affect you, and that's easier said than done, obviously. If you have something to focus upon when tragedy happens, it makes it a little easier. That's a lesson for everybody."

Long allowed, "It's my fault and I take full responsibility." He and teammate Tim Worley, who was found to be using cocaine, were the only two players suspended for violating the NFL's drug policy during the 1991 season, and they were the first Steelers ever to be punished in this manner.

Steve Courson, who had just published a book called *False Glory* about his own problems with alcohol and anabolic steroids, was called by Long's girlfriend before the suicide attempt. She told Courson that Long had been found to have high levels of ester, a synthetic derivative of testosterone. It is illegal when not prescribed for medical uses. It is banned by the NFL because it creates muscle mass. Long had gotten his steroid supply from his native South Carolina. He had taken a urine test on July 11, the day after reporting to St. Vincent, and that's when he tested positively.

Courson, who needs a heart transplant because of his physical problems, thought Long over-reacted. "Testing positive obviously is not going to make your day," Courson told Steve Hubbard of *The Pittsburgh Press*. "Football's important to us. But life is a lot more important. You're got to put it all in perspective. I just hope he didn't do anything stupid."

Long did succeed in making the team as the third guard. Then Brian Blankenship suffered an injury that shelved him, and it provided an opportunity for Long.

But Long was not able to take full advantage of the opening. Long was sidelined by a suspension from the league office — he had to sit out four weeks — and then by an injury soon after returning to the lineup. He required surgery in December. "It just hasn't been my year," he said. "At the end of January, I got my knee fixed. Then I got put on Plan B and found out I could lose my job. Then I found out I could compete for a job, only to tear my hamstring. Then the steroid thing and the alleged suicide. Then the suspension. Now a torn tricep."

He said his difficulties made him look elsewhere for support. "It brought me closer to the Lord," he said. "He's given me a second chance. It has opened my eyes to a lot of things that we each take for granted, such as playing and life itself."

Long said he had used the steroids to help him recover from off-season surgery. He insisted that he did not use them as part of his body-building process while he was in the military service or during his stay at East Carolina University.

In a revealing interview with Ed Bouchette of the *Pittsburgh Post-Gazette*, Long said when he learned of his failing the drug test he went off the deep end. "I kept thinking, 'How am I going to deal with this situation?' It just wouldn't go away. So I just went home and planned to do a few stupid things."

He had a gun and considered shooting himself, but instead took other measures.

"I figured I would take the sleeping pills, and with the other things that I had accumulated in my body, it would 'off' me, you know, get the job done," Long told Bouchette. "I seriously wanted to check out because I thought I had really destroyed everything I stood for in my life."

After Long's suicide attempt, his mother suffered a minor heart attack in October. Long felt he had contributed to his mother's anxiety and illness.

"She said, 'I'm fine, don't worry about it.' I said, 'I'm sorry if I was part of this problem.' She said, 'You did nothing but good things. You always sent money home and have taken care of the house. You've done your part to make sure that I was OK.'"

Long also told Bouchette he was worried that his well-publicized actions might have hurt his relationship with John Miller, a former high school football player from Bellaire, Ohio, who was paralyzed from the neck down after making a tackle. The two usually talked about twice a week. "I was his hero," said Long.

In another *Post-Gazette* story by Bouchette, Joe Greene, then serving as an assistant coach with the Steelers and a Hall of Fame defensive tackle, charged that people were "dumb" who took steroids.

"I'm basically as ignorant to steroids now as I was when I was playing," said Greene. "I think it's tragic that guys feel they have to have that to play. There was no information about it (when I played). People who do it now, it's not tragic, it's dumb."

The NFL first banned steroids in 1989, and steroids were classified as an illegal controlled substance in February, 1991 when a federal law took effect.

"I've always been a big guy," Greene said, "but if someone had told me back then that they (steroids) would help me, then maybe I would have tried it. I don't know. I like to think I wouldn't have. People who love the sport . . . we do dumb things.

"Through my generation, professional sports definitely has been glamorized. Those who play it and live with it 24 hours a day know that it's not all that glamorous. There were guys who loved to play it who will pay the ultimate price.

"Yes, I'm concerned. I've read over the past four, five years of people I played with, guys younger than me or slightly older, who are not with us anymore . . . whether from obesity, cirrhosis of the liver, heart attack and this stuff here (steroids)."

Long, understandably, declined to discuss his situation for nearly two months, but broke his silence on September 18 in an article by Bob

Labriola in *Steelers Digest*. Long told Labriola he had received a lot of supportive mail, and was thrilled by the cheers he heard from the crowd at Three Rivers Stadium when he went in to replace the injured Brian Blankenship in a game against the New England Patriots.

"The feeling I had from that game when I went in and the crowd cheered me . . . it just reinforced what I thought about Pittsburgh the whole time," said Long. "If it isn't the No. 1 city, it should be because they are a great bunch of people. They've always treated me with the utmost respect. I really appreciate that from the fans, that they have supported me through this whole situation.

"I would like to think that a man who has been through as much as I have been through in the last two or three months has learned something from it and gained a little wisdom about it. The biggest thing my situation has done is it's brought me closer to the Lord and made me realize He is real and has given me a second chance.

"It has opened my eyes to a lot of things we each take for granted, such as playing and life itself."

During the winter of 1992, Long was again put on the Steelers Plan B Free Agent list, and the Steelers later announced that he would not be offered a new contract. But Long continued to play for the Steelers' basketball team in high school gyms around the tri-state area.

Chuck Lanza, coach Hal Hunter and Long listen to captain Mike Webster.

Chuck Noll

"Travelin' at trawler speed"

*"Football is not a normal existence . . . the family
ends up on the short end quite a bit."*
—Chuck Noll
Upon turning 60

*"At 59 you're still in the game, still racing down the field
to catch the pass, mud on your cleats, but at 60 you're
in the stands, covered with a lap robe and forgetting
the score."*
—John Updike
Upon turning 60

Chuck and Marianne Noll were sitting across a table from me in the spacious family room of their home in Upper St. Clair, sorting out story details, smiling, and playing off one another. They are a good team. Both seemed to be in the best of spirits. They looked relaxed, indeed, they looked relieved. I envied them their tranquil appearance and setting and security.

Chuck wore a white jersey and beige slacks, Marianne wore a white blouse with the collar turned up, and beige slacks, and they went well with the beige berber wall-to-wall carpeting in the room. Beige is a good color for the Nolls.

It had been just over three months since Noll announced his retirement as head coach of the Pittsburgh Steelers, and the couple had spent most of that time touring Florida on their boat and visiting family and friends. This may also have accounted for their sunny disposition. Chuck's brother, Bob, lives in Tampa, and there's a niece and a nephew down there. Chuck also has a sister, Rita, who lives in Cleveland, and her children lived with Chuck and Marianne quite a bit through difficult times.

The Nolls have a getaway place in Hilton Head, and a slip with a new 40-foot boat.

During the previous 23 years, Noll would have spent the winter studying scouting reports from his personnel department, trying to determine whom the Steelers should select in the college draft. He was paying absolutely no attention to such activity now. It did not concern him. That was now Bill Cowher's concern.

"I haven't spent a great deal of time with Bill," said Noll when I asked him what he thought of his successor. "He's a bright young man, and there's no reason why he shouldn't be successful."

"Are you still a draftnik? Have you paid any attention to what's been going on in the all-star games and the scouting camp workouts?"

Jim O'Brien

Mike Fabus

George Gojkovich

"I frankly haven't seen them play," he said. "I haven't got that day-to-day obligation, or decisions to make. I don't have that big decision to make. My next decision is what port of call to make in our boat."

The only chore he had been asked to do since he retired was to flip the coin to start the Super Bowl. The coin had taken a bad bounce for him. In a few days, he would perform another honorary function, as he had been asked to throw out the first pitch for the Pirates' opener against the Montreal Expos at Three Rivers Stadium. Hopefully, he wouldn't bounce the ball. It was just the sort of spotlight duty Noll had always avoided when he was the field boss of the Steelers. (It turned out that he threw a strike over the outside corner, down and away, a much better effort than President Bush who bounced one in front of the plate for the second year in a row to open the baseball season).

Chuck and Marianne had been asking me some questions about the whereabouts and recent activities of some of the former Steelers I had been interviewing. I was mentioning names from the past, when the name of Bobby Layne came up. It brought a smile and a memory forth from Noll, and he repeated the name.

"I remember when I was playing for the Cleveland Browns and we came to play the Steelers at Forbes Field," said Noll. "Our team was staying at the Schenley Hotel. Marianne came in for the game, and we went out to dinner together at the Park Schenley. It was owned by Jim Blandi, who now owns LeMont. As I was coming out the door of the restaurant, someone approached me and held out a hand to shake mine. 'I know you,' he said, 'you're Bobby Layne.' I told him, 'You don't know me that well.'"

Chuck Noll, it seems, has always had an identity problem in Pittsburgh. He was mistaken for Bobby Layne back in 1958, and is often overlooked today when he is passing through a shopping mall near his home. He doesn't have the kind of face that cartoonists crave because there are no outstanding features — no big nose, no big ears, no long chin, dark brows or mole. Noll is a nice looking man, that's it. Not too many people know him that well. Despite his long and successful stay with the Steelers, Noll is an enigma to most. Neither he nor Marianne ever sought the spotlight. They guarded their private life. Noll turned down offers for TV and radio shows, and commercials, public appearances, speaking engagements and disappointed sportswriters seeking a more colorful coach. Noll was never regarded as a good interview. But he was better than most people realized, and he was generally always available. His door was usually open.

Chuck and Marianne did not say anything startling or especially revealing during my lengthy visit to their home in early April, 1992, but they did offer insights, sometimes subtle, that help explain why they were the way they were. It was a pleasant time and, as always, I learned something I didn't know before I knocked on his door. I thought there was a great deal of substance to what was said, as is often the case when anyone gives Noll a chance to speak his mind.

There was only one uncomfortable moment in our interview, when I asked him if he thought he had surprised Dan Rooney when he

460

decided to retire. Now wanting to deal with that, he simply shrugged it off, and muttered something unintelligible. "I don't know," he finally surrendered.

The Nolls spoke of being in Baltimore a few weeks earlier, at an awards dinner attended by several of the players Noll knew when he was an assistant coach with the Colts prior to his Pittsburgh Steelers assignment. He and Marianne took turns mentioning Colts who came, such as Tom Matte, Rick Volk, Artie Donovan, Ordell Brasse, John Mackey and Jim Parker. Rocky Bleier was there, too.

"Is that what you're going to be doing now . . . going to reunions?" I asked Noll.

"Going backwards," said Noll in a slow drawl with a slow smile.

The Nolls have lived in the same house ever since they moved to Pittsburgh from Baltimore back in 1969. It is a home near South Hills Village in a neighborhood that was recommended to them by Steelers' president Dan Rooney. In fact, Rooney introduced them to a couple he thought they would like, Pat and John "Red" Manning — he is the former basketball coach and athletic director at Duquesne University — and the Nolls and Mannings remain the closest of friends.

There is a sense of permanency that appeals to Noll. During his reign, the Steelers always conducted their pre-season camp at St. Vincent College in Latrobe. He never considered moving the camp to a different site. He liked its layout, its simplicity, its spirituality — its Benedictine priests were the same he had as a high school student back in Cleveland —and its closeness to home.

"Pittsburgh has been great for Marianne and I," noted Noll during our visit. "We've been to different parts of the country. We lived, at the outset of my coaching career, in San Diego. Nobody's a native and everybody is 'where are you from?' Baltimore was a different scene. Pittsburgh is loaded with good, caring, very responsive people. Hopefully, we've been good for Pittsburgh. It's been a great place to raise a family. To mature.

"Being with the Steelers has been an outstanding experience. Being able to do what we've done comes from association with people. Good people. We've had those. People with commitment and focus."

"What have you heard from some of these people since you announced your retirement?" I asked Noll.

"I can't believe the letters we've gotten from people," he said. "It's really been great. And people we've run into on our sojourn. We think we're lost in a foreign part of the country, and somebody from Pittsburgh is always there. It's great."

While the Nolls have remained in the same house in Upper St. Clair, they did have a major renovation about a year earlier, extending the back of the house to give them a larger family room and an atrium deck off it, overlooking a large wooded area, and allowing them plenty of privacy if they want to dine under natural skylight.

461

The atrium contains an assortment of colorful flowers, mostly miniature red roses and violets. "We want to get in some orchids," said Noll. There was a small fan turning from side to side in a slow, lazy manner, and a mister sending out a fine spray. Both the fan and the spray are necessary to grow flowers and the like in the enclosed atrium. "It's nice to have a little green in the wintertime," said Noll. "It's a great spot. We put a little table out there, and we like to go out there once in a while to eat." It's an appealing place, with a Mexican tile floor, a lot of natural light, and a great view of woods and bordering farmland.

It is what a science teacher in Upper St. Clair named Howard O'Shell who loves field trips would call a "magic spot." Sit out there long enough, and the woods will come alive around you.

"My wife sat down there one day," said Noll, pointing to a cleared-out area below the atrium, "and counted 32 different kinds of birds. You don't have to go far to enjoy Mother Nature."

One night, Chuck and Marianne were sitting out on the deck, and Marianne had the lights on below.

Chuck said, "What do you have the lights on for?"

"Maybe something will come by," said Marianne.

"The lights will scare them away," said Chuck.

Recalling that night, Chuck said, "I didn't get it out of my mouth when seven deer walked by. I was wrong again."

And their home is only 11 miles from Three Rivers Stadium. Pittsburgh is not New York.

Noll is not as complex as many people think. He is just different, as far as football coaches go. He is a man of many interests. There is a piano in the family room, and a guitar and ukelele lean against it on the left side. I had heard stories about Noll playing the guitar or the ukelele at parties with close friends, sometimes in the presence of his players.

"When I went to the University of Dayton, we had some Hawaiian students and they taught me how to play the ukelele," said Noll. He is always trying to learn how to do new things.

There were no signs about the family room that I saw that would indicate that a man lived there who had coached the Steelers. I saw lots of books, and a few large modern paintings. I saw no photos or football memorabilia.

"What there is," said Marianne at a later meeting, "is downstairs in the basement, in our game room. There's more stuff up now than there was before because I cleared out his closet down at the Stadium. There are some trophies and some photos, and that's a mixture of family and Steeler stuff. Chuck's never been big on that sort of thing."

When I spoke to him about his boating activity, Noll brought me a batch of recently-developed photos, taken during the time he spent in Florida following his retirement.

He showed me photos he had taken of herons and manatee — so-called "sea cows" — and his boat, a white 40-foot trawler called the *HNS Seascape*. The H is for Hanes, Marianne's maiden name. The N is for Noll. The S is for Ship.

462

"And you're the captain?" I asked Noll.

"Yes, I'm the captain," he said, and noting Marianne coming out of the kitchen and back into the family room, he continued, "And here comes the crew, as they say in South Carolina."

I told him I had seen TV shows about the manatee, which looks like a small whale, and is an endangered species. "I thought you were going to tell me," he said, laughing at his own line, "that they were related to mermaids. That's an old sea tale. You have to be at sea a long time before they look like mermaids."

A trawler is a slow-moving boat. "People let out a net behind the boat and drag it through the water for fish," explained my brother-in-law, Harvey Churchman, who lives in North Carolina and has a boat of his own, "and sit back and relax and enjoy a beer. It's the good life."

For Noll, it represents a pace that appeals to him. "I'm traveling at trawler speed right now," he said. "It's a slow boat; you don't go fast. It's a slow rhythm. It's helped my golf swing. It's slowed it down. I used to come away from football, and get out on the golf course, and I used to swing as hard as I could. Just like a football player. But now I've gotten into a different groove. Now I do it naturally. I've gotten into a trawler mode."

When Noll showed me the photos of herons and manatees and boats, I told him that Jack Lambert was now showing people pictures of his three children.

"I was talking to Jack about that," said Noll. "He told me if he had been married when he was playing with the Steelers that he couldn't have done it as well as he did. He said he'd have had to give it up. He said he couldn't have done the things he did. His family is so important to him. He couldn't have given the attention to football and given the attention to his family. He said both are full-time jobs."

I told Noll I had seen him twice at the Steelers' offices since he retired, and that, to me, he appeared awkward, like he was suddenly out of place. He nodded affirmatively. "There's a transition, no doubt about it," he said. "The people there are in a different situation, too. They feel a little awkward around me, I'm sure. It'll fall into place."

"Have you and Dan Rooney determined yet exactly what your role with the team will be?"

"No, we haven't. It's open-ended. I don't know what he expected when I told him I didn't want to coach any longer. It was something Marianne and I talked about. We felt it was time."

Instead of reading scouting reports, Noll has been reading waterway guides, and "nautical life," as he puts it. "I want to know how to navigate my boat properly, and stay out of trouble."

I mentioned that I had just watched a PBS documentary about the Titanic. "Well, you have to watch out for icebergs in the north seas. We try to go south. The only thing we had to dodge were the manatees."

I mentioned that I had recently spoken to one of his former players, Jim Clack, during a visit to North Carolina. Clack is a motivational speaker and told me he repeats his personal goals each morning before starting his work day.

"Do you have any goals?" I asked Noll.

"Not really," he said. "Our biggest goal now is to spend some time with the family. My son, Chris, is going to get away in June, and I'm looking to having him and his wife, Linda, and my wife, Marianne, all together on our boat in South Carolina and Florida.

"The family suffers when you're coaching football seven days a week for as long as I did. That was the biggest factor in my decision to retire.

"Football is not a normal existence. There's obviously a tradeoff, as far as finances are concerned, and doing something I wanted to do and enjoyed very much. But the family ends up on the short end quite a bit. It's one of the things you have to recognize right at the start. You know the price.

"Maybe you can make up for it now, just a little bit."

I mentioned to Noll that Frenchy Fuqua had told me about a pregame speech Noll had once rendered, in which he talked about how his father-in-law often talked about what he and his wife wanted to do when he retired. But he kept putting off his retirement. Then his wife — Marianne's mother — died before he had a chance to realize his dream. Did that enter into his thinking. "I think so," said Noll.

He said he was playing some golf and a little tennis.

"Have you second-guessed yourself at all about your retirement decision?" I asked.

"No second guessing," he said. "I don't know what will happen down the road. This is important."

I told him of an interview I had a month earlier with one of his former assistant coaches, George Perles, now the head coach at Michigan State University. "George says that you're going to spend this year sailing and golfing and playing tennis, and taking it easy," I said, "and that you're going to come back, as big as Vince Lombardi, to the NFL a year from now."

Noll smiled broadly, and his blue eyes positively lit up in amusement, as I spoke.

"I'm not looking at it that way," said Noll. "That's not my intent. Who knows? You should never say never."

I said I had told Marianne about this theory when I bumped into her at lunch one day at the St. Clair Country Club, and she was not pleased with the suggestion. "It's not her intention, either," said Noll.

"How about coaching, or being an athletic director at a prep school?" I said. "You have often said you'd like to teach at a prep school someday."

Noll wagged his head in a negative manner. "My son is doing that," he said. "I don't want to crowd his turf.

"My intent was to retire, to relax, and to enjoy it. I want to see what the falls are like. What the springs are like. Those are things I haven't had a chance to enjoy."

464

Mike Fabus

Bill Amatucci

George Gojkovich

Chuck Noll

Pittsburgh Steelers

Fourth Super Bowl victory was turned in by 1979 coaching staff (from left): Paul Uram, Tom Moore, Dick Walker, Rollie Dotsch, Chuck Noll, George Perles, Woody Widenhofer and Dick Hoak.

I traveled with sports teams during the first 15 years of my marriage to my wife, Kathie, and she never complained once about the hectic schedule, or my long absences. I always appreciated that. I saw young sportswriters forced to quit major league beats because their young wives didn't want them out on the road. I didn't think I wanted to continue to travel as much when my children grew up, and was glad I could make that choice.

I asked Chuck how Marianne had been in that regard. "I never had a complaint," he said. "She's been very much a fan. She was more than a fan. We had a lot at stake. It was her life, too. She has been very supportive to me. She understood what coaching was all about. She knew the time it takes."

I mentioned to Noll that I had attended a sports banquet the weekend before at St. Vincent College where the former athletic director there, Olan "Dodo" Canterna, was honored upon his retirement. There were lots of Canterna's colleagues present, former area college basketball and baseball coaches. "They were a different breed from most of today's coaches," I noted. "They were teachers as well as coaches. They taught young people things that they carried with them throughout their lives. Do you think that's gone from the game now?"

"If you're going to be successful in coaching," said Noll, "you have to be a teacher. You're going to influence young people, one way or another. You have so much contact. You're going through an emotional experience together. How you handle that, ultimately, is something that has to be controlled. An example has to be set. You have to teach people how to stay focused when everybody else loses their perspective and cool. Hopefully, you make them aware of what's important. And you can sort out the fluff from the substance of what's really important. You've heard me say before that you have to learn to keep your eye on the donut and not on the hole."

I asked Noll about another of his favorite phrases, that is, "It's not my job to motivate people; it's my job to direct motivated people." I told him I came to appreciate that the more I was involved in teaching college students.

"You don't change people," said Noll. "You have to pick the right kind of people. When you have a lot of people, you're going to have some people who don't get the message. They're going to hear what they want to hear.

"To me, football is the greatest learning experience. But you can't force it. The basics are so important. Talk about fluff and substance."

I mentioned to Noll that Ray Mansfield, who admires him so much, had told me he has this dream of going out in the wildnerness with his buddy, Andy Russell, and some other Steelers from the Super Bowl years, and having Noll lead the expedition.

Noll smiled knowingly. "I got a letter from Andy asking me to do just that," he said. "He wants to get a whole gang together in August, when we normally would be going off to training camp. They want to go mountain climbing. I don't know if they'd want to see their leader falling out from fatigue, or having a heart attack midway up the mountain.

I don't know if they're considering the physical aspects of it. They don't want to cart me off. I'm going to see what happens."

"Are you open to the idea?" I asked. "Is it something you might really consider doing?"

"We'll see," he said. "We'll see what happens."

"What do they want you to do?"

"Tell stories. Play my guitar and ukelele."

I told him that players like Rocky Bleier, Lynn Swann and Mike Wagner, as well as Russell and Mansfield, had expressed a need to sit down with him, and reflect on their days with the Steelers.

"I understand that," said Noll. "That's neat. We spent a lot of time together. You go through a lot of emotional experiences together, triumphs and joys. All the things you remember. I guess when you finish up you want to relive them again."

"Many of them, including Russell, characterized you as aloof when they were playing for you. You have been portrayed as others, like Terry Bradshaw, as being cold and distant."

"That was a part of being the head coach, and being responsible for them," said Noll. "I was so focused, so goal-oriented. There was no time or room for social niceties. It takes up all your energies staying focused."

Some of the players have said that Noll communicated with them through his assistants. They tend to be the good guys, the go-betweens, the back-patters. Was Noll any different when he was an assistant coach with the Colts or the Chargers?

"I was the same way," said Noll. "It's not a social situation. I'm not there to have fun. It's business. I always tried to keep a business attitude. Pro football is a difficult situation. You can't do it alone. Assistant coaches are a big part of it. It's not just one guy. It all comes down to people. The assistant coaches. The players. Management. You have to work together. All their input and feelings. If people can't carry their load, then you have a problem.

"I've been fortunate to know a lot of good people through the years. Good players, good coaches, good management — people who were focused."

I had interviewed many of his former players from the Super Bowl period who expressed comments that things had changed in the Emperor's empire. They saw and read about behavior he would not have tolerated when they were on the team. They thought he might have mellowed.

"No, not really," Noll said. "That's people. That's the individual. They had a lot of pride. When you don't have those kind of people you don't have the same environment. When they say they were never late for meetings, and stuff like that, well, that didn't come from me. That came from them.

"You have to have people who are motivated themselves. You can't stand over people with a whip and make them do something. When you talk to them, they may think it is a power that I had. When you have people who want to do it right, it's a helluva lot easier.

"It's the same thing. You don't win unless you have good people. I always told them, 'We have rules and we have fines. But I don't want your money. If have to fine somebody quite a bit, they'll find themselves somewhere else. I don't want to do that; I don't want people like that.'

"You have all kinds at all times. You have to have guys who are carrying the load. You can put up with a few who are not as naturally dedicated or motivated. They'll go along with the guys who have it. When you're overbalanced on the other side it's not going to work out very well.

"We had dozens who were great people, who were focused. To them, the biggest thing was to get ready for a game and to win. They were embarrassed if they didn't."

"That's the synergism you often spoke about?"

"There's no one way to do it," said Noll. "You're getting yourself ready, and you can't interfere with the other guys getting ready. We had people who rubbed off on one another.

"You don't have all of them who have that great focus. Some of them would rather socialize instead of getting themselves ready. You have a lot of different personalities on a team, but it's very much a team thing. It comes down to people. You have to have a lot of them pulling in the same direction. It's the old tug-of-war games."

Noll has often been criticized for failing to inspire his players, for not having the ability to get them pumped up to play, for not being a fiery speechmaker in the clubhouse.

"The true motivation in football is showing them how to get the job done," said Noll. "There is a how-to, showing them how to do it, talking about techniques that are involved in the minutia of football. There's a resistance to get involved.

"Once they have some success, people will be motivated to do more, to have more success. You can stand there and holler at guys and people will think you're the great motivator. In a tackling drill, for instance, a kid's getting beat to hell. He's hurting himself and not doing well. You haven't taught him how to defend himself, how to handle contact, the proper techniques. You've turned him off on football. That's not motivation. If you show him how to do it, and he's going to have some success, he'll enjoy doing it.

"I don't think people know what motivation is. You have to help them have success.

"Some of the lessons I've learned are pretty simple. When you go in on Monday and review the game with the press, one of the things that keeps popping up are the problems, the obvious mistakes that were made in the game.

"When we're basically sound, things go pretty well. It's hard not to recognize that. I've talked about this to a group of businessmen in town. Businessmen say to me, 'You're lucky you have a scoreboard in your business.' But, in life, you do have a scoreboard. When you get off the path you ought to know it. In life, you have a scoreboard. Sometimes you don't pay attention to it. Sometimes you focus on symptoms and not the disease."

One of Chuck Noll's greatest admirers, Bill Priatko, sent me an article about Paul Brown that appeared in the game program for Super Bowl XXVI in 1992. Priatko played a year for both the Browns and the Steelers, and always thought that Noll had patterned his style after that of his boss in Cleveland.

In the article about Paul Brown, Noll, who played guard and linebacker for the Browns (1953-59), is quoted as saying: "Paul was a determined and single-minded individual when it came to football. He didn't see it as a jolly, fun time. He took it as a job, and he was very serious. Personally, I found him easy to play for. If you were prepared and you played hard, you usually didn't have too many problems.

"The year after Otto (Graham) retired, we went from league champions to 5-7. That was the only losing season Paul ever had in Cleveland, and he was miserable. After the last game, when everyone was getting ready to leave, I remember Paul saying, 'Have a merry Christmas . . . if you can.'

"I listened to Paul's football philosophy for so long that I simply took it on as my own. Now that I'm a coach, I hear myself mouthing the same things Paul said about football being a game of mistakes and preparation being the key to success.

"I also picked up a few things from Paul that got me in trouble. When I talked about the 'criminal element' in football . . . I heard Paul say that originally. He was just smarter than me. He never said it around the press."

Bob Williams/Advertiser, Almanac

Marianne and Chuck Noll at Premier Performance banquet on May 17, 1992.

Gary Anderson
The soccer star from South Africa

"All I have to do is kick the ball through the uprights and everybody's happy. That shouldn't be too hard to do."
—Anderson, at age 18

"Sometimes you have a bad day."
—Roy Gerela

"I like The Organization. Some players knock it. But they're part of the new breed. They don't want to work for a thing. They want it all passed out to them. I could have quit a dozen times. I damn near did. The Raiders give you a job and even if you have a bad day and have to come out, you know you'll be back in the next week. They don't panic. So the ballclub doesn't panic."
—George Blanda

Gary Anderson has always seemed out of place on the Pittsburgh sports scene. At 5-10, 175 pounds, he has been the smallest of the Steelers since he first reported for duty in 1982. He is cute, has chipmunk cheeks, an accent, and comes off as a choir boy touring the U. S. with a foreign troupe. He was born in Parys, Orange Free State, South Africa, so his accent remains strange to the Pittsburghese-trained ear. He still thinks football refers to soccer, the sport he first embraced, and starred in as a high schooler in Durban, South Africa.

He shows up at the Civic Arena whenever his alma mater, Syracuse University, comes to play Pitt, and sits in the front row behind the Orangemen's bench, and seems even smaller alongside the young basketball giants than he does in the Steelers' clubhouse. He does not create much of a stir among the sports fans because he can get lost in the crowd. In short, he looks as normal as the next guy at the game.

Anderson has been among the most successful Steelers during the past decade, and set team place-kicking marks en route to establishing a record as one of the National Football League's all-time most consistent kickers. He replaced Roy Gerela as the top toe in team history.

Not even Anderson escaped the woes of the 1991 campaign, however, and he had one of his worst seasons in his tenth year in Pittsburgh. "It was my most frustrating, for sure," he told us during the off-season. He was plagued by the lack of an experienced or efficient long-snapper much of the season, and it hurt his accuracy and confidence. He missed field goals that have always been almost automatic for him. He scored 100 points, but his percentage of .697 was his lowest since he had a .656 percentage in 1986.

470

Gary and Carol with sons Austin and Douglas Jordan.

Gary golfs with Bubby Brister and Arnold Palmer.

Even so, Anderson must have felt particularly devalued as he sat on a raised platform alongside Pro Bowl teammate Rod Woodson at the U.S.A. Celebrity Sports Trading Card Show on Sunday, March 29 at Duquesne University's A.J. Palumbo Center.

Among the items up for sale that weekend were the autographs of sports stars. Baseball's all-time home run hitter Henry Aaron's autograph commanded $25 per customer, while baseball's all-time hitter Pete Rose was getting $20 the day before at the same stand. Hall of Fame pitcher Ferguson Jenkin's signature was for sale at $12. Former slugger George Foster was getting $5. Anderson's was available for $3. Talk about bargain basement prices. These trading card shows simply attract more baseball buffs than football, hockey or basketball fans. Aaron and Rose both attracted more than a thousand takers at those steep prices, and Anderson attracted the spilloff.

He must have felt a little better because Woodson was signing scraps of paper, pictures and game programs for free, as Woodson was appearing to promote a nationally-syndicated football camp he represents.

"It was a real eye-opener for me; I'd never been involved in one of those card trading shows before," Anderson said. "It was a nothing-but-money deal. It was just signing so many signatures per minute, right on the clock. There was no eye contact whatsoever, no personal interaction.

"I always try to give people as much attention as possible. I kinda winced when I saw what was going on there. I do so many things around town that anybody who wants my autograph had to be crazy to pay $3. They can get it for free anytime. It was really odd for me. It left me with an uncomfortable feeling."

Anderson still appears at more places than just about anybody on the Steelers' team. Woodson, Bubby Brister, Merril Hoge and Louis Lipps have commanded more requests for appearances in recent seasons, though the demands have dwindled a bit because of diminished performances. But Anderson shows up at more sports banquets, luncheons, schools, and fund-raising affairs. He has a reputation for being reliable and well received. Anderson spends much of the off-season speaking to school students for the Blue Cross of Western Pennsylvania Drug and Alcohol Awareness program. "We have been very pleased with the efforts of Gary Anderson," said Blue Cross president Eugene J. Barone, a former collegiate athlete at Pitt who serves on the U.S. Olympic Committee. "He does a great job for us. And you can count on him."

Chuck Noll and Steelers fans always felt the same way. Anderson is comfortable in Pittsburgh. His wife, Carol, grew up in Shaler Township, a suburb just north of Pittsburgh. They have two sons, Austin, 3, and Douglas Jordan, almost 2. The Andersons are at home in Wexford. Gary has worked in commercial and real estate development in preparation perhaps for his "life's work," and is active in many local charities, including Spina Bifida, Mercy Hospital and Youth Guidance. Carol was the 1989 recipient of Childhelp USA/NFL Players Association Humanitarian Woman of the Year Award. She is a graduate of the Art Institute of Pittsburgh and has worked as a graphics designer and part-time aerobics instructor.

When I spoke to Anderson about the high regard Eugene Barone, as well as John McGrady Jr. of Blue Cross had for him, he said, "I've been doing that for them for about six years now. I'm pleased that they're pleased. To me, it's just doing what I ought to be doing. That's the way I was brought up. It's not just my attitude toward the Steelers.

"If I'm supposed to do something, I do my best to be on time, and to do the best I can. I always have that perspective wherever I am. To me, it doesn't matter what I am doing, I am always representing the Steelers.

"I've always considered it a real honor and privilege to play for the Steelers football team. It's very sad for me to hear stories about guys showing up late or not showing up at all for appearances. It really annoys me.

"My dad passed away a few years ago. But if he found out I failed to do something, or didn't show up for an appearance as scheduled, he'd kick me in the tail. That's the way I was raised."

I mentioned to Anderson that one of the Steelers' pioneer performers, "Bullet Bill" Dudley, had recently asked me about the attitudes of today's players, and wanted to know if they had become more selfish and less conscious of their responsibilities as role models.

"It's tough to make generalizations," Anderson said, "but I know why he's asking those questions. His perspective is my perspective to a T. I'm sure there were some guys who were different from him in his day, too. But we do have guys who care.

"It annoys me tremendously if I hear of an athlete doing something wrong, or where they feel they do not have a responsibility toward young people. You have to feel a responsibility. Over the years, it has been exciting for me to be seen in that light by the public.

"When I first came to the Steelers ten years ago, I was really impressed with the guys on our team. One of my first impressions was that they were decent fellows.

"I think that is one of our problems with the present day squad. I was around those Super Bowl guys, and there was a huge difference between the way those guys looked at life, and they way these guys look at life.

"Those guys did the right things. And it's worked its way over into their careers after football. They had good work habits. They were on time for practice and for team meetings. The team concept was more meaningful to them.

"From that aspect, I have seen football change in recent years. It has changed, there's no doubt about that. What's the difference? Those Super Bowl players were a special group of guys. They saw the big picture. One of the things that Chuck Noll always preached was how close teams were when they were winning."

473

I suggested to Anderson that Noll was hastened into retirement by all the things that went wrong with his players the past season, plus a critical media that was coming down hard on his head.

"I agree with you," Anderson said. "I made a side hobby of watching Chuck Noll. I could do it. I know one thing: Chuck really believed we had a good team last year. He was frustrated that we didn't do better.

"All that nonsense that we had on the team got to him, I think. We had more things go sour; I never saw it like that in my ten years. I was one of the few people who predicted he would retire. Peter King of *Sports Illustrated* told me I was the only person in Pittsburgh who told him that Chuck was going to retire.

"When he was winning Super Bowls, he was dealing with motivated people. I'm not sure that's the case these days. It's easy now to be a Monday morning quarterback, but I saw a few things that I hadn't seen Chuck do in the ten years I'd been here."

"I think he's relaxed now," I said. "He seems to be at peace with himself."

"I agree," Anderson said. "I saw him on TV after he had thrown out the first ball in the Pirates' opener. He was beaming.

"He was the perfect coach for me. He reinforced everything I had been brought up with, as far as values are concerned. The things he preached all rang familiar bells in my mind. And keep in mind my dad was a minister as well as a former professional soccer player.

"I think Chuck felt that you had to have quality people to win. Those are the guys who will win for you.

"One of the problems in the game, and one of the things that, in my mind, I struggle the most with psychologically, is the system the owners have gotten into where the biggest money goes to the new and unproven players. They end up paying the young guys the most money. That's really a fundamental problem. It doesn't need to be like that. It makes no sense to be like that. The high round draft choices show up and they have a superior attitude. It's not my job to mention names, but you know who I'm talking about. You can look back over the last ten years and see how many top draft choices came in here with the attitude that they had it made.

"They get a big signing bonus, and it ruins the whole motivational thing. I look back at some of the older guys on our team when I first got here, and it's not hard to see the difference.

"It was something I noticed right away. I was shocked. I thought some of those Super Bowl guys would have an attitude, but they had won four Super Bowls, and guys like Mike Webster, Donnie Shell and John Stallworth busted their tails every day at practice. They didn't have the attitude like so many of our guys today: I'm not going to put out in practice; I'll play on Sunday."

Even Anderson, however, was critical of Noll in 1991 for not getting the long snapper the Steelers needed for their punting and placekicking game. "Brian Blankenship got hurt in the second game of the season, and Dermontti Dawson drew the assignment. And he told me he hated it. It affected his overall game. He said it would be second down, and he would start getting anxious about having to snap the ball.

"I think it cost us some games. It cost me some field goals and some balls were snapped over the head of our punter, Dan Stryzinski, and they hurt us, too. I told Tom Donohoe we had to get a long snapper.

"Most teams have a specialist. You have to have someone who can snap the ball. I don't know how many times the ball came bouncing back when I was kicking field goals. But Noll would not get a snapper. To him, it was wasting a spot on the roster."

I mentioned to Anderson that Noll had played professionalally with the Cleveland Browns, and their punter was Horace Gillom, who was a terrific end, and their placekicker was Lou Groza, who was an All-Pro offensive tackle. That's the way it would have been on a perfect football team.

"I recall during the season that he had some of our linemen practicing snapping the ball for the first time in their lives," Anderson said. "I couldn't believe it. It was like having me be a wide receiver.

"This is the NFL, not high school. Everyone was fighting with him to get us a solid long snapper. On Thanksgiving, we had a lot of problems with our long snapping and Bill Walsh was highly critical of it on TV. My wife taped it for me, and she said, 'Wait till you hear what Walsh said.' Walsh said, 'Hey, folks, this is a problem. This is not close to NFL caliber when it comes to special teams play.' I'm hoping that Noll will hear what Walsh had to say."

I told Anderson that the last guy who could influence Noll's outlook on football would be Walsh. Noll always felt that Walsh was responsible for labeling himself a "football genius," so this wasn't the man Anderson needed to lobby on his behalf for a long snapper.

"It was just so blatant," Anderson said. "Bad snaps are part of the game, but this was getting out of hand.

"And I felt sorry for Dermontti Dawson. He is one of the best guys on the team. He would have fitted in perfectly with those guys from the Super Bowl teams. He is a great guy, and his poor snapping was killing him."

I have heard Anderson tell the story of how he got his start in football on many occasions, but remain fascinated by it. The most recent occasion was when Anderson served as the featured speaker at a high school sports banquet sponsored by *The Almanac* and *The Advertiser*, weekly newspapers in Pittsburgh's South Hills, at the Green Tree Marriott.

As a high school student in South Africa, Anderson excelled in rugby and soccer. His father, Dick, was a professional soccer player in England and Ireland. His dad started teaching Gary how to play soccer "as soon as I could walk." He saw his first American football game in a movie, "The Longest Yard," starring Burt Reynolds, during his senior year in high school.

"I thought," Anderson said, "what kind of crazy game is this where they talk for five minutes and then play for a few seconds and then talk again?"

Anderson had never seen a football game in person until he came to the U.S. The Andersons — Gary was one of five children — moved to Downington, Pennsylvania, near Philadelphia, after he graduated from high school. The father was a Baptist minister. Even after the family had moved to America, Gary still dreamed of someday playing soccer in Europe.

Asked why they left South Africa, Anderson said, "Basically, we didn't agree with the political situation." He was referring, of course, to South Africa's apartheid policy, segregation in a nation with a small white population in control of state affairs.

He was fooling around one day at a ballfield near his home, kicking a football, and he quickly displayed a natural ability to boot a football long and high. He was encouraged to attend a kickers' tryout nearby that was being held by the Philadelphia Eagles.

Dick Vermeil was the Eagles' coach, but felt that Anderson, at 18, was too young and lacked the experience to rate an invitation to his team's training camp.

Several college coaches attended the tryout, however, and were impressed with Anderson's accuracy, and moreso by his strong leg. "They told me I had to go to college first, that it would be good," recalled Anderson. "They explained to me about field goals, kickoffs and extra points. I didn't know a thing.

"I had kicked a rugby ball all my life, so nobody had to teach me how to kick. It was natural for me. And I knew that all I had to do was kick the ball through the uprights, and everybody's happy. I figured that shouldn't be too difficult to do."

Anderson visited all four schools that were interested in him, namely Indiana, Tennessee, Georgia Tech and Syracuse.

A Syracuse assistant signed Anderson to attend school in upstate New York. Frank Maloney was the head coach at the time. Dick MacPherson, now the head coach of the New England Patriots, was an assistant coach at Syracuse back then. He was Anderson's special teams coach. Both were bound for bigger and better things, but surely helped get each other's careers successfully launched.

"My father was amazed," Anderson said. "He said, 'What kind of game is this where they see you kick two balls and offer you a $40,000 scholarship?' "

In addition to earning a b.s. degree in business management-accounting in 1982, Anderson completed his college career with an NCAA-record 87.4 per cent accuracy rate as a field goal kicker. He made 18 of 19 field goal tries as a senior — his only miss was a 48-yarder against Navy — and 42 of 56 altogether. He was 72 of 72 on points after touchdowns in his career. A sidenote: he roomed with Joe Morris, a running back who would go on to star for the New York Giants. He also played rugby and was the soccer team's leading scorer as a freshman.

Gary Anderson

As a senior, Anderson was an AP first team All-American. He had come a long way from South Africa.

"There can't be many college kickers in the country as trustworthy as Gary," said MacPherson. "He has that light touch. Everything's a chip shot for him; he has such power in that leg."

Anderson was selected on the seventh round by the Buffalo Bills, just before the Steelers planned to draft him. He was the 171st player picked in that 1982 draft, and it appeared the Steelers had waited too long to take him. But their seventh round choice that year, defensive lineman Edmund Nelson of Auburn, ended up playing six solid seasons for them, so they can't kick themselves too much. And, as it turned out, they added Anderson to their squad five days before the season opener.

"He wasn't our draft pick," said Dick Haley, who was the director of player personnel for the Steelers at the time, "but he has to be one of the most important players we've ever brought here. We wish we would've drafted him."

Haley had personally scouted Anderson in three of Buffalo's four pre-season games. Anderson missed all five field goals he attempted, yet Anderson still thought he was better than Nick Mike-Mayer.

"If I don't make it here," Anderson told Craig Stolze, a sports writer for the *Rochester Times-Union*, "I'll go somewhere else and make it. I can be a star in this league and I think the Bills know it."

Not really. Chuck Knox was the head coach of the Bills when Anderson was put on waivers. Haley signed Anderson as a free agent. He had also watched Anderson kick in practice, and liked what he saw.

The Steelers had become disenchanted with David Trout, whom they had signed the year before to replace the incumbent Matt Bahr. Letting Bahr go was a bad move, but the Steelers haven't suffered from it long term. After all, Anderson has been referred to as "maybe the best place-kicker in NFL history" by pro football expert Paul Zimmerman of *Sports Illustrated.*

Trout missed three of 12 extra point attempts during the pre-season schedule. The Steelers had seen enough to know they were ready to make a change. Haley assured everybody that Anderson was equal to the task.

Gary Tuma of the *Pittsburgh Post-Gazette* wrote: "The Steelers yesterday got rid of a kicker who couldn't make extra points in the pre-season and picked up one who couldn't make field goals."

"It was a matter of who we had the best feel for," said Haley, who moved on to the New York Jets following the 1991 season after 21 years in the Steelers' scouting department and 25 years in the organization. "We liked Anderson off last spring and his college career. We had the conviction that we thought he could kick in this league."

In his first regular season game with the Steelers, Anderson was standing on the sideline next to Chuck Noll in the late going of a game at Dallas. Noll turned to Anderson and asked him a question: "Can you make it?"

Anderson simply nodded.

"Then go do it!" Noll said.

And Anderson kicked a 40-yard field goal to seal the verdict in a 36-28 victory over the Cowboys.

The first words from Noll in the post-game press conference were: "Looks like we've found ourselves a kicker."

In that first outing, Anderson kicked field goals of 26, 43 and 40 yards, but he kicked them after a bad snap cost him his first extra point attempt, and a missed block cost him his first field goal attempt. It was blocked by John Dutton.

Terry Bradshaw was quick to assure Anderson that things would get better before they got worse.

"I made sure I told him, 'That's not your fault. That's their fault,'" said Bradshaw. "We tried to take the pressure off him. But it didn't bother him. He's South African. He doesn't know any better."

It sounds just like the sort of thing Bradshaw might say now on a CBS telecast of NFL action. A typical Bradshaw soundbite.

Anderson converted 10 of 12 field goals and all 22 extra points on which he actually kicked the ball in the strike-shortened 1982 season to gain all-rookie honors.

In 1983, he was named to the Pro Bowl for the first time, and won the first of three straight AFC scoring titles. He was voted the team's MVP and the NFL Alumni Association's kicker of the year. He scored 119 points on 27 of 31 field goals, and 38 of 39 PATs, setting a team record of 87.1 per cent field goal accuracy, including a streak of 13 straight.

In 1984, he led the AFC with 117 points and nailed a 53-yard field goal at Indianapolis to break Lou Michael's team record for longest field goal, and topped his own record five weeks later with a 55-yarder against San Diego.

In 1985, he set a team record with 139 points, and became the first AFC player to win three consecutive scoring titles since Gino Cappelletti won four (1963-66), and Anderson had a streak of 18 straight field goals.

He continued to set one record after another in the years that followed. He became one of the NFL's most productive and consistent kickers. He erased most of Gerela's records from the Steelers' books, and became the greatest scorer in Steelers' history.

At practice, Anderson is the guy off by himself. If he wants a conversation, he has to seek out the punter. "I'm by myself a majority of the time," he said. "You don't want to do too little or too much. It can hurt you if you kick too much, but I don't count them.

"I don't think about the fine mechanics of kicking. I just step back to where it seems right, look at the ball and kick. If I miss, I know what was wrong."

From start to finish, football has been a simple game for Gary Anderson.

Postscript

"No one taught us more about the
value of teamwork than Chuck Noll."
—Ray Mansfield

Soon after he retired as coach of the Pittsburgh Steelers, Chuck Noll began making more public appearances around Pittsburgh and the nation than he may have made during his 23 years on the job. Or so it seemed, anyhow.

His behavior was so atypical. He was flipping a coin to start the Super Bowl, throwing out the first pitch for the Pirates' opener. The sort of stuff, or showcase situations, he once dreaded.

All of a sudden he was showing up at sports banquets all over town, waving to the crowd in a community parade, gladly agreeing to participate in fund-raising golf outings, accepting honorary degrees, and doing sports talk shows.

This was not the Noll we knew and were mystified by during his long spell as the head coach of the Steelers.

But, indeed, it was. Now that he has retired, Noll has the time to be a good guy. Noll will no longer be an enigma. He can afford to spend an evening or an afternoon at a hotel, church or golf course, and not fret about the time sacrificed from his main mission: how to win the next football game.

No, this is not a new Noll that has emerged from the closet since he called it quits as the head coach the day after Christmas.

He simply switched his enthusiasm and dedication from one task to another, while making sure he still had more time for his wife, Marianne, and their son, Chris, and for doing the recreational and educational things that interest him. He has become a statesman for the Steelers.

Chuck and Marianne graced the dais on a Sunday evening in mid-May, 1992, at the second annual Premier Performers sports awards banquet sponsored by *The Almanac* and *The Advertiser* weekly newspapers at the Green Tree Holiday Inn. They were a big hit. They posed for photos, presented plaques, signed autographs, and talked with everyone.

The best and brightest of the young women and young men who play sports for high schools in the suburbs south of Pittsburgh were honored. Having the Nolls there to acknowledge their achievements added something special to the evening.

Earlier in the day, the Nolls were together at their church, St. John Capistran Catholic Church in Upper St. Clair, where Chuck delivered a message at a special recognition service for the graduating high school senior members.

"Chuck wants to do this now," said Marianne. "He has a message. He has something to say. And he likes the banquets where he has an opportunity to talk to the young people."

The Nolls were a week away from celebrating their 35th wedding anniversary (May 25) and they appeared to be enjoying their new, more relaxed, role as ambassadors for the Steelers. "We're both enjoying this new situation," he said.

Chuck's message was familiar to those of us who have followed his career closely, while he was winning four Super Bowls and struggling in the years since to live up to the high standards he had set for himself, the Steelers and the City of Champions.

He preaches about old-fashioned values, about teamwork, fundamentals, not straying from the basics, about the whole being greater than the sum of its parts — despite what you learned in math class — about staying free of drugs and steroids ("there are no shortcuts"), about desire and dedication, and about the special people who played for him. He told the young people the qualities needed to be a winner.

Only he was doing it publicly and this meant a great deal to those in attendance at such gatherings.

"These are the things I really couldn't do when I was coaching," he explained. "They would have been a distraction, and I didn't want any distractions. Talk is cheap. Action is what it's all about. Action is what I've been all about for 23 years."

The week before, Noll was honored as the Man of the Year by the Downtown YMCA. His former ballplayers fawned over him that evening at the Hilton. Ray Mansfield said, "No one taught us more about the value of teammwork than Chuck Noll." And Mansfield kissed Noll on top of his head, stunning sportscaster Sam Nover of WPXI-TV with his show of affection. "I never saw anything like that before," noted Nover.

Hall of Famer Mel Blount said, "Coach, I love you. God bless you."

I have a theory that Noll will become a beloved figure in Pittsburgh. He has no real responsibilities for running the Steelers operation. Like Art Rooney, he can take advantage of his newfound freedom to be a goodwill ambassador for the organization. He can lighten up.

Some people retire and do nothing. Others take the opportunity to play catch-up on correspondence and communication, and they provide service in their community.

When I asked Noll once what he had learned from the former owner of the Steelers, he said, "I learned a lot from him. He was so great with people."

Noll can be the same way, only in a different way. His way. I predict he will get closer to his former players, and probably go hiking with them, and be a catalyst for reunions. Already, he has traveled around the country, to places where he once coached, Baltimore and San Diego, and spent time with old colleagues. He is even into reminiscing now.

On Draft Day, April 26, he received an honorary doctorate degree at his alma mater, the University of Dayton, to go along with ones he previously received at Robert Morris and Duquesne. He paid no attention to the NFL draft.

On May 9, 1992, I was among those who stood in the rain as Noll rode by in a stretch white limousine as the grand marshal of the

Community Day parade in Upper St. Clair, where the Nolls have lived since they moved from Baltimore.

He had shunned sports talk shows successfully for 23 years and, suddenly, he agreed to go on with sportscasters Stan Savran and Guy Junker on KBL, the Pittsburgh-based regional sports cable channel, and, a few days later, with Myron Cope on WTAE Radio.

Both appearances created a flap, and it must have reaffirmed why Noll was always wary of such shows in the first place. For starters, Cope was upset that Noll was not making his sports show debut with him — after all, they had worked together for more than 20 years. Then when he got Noll on his show, Cope kept asking him questions regarding why the Steelers and most other NFL teams passed on Danny Marino in the draft after his senior season at Pitt. Cope rekindled the unsubstantiated drug rumors that whirled around Marino's handsome head back then.

Noll did his best to tap dance around an issue he was not comfortable in discussing, but still ended up looking bad in a wire service story about his remarks regarding Marino. Noll ended up being blasted by an irresponsible journalist in Miami who said Noll was still bitter about not getting Marino.

I met a man around the same time named George Rose, who is the president of the AARP club in Mt. Lebanon. He used to be a salesman at Sears in South Hills Village, just a block away from Noll's home.

He recalled how he once talked to the Nolls about the pros and cons of a gas range versus an electric range when they first moved here in 1969. "If you're going to move around," Rose told the new couple in town, "you can take the electric range with you. It's more mobile. But gas is a better buy if you're going to be here awhile."

Rose didn't know who the Nolls were at the time, but another salesman told him afterward. "We're planning on being here for the long term," Noll told Rose.

Pittsburghers were lucky that the Nolls found a home in their city's suburbs, that they remained in it, and that they now have the time to become part of the community.

Another former Steeler, Andy Russell, received the St. Barnabas Hance Award for community service the same month of May as Noll was making the rounds of the local banquet circuit.

"This town never ceases to amaze me," Russell said. "Just the way the city reacts to the old Steelers. It's a little weird, to tell you the truth. I've been out of it since 1976, and even though I'm very proud of the things we accomplished, I don't want to live in the past. I think that there is more to the mountain climbing and the things I'm trying to do today.

"But I'm always amazed at how well the Steelers are treated and how much we mean to the city. I guess it helps (in terms of community involvement) because people are very responsive. I think it helps you get in to see people.

"But the city really embraces the Super Bowl Steelers, and I'm proud to be one of a lot of them. Guys like Mansfield and I are thrilled to be included. There were a lot of young guys there who did us a great service."

Sam Davis spent about seven months in health care and rehabilitation facilities before going home in May of 1992. He was making progress, but it was slow and painful, for all who are close to him. He has had his good days and bad days.

Franco Harris came to see him, and John Brown took him to lunch at the Allegheny Club. Jon Kolb kept in close contact, as did other Steelers. "Jon Kolb kept a vigil at his bedside in the beginning when Sam was at Allegheny General," said Tammy Davis, Sam's wife. "He's been unbelievable. They were roommates and Jon really cares."

Tammy was hopeful that her husband would eventually make a major breakthrough, but he was still falling into periods of confusion and depression. He told me on the telephone, for instance, that Chuck Noll had taken a new job in Miami when it was Joe Greene who had gone to work for the Dolphins. Sam had asked his wife to call the Steelers to set up a retirement announcement for him.

"I wasn't married to Sam during his days with the team," she said, "but the Steelers have all been great through this whole thing. The Steelers have been a Godsend."

The Penguins won a second straight Stanley Cup in June, 1992, and everybody was celebrating another sports triumph in Pittsburgh. It could still claim the title as "The City of Champions."

But I felt badly for a friend, a former college classmate. Paul Martha was nowhere to be seen in the post-Stanley Cup celebrations. Nobody mentioned him when praise was passed around about the achievement.

The morning after the Penguins put away the Chicago Black Hawks in a four-game sweep, there was an announcement that Martha had joined the Pittsburgh law firm of Eckert, Seamans, Cherin and Mellott. He would work as a consultant in the sports and entertainment division. Carl Barger brought him into the firm. Barger had headed the Pirates' organization, and was now the boss of the Miami franchise in Major League Baseball, as well as being a partner in the law firm.

"I've always wanted to do something like this," said Martha, who remained as the legal counsel and alternate governor for the Penguins.

But he was already, one day after the Cup chase was completed, in his new office on the 42nd floor of the USX Tower, just across the way from his former office at the Civic Arena.

"I enjoyed us winning the Stanley Cup," he said. "I was there in Chicago. I just didn't go down onto the ice afterward. That's not me. It wasn't as tumultuous as the first time, but it felt good to see the guys winning it again. It's great for Pittsburgh."

What readers say about "Doing It Right"

"Our whole family enjoyed it. Anybody who's a Steelers fan would love this book."
—Lisa Holmes, Pleasant Hills, Pa.

"Having been raised in Oakland (Lawn Street), the names were very familiar to me and brought back many fond memories."
—Bill Lindner, Danbury, Conn.

"These last few days have been pure bliss, reading your book, and remembering all those great moments with the Steelers then and now. Your book is a masterpiece. Your portrayal and description of Art Rooney, Dan Rooney, Chuck Noll, the other coaches and players was so revealing and genuine. If people want to know what the Pittsburgh Steelers' organization is all about, they should read your book!"
—Don Siebert, Hastings, Pa.

"It's a good read. I'd recommend it."
—Doug Hoerth, WTAE Radio

"I have read that marvelous book, 'Doing It Right,' and found it absolutely superb reading. I have recommended it for all the fans over here who get my biweekly Steelers' newsletter."
—Gordon Dedman, Fareham, England

"It's like a family album of the Pittsburgh Steelers. It is full of wonderful stories and, in a sense, they are all parables to help us in our own lives. I believe you did it right."
—Rev. Laird Stuart, Pastor
Westminster Presbyterian Church
Pittsburgh, Pa.

"Once you started it, you can't put it down. The joy of the book . . . it brings back so many good times."
—Ralph Conde, WHJB Radio, Greensburg, Pa.

484

"You certainly know how to tug at the skirts of Mother History and compel her to come out and play. It's interesting and pleasant reading."
—John G. Brosky, Senior Judge
Superior Court of Pennsylvania

"I was born at McKeesport Hospital. I ended up playing for Vince Lombardi and the Green Bay Packers in the last world championship (Jim Brown's last game in 1965) and the first two Super Bowls. So I can appreciate these stories about a similarly great team, the Pittsburgh Steelers."
—Robert A. Long, Waukesha, Wisc.

"I am a huge Pittsburgh Steelers fan and enjoy anything I can get on the Steelers. I absolutely loved it. Your writing brought the players and organization closer to me, and now I feel like I know both better."
—Ricky Wilson, Independence, Va.

"I enjoyed 'Doing It Right.' You did a wonderful job in writing about the Steelers. I felt as though I was reading about my friends."
—Philip Ahesh, Canonsburg, Pa.

"I am the son of 'the first professional football player,' and really enjoyed your book 'Doing It Right.' Since I was born and raised in Latrobe, I enjoyed your comments about the Steelers training camp at St. Vincent. I don't think I ever drive past the school that it doesn't bring back memories of my father."
—Dr. John K. Brallier, Ligonier, Pa.

"I wanted to commend you on an outstanding effort to capture the image of the Pitsburgh Steelers. It brought back fond memories, especially of Art Rooney. He was a legend and he was truly one of a kind."
—D. Michael Fisher, Harrisburg, Pa.
Pennsylvania State Senator

"The people that I have given it to as gifts have raved about it. They were great Christmas gifts for my customers."
—Tom Hayes, Pittsburgh, Pa.

485

Acknowledgements

Writing and publishing books on an independent basis can be a risky business, unless you are also independently wealthy and want to do it to indulge your fancy.

I wish to thank the following patrons: AEG Westinghouse Transportation, Baierl Chevrolet, Black Box Corp., Blue Cross of Western Pennsylvania, Bowne of Pittsburgh, The Brooks Performance Group, Cold-Comp, Community Savings Bank, Compucom, Continental Design and Management Group, Desks Inc., Equibank, Feldstein Grinberg Stein & McKee, Frank B. Fuhrer Wholesale Company, H.J. Heinz Company, Hilden Enterprises Inc., Industrial Metals and Minerals Co., Integra Financial Corp., Investment Corporation of West Palm Beach, J&L Structural Inc., Jessop Steel Co., Mascaro Inc., Meridian Exploration Corp., Merna Corp., Miles Inc., North Side Deposit Bank, Nortim Corp., Pittsburgh Brewing Co., Pittsburgh National Bank, PPG Industries, Inc., Reed Smith Shaw & McClay, Sargent Electric, The Gustine Company, Tomsin Steel, Waddell & Reed Inc. Financial Services, Westinghouse Electric Corp., West Penn Wire Corp., Zimmer Kunz Loughren.

I wish to thank the following individuals for their support: Bill Baierl, Andrea and Jack Barnes, Eugene J. Barone, Jeffery M. Boetticher, Howell Breedlove, Dave Brown, R. Everett Burns, Jim Clack, Renny Clark, Ray Conaway, Gregory W. Fink, Patrick Fleming, Frank B. Fuhrer Sr., Marshall Goldstein, Frank W. Gustine Jr., F. Edwin Harmon, Donald J. Hastings, Jim Hesse, Darrell J. Hess, Karen Horvath, Bob Keaney, Andy Komer, Jim Kozak, Michael C. Linn, Robert Lovett, Jack Mascaro, John E. McGrady, Jr., Del Miller, Don Miller, Clark Nicklas, Dom Palombo, Alex Pociask, Charlie and Steve Previs, Joe Reljac, Arthur J. Rooney Jr., Patrick J. Rooney, Ed Ryan, Frederick B. Sargent, Vince Sarni, Vince R. Scorsone, Stanley M. Stein, Joyce Stump, Dick Swanson, Tom Sweeney, Steve Szemes, Larry Werner, John Williams and Lester E. Zittrain.

Special thanks goes to my friends, Bill Priatko, John Fadool, Bill Haines, Walt Becker, Jim Broadhurst, Henry Suffoletta, Richard Newton, Marty Wolfson and Walter Stockdale for their support.

Once again, Ed Lutz of Cold-Comp and Stanley Goldmann of Geyer Printing and their staffs proved what caring professionals they are, and brought special pride to their performance in setting the type and printing the book.

Thanks to the Pittsburgh Steelers for their cooperation, especially Dan Rooney, Joe Gordon, Dan Edwards and Ron Miller.

Thanks to Shelley Urbank of Waldenbooks, Diane Simowski of B. Dalton Booksellers and Gary Morton of Central Wholesale Inc. for getting my books to the marketplace.

Thanks to my wife Kathleen, my daughters Sarah and Rebecca, and my sister Carole Cook for their special assistance.

— Jim O'Brien

Tunch Ilkin 62   John F. Rowser

John Stallworth   Andy Russell

Larry "Moon" Mullins

Rocky Bleier

Pat Brady   Gary Anderson